PATENT LITIGATION AND STRATEGY

By

Kimberly Pace Moore
Assistant Professor of Law
University of Maryland School of Law

The Honorable Paul R. Michel
Circuit Judge
United States Court of Appeals
for the Federal Circuit
Lecturer in Law
John Marshall Law School
George Washington University
National Law Center

Raphael V. Lupo
Partner and Head
of the Intellectual Property Group
of McDermott, Will & Emery
Adjunct Professor
George Washington University
National Law Center

AMERICAN CASEBOOK SERIES®

WEST GROUP

ST. PAUL, MINN., 1999

*TEXT IS PRINTED ON 10% POST
CONSUMER RECYCLED PAPER*

Acknowledgments

The authors wish to acknowledge that in the writing of this casebook we have been assisted by many people. Of course, the errors are entirely our own.

Acknowledgments By Kimberly Pace Moore

I would like to give special thanks to the support given to me by Chicago-Kent College of Law in the preparation of these materials. In particular I would like to recognize the contributions by the Associate Director of the Intellectual Property Program, Andrew Dallmann, who performed extensive research, drafted chapters and tirelessly proofread this casebook. I would also like to thank the many students at Chicago-Kent College of Law who performed research for the chapters contained herein. Finally, I would like to thank my spouse, Matthew J. Moore, a patent attorney at Howrey & Simon, for sharing in this endeavor with me. He contributed substantively to many of the chapters and has been my greatest resource in the completion of this text.

Acknowledgments By Ray Lupo

I wish to acknowledge several individuals at my law firm who provided great assistance to me in connection with my co-authoring activities. First, Wendy Weinburger performed extensive research and analysis and helped organize and draft several of the chapters. I also wish to acknowledge the considerable work done by Debbie Johnson who prepared the materials drafted by me. I also wish to thank Donna Tanguay, my partner and Co-Professor at George Washington University Law School, who generously shared her teaching materials for our Patent Enforcement course. Lastly, I wish to acknowledge the contributions of my partners, Jack Lever, Mark Davis and Brian Ferguson who also gave advice and contributed materials for consideration.

*

Summary of Contents

*

Table of Contents

*

Table of Cases

The principal cases are in bold type. Cases cited or discussed in the text are roman type. References are to pages. Cases cited in principal cases and within other quoted materials are not included.

xix

Table of Statutes

PATENT LITIGATION AND STRATEGY

*

Chapter One

INTRODUCTION

In deciding whether to sue for patent infringement, keep in mind that patent litigation is an expensive endeavor.[1] In addition to the financial expense incurred in bringing a patent infringement action, the patentee must also be aware of the risk to her property right. If the defendant challenges the validity of the patent (and they almost always do), the patent could be invalidated or rendered unenforceable. Accordingly, licensing provides an excellent alternative to litigation. The patentee should always be cognizant of reexamination and reissue options as alternatives to litigation, especially where validity is a concern. Finally, both parties ought to consider alternative dispute resolution options before proceeding to trial. Mediation or binding arbitration are effective, efficient alternatives to protracted litigation. Parties to a patent litigation often express concern over the abilities of lay persons (judges and juries) to comprehend and resolve the complex technical issues in a patent dispute. Because the parties jointly select an arbitrator or mediator, they can chose someone with a technical degree in the subject matter of the patent and with knowledge and experience in patent law. Experienced lawyers or law professors make ideal arbitrators. A problem in the selection process is choosing an unbiased arbitrator who is not conflicted out of working on the case.

A. OVERVIEW OF THE CASEBOOK

This casebook concentrates on the unique aspects of a patent litigation, weaving in strategic considerations that litigants are faced with in patent suits. The book sets out governing statutes and rules at

---

1. The American Intellectual Property Law Association conducted an economic survey in 1995 which examined the total cost of a patent infringement suit from filing to final adjudication including all attorneys fees, court costs and other expenses. The analysis was broken down by geographic area and amount of money at stake in the trial. In 46 percent of the cases the amount at stake in the litigation was between $1 million and $10 million. In these cases, the median legal cost for a litigation conducted in California was $999,000. In the $10 million to $100 million range, where 32 percent of the patent litigations fell, the median cost in California was $1.2 million. *See* American Intellectual Property Law Association, *Report of Economic Survey* 1995, 70.

the beginning of each chapter and includes sample litigation documents where possible. The chapters also contain problems, many of which build on a single fact pattern involving a patent issued for an electronic autopilot system for a trolling motor (used for fishing). The patent appears in the chapter on claim construction (Chapter 8).

Generally, the book proceeds through a litigation in the order the parties would. The book begins with the same considerations that a potential plaintiff would have: who to sue (Chapter 2); and where to sue (Chapter 3). The pleading requirements are addressed (Chapter 4) as are the various manners of discovery available to the litigants, the need for protective orders, and the attorney/client privilege issues that typically arise in patent litigation (Chapter 5). The book next turns to strategy issues in preparation for trial, selecting and preparing witnesses and experts for trial, the need to tell a story, dispositive motions to limit the issues to be tried, and bifurcation (Chapters 6 and 7).

The next section of the casebook moves into the substantive legal issues at trial. The liability case-in-chief for the plaintiff (patent owner) includes claim construction (Chapter 8) and proving infringement literally and under the doctrine of equivalents (Chapter 9). This section also addresses in detail the treatment of means-plus-function clauses (Chapter 9). The case-in-chief for the defendant (accused infringer) includes the possible non-infringement defenses (Chapter 10), invalidity defenses (Chapter 11), and unenforceability defenses (Chapter 12).

The book focuses on litigating remedies issues including injunctive relief and contempt proceedings (Chapter 13) and damages (Chapter 14). The damages chapter explores the time limitations for damages due to statutory constraints such as notice requirements and limitations periods, proving lost profits and reasonable royalties, enhanced damages for willful infringement, attorney's fees, and interest. Rather than simply stating the governing law, the book explains the law and focuses on the ways to prove entitlement to the various forms of damages and the types of evidence which will build a winning case.

The next section focuses on post-trial matters including jury instructions, special verdict forms, the judgment, judgment as a matter of law (JMOL) and new trial motions (Chapter 15). Do not be confused by the fact that jury instructions, special verdict forms, and JMOL motions are covered in this section on post-trial matters. Attorneys should start working on them early in the trial process. Since you never know exactly how long the trial will take, the jury instructions, special verdict forms, and JMOL motions should be prepared well in advance. As the defendant, you should have your JMOL motion prepared so that when the patent owner rests her case, you can jump to your feet and move for judgment as a matter of law presenting the court with a written brief to support your oral motion.

The final section of the book contains chapters on the appeal process (chapter 16) and unique issues in litigations involving assignees/assignors and licensees/licensors (Chapter 17) and reexamination and reissue proceedings (Chapter 18). Although we tried to incorporate issues with respect to licensees and assignees in the substantive chapters in which they would arise (i.e., licensee marking is covered in the marking section), there are some unique estoppel issues that warrant a separate chapter. Although the reissue and reexamination chapter is the last in the book, it is extremely important throughout the litigation process to consider the PTO as an alternative forum to resolve potential issues with the patent. Taking advantage of this forum will help simplify the issues that need to be tried and could save a potentially invalid patent.

B.   THE CONTENTS AND TERM OF A PATENT

STATUTORY PROVISION—35 U.S.C. § 154(a):

Contents and term of patent

(1) *Contents.*—Every patent shall contain a short title of the invention and a grant to the patentee, his heirs or assigns, of the right to exclude others from making, using, offering for sale, or selling the invention throughout the United States or importing the invention into the United States, and, if the invention is a process, of the right to exclude others from making, using, offering for sale, or selling throughout the United States, or importing into the United States, products made by that process, referring to the specification for the particulars thereof.

(2) *Term.*—Subject to the payment of fees under this title, such grant shall be for a term beginning on the date on which the patent issues and ending 20 years from the date on which the application for the patent was filed in the United States or, if the application contains a specific reference to an earlier filed application or applications under section 120, 121, or 365(c) of this title, from the date on which the earliest such application was filed.

Patents based on an application filed on or after June 8, 1995 have the right to exclude for a period of twenty years measured from the application filing date. For patents based on applications filed before June 8, 1995, a patent confers the right to exclude for a period of seventeen years measured from the date the patent issues or twenty years measured from the application filing date, whichever is greater. In 1994, the patent term was changed from seventeen years from date of issuance to twenty years from the application filing date. Why do you think the patent term was changed? Although a patent ceases to be effective upon its expiration date and the invention is dedicated to the public, the patentee may bring an action for past infringement even after the expiration of the patent, subject to the six year statute of limitations in 35 U.S.C. § 286. A patent becomes enforceable only upon issuance by the Patent and Trademark Office (PTO). Hence no remedies for patent infringement are available prior to the patent issuance. However, in limited situations a patentee may be able to recover damages for activities that occurred prior to the issuance of the patent under state trade secret laws.

Notice that a patent does not grant an inventor the right to make, use, or sell her invention. It grants the right to exclude others from making, using, or selling. Can you think of any circumstances where the patent owner may not be permitted to make, use, or sell her patented invention?

C. OVERVIEW OF THE UNITED STATES PATENT SYSTEM

Article I, Section 8, Clause 8 of the United States Constitution states:

> The Congress shall have power . . . to promote the progress of . . . the useful arts, by securing for limited times to . . . inventors the exclusive right to their . . . discoveries.

1. INCENTIVES UNDERLYING THE PATENT LAWS

The patent laws which Congress has enacted pursuant to this constitutional grant are codified at 35 U.S.C. There are three basic incentives that the patent laws provide: the incentive to invent; the incentive to disclose; and the incentive to risk capital. First, the patent laws provide an incentive to invent by offering the possibility of reward to the inventor (exclusive rights) for new inventions. Second, the patent laws promote early public disclosure of technological advances, which in turn can serve as the basis for further advances. In the absence of patent protection, many inventions would be maintained in secret in order to preserve some advantage for the inventor. Third, the patent laws provide the stimulus for investment and capital funding that is necessary for complete development and marketing of the invention. In the absence of the promise of exclusive rights, companies would not risk the capital expenditures in research and development and fewer inventions would reach the public. Courts, and in particular the Federal Circuit, will often consider these incentives when interpreting the patent laws.

2. PATENT PROSECUTION—THE PATENT APPLICATION PROCESS.

The process of receiving a patent from the PTO is called "prosecution." Prosecution times vary depending upon a number of factors, including the complexity of the technology and claims to the same invention by multiple inventors. Presently, patent applications take on average 18 months to prosecute. Under 35 U.S.C. § 131, when the application is filed with the PTO it is assigned to an examiner from the art group responsible for the technology or subject matter to which the patent application is directed. This examiner determines whether the claimed invention meets the requirements for patentability (§ 101–103) and whether the patent application meets the disclosure and format requirements for patentability (§ 112). If the examiner determines that the invention does not meet these patentability requirements, she rejects the claims specifying the grounds upon which the claims are rejected in an Office Action. The attorney prosecuting the application can file an amendment altering the claims or a response explaining why the examiner's rejection is improper. The examiner reviews the amendment and response and determines whether it overcomes her rejection. If so, a patent is issued. If not, the examiner can issue a final rejection.

The final rejection is not absolute. The applicant can submit a response to the final rejection, which may be accepted if the response places the application in condition for allowance or a better position for appeal. The applicant can also request an interview with the examiner where they can meet face-to-face or over the phone to discuss how to overcome the rejection. If none of these options proves successful, the applicant can appeal the examiner's final rejection to the Board of Patent Appeals and Interferences. If the Board finds for the applicant, the patent issues. If the Board agrees with the examiner's rejection, then the applicant can appeal this decision to the United States Court of Appeals for the Federal Circuit or the United States District Court for the District of Columbia.

As you can see from this brief overview, patent prosecution can be a lengthy affair with an extensive written record. It is important in a patent litigation or when threatened with a patent litigation to obtain the prosecution history as it can weigh heavily on how the claims will be construed and what will amount to infringement.

D.   WHOSE LAW TO APPLY?: GRAPPLING WITH PROCEDURAL ISSUES

In a patent trial, what law should apply to procedural or substantive issues: the law of the regional circuit where the district court sits or the law of the Federal Circuit? The answer is highly fact dependent but the basic rule is when the procedural issues are not unique to patent law, regional circuit law will apply, otherwise Federal Circuit law will apply. The following case considers what procedural law ought to apply in a patent trial.

BIODEX CORP. v. LOREDAN BIOMEDICAL, INC.
946 F.2d 850, 20 USPQ2d 1252 (Fed. Cir. 1991)

Before RICH, MICHEL, and CLEVENGER, Circuit Judges.

CLEVENGER, Circuit Judge.

Biodex Corporation ("Biodex") appeals the judgment of the U.S. District Court for the Eastern District of California entered on a jury verdict that found U.S. Patent No. 4,691,694 ("694 patent") invalid and U.S. Patent No. 4,628,910 ("910 patent") not infringed by devices manufactured by defendants, Loredan Biomedical, Inc., and its chief executive, Malcolm Bond (collectively, "Loredan"). We affirm.

I

Biodex is the assignee of both patents in suit which claim certain muscle exercise and rehabilitation devices. The 910 patent issued December 16, 1986. After notice of allowance, Biodex had filed a continuation-in-part application on September 15, 1986, which later matured into the 694 patent upon issuance on September 9, 1987. Biodex filed suit asserting that devices manufactured by Loredan infringed various claims of the patents.

At trial before a jury, Loredan contended, *inter alia*, that the 694 patent was invalid under 35 U.S.C. § 102(b) because the subject matter of the claimed invention had been offered for sale in the spring and summer of 1985, more than one year before the filing date. Biodex argued that the invention claimed in the 694 patent had not been satisfactorily tested so as to be safe for human use until after the critical date of September 15, 1985, and, therefore, could not have been on sale. On the 910 patent, Loredan argued that two terms in the asserted claims, written in means-plus-function language, did not read on the alleged devices because the corresponding structures found in the Loredan devices were not equivalent to the structures disclosed in the specification. Loredan contended that the inventor had expressly conceded this fact before the U.S. Patent and Trademark Office ("PTO"). Biodex responded, first, that the jury need only consider the plain language of the terms in question which read on the Loredan devices; second, that Loredan misconstrued the inventor's concession during prosecution; and, third, that the structures in the accused devices were equivalents.

In its appellate briefs, Biodex recognizes that resolution of these issues required the jury to decide questions of fact. For instance, in its opening brief, Biodex contests that "the jury verdict of noninfringement of the '910 patent was supported by substantial evidence." In its reply brief, Biodex argues that the special verdict of invalidity of the 694 patent was not "supported by the evidence." We read both references to evidentiary support to concede that the verdicts were based upon factual determinations made by the jury. In any event, while we agree with Biodex's initial contention that an ultimate conclusion as to an on-sale bar is a question of law, the inquiry does not end there, as noted by Loredan. The many factors that enter into the "totality of the circumstances" underlying the legal conclusion of an on-sale bar involve exploration and resolution of questions of fact. Both parties agree that an operable physical embodiment of the invention was not in existence before the critical date. Therefore, the only question for the jury to resolve on the contested validity issue, which the parties treated as the determinative factor underlying validity, was whether the subject matter of the 694 patent was sufficiently tested by the spring and summer of 1985 so that the invention could be on sale. Evidence was provided that some testing had been undertaken prior to the critical date and the only disputed issue, then, was the adequacy of that testing, which is a question of fact. Similarly, "whether an accused device is a section 112 equivalent of the described embodiment is a question of fact." *Durango Assoc., Inc. v. Reflange, Inc.*, 843 F.2d 1349, 1357, 6 USPQ2d 1290, 1295 (Fed. Cir. 1988).

At the conclusion of testimony, Biodex orally moved for a directed verdict. Review of a transcript of that motion does not reveal a specific allegation that Loredan's evidence in support of the contested validity or infringement issues was insufficient although judgment was requested on those issues as a matter of law. The district court never ruled upon the motion. The case was submitted to the jury with multiple special verdicts forms. In the verdicts, the jury found that all the asserted claims of the 694 patent were proved invalid and that none of the claims of the 910 patent were infringed by Loredan. The district court entered judgment on the jury verdicts. Biodex made no post-verdict motions either by renewing its motion for a directed verdict, moving for a new trial, or by moving for judgment *non obstante veredicto* ("JNOV").

On appeal, Biodex contends...that neither special verdict, of invalidity of the one patent nor of non-infringement of the other, was supported by substantial evidence. On the special verdicts, Loredan argues that, while there was sufficient evidentiary support, Biodex did not preserve the issues for appellate review by filing a post-verdict motion in the district court.

IV

The extent to which we may review the special verdicts is not so readily apparent. Quite clearly, the only available remedy upon finding error in a judgment entered on a jury verdict where there has been no motion for JNOV is limited to a remand for a new trial. Whatever the remedy, however, we must first respond to the contention of Loredan and determine whether there is any limitation on our review for error in these circumstances, i.e., whether and to what degree a jury verdict on a factual issue is reviewable on appeal. When no motion challenging the legal sufficiency of the evidence has been made at any stage in the district court, the law is uniform in all circuits that review is limited to plain error. In this case, Biodex did make an oral motion for directed verdict at the conclusion of the evidence, although this motion was not resubmitted or renewed in any form after the verdict. Our case law does not address whether jury verdicts, in such circumstances, may lack reviewability for sufficiency of the evidence. Furthermore, our case law has not been clear on whether we should or must defer to the law of the regional circuit on this kind of issue. An added difficulty, as noted by both parties, is that the law of the U.S. Court of Appeals for the Ninth Circuit, whence this case originates, on this point is not clearly discernable. The parties do not cite, and we have not identified, a Ninth Circuit case that addresses and decides this issue. Moreover, regional circuit law as to whether appellate review for sufficiency of the evidence is precluded absent a motion for JNOV is neither uniform nor clear, which makes either discerning Ninth Circuit law or stating our own more difficult. Indeed, this Court has previously noted that the law on the reviewability of a jury verdict for sufficiency of the evidence absent a post-verdict motion is unsettled.

V

We first address whether deference to regional circuit law is appropriate in deciding if a post-verdict motion is a prerequisite to appellate review of the sufficiency of the evidence underlying a jury verdict. In general, our initial inquiry in determining whether deference to regional circuit law is due has been to decide whether the law that must be applied, whether procedural or substantive, is one "over which this court does not have exclusive appellate jurisdiction." *Cicena Ltd. v. Columbia Telecommunications Group*, 900 F.2d 1546, 1548, 14 USPQ2d 1401, 1403 (Fed. Cir. 1990) (unfair competition law). This test has been variously and inconstantly phrased. The court has recently stated the relevant test as whether the issue concerns a "subject which is not unique to patent law," or which is "not specific to our statutory jurisdiction," in which event we have deferred. Alternatively, we have looked to whether the procedural issue may be "related" to "substantive matters unique to the Federal Circuit" and thus committed to our law. Furthermore, no matter how phrased, this particular test has not always ended our inquiry. We have considered, secondarily, whether "[m]ost cases [involving the issue] will come on appeal to this court," thereby putting us in a "good position to create a uniform body of federal law" on the issue. Finally, we have generally conformed our law to that of the regional circuits, without regard to the relationship of the issue to our exclusive jurisdiction, when there is existing and expressed uniformity among the circuits. Indeed, in such circumstances, a choice of different law might have been problematic.

Our inquiry into this question will benefit from an examination of the origins of our rule of deference. In *Atari, Inc. v. JS & A Group, Inc.*, 747 F.2d 1422, 1439, 223 USPQ 1074, 1087 (Fed. Cir. 1984), which dealt with a substantive legal issue under copyright, this Court noted that "[i]t would be at best unfair to hold in this case that the district court, at risk of error, should have 'served two masters', or that it should have looked, Janus-like, in two directions in its conduct of that judicial process." On a procedural issue, attorney disqualification, this Court remarked that, in "[d]ealing daily with such procedural questions in all types of cases, a district court cannot and should not be asked to answer them one way when the appeal on the merits will go to the regional circuit in which the district court is located and in a different way when the appeal will come to this circuit." *In re International Medical Prosthetics Research Assoc.*, 739 F.2d 618, 620 (Fed. Cir. 1984). In short, the policy of achieving uniformity in district court management of trials has been a significant factor in our occasional deference to regional circuit law. This Court stated the importance of this factor, as a rule, in *Panduit Corp. v. All States Plastic Mfg. Co.*, 744 F.2d 1564, 223 USPQ 465 (Fed. Cir. 1984):

> We, therefore, rule, as a matter of policy, that the Federal Circuit shall review procedural matters, that are not unique to patent issues, under the law of the particular regional circuit court where appeals from the district court would normally lie. This policy is

within the intent and spirit of not only our enabling statute but also the general desire of the federal judicial system to minimize confusion and conflicts. Since our mandate is to eliminate conflicts and uncertainties in the area of patent law, we must not, in doing so, create unnecessary conflicts and confusion in procedural matters.

In the very next sentence, with prescience, the Court recognized that the relationship between the particular issue at hand and the exercise of our exclusive statutory jurisdiction could not then be expressed in fixed language, by stating that "[t]he exact parameters of this ruling will not be clear until such procedural matters are presented to this court for resolution." *Id.* The *Panduit* Court itself further phrased the relevant line of demarcation in fluid language, noting that the resolution of the issue of deference in particular cases would depend on whether the procedural matter should "pertain to" or be "related to" patent issues, [such that] they have a direct bearing on the outcome." *Id.* at n.14 (citing *Barmag Barmer Maschinenfabrik AG v. Murata Machinery, Ltd.*, 731 F.2d 831, 839, 221 USPQ 561, 567–68 (Fed. Cir. 1984)). Although not at issue in *Panduit*, the Court additionally noted the potential applicability of a comparable rule to the review of Little Tucker Act cases. Subsequently, again citing the implicated policy of achieving uniformity in the law, this Court held that "[i]t would contravene the intent of Congress to achieve uniformity in the adjudication of Tucker Act claims for us to apply regional circuit law in appeals from district court Little Tucker Act decisions, since those cases usually involve the same legal issues as do appeals from the Claims Court." *United States v. One (1) 1979 Cadillac Coupe De Ville*, 833 F.2d 994, 998 (Fed. Cir. 1987). The Court has thus cautioned that our deference to regional circuit law in the interest of uniformity was not applicable when we would be called upon to resolve either procedural or substantive matters that were essential to the exercise of our exclusive statutory jurisdiction.

In sum, *Panduit* did not engrave a fixed meaning to the terms "unique to," "related to," or "pertain[ing] to," our exclusive statutory subject matter jurisdiction, but instead recognized that each case must be decided by reference to the core policy of not creating unnecessary conflicts and confusion in procedural matters. Moreover, *Panduit* expressly directs us to a review of our subsequent cases, in which deference has been applied, to clarify the parameters of the rule.

In reviewing our subsequent cases, we note that our practice has been to defer to regional circuit law when the precise issue involves an interpretation of the Federal Rules of Civil Procedure or the local rules of the district court. Resolution of such issues manifestly implicates the consistency of future trial management. Similarly, with regard to substantive legal issues not within our exclusive subject matter jurisdiction, our practice has been to defer to regional circuit law when reviewing cases arising under the patent laws.

However, we have not deferred in the resolution of all procedural issues merely because that issue might separately arise in a case having nothing to do with the patent laws. Such an application of the rule in

Panduit would be too expansive. For instance, in *Chrysler Motors Corp. v. Auto Body Panels of Ohio, Inc.*, 908 F.2d 951, 15 USPQ2d 1469 (Fed. Cir. 1990), we confronted the applicable standard for the issuance of a preliminary injunction, a procedural issue not necessarily limited to patent law. We stated then that, "when the question on appeal is one involving substantive matters unique to the Federal Circuit, as in this case, we apply to *related procedural issues* the law of this circuit," echoing the language from *Panduit* itself. *Chrysler*, 908 F.2d at 953, 15 USPQ2d at 1470 (emphasis added) (adopting language of *Panduit*, 744 F.2d at 1575 n.14, 223 USPQ at 471 n.14).

Furthermore, in *Sun-Tek Indus., Inc. v. Kennedy Sky Lites, Inc.*, 856 F.2d 173, 175, 8 USPQ2d 1154, 1155–56 (Fed. Cir. 1988), we confronted the issue of whether an order increasing a supersedeas bond was a final appealable order. Although this procedural issue also is not confined to patent law, we declined to defer because the issue went to our own appellate jurisdiction.

Where there is an essential relationship between our exclusive statutory mandate or our functions as an appellate court and the relevant procedural issue, that relationship provides an additional reason why resolution of the procedural issue may be committed to our jurisprudence. No offense would be taken were we to apply the law of our circuit, with due regard for established regional circuit law, to other issues that are essential to our statutory function such as the interpretation of the Federal Rules of Appellate Procedure or the promulgation of our Rules of Practice.

VI

The precise issue before us, not jurisdictional but closely related to the exercise of our mandate, is the reviewability on appeal of fact findings made by a jury in a patent trial absent any post-verdict motions. Determination of the prerequisites to appellate review of legal issues, here sufficiency of the evidence, is committed to this Court by statute, which expressly includes all "appeal[s] from a final decision of a district court . . . if the jurisdiction of that court" arose under an Act of Congress relating to patents. 28 U.S.C. §§ 1295(a)(1), 1338 (1988). The issue at hand, albeit procedural, bears an essential relationship to matters committed to our exclusive control by statute, the appellate review of patent trials.

Uniformity in the review of patent trials is enhanced, rather than hindered, by our adoption of a single position, rather than applying varying regional law to the issue before us. Indeed, an opposite rule would be confusing, as the same patent, asserted in different district court jurisdictions, might have the same dispositive factual finding reviewed or not depending upon which of differing regional circuit laws was applicable. Moreover, concern that district courts not be required to apply two sets of substantive or procedural laws during trial, depending on the appellate path ultimately taken, is not at issue. The extent to which the underlying factual findings of a judgment on a verdict are reviewed on appeal, absent a motion for JNOV, is an issue that can only arise after all the evidence is submitted and the verdict rendered. A district court would not, therefore, be required to have "served two masters" since the availability of appellate review is irrelevant to the conduct of the trial or to any decision on substantive legal issues that may arise during trial. Furthermore, our national jurisdiction provides a good position from which to establish uniform rules for the reviewability of factual issues in civil litigation under federal question jurisdiction in the absence of a post-verdict motion. Finally, predictability in the later application of the law in a circuit or other circuits is improved by the adoption of a single nationwide standard for preserving the reviewability of sufficiency of the evidence in a case arising under the patent laws. Thus, applying *Panduit*, in considering the application of the longstanding policies of promoting uniformity and minimizing confusion and recognizing the essential relationship of the issue before us to the exercise of our statutory authority, we conclude that deference to regional circuit law is not appropriate in this case.

VII

In order to state the law of this circuit on the issue, we turn first to the meaning of substantial evidence in the context of appellate review of sufficiency of the evidence. "Substantial evidence is more than a mere scintilla. It means such relevant evidence as a reasonable mind might accept as adequate to support a conclusion." *Consolidated Edison Co. v. NLRB*, 305 U.S. 197, 229 (1938). In general, an appellate court performing this task must consider all the evidence in a light most favorable to the nonmover without determining the credibility of witnesses and without substituting its judgment for that of the jury in deciding contested factual issues.

In that light, a requirement for an express post-verdict motion by the potential appellant assists appellate review in several ways. First, in the preferred and best of circumstances, the district court will produce a thorough written or oral opinion on the motion for JNOV. The trial judge is best positioned to review impartially and in detail the evidence and events at trial, and, "our decisional approach is aided by the trial judge's review ... setting forth his [or her] reasons for denying the motion for JNOV." *Railroad Dynamics, Inc. v. A. Stucki Co.*, 727 F.2d 1506, 1513, 220 USPQ 929, 936 (Fed. Cir. 1984). The appellate process materially benefits by a comprehensive summary of the course of proceedings below and an impartial review of the evidence supporting a verdict. The appellant is directed to the probative evidence contrary to his or her position and the appellate court need not sift through the entire record searching for such contrary evidence.

Second, the jury may have been persuaded by many considerations beyond just the credibility of a witness that are not always adequately reproduced in a transcript. The district court "has the same opportunity that jurors have for seeing the witnesses [and] for noting all those matters in a trial not capable of record." *Patton v. Texas & Pacific Ry.*

Co., 179 U.S. 658, 660 (1901). "The trial judge sits as the '13th juror' in evaluating the weight" to be given to all of the evidence, *Menefield v. Borg*, 881 F.2d 696, 699 (9th Cir. 1989), or in determining that a particular witness's testimony is so inherently incredible that a reasonable mind could not accept it. Beyond credibility, the weight given to particular testimony by the jury can be affected by the demeanor and responsiveness of a witness during direct testimony and upon cross-examination. These concerns are equally applicable to trials of patent issues as to any other. For instance, testifying corporate executives may be biased by a financial interest. Expert witnesses, frequently necessary to explain terminology or the general teachings of the art, may also be similarly biased. Courts have commented on the inherent discredit that may be placed upon an inventor's testimony, especially when relating to the teachings of the prior art or to the inventor's recollection of the act of invention. These considerations focus on the weight to be given to testimonial evidence and go beyond an assessment of adherence to truth. Thus, a juror's adverse appraisal of particular testimony need not rise to the level of general credibility. These issues, ostensibly a part of the record submitted for review in a sufficiency of the evidence determination, are not accessible to the appellate court unless attention is directed to them by the district court or the appellee. In short, the printed record on appeal more often than not will not reflect all the persuasive issues that may have determined the course of events at trial, even when that record is reviewed in its entirety by the appellate court. Thus, denial of a post-verdict motion, even in summary fashion, perforce provides the appellate court with the district court's overall assessment of the events at trial.

Third, a rule requiring presentation before the district court of a party's contention that a judgment lacks sufficient evidence promotes fair and equitable jurisprudence. The district court may take corrective action when confronted with error before an appeal is taken. "By failing to move for JNOV, the trial judge was denied the chance to correct any error by the jury." *Coffman v. Trickey*, 884 F.2d 1057, 1064 (8th Cir. 1989). Surely, avoidance of unnecessary appeals is to be encouraged. Additionally, when an appeal is taken based upon a contention of insufficient evidence, the appellee is afforded more timely notice by a previous post-verdict motion. Under the Federal Rules of Appellate Procedure, an appellant urging that "a finding or conclusion is unsupported by the evidence," Rule 10(b)(2), must either order an entire transcript within 10 days after filing the notice of appeal, Rule 10(b)(1), or notify the appellee of the issue presented for appeal in the same time period. Rule 10(b)(3). If no post-verdict motion has raised issues of sufficiency of the evidence, an appellant can, by including in the record a transcript of all evidence, as happened in this case, first provide the appellee with notice of the specific factual issues in its appeal in its opening appellate brief. In such circumstances, the appellee's opportunity to respond to these specific factual issues is foreshortened as compared to the opportunity to have joined the issue earlier during the period after the verdict. When, as here, the appellant cites only testimony in support of its position, this disparity in opportunities is exacerbated. The post-verdict motion thus functions as a timely notice to benefit the appellate process, because briefing and argument are more likely to be informed and informative when the issue has already been joined in post-verdict argument.

Fourth, a rule requiring formal post-verdict presentation of contested issues is not burdensome. For instance, local rules in district courts may similarly require early and explicit formulation and substantiation of contentions that have been made in conclusory fashion in pleadings. Submission of statements identifying genuine issues of material fact with accompanying substantiating affidavits may be required when opposing a motion for summary judgment. As noted by the Supreme Court, "Rule 56(e) provides that, when a properly supported motion for summary judgment is made, the adverse party 'must set forth specific facts showing that there is a genuine issue for trial.' "*Anderson v. Liberty Lobby, Inc.*, 477 U.S. 242, 250, (1986). The efficient resolution of controversies at a time of increased filings and overburdened dockets is further served by a standard for reviewability that requires a party to have set forth the specific defects in the evidentiary support for a judgment in the district court in order to obtain appellate review.

Adoption of such a rule would not deny an appellant its right to appeal. The law has long been that appellate review is not available for issues not preserved at trial. A rule that requires explicit formulation and specification of the preserved issues after the verdict does not limit the scope of appeal but merely requires the prospective appellant to present the preserved issues to the district court in a well-known and defined format after the verdict.

The rule, furthermore, stands in harmony with Rule 50 of the Federal Rules of Civil Procedure. Rule 50(b) states that "[w]henever a motion for a directed verdict ... is denied or for any reason not granted, the [district] court is deemed to have submitted the action to the jury subject to a later determination of the legal questions raised by the motion." Although a later determination of the legal question of sufficiency of the evidence by this Court would be predicated upon the filing of the post-verdict motion which renewed the contention, that predicate would not interfere with interpretation of Rule 50(b) by the district court in accordance with the procedural law of its regional circuit. The precise methodology of the district court's treatment of a previous directed verdict motion after the verdict is not a matter for us to decide. The district court remains free to defer action upon a motion for directed verdict until after the jury's deliberations. A district court may choose not to rule on a directed verdict motion made at the close of the evidence, and may, instead, under Rule 50(b), make a later determination of the legal question raised by the motion without first receiving a motion for JNOV. In such circumstances, the ruling by the district court on the deferred motion, whether by grant or denial, will have the legal consequence on appellate review of a similar ruling by the district court on a motion for JNOV, because the court's deferred consideration effectively converts the motion into a post-verdict motion. Thus, a requirement for a post-verdict motion does not affect the manner in which a district court chooses to determine legal questions raised on motions.

In sum, we conclude that we cannot review the sufficiency of the evidence after a jury verdict absent some post-verdict disposition, either by a deferred ruling or upon a post-verdict motion. Biodex's failure to present the district court with a post-verdict motion precludes appellate review of sufficiency of the evidence. Our resolution of the standard for establishing reviewability of the sufficiency of evidence in a patent case by requiring a post-verdict motion is, therefore, dispositive of that portion of the appeal directed to whether there was substantial evidence to support the special verdicts.

Notes

1. **The Federal Circuit.** What are the benefits of having a single appellate court resolve all patent appeals? What are the drawbacks of such a specialized court? Do you think there ought to be a specialized trial court which handles patent trials?

2. What are the reasons in favor of applying regional circuit law to procedural issues in patent cases in district courts? What are the arguments in favor of applying Federal Circuit law? Do you think the Federal Circuit's compromise that it will sometimes apply regional circuit law and sometimes apply Federal Circuit law is workable?

3. **What if there is no regional circuit precedent on a procedural issue?** In *Panduit Corp. v. All States Plastic Mfg. Co.,* 744 F.2d 1564, 223 USPQ 465 (Fed. Cir. 1984), the Court held that when the issue is not unique to patent law, the law of the regional circuit should be applied. What should be done if the regional circuit has not spoken to a particular issue?

> When we review procedural matters that do not pertain to patent issues, we sit as if we were the particular regional circuit court where appeals from the district court we are reviewing would normally lie. We would adjudicate the rights of the parties in accordance with the applicable regional circuit law. Where the regional circuit court has spoken on the subject, we must apply the law as stated. Where the regional circuit court has not spoken, we need to predict how that regional circuit would have decided the issue in light of the decisions of that circuit's various district courts, public policy, etc.

Id. at 1575, 223 USPQ at 472. Do you think the Federal Circuit will be good at guessing how the regional circuit would have dealt with a procedural issue? How often do you think this will arise?

E. WHOSE SUBSTANTIVE LAW TO APPLY?

How should the Federal Circuit deal with substantive issues that do not pertain to patent law? Whose substantive law should apply to an antitrust counterclaim pled in a patent infringement suit. The well-pled complaint rule dictates that such a counterclaim would fall within the Federal Circuit's jurisdiction on appeal. Does this mean that Federal Circuit law rather than regional circuit law should apply? If the patent infringement claim was dismissed early in the suit and the only issue on appeal was the antitrust counterclaim, should Federal Circuit law apply?

1. COPYRIGHT CLAIMS

In *Atari, Inc. v. JS & A Group, Inc.*, 747 F.2d 1422, 223 USPQ 1074 (Fed. Cir. 1984) (*en banc*), the Federal Circuit denied a petition to transfer to the Seventh Circuit the appeal from a district court order on a copyright count that was joined with a patent count even though the district court had granted the appellee's Rule 42(b) motion for separate trials. The sole purpose of the appellee's motion was to funnel any potential appeal of the non-patent issues to the Seventh Circuit rather than the Federal Circuit.

Atari had filed a complaint against JS & A alleging patent infringement, contributory copyright infringement, and unfair competition under both state and federal law. The district court granted a preliminary injunction on the copyright count. JS & A appealed to the Federal Circuit after the district court granted the Rule 42(b) motion for separate trials. The Federal Circuit, sitting *en banc*, rejected Atari's claim that the separation order removed jurisdiction from the Federal Circuit. The court held that a denial of the transfer motion would be consistent with legislative history and purposes for creating the Federal Circuit. The court noted that Congress explicitly rejected "issue jurisdiction" and instead chose "arising under jurisdiction" where the Federal Circuit had jurisdiction over an appeal if the statutory basis for the district court's jurisdiction was the patent segment of 35 U.S.C. § 1338(a).

> Congress recognized that non-patent claims might accompany a patent claim in a single complaint. It could have provided appellate jurisdiction in this court only over judgments entered on the patent claim. It did not. It designed and enacted a statute that provided jurisdiction in this court over appeals from decisions in "cases" in which the district court's jurisdiction "was based, in whole *or in part*, on Section 1338." [Emphasis added]. Thus our jurisdiction here is mandated by the plain language of the statute, the best indication of the scope of a court's jurisdiction.

Atari, 747 F.2d at 1429, 223 USPQ at 1079. Although jurisdiction over the appeal resides with the Federal Circuit, the Court held that it would apply regional circuit law to the non-patent law issues in cases appealed to the Federal Circuit. *Id.* at 1438–39, 223 USPQ at 1086–87.

2. TRADEMARK OR TRADE DRESS ISSUES

In *Elmer v. ICC Fabricating, Inc.*, 67 F.3d 1571, 36 USPQ2d 1417 (Fed. Cir. 1995), the Federal Circuit held that regional circuit law applies when deciding trademark, trade dress, and other unfair competition claims under Section 45 of the Lanham Act. In another 1995 decision emanating from a Lanham Act claim, the Federal Circuit stated, "a district court judge should not be expected to look over his shoulder to the law in this circuit, save as to those claims over which our subject matter jurisdiction is exclusive." *Imagineering, Inc. v. Van Klassens, Inc.*, 53 F.3d 1260, 1268, 34 USPQ2d 1526, 1533 (Fed. Cir. 1995).

3. ANTITRUST CLAIMS

In *Nobelpharma AB v. Implant Innovations, Inc.*, 141 F.3d 1059, 1067–68, 46 USPQ2d 1097, 1103–04 (Fed. Cir. 1998) (*en banc*) (citations omitted), the Federal Circuit held:

> As a general proposition, when reviewing a district court's judgment involving federal antitrust law, we are guided by the law of the regional circuit in which that district court sits. However, we apply our own law, not regional circuit law, to resolve issues that clearly involve our exclusive jurisdiction.

> Whether conduct in the prosecution of a patent is sufficient to strip a patentee of its immunity from the antitrust laws is one of those issues that clearly involves our exclusive jurisdiction over patent cases. It follows that whether a patent infringement suit is based on a fraudulently procured patent impacts our exclusive jurisdiction.

> Moreover, an antitrust claim premised on stripping a patentee of its immunity from the antitrust laws is typically raised as a counterclaim by a defendant in a patent infringement suit. Because most cases involving these issues will therefore be appealed to this court, we conclude that we should decide these issues as a matter of Federal Circuit law, rather than rely on various regional precedents. We arrive at this conclusion because we are in the best position to create a uniform body of federal law on this subject and thereby avoid the "danger of confusion [that] might be enhanced if this court were to embark on an effort to interpret the laws" of the regional circuits. Accordingly, we hereby change our precedent and hold that whether conduct in procuring or enforcing a patent is sufficient to strip a patentee of its immunity from the antitrust laws is to be decided as a question of Federal Circuit law. This conclusion applies equally to all antitrust claims premised on the bringing of a patent infringement suit. Therefore, *Cygnus*, 92 F.3d at 1161, 39 USPQ2d at 1672 , *Loctite*, 781 F.2d at 875, 228 USPQ at 99 , and *Atari*, 747 F.2d at 1438–40, 223 USPQ at 1086–87, are expressly overruled to the extent they hold otherwise. However, we will continue to apply the law of the appropriate regional circuit to issues involving other elements of antitrust law such as relevant market, market power, damages, etc., as those issues are not unique to patent law, which is subject to our exclusive jurisdiction.

Problems

Whose law should apply to the following issues?

1.   Grant of a preliminary injunction against patent infringement. *See Reebok Int'l Ltd. v. J. Baker, Inc.*, 32 F.3d 1552, 31 USPQ2d 1781 (Fed. Cir. 1994).

2.   Grant of preliminary injunction against trademark infringement. *See Black & Decker, Inc. v. Hoover Serv. Ctr.*, 886 F.2d 1285, 12 USPQ2d 1250 (Fed. Cir. 1989).

3.   Determining the amount of damages to award for contempt in a patent infringement suit (violating the injunctions). *See Graves v. Kemscop Group, Inc.*, 864 F.2d 754, 9 USPQ2d 1404 (Fed. Cir. 1988).

4.   Measuring relevance for discovery in a patent infringement suit. *See Micro Motion, Inc. v. Kane Steel Co.*, 894 F.2d 1318, 13 USPQ2d 1696 (Fed. Cir. 1990).

5.   Review of jury finding in a patent infringement suit. *See Biodex Corp. v. Loredan Biomedical, Inc.*, 946 F.2d 850, 20 USPQ2d 1252 (Fed. Cir. 1991).

6.   Standard of appellate review on denial of motion for JNOV. *See Moxness Prods., Inc. v. Xomed, Inc.*, 891 F.2d 890, 13 USPQ2d 1169 (Fed. Cir. 1989).

7.   Whether a party is a "prevailing party" and therefore entitled to costs pursuant to Federal Rule of Civil Procedure 54(d). *See Manildra Mill. Corp. v. Ogilvie Mills, Inc.*, 76 F.3d 1178, 37 USPQ2d 1707 (Fed. Cir. 1996).

8.   Disqualification of attorneys for conflicts. *See Panduit Corp. v. All States Plastic Mfg. Co.*, 744 F.2d 1564, 223 USPQ 465 (Fed. Cir. 1984).

9.   When a district court can award sanctions for discovery abuses. *See Refac Int'l, Ltd. v. Hitachi, Ltd.*, 921 F.2d 1247, 16 USPQ2d 1347 (Fed. Cir. 1990).

10.   Whether a court has personal jurisdiction over a defendant. *See Beverly Hills Fan Co. v. Royal Sovereign Corp.*, 21 F.3d 1558, 30 USPQ2d 1001 (Fed. Cir. 1994).

Chapter Two

THE PARTIES: WHO CAN BRING SUIT?

INTRODUCTION

A patent infringement suit is brought when two parties dispute the validity and scope of a patent. The suit may be brought by the owner of the patent (the inventor or assignee or in some cases the exclusive licensee) charging the defendant with infringing the patent. Suit may also be brought by a potential infringer seeking a declaratory judgment as to the scope and validity of the patent. If the patent is issued to two persons jointly, each has a one-half undivided interest in the patent. Each co-owner is free to operate, assign or license under the patent without an accounting to the other co-owners. For example, if Pete Rose and Cal Ripkin jointly invent and patent a new baseball glove, Pete can license the glove to Roberto Alomar or anyone else without consulting Cal and he does not have to share the royalties with Cal. However, co-owners may not act independently of each other with respect to infringement suits. In order to maintain an infringement action, all co-owners must voluntarily join the suit. If Brady Anderson makes a glove that infringes the patent, Pete cannot sue Brady unless Cal agrees to bring suit.

A. RUN OF THE MILL INFRINGEMENT SUITS

Under 35 U.S.C. § 271, the patentee can bring suit against anyone who makes, uses, offers for sale, or sells the patented invention, actively induces or contributes to infringement. Consequently, several different parties may be liable for infringement. The patent owner can chose whom to sue from amongst these potential defendants based on a number of factors such as the financial interest in the infringing activity, the ability to pay damages, or the location of the parties. Ordinarily it is advisable to sue the party with the greatest financial interest in the infringing activity first to resolve the bulk of the dispute. If successful, the parties with lesser interests can often be persuaded to settle or take a license. However, it may be in the patentee's best interest to sue smaller infringers or infringers with smaller interests first because these parties would not have the resources to mount as significant a defense. This could result in binding precedent regarding issues like construction of the patent claims and validity which would assist the patentee in later suits.

1. DIRECT INFRINGEMENT

STATUTORY PROVISION—35 U.S.C. § 271 (a):

Except as otherwise provided in this title, whoever without authority makes, uses, offers to sell or sells any patented invention, within the United States or imports into the United States any patented invention during the term of the patent therefor, infringes the patent.

2. INDUCED AND CONTRIBUTORY INFRINGEMENT

STATUTORY PROVISION—35 U.S.C. § 271 (b):

Whoever actively induces infringement of a patent shall be liable as an infringer.

Inducement to infringe is when one causes, urges, encourages, or aids another in the infringement of a patent. Inducement under § 271(b) is often described as activity that "aids and abets" infringement. In order to succeed in a suit for inducement to infringe, the inducer must specifically intend to induce direct infringement of the patent and a direct infringement must result. The intent does not have to be proven by direct evidence; circumstantial evidence is sufficient. The elements for inducement to infringe are:

(i) direct infringement by another;

(ii) specific intent to cause the acts which constitute infringement; and

(iii) an affirmative act.

Although the sellers of a device with substantial noninfringing uses will not be liable under § 271(c), they may still be liable for inducement to infringe if active steps are taken to encourage direct infringement. Examples of such active steps include: providing instructions and plans through labels or advertising that enable the buyer to use the product in an infringing manner. The defendant must have knowledge of the patent to be liable for inducing infringement. *See Insituform Tech., Inc. v. Cat Contracting, Inc.,* 161 F.3d 688, 48 USPQ2d 1610 (Fed. Cir. 1998).

STATUTORY PROVISION—35 U.S.C. § 271 (c):

Whoever offers to sell or sells within the United States or imports into the United States a component of a patented machine, manufacture, combination or composition, or a material or apparatus for use in practicing a patented process, constituting a material part of the invention, knowing the same to be especially made or especially adapted for use in an infringement of such patent, and not a staple article or commodity of commerce suitable for substantial noninfringing use, shall be liable as a contributory infringer.

Contributory infringement makes someone liable who makes, uses or sells less than the whole invention; for example, someone who is selling a non-staple article of commerce which she knows to be specially designed for an infringing use. A component is not a staple article of commerce if it has substantial noninfringing uses. Direct infringement must be proven to succeed on a claim for contributory infringement. *Met-Coil Sys. Corp. v. Korners Unlimited, Inc.*, 803 F.2d 684, 687, 231 USPQ 474, 477 (Fed. Cir. 1986). To maintain an action for contributory infringement, the patentee must be able to identify a direct infringer. Finally, the person supplying the non-staple materials must have knowledge of the patent. The elements for contributory infringement are:

(i) direct infringement by another;

(ii) knowledge of the patent;

(iii) knowledge that the component was designed for an infringing use;

(iv) the component is a material part of the patented product; and

(v) the component is not a staple article of commerce.

The following case highlights the different levels of intent required for contributory and induced infringement.

HEWLETT-PACKARD CO. v. BAUSCH & LOMB INC.

909 F.2d 1464, 15 USPQ2d 1525 (Fed. Cir. 1990)

Before RICH and NEWMAN, Circuit Judges, and COWEN, Senior Circuit Judge.

RICH, Circuit Judge.

Bausch & Lomb Incorporated (B & L) appeals from the September 13, 1989 Judgment of the United States District Court for the Northern District of California, holding U.S. Pat. No. 4,384,298 (LaBarre) valid and infringed by B & L. Hewlett–Packard Company (HP) cross-appeals from that portion of the Judgment holding that B & L had not actively induced infringement of the LaBarre patent subsequent to September of 1985. We affirm.

Background

Two patents are discussed extensively throughout this opinion. The first is the patent in suit, LaBarre, which is assigned to HP. The second is U.S. Pat. No. Re 31,684 (Yeiser), which is assigned to B & L and which is the sole piece of prior art argued by B & L to invalidate the LaBarre patent. Both patents relate to X–Y plotters used to create a two-dimensional plot, such as a chart or a graph, on a sheet of paper. Such plotters can be broadly divided into two categories: one in which the paper is held stationary and a pen is attached to a gantry movable in one direction (the Y-direction) and a carriage movable in a second, orthogonal direction (the X-direction); and another in which the paper is moved in the Y-direction, while the pen is attached to a carriage movable in the X-direction. Both LaBarre and Yeiser relate to this second type of plotter, and both show that the movement of the paper in the Y-direction can be effectuated by one or more pairs of pinch rollers between which the paper is placed.

In order to draw accurate plots, it is critical in devices like those disclosed in Yeiser and LaBarre that the paper be moved back and forth without slippage between the paper and the pinch rollers. With this in mind, Yeiser teaches that at least one of the pinch wheels should have a surface with a high coefficient of friction formed "by knurling or by a layer of rubber or the like." LaBarre, on the other hand, teaches that an efficient way to effectively eliminate slippage between the rollers and the paper is to simply cover one of the pinch wheels with silicon carbide grit. The grit not only increases the friction between the pinch wheels and the paper, but also causes small indentations to be formed in the paper. These indentations repeatedly mate with the grit as the paper is moved back and forth in the Y-direction, thus further inhibiting slippage between the pinch wheels and the paper. Due to this mating effect between the grit and the indentations in the paper, HP urges that the LaBarre printer should be considered to be a "positive drive" plotter, wherein the paper is drawn along using "teeth" (i.e., the grit) which engage in "holes" (i.e., the indentations) in the paper, as opposed to a "friction drive" plotter, wherein the moving force on the paper is caused simply by the friction between the wheels and the paper.

B & L, through a division called Houston Instruments, began selling plotters having grit-covered pinch wheels ("grit wheel plotters") sometime in late 1982 or early 1983. However, in September of 1985, B & L entered into a "PURCHASE AGREEMENT" with Ametek, Inc. (Ametek) pursuant to which B & L sold the Houston Instruments division (including all "assets, properties, rights and business") to Ametek for a total purchase price of $43,000,000. Concurrent with execution of the PURCHASE AGREEMENT, B & L and Ametek also entered into an "AGREEMENT WITH RESPECT TO PATENTS," in which the parties agreed that, among other things, (1) B & L would grant Ametek a license under the Yeiser patent; (2) B & L would indemnify Ametek against liability for infringing the LaBarre patent up to a cap of $4.6 million; (3) B & L and Ametek would jointly work toward developing a plotter which would not infringe the LaBarre patent; and (4) Ametek would comply with a so-called "gag order;" (i.e., would not communicate with HP concerning the LaBarre patent).

HP brought the present suit against B & L in May of 1986, accusing B & L of direct infringement of the LaBarre patent for the time period prior to the sale of Houston Instruments to Ametek, and of active inducement of infringement under 35 U.S.C. § 271(b) for the period subsequent to the sale of Houston Instruments. As to the charge of direct infringement, B & L admitted infringement, but defended on the grounds that, among other things, the asserted claims of LaBarre were invalid for obviousness under 35 U.S.C. § 103 in view of the Yeiser patent. As to the charge of inducing infringement, B & L denied that its activities surrounding the sale of Houston Instruments to Ametek in September of 1985 constituted active inducement of infringement.

The district court, in an extensive Findings of Fact, Conclusions of Law and Order Thereon, found claim 1 of LaBarre would not have been obvious in view of Yeiser and that B & L was liable for infringement prior to the sale of Houston Instruments in September of 1985. However, the district court further found that B & L did not actively induce infringement of the LaBarre patent by Ametek under 35 U.S.C. § 271(b), and so found no liability subsequent to the 1985 sale.

OPINION

B. Active Inducement—35 U.S.C. § 271(b)

Section 271(b) provides that "Whoever actively induces infringement of a patent shall be liable as an infringer." At the outset, we feel that it is necessary to make clear the distinction, often confused, between active inducement of infringement under § 271(b) and contributory infringement under § 271(c). Prior to the enactment of the Patent Act of 1952, there was no statute which defined what constituted infringement. However, infringement was judicially divided into two categories: "direct infringement," which was the unauthorized making, using or selling of the patented invention, and "contributory infringement," which was any other activity where, although not technically making, using or selling, the defendant displayed sufficient culpability to be held liable as an infringer. Such liability was under a theory of joint tortfeasance, wherein one who intentionally caused, or aided and abetted, the commission of a tort by another was jointly and severally liable with the primary tortfeasor.

The most common pre–1952 contributory infringement cases dealt with the situation where a seller would sell a component which was not itself technically covered by the claims of a product or process patent but which had no other use except with the claimed product or process. In such cases, although a plaintiff was required to show intent to cause infringement in order to establish contributory infringement, many courts held that such intent could be presumed because the component had no substantial non-infringing use.

The legislative history of the Patent Act of 1952 indicates that no substantive change in the scope of what constituted "contributory infringement" was intended by the enactment of § 271. *See Aro Mfg. Co. v. Convertible Top Replacement Co.*, 377 U.S. 476, 485–86 (1964) ("*Aro II*"). However, the single concept of "contributory infringement" was divided between §§ 271(b) and 271(c) into "active inducement" (a type of direct infringement) and "contributory infringement," respectively. Section 271(c) codified the prohibition against the common type of contributory infringement referred to above, and made clear that only proof of a defendant's knowledge, not intent, that his activity cause infringement was necessary to establish contributory infringement.[3] Section 271(b) codified the prohibition against all other types of activity which, prior to 1952, had constituted "contributory infringement."

That, however, leaves open the question of what level of knowledge or intent is required to find active inducement under § 271(b). On its face, § 271(b) is much broader than § 271(c) and certainly does not speak of any intent requirement to prove active inducement. However, in view of the very definition of "active inducement" in pre–1952 case law and the fact that § 271(b) was intended as merely a codification of pre–1952 law, we are of the opinion that proof of actual intent to cause the acts which constitute the infringement is a necessary prerequisite to finding active inducement.[4] And it is proof of that intent which is missing in the present case.

Looking at the totality of events surrounding the sale of Houston Instruments, it is clear that B & L was merely interested in divesting itself of Houston Instruments at the highest possible price. B & L had no interest in what Ametek did with Houston Instruments and certainly did not care one way or the other whether Houston Instruments, under Ametek's ownership, continued to make grit wheel plotters. HP attempts to make much of the fact that part of the sale of Houston Instruments included the sale of specific plans for making grit wheel plotters as well as key personnel knowledgeable in this area. However, this is simply a result of the fact that Houston Instruments was sold "lock, stock and barrel" (i.e. with all "assets, properties, rights and business" included). B & L had no interest in nor control over what Ametek chose to do with the plans or the personnel. In this regard, it should also be kept in mind that grit wheel plotters constituted only a portion of Houston Instruments' sales. The PURCHASE AGREEMENT between B & L and Ametek indicates that Houston Instruments was also in the business of developing, manufacturing and selling analog and digital recorders, digitizers, computer-assisted drafting equipment, and other products.

We do not find any of the remaining details of the agreement between B & L and Ametek to be sufficiently probative of intent to induce infringement. The grant of a license from B & L to Ametek under the Yeiser patent is not probative of any intent to induce infringement. The license agreement between B & L and Ametek did not purport to give Ametek the right to make, use and sell X–Y plotters; it merely freed Ametek from whatever bar the Yeiser patent would have been to such activity. Both parties clearly knew, as evidenced by their discussion of the LaBarre patent in the AGREEMENT WITH RESPECT TO PATENTS, that other patents could still be a bar to making, using and

---

3. Although not clear on the face of the statute, subsequent case law held that § 271(c) required not only knowledge that the component was especially made or adapted for a particular use but also knowledge of the patent which proscribed that use. *See Aro II*, 377 U.S. at 488.

4. *See Water Techs. v. Calco, Ltd.,* 850 F.2d 660, 668, 7 USPQ2d 1097, 1103 (Fed. Cir. 1988), holding such intent is necessary and that it may be shown by circumstantial evidence.

selling X–Y plotters. The agreement between B & L and Ametek to work together to find a way to avoid infringement of the LaBarre patent establishes, if anything, an intent by B & L not to induce infringement by helping Ametek to develop a plotter which would not infringe.

The most troubling aspect of the agreement between B & L and Ametek is the indemnification clause. Cases have held that an indemnification agreement will generally not establish an intent to induce infringement, but that such intent can be inferred when the primary purpose is to overcome the deterrent effect that the patent laws have on would-be infringers. *See* Miller, "Some Views on the Law of Patent Infringement by Inducement," 53 J. Pat. Off. Soc'y 86, 150–51 (1971), and the cases cited therein. While overcoming the deterrent of the patent laws might have been the ultimate effect of the indemnification agreement in the present case, we cannot say that that was its purpose. We are once again led back to our conclusion that what B & L really wanted out of this agreement was the sale of Houston Instruments at the greatest possible price. Therefore B & L agreed that, if Ametek should wish to continue the manufacture and sale of grit-wheel plotters, B & L would bear the risk of those plotters ultimately being found to infringe the LaBarre patent. The indemnification agreement certainly facilitated the sale of Houston Instruments at the particular price at which it was sold, but we cannot agree that B & L used it to induce infringement by Ametek.

Conclusion

The district court's decision holding the LaBarre patent valid and holding B & L not liable for the period subsequent to the sale of Houston Instruments is affirmed.

Notes

1. As the preceding case demonstrates, a standard agreement to indemnify another for liability for patent infringement does not normally constitute active inducement. Can you think of examples of behavior that would constitute inducement to infringe?

2. Despite the fact that direct infringement is required in order to succeed in a claim for either contributory or induced infringement, courts have held that the direct infringer does not have to be joined in a suit against a contributory infringer. *Upjohn Co. v. Syntro Corp.,* 14 USPQ2d 1469, 1473 (D. Del. 1990).

3. **Repair/Reconstruction Doctrine**: Direct infringement includes the making of a patented article without authority. After purchasing a patented product from the patentee, the buyer has authority to use and to resell the item. The buyer also has the right to repair the patented article if it breaks down, but she is not entitled to reconstruct the article. Such a reconstruction would constitute direct infringement because the buyer would be making the patented product. The doctrine of repair/reconstruction often arises when a manufacturer is charged with contributory infringement because it is selling a component part of the patented invention. Contributo-

ry infringement requires that a direct infringement occur with the product. The buyer's reconstruction is that direct infringement. In *Sandvik Aktiebolag v. E.J. Co.*, 121 F.3d 669, 43 USPQ2d 1620 (Fed. Cir. 1997), the Federal Circuit for the first time held that replacement of a part constituted an infringing reconstruction. The court articulated the following factors that should be considered in determining whether an action is a repair or reconstruction:

> There are a number of factors to consider in determining whether a defendant has made a new article, after the device has become spent, including the nature of the actions by the defendant, the nature of the device and how it is designed (namely, whether one of the components of the patented combination has a shorter useful life than the whole), whether a market has developed to manufacture or service the part at issue and objective evidence of the intent of the patentee.

In *Sandvik*, the court held that replacing a carbide drill tip constituted an impermissible reconstruction.

> Under the totality of the circumstances, we hold in this case that E.J.'s actions are a reconstruction. By E.J.'s own admission, the drill is "spent" when the tip can no longer be resharpened unless it is retipped. In fact, the record reveals that E.J.'s customers may elect not to retip and inform E.J. to discard the drill instead.
>
> Moreover, the nature of the work done by E.J. shows that retipping is more like reconstruction than repair. E.J. does not just attach a new part for a worn part, but rather must go though several steps to replace, configure and integrate the tip onto the shank. It has to break the worn or damaged tip from the shank by heating it to 1300 degrees Fahrenheit. It brazes to the shank a new rectangular block of carbide and grinds and machines it to the proper diameter and creates the point. Thereafter, the tip is honed and sharpened, grinding the rake surfaces and the center of the point and honing the edges. These actions are effectively a re-creation of the patented invention after it is spent. This is not a case where it is clear that the patented device has a useful life much longer than that of certain parts which wear out quickly.... The drill tip was not manufactured to be a replaceable part, although it could be resharpened a number of times to extend its life. It was not intended or expected to have a life of temporary duration in comparison to the drill shank. And finally, the tip was not attached to the shank in a manner to be easily detachable ...
>
> Evidence of development in the industry could also be a factor tending to prove that there is a reasonable expectation that the part of the patented combination wears out quickly and requires frequent replacement. In this case, there is no evidence of a substantial market for drill retipping of the sort required for the Sandvik drill. There is no evidence of large numbers of customers retipping these drills or of companies (other than E.J.) offering to retip these drills. No one manufactures replacement tips for Sandvik's drill and

although some customers opt to retip the drill only a small percentage of all drills manufactured are retipped.

Finally, there was no intent evidenced by the patentee that would support E.J.'s argument that replacement of the tips is a repair. The evidence shows that Sandvik never intended for its drills to be retipped. It did not manufacture or sell replacement drill tips. It did not publish instructions on how to retip its patented drills or suggest that the drills could or should be retipped. Sandvik was aware that the drill tip would need occasional resharpening and instructed its customer on how to resharpen the tip. There is, therefore, no objective evidence that Sandvik's drill tip was intended to be a replaceable part. Although the repair or reconstruction issue does not turn on the intention of the patentee alone, the fact that no replacement drill tips have ever been made or sold by the patentee is consistent with the conclusion that replacement of the carbide tip is not a permissible repair.

Although there is no bright-line test for determining whether reconstruction or repair has occurred, we conclude based on all of the facts in this case that E.J. is reconstructing an otherwise spent device when it retips Sandvik's drills.

121 F.3d at 673–74, 43 USPQ2d at 1623–24 (citations omitted).

Compare *Sandvik* with *Aro Mfg. Co. v. Convertible Top Replacement Co.*, 365 U.S. 336, 128 USPQ 354 (1961) (replacement of the fabric on a convertible top is a repair); *Porter v. Farmers Supply Serv., Inc.*, 790 F.2d 882, 229 USPQ 814 (Fed. Cir. 1986) (replacing cutting discs on a tomato harvester is a repair); *FMC Corp. v. Up–Right, Inc.*, 21 F.3d 1073, 30 USPQ2d 1361 (Fed. Cir. 1994) (sequential replacement of parts in a patented machine was permissible repair); *Sage Products, Inc. v. Devon Indus., Inc.*, 45 F.3d 1575, 33 USPQ2d 1765 (Fed. Cir. 1995) (replacement of a removable inner container in the patented contaminated surgical instrument disposal system was a permissible repair).

4. **The Exhaustion Doctrine.** Whether there is patent infringement will also turn on whether the patentee has already received compensation for the accused infringing act such that an "exhaustion" of the patentee's remedies has occurred. Under the exhaustion doctrine, the patent owner's exclusive rights are "exhausted" upon the first authorized sale of the patented product. *See Mallinckrodt, Inc. v. Medipart, Inc.*, 976 F.2d 700, 24 USPQ2d 1173 (Fed. Cir. 1992). When a patentee sells a product without restriction, the patentee in effect, promises not to interfere with the purchaser's full enjoyment of the purchased product in exchange for the paid price, thereby entering into an implied license agreement. *See Hewlett–Packard Co. v. Repeat–O–Type Stencil Mfg. Corp.*, 123 F.3d 1445, 1451, 43 USPQ2d 1650, 1655 (Fed. Cir. 1997). A complaint should not be filed against a party acting under an implied license allowing use of the patented device or for re-sale of the product to a subsequent purchaser.

3. EXPORTATION AND IMPORTATION

As commerce becomes increasingly global, a patentee needs to be aware of his rights regarding an infringer's exporting and importing activities.

a.   *Exportation*

STATUTORY PROVISION—35 U.S.C. § 271 (f):

(1) Whoever without authority supplies or causes to be supplied in or from the United States all or a substantial portion of the components of a patented invention, where such components are uncombined in whole or in part, in such manner as to actively induce the combination of such components outside of the United States in a manner that would infringe the patent if such combination occurred within the United States, shall be liable as an infringer.

(2) Whoever without authority supplies or causes to be supplied in or from the United States any component of a patented invention that is especially made or especially adapted for use in the invention and not a staple article or commodity of commerce suitable for substantial noninfringing use, where such component is uncombined in whole or in part, knowing that such component is so made or adapted and intending that such component will be combined outside of the United States in a manner that would infringe the patent if such combination occurred within the United States, shall be liable as an infringer.

In *Deepsouth Packing Co. v. Laitram Corp.*, 406 U.S. 518, 173 USPQ 769 (1972), the Supreme Court held that an American company does not infringe a patent for a shrimp deveiner when it manufactures all of the parts and exports them to foreign buyers with instructions on how to assemble the two unassembled parts (assembly abroad took less than an hour). The Court held that such conduct did not technically fall within the § 271(a) prohibition against making a patented invention. In 1984, Congress responded by enacting § 271(f)(1) to make liable as an infringer anyone who supplies all or a substantial portion of a patented combination that if put together in the United States would constitute infringement. Section 271(f)(1) is similar to active inducement.

Section 271(f)(2), like contributory infringement, makes liable for infringement anyone who exports a component of a patented invention which is not a staple article of commerce *intending* that the component will be combined in a foreign country in a manner that would infringe the patent if the combination had occurred in the United States. Notice that § 271(f)(2), unlike contributory infringement under § 271(c), requires a showing of intent.

b.   *Process Patents and Importation*

STATUTORY PROVISION—35 U.S.C. § 271 (g):

Whoever without authority imports into the United States or offers to sell, sells, or uses within the United States a product which is made if the importation, offer to sell, sale, or use of the product occurs during patent, no remedy may be granted for infringement on account of the noncommercial use or retail sale of a product unless there is no adequate remedy under this title for infringement on account of the importation or other use, offer to sell, or sale of that product. A product which is made by a patented process will, for purposes of this title, not be considered to be so made after—

(1) it is materially changed by subsequent processes; or

(2) it becomes a trivial and nonessential component of another product.

Section 271(g) closes another loophole which had allowed defendants to avoid direct infringement. Prior to the enactment of § 271(g), a defendant could import into the United States products made by a patented process (as long as the process was performed abroad) and sell them in the United States without infringing the process patent. Under § 271(g), this action now constitutes infringement unless the product which is made by the patented process is materially changed by subsequent processes or becomes a trivial and nonessential component of another product. Do you think that a company importing camcorders which contain a semiconductor imaging chip manufactured by a semiconductor fabrication process patented in the United States will be liable for infringement? What if the performance of the imaging chip is what makes the camcorder commercially successful?

B. DECLARATORY JUDGMENT ACTIONS

STATUTORY PROVISION—28 U.S.C. § 2201 (a):

In a case of actual controversy within its jurisdiction, . . . any court of the United States, upon the filing of an appropriate pleading, may declare the rights and other legal relations of any interested party seeking such declaration, whether or not further relief is or could be sought. Any such declaration shall have the force and effect of a final judgment or decree and shall be reviewable as such.

The single largest use of declaratory judgment actions in patent infringement suits is in the form of a counterclaim brought by the alleged infringer for a declaration of invalidity, unenforceability, and noninfringement.

1. DECLARATORY JUDGMENT ACTION BROUGHT BY IN-FRINGER

Declaratory judgment actions can be a sword for the alleged infringer as well as a shield. In addition to resolving the infringement issue so that the alleged infringer can resume its normal business activities without the threat of an infringement action looming over it, the declaratory judgment gives the alleged infringer the additional benefit of choosing the forum and the time of the suit. This can be a strategic benefit in a litigation. By controlling the forum, the alleged infringer can choose what it perceives to be the most favorable locale. If the alleged infringer is a large corporation, it may want to bring suit in a locale where it employs a large number of people, or where jurors are more likely to have more technical skills (such as the Northern District of California) or where the trial will proceed quickly (like the Eastern District of Virginia, affectionately known as the Rocket Docket). A speedy trial may be important to a defendant who wishes to avoid investing additional resources in further development or manufacture of a potentially infringing product. Sometimes, being able to get a quick decision is as important as the outcome to a company which needs to make investment decisions. Of course the alleged infringer may be limited as to where suit can be brought by jurisdictional and venue issues discussed in Chapter Three. By controlling the timing, the alleged infringer could catch the patentee off-guard.

Courts are not in the business of issuing advisory opinions. Accordingly, the alleged infringer can only bring a declaratory judgment action against the patentee if an actual controversy exists. Whether an actual controversy exists is a question of law the declaratory plaintiff bears the burden of proving. An actual controversy is said to exist in a patent case when there is:

1. an explicit threat or other action by the patentee, which creates an objectively reasonable apprehension on the part of the declaratory plaintiff that it will face an infringement suit; and

2. present activity which could constitute infringement or concrete steps taken with the intent to conduct such activity.

As you might imagine, difficulty arises in establishing that there was action by the patentee which gave the alleged infringer a reasonable apprehension of being sued. If there is no express threat, such as a cease and desist letter, then the court will consider the totality of the circumstances to determine whether there is a reasonable apprehension. Whether there is a reasonable apprehension of suit is an objective test. The alleged infringer's subjective belief is irrelevant. The burden of proving that an actual controversy exists at the time the suit is filed is on the person bringing the action (action taken by the patentee after the suit is filed cannot be used to establish an actual controversy).

Some of the factors which have been found to influence whether the declaratory judgment plaintiff had a reasonable apprehension of suit include: (1) patentee's willingness and capacity to engage in litigation to enforce its patent rights: has the patentee been involved in many patent suits, has the patentee filed other suits against the declaratory judgment plaintiff or against the declaratory judgment plaintiff's customers or competitors, how long ago were these suits (the further in the past, the less relevant); (2) the relationship between the parties when the suit was filed, were the parties involved in on-going negotiations, who prompted the negotiations; and (3) the nature of any contact between the parties regarding the patent in suit: did the patentee offer a license to the declaratory judgment plaintiff, did the patentee accuse the declaratory judgment plaintiff of infringement, did the patentee threaten suit, was this letter sent only to the declaratory judgment plaintiff or was it part of a mass mailing.

The following case discusses the discretionary nature of declaratory judgment jurisdiction as well as what constitutes a reasonable apprehension of suit. Do you agree that there was a reasonable apprehension of suit in the following case?

EMC CORP. v. NORAND CORP.

89 F.3d 807, 39 USPQ2d 1451 (Fed. Cir. 1996)

Before MAYER, SCHALL, and BRYSON, Circuit Judges.

BRYSON, Circuit Judge.

EMC Corporation filed an action in the United States District Court for the District of Massachusetts seeking a declaratory judgment against Norand Corporation. EMC requested that the court declare certain patents owned by Norand to be invalid and to declare that EMC did not infringe those patents. The district court dismissed the action, exercising its discretion to decline jurisdiction under the Declaratory Judgment Act, 28 U.S.C. § 2201(a). Because we conclude that the district court did not abuse the broad discretion accorded it by the Act, we affirm.

I

The parties present widely divergent versions of the circumstances that led to EMC's filing of its request for a declaratory judgment. Because the district court decided this case without making findings of fact, we confine ourselves to those facts that are undisputed.

EMC manufactures disk drive storage subsystems. Norand does not manufacture or sell such devices but holds four United States patents on technology in that general field. In August 1994, W. Mark Goode, the president of a consulting company representing Norand, wrote to an EMC vice president suggesting that Norand and EMC initiate license negotiations related to Norand's patents. After receiving no reply to his letter, Goode sent a letter to Paul Dacier, EMC's General Counsel, again suggesting license negotiations. In the letter, Goode stated that Norand had "requested that we simply turn the matter over to McAndrews, Held & Malloy [Norand's outside patent counsel] for action," but that he wanted to have a preliminary business discussion, "perhaps avoiding this matter escalating into a contentious legal activity."

EMC officials agreed to meet with Norand. Norand's outside patent counsel then contacted EMC and requested that the meetings not be used as a basis for filing a declaratory judgment action. EMC and Norand held meetings in September and October 1994 in which the parties discussed the potential sale or license of the patents. EMC alleges that Norand's representatives made explicit claims of infringement by EMC at the meetings; Norand denies that its representatives made any such claims or otherwise threatened suit.

At the parties' third meeting, held on January 19, 1995, Norand informed EMC that there were six other companies in EMC's market that Norand was approaching regarding the sale or licensing of its patents. Goode subsequently sent a letter to EMC officials confirming plans for a fourth meeting and assuring EMC that he would call later in the week to arrange a time for the meeting. Three days later, however, EMC filed its declaratory judgment action in the United States District

Court for the District of Massachusetts. A telephone message left by an EMC attorney on the day after the filing indicated that EMC had taken the step because its management "thought it was in their interest to protect themselves first and continue discussions." The parties held two further meetings while the action was pending and scheduled a third meeting, but that meeting was later canceled.

Norand moved to dismiss the complaint for lack of jurisdiction on the ground that EMC had failed to establish that there was a justiciable case or controversy between the parties. In addressing the motion, the district court first considered whether Norand's conduct gave rise to a reasonable apprehension that Norand would sue EMC for patent infringement. The court found that making that determination would be a significant undertaking and would involve a close question. The court therefore decided that it would not determine whether EMC could prove a case or controversy for jurisdictional purposes, but that it would exercise its discretion under the Declaratory Judgment Act to decline to entertain the action.

The court found that the parties were still in active license or sale negotiations, that Norand was not a competitor of EMC, and that it was considering entering negotiations with others as well. Under those circumstances, the court concluded, to entertain the declaratory judgment action would be inconsistent with the purposes of the Declaratory Judgment Act. In particular, the court found, to allow a declaratory judgment action to proceed under such circumstances would encourage parties who were negotiating with patentees to use the declaratory judgment procedure to improve their bargaining positions and to impede negotiations between patentees and other potential licensees or buyers. The court explained that a plaintiff in EMC's position

> may be able to obtain a more favorable bargaining position with the defendant [patentee] by filing a declaratory judgment action, thereby inducing if not virtually forcing defendant [patentee] to consider whether as a practical matter it would be better to avoid litigation costs and any risk of adverse rulings that might render their patents less valuable. It would be reasonable to expect that, if there is in fact a market for the patents, the mere pendency of the lawsuit may negatively affect the value of the defendant's patents in that market and the price any potential purchaser, either the plaintiff or another prospective purchaser, might be willing to pay.

The court added that a plaintiff such as EMC "may prefer that a defendant, such as Norand, own a patent rather than that a competitor of the plaintiff own the patent," as a competitor might be more likely to try to enforce the patent against EMC than Norand would. In that setting, the district court concluded, the pendency of a declaratory judgment action might have the effect of impeding the sale of the patent to the plaintiff's competitor, regardless of whether it was filed for that reason. The court therefore determined that to exercise its discretionary jurisdiction in this case would create "an incentive structure that is inconsistent with the public interest in preserving declaratory proceedings for cases closer to the central objectives of declaratory proceedings.''

II

The Declaratory Judgment Act, 28 U.S.C. § 2201(a), provides in pertinent part:

> In a case of actual controversy within its jurisdiction ... any court of the United States, upon the filing of an appropriate pleading, may declare the rights and other legal relations of any interested party seeking such declaration, whether or not further relief is or could be sought.

The Act, paralleling Article III of the Constitution, requires an actual controversy between the parties before a federal court may exercise jurisdiction over an action for a declaratory judgment. In general, the presence of an "actual controversy" within the meaning of the statute depends on "whether the facts alleged, under all the circumstances, show that there is a substantial controversy, between parties having adverse legal interests, of sufficient immediacy and reality to warrant the issuance of a declaratory judgment." *Maryland Casualty Co. v. Pacific Coal & Oil Co.*, 312 U.S. 270, 273, (1941); *Arrowhead Indus. Water, Inc. v. Ecolochem, Inc.*, 846 F.2d 731, 735, 6 USPQ2d 1685, 1688 (Fed. Cir. 1988).

Even if there is an actual controversy, the district court is not required to exercise declaratory judgment jurisdiction, but has discretion to decline that jurisdiction. As this court summarized in *Spectronics Corp. v. H.B. Fuller Co.*, 940 F.2d 631, 634, 19 USPQ2d 1545, 1547 (Fed. Cir. 1991): "When there is no actual controversy, the court has no discretion to decide the case. When there is an actual controversy and thus jurisdiction, the exercise of that jurisdiction is discretionary."

The district court did not decide whether this case presented an actual case or controversy, as it concluded that it would dismiss as a discretionary matter even if it found that it had jurisdiction. EMC argues that the district court erred in bypassing the question of jurisdiction and contends that there is a sufficient case or controversy as a matter of law. In addition, EMC argues that the district court abused its discretion by not relying on any of the "legitimate bases for exercising discretion not to hear a declaratory judgment action."

A

We agree with EMC that the undisputed facts establish a sufficient controversy between the parties to give the district court statutory and constitutional authority to hear this declaratory judgment action. We therefore find it unnecessary to decide whether it was appropriate for the district court to bypass the issue of jurisdiction without deciding that issue.

This court has developed a two-part inquiry to determine whether there is an actual controversy in suits requesting a declaration of patent non-infringement or invalidity. First, the plaintiff must actually produce

or be prepared to produce an allegedly infringing product. Second, the patentee's conduct must have created an objectively reasonable apprehension on the part of the plaintiff that the patentee will initiate suit if the activity in question continues. *Spectronics*, 940 F.2d at 634, 19 USPQ2d at 1548.

The parties do not dispute that EMC satisfies the first part of the test. We therefore address only the question whether Norand's conduct placed EMC in reasonable apprehension that it would be sued for infringing Norand's patent rights. To put a putative infringer in reasonable apprehension of suit does not require an express charge of infringement and threat of suit; rather, such apprehension may be induced by subtler conduct if that conduct rises "to a level sufficient to indicate an intent [on the part of the patentee] to enforce its patent," i.e., to initiate an infringement action. *Shell Oil*, 970 F.2d at 887, 23 USPQ2d at 1629–30.

A certain minimum degree of adverseness must be present in order to establish the requisite controversy. Thus, "more is required than the existence of an adversely held patent." *BP Chemicals Ltd. v. Union Carbide Corp.*, 4 F.3d 975, 978, 28 USPQ2d 1124, 1126 (Fed. Cir. 1993). A patentee's offer of a license, without more, is insufficient to establish the predicate for declaratory judgment jurisdiction, *Indium Corp. v. Semi–Alloys, Inc.*, 781 F.2d 879, 883, 228 USPQ 845, 848 (Fed. Cir. 1985), and merely "proposed or ongoing license negotiations" are likewise insufficient, *Phillips Plastics Corp. v. Kato Hatsujou Kabushiki Kaisha*, 57 F.3d 1051, 1053, 35 USPQ2d 1222, 1224 (Fed. Cir. 1995). But when the patentee takes steps that create a reasonable apprehension that he will seek redress through the courts, the alleged infringer is not required to wait for the patentee to decide when and where to sue, but can take the initiative and seek declaratory relief.

To be sure, any time parties are in negotiation over patent rights, the possibility of a lawsuit looms in the background. No patent owner with any sense would open negotiations by assuring his opposite party that he does not intend to enforce his patent rights under any circumstances. The threat of enforcement—either directly by the patentee or indirectly by a third party to whom the patentee licenses or sells the patent—is the entire source of the patentee's bargaining power. *See Shell Oil*, 970 F.2d at 888, 23 USPQ2d at 1631 (patentee, if asked whether it intends to enforce its patent must answer "yes" if it hopes to negotiate a license). Thus, it is unrealistic to suggest that some negotiating patentees intend to enforce their patents while some do not, and that the first group is subject to declaratory judgment actions while the second is not.

This court's two-part test for declaratory judgment jurisdiction is designed to police the sometimes subtle line between cases in which the parties have adverse interests and cases in which those adverse interests have ripened into a dispute that may properly be deemed a controversy. The test for finding a "controversy" for jurisdictional purposes is a pragmatic one and cannot turn on whether the parties use polite terms in dealing with one another or engage in more bellicose saber rattling. The need to look to substance rather than form is especially important in this area, because in many instances (as in this case) the parties are sensitive to the prospect of a declaratory judgment action and couch their exchanges in terms designed either to create or defeat declaratory judgment jurisdiction. In the end, the question is whether the relationship between the parties can be considered a "controversy," and that inquiry does not turn on whether the parties have used particular "magic words" in communicating with one another. *See Phillips Plastics*, 57 F.3d at 1053, 35 USPQ2d at 1223 ("one who may become liable for infringement should not be subject to manipulation by a patentee who uses careful phrases in order to avoid explicit threats").

In this case, we conclude that an "actual controversy" was present. In particular, the undisputed evidence makes it clear that Norand's conduct created a reasonable apprehension on EMC's part that Norand would sue if EMC did not satisfy Norand's economic demands. The most telling evidence on that issue is the August 19, 1994 letter that Goode sent to Dacier, EMC's general counsel. The letter referred to Norand's inclination to "turn the matter over to" Norand's litigation counsel "for action," and urged a "preliminary business discussion," "perhaps avoiding this matter escalating into a contentious legal activity." That language plainly suggested that Norand's management favored filing suit immediately and had to be persuaded by its consultant to hold off for a period of time necessary to seek a solution short of litigation. An objective reader of Goode's August 19 letter could only conclude that Norand had already decided EMC was infringing its patents and that Norand intended to file suit unless it could obtain satisfaction without having to sue.

Norand argues that the August 19 letter was merely an invitation to engage in a licensing discussion, of the sort that was held not to create a justiciable controversy in *Phillips Plastics Corp. v. Kato Hatsujou Kabushiki Kaisha, supra*. In *Phillips Plastics*, however, the patentee had not stated or even hinted that it would pursue legal recourse if it were not satisfied with the outcome of the proposed licensing negotiations. This court held that where all that is present is negotiation unaccompanied by threats of legal action, the setting is not sufficiently adverse to create a justiciable controversy. That principle, however, is inapplicable in a case such as this one, where the patentee has made explicit references to the prospect of initiating legal action.

This case is also unlike those in which it was the declaratory judgment plaintiff, not the patentee-defendant, who first approached the opposing party. *See Shell Oil*, 970 F.2d at 888, 23 USPQ2d at 1630–31 (no apprehension of suit where patentee was approached by declaratory judgment plaintiff, and patentee merely defended the validity of its patent in negotiations). Unlike in *Shell Oil*, it was Norand, the patentee, that approached EMC, not the reverse. Moreover, in making that contact, Norand did not simply invite EMC to engage in licensing negotiations, but specifically alluded to the prospect of "contentious legal activity."

The *Shell Oil* case exemplifies the broader principle that a declaratory judgment action should not be used to force unwanted litigation on "quiescent patent owners." *Arrowhead*, 846 F.2d at 736, 6 USPQ2d at 1689; *see also West Interactive Corp. v. First Data Resources, Inc.*, 972 F.2d 1295, 23 USPQ2d 1927 (Fed. Cir. 1992) (no apprehension of suit where patentee made no contact with declaratory judgment plaintiff, and sole source of plaintiff's apprehension was patentee's alleged statement to an unrelated party that plaintiff was infringing the patents at issue). That principle is inapplicable here, as Norand certainly does not qualify as a "quiescent" patentee.

In the weeks following Goode's August 19 letter, EMC and Norand held three meetings at which they discussed the possibility of licensing the Norand patents. Norand's outside litigation counsel was present at each meeting. Although the parties dispute whether Norand made any charges of infringement or threats of suit during that period, we do not regard the resolution of that question to be essential to determining whether there was an actual controversy between the parties at the time EMC filed suit. Goode's letter made it reasonably clear that Norand intended to resort to litigation if it were not satisfied with the results of the parties' negotiations. Nothing that EMC offered by way of evidence suggested that Norand had abandoned that posture during the ensuing weeks. Moreover, the amount of Norand's licensing offer—$1.5 million plus two percent of sales for a nonexclusive license—was sufficiently large to make the prospect of ultimate litigation even more realistic.

We conclude from the undisputed evidence before the district court that Norand and EMC had adverse interests and that those adverse interests had ripened into a concrete dispute by the time EMC filed its complaint. EMC's complaint therefore satisfied the case or controversy requirement of the Constitution as well as the "case of actual controversy" requirement of the Declaratory Judgment Act.

B

Simply because there is an actual controversy between the parties does not mean that the district court is required to exercise that jurisdiction. The Act states that a court may grant declaratory relief. The Supreme Court recently reaffirmed that the Declaratory Judgment Act thereby accords district courts a "unique breadth of . . . discretion to decline to enter a declaratory judgment." *Wilton v. Seven Falls Co.*, 115 S. Ct. 2137, 2143, (1995) (rejecting the argument that district courts are authorized to decline to exercise declaratory judgment jurisdiction only in "exceptional circumstances"). The Court noted that the Declaratory Judgment Act is "an enabling Act" that confers on district courts "unique and substantial discretion in deciding whether to declare the rights of litigants." 115 S. Ct. at 2142. The Court characterized the Act as "plac[ing] a remedial arrow in the district court's quiver" and as "creat[ing] an opportunity, rather than a duty, to grant a new form of relief to qualifying litigants." 115 S. Ct. at 2143. In expounding on the "unique breadth" of the district court's discretion, the Court explained that "[t]he statute's textual commitment to discretion, and the breadth of leeway we have always understood it to suggest, distinguish the declaratory judgment context from other areas of the law in which concepts of discretion surface." 115 S. Ct. at 2142.

The Court in Wilton also addressed the appropriate standard of review by appellate courts of a district court's exercise of its discretion to decline jurisdiction under the Declaratory Judgment Act. Recognizing a difference of approach among the circuits, the Court adopted a deferential "abuse of discretion" standard and explicitly rejected the more probing review previously practiced by this court. In particular, the Court concluded that it was appropriate to vest district courts with discretion "in the first instance, because facts bearing on the usefulness of the declaratory judgment remedy, and the fitness of the case for resolution, are peculiarly within their grasp." *Wilton*, 115 S. Ct. at 2143. In light of the clear directions from the Supreme Court, we must limit our review of the district court's decision to decline jurisdiction in this case to whether the court abused the "unique and substantial discretion" granted it under the Declaratory Judgment Act.

EMC is correct in contending that the district court's discretion is not unfettered. A district court, for example, "cannot decline to entertain [a declaratory judgment] action as a matter of whim or personal disinclination." *Public Affairs Assocs., Inc. v. Rickover*, 369 U.S. 111, 112 (1962). Nor can a district court dismiss a declaratory judgment action merely because a parallel patent infringement suit was subsequently filed in another district; to take such action without any other reasons, this court has held, would be contrary to the general rule favoring the forum of the first-filed action. On the other hand, as long as the district court acts in accordance with the purposes of the Declaratory Judgment Act and the principles of sound judicial administration, the court has broad discretion to refuse to entertain a declaratory judgment action. *See Serco Servs. Co., L.P. v. Kelley Co.*, 51 F.3d 1037, 1039, 34 USPQ2d 1217, 1218 (Fed. Cir. 1995) (court may dismiss declaratory judgment action if its action is based on "a reasoned judgment whether the investment of time and resources will be worthwhile").

EMC argues that it should be an abuse of discretion for a district court to dismiss a declaratory judgment action except when special circumstances are present, such as when the court lacks jurisdiction over all the necessary parties, when the suit is filed in an inconvenient forum, or when the declaratory judgment action would interfere with proceedings in another forum. We disagree. We detect no such implied restriction on the scope of the district court's discretion, as described by the Supreme Court in *Wilton*. Rather, we heed the Supreme Court's instruction that special flexibility is called for in the declaratory judgment context, where "the normal principle that federal courts should adjudicate claims within their jurisdiction yields to considerations of practicality and wise judicial administration." *Wilton*, 115 S. Ct. at 2143. It is appropriate, therefore, for a district court to examine whether hearing the declaratory judgment action would serve the objectives for which the Declaratory Judgment Act was created.

In this case, the district court based its decision to decline jurisdiction on its conclusion that allowing the declaratory judgment action to proceed would "creat[e] an incentive structure that is inconsistent with the public interest in preserving declaratory proceedings for cases closer to the central objectives of declaratory proceedings...." The court explained that a party in EMC's position could abuse the declaratory judgment device to obtain a more favorable bargaining position in its ongoing negotiations with the patentee and also to undermine the value of the patent so as to impede its sale or licensing to a third party.

In addition, in explaining the reasons for its discretionary dismissal, the district court cited *Davox Corp. v. Digital Systems International, Inc.*, 846 F. Supp. 144, 26 USPQ2d 1231 (D. Mass. 1993). There, the court declined to exercise jurisdiction over a declaratory judgment action in which the plaintiff filed suit while still engaged in negotiations with the patentee. Dismissal was proper there, the court observed, because "it would be inappropriate to reward—and indeed abet—conduct which is inconsistent with the sound policy of promoting extrajudicial dispute resolution, and conservation of judicial resources." *Davox Corp.*, 846 F. Supp. at 148, 26 USPQ2d at 1234. We agree that a court may take into account the pendency of serious negotiations to sell or license a patent in determining to exercise jurisdiction over a declaratory judgment action. While a court may conclude that ongoing negotiations do not negate the presence of a controversy for jurisdictional purposes, the court may nonetheless find, in deciding whether to hear the declaratory judgment action, that the need for judicial relief is not as compelling as in cases in which there is no real prospect of a non-judicial resolution of the dispute. *See NSI Corp. v. Showco, Inc.*, 843 F. Supp. 642, 645–46, 30 USPQ2d 1546, 1549 (D. Or. 1994) (declaratory judgment plaintiff "took advantage of the fact that [patentee] had deferred the filing of expensive and probably protracted litigation because of its belief that settlement negotiations were under way"); *Bausch & Lomb Inc. v. Alcide Corp.*, 684 F. Supp. 1155, 1160, 5 USPQ2d 1612, 1616 (W.D. N.Y. 1987) (dismissing declaratory judgment action filed just after defendant sent letter offering to resolve the dispute without resorting to litigation; "[t]o allow this action to proceed would be to discourage such good faith effort to negotiate").

In *Arrowhead Industrial Water, Inc. v. Ecolochem, Inc.*, 846 F.2d at 734–35, 6 USPQ2d at 1688, this court described the type of situation the Declaratory Judgment Act was intended to address:

> [A] patent owner engages in a danse macabre, brandishing a Damoclean threat with a sheathed sword.... Guerilla-like, the patent owner attempts extra-judicial patent enforcement with scare-the-customer-and-run tactics that infect the competitive environment of the business community with uncertainty and insecurity.... Before the Act, competitors victimized by that tactic were rendered help-

less and immobile so long as the patent owner refused to grasp the nettle and sue. After the Act, those competitors were no longer restricted to an in terrorem choice between the incurrence of a growing potential liability for patent infringement and abandonment of their enterprises; they could clear the air by suing for a judgment that would settle the conflict of interests.

See also BP Chemicals, 4 F.3d at 977, 28 USPQ2d at 1126 ("The purpose of the Act is to enable a person who is reasonably at legal risk because of an unresolved dispute, to obtain judicial resolution of that dispute without having to await the commencement of legal action by the other side. It accommodates the practical situation wherein the interests of one side to the dispute may be served by delay in taking legal action."). In the terms used in *Arrowhead* and *BP Chemicals*, a patentee in the midst of active negotiations may not be leaving the other party "immobile" or "helpless" and may not be benefitting from the delay. Instead, the patentee may be attempting to avoid litigation by engaging the other party in extra-judicial dispute resolution.

Of course, there may be situations in which the patentee has entered negotiations with an alleged infringer but nonetheless is engaging in the "danse macabre" referred to in *Arrowhead*, feigning interest in continued negotiations merely to deflect a declaratory judgment action. Such manipulation could well justify a district court's decision to accept a declaratory judgment action. In any event, the alleged infringer can usually avoid that problem altogether simply by cutting off negotiations if it appears that the patentee is not negotiating in good faith.

In this case, EMC and Norand were involved in negotiations over the sale or licensing of Norand's patents up to the time the complaint was filed. Although EMC complains that Norand's position in the negotiations was unreasonable, there is no suggestion in any of the evidence proffered by EMC that Norand's participation in the negotiations was merely a pretext designed to give Norand a basis for keeping EMC from obtaining declaratory judgment relief.

Moreover, the circumstances surrounding and immediately following the filing of the complaint lend further support to the district court's decision not to exercise its jurisdiction in this case. The complaint was filed shortly after Norand informed EMC of its plans to enter negotiations with EMC's competitors. The day after the complaint was filed, EMC's senior intellectual property counsel called Norand's outside patent counsel and explained that the declaratory judgment complaint had been filed as "merely a defensive step" and that EMC "would like to continue to discuss with you all the options hopefully in a more meaningful manner over the near term." By way of explaining why the complaint was filed, EMC's counsel added that EMC's management decided to file suit because "they just thought it was in their interest to protect themselves first and continue discussions." Under these circumstances, the district court could properly view the declaratory judgment complaint as a tactical measure filed in order to improve EMC's posture in the ongoing negotiations—not a purpose that the Declaratory Judgment Act was designed to serve.

In sum, the district court was able to determine from the undisputed facts that this case was not one that furthered the objectives of the Declaratory Judgment Act. In light of the limited scope of our review, we cannot conclude that the district court's decision on that issue was so contrary to "the teachings and experience concerning the functions and extent of federal judicial power," *Public Serv. Comm'n v. Wycoff Co.*, 344 U.S. at 243, that it constituted an abuse of discretion.

AFFIRMED.

Notes

1. Would it have made a difference to the court if EMC had explicitly withdrawn from the negotiations prior to filing its declaratory judgment action? What if neither party had withdrawn, but it was clear that they had reached an insurmountable impasse? Notice Judge Bryson relies heavily on the fact that the negotiations were on-going. There was plenty of evidence to support the fact that the negotiations were on-going including the statement by EMC management that EMC filed the declaratory judgment action because management "thought it was in their interest to protect themselves first and continue discussions" and the fact that additional negotiation sessions were scheduled. This fact led the court to conclude that EMC was simply filing suit in an attempt to improve it bargaining position. How would filing the suit have improve the bargaining strength of EMC in this case?

2. A cease and desist letter sent by the patentee usually states that the patentee will be forced to bring suit if the alleged infringer does not discontinue the activities that the patentee deems infringing. This type of letter is an express threat of suit sufficient to bring a declaratory judgment action. As the *EMC* case demonstrates, a letter which contains something less that an express threat can be sufficient to create a reasonable apprehension of suit. At the opposite end of the spectrum, however, courts have repeatedly held that an offer to license alone by the patentee does not create a reasonable apprehension of harm.

3. Should the court look at the parties actions after the suit was filed to help in its determination of whether the declaratory judgment plaintiff had a reasonable apprehension of being sued? *See West Interactive Corp. v. First Data Resources, Inc.*, 972 F.2d 1295, 1297, 23 USPQ2d 1927, 1929 (Fed. Cir. 1992) (holding that "because this court examines [plaintiff's] declaratory judgment action at the time of its filing, [defendant's] subsequent action is irrelevant"); *Spectronics Corp. v. H.B. Fuller Co., Inc.*, 940 F.2d 631, 634–35, 19 USPQ2d 1545, 1548 (Fed. Cir. 1991) ("We agree wholeheartedly that in personam and subject matter jurisdictional facts must be pleaded and proved when challenged, and that later events may not create jurisdiction where none existed at the time of filing."); *Arrowhead Indus. Water, Inc. v. Ecolochem, Inc.*, 846 F.2d 731, 734 n. 2, 6 USPQ2d 1685, 1687 n. 2 (Fed. Cir. 1988) (disregarding defendant's letter to plaintiff's customer from the analysis because "the presence or absence of jurisdiction must be determined on the facts existing at the time the complaint under consideration was filed"); *International Med. Prosthetics Research Assocs.,*

Inc. v. Gore Enter. Holdings, Inc., 787 F.2d 572, 576 n. 8, 229 USPQ 278, 281 n. 8 (Fed. Cir. 1986) ("The basis for jurisdiction, i.e., facts showing a justiciable controversy, and notice of the case to be tried, should be found in the complaint."); *Performance Abatement Servs., Inc. v. GPAC, Inc.*, 733 F. Supp. 1015, 1019, 17 USPQ2d 1561, 1564 (W.D. N.C. 1990) (prohibiting plaintiff from justifying its claimed reasonable apprehension on, among other things, defendant's "institution of a patent infringement suit two weeks after [plaintiff] filed its action").

MOTIONS TO DISMISS

When the patentee believes that the declaratory judgment action should never have been brought, that there is no justiciable controversy between the parties at the time the suit was filed, the patentee should file a Rule 12(b)(1) motion to dismiss for lack of subject matter jurisdiction. Do you agree with the court's denial of the patentee's motion to dismiss in the following case? Did Oce have a reasonable apprehension of being sued?

OCE-OFFICE SYS., INC. v. EASTMAN KODAK CO.

805 F. Supp. 642, 25 USPQ2d 1370 (N.D. Ill. 1992)

ALESIA, District Judge.

Plaintiffs, Oce–Office Systems, Inc. and Oce–Nederland B.V. ("Oce"), filed this action against the defendant, Eastman Kodak Co. ("Kodak"), seeking a declaratory judgment that plaintiffs' Oce 2500 Copier–Duplicator (hereinafter "Oce 2500") does not infringe any claim of United States Letters Patent 4,140,387 (hereinafter the '387 patent), which is owned by Kodak, or alternatively that no claim of the '387 patent is valid. Presently before the court is defendant's motion to dismiss plaintiffs' complaint pursuant to Rule 12(b)(1) of the Federal Rules of Civil Procedure, alleging that this Court lacks subject matter jurisdiction because no justiciable controversy exists between the parties. For the reasons set forth below, defendant's motion is denied.

I. JURISDICTION OF FEDERAL COURTS UNDER THE DECLARATORY JUDGMENT ACT

The Declaratory Judgment Act, 28 U.S.C. § 2201, provides that federal courts may issue declaratory judgments only in cases of "actual controversy." 28 U.S.C. § 2201. This requirement is a jurisdictional prerequisite. Therefore, the complaint in a declaratory judgment action must allege facts sufficient to establish such an actual controversy.

Furthermore, when the jurisdictional sufficiency of a complaint is challenged, as here, the burden is on the plaintiff to establish jurisdiction affirmatively with competent proof. And where the facts presented in support of, and in opposition to, a motion to dismiss present a factual controversy, the resolution requires the court to "weigh the conflicting evidence in arriving at the factual [foundation] upon which to base the legal conclusion that subject matter jurisdiction either exists or does not." *Grafon Corp. v. Hausermann*, 602 F.2d 781, 783 (7th Cir. 1979). The court will, however, resolve all conflicts in the evidence in the favor of the plaintiff.

Specifically, in declaratory judgment actions concerning patents, there are two prerequisites to establishing an actual controversy. First, the plaintiff must have a reasonable apprehension, based on defendant's conduct, that it will face an infringement suit or the threat of one if it commences or continues the activity in question. Secondly, the plaintiff must have actually produced the accused article or have engaged in preparations for production. This test is objective and is applied to the facts in existence at the time the complaint is filed. Oce has obviously satisfied the second prong of the "actual controversy" test in that production and sales of the Oce 2500 in the United States have been ongoing since 1989. Thus, the only remaining issue pending before the court is whether Oce had a reasonable apprehension of an infringement suit or the threat of one based on defendant's conduct. Applying the standard set forth above to the evidence presented, the court finds that a justiciable controversy existed at the time the suit was filed.

A.   *Facts Establishing Jurisdiction*

In challenging jurisdiction, Kodak submitted an affidavit by Ronald P. Hilst, Senior Director of Business Development for Kodak, and various correspondence between the two parties. In opposition to Kodak's motion to dismiss, Oce submitted a declaration by Johannes M.M. van der Velden, Assistant Director and Legal Counsel for Oce, affidavits by William O. Bittman and Bernard L. Sweeney, both attorneys representing Oce in this action, as well as various correspondence between the parties. These materials established the facts as set out below.

In 1984, Oce initially contacted Kodak regarding licenses under the '387 patent with the intent to use the '387 patent technology in as yet undeveloped Oce copier systems. At that point in time, the Oce 2500 was beyond this stage in its development and, therefore, these discussions did not include this copier. These licensing discussions continued until 1987 when they were terminated without Oce ever acquiring a license under the '387 patent. According to Oce, the terms offered by Kodak were unacceptable and Kodak would not consider granting a license under the '387 patent with respect to high speed copiers.

With regard to the Oce 2500, it was Kodak that initiated contact with Oce in a letter dated August 5, 1991. In this letter, Kodak expressed its belief that the Oce 2500 infringed the '387 patent and stated that if Oce disagreed, it was to provide a written explanation which conclusively established that there was no infringement. Kodak then stated that failure of Oce to provide such an analysis would indicate to Kodak that its belief regarding infringement was correct and that Oce should either take a license under the patent or immediately terminate its infringing activity and compensate Kodak for any damages resulting from the infringement.

Oce responded on September 25, 1991, with a letter to Kodak explaining why the Oce 2500 did not infringe the claims of the '387 patent. In the last paragraph of the letter, Oce requested that Kodak specify the terms under which it would be willing to license the '387 patent for future Oce machines. Nowhere in this letter to Kodak did Oce offer to discuss licensing the '387 invention for use in the Oce 2500 copier.

On November 18, 1991, Kodak responded by letter, stating that it still believed the Oce 2500 infringed the '387 patent. Additionally, Kodak enclosed with this letter a statement, prepared by Kodak's Patent Legal Staff, explaining why they believed the Oce 2500 copier directly infringed the '387 patent. Kodak then outlined the terms under which it would be willing to grant Oce a license under the '387 patent for high-speed copiers. Kodak further stated its intention that any such licenses would apply to the Oce 2500 as well as other relevant copiers. Kodak elaborated that it must hear from Oce regarding this matter on or before December 15, 1991 or else Kodak would "assume that Oce intend[ed] to continue its infringing activities, and ha[d] no interest in pursuing [the] license discussions." Kodak explained that if it did not hear from Oce, it would then proceed "with consideration of other appropriate actions to protect Kodak's patent rights."

The parties subsequently met on March 31, 1992. According to plaintiff's brief in opposition to Kodak's motion to dismiss, Oce agreed to hold such a meeting to further try to convince Kodak that the Oce 2500 did not infringe the '387 patent. At the start of this meeting, Kodak reiterated its belief that the Oce 2500 infringed the '387 patent. Oce then explained why the Oce 2500 did not infringe the '387 patent based on the two position papers Oce had sent to Kodak prior to this meeting. Kodak responded that despite Oce's explanations, Kodak still believed that the Oce 2500 literally infringed the patent. Furthermore, during these discussions, Kodak made reference to the fact that it believed that a jury would decide this controversy in its favor.

When Oce suggested that the matter be sent to arbitration for resolution, Kodak responded that it did not favor arbitration because it found arbitration to be more expensive and time-consuming than litigation. Kodak also indicated that arbitration would deprive it of the opportunity to have a jury decide the liability issues. And while Ronald P. Hilst stated in his affidavit that no one at Kodak ever directly or indirectly threatened to file an infringement action against Oce, Kodak has not denied that the above statements were made. And although these statements may not have been meant to threaten litigation, that was the effect that they had on the Oce representatives. Furthermore, in light of the ongoing series of communications between these two parties, the court finds that such an interpretation was reasonable under the circumstances.

The Oce representatives then terminated these discussions. They did so based on defendant's conduct at the meeting and their belief that the two parties were not going to be able to agree on the relationship between the Oce 2500 and the '387 patent. It was after the breakdown of these discussions that Oce filed this declaratory judgment action seeking a final determination of this issue, rather than having Kodak's charges of infringement continue indefinitely.

B. *Establishing Reasonable Apprehension*

As the main thrust of its argument that there was no reasonable apprehension of suit, Kodak repeatedly relies on the fact that it never directly or indirectly threatened to sue Oce for infringement. However, this reliance is misplaced because an express threat to sue is not necessary in order for there to be a justiciable controversy in such patent cases. Requiring an express charge of litigation would destroy the purpose of the Declaratory Judgment Act, which in patent cases is to provide the allegedly infringing party relief from uncertainty and delay with regard to its legal rights.

In fact, there does not even need to be an express charge of infringement in order for a justiciable controversy to exist. "We must [first] look for any express charges of infringement, and if none, then to the totality of the circumstances." *Shell Oil Co.*, 970 F.2d at 886. And the totality of the circumstances, with regard to defendant's conduct, must be such as to indicate defendant's intent to enforce its patent. The Federal Circuit Court in *Arrowhead* specifically stated that "[i]f defendant has expressly charged a current activity of the plaintiff as an infringement, there is clearly an actual controversy, [and] certainty has rendered apprehension irrelevant." *Arrowhead*, 846 F.2d at 736. Therefore, based on Kodak's express charges of infringement, as well as its intent to enforce its patent rights as expressed in its letter of November 18, 1991, combined with its conduct at the March 31, 1992 meeting, it was reasonable for Oce to anticipate the threat of an infringement suit.

In rebuttal, Kodak additionally argues that Oce has never apprehended an infringement suit; rather, it contends Oce is just using this action to further its bargaining position in what is a continuing series of business negotiations. It supports this contention with an April 3, 1992 letter from Oce to Kodak stating that Oce hoped that this matter could be resolved without the litigation going to conclusion. Kodak argues that this letter was essentially a counteroffer to the terms proposed by Kodak at the March 31 meeting. Oce states that this letter was no more than a transmittal letter sent to Kodak with a courtesy copy of the complaint, and that the portion of the letter to which Kodak refers was an attempt to keep open the possibility that any litigation might be resolved out of court.

The court finds Kodak's position unpersuasive. While the April 3, 1992 letter seems to indicate a willingness on the part of Oce to continue negotiations, the affidavits of both Mr. Hilst and Mr. Bittman state that in no way should the letter be construed to indicate that Oce wishes to continue negotiations. Oce further maintains that it never negotiated licensing conditions for the Oce 2500 under the '387 patent. Therefore, based on the material submitted and supported by the fact that Oce has unwaveringly maintained since the beginning of these communications that the Oce 2500 does not infringe the '387 patent, it is unlikely that the April 3 letter evinces a wish on Oce's behalf to continue negotiations for a license for their copier under this patent.

Kodak additionally finds fault with Oce filing a declaratory judgment action in order to not let this matter "languish indefinitely." The court does not agree. In fact, as stated above, the aim of a declaratory judgment is to relieve the plaintiff from uncertainty and delay regarding its legal rights. It would be unfair to require imminent apprehension of an infringement suit when a defendant could delay such suit until all other enforcement efforts had failed. Resolving the uncertainty and anxiety resulting from a looming lawsuit is, indeed, the purpose of the Declaratory Judgment Act. Hence, the court finds no fault with Oce wishing to determine this real and tangible issue in a prompt fashion.

Lastly, Kodak argues in its brief supporting its motion to dismiss that it had fully intended licensing discussions to continue after the March 31, 1991 meeting, and that Kodak would only begin "consideration of other appropriate actions" once licensing discussions had failed. Licensing discussions did fail. Oce steadfastly maintained its position that its 2500 copier did not infringe Kodak's § 387 patent. And Kodak equally tenaciously maintained its infringement position and the requirements for a license. So, at the conclusion of the March 31 meeting, Oce determined that the discussions were fruitless and ended the negotiations. And, while it was Oce who terminated these discussions, it is not a prerequisite that negotiations must terminate naturally or amicably, nor that the defendant must be the party to terminate negotiations, for a declaratory judgment plaintiff to establish jurisdiction. It is enough that the defendant's conduct "be such as to indicate defendant's intent to enforce its patent." *Arrowhead*, 846 F.2d at 736. Therefore, Kodak's argument that it had intended negotiations to continue does not work to defeat jurisdiction.

II. CONCLUSION

Based on Kodak's express charges of infringement, the conclusions of Kodak's legal staff regarding Oce's alleged infringement, Kodak's refusal to modify its position regarding the '387 patent, Kodak's statement in its November 18, 1991 letter that it would consider other appropriate action if license discussions broke down, and Kodak's reference to a recent case where a jury had found in favor of the patent holder, Oce has established that it had a reasonable apprehension of litigation or the threat of litigation if it continued its activities with regard to the Oce 2500. Hence, a justiciable controversy is present here and Kodak's motion to dismiss is denied.

Notes

1. Can an alleged infringer bring a declaratory judgement action after being expressly threatened by a patent applicant? Read the following excerpt

from *GAF Building Materials Corp. v. Elk Corp.*, 90 F.3d 479, 481–82, 39 USPQ2d 1463, 1465–66 (Fed. Cir. 1996):

> We agree that when GAF commenced the declaratory judgment action it had a reasonable apprehension that it would be sued for patent infringement. Elk's December 1993 letter unmistakably notified GAF that Elk intended to sue GAF for infringement if GAF did not stop marketing the accused product. A demand to cease and desist is a threat. Furthermore, GAF had reason to believe that the PTO had allowed Elk's design patent application and that Elk had paid the issue fee. Thus, it was likely that a patent would issue. In addition, the parties do not dispute that GAF was (and is) manufacturing and marketing the accused product. Therefore, we agree that the two established criteria for an "actual controversy" described in Jervis B. Webb and other cases were satisfied under the facts of this case. However, the cases which have discussed only these two requirements have involved a granted patent, such that further issues which arise in the absence of a patent were not discussed. A broader inquiry than our two-part "test" is required here because no patent had issued when the complaint was filed.
>
> Using these guidelines, it is clear that GAF's complaint did not present a justiciable case or controversy under Article III and § 2201 when it was filed. The complaint alleged a dispute over the validity and infringement of a possible future patent not then in existence. The district court did not know with certainty whether a patent would issue or, if so, what legal rights it would confer upon Elk. Thus, the dispute was purely hypothetical and called for an impermissible advisory opinion. Furthermore, the court could not have provided "specific relief through a decree of a conclusive character," since there was no issued patent for the court to declare "invalid" or "not infringed." A declaratory judgment of "invalidity" or "noninfringement" with respect to Elk's pending patent application would have had no legal meaning or effect. The fact that the patent was about to issue and would have been granted before the court reached the merits of the case is of no moment. Justiciability must be judged as of the time of filing, not as of some indeterminate future date when the court might reach the merits and the patent has issued.
>
> We therefore hold that a threat is not sufficient to create a case or controversy unless it is made with respect to a patent that has issued before a complaint is filed. Thus, the district court correctly held that there was no justiciable case or controversy in this case at the time the complaint was filed.

2. **Choice of Forum.** Prior to sending a cease-and-desist letter, a patentee may want to offer a license. If this is unsuccessful, the patentee may want to consider filing a complaint without serving it against an alleged infringer before sending a cease and desist letter. This will preserve the patentee's choice of forum. If the patentee does not file a complaint prior to sending the cease and desist letter, it should be prepared to litigate.

3. **Concrete Steps.** Declaratory judgments are not advisory. A manufacturer cannot bring a declaratory judgment action prior to taking infringing activity. The alleged infringer does not need to demonstrate that it is actually infringing already in order to bring suit. The test is whether the alleged infringer has taken any present activity which could constitute infringement or concrete steps taken with the intent to conduct such activity. It is enough if the manufacturer has taken meaningful preparation toward infringing. For example, concrete steps toward infringing may have been taken if the manufacturer has made a significant expenditure such as bought equipment for its plant that it will use to manufacture the infringing product or expended capital on marketing or advertising or made more than a de minimis effort to secure FDA approval. A declaratory judgment action may be brought under these circumstances, even though the manufacturer has not actually begun making the infringing product.

4. A patentee defending against an action for a declaratory judgment of invalidity or noninfringement can divest the trial court of jurisdiction over the case by filing a covenant not to assert the patent at issue against the putative infringer with respect to any of its past, present, or future acts or by promises not to sue made by patentee's counsel in motions or brief submitted to the court. *Super Sack Mfg. Corp. v. Chase Packaging Corp.*, 57 F.3d 1054, 1058, 35 USPQ2d 1139, 1143 (Fed. Cir. 1995). By agreeing not to bring suit against the alleged infringer the patentee has eviscerated any apprehension of suit and accordingly, there is no actual controversy between the parties. The patentee can, however, bring suit against the allegedly infringing defendant if it makes a different product in the future which the patentee claims infringes. *Id.* at 1059, 35 USPQ2d at 1144. The promise not to sue only prevents the patentee from suing the defendant over the products at issue in that suit. The development by the alleged infringer of different potentially infringing products in the future could result in suit. This possibility does not create an actual controversy such that the declaratory judgment action could go forward because it would fail the second part of the test: that the alleged infringer has undertaken present activity which puts it at risk for infringement liability. *Id.*

5. Evidence that the patent owner has sued others on the same patent or that the patent owner brings infringement suits often to enforce its patent rights is relevant to an objective determination of whether there is a reasonable apprehension of being sued. A patent owner's willingness and capacity to enforce its patent rights is pertinent to the inquiry concerning the existence of an actual controversy. *West Interactive Corp. v. First Data Resources, Inc.*, 972 F.2d 1295, 1298, 23 USPQ2d 1927, 1939 (Fed. Cir. 1992). Such a showing will be stronger evidence if the other infringement suits involve the same patent, technology similar to the defendants, and are close in time.

6. Threats of suit made by a non-exclusive licensee under a patent cannot expose the patentee to a declaratory judgment action, but threats made by an exclusive licensee who owns all the substantive rights under the patent can.

7. A patentee cannot divest a declaratory judgment plaintiff of his choice of forum by filing an infringement suit. The general rule favors the

forum of the first-filed action regardless of whether it is a declaratory judgement. If there is sound reason that would make it unjust or inefficient to continue the first-filed action such as the convenience and availability of witnesses, or absence of jurisdiction over all necessary or desirable parties, or the possibility of consolidation with related litigation, or considerations relating to the real party in interest then the court could exercise its discretion and dismiss the suit. *See Kahn v. General Motors Corp.*, 889 F.2d 1078, 1081–83, 12 USPQ2d 1997, 1999–2001 (Fed. Cir. 1989). When a declaratory judgment action is dismissed simply because a patent infringement suit is filed the next day, the court has abused its discretion. *Genentech, Inc. v. Eli Lilly & Co.,* 998 F.2d 931, 27 USPQ2d 1241 (Fed. Cir. 1993).

2. DECLARATORY JUDGMENT ACTION BROUGHT BY PATENTEE TO PREVENT FUTURE INFRINGEMENT

LANG v. PACIFIC MARINE & SUPPLY CO.

895 F.2d 761, 13 USPQ2d 1820 (Fed. Cir. 1990)

Before FRIEDMAN, Senior Circuit Judge, and BISSELL and MAYER, Circuit Judges. BISSELL, Circuit Judge.

BISSELL, Circuit Judge.

Thomas G. Lang and Swath Ocean Systems, Inc. (Swath Ocean) (collectively Lang) appeal the order of the United States District Court for the District of Hawaii dismissing Lang's complaint against Pacific Marine and Supply Co., Ltd. (Pacific Marine & Supply), Pacific Marine and Engineering Science Corp., and Thompson Metal Fabricators, Inc. (Thompson Metal) (collectively Pacific Marine). We affirm.

BACKGROUND

Thomas Lang and Swath Ocean are patentee and licensee, respectively, of United States Patents No. 3,897,744 ('744) and No. 3,623,444 ('444) which claim certain features of a ship's hull. Lang sued Pacific Marine on April 25, 1988, asserting five counts as grounds for relief. At the time suit was filed, Thompson Metal was in the process of manufacturing a hull structure for Pacific Marine & Supply that Lang contends would, when finished, infringe its patent. The vessel was not scheduled to be completed and ready for final Coast Guard inspection until February 1989.

In Count I of the complaint, Lang sought a declaratory judgment that Pacific Marine's acts constituted patent infringement and/or threatened infringement.... Pacific Marine moved to dismiss all the counts for lack of subject matter jurisdiction and/or failure to state a claim under Federal Rules of Civil Procedure 12(b)(1) and (6). The district court granted the motion and dismissed Lang's complaint. Lang appeals the dismissal of Counts I through IV.

ISSUES

Whether the district court erred in dismissing Counts I through IV of Lang's complaint for either lack of subject matter jurisdiction or failure to state a claim.

Count I—Declaratory Judgment of Threatened Infringement

Declaratory judgment actions in the patent area are most commonly brought by potential infringers against patentees seeking a declaration of noninfringement or invalidity or both. Declarations of infringement sought by patentees against parties who will allegedly infringe in the future have been less frequently requested, but have nevertheless been allowed to proceed. *See, e.g., Erbamont Inc. v. Cetus Corp.,* 720 F. Supp. 387, 390, 12 USPQ2d 1344, 1347 (D. Del. 1989); *Westnofa USA Inc. v. British Design (U.S.A.) Corp.,* 222 USPQ 136, 138 (N.D. Ill. 1983). Lang's Count I seeks a declaration of the second type—"that any ship constructed in accordance with the disclosure of said Pacific Marine '671 patent will of necessity, infringe one or more claims of the Lan '444 and '744 patents." Whether a patentee may maintain such an action is a question of first impression for this court.

The Declaratory Judgment Act, 28 U.S.C. § 2201 (1982 & Supp. V 1987), "enlarge[s] the range of remedies available in the federal courts but d[oes] not extend their jurisdiction." *Skelly Oil Co. v. Phillips Petroleum Co.,* 339 U.S. 667, 671–72 (1950). "The sole requirement for jurisdiction under the Act is that the conflict be real and immediate, i.e., that there be a true, actual 'controversy' required by the Act." *Arrowhead Indus. Water, Inc. v. Ecolochem, Inc.,* 846 F.2d 731, 735, 6 USPQ2d 1685, 1688 (Fed. Cir. 1988).

If the controversy requirement is met by a sufficient allegation of immediacy and reality, we see no reason why a patentee should be unable to seek a declaration of infringement against a future infringer when a future infringer is able to maintain a declaratory judgment action for noninfringement under the same circumstances. *Id.* at 736, 6 USPQ2d at 1689 (explaining that meaningful preparation for infringing activity coupled with acts of the patentee indicating an intent to enforce its patent will meet the controversy requirement); *see Erbamont,* 720 F. Supp. at 391, 12 USPQ2d at 1348 (recognizing that "the better view is that the patent owner may, in certain circumstances, seek a declaratory judgment as to infringement" prior to the defendant actually committing an act of infringement). A concern that the alleged future infringer might alter its course of conduct or discontinue it altogether should not cause a dismissal any more than it should in a suit by the accused infringer. Furthermore, the fact that the patent owner, unlike the accused infringer, will have an express statutory remedy for infringement at a later time is irrelevant. The Declaratory Judgment Act applies "whether or not further relief is or could be sought." 28 U.S.C. § 2201; 10A Wright & Miller § 2758, at 620, 621 (explaining that "declaratory relief is alternative and cumulative" and "that the existence of another adequate remedy does not bar a declaratory judgment").

To meet the controversy requirement in a declaratory judgment suit by a patentee against an alleged future infringer, two elements must be present: (1) the defendant must be engaged in an activity directed

toward making, selling, or using subject to an infringement charge under 35 U.S.C. § 271(a) (1982), or be making meaningful preparation for such activity; and (2) acts of the defendant must indicate a refusal to change the course of its actions in the face of acts by the patentee sufficient to create a reasonable apprehension that a suit will be forthcoming. The first prong is identical to one of the requirements in a patent declaratory judgment action where the threatened infringer is the plaintiff. It looks to the accused infringer's conduct and ensures that the controversy is sufficiently real and substantial. The second prong requires conduct by both the accused infringer and the patentee and is similar to the reasonable apprehension prong in the normal action. It ensures that the controversy is definite and concrete between parties having adverse legal interests.

Here, Lang failed to meet the actual controversy requirement necessary to maintain Count I under the Declaratory Judgment Act. The accused infringing ship's hull would not be finished until at least 9 months after the complaint was filed. Unlike the plaintiff in *Automation Systems, Inc. v. Intel Corp.*, 501 F. Supp. 345, 348, 209 USPQ 573, 575 (S.D. Iowa 1980), the accused infringers had not distributed sales literature, prepared to solicit orders, or engaged in any activity indicating that the ship would soon be ready for sea. As the district court correctly held, "there is no 'substantial controversy ... of sufficient immediacy and reality to warrant' consideration of [Lang's] claim for declaratory relief."

AFFIRMED.

C. PRE–SUIT INVESTIGATIONS

FEDERAL RULES OF CIVIL PROCEDURE—RULE 11:

Rule 11. Signing of Pleadings, Motions, and Other Papers; Representations to Court; Sanctions

(a) Signature. Every pleading, written motion, and other paper shall be signed by at least one attorney of record in the attorney's individual name, or, if the party is not represented by an attorney, shall be signed by the party. Each paper shall state the signer's address and telephone number, if any. Except when otherwise specifically provided by rule or statute, pleadings need not be verified or accompanied by affidavit. An unsigned paper shall be stricken unless omission of the signature is corrected promptly after being called to the attention of the attorney or party.

(b) Representations to Court. By presenting to the court (whether by signing, filing, submitting, or later advocating) a pleading, written motion, or other paper, an attorney or unrepresented party is certifying that to the best of the person's knowledge, information, and belief, formed after an inquiry reasonable under the circumstances,—

    (1) it is not being presented for any improper purpose, such as to harass or to cause unnecessary delay or needless increase in the cost of litigation;

    (2) the claims, defenses, and other legal contentions therein are warranted by existing law or by a nonfrivolous argument for the

extension, modification, or reversal of existing law or the establishment of new law;

    (3) the allegations and other factual contentions have evidentiary support or, if specifically so identified, are likely to have evidentiary support after a reasonable opportunity for further investigation or discovery; and

    (4) the denials of factual contentions are warranted on the evidence or, if specifically so identified, are reasonably based on a lack of information or belief.

(c) Sanctions. If, after notice and a reasonable opportunity to respond, the court determines that subdivision (b) has been violated, the court may, subject to the conditions stated below, impose an appropriate sanction upon the attorneys, law firms, or parties that have violated subdivision (b) or are responsible for the violation.

Rule 11 traces back to 1937 and has had several amendments in the course of its life. Until the 1993 adoption of the rule (see above), it had generally been applied with mixed results. Rule 11 has always been directed to improper litigation conduct involving a lack of good faith basis for filing a pleading or a motion. The Rule is mandatory as the court also " ... shall impose ..." a sanction on the person responsible for the improper conduct. The Rule not only applies to counsel, but also local counsel and the client. The 1993 revision also provided for a "safe harbor" of 21 days in which the accused litigant could withdraw the pleading without penalty after motion by the aggrieved party. Fed. R. Civ. P. 11(c)(1)(A).

JUDIN v. UNITED STATES

110 F.3d 780, 42 USPQ2d 1300 (Fed. Cir. 1997)

Before ARCHER, Chief Judge, PLAGER and SCHALL, Circuit Judges.

PLAGER, Circuit Judge.

Hewlett–Packard Company ("HP") appeals from a decision of the Court of Federal Claims denying HP's motion for sanctions under Rule 11, Rules of the Court of Federal Claims ("RCFC"). HP alleged that plaintiff Judin and his attorneys failed to perform a reasonable inquiry prior to filing Judin's patent infringement complaint. Because we find a clear violation of Rule 11, we hold that the trial court abused its discretion in determining otherwise. We vacate the decision of the court and remand the case for further proceedings.

Discussion

Rule 11, RCFC, which is patterned after Rule 11, Fed. R. Civ. P., provides that every pleading filed by a party shall be signed by the party's attorney. The rule also provides:

    The signature of an attorney or party constitutes a certificate by the attorney or party that ... to the best of the attorney's or party's knowledge, information and belief formed after reasonable inquiry

it is well grounded in fact and is warranted by existing law or a good faith argument for the extension, modification, or reversal of existing law; and that it is not interposed for any improper purpose. . . . If a pleading, motion, or other paper is signed in violation of this rule, the court, upon motion or upon its own initiative, shall impose upon the person who signed it, a represented party, or both, an appropriate sanction, which may include an order to pay . . . a reasonable attorney's fee.

Rule 11, RCFC (emphasis added).

In interpreting Rule 11, RCFC, "[p]recedent illuminating [Rule 11, Fed. R. Civ. P.] is applicable." *Doe v. United States*, 16 Cl. Ct. 412, 414 (1989). In general, a trial court's Rule 11 determinations are reviewed under an abuse-of-discretion standard.

Rule 11 is aimed at curbing baseless filings, which abuse the judicial system and burden courts and parties with needless expense and delay. Rule 11 was amended in 1983 to provide that courts "shall impose" sanctions if the rule is violated, and the purpose of this mandatory language was to "reduce the reluctance of courts to impose sanctions." *Refac Int'l, Ltd. v. Hitachi, Ltd.*, 921 F.2d 1247, 1257, 16 USPQ2d 1347, 1355 (Fed. Cir. 1990). The purpose of imposing Rule 11 sanctions is to deter the misconduct addressed by the rule.

The issue in this case is whether the trial court abused its discretion in determining that Judin and his attorney, before filing the complaint, made reasonable inquiry to determine that the complaint was well grounded in fact. As noted, prior to filing the complaint, Judin and Van Der Wall observed an accused device from a distance while it was in use at a post office, but neither Judin nor his attorney attempted to obtain a device from the Postal Service or the manufacturer so that they could more closely observe the device, nor was any attempt made to dissect or "reverse-engineer" a sample device.

Attorney Van Der Wall reviewed one of the asserted patent claims and stated that he "saw no problem with it." "Determining infringement, however, requires that the patent claims be interpreted and that the claims be found to read on the accused devices." *S. Bravo Systems, Inc. v. Containment Technologies Corp.*, 96 F.3d 1372, 1375, 40 USPQ2d 1140, 1143 (Fed. Cir. 1996). As in *S. Bravo Systems*, there is no evidence that Judin or his attorneys "compared the accused devices with the patent claims" prior to filing the complaint. *See id.* (holding that trial court abused its discretion by denying a motion for Rule 11 sanctions without adequate explanation).

By viewing the accused devices at a distance Judin was able to determine that they had a light source and a rounded tip through which the light passed, and that the light was focused in a pinpoint. That may have been sufficient to put Judin on inquiry about whether the Government was using a device that infringed his patent. But Rule 11 requires more. It requires that the inquiry be undertaken before the suit is filed, not after. Defendants have no choice when served with a complaint if they wish to avoid a default. They must undertake a defense, and that necessarily involves costs. Rule 11 prohibits imposing those costs upon a defendant absent a basis, well-grounded in fact, for bringing the suit.

In this case, prior to the filing of the suit, neither Judin or his counsel had made a reasonable effort to ascertain whether the accused devices satisfied the two key claim limitations, either literally or under the doctrine of equivalents. No adequate explanation was offered for why they failed to obtain, or attempted to obtain, a sample of the accused device from the Postal Service or a vendor so that its actual design and functioning could be compared with the claims of the patent. Under these circumstances, there is no doubt that Judin failed to meet the minimum standards imposed by Rule 11, and his attorney acted unreasonably in giving blind deference to his client and assuming his client had knowledge not disclosed to the attorney. The trial court's determination to the contrary is an abuse of its discretion. *Cf. Refac Int'l, Ltd. v. Hitachi, Ltd.*, 141 F.R.D. 281, 286–88, 19 USPQ2d 1855, 1857–59 (C.D. Cal. 1991) (imposing Rule 11 sanctions on patent infringement plaintiff that failed to reverse engineer or examine accused products prior to filing complaint). Because Rule 11 is not about after-the-fact investigation, Judin and Van Der Wall's violation of Rule 11 was not cured by the fact that, after filing the complaint, Judin consulted with an expert and was able to make "colorable" arguments in response to a motion for summary judgment of noninfringement.

Rule 11 requires the court to impose "an appropriate sanction" for a pleading filed in violation of the rule, "upon the person who signed it, a represented party, or both." For a party represented by an attorney, the "person who signed" the pleading refers to the individual attorney who signed the pleading, not the attorney's firm. In imposing Rule 11 sanctions, a court may allocate sanctions between an attorney and client according to their relative fault. Attorneys are usually held solely responsible for Rule 11 sanctions when the filing violating Rule 11 is unwarranted by existing law, or a good faith argument for extension, modification, or reversal of existing law. However, an attorney and client may be held jointly and severally liable for filings that are not well grounded in fact.

On the record before us, we would have no hesitancy to impose on Mr. Judin and Mr. Van Der Wall, as a Rule 11 sanction in favor of HP, "the amount of the reasonable expenses incurred because of the filing of the [complaint], including a reasonable attorney's fee." Rule 11, RCFC. Further, even though Mr. Van Der Wall was not Mr. Judin's attorney of record for this Rule 11 proceeding, the record indicates that: Mr. Van Der Wall appeared at the Rule 11 sanctions hearing before the trial court; he filed an affidavit relating to HP's motion for sanctions; and he was served with the brief and related papers filed by Judin in this appeal.

Nevertheless, because determining what sanction to impose for a Rule 11 violation initially is a matter within the discretion of the trial court, we remand the case to the trial court for a determination of an appropriate sanction, and to determine whether in the interest of justice a further opportunity to be heard need be accorded to Mr. Van Der Wall.

As for the two other attorneys who represented Mr. Judin after Mr. Van Der Wall, the trial court declined to impose sanctions on them in order to avoid being inconsistent with its decision not to impose sanctions with respect to the filing of the complaint. In view of our ruling to vacate the decision with respect to the complaint, on remand the trial court should reconsider its decision with respect to later filings made by the other two attorneys. The court should consider that "reliance on forwarding co-counsel may in certain circumstances satisfy an attorney's duty of reasonable inquiry[,] ... [although a]n attorney who signs a pleading cannot simply delegate to forwarding co-counsel his duty of reasonable inquiry." *Unioil, Inc. v. E.F. Hutton & Co.*, 809 F.2d 548, 558 (9th Cir. 1986); *see* Fed. R. Civ. P. 11, Advisory Committee Notes to 1983 Amendment.

Notes

1. **Discovery Abuses.** Rule 11 in its current form excludes consideration of discovery abuses which are treated under Rule 37(a)(4). Fed. R. Civ. P. 11(d). *Loctite Corp. v. Fel–Pro*, 667 F.2d 577 (7th Cir. 1981), exemplifies extreme discovery abuses in the patent litigation context. In *Loctite,* the plaintiff filed suit with only unconfirmed data to support patent infringement. Under today's version of Rule 11, that failure by itself could have constituted grounds sufficient for a court to award Rule 11 sanctions. But Loctite's conduct progressively worsened during discovery. First, Loctite refused to produce test reports which would substantiate the infringement charges. Second, Loctite concealed a suspicion, later proven as a fact, that the test data was tainted and unreliable. In addition, Loctite repeatedly impeded discovery in various ways including instructions by Loctite to its personnel not to record written reports of test results. Also, Loctite only partially answered interrogatories and concealed evidence. Material misrepresentations in briefs and affidavits were also left uncorrected. Finally, Loctite failed to obey several court orders directing it to comply with its discovery obligations.

2. *Loctite* is also cited for the proposition that in suits where alleged infringement involves chemical patents or sophisticated technology, testing by experts prior to filing is usually required.

3. In *S. Bravo Systems, Inc. v. Containment Tech. Corp.*, 96 F.3d 1372, 40 USPQ2d 1140 (Fed. Cir. 1996), the Court held that when a party proffered substantial evidence of Rule 11 violations, the district court should provide some explanation when choosing to deny the request for sanctions. The Court explained:

> Rule 11 calls for sanctions to be imposed on a party for making arguments or filing claims that are frivolous, legally unreasonable, without factual foundation, or asserted for an "improper purpose."
> A "frivolous" argument or claim is one that is "both baseless and made without a reasonable and competent inquiry."

Id. at 1374–75, 40 USPQ2d at 1142–43 (citations omitted). *S. Bravo Systems* illustrates the necessity for infringement analysis and general pre-suit investigation as well as how Rule 11 requirements and sanctions intertwine with these investigations.

4. **A patentee is not normally required to obtain a validity opinion before filing suit.** Under 35 U.S.C. § 282, a patent is presumed to be valid. A patentee may rely on that presumption and is not typically required to obtain a validity opinion to satisfy its Rule 11 obligations. However, there may be a requirement for the patentee in certain situations to acquire a validity opinion if the patentee has been put on notice of potential invalidity. For example, if an accused infringer asserted invalidity by offering prior art in earlier license discussions, then the patentee may be advised to obtain a validity opinion over that prior art, unless, of course, it is clearly a frivolous assertion. *See* Robert L. Harmon, *Patents and the Federal Circuit*, § 1.5 (3d ed. 1984 and Supp. 1996).

5. **An accused infringer who intends to assert invalidity as a basis for a declaratory judgment should conduct a pre-suit validity study.** Rule 11 can also apply to a declaratory judgment plaintiff. It can be argued that under 35 U.S.C. § 282, an accused infringer should conduct a validity study when a declaratory judgment action is undertaken if the accused infringer is contemplating an assertion of invalidity and/or non-infringement.

Problems

1. Can you imagine any circumstances where pre-suit infringement testing would be unnecessary? Would pre-suit infringement testing be necessary where a licensee suddenly refused to pay while continuing to manufacture licensed product?

2. You are counsel to FAST SEMICONDUCTOR CORP. which makes and sells semiconductor chips. The President of FAST brings you a letter that he received from BIPOLAR CORP. The letter reads as follows:

President

FAST SEMICONDUCTOR CORPORATION

Dear President:

Bipolar is the assignee of the Smith patents on semiconductors and their fabrication process. These are U.S. Patent Numbers 6,000,000 and 6,000,001 issued last December.

We wish to let you know that the patents are available for licensing on a non-exclusive basis. If FAST does have an interest in obtaining a license, I would be pleased to discuss the matter with you.

Yours very truly,

Vice President,

BIPOLAR CORP.

FAST informs you that it discovered that BIPOLAR has already filed patent infringement suits against two other semiconductor manufacturers who are making similar products. These suits both settled out of court when the manufacturers took licenses from BIPOLAR. FAST also informs you that BIPOLAR is suing them in state court over a trade secret matter that is unrelated to the semiconductor patents.

The President says to you, "Look, we know we are making semiconductors that probably fall within the claims of the BIPOLAR patents. But, we have been making these products for years. In fact, I think that BIPOLAR may have stolen the idea from us. I have no doubt BIPOLAR plans on suing us next—just look at this baseless trade secret claim they just brought. What can we do?" How would you advise your client?

Would you advice change if the BIPOLAR letter had also stated: "BIPOLAR intends to enforce its patents to the maximum extent of the law against anyone who it determines is infringing and who refuses to take a license" and the President of FAST tells you that they just hired an ex-employee of BIPOLAR, a technician, who says that he heard that FAST is planning a big suit against BIPOLAR. Finally, the President got a call from one of FAST's semiconductor customers who asked if FAST was still going to manufacture semiconductors. Apparently, a semiconductor salesman from BIPOLAR had stopped by and suggested that the customer start buying semiconductors from BIPOLAR now because FAST may not be allowed to keep making them.

How would you advise your client?

The President also mentions that he called FAST after he received the letter to discuss licensing the semiconductor patents, but that FAST's proposed royalty rate was ridiculously high. The President said that if they agreed to FAST's terms they would actually lose money by manufacturing the semiconductors. A face-to-face licensing negotiation is scheduled for next week.

How would you advise your client?

3. Wayne Crow, a farmer from Illinois, owns a patent on a tractor with an improved grooved cutting blade (the '001 patent). He does not own a patent on the improved grooved cutting blade itself. Wayne has never sold any of his tractors but uses them at home. He believes that Tractors–R-Us may be infringing his patent by selling similar tractors. He sends them a letter, requesting information on the Tractors–R–Us Green I tractor. He explains in the letter that he believes that it may infringe his '001 patent, and he would like more information on it in order to reach a conclusion on infringement. He explains that he is not a lawyer but thinks that the two tractors are very similar. He also offers Tractors–R–Us a license under the '001 patent. Wayne never hears back from Tractors–R–Us.

Several months later, Wayne decides to drive down to his local Tractors–R–Us distributor, John Smith. He tells Mr. Smith that he is interested in buying a Tractors–R–Us tractor and he asks him about the Green I Model. Mr. Smith gives Wayne a brochure on the Green I model and explains that he may want to hold off on buying a new tractor now because Tractors–R–Us will be coming out with a Green II in about six months, which will be even better than Green I. According to Mr. Smith, the Green II will have an improved grooved cutting blade. Mr. Smith also explains that if Wayne is interested in buying the Green I model now, he could sell him one of the improved grooved cutting blades and give him written instructions on how to install the grooved cutting blade. He says that Tractors–R–Us started manufacturing and selling the improved cutting blades a month ago. He says he has been offering this service to everyone interested in tractors and has sold several of these enhanced cutting blades already. According to Mr. Smith, the customers just love them.

Angry that Tractors–R–Us may have stolen his idea, Wayne fires off a letter to Tractors–R–Us claiming that they are definitely infringing his '001 patent, that he knows about the Green II model and is sure that it will infringe his patent. He writes that if Tractors–R–Us does not take a license from him for both the Green I and the Green II—he will see them in court.

What are the litigation options for each side?

Chapter Three

THE PROPER COURT: WHERE CAN YOU BRING SUIT?

INTRODUCTION

A suit that litigates patent rights must be filed in the proper court. There are three basic requirements that dictate what court a patent suit should be filed in: (1) subject matter jurisdiction; (2) personal jurisdiction; and (3) venue.

Subject matter jurisdiction is the power of a court to decide a particular claim. By statute (28 U.S.C. § 1338), Congress mandated that only federal courts may resolve disputes "arising under" the patent laws. However, this does not mean that state courts never decide patent law issues. For example, if a plaintiff brings a suit for breach of a licensing agreement (where the subject of the license is patented technology) and the defendant defends his actions on the ground that the patent is invalid, the state court may have to resolve the patent's validity. Breach of a patent licensing or assignment agreement has no statutory basis; therefore, unless there is diversity of citizenship, state courts decide these issues because they arise under state contract law rather than federal patent law. Similarly, a dispute over title or ownership of a patent arises under state property law, even though the validity of the patent may be affected by resolution of these issues. However, do not confuse this with inventorship, which definitively arises under the patent laws, and therefore, requires resolution by a federal tribunal.

How the plaintiff pleads the action, rather than the nature of the underlying dispute, dictates which court has jurisdiction. The Supreme Court recently indicated that a case "arises under" the patent laws pursuant to § 1338 when "a well-pleaded complaint establishes either that federal patent law creates the cause of action or that the plaintiff's right to relief necessarily depends on resolution of a substantial question of federal patent law, in that patent law is a necessary element of one of the well-pleaded claims."[1] Therefore, it is the plaintiff, not the defendant

---

1. *Christianson v. Colt Indus. Operating Corp.*, 486 U.S. 800, 801 (1988).

who controls which forum will adjudicate a claim involving issues related to a patent.

Personal jurisdiction is the power of the courts over the parties involved in the dispute. The Supreme Court stated in *International Shoe Co. v. Washington*, 326 U.S. 310, 316 (1945), "due process requires ... that in order to subject a defendant to a judgment *in personam,* if he be not present within the territory of the forum, he have certain *minimum contacts* with it such that the maintenance of the suit does not offend 'traditional notions of fair play and substantial justice.' " In this respect, a patent case is no different than any other type of case.

Venue is appropriate if the forum is convenient for the parties, especially the defendant. "[T]he fundamental and historical purpose of venue ... is that there is a particular court or courts in which an action 'should be brought' for the convenience of the parties, particularly that of defendant." *Delta Air Lines, Inc. v. Western Conference of Teamsters,* 722 F. Supp. 725, 727 (D.Ga.1989).

A patent holder can bring suit in any federal district court where jurisdiction and venue requirements can be met and the defendant can be served. There will often be several forums available to the patentee in which to bring suit. The patentee should consider the following factors when deciding where to bring suit: (1) convenience issues; (2) the docket of the court; and (3) the relative competence and predisposition of the judge and potential jury.

Convenience issues include matters such as location of counsel, proximity to the court, location of the documents or other evidence, and location of the witnesses. The court's docket may be important to a patentee who is seeking expeditious resolution of his case in order to compel others to license the technology. The Eastern District of Virginia, which is affectionately known as the "rocket docket" because of its speedy trials, provides an excellent forum for such a plaintiff. The Eastern District of Wisconsin has also garnered a reputation with the patent community as having a fast docket. You cannot ignore the experiences of the judges and juries in a given district when choosing where to bring suit. For instance, the District of Delaware and the Northern District of California conduct more patent trials than other districts. If it is important to the patentee's case to have a court that is skilled in dealing with the complexities of patent law and the technology at issue, one of these districts would be a good choice. The attitudes of the judges in a district should be considered as well. Do the judges appear to consistently invalidate patents? The competence and attitudes of prospective jurors will also vary by jurisdiction. For example, you are more likely to get a jury with technical training in the Northern District of California then some other jurisdictions. Finally, you probably would not want to choose the district in which the defendant employs a large segment of the population. You would likely get a jury that favors the defendant because the defendant provides jobs to the community or sponsors the local little league teams.

A. JURISDICTION OF PATENT CASES

1. SUBJECT MATTER JURISDICTION

STATUTORY PROVISION— 35 U.S.C. § 1338:

(a) The district courts shall have original jurisdiction of any civil action arising under any Act of Congress relating to patents, plant variety protection, copyrights and trademarks. Such jurisdiction shall be exclusive of the courts of the states in patents, plant variety protection and copyright cases.

This provision grants federal courts original and exclusive jurisdiction over patent cases. As discussed above, this does not mean that federal courts have jurisdiction over every case involving patent law. For more information *see* Emmette F. Hale, III, *The "Arising Under" Jurisdiction of the Federal Circuit: An Opportunity For Uniformity in Patent Law*, 14 FLA. ST. U. L. REV. 229, 242–43 (1986) (noting that use of the well-pleaded complaint rule to determine jurisdiction ensures that state courts will have significant input into federal patent law); Donald Chisum, *The Allocation of Jurisdiction Between State and Federal Courts in Patent Litigation*, 46 WASH.L.REV. 633, 670 (1970).

2. PERSONAL JURISDICTION

Personal jurisdiction requires that the defendant have sufficient minimum contacts with the federal district in which the case is being brought. Whether the defendant has purposefully established minimum contacts with a forum is determined under a three prong test set out in *Akro Corp. v. Luker*, 45 F.3d 1541, 1545–46, 33 USPQ2d 1505, 1508–09 (Fed. Cir. 1995):

1. did the defendant purposefully direct activities at residents in the forum;

2. did the cause of action or claim arise out of, or relate to, those activities directed at the forum; and

3. is the assertion of personal jurisdiction in that forum fair and reasonable.

The underlying question is whether it would be fair for the defendant to be hauled into court in that federal district. The court begins by looking at the state's long arm statute in order to determine whether a defendant is subject to personal jurisdiction in that district. The long arm statute will usually define what amounts to minimum contacts.

BEVERLY HILLS FAN CO. v. ROYAL SOVEREIGN CORP.

21 F.3d 1558, 30 USPQ2d 1001 (Fed. Cir. 1994)

Before NEWMAN, Circuit Judge, SMITH, Senior Circuit Judge, and PLAGER, Circuit Judge.

PLAGER, Circuit Judge.

BACKGROUND

Beverly is the current owner of U.S. Design Patent No. 304,229 (the '229 patent), which issued on October 24, 1989. That patent is directed to the design of a ceiling fan. Beverly is incorporated in Delaware and has its principal place of business in California. Ultec is the manufacturer of a ceiling fan which Beverly alleges infringes the '229 patent. Ultec is incorporated in the People's Republic of China (PRC) and manufactures the accused fan in Taiwan. Royal imports into and distributes the accused fan in the United States. It is incorporated in New Jersey.

On December 11, 1991, Beverly filed suit against Ultec and Royal in the United States District Court for the Eastern District of Virginia. Beverly's complaint alleged in relevant part that both defendants are infringing and inducing infringement of the '229 patent by selling the accused fan to customers in the United States, including customers in Virginia; and that defendants are selling the accused fan to the Virginia customers through intermediaries.

Ultec and Royal subsequently filed a motion to dismiss for lack of personal jurisdiction pursuant to Rule 12(b)(2) of the Federal Rules of Civil Procedure. In support of their motion, defendants submitted several declarations. A first declaration was from James Cheng (the Cheng Declaration), the President of Ultec. In that declaration, Mr. Cheng stated that Ultec has no assets or employees located in Virginia; has no agent for the service of process in Virginia; does not have a license to do business in Virginia; and has not directly shipped the accused fan into Virginia. A second declaration was from T.K. Lim (the Lim Declaration), the President of Royal. In that declaration, Mr. Lim stated that Royal, as well, has no assets or employees in Virginia; has no agent for the service of process in Virginia; does not have a license to do business in Virginia; made a one-time sale of unrelated goods to Virginia in 1991 which represented less than three percent of Royal's total sales that year; and has not sold the accused fan to distributors or anyone else in Virginia.

Beverly then submitted several declarations in opposition to the motion. A first declaration was from Lyndal L. Shaneyfelt (the first Shaneyfelt Declaration), a private investigator. In that declaration, Mr. Shaneyfelt stated that, on December 4, 1991, he purchased one of the accused fans from the Alexandria, Virginia outlet of a company known as Builder's Square; that a manual accompanying the fan identified Royal as the source of the fan; that the fan was accompanied by a warranty which Royal would honor; and that Builder's Square has approximately six retail outlets located throughout Virginia. A second declaration was from Shelley A. Greenberg (the Greenberg Declaration), the President of Beverly. In that declaration, Mr. Greenberg stated that Beverly does a substantial amount of business in Virginia; that Beverly's Virginia customers include all six Builder's Square outlets; and that Beverly sells a commercial embodiment of the '229 patent to customers in Virginia through these outlets.

The trial court, after argument from the parties and consideration of their written submissions, ruled on the motion. The court correctly recognized that there were two limits to its jurisdictional reach: Virginia's long-arm statute and the Due Process Clause of the U.S. Constitution. The court found its analysis of the limits imposed by the Due Process Clause conclusive of the matter.

[T]he court concluded that the relevant inquiry was whether defendants' contacts with the forum were sufficiently purposeful that litigation in the forum could reasonably have been foreseen. The only purposeful contact the court considered relevant was the one-time shipment of unrelated goods referred to in the Lim Declaration. Finding that such contact was not sufficient to make litigation in Virginia reasonably foreseeable, the court granted the motion to dismiss. On March 6, 1992, an order granting judgment for defendants was entered consistent with the court's ruling.

Discussion

In light of the trial court's conclusion to the contrary, based in part on a failure to draw the proper inferences from the undisputed facts, we must disapprove the court's granting of the motion to dismiss. No additional development of the record is necessary for a decision on defendants' jurisdictional motion. The matter presents a pure question of law. The specific question on which the matter turns is whether the Due Process Clause of the Federal Constitution or specific limiting provisions in Virginia's long-arm statute preclude the exercise of jurisdiction in a case in which an alleged foreign infringer's sole contact with the forum resulted from indirect shipments through the stream of commerce.

As a preliminary matter, we consider whether we are bound to apply Fourth Circuit law to this question. As previously noted, the Fourth Circuit is where the case arose; under *Panduit Corp. v. All States Plastic Manufacturing Co.*, 744 F.2d 1564, 1574–75, 223 USPQ 465, 471 (Fed. Cir. 1984), we apply the law of the Fourth Circuit to procedural matters that are not unique to patent law. Beverly argues that we are not bound to apply Fourth Circuit law in this case because the issue here is intimately related to substantive patent law. Thus, argues Beverly, we are free to develop our own law on this issue.

Beverly is correct. Although in one sense the due process issue in this case is procedural, it is a critical determinant of whether and in what forum a patentee can seek redress for infringement of its rights. As we explain more fully below, the stream of commerce theory has achieved fairly wide acceptance in the federal courts. But even when followed, the theory comes in several variants. The regional circuits have not reached a uniform approach to this jurisdictional issue. *See, e.g., Max Daetwyler Corp. v. R. Meyer*, 762 F.2d 290, 226 USPQ 305 (3d Cir. 1985) (no jurisdiction found); *Honeywell, Inc. v. Metz Apparatewerke*, 509 F.2d 1137, 184 USPQ 387 (7th Cir. 1975) (jurisdiction found). Nor is there any apparent uniformity on the issue within the Fourth Circuit. The application of an assumed Fourth Circuit law, or for that matter, the law of any particular circuit, would thus not promote our mandate of achieving national uniformity in the field of patent law.

The creation and application of a uniform body of Federal Circuit law in this area would clearly promote judicial efficiency, would be consistent with our mandate, and would not create undue conflict and confusion at the district court level. Under circumstances such as these, we have held we owe no special deference to regional circuit law. *See, e.g., Biodex Corp. v. Loredan Biomedical, Inc.*, 946 F.2d 850, 855–59, 20 USPQ2d 1252, 1256–61 (Fed. Cir. 1991).

The Supreme Court stated in *International Shoe Co. v. Washington*, 326 U.S. 310 (1945), "due process requires . . . that in order to subject a defendant to a judgment in personam, if he be not present within the territory of the forum, he have certain minimum contacts with it such that the maintenance of the suit does not offend 'traditional notions of fair play and substantial justice.' "*Id.* at 316 (quoting *Milliken v. Meyer*, 311 U.S. 457, 463 (1940)). Later cases have clarified that the minimum contacts must be 'purposeful' contacts. *Burger King Corp. v. Rudzewicz*, 471 U.S. 462, 474 (1985) (purposeful minimum contacts the 'constitutional touchstone' of the due process analysis). The requirement for purposeful minimum contacts helps ensure that non-residents have fair warning that a particular activity may subject them to litigation within the forum. Fair warning is desirable for non-residents are thus able to organize their affairs, alleviate the risk of burdensome litigation by procuring insurance and the like, and otherwise plan for the possibility that litigation in the forum might ensue.

Defendants argue that their contacts with Virginia were insufficient to give them warning that litigation in Virginia might ensue. We disagree. The allegations are that defendants purposefully shipped the accused fan into Virginia through an established distribution channel. The cause of action for patent infringement is alleged to arise out of these activities. No more is usually required to establish specific jurisdiction.

Defendants argue that the exercise of jurisdiction over them is foreclosed by the holding in *World-Wide Volkswagen*. In *World-Wide Volkswagen*, jurisdiction did not lie over an alleged foreign tortfeasor whose product was transported into the forum state through the unilateral actions of a third party having no pre-existing relationship with the tortfeasor. There was thus no purposeful contact by the tortfeasor with the forum, and thus no basis for exercising personal jurisdiction over the defendants. Here, by contrast, the allegations are that the accused fan arrived in Virginia through defendants' purposeful shipment of the fans through an established distribution channel.[2] The Court in *World-Wide*

---

2. The presence of an established distribution channel is a significant factor in the cases cited by the parties involving the stream of commerce theory. In plaintiff's cases, in which jurisdiction over the nonresident was found to exist, there was an established distribution channel into the forum. In defendants' cases, in which jurisdic-

Volkswagen specifically commented on the significance of this factual pattern: "[I]f the sale of a product of a manufacturer or distributor ... is not simply an isolated occurrence, but arises from the efforts of the [defendants] to serve, directly or indirectly, the market for its product ..., it is not unreasonable to subject it to suit." *Id.* at 297. And "[t]he forum State does not exceed its powers under the Due Process Clause if it asserts personal jurisdiction over a corporation that delivers its products into the stream of commerce with the expectation that they will be purchased by consumers in the forum State." *Id.* at 297–98.

Since the decision in *World-Wide Volkswagen*, lower courts have split over the exact requirements of the stream of commerce theory. In *Asahi Metal Industry Co. v. Superior Court*, 480 U.S. 102 (1987), the Supreme Court reflected that split in the context of a case in which jurisdiction in California state courts was asserted for the purpose of requiring a Japanese corporation to indemnify a Taiwanese corporation on the basis of a sale made in Taiwan and a shipment of goods from Japan to Taiwan.

All of the Justices agreed that on the facts of the case before them, jurisdiction did not lie in California; and apparently all of the Justices agreed that the stream of commerce theory provides a valid basis for finding requisite minimum contacts. The split was over the exact requirements for an application of the theory.

We need not join this debate here, since we find that, under either version of the stream of commerce theory, plaintiff made the required jurisdictional showing. When viewed in the light of the allegations and the uncontroverted assertions in the affidavits, plaintiff has stated all of the necessary ingredients for an exercise of jurisdiction consonant with due process: defendants, acting in consort, placed the accused fan in the stream of commerce, they knew the likely destination of the products, and their conduct and connections with the forum state were such that they should reasonably have anticipated being brought into court there.

Notwithstanding the existence of purposeful minimum contacts, a due process determination requires one further step. As Justice Stevens put it in his concurrence in *Asahi*, " 'minimum requirements inherent in the concept of "fair play and substantial justice" may defeat the reasonableness of jurisdiction even if the defendant has purposefully engaged in forum activities.' " 480 U.S. at 121–22 (Stevens, J., concurring in part and concurring in the judgment) (quoting *International Shoe*, 326 U.S. at 320). In other words, even if the requisite minimum contacts have been found through an application of the stream of commerce theory or otherwise, if it would be unreasonable for the forum to assert jurisdiction under all the facts and circumstances, then due process requires that jurisdiction be denied.

In general, these cases are limited to the rare situation in which the plaintiff's interest and the state's interest in adjudicating the dispute in

tion was found not to exist, there was no such channel in place.

the forum are so attenuated that they are clearly outweighed by the burden of subjecting the defendant to litigation within the forum.

We conclude this is not one of those rare cases. Virginia's interests in the dispute are significant. Virginia has an interest in discouraging injuries that occur within the state. That interest extends to design patent infringement actions such as the one here.

Virginia also has a substantial interest in cooperating with other states to provide a forum for efficiently litigating plaintiff's cause of action. Beverly will be able to seek redress in Virginia for sales of the accused fan to consumers in these other states.[3] These other states will thus be spared the burden of providing a forum for Beverly to seek redress for these sales. And defendants will be protected from harassment resulting from multiple suits.

That it is to plaintiff's advantage to adjudicate the dispute in the district court for the Eastern District of Virginia does not militate against its right to have access to that court. The court is part of the exclusive mechanism established by Congress for the vindication of patent rights. The fact that it has unique attributes of which plaintiff apparently has an interest in taking advantage does not change the case.

The burden on Royal does not appear particularly significant. Royal, being incorporated in New Jersey, is not located that far from Virginia. This is not a burden sufficiently compelling to outweigh Beverly's and Virginia's interests. Ultec, on the other hand, will be required to traverse the distance between its headquarters in the PRC and the district court in Virginia, and will also be required to submit itself to a foreign nation's judicial system. However, it is recognized that " 'progress in communications and transportation has made the defense of a lawsuit in a foreign tribunal less burdensome.' "*World-Wide Volkswagen*, 444 U.S. at 294 (quoting *Hanson v. Denckla*, 357 U.S. 235 (1958)). And Ultec, through its business dealings with Royal, cannot profess complete ignorance of the judicial system of the United States. Accordingly, we conclude that the burden on Ultec, as well, is not sufficiently compelling to outweigh Beverly's and Virginia's interests.

The final issue we must address is the applicability of Virginia's long-arm statute. Federal courts apply the relevant state statute when determining whether a federal court, sitting in a particular case, has personal jurisdiction over a defendant, even when the cause of action is purely federal. *See* Fed.R.Civ.P. 4(e)-(f).

Subsections A.3 and A.4 of the Virginia statute read:

A. A court may exercise personal jurisdiction over a person, who acts directly or by an agent, as to a cause of action arising from the person's:

---

3. Beverly is not precluded from bringing suit in Virginia just because the bulk of the harm inflicted on it may occur through sales in these other states. *See Keeton*, 465 U.S. at 779–80.

    3. Causing tortious injury by an act or omission in this Commonwealth;

    4. Causing tortious injury in this Commonwealth by an act or omission outside this Commonwealth if he ... derives substantial revenue from goods used or consumed or services rendered, in this Commonwealth.

Beverly first argues that subsection A.3, the 'single act' provision of Virginia's long-arm statute, applies. That provision requires "an act or omission in this Commonwealth," i.e., a tortious act or omission within Virginia. But jurisdiction here cannot be based on a tortious omission, since active inducement of infringement requires the commission of an affirmative act. Nor is there support for finding such an affirmative act to have occurred in Virginia—there is nothing in the record suggesting that either defendant necessarily committed any affirmative act there.

The other relevant subsection of Virginia's long-arm statute, subsection A.4, also requires that a tortious injury occur in the state, but here the act or omission causing the injury can take place outside the state. The question, then, in determining whether subsection A.4 is applicable to the facts of this case, is whether a 'tortious injury' occurred in the Commonwealth of Virginia.

Beverly contends that *Honeywell, Inc. v. Metz Apparatewerke*, 509 F.2d 1137, 184 USPQ 387 (7th Cir. 1975) supports jurisdiction over defendants. In *Honeywell*, plaintiff brought suit in the Northern District of Illinois against a U.S. retailer, two U.S. distributors, and the foreign manufacturer of a product the sale of which in Illinois was alleged to infringe Honeywell's patent. The district court, applying the Illinois statute, dismissed the suit against the foreign manufacturer. On appeal, the Seventh Circuit reversed, holding that Honeywell had suffered a tortious injury in Illinois and, under that state's statute, jurisdiction was proper.

The *Honeywell* decision can be read as holding that the injury occurred where infringing sales were made. Alternatively, however, *Honeywell* can also be read to mean that the situs of the injury is the situs of the intangible property interest, which is determined by where the patent owner resides (Honeywell's principal place of business was in Illinois). The law is unsettled on this question; the district courts have read the case both ways.

As noted, in a case such as this some courts consider the legal situs of an injury to intellectual property rights to be the residence of the owner of the interest. The theory is that, since intellectual property rights relate to intangible property, no particular physical situs exists. If a legal situs must be chosen, it is not illogical to pick the residence of the owner.

At first glance this rule may not seem illogical, but there are good arguments against it. Among the most important rights in the bundle of rights owned by a patent holder is the right to exclude others. This right is not limited to a particular situs, but exists anywhere the patent is recognized. It seems questionable to attribute to a patent right a single situs. A patent is a federally created property right, valid throughout the United States. Its legal situs would seem to be anywhere it is called into play. This point is illustrated by the fact that, when an infringement occurs by a sale of an infringing product, the right to exclude is violated at the situs where the sale occurs.

Other courts have avoided the problems created by the single-situs/place of residence idea, and found the situs of injury to intellectual property in an appropriate case to be the place of the infringing sale. Although economic harm to the interests of the patent holder is conceptually different from the tortious injury to the patent holder's right to exclude others, recognizing the relationship between these concepts permits the court to assess realistically the legal situs of injury for purposes of determining jurisdiction over the patent holder's infringement claim.

Economic loss occurs to the patent holder at the place where the infringing sale is made because the patent owner loses business there. This loss is immediate when the patent holder is marketing a competing product. Even if the patent holder is not, the loss may be no less real since the sale represents a loss in potential revenue through licensing or other arrangements. Furthermore, analysis of long-arm jurisdiction has its focus on the conduct of the defendant. Plaintiff's contacts with the forum—such as where the plaintiff resides—as a general proposition are not considered a determinative consideration. Additionally, a focus on the place where the infringing sales are made is consistent with other areas of intellectual property law—it brings patent infringement actions into line with the rule applied in trademark and copyright cases.

As we observed earlier in connection with the stream of commerce theory, we believe a uniform body of Federal Circuit law in this area would clearly promote judicial efficiency, would be consistent with our mandate, and would not create undue conflict and confusion at the district court level. Accordingly we hold that, in a case such as this, the situs of the injury is the location, or locations, at which the infringing activity directly impacts on the interests of the patentee, here the place of the infringing sales in Virginia.

We conclude that the 'tortious injury' requirement of subsection A.4 has been met. The 'act or omission outside this Commonwealth' requirement is likewise satisfied given our previous conclusion that defendants purposefully shipped the accused fan into Virginia through an established distribution channel.

This leaves the 'substantial revenue' requirement. We conclude that this requirement is also satisfied. It can be inferred from plaintiff's allegations that defendants, by making through distribution channels ongoing and continuous shipments into Virginia, have derived substantial revenue, at least in absolute terms, from sales in Virginia. Although it is uncertain whether these sales have been substantial in percentage terms, the statute does not require that.

Royal derived revenue from the one-time sale referred to in the Lim Declaration. There is evidence in the record that this revenue was substantial given that the underlying sale represented something in the range of 3% of Royal's total sales in 1991.[4] This revenue is relevant even though it resulted from the sale of unrelated goods.

For all the foregoing reasons, we conclude that the requirements of subsection A.4 have been satisfied, and that defendants were subject to personal jurisdiction under Virginia's long-arm statute.

GENETIC IMPLANT SYSTEMS, INC. v. CORE–VENT CORP.

123 F.3d 1455, 43 USPQ2d 1786 (Fed. Cir. 1997)

Before PLAGER, Circuit Judge, SMITH, Senior Circuit Judge, and LOURIE, Circuit Judge.

LOURIE, Circuit Judge.

BACKGROUND

This appeal is from an action involving U.S. Patent 4,960,381, which issued on October 2, 1990 and claims dental implants. Niznick is the sole inventor named on the patent and he assigned the patent to Core–Vent, which is a Nevada corporation with its principal place of business in California. Niznick is the president, chief executive officer, sole shareholder, and sole board member of Core–Vent.

Core–Vent directly sold its dental implant products in the state of Washington until the issuance of the '381 patent in 1990. In April 1991, it entered into an exclusive worldwide marketing and distribution agreement with Dentsply International, Inc., a Delaware corporation with its principal place of business in Pennsylvania. Since 1991, Dentsply has made substantial sales of Core–Vent products in Washington, a significant portion of which are attributable to products covered by the '381 patent.

Genetic, a Washington corporation, alleges that after the patent issued, Niznick repeatedly and publicly threatened to sue Genetic and Stanley W. Sapkos, Genetic's chief executive officer, for infringement. In 1994–95, Core–Vent sent Genetic three letters accusing it of infringing the '381 patent and, in the third letter, it refused an offer of settlement by Genetic. Genetic alleges that Core–Vent also communicated its threats of infringement to others in the industry. According to Genetic, these threats have had a detrimental effect on its ability to market and sell its implants, in that potential customers have refused to purchase the implants due to fear of litigation. It also alleges that the threats successfully discouraged investment in Genetic. Accordingly, Genetic sued Core–Vent and Niznick on May 5, 1995, in the United States District Court for the Western District of Washington, requesting a

---

4. That evidence shows that Royal had $10,000,000 in gross sales in 1991. Assuming that figure is correct, in dollar terms, the 3% figure represents $300,000.

declaratory judgment of noninfringement and invalidity of the '381 patent. Core–Vent and Niznick moved to dismiss on the ground of lack of personal jurisdiction.

The district court granted the motion. The court found that Core–Vent's threats of infringement, in view of the fact that Core–Vent had only a distributorship agreement with an out-of-state company, were insufficient to establish purposeful availment of the privileges and benefits of the state of Washington. It found that, even if Core–Vent's activities did constitute purposeful availment, it would be unreasonable to force Core–Vent to defend itself in the state of Washington. The court thus dismissed the action against Core–Vent. Genetic now appeals to this court. We have jurisdiction pursuant to 28 U.S.C. § 1295(a)(1) (1994).

Discussion

Whether a court has personal jurisdiction over a defendant is a question of law that we review de novo.

Genetic argues that Core–Vent initiated and maintained sufficient minimum contacts with the state of Washington to subject itself to personal jurisdiction. Genetic asserts that Core–Vent purposefully directed its sales and marketing activities to residents of the state, and that the present declaratory judgment action arises out of or relates to those activities. Core–Vent responds that it does not maintain contacts with and does not direct sufficient commerce into Washington to justify assertion of personal jurisdiction over the company. It argues that sending cease-and-desist letters into the forum is not sufficient to establish personal jurisdiction. It asserts that the combination of sales of its products in Washington and the warning letters still do not establish personal jurisdiction, as the sales occurred prior to issuance of the patent and thus are irrelevant to a determination of jurisdiction.

Determining whether jurisdiction exists over an out-of-state defendant involves two inquiries: whether a forum state's long-arm statute permits service of process and whether assertion of personal jurisdiction violates due process. *See Burger King Corp. v. Rudzewicz*, 471 U.S. 462, 471–76 (1985). The relevant provision of the Washington long-arm statute identifying acts that may subject a defendant to jurisdiction reads as follows:

4.28.185. Personal service out of state—Acts submitting person to jurisdiction of courts—Saving

(1) Any person, whether or not a citizen or resident of this state, who in person or through an agent does any of the acts in this section enumerated, thereby submits said person, and, if an individual, his personal representative, to the jurisdiction of the courts of this state as to any cause of action arising from the doing of any of said acts:

(a) The transaction of any business within this state;

Wash. Rev.Code § 4.28.185 (1996). The scope of the "transaction of any business" criterion set forth in the statute is co-extensive with the limits of due process. The focus of the inquiry in this case is therefore whether assertion of jurisdiction over Core–Vent in Washington comports with due process. That inquiry involves consideration of three factors: whether the defendant purposefully directed its activities at residents of the forum, whether the claim arises out of or relates to the defendant's activities with the forum, and whether assertion of personal jurisdiction is reasonable and fair. *Akro Corp. v. Luker*, 45 F.3d 1541, 1545–46, 33 USPQ2d 1505, 1508–09 (Fed. Cir. 1995) (citing *Burger King*, 471 U.S. at 471–76).

We agree with Genetic that Core–Vent has had sufficient minimum contacts with the state of Washington. We have held that sending infringement letters, without more activity in a forum state, is not sufficient to satisfy the requirements of due process. Other activities are required in order for a patentee to be subject to personal jurisdiction in the forum. Here, however, Core–Vent did more than send cease-and-desist letters to Genetic in Washington. In particular, it engaged in a program to develop a market in Washington, including founding teaching centers in Seattle staffed by local periodontists, developing Washington customer lists through the teaching centers, and advertising in publications distributed to potential Washington customers. These pre–1991 activities resulted in substantial revenue from sales in Washington and contributed to Core–Vent's presence in Washington by producing a customer base in the state that may result in or enhance future sales. The fact that they may have occurred before the grant of the patent is irrelevant since they do show that Core–Vent engaged in substantial activities in the state. It is jurisdiction that is at issue, not liability for patent infringement. In addition, and most significant, since 1991, Core–Vent and Niznick have contracted with Dentsply to sell Core–Vent's patented products in Washington. Dentsply has two sales representatives in Washington and, since 1991, has sold in the state a substantial dollar amount of Core–Vent products covered by the '381 patent.

We concluded in *Akro* that infringement letters sent into a forum state accompanied by the grant of a license to an in-state competitor doing business in the state were sufficient to justify assertion of personal jurisdiction against an out-of-state patentee. The appointment of a distributor to sell a product covered by a patent is analogous to a grant of a patent license. Such an action conveys an implied license to the distributor, thereby surrendering the patentee's right to exclude the distributor under the patent. *See* 35 U.S.C. § 154(a)(1) (1994) ("Every patent shall contain ... a grant to the patentee, his heirs or assigns, of the right to exclude others from making, using, offering for sale, or selling the invention throughout the United States...."). In the Dentsply agreement Core–Vent appointed Dentsply as the "exclusive world-wide distributor" of its dental implant products. It granted Dentsply the right to distribute the products, and it agreed not to appoint "any other person, firm or entity to sell or otherwise distribute" the products, which includes dental implants covered by the '381 patent.

The agreement contained other provisions similar to those typically found in a patent license agreement. Core–Vent agreed to maintain all patents covering the products and it agreed to file and prosecute applications for patents covering new products. Core–Vent also retained the right to pursue claims for infringement and it agreed to indemnify Dentsply for liability arising from any third party patent infringement action related to Dentsply's sale, use, or making of the products. Finally, Core–Vent authorized Dentsply to use Core–Vent's trademarks in marketing and distributing the products. Accordingly, Core–Vent purposefully availed itself of the facilities of the state of Washington; moreover, the cause of action is clearly related to or arises out of its activities in Washington.

Core–Vent argues nonetheless that it cannot be subject to personal jurisdiction as a result of Dentsply's sales of its products in Washington because Dentsply is not its agent and is not an in-state licensee. We do not agree. Core–Vent's distinction between in-state and out-of-state distributors is not tenable; the fact that Dentsply is not a Washington corporation is not determinative. Dentsply is present in Washington in the sense that it promotes and sells Core–Vent's patented products in the state; thus, it is transacting business "in-state."

Core–Vent argues that, although the first two factors in the personal jurisdiction inquiry may be satisfied, assertion of jurisdiction over it would not be reasonable and fair. It asserts that a defendant's minimum contacts may be considered in light of additional factors to "determine whether the assertion of personal jurisdiction would comport with 'fair play and substantial justice.'" *Burger King*, 471 U.S. at 476 (quoting *International Shoe Co. v. Washington*, 326 U.S. 310, 320 (1945)). "[W]here a defendant who purposefully has directed his activities at forum residents seeks to defeat jurisdiction, he must present a compelling case that the presence of some other considerations would render jurisdiction unreasonable." *Id.* at 477; *see World–Wide Volkswagen Corp. v. Woodson*, 444 U.S. 286, 292 (1980) (listing factors to consider in determining the reasonableness of asserting jurisdiction over a defendant).

Core–Vent has not shown that requiring it to defend itself in Washington would be unreasonable or unfair. It has not shown, for example, that it would be inconvenient for it to litigate in Washington or that the forum state does not have a sufficient interest in resolving the dispute. Entering into an exclusive distributorship agreement authorizing the distribution of its trademarked and patented products in Washington is sufficiently analogous to entering into a patent license agreement, which we have previously concluded is a sufficient contact, in combination with cease-and-desist letters, to comply with the requirements of due process. Accordingly, the district court erred in dismissing the complaint on the ground of lack of personal jurisdiction over Core–Vent.

CONCLUSION

The district court erred in holding that it did not have jurisdiction over Core–Vent. Core–Vent has had sufficient minimum contacts with the state of Washington, and the exercise of jurisdiction over it is reasonable and fair in light of its exclusive distributorship agreement with Dentsply. Accordingly, we reverse the judgment of the district court dismissing Genetic's complaint against Core–Vent, and remand for further proceedings.

Notes

1. **Long Arm Statute.** The patent code has its own form of long arm statute to allow declaratory judgments against foreign patentees. *See* 35 U.S.C. § 293. When the patentee is a foreign party, it can designate a person residing in the United States on whom process or notice of proceedings may be served. Such a designation is made pursuant to 35 U.S.C. § 293, by filing a written designation with the PTO. If there is no designation on file or if the designated person cannot be found, the United States District Court for the District of Columbia shall have jurisdiction and a summons can be served by publication.

2. **Federal Circuit Law Applies to Personal Jurisdiction Issues.** The procedural law of the Federal Circuit, rather than that of the regional circuit in which the case arose, applies when determining whether the district court properly declined to exercise personal jurisdiction over an out-of-state accused infringer. *See Beverly Hills Fan Co. v. Royal Sovereign Corp.*, 21 F.3d 1558, 1564, 30 USPQ2d 1001, 1006 (Fed. Cir. 1994). Do you agree that this issue is "unique to" patent law or "relates to" the Federal Circuit's exclusive jurisdiction?

3. **Stream of Commerce Theory**. The Federal Circuit has endorsed the stream of commerce theory, regular and anticipated flow of products from the manufacturer to distribution to retail sale, for establishing the minimum contacts required for personal jurisdiction. *See Beverly Hills Fan Co. v. Royal Sovereign Corp.*, 21 F.3d 1558, 1566, 30 USPQ2d 1001, 1008 (Fed. Cir. 1994) (a forum state does not exceed its powers under the Due Process Clause if it asserts personal jurisdiction over a corporation that delivers its products into the stream of commerce with the expectation that they will be purchased by consumers in the forum State). The presence of an existing distributional channel in a state is a significant factor in the stream of commerce analysis. The Federal Circuit, however, has declined to take a position on whether placing a product in the stream of commerce alone is sufficient for minimum contacts or whether additional conduct is necessary. *Viam Corp. v. Iowa Export–Import Trading Co.*, 84 F.3d 424, 428, 38 USPQ2d 1833 (Fed. Cir. 1996) ("we need not join the debate in *Asahi* as to which version of the stream of commerce theory is the correct one, because under either theory the result we reach here would be the same").

4. **Cease and Desist Letters Alone are Insufficient to Create Personal Jurisdiction.** Assertions of infringement and the negotiations of a licensing agreement are not sufficient to exercise personal jurisdiction over a defendant. Correspondence such as letters, facsimiles, and telephone conversations alone do not establish personal jurisdiction. *Red Wing Shoe*

Co. v. Hockerson–Halberstadt, Inc., 148 F.3d 1355, 47 USPQ2d 1192 (Fed. Cir. 1998). In *Red Wing Shoe*, the court held that there was no personal jurisdiction in Minnesota despite the fact that the patentee had contacted the defendant in Minnesota claiming infringement, engaged in licensing and settlement negotiations with the defendant in Minnesota, and had over 30 licensees—some of which sold shoes in Minnesota. How can this be reconciled with *Viam* which held that there was personal jurisdiction when the patentee had a distribution agreement for a distributor to sell in the state and knew that its products were being sold in the state? What is the difference between a distributor and a licensee? Would it matter if the patentee knew that the licensee was located in the state and the licensing agreement granted it the right to sell the patented product in the state? Should it turn on how much control the patentee has over the licensee?

5. **Price Quotation Letters Can Form the Basis for Personal Jurisdiction as Offers to Sell.** In *3D Systems Inc. v. Aarotech Labs. Inc.*, 160 F.3d 1373, 48 USPQ2d 1773 (Fed. Cir. 1998), the court held that Aarotech purposefully directed activities at California because it sent residents price quotes, promotional letter, videos, and sample parts even though it never sold any equipment to anyone in California. Aarotech also responded to e-mail requests from California companies and discussed the use of a California company's software with its hardware. In addition, the court held that the cause of action (patent infringement) arose from Aarotech's activities with California residents (offers to sell). If a defendant has contacts with a state, the fact that it did not sell the product at issue in the state is not sufficient to defeat personal jurisdiction. *Akro Corp. v. Luker*, 45 F.3d 1541, 1547, 33 USPQ2d 1505 (Fed. Cir. 1995).

6. **The "Chutzpah" Award.** In *Dainippon Screen Mfg. Co. v. CFMT, Inc.*, 142 F.3d 1266, 46 USPQ2d 1616 (Fed. Cir. 1998), the court reversed the district court's dismissal of a declaratory judgment action brought against CFMT for lack of personal jurisdiction. CFMT was a wholly owned subsidiary of CFM incorporated in order to hold CFM's intellectual property assets and license them back. CFMT licensed CFM to make, use, and sell the patented product in California and derived substantial revenues from CFM's California sales. CFM had sales agents in California. CFMT itself issued threats of infringement in California and tried to negotiate a license with Dainippon in California. The Federal Circuit held that in light of its own activities and the activities of its parent in California there was personal jurisdiction over CFMT in California stating:

> Stripped to its essentials, CFM contends that a parent company can incorporate a holding company in another state, transfer its patents to the holding company, arrange to have those patents licensed back to itself by virtue of its complete control over the holding company, and threaten its competitors with infringement without fear of being a declaratory judgment defendant, save perhaps in the state of incorporation of the holding company. This argument qualifies for one of our "chutzpah" awards.

Id. at 1271, 46 USPQ2d at 1621. The court noted that " 'chutzpah' describes 'the behavior of a person who kills his parents and pleads for the court's mercy on the ground of being an orphan' " *Id.*

7. **Motions to Dismiss**. A defendant challenges personal jurisdiction by filing a motion to dismiss pursuant to Federal Rule of Civil Procedure 12(b)(2).

8. **ITC Proceedings.** The International Trade Commission (ITC) is the appropriate forum for bringing an unfair competition or patent suit against one who imports articles that may be covered by a patent into the United States. *See* 19 U.S.C. § 337. If the unfair acts pertain to a United States patent, the ITC complaint must establish a domestic industry exists or is in the process of being established. This can be proven with evidence of: significant investment in a plant, equipment, labor or capital, or substantial investment in the exploitation of intellectual property, including engineering, research and development, or licensing. The plaintiff who brings suit in the ITC had better be prepared to move quickly.

9. **Internet.** The Internet has raised some interesting jurisdiction questions. Does a defendant have minimum contacts with Illinois when she creates a Web page and residents from Illinois can access it? Should advertising on the Internet be sufficient to establish personal jurisdiction? In *CompuServe, Inc. v. Patterson,* 89 F.3d 1257, 39 USPQ2d 1502 (6th Cir. 1996), the court considered the impact of operating a business on the Internet on the personal jurisdiction analysis. The court noted that:

> The Internet represents perhaps the latest and greatest manifestation of these historical, globe-shrinking trends. It enables anyone with the right equipment and knowledge . . . to operate an international business cheaply, and from a desktop. That business operator, however, remains entitled to the protection of the Due Process Clause, which mandates that potential defendants be able "to structure their primary conduct with some minimum assurance as to where the conduct will and will not render them liable to suit."

CompuServe, 89 F.3d at 1262. In *Compuserve*, Patterson had established contacts with Ohio where Compuserve brought the suit. Patterson had:

> subscribed to CompuServe, and then he entered into the Shareware Registration Agreement when he loaded his software onto the CompuServe system for others to use and, perhaps, purchase. Once Patterson had done those two things, he was on notice that he had made contracts, to be governed by Ohio law, with an Ohio-based company. Then, he repeatedly sent his computer software, via electronic links, to the CompuServe system in Ohio, and he advertised that software on the CompuServe system. Moreover, he initiated the events that led to the filing of this suit by making demands of CompuServe via electronic and regular mail messages.

Id. at 1264. The court held that Patterson had established the required minimum contacts with Ohio for that court to assert personal jurisdiction over him. *Id.* at 1264. The court found that Compuserve had effectively acted as Patterson's distributor. *Id.* at 1265. The court held that jurisdiction was not defeated by the fact that Patterson had only a de minimus amount of actual sales in Ohio. *Id.*

In *Zippo Manufacturing Co. v. Zippo Dot Com, Inc.*, 952 F. Supp. 1119, 42 USPQ2d 1062 (W.D. Pa. 1997), the court discussed in detail the impact of the Internet on personal jurisdiction. The court stated that its review of the cases addressing the Internet and personal jurisdiction:

> reveals that the likelihood that personal jurisdiction can be constitutionally exercised is directly proportionate to the nature and quality of commercial activity that an entity conducts over the Internet. This sliding scale is consistent with well developed personal jurisdiction principles. At one end of the spectrum are situations where a defendant clearly does business over the Internet. If the defendant enters into contracts with residents of a foreign jurisdiction that involve the knowing and repeated transmission of computer files over the Internet, personal jurisdiction is proper. At the opposite end are situations where a defendant has simply posted information on an Internet Web site which is accessible to users in foreign jurisdictions. A passive Web site that does little more than make information available to those who are interested in it is not grounds for the exercise of personal jurisdiction. The middle ground is occupied by interactive Web sites where a user can exchange information with the host computer. In these cases, the exercise of jurisdiction is determined by examining the level of interactivity and commercial nature of the exchange of information that occurs on the Web site.

Id. at 1124 (citations omitted).

In *Bensusan Restaurant Corp. v. King*, 937 F. Supp. 295, 40 USPQ2d 1519 (S.D. N.Y. 1996), *aff'd,* 126 F.3d 25 (2d Cir. 1997), the court held that the defendant did not purposefully avail himself of the laws of the state when the defendant had a Web site and left a phone number to call. *See also Hearst Corp. v. Goldberger*, 1997 WL 97097, at * 1 (S.D.N.Y. Feb.27, 1997) (merely advertising a product on a Web site is not sufficient to establish personal jurisdiction); *Smith v. Hobby Lobby Stores, Inc.*, 968 F. Supp. 1356 (W.D. Ark. 1997) (same); *Weber v. Jolly Hotels*, 977 F. Supp. 327 (D.N.J. 1997) (same). On nearly identical facts, however, other courts have held that there was a basis for jurisdiction. *Inset Systems, Inc. v. Instruction Set*, 937 F. Supp. 161, 165 (D. Conn. 1996) (maintaining a toll free number on a continuous Internet Web site did provide a basis for jurisdiction); *Telco Communications v. An Apple A Day*, 977 F. Supp. 404 (E.D. Va. 1997) (conducting advertising and soliciting over the Internet via a Web site (by posting two or three press releases), which could be accessed by a Virginia resident 24 hours a day, constitutes a persistent course of conduct sufficient for personal jurisdiction in Virginia). For more information *see* David L. Stott, Comment, *Personal Jurisdiction in Cyberspace: The Constitutional Boundary of Minimum Contacts Limited to a Web*, 15 J. Marshall J. Computer & Info. L. 819 (1997); Corey B. Ackerman, Note, *World-Wide Volkswagen, Meet the World Wide Web: An Examination of Personal Jurisdiction Applied to a New World*, 71 St. John's L. Rev. 403 (1997).

10. Issues of personal jurisdiction and the Internet arise frequently in all types of intellectual property litigations. The issues are simple to frame: if a bulletin board service (BBS) provider in Pakistan posts an article that infringes a U.S. copyright and a user in New York accesses the BBS, does a New York court have personal jurisdiction over the Pakistani BBS? Similar-

ly, if a company held a United States trademark could they post it on the Internet even if it would infringe another's trademark if used abroad? Does use of the mark on a web site that can be accessed abroad constitute trademark infringement? *See Playboy Enters., Inc. v. Chuckleberry Publ'g, Inc.*, 939 F. Supp. 1032, 39 USPQ2d 1746 (S.D.N.Y. 1996) (personal jurisdiction is established when an Italian publisher actively solicits U.S. customers on the Internet via a Web site to subscribe to view on-line images that infringed plaintiff's trademark rights).

11. **Service of Process**. The existence of the Internet may affect service of process as well. Can service of process be effectuated via e-mail? *See* Wendy R. Leibowitz, *Geography Isn't Destiny, High Tech is Reshaping Legal Basics; Bit By Bit, Computers and the Internet are Changing the Nuts and Bolts of Law*, Nat'l L.J., Sept. 23, 1996, at A1.

B. VENUE IN PATENT CASES

Statutory Provision— 28 U.S.C. § 1391:

(b) A civil action wherein jurisdiction is not founded solely on diversity of citizenship may, except as otherwise provided by law, be brought only in (1) a judicial district where any defendant resides, if all defendants reside in the same State, (2) a judicial district in which a substantial part of the events or omissions giving rise to the claim occurred, or a substantial part of property that is the subject of the action is situated, or (3) a judicial district in which any defendant may be found, if there is no district in which the action may otherwise be brought.

(c) For purposes of venue under this chapter, a defendant that is a corporation shall be deemed to reside in any judicial district in which it is subject to personal jurisdiction at the time the action is commenced. In a State which has more than one judicial district and in which a defendant that is a corporation is subject to personal jurisdiction at the time an action is commenced, such corporation shall be deemed to reside in any district in that State within which its contacts would be sufficient to subject it to personal jurisdiction if that district were a separate State, and, if there is no such district, the corporation shall be deemed to reside in the district within which it has the most significant contacts.

Statutory Provision— 28 U.S.C. § 1400(b):

Any civil action for patent infringement may be brought in the judicial district where the defendant resides, or where the defendant has committed acts of infringement and has a regular and established place of business.

Venue in a patent infringement action is controlled by 28 U.S.C. § 1400(b). Under this section, the plaintiff has the burden of proving that venue is proper by showing that the action has been brought in a jurisdiction either: (1) where the defendant resides; or (2) where the defendant committed acts of infringement *and* has a regular and established place of business (this is normally defined as where the defendant conducts a substantial part of its ordinary business in a fixed location). With respect to individuals, the defendant resides where he is domiciled.

Fourco Glass Co. v. Transmirra Prods. Corp., 353 U.S. 222, 226, 113 USPQ 234 (1957). With respect to corporations, the meaning of the term "reside" has undergone significant evolution. Currently, corporate defendants are deemed to reside in any judicial district in which they are subject to personal jurisdiction. Do you agree with the action the court took in *VE Holding*?

VE HOLDING CORP. v. JOHNSON GAS APPLIANCE CO.

917 F.2d 1574, 16 USPQ2d 1614 (Fed. Cir. 1990)

Before ARCHER, PLAGER and CLEVENGER, Circuit Judges.

PLAGER, Circuit Judge

For almost one hundred years, a specific statutory provision, currently section 1400(b) of chapter 87, title 28, U.S. Code, has set forth the bases for establishing venue in patent infringement actions. Where the defendant 'resides' is one of those bases. Supreme Court decisions, with one exception, have maintained that provision is unaffected by other statutory provisions governing venue.

In 1988 Congress adopted a new definition of reside as it applies to venue for corporate defendants. This case requires us to decide whether, by that amendment to § 1391(c) of chapter 87, Congress meant to apply that definition to the term as it is used in § 1400(b), and thus change this long-standing interpretation of the patent venue statute. The district courts addressing this question have arrived at conflicting results.

This is a case of first impression. We hold that Congress by its 1988 amendment of 28 U.S.C. § 1391(c) meant what it said; the meaning of the term 'resides' in § 1400(b) has changed. We therefore reverse the judgment in VE Holding II and remand the case for further proceedings consistent with this opinion.

II.

Venue, which connotes locality, serves the purpose of protecting a defendant from the inconvenience of having to defend an action in a trial court that is either remote from the defendant's residence or from the place where the acts underlying the controversy occurred. The venue statutes achieve this by limiting a plaintiff's choice of forum to only certain courts from among all those which might otherwise acquire personal jurisdiction over the defendant.

The first statute specifically addressed to venue in patent infringement suits was enacted in 1897. The current version of this Act is found in § 1400(b) of the venue chapter (chapter 87 of title 28). Section 1400(b), which has been in its present form since 1948, reads:

(b) Any civil action for patent infringement may be brought in the judicial district where the defendant resides, or where the defendant has committed acts of infringement and has a regular and established place of business.

Patent law is not alone in having a particular venue statute that differs in its terms from the general venue provisions applicable to other federal causes of action. For example, in addition to sections dealing with venue in diversity jurisdiction cases, federal question cases, and venue regarding suits against aliens, the venue chapter contains provisions for suits in certain cases by a national banking association, for suits for collection of internal revenue taxes, for suits regarding Interstate Commerce Commission orders, and for stockholder's derivative actions. Other particular venue provisions appear elsewhere in the Code, accompanying the substantive law provisions governing specific areas. *See, e.g.*, 46 U.S.C. App. § 688 applying to Jones Act cases; 15 U.S.C. §§ 15, 22 applying to antitrust actions.

In all of these areas in which particular venue statutes apply, the question can be raised—to what extent do the general venue provisions of chapter 87 supplement what is contained in the special provision, whether that special provision is contained in chapter 87 or elsewhere. The issue appears to arise infrequently; the few decisions suggest that the answer depends very much on the precise language of the relevant statutes along with, in appropriate cases, other evidence of Congressional intent. Facially, there is little consistency from area to area.

In the Jones Act and antitrust areas, for example, the courts have read the general venue provisions into the special provisions. In applying these particular venue provisions, courts have concluded that the Congressional intent was to 'enlarge' the plaintiff's choice of forum by reading the special venue provisions as supplemental to, rather than superseding, the general venue provisions. *See Pure Oil*, 384 U.S. at 206 ("there is nothing to show a congressional purpose negativing the more natural reading of the two [Jones Act and general] venue sections together"); *Delong Equip. Co. v. Washington Mills Abrasive Co.*, 840 F.2d 843, 855 (11th Cir. 1988) ("In a federal antitrust case, venue may be established under [15 U.S.C. § 15 or § 22], or the general federal venue statute, 28 U.S.C. § 1391(b).").

In the patent field, that has not been the case. The Supreme Court in 1942 and again in 1957 took a restrictive view of venue in patent infringement cases, holding in effect that the meaning of the terms used in § 1400(b) was not to be altered or supplemented by other provisions found in the venue statutes. *Fourco Glass Co. v. Transmirra Prods. Corp.*, 353 U.S. 222 (1957); *Stonite Prods. Co. v. Melvin Lloyd Co.*, 315 U.S. 561 (1942); followed in *In re Cordis*, 769 F.2d 733, 226 USPQ 784 (Fed. Cir. 1985). *But see, Brunette Mach. Works, Ltd. v. Kockum Indus., Inc.*, 406 U.S. 706 (1972), discussed below.

As written, section 1400(b) dictates that venue is proper when either of two tests is satisfied: (1) the defendant resides in the judicial district, or (2) the defendant has committed acts of infringement and has a regular and established place of business in the judicial district. The Supreme Court in *Fourco* confirmed that for defendants that are corporations, 'resides' meant the state of incorporation only. Section 1391(c), the general venue section which addressed the question of where corporations may be sued, and which contained language about the residence of corporations, did not supplement the specific provisions of § 1400(b). 353 U.S. at 229.

At the time the Supreme Court's decision in *Fourco* was handed down, § 1391(c) consisted of one sentence which read:

> (c) A corporation may be sued in any judicial district in which it is incorporated or licensed to do business or is doing business, and such judicial district shall be regarded as the residence of such corporation for venue purposes.

The first clause (up to the comma) established venue for corporations. The second clause either was surplusage since the term 'residence' was not used in the first clause as one of the bases for venue or, if it applied to plaintiffs as well as defendants was at best confusing.

In response to pressure from the bar and the courts, in 1988 Congress amended § 1391(c). The former one sentence subsection now consists of two sentences. The new second sentence of subsection (c) applies when a defendant corporation is amenable to federal jurisdiction in a state having several judicial districts. It prescribes which of them shall be the proper venue, and is not at issue in this case.

The new first sentence of amended § 1391(c) reads:

> (c) *For purposes of venue under this chapter,* a defendant that is a corporation shall be deemed to reside in any judicial district in which it is subject to personal jurisdiction at the time the action is commenced.

28 U.S.C. § 1391(c) (1988) (emphasis added). The phrase "this chapter" refers to chapter 87 of title 28, which encompasses §§ 1391–1412, and thus includes § 1400(b). On its face, § 1391(c) clearly applies to § 1400(b), and thusredefines the meaning of the term 'resides' in that section.

However, one familiar with the judicial history of § 1400(b) may be tempted to disregard the clear language of § 1391(c) and maintain the independence of that section from § 1400(b). The lack of express legislative history indicating that the 1988 amendment of § 1391(c) was intended to change the scope of venue in patent infringement cases, and the fact that such a conclusion would seem to fly in the face of thirty years of Supreme Court law, strengthens the temptation.

In *Fourco*, the Supreme Court addressed the same question presently before this court. "The question is ... whether § 1391(c) supplements § 1400(b), or, in other words, whether the latter is complete, independent and alone in controlling in its sphere as was held in *Stonite*, or is, in some measure, dependent for its force upon the former." *Fourco*, 353 U.S. at 228. In deciding that it was not so intended, the Supreme Court stated:

> We think it is clear that § 1391(c) is a general corporation venue statute, whereas § 1400(b) is a special venue statute applicable,

specifically, to all defendants in a particular type of actions, i.e., patent infringement actions. In these circumstances the law is settled that "However inclusive may be the general language of a statute, it 'will not be held to apply to a matter specifically dealt with in another part of the same enactment.... Specific terms prevail over the general in the same or another statute which otherwise might be controlling.' "

Fourco, 353 U.S. at 228–29.

III.

The Supreme Court's decision in *Fourco* is generally viewed as holding that § 1400(b) is the exclusive venue statute in patent infringement actions. Thus it is sometimes said that, since *Fourco*, the only way to change the way that venue in patent infringement actions is determined is to change § 1400(b). This argument fails, however, because the Supreme Court, in *Brunette*, 406 U.S. 706, refused to impose such a disablement upon the Congress' ability to enact or amend legislation. The issue in *Brunette* was whether § 1400(b) governed venue in a patent suit involving a foreign corporation, or whether the general venue provision applicable to aliens, 28 U.S.C. § 1391(d), governed. The Court held § 1391(d) applied, and that § 1400(b) was supplemented by the provision governing suits against aliens. *Fourco* and *Stonite* were distinguished.

The specific question in *Fourco* was whether the statutory language previously enacted by the Congress as § 1391(c) supported a conclusion that Congress intended to have §§ 1391(c) and 1400(b) read together. On the basis of the nonspecific language of § 1391(c) and prior history as the Court read it, the Court concluded the answer was no.

Section 1391(c) as it was in *Fourco* is no longer. We now have exact and classic language of incorporation: "For purposes of venue under this chapter...." Congress could readily have added "except for section 1400(b)," if that exception, which we can presume was well known to the Congress, was intended to be maintained. Certainly it would not be sensible to require Congress to say, "For purposes of this chapter, and we mean everything in this chapter ...," in order to ensure that it has covered everything in a chapter of the statutes.

The issue, then, is not whether the prior cases, including Supreme Court cases, determined that under different statutory language Congress' intent was that § 1400(b) stood alone. The issue is, what, as a matter of first impression, should we conclude the Congress now intends by this new language in the venue act.

In the case before us, the language of the statute is clear and its meaning is unambiguous. Absent extraordinary circumstances, our inquiry must end here. *Ron Pair Enters.*, 489 U.S. at 241–42 (where statute's language is plain, the court's sole function is to enforce it according to its terms—the words express Congress' intent and so reference to legislative history is unnecessary). Section 1391(c) applies to all of chapter 87 of title 28, and thus to § 1400(b), as expressed by the words "For purposes of venue under this chapter." There can be no mistake about that.

It is true that § 1391(c) is a general venue statute and that § 1400(b) is a specific one. But the general rule that a specific statute is not controlled or nullified by a general statute regardless of priority of enactment, absent a clear intention otherwise, does not govern the present situation. This is for two reasons. First, in this case the general statute, § 1391(c), expressly reads itself into the specific statute, § 1400(b). Second, § 1391(c) only operates to define a term in § 1400(b)—it neither alone governs patent venue nor establishes a patent venue rule separate and apart from that provided under § 1400(b). Nor does it conflict with § 1400(b). Furthermore, even were the rule applicable to the issue at hand, the language of the statute would reveal "a clear intention" that § 1391(c) is to supplement § 1400(b).

VI.

Thus, the first test for venue under § 1400(b) with respect to a defendant that is a corporation, in light of the 1988 amendment to § 1391(c), is whether the defendant was subject to personal jurisdiction in the district of suit at the time the action was commenced. 28 U.S.C. §§ 1391(c) & 1400(b) (1988). Since Johnson has conceded that VE obtained personal jurisdiction over it in the Northern District of California Johnson "resides" in that district, within the meaning of the first test of § 1400(b), and venue properly lies in the Northern District of California. The District Court's determination that venue with regard to Johnson did not lie in the Northern District of California was error.

Notes

1. The new definition of "resides" mandates that we treat each district as a separate state, and determine if the defendant has "minimum contacts" with that "state." The case law on personal jurisdiction now resolves venue issues.

2. **Declaratory Judgment Action**. A declaratory judgment action alleging that a patent is invalid and not infringed is governed by the general venue statute—§ 1391, not by § 1400(b), even though it is the mirror-image of a patent infringement suit.

3. **Motions to Transfer Venue.** Motions to transfer venue can be brought under 28 U.S.C. § 1404(a). Section 1404(a) provides: "For the convenience of parties and witnesses, in the interest of justice, a district court may transfer any civil action to any other district or division whether it might have been brought." Such motions are committed to the discretion of the trial court and are not frequently granted. When deciding a motion to transfer, a court should consider the availability and convenience of witnesses and parties, location of counsel, location of books and records, location of manufacturing facilities, costs of obtaining attendance of witnesses and other trial expenses, place of the alleged wrong, related litigations, the possibilities of trial delay and the seriousness of the resulting prejudices arising from it if the transfer is granted, and plaintiff's choice of

forum. The plaintiff's choice of forum is the most influential factor and should rarely be disturbed unless the balance is strongly in favor of the defendant.

Problems

A patent dispute has arisen between ON–LINE corporation which owns the '111 patent (issued on January 1, 1998) on Internet connection software that allows for faster Internet connections and MICRONET. ON–LINE was formed by several MIT graduates as a Delaware corporation with its only place of business in Massachusetts. MICRONET is the largest Internet service provider and a leader in the software industry. It was incorporated in California and is headquartered in Palo Alto, California. It employs a large number of people in Palo Alto and San Jose. Moreover, it has become the darling of the Internet Service Provider community and most of people in California who use the Internet subscribe to MICRONET because they offer the best prices around. MICRONET has stores in Washington, California, and New York. Most of its sales business, however, comes from the Internet, which allows it to make software sales all over the world. It has a Web page in which it posts advertisements and which Internet users can access to get more information on MICRONET and its products. An interested customer can use a credit card to buy its software right off the Web page.

ON–LINE discovered that MICRONET could be using its software when a recent Cal-tech graduate, who had worked at MICRONET during his summers joined ON–LINE after graduation. ON–LINE immediately sent a cease-and-desist letter to MICRONET stating that it believed MICRONET could be infringing its '111 patent and that it was willing to license the patent at a reasonable royalty rate. ON–LINE sent this letter to each of MICRONET's stores and to its headquarters. ON–LINE's president and lawyer flew out to MICRONET's headquarters to negotiate a license. They were unable to reach any agreement during the negotiations. As ON–LINE left the negotiation its President told MICRONET that if MICRONET did not accept its offer to license by January 1, 1999, ON–LINE would be forced to take legal action. Today is January 15, 1999 and MICRONET has not responded.

What are the litigation options for each side? Who can bring suit and where? Is there any additional information you would like to know?

To complicate matters further, ON–LINE tells you that it once considered opening an office in Palo Alto. In fact, in 1997, the President of ON–LINE flew to California and even signed a six-month lease with a real estate agent for a store. They opened this small store, but business was terrible. Realizing that they could not compete with MICRONET, they closed the office after only four months. The Cal tech grad that ON–LINE just hired is trying to convince them to try the California market again, but they have not taken any actions toward this end yet.

Does this alter the litigation options for either side?

Chapter Four

THE PLEADINGS

A. THE PATENT INFRINGEMENT COMPLAINT

FEDERAL RULES OF CIVIL PROCEDURE—RULE 8:

General Rules of Pleading

(a) **Claims for Relief.** A pleading which sets forth a claim for relief, whether an original claim, counterclaim, cross-claim, or third-party claim, shall contain (1) a short and plain statement of the grounds upon which the court's jurisdiction depends, unless the court already has jurisdiction and the claim needs no new grounds of jurisdiction to support it, (2) a short and plain statement of the claim showing that the pleader is entitled to relief, and (3) a demand for judgment for the relief the pleader seeks. Relief in the alternative or of several different types may be demanded.

* * *

(e) **Pleading to be Concise and Direct; Consistency.**

(1) Each averment of a pleading shall be simple, concise and direct. No technical forms of pleading or motions are required.

(2) A party may set forth two or more statements of a claim or defense alternately or hypothetically, either in one count or defense or in separate counts or defenses. When two or more statements are made in the alternative and one of them if made independently would be sufficient, the pleading is not made insufficient by the insufficiency of one or more of the alternative statements. A party may also state as many separate claims or defenses as the party has regardless of consistency and whether based on legal, equitable, or maritime grounds. All statements shall be made subject to the obligations set forth in Rule 11.

Rule 8 of the Federal Rules of Civil Procedure sets forth a number of procedural requirements for filing any pleading and applies to all patent complaints. Specifically, a claim for relief must be set forth whether or not the pleading is a claim, a counterclaim, a cross-claim, or a third-party claim. Additionally, Rule 8 requires: (1) a short and plain statement of the grounds upon which the court's jurisdiction depends; (2) a short and plain statement of the claim showing the pleader is entitled to relief; (3) and a demand for judgment.

1. PROCEDURAL REQUIREMENTS

a. *Jurisdictional Statement*

Rule 8 requires a statement of the grounds for jurisdiction. This statement should address the grounds for subject matter jurisdiction and personal jurisdiction. (*see* sample complaint ¶ 4, 5). This statement should also assert that the forum is the proper venue for the action to be brought. (*see* sample complaint ¶ 4).

b. *Statement of the Claim in a Patent Case*

Where the plaintiff-patentee sues for infringement of its patent rights, a statement of the infringement claim will be governed by the statutory definition of infringement found in 35 U.S.C. § 271 as well as case law interpretation. A complaint filed for patent infringement need only be based on a single sale, offer for sale, use, manufacture or importation into the United States. *See Water Techs. Corp. v. Calco, Ltd.*, 658 F. Supp. 961, 1 USPQ2d 1178 (N.D. Ill. 1986), *modified*, 850 F.2d 660, 7 USPQ2d 1097 (Fed. Cir. 1988) ("Under the law, even a single sale or use can constitute infringement."). There are additional considerations to undertake when assessing the need to file a patent infringement complaint, including whether the act constituting the alleged infringement was done under the patentee's authority, even if that authority was indirect and whether the act amounts to a permissible repair of the patented product. *See* Chapter 2 for a discussion of who can be sued and what behavior amounts to infringement.

A claim of patent infringement should identify the patent or patents which form the basis for the infringement assertion. It is customary to attach a copy of the patent to the complaint. (*see* sample complaint ¶ 6). It should also include a statement of ownership and an indication that the pleader has the right to sue for infringement. (*see* sample complaint ¶ 6). The complaint should also identify the accused infringer and contain a brief statement of the alleged infringing act or acts. (*see* sample complaint ¶ 8). Finally, if the patent owner's product is marked, there should be a statement indicating compliance with 35 U.S.C. § 287 or a statement of whether actual notice of infringement was given to the defendant. (*see* sample complaint ¶ 7). Where actual notice has not previously been given, the complaint will act as notice.

If the action is a declaratory judgment action, the complaint will typically be broader in scope. A plaintiff may request a declaration that the patent involved is invalid or not infringed, or that it is unenforceable. In order for a declaratory judgment action to commence, there must be a threat of suit by the patentee. In other words, there must be an actual controversy where the patentee has indicated an intent to enforce its patent and the defendant's activities are accused of constituting an infringing act or otherwise exhibit an intent to conduct such an activity. Thus, an accused infringer may request a declaratory judgment even where the device has not yet been made, used or sold, but where the accused infringer has the intention to do so. Where a plaintiff seeks a declaratory judgment order alleging unenforceability based on fraud or inequitable conduct, Rule 9 of the Federal Rules of Civil Procedure requires pleading "the circumstances constituting fraud ... with particularity."

c. *Demand For Judgment*

There must also be a demand for judgment stated in the complaint. Title 35 provides for injunctive relief and payment of damages. Attorneys' fees may also be awarded in exceptional cases and the court has the discretion to increase thedamage award. The scenario for increased damages usually occurs in the context of a claim for willful infringement. *See* Chapter 14. A complaint should allege acts causing damage and irreparable harm (*see* sample complaint ¶ 9) and should state an allegation of willful infringement (*see* sample complaint ¶ 8). It should pray for damages, injunctive relief, and under the appropriate facts and circumstances, increased damages, attorney's fees and any other relief the court may deem "just and proper" (*see* sample complaint ¶ A–F).

d. *Demand For Jury*

A jury demand is a matter of right for both parties on legal issues. Rule 38(b) of the Federal Rules of Civil Procedure sets forth the requirements for a jury trial demand. The rule states that "after the commencement of the action and not later than 10 days after the service of the last pleading directed to such issue," a party may demand a jury trial. It is not necessary to request a jury trial on all the legal issues in the case. The requesting party may ask for a jury trial on only some of the legal issues. If the requesting party does not designate which issues it wishes to be tried to a jury, it is presumed that the request for a jury trial is on all legal issues. If a party requests a jury trial on only selected legal issues, Rule 38(c) affords the opposing party ten additional days to designate other issues for the jury trial. Under Rule 38(d), it is important to remember that if the ten days pass and neither party requests a jury trial, then the right is waived. Parties normally include their jury trial demands in their initial pleadings. (*see* sample complaint).

A complaint alleging patent infringement may plead other allegations such as unfair competition or misappropriation of trade secret, breach of contract or tortious interference with business relations or tortious interference with prospective business relations.

2. JURY TRIAL VERSUS BENCH TRIAL

Over the past twenty years, jury trials have become very popular in patent infringement cases. Jury trials were rare as late as the early 1980s. Today over 70%, of patent cases are tried before juries. This sharp increase is due to the perception by many plaintiff-patentees that juries generally respond favorably to a patentee's case. Juries often find the inventor's quest in developing the patented technology to be a good human interest story and are also impressed with the fact that the United States Government issued a patent to reward the inventor's hard work. In short, the concept of the inventor working diligently to improve technology and being rewarded for her efforts is consistent with the American dream. Juries also react negatively to the concept of theft of the patented technology by an accused infringer. As a result, plaintiff-patentees are said to prevail in the majority of patent infringement trials before juries.

It is important for the defendant to attempt to negate the impression of theft of the patented technology if confronted with a jury trial demand from the plaintiff. One way of doing that is by proving non-infringement. In other words, the defendant could not have stolen the patented technology, since the defendant's technology is different. The defendant's story is often one that also indicates independent development of the technology with significant investment of time and resources. Further, an equalization of jury perception can occur in those situations where there appears to have been inequitable conduct on the part of the patentee in procuring the patent. Juries also understand theft of the patent grant from the public where the patentee was not candid with the Patent Office and withheld critical prior art or misrepresented critical facts. Defenses such as a failure to disclose the best mode or to enable will also garner some sympathy for the defendant with the jury because they are premised on the fact that the patentee withheld information from the Patent Office.

The jury trial generally yields a quicker result than the typical bench trial as the jury deliberates immediately at the close of trial. The parties know the verdict within days. In contrast, a bench trial often ends with the judge asking for briefs to summarize what was presented during the trial and the applicable legal principles. It is not unheard of in a bench trial to have the court decide the matter one year after the close of evidence. This delay can be quite damaging since businesses usually want certainty so that manufacturing and marketing decisions may be made in the context of intellectual property rights.

B. ANSWERING THE COMPLAINT: MOTIONS, ANSWERS, COUNTERCLAIMS

1. MOTIONS TO DISMISS

In most cases, the defendant files an answer to the patent complaint. But as a preliminary matter, consideration may be given to filing a motion for dismissal in lieu of an answer. Seven specific grounds are available to support a motion to dismiss under Rule 12 of the Federal Rules of Civil Procedure.

FEDERAL RULES OF CIVIL PROCEDURE—RULE 12:

Defenses and Objections—When And How Presented By—Pleading or Motion—Motion for Judgment on Pleadings.

(b) **How Presented.** Every defense, in law or fact, to a claim for relief in any pleading, whether a claim, counterclaim, cross-claim, or third-party claim, shall be asserted in the responsive pleading thereto if one is required, except that the following defenses may at the option of the pleader be made by motion: (1) lack of jurisdiction over the subject matter, (2) lack of jurisdiction over the person, (3) improper venue, (4) insufficiency of process, (5) insufficiency of service of process, (6) failure to state a claim upon which relief can be granted, (7) failure to join a party under Rule 19. A motion making any of these defenses shall be made before pleading if a further pleading is permitted. No defense or objection is waived by being joined with one or more other defenses or objections in a responsive pleading or motion. If a pleading sets forth a claim for relief to which the adverse party is not required to serve a responsive pleading, the adverse party may assert at the trial any defense in law or fact to that claim for relief. If, on a motion asserting the defense numbered (6) to dismiss for failure of the pleading to state a claim upon which relief can be granted, matters outside the pleading are presented to and not excluded by the court, the motion shall be treated as one for summary judgment and disposed of as provided in Rule 56, and all parties shall be given reasonable opportunity to present all material made pertinent to such a motion by Rule 56.

One of the more prevalent bases for a motion to dismiss is Rule 12(b)(6) for a "failure ... to state a claim upon which relief can be granted."

AMERICAN TECHNICAL MACHINERY CORP. v. MASTERPIECE ENTERPRISES, INC.

235 F. Supp. 917, 143 USPQ 19 (M.D. Pa. 1964)

NEALON, District Judge.

In this action, plaintiff, American Technical Machinery Corporation, seeks injunctive relief and damages from Masterpiece Enterprises, Inc., and Norris Machine Company, Inc., and also against Percy Dieffenbach, President of Masterpiece, individually, and Alfred Norris, President of Norris, individually. It is plaintiff's contention that the defendants have infringed with plaintiff's patent. The defendant, Percy Dieffenbach, has moved under Federal Rules of Civil Procedure 12(b), 28 U.S.C.A., to dismiss the action, asserting that the complaint fails to state a claim against him upon which relief can be granted.

The pertinent allegation of the complaint avers that the defendant, Percy Dieffenbach, with knowledge of plaintiff's patent, induced and conspired with Masterpiece Enterprises, Inc., to infringe the aforesaid patent, thereby causing plaintiff substantial damage. It is defendant's contention that this allegation does not raise a prima facie presumption of liability on his part as an individual. He argues, rather, that the alleged acts of infringement in the complaint were the acts of the corporate defendants and, in the absence of special circumstances, managing officers of a corporation are not liable for the infringing acts of the corporation though committed under their general direction.

Under the Patent Statute, 35 U.S.C.A. § 271(b), anyone who "actively induces infringement of a patent shall be liable as an infringer."

The decisions in patent infringement cases are clear that where an individual is an organizer, president and dominant spirit of an infringing company, then he is personally liable. This rule was applied in *Upjohn Company v. Italian Drugs Importing Co.*, 190 F. Supp. 361 (S.D.N.Y. 1961):

> where a corporate officer exceeds his executive duties and deliberately organizes a corporation for the purpose of infringing a patent, or where he *otherwise* acts as the moving, active, conscious force behind an infringement, he may be held personally liable. (Emphasis supplied)

A motion to dismiss a complaint for failure to state a claim upon which relief can be granted admits the facts alleged in the complaint, but challenges the plaintiff's right to relief. The complaint should not be dismissed unless it appears to be a certainty that the plaintiff would not be entitled to relief under any state of facts which could be proved in support of the claim. All that is usually required in the complaint is a generalized statement of the facts from which the defendant may form a responsive pleading; thus if a bona fide complaint is filed that charges every element necessary to recover, summary dismissal for failure to set out evidential facts is not justified. The United States Supreme Court in *Conley v. Gibson*, 355 U.S. 41, 46 (1957), has endorsed "the accepted rule that a complaint should not be dismissed for failure to state a claim unless it appears beyond doubt that the plaintiff can prove no set of facts in support of his claim which would entitle him to relief." Pleadings must be construed liberally and, with that precept in mind, I am satisfied that the complaint charging Dieffenbach with knowingly inducing and conspiring with Masterpiece to infringe the patent is a sufficient foundation upon which further proof may be offered to show that he was the organizer, president and dominant spirit of an infringing company or that he otherwise acted as the moving, active, conscious force behind an infringement. The motion will be denied.

2. THE ANSWER

Typically, the patent complaint is responded to by the defendant's answer, which is governed by Rule 12(1) and Rule 8(b) of the Federal Rules of Civil Procedure.

FEDERAL RULES OF CIVIL PROCEDURE—RULE 12:

Defenses and Objections—When And How Presented—By Pleading or Motion—Motion for Judgment on Pleadings

(1) Unless a different time is prescribed in a statute of the United States, a defendant shall serve an answer

(A) within 20 days after being served with the summons and complaint, or

(B) if service of the summons has been timely waived on request under Rule 4(d), within 60 days after the date when the request for waiver was sent, or within 90 days after that date if the defendant was addressed outside any judicial district of the United States.

FEDERAL RULES OF CIVIL PROCEDURE—RULE 8:

General Rules Of Pleading

(b) **Defenses; Forms of Denials.** A party shall state in short and plain terms the party's defenses to each claim asserted and shall admit or deny the averments upon which the adverse party relies. If a party is without knowledge or information sufficient to form a belief as to the truth of an averment, the party shall so state and this has the effect of a denial. Denials shall fairly meet the substance of the averments denied. When a pleader intends in good faith to deny only a part or a qualification of an averment, the pleader shall specify so much of it as is true and material and shall deny only the remainder. Unless the pleader intends in good faith to controvert all the averments of the preceding pleading, the pleader may make denials as specific denials of designated averments or paragraphs or may generally deny all the averments except such designated averments or paragraphs as the pleader expressly admits; but, when the pleader does so intend to controvert all its averments, including averments of the grounds upon which the court's jurisdiction depends, the pleader may do so by general denial subject to the obligations set forth in Rule 11.

When answering a complaint, the defendant must either admit or deny the specific allegations of the complaint. It is also acceptable for a party to state that it is without sufficient knowledge to form a belief. (*see* sample answer ¶ 7). This is treated as a denial. Another alternative is that a party may admit or deny portions of an allegation. If a party elects to do so, the party should admit or deny by specifically indicating which portions are admitted, and which are denied. Affirmative defenses and counterclaims are also available and must be set forth at the time of answering the complaint.

3. AFFIRMATIVE DEFENSES

The defendant also has the option of pleading affirmative defenses in his answer under Rule 8 of the Federal Rules of Civil Procedure.

FEDERAL RULES OF CIVIL PROCEDURE—RULE 8:

General Rules Of Pleading

(c) **Affirmative Defenses.** In pleading to a preceding pleading, a party shall set forth affirmatively accord and satisfaction, arbitration and award, assumption of risk, contributory negligence, discharge in bankruptcy, duress, estoppel, failure of consideration, fraud, illegality, injury by fellow servant, laches, license, payment, release, res judicata, statute of frauds, statute of limitations, waiver, and any other matter constituting an avoidance or affirmative defense. When a party has mistakenly designated a defense as a counterclaim or a counterclaim as a defense, the court on terms, if justice so requires, shall treat the pleading as if there had been a proper designation.

Affirmative defenses must be set forth at the time of answering the complaint. In the patent context, Rule 8(c) is to be interpreted as requiring the answering party to plead laches, estoppel, intervening rights or other equitable defenses, or it may waive its opportunity to plead these defenses at a later time. It is important to note that Rule 8(c) states that when a party mistakenly designates an affirmative defense as a counterclaim or a counterclaim as an affirmative defense, the court may apply "justice" and treat the pleading as if it were properly designated.

STATUTORY PROVISION—35 U.S.C. § 282:

Presumption of validity; defenses

* * *

The following shall be defenses in any action involving the validity or infringement of a patent and shall be pleaded:

(1) Noninfringement, absence of liability for infringement or unenforceability,

(2) Invalidity of the patent or any claim in suit on any ground specified in part II of this title as a condition for patentability,

(3) Invalidity of the patent or any claim in suit for failure to comply with any requirement of sections 112 or 251 of this title,

(4) Any other fact or act made a defense by this title.

In actions involving the validity or infringement of a patent the party asserting invalidity or noninfringement shall give notice in the pleadings or otherwise in writing to the adverse party at least thirty days before the trial, of the country, number, date, and name of the patentee of any patent, the title, date, and page numbers of any publication to be relied upon as anticipation of the patent in suit or, except in actions in the United States Claims Court, as showing the state of the art, and the name and address of any person who may be relied upon as the prior inventor or as having prior knowledge of or as having previously used or offered for sale the invention of the patent in suit. In the absence of such notice proof of the said matters may not be made at the trial except on such terms as the court requires.

Invalidity of the extension of a patent term or any portion thereof under section 156 of this title because of the material failure—

(1) by the applicant for the extension, or

(2) by the Commissioner,

to comply with the requirements of such section shall be a defense in any action involving the infringement of a patent during the period of the extension of its term and shall be pleaded. A due diligence determination under section 156(d)(2) is not subject to review in such an action.

Hence the statutory defenses set forth in § 282 including noninfringement, invalidity, and unenforceability will be waived if not pled in answering the complaint.

4. COUNTERCLAIMS AND CROSS–CLAIMS

FEDERAL RULES OF CIVIL PROCEDURE—RULE 13:

Counterclaim and Cross–Claim

(a) Compulsory Counterclaims. A pleading shall state as a counterclaim any claim which at the time of serving the pleading the pleader has against any opposing party, if it arises out of the transaction or occurrence that is the subject matter of the opposing party's claim and does not require for its adjudication the presence of third parties of whom the court cannot acquire jurisdiction. But the pleader need not state the claim if (1) at the time the action was commenced the claim was the subject of another pending action, or (2) the opposing party brought suit upon the claim by attachment or other process by which the court did not acquire jurisdiction to render a personal judgment on that claim, and the pleader is not stating any counterclaim under this Rule 13.

(b) Permissive Counterclaims. A pleading may state as a counterclaim any claim against an opposing party not arising out of the transaction or occurrence that is the subject matter of the opposing party's claim.

* * *

(f) Omitted Counterclaim. When a pleader fails to set up a counterclaim through oversight, inadvertence, or excusable neglect, or when justice requires, the pleader may by leave of court set up the counterclaim by amendment.

(g) Cross–Claim Against Co–Party. A pleading may state as a cross-claim any claim by one party against a co-party arising out of the transaction or occurrence that is the subject matter either of the original action or of a counterclaim therein or relating to any property that is the subject matter of the original action. Such cross-claim may include a claim that the party against whom it is asserted is or may be liable to the cross-claimant for all or part of a claim asserted in the action against the cross-claimant.

Rule 13 of the Federal Rules provides for counterclaims and cross-claims. Counterclaims may be either compulsory or non-compulsory. Compulsory counterclaims, such as invalidity and non-infringement of the patent, generally present the same issues as those asserted by the plaintiff in the complaint. An additional requirement for a compulsory counterclaim is that adjudication of it does not require the presence of third parties over whom the court cannot acquire jurisdiction. If the counterclaim urged by the defendant asserts infringement by the plaintiff of defendant's patent, the counterclaim will probably not be deemed compulsory as the issues litigated are not the same ones created by the complaint. The main criterion for deciding whether a counterclaim is compulsory is whether the causes arose out of the same transaction or occurrence and in the interests of judicial economy should reasonably be litigated in the same suit. Failure to bring a compulsory counterclaim, usually bars bringing the action in a subsequent litigation.

Thus, in answering the complaint, the accused infringer may have several options with respect to counterclaims. First, the defendant may assert a declaratory judgment counterclaim that the plaintiff's patent(s) is not infringed, or is invalid or unenforceable. This counterclaim need not be limited to adjudication of just the claim(s) selected by the plaintiff. Thus, the defendant can gain an opportunity to contribute to defining the battlefield for the litigation, and can place the entire patent of the plaintiff at risk where the plaintiff had carefully selected only its strongest claims as the basis for the infringement allegation. The presence of a counterclaim asserting non-infringement and invalidity of different claims means that the defendant has the opportunity to continue pursuit of its claims, and thus provides an added settlement dimension. Second, the defendant may counterclaim by asserting its own patents and claiming infringement by the plaintiff's products. This would be a permissive counterclaim. Obviously, such a counterclaim significantly alters the equation for the litigation. And of course, the defendant's counterclaims for infringement provide the plaintiff with the opportunity to counter or cross-claim for a declaratory judgment of non-infringement and invalidity of the defendant's (counterclaim-plaintiff's) patents. Third, the defendant could counterclaim that the plaintiff's infringement allegations are an antitrust violation or that the patentee committed an antitrust violation in the procurement of the patent. Would these antitrust counterclaims be compulsory or permissive?

C. AMENDING THE PLEADINGS

FEDERAL RULES OF CIVIL PROCEDURE—RULE 15:

Rule 15. Amended and Supplemental Pleadings

(a) Amendments. A party may amend the party's pleading once as a matter of course at any time before a responsive pleading is served or, if the pleading is one to which no responsive pleading is permitted and the action has not been placed upon the trial calendar, the party may so amend it at any time within 20 days after it is served. Otherwise a party may amend the party's pleading only by leave of court or by written consent of the adverse party; and leave shall be freely given when justice so requires. A party shall plead in response to an amended pleading within the time remaining for response to the original pleading or within 10 days after service of the amended pleading, whichever period may be the longer, unless the court otherwise orders.

The federal rules have very liberal pleading requirements and generally allow amendments to the pleadings especially when discovery reveals new claims of infringement or defenses. However, the district court has the discretion to deny a motion to amend especially where the motion is made in bad faith, after undue delay, causes prejudice to the opposing party, or the amendment is futile.

SAMPLE PLEADINGS

IN THE UNITED STATES DISTRICT COURT
FOR THE NORTHERN DISTRICT OF CALIFORNIA

MIKE'S FISHING, INC.,)	
)	
Plaintiff,)	Civil Action No. 99
)	
v.)	(Demand For Jury Included)
)	
MARK'S BOATS, INC.,)	
)	
Defendant.)	

COMPLAINT FOR PATENT INFRINGEMENT

Plaintiff, Mike's Fishing, Inc., by its attorneys, sues Defendant, Mark's Boats, Inc. for infringing U.S. Patent No. 5,551,835 ("the '835 patent") and alleges as follows:

PARTIES

1. Plaintiff Mike's Fishing, Inc. ("Mike's Fishing") is a corporation organized under the laws of the State of Blackstone, and has a principal place of business at 47 Ahab Lane, Naperville, Illinois.

2. Defendant Mark's Boats, Inc. ("Mark's Boats") is a corporation organized under the laws of the State of Blackstone, and upon information and belief has a principal place of business at 11 North Beach Drive, Mountain View, Blackstone.

JURISDICTION AND VENUE

3. This is an action for pecuniary and injunctive relief from patent infringement arising under the Patent Laws of the United States, Title 35 of the United States Code.

4. This Court has jurisdiction over the subject matter of this action as provided for in 28 U.S.C. § 1331 and § 1338. Venue is proper in this District pursuant to 28 U.S.C. § 1391 and § 1400.

5. This Court has jurisdiction over Mark's Boats because Mark's Boats is a citizen of Blackstone by virtue of being incorporated in Blackstone, and because Mark's Boats has committed acts of patent infringement during the course of its business in this District.

THE PATENTS IN SUIT

6. On April 1, 1995, U.S. Patent No. 5,551,835 ("the '835 patent"), entitled "Trolling Motor" was duly and legally issued to Michael J. Perch, who has assigned his rights in the '835 patent to Mike's Fishing. Mike's Fishing has been and is still the owner of the entire right, title,

and interest in and to the '835 patent. A copy of the '835 patent is attached as Exhibit A.

7. Mike's Fishing has fully complied with the requirements of 35 U.S.C. § 287(a) by affixing the word "patent" or the abbreviation "pat", together with the number of the patent (5,551,835), on all apparatuses manufactured or sold by Mike's Fishing which embody the patented invention.

INFRINGEMENT OF THE '835 PATENT

8. Mark's Boats has infringed and continues to infringe; has induced and continues to induce others to infringe; and/or has committed and continues to commit acts of contributory infringement of, one or more of the claims of the '835 patent. Mark's Boats' infringing activities in the United States and this District include development, manufacture, use, sale, and/or offer for sale of certain bow-mounted trolling motors having auto pilot controls. Such infringing activities violate 35 U.S.C. § 271. Upon information and belief, such infringement has been, and continues to be, willful.

9. As a consequence of the infringing activities of Mark's Boats regarding the '835 patent as complained of herein, Mike's Fishing has suffered monetary damages in an amount not yet determined, and Mike's Fishing will continue to suffer such damages in the future unless and until Mark's Boats' infringing activities are enjoined by this Court.

REQUESTED RELIEF

WHEREFORE, Mike's Fishing prays for judgment against Mark's Boats as follows:

A. That Mark's Boats be declared to have infringed, induced others to infringe, and/or committed acts of contributory infringement with respect to the claims of the '835 patent;

B. That Mark's Boats, its officers, agents, servants, employees, attorneys, parents, subsidiaries, affiliates, successors, and all others in active concert or participation with them or acting on their behalf be permanently enjoined from further infringement of the '835 patent;

C. That Mark's Boats be ordered to account for and pay to Mike's Fishing all damages caused to Mike's Fishing by reason of Mark's Boats' infringement of the '835 patent pursuant to 35 U.S.C. § 284, including any enhanced damages;

D. That Mike's Fishing be granted pre-judgment and post-judgment interest on the damages caused to it by reason of Mark's Boats' infringement of the '835 patent;

E. That this be declared an "exceptional case" pursuant to 35 U.S.C. § 285 and that Mark's Boats be ordered to pay Mike's Fishing's attorney fees and costs; and

F. That Mike's Fishing be granted such other and further relief as the case may require and the Court may deem just and proper.

JURY DEMAND

Mike's Fishing demands a jury trial on all issues triable to a jury in this matter.

Dated: _____   _____

IN THE UNITED STATES DISTRICT COURT
FOR THE NORTHERN DISTRICT OF CALIFORNIA

MIKE'S FISHING, INC.,	)	
	)	
Plaintiff,	)	Civil Action No. 99
	)	
v.	)	
	)	
MARK'S BOATS, INC.,	)	
	)	
Defendant.	)	

ANSWER AND COUNTERCLAIM OF MARK'S BOATS, INC.

Defendant, Mark's Boats, Inc. ("Mark's Boats"), answers the Complaint filed by Mike's Fishing, Inc. ("Mike's Fishing") as follows:

1. Defendant is without knowledge or information sufficient to form a belief as to the truth of the allegations in paragraph 1 of the Complaint.

2. Defendant admits the allegations in paragraph 2 of the Complaint.

3. Defendant admits the allegations in paragraph 3 of the Complaint.

4. Defendant admits the allegations in paragraph 4 of the Complaint.

5. Defendant admits the allegations in paragraph 5 of the Complaint to the extent that there is jurisdiction but denies that it has committed acts of infringement during the course of its business in the District.

6. Defendant admits that U.S. Patent No. 5,551,835 ("the '835 patent") bears an issue date of April 1, 1995, and further admits that Exhibit A attached to the Complaint is a true and correct copy of the '835 Patent. Defendant is without knowledge or information sufficient to form a belief as to the truth of the remaining allegations in paragraph 6 of the Complaint.

7. Defendant is without knowledge or information sufficient to form a belief as to the truth of the allegations in paragraph 7 of the Complaint.

8. Defendant denies the allegations in paragraph 8 of the Complaint.

9. Defendant denies the allegations in paragraph 9 of the Complaint.

AFFIRMATIVE DEFENSES

First Affirmative Defense

10. The '835 Patent, and each claim thereof, is invalid for failing to comply with the requirements of the patent laws of the United States, specifically 35 U.S.C. §§ 102, 103, 112, and/or 132.

Second Affirmative Defense

11. Defendant has not directly infringed, has not contributorily infringed, and has not induced infringement of, any claim of the '835 Patent, and is not liable for any acts of infringement of the '835 Patent.

Third Affirmative Defense

12. Plaintiff's claim is barred by equitable estoppel.

Fourth Affirmative Defense

13. Plaintiff's claim is barred by Plaintiff's unclean hands.

Fifth Affirmative Defense

14. The '835 Patent is unenforceable because Defendant has misused that patent by attempting to enforce a knowingly invalid and unenforceable patent.

Sixth Affirmative Defense

15. Defendant has not willfully infringed the '835 Patent.

Seventh Affirmative Defense

16. The Complaint fails to state a claim upon which relief can be granted.

COUNTERCLAIM FOR DECLARATORY JUDGMENT OF PATENT INVALIDITY, UNENFORCEABILITY, AND NONINFRINGEMENT

17. Defendant brings this counterclaim pursuant to the Declaratory Judgment Act, 28 U.S.C. §§ 2201 and 2202. This counterclaim arises under the patent laws of the United States. 35 U.S.C. § 1, *et seq*.

18. This Court has subject matter jurisdiction pursuant to 28 U.S.C. §§ 1331 and 1338.

19. Plaintiff has charged Defendant *inter alia* with infringement, willful infringement, contributory infringement, and inducing infringement of the '835 Patent. Defendant has denied that it has committed any of the alleged acts of infringement, willful infringement, contributo-

ry infringement, or inducing infringement, and Defendant has further asserted that the '835 Patent is invalid and unenforceable.

20.   There is an actual controversy between Plaintiff and Defendant with respect to the validity and enforceability of the '835 Patent, and with respect to alleged infringement of the '835 Patent by Defendant.

21.   Defendant has not infringed, willfully infringed, contributorily infringed, or induced others to infringe, any claim of the '835 Patent.

22.   The '835 Patent is invalid for failing to comply with the patent laws of the United States, specifically 35 U.S.C. §§ 102, 103, 112, and/or 132.

23.   The '835 Patent is unenforceable because of Plaintiff's misuse of that patent in knowingly attempting to enforce an invalid and unenforceable patent.

CLAIMS FOR RELIEF

WHEREFORE, Defendant Mark's Boats requests the following relief:

A.   The Court enter judgment in Defendant's favor and against Plaintiff Mike's Fishing on the claim for patent infringement alleged in the Complaint;

B.   The Court declare that the '835 Patent, and each claim thereof, is invalid;

C.   The Court declare that Defendant has not infringed any claim of the '835 Patent, and declare that Defendant is not liable for any acts of infringement, contributory infringement, or inducing infringement of the '835 Patent;

D.   The Court declare that the '835 Patent is unenforceable;

E.   The Court find this case to be exceptional and award Defendant its costs, expenses, and attorneys' fees; in accordance with 35 U.S.C. § 285; and

F.   The Court grant Defendant such other and further relief as may be deemed appropriate and just.

Date: _____   Respectfully submitted,

_____

A. Head Charger
Moore, Michel & Lupo
1650 Dead Patent Road
Coal Dust Township, Blackstone

Chapter Five

DISCOVERY

Introduction

Discovery is the most tedious, burdensome, and expensive part of patent litigation. However, it is necessary to obtain facts to support your case and understand your opponent's case. Discovery will help prevent surprises at trial. Planning is the key to discovery. During discovery, each party should develop: a plan to get facts for your case, a plan to learn about your opponent's case, and a strategy to prepare your client for discovery. To prepare your client for your opponent's discovery requests you should identify and interview key witnesses and locate key documents.

A. THE SCOPE OF DISCOVERABLE MATERIAL IN A PATENT LITIGATION

Federal Rules of Civil Procedure—Rule 26:

(b) Discovery Scope and Limits. Unless otherwise limited by order of the Court in accordance with these rules, the scope of discovery is as follows:

(1) In General. Parties may obtain discovery regarding any matter, not privileged, which is relevant to the subject matter involved in the pending action, whether it relates to the claim or defense of the party seeking discovery or to the claim or defense of any other party, including the existence, description, nature, custody, condition, and location of any books, documents, or other tangible things and the identity and location of persons having knowledge of any discoverable matter. The information sought need not be admissible at the trial if the information sought appears reasonably calculated to lead to the discovery of admissible evidence.

(2) Limitations. By order or by local rule, the court may alter the limits in these rules on the number of depositions and interrogatories and may also limit the length of depositions under Rule 30 and the number of requests under Rule 36. The frequency or extent of use of the discovery methods otherwise permitted under these rules and by any local rule shall be limited by the court if it determines that: (i) the discovery sought is unreasonably cumulative or duplicative, or is obtainable from some other source that is more convenient, less burdensome, or less expensive; (ii) the party seeking discovery has had ample opportunity by discovery in the action to obtain the information sought; or (iii) the burden or expense of the proposed discovery outweighs its likely benefit, taking into account the needs of the case, the amount in controversy, the parties' resources, the importance of the issues at stake in the litigation, and the importance of the proposed discovery in resolving the issues. The court may act upon its own initiative after reasonable notice or pursuant to a motion under subdivision (c).

(3) Trial Preparation: Materials. Subject to the provisions of subdivision (b)(4) of this rule, a party may obtain discovery of documents and tangible things otherwise discoverable under subdivision (b)(1) of this rule and prepared in anticipation of litigation or for trial by or for another party or by or for that other party's representative (including the other party's attorney, consultant, surety, indemnitor, insurer or agent) only upon a showing that the party seeking discovery has substantial need of the materials in the preparation of the party's case and that the party is unable without undue hardship to obtain the substantial equivalent of the materials by other means. In ordering discovery of such materials when the required showing has been made, the court shall protect against disclosure of the mental impressions, conclusions, opinions or legal theories of an attorney or other representative of a party concerning the litigation.

A party may obtain without the required showing a statement concerning the action or its subject matter previously made by that party. Upon request, a person not a party may obtain without the required showing a statement concerning the action or its subject matter previously made by that person. If the request is refused, the person may move for a court order. The provisions of rule 37(a)(4) apply to the award of expenses incurred in relation to the motion. For purposes of this paragraph, a statement previously made is (A) a written statement signed or otherwise adopted or approved by the person making it, or (B) a stenographic, mechanical, electrical, or other recording, or a transcription thereof, which is a substantially verbatim recital of an oral statement by the person making it and contemporaneously recorded.

(4) Trial Preparation: Experts.

    (A) A party may depose any person who has been identified as an expert whose opinions may be presented at trial. If a report from the expert is required under subdivision (a)(2)(B), the deposition shall not be conducted until after the report is provided.

    (B) A party may, through interrogatories or by deposition, discover facts known or opinions held by an expert who has been retained or specially employed by another party in anticipation of litigation or preparation for trial and who is not expected to be called as a witness at trial, only as provided in Rule 35(b) or upon a showing of exceptional circumstances under which it is impracticable for the party seeking discovery to obtain facts or opinions on the same subject by other means.

(C) Unless manifest injustice would result, (i) the court shall require that the party seeking discovery pay the expert a reasonable fee for time spent in responding to discovery under this subdivision, and (ii) with respect to discovery obtained under subdivision (b)(4)(B) of this rule the court shall require the party seeking discovery to pay the other party a fair portion of the fees and expenses reasonably incurred by the latter party in obtaining facts and opinions from the expert.

(5) Claims of Privilege or Protection of Trial Preparation Materials. When a party withholds information otherwise discoverable under these rules by claiming that it is privileged or subject to protection as trial preparation material, the party shall make the claim expressly and shall describe the nature of the documents, communications, or things not produced or disclosed in a manner that, without revealing information itself privileged or protected, will enable other parties to assess the applicability of the privilege or protection.

Discovery in a patent infringement case is conducted through the same discovery mechanisms available in all civil litigation cases. This chapter is not intended to present the basics of civil litigation discovery techniques and knowledge thereof is presumed. Instead, this chapter addresses several areas that arise frequently in patent cases.

A brief overview of discovery basics may nevertheless be helpful. As a general rule, a party may obtain discovery on any non-privileged matter relevant to the subject matter of the civil action. The Federal Circuit has consistently interpreted the language "relevant to the subject matter involved" broadly. *See Micro Motion Inc. v. Kane Steel Co.*, 894 F.2d 1318, 1326, 13 USPQ2d 1696, 1701 (Fed. Cir. 1990) ("while the requirement that discovery be 'relevant to the subject matter involved' is to be broadly construed, the divergent situations to which it must apply makes it impossible to provide a rigid definition of this phrase"); *Truswal Systems Corp. v. Hygro–Air Eng'g, Inc.*, 813 F.2d 1207, 1211, 2 USPQ2d 1034, 1038 (Fed. Cir. 1987) (discovery allows for a broader interpretation of relevance than trial). In general, discovery is permitted to ascertain information that seems likely to lead to admissible evidence. Rule 26(b) allows for discovery of matters relating to any claims or defenses by any party. In addition, discovery is allowed where it may lead to information and ultimately admissible evidence to a counterclaim, even where the counterclaim is arguably not relevant to the issues raised in the complaint.

Since unrestrained liberal discovery can lead to abuse, the courts have been afforded the power to monitor the limits of discovery on a case-by-case basis. For example, courts may place limitations on the number of depositions, interrogatories or requests for admissions. Of course, courts resolve discovery disputes. In all of these instances, the court is given wide discretion in discovery management. Discovery may also be denied where the burden on the party outweighs the need of the requesting party.

In interpreting the proper bounds for discovery in the context of patent litigation, courts have held that certain types of information are relevant including evidence of commercial success, foreign sales information, prior art relied upon to invalidate a patent, information relating to the uniqueness, superiority and marketability of a patented product, documents reflecting the level of skill in the art, direct evidence of obviousness, documents reflecting infringers' profits, and evidence of long-felt need for the invention.

Resolution of discovery disputes should first be attempted through negotiations between the parties. When all else fails, the court's intervention is necessary. Often, the matter is referred to a magistrate for decision.

CHUBB INTEGRATED SYSTEMS LTD. v. NATIONAL BANK

103 F.R.D. 52, 224 USPQ 1002 (D. D.C. 1984)

JEAN F. DWYER, Magistrate.

The parties are before the Court to resolve certain discovery disputes; specifically, defendants' motion to compel production of documents and answers to interrogatories, and plaintiff's response and objections thereto. The production of documents issue involves a question of privilege. This Court will deal with that issue separately after an in camera inspection of the documents in question. Accordingly, we consider only the outstanding interrogatories.

This case arises out of a complaint for alleged infringement of several patents held by plaintiff, Chubb Integrated Systems Limited (Chubb). For their part, defendants, National Bank of Washington and Docutel/Olivetti Corp. (NBW/Olivetti), maintain that for a variety of reasons, there has been no patent infringement. For example, they argue the patents are invalid, and accordingly there was no infringement. Alternatively, they contend that any recovery is barred by laches or estoppel. In this regard, defendants seek to compel discovery in three broad categories: (1) sales information relevant to the commercial success of plaintiff's patented inventions; (2) use, sales and publication information relevant to the requirements of patentability under Title 35 of the United States Code; and (3) the basis for plaintiff's belief that the patents had been infringed and when that conclusion was first reached.

I

A. SALES INFORMATION

Defendants' interrogatories nos. 87(a-i) and 89(a-i) seek information about the sales of machines embodying the inventions of the patents in suit. Plaintiff refuses to supply any information of its sales in the United States. Plaintiff contends it will not rely on its U.S. sales as an element of proof of the non-obviousness of the inventions claimed in the patents. Plaintiff further observes that if it chooses to use its European sales figures in support of non-obviousness, it will provide answers only to certain subparts (a, g, h, and i). Chubb maintains that the remaining subparts (b-f) are not properly discoverable. Plaintiff's objection is based on two grounds. Initially, plaintiff argues that information such as identification of customers, and sales to each customer, are not relevant to establishing commercial success. Plaintiff also contends that such information is highly proprietary.

The U.S. sales figures are clearly discoverable. The fact that plaintiff does not plan to use them to support its case does not prevent defendants from obtaining discovery of those figures, so long as they are relevant to any part of the litigation. Fed. R. Civ. P. 26(b)(1) provides in pertinent part "parties may obtain discovery regarding any matter . . . relevant to the subject matter involved in the pending action, whether it relates to a claim or defense of the party seeking discovery or the claim or defense or defense of any other party. . . ." In the instant case, plaintiff's United States sales figures may be relevant to one of the defenses asserted by defendants.

NBW/Olivetti raise the affirmative defense of patent invalidity. They allege the invention was obvious. Case law and statutes make it clear that "obviousness" of patent claims is relevant to patent invalidity. *See* 35 U.S.C. § 103 (1982); *Graham v. John Deere Co.*, 383 U.S. 1, 12 (1966). It is equally well settled that commercial success of an alleged invention is an indicium of "obviousness" or "non-obviousness", albeit a secondary consideration. *Graham v. John Deere Co.*, 383 U.S. at 17. Sales information is a relevant factor in a determination of commercial success or a lack thereof. *See Kansas Jack, Inc. v. Kuhn*, 719 F.2d 1144, 1151 (Fed. Cir. 1983) (Markey, C.J.) (the court noted that the number of units sold is some evidence of commercial success, as well as market share and market growth); *In re Sernaker*, 702 F.2d 989, 996 (Fed. Cir. 1983) (in an appeal from a patent rejection the court found sales to be an element of commercial success and evidence of non-obviousness). Accordingly, Chubb's sales are relevant to its commercial success and therefore relevant to defendants' claim of obviousness.

Determining that sales information is generally relevant to "obviousness" does not end our inquiry. We must consider whether the specific information sought in the various subparts is relevant to commercial success. Courts have indicated that the following areas of inquiry are probative of commercial success: volume of sales, evidence of share in the market place, growth in market share, replacing earlier units sold by others, dollar amounts, nexus between sales and the merits of the invention, evidence that the applicant has been able to license the invention and evidence that the licensees have been able to sell the product. With this in mind, we consider the subparts in question.

Only subpart (a), which seeks volume of sales, falls squarely within the type of information discussed in *Kansas Jack* and *In re Sernaker*. Accordingly, that information should be provided. Subpart (b) seeks to determine without description or limitation, "each customer". The request is ambiguous at best. However, to the extent that it seeks the number of customers, but not the names, it is an appropriate inquiry. On the other hand, subparts (c), (d), and (e) (which seek yearly sales broken down by customer, yearly profit from sales, and all contracts relating to sales), are not likely to lead to evidence of market share, growth in the market place, etc., and therefore they are not probative of commercial success. We will not require Chubb to answer subparts (c), (d) and (e) at this time. Consistent with this rule, plaintiff's response to subpart (f) (which requests each document relating to or identifying persons having knowledge of subparts (a)-(e)), shall be limited to documents relating to or identifying persons having knowledge of annual volume of sales under subpart (a) and the number of customers under subpart (b).

We believe that the limitations we have placed on the foregoing interrogatories should assuage plaintiff's concerns about the proprietary nature of the information requested. In the future, if the names of the customers, or the other information, become of consequence to the litigation, the parties may advise the court and we will proceed accordingly.

Defendants' interrogatories nos. 134 and 136 inquire whether Chubb is currently selling automated teller machines (ATMs) covered by the patents in suit. Chubb objects to the interrogatories claiming that the requested information is not relevant to any issue in the litigation, nor is it likely to lead to relevant information. We think plaintiff takes too narrow a view of relevance.

"A request for discovery should be considered relevant if there is any possibility that the information sought may be relevant to the subject matter of the action." *In re Folding Carton Antitrust Litigation*, 83 F.R.D. 251, 254 (N.D. Ill. 1978). Unquestionably, information regarding Chubb's current sales of ATMs is relevant to the subject matter of the pending action. Current sales are indicative of the commercial success of plaintiff's inventions. This alone marks the inquiry as relevant to the issue of patent validity.

Interrogatories nos. 115 and 116 request the identity of every model of ATMs manufactured by Chubb or for Chubb, and the beginning and ending dates of the manufacture, use, sale and/or lease of each model, since 1965. Chubb answered in part, supplying the information for the period 1965–1970. However, plaintiff refuses to supply any information after 1970. Plaintiff argues that the information is not relevant. Once again, we find plaintiff's view of relevancy is too restrictive.

In *Roesberg v. Johns–Manville Corp.*, 85 F.R.D. 292 (E.D. Pa. 1980), the court considered an objection to an interrogatory which spanned more than fifty years. The court allowed the discovery stating "the selected time frame is not wholly unreasonable or irrelevant". *Id.* at 296. The court concluded that where these tests are satisfied, a request for information should be considered relevant and therefore discoverable. *Id.* In the case at bar, these tests are satisfied.

We cannot find the period after 1970 wholly unreasonable or irrelevant. Post patent commercial success is a common area of inquiry in patent infringement litigation. Here, patents '904 and '527 were issued in 1970. It follows that production and sales of ATMs after 1970 are both reasonable and relevant.

Furthermore, plaintiff does not explain why the period after 1970 is irrelevant or wholly unreasonable. General objections are not useful to the court ruling on a discovery motion. Nor does a general objection fulfill plaintiff's burden to explain its objections. *See Fonseca v. Regan*, 98 F.R.D. 694, 700 (E.D. N.Y. 1983) (the party resisting discovery must explain and support its objections). Chubb's bare objection, that the requested information is "irrelevant", does not meet the standard for a successful objection. Accordingly, plaintiff is directed to answer fully interrogatories nos. 115 and 116.

B. INTERROGATORIES RELEVANT TO PATENTABILITY UNDER 35 U.S.C. § 102

Defendants' interrogatories nos. 30 and 32 request information about the uses and sales of machines covered by the patents '904 and '527 prior to the dates plaintiff filed for U.S. patents. To the extent that these interrogatories request information relative to a first sale occurring after the filing dates of plaintiff's United Kingdom patent applications, but before its corresponding United States filing dates, plaintiff makes three objections—relevancy, repetition, and burdensomeness.

(1) Relevancy

Plaintiff argues that the information defendants seek cannot invalidate the patent under 35 U.S.C. § 102. Plaintiff contends it is *prima facie* entitled to the benefit of the U.K. filing dates. Chubb further argues that as a matter of law, defendants would have to rebut plaintiff's entitlement to the U.K. filing dates before the information could be admitted at trial. Based on this reasoning, plaintiff concludes the interrogatories are irrelevant. We disagree.

We are unpersuaded by plaintiff's argument for two reasons. Initially, we note that defendants' request falls within the scope of discovery permitted by the Federal Rules of Civil Procedure. The concept of relevancy is broadly construed at the discovery stage of an action, and discovery rules are to be accorded liberal treatment. Rule 26(b) provides that information is discoverable if it is "relevant to the subject matter involved in the pending action. . . ." Unquestionably, defendants' interrogatories nos. 30 and 32 are relevant to the subject matter of the action. The questions seek information to support the allegations in paragraphs 16 and 18, affirmative defenses of defendant NBW's answer and in the same paragraphs of defendant Docutel/Olivetti's answer.

Whether this information is found to be admissible at trial has little bearing on the issue of discoverability. Rule 26(b) makes a clear distinction between information that is relevant to the subject matter for pretrial discovery and the ultimate admissibility of that information at trial. *See* Fed. R. Civ. P. 26(b)(1), advisory committee note, 1970 Amendment. Admissibility at trial is not the yardstick of permissible discovery.

We are troubled by a second aspect of Chubb's objection. While plaintiff's argument is couched in terms of relevance, we feel that plaintiff implicitly challenges the sufficiency of defendants' affirmative defense. In ruling on questions of discovery, typically, courts do not determine the legal sufficiency of claims and defenses. The legal sufficiency of a claim or defense is appropriately challenged in a motion to strike, and a defense, until stricken, is valid.

It is, of course, within the court's discretion to deny discovery related to a patently insubstantial claim, for example, where the claim or defense appears baseless and the discovery would work a hardship on the answering party. We see no reason to bar discovery on these grounds in this case.

In the instant case, plaintiff does not assert that the defense is baseless. Rather, plaintiff claims that *prima facie* entitlement to the benefits of the U.K. filing dates renders the information inadmissible. This is an issue that will be resolved at trial. At this point in the litigation, we do not regard the defense proffered under 35 U.S.C. § 102 as "baseless".

Plaintiff makes an independent objection to this discovery on grounds of burdensomeness. We address it below.

(2) Repetition and Burdensomeness

Chubb contends that the information sought in these interrogatories nos. 30 and 32 has long been made available to defendants during defendants' search of Chubb's document files in the U.K. during October–November, 1983. Chubb bases its objections of repetition and burden on this search. However, we do not think the mere fact that defendants undertook a document search supports plaintiff's claim.

Labeling plaintiff's effort as repetitious, does not support its objection. Standing alone, the fact that defendants conducted a search does not support plaintiff's claim of burdensomeness. An objection must show specifically how an interrogatory is overly broad, burdensome or oppressive, by submitting affidavits or offering evidence which reveals the nature of the burden. Plaintiff's objections do not reveal the nature of its burden. Without more, this Court cannot conclude that Chubb will be unduly burdened by the interrogatories. Accordingly, we reject this argument.

Finally, we note that plaintiff's refusal to respond to the above-mentioned interrogatories will effectively prevent defendants from pursuing a potential legal theory at trial. Our denial of defendants' discovery request would have a similar effect. We decline to do so. It is well settled that the court's decision should not have the effect of completely denying a party information that would be useful at trial.

Because we reject Chubb's objections of relevancy, repetition, and burdensomeness, plaintiff is directed to provide a response to interrogatories nos. 30 and 32.

C. Basis of Plaintiff's Infringement Claim

Defendants' interrogatories nos. 8(a, b, c) and 10(a, b, c) ask plaintiff to (a) identify the patent claims which plaintiff contends have been infringed by defendant Docutel/Olivetti; (b) the facts known to plaintiff supporting the infringements alleged in (a); and (c) the identity of any documents supporting or referred to in subparts (a) and (b). Plaintiff answered subpart (a), providing a list of those patent claims which it believes the defendants' models infringe. Plaintiff did not answer subparts (b) and (c). Instead, plaintiff stated that it did not have specific information concerning the structure and mode of operation of defendants' machines, products, or apparatuses to identify with certainty those claims which are infringed. In plaintiff's response to defendants' motion to compel, plaintiff added that it had just received from defendant, a few days prior to its answer, a replacement set of the materials from which the answer to subparts (b) and (c) would be deduced. Plaintiff requests that it be given sufficient time to examine the materials and to provide a supplement to its answer.

Chubb's answer and reply is not responsive to the question. Fairly read, the question seeks facts within the knowledge of plaintiff at the time it answered the interrogatories. There should be no question that Chubb has information to support the allegation. Chubb must therefore disclose the information in answer to an interrogatory seeking the basis of the allegation. Accordingly, plaintiff shall answer interrogatories 8(b, c) and 10(b, c). Further, this Court directs plaintiff to supplement its response to these interrogatories.

Note

1. Material is discoverable if there is any possibility that the information is relevant or will lead to relevant information regarding the subject matter of the litigation. Discoverable material is not necessarily the same as admissible material at trial. The scope of discoverable material is broader and covers information that may lead to admissible trial evidence. To object to the discovery of relevant materials, the objecting party must show how the request is overly broad, burdensome or oppressive. A mere assertion of irrelevancy is insufficient.

B.   DISCOVERY MECHANISMS

1.   PARTY DISCOVERY MECHANISMS

No discovery may be taken until after the parties have their discovery planning meeting as required by Rule 26(f). Party discovery mechanisms include:

1. interrogatories;
2. document requests;

3. requests for admissions; and

4. depositions.

When a party is served with discovery, it has three options: respond within the time allotted; move for an extension of time; or move for a protective order if the information sought is confidential or is sought for harassment purposes. If the served party does not use one of these three options, a motion to compel and/or a motion for sanctions may be filed pursuant to Rule 37.

a. Interrogatories

Rule 33 governs the use of interrogatories in discovery. Interrogatories may be served on parties. The rules limit each party to 25 interrogatories; although this number can be changed by local rule, stipulation, or court order. Interrogatories should be used to clarify the issues (*see, e.g.,* sample interrogatories nos. 2 and 4), identify witnesses (*see, e.g.,* sample interrogatories nos. 3 and 6), and uncover your opponent's case (*see, e.g.,* sample interrogatories nos. 3 and 9). Interrogatories should be narrow and specific. Since the number of interrogatories is limited, you should always check to see if the interrogatory can be drafted as a document request. For example, it is a waste of an interrogatory to ask your opponent "to identify all prior art known to the defendant prior to or at the time of issuance" when such a request can easily be framed as a document request. Answers to interrogatories may be narrative or reference a document which contains the answer. Sample interrogatories appear at the end of this chapter.

b. Document Requests

Rule 34 governs document requests. Document requests may only be served on parties. Documents may be obtained from third parties by subpoena using Rule 45. Document requests should be coordinated with the interrogatories. Compare sample document request nos. 10 and 13 with interrogatory no. 2. Be careful not to draft the requests too broad because you will have to review all the documents produced. Documents which correspond to document requests must be delivered in the same manner they are kept in business. For example, if the documents are contained in a file or labeled, they should be produced this way. Sample document requests appear at the end of this chapter.

c. Requests for Admissions

Rule 36 governs requests for admissions. Requests for admission should be used for the facts that are not in dispute in order to limit the issues for trial. Requests for admission are valuable for document authentication. In a patent case, they can be used to eliminate infringement issues. For example, if a claim covers "an apparatus comprising A, B, and C," there may be no dispute that the accused device has A and B. Use a request to admit with respect to A and B and then you need only focus on proving C. In response to a request to admit, the party served must admit, deny, or specify that it does not have sufficient information to admit or deny the allegation.

d. Depositions

Depositions are governed by Rule 30. The rules limit the parties to 10 depositions. Once you have identified the people you would like to depose, you need to file a notice of the deposition which must specify how the deposition will be recorded. Usually, a court reporter records the deposition; however, videotaped depositions are also permitted. Why would you want to videotape a deposition? Objections during a deposition must be concise and not suggestive (coaching the witness is not permitted). The witness must still answer the objected to question unless it is privileged. What is the purpose then of the objection? If the opposing party is a corporation, a Rule 30(b)(6) notice can be filed. In the notice, the party requesting discovery identifies subject matter on which it wishes to take discovery (for example, damages) and the corporation must identify and produce a witness with knowledge of that subject matter.

2. THIRD PARTY DISCOVERY

Rule 45 governs discovery of non-parties. Parties can seek discovery of third parties by deposition or document request. Third party discovery is often necessary in a patent case to determine lost profits and reasonable royalty calculations. If competing products are sold by third parties, discovery may be necessary to prove the patent owner's market share or an established industry royalty rate. Can you think of other circumstances when third party discovery may be necessary?

Depositions of quasi judicial officers such as U.S. patent examiners relating to their decisions are not favored. Although oral examination of patent examiners is sometimes allowed, it is permitted reluctantly by the U.S. Patent and Trademark Office and with strict limitations placed on the scope of subject matter open for examination. The general rule is that patent examiners may be questioned as to factual matters only (such as whether they considered a reference) and may not be questioned about the underlying mental processes or reasons for their actions. Can you think of any reason why the plaintiff-patentee would want to take the deposition of a patent examiner for use at trial?

C. THE IMPACT ON DISCOVERY FROM AN ASSERTION OF ATTORNEY CLIENT PRIVILEGE OR WORK PRODUCT IMMUNITY IN PATENT LITIGATION

In general, under Federal Rule of Civil Procedure 26(b), a party may obtain discovery regarding any nonprivileged communication which is relevant to the subject matter of a civil litigation. Federal Rule of Civil Procedure 26(b)(1) excludes "privileged" communications from discoverable material. Claims of attorney-client privilege and work product immunity are often used to attempt to protect sensitive communications from discovery. These communications are potentially damaging as they involve the most critical analysis of one's case or lay out trial or discovery strategy. The burden of establishing the privilege or immunity is on the party asserting it.

Attorney-client privileged materials are communications between the attorney and client that are made for the purpose of obtaining legal advice. Their purpose is to protect confidences made by the client to the attorney, and thereby allow full and frank discussions. Rule 26(b)(3) of the Federal Rules of Civil Procedure also protects attorney work product from discovery, *i.e.*, trial preparation materials. The rule's purpose is to prevent opposing parties and counsel from interfering with an attorney performing the necessary duties involved in litigating a case as well as those materials prepared in anticipation of the litigation.

Under Federal Rule of Civil Procedure 26(b)(5), a party withholding information subject to a privilege must specifically claim the privilege. The claim must include a description of the document, communication, or other item to be withheld without disclosing its substance. A "privilege log" of the withheld documents should be provided to the opponent to describe the withheld documents to enable the opponent to assess the applicability of the privilege. This log is often called a *Duplan* log to indicate that it is intended to convey the information categorized in *Duplan Corp. v. Deering Milliken*, 397 F. Supp. 1146, 184 USPQ 775 (D.S.C. 1974).[1]

In the following patent case, the court was presented with defendant's Motion to Compel the Production of Documents to which plaintiff alleged both attorney client privilege and work product immunity. Defendants asserted that any privilege or immunity was eliminated by the fraud or waiver of the plaintiff.

HERCULES INC. v. EXXON CORP.

434 F. Supp. 136, 196 USPQ 401 (D. Del. 1977)

CALEB M. WRIGHT, Senior District Judge.

Presently before the Court are two discovery motions filed by defendant, Exxon Corp., to compel production of plaintiff's withheld documents and to compel answers to interrogatories. The motions arise out of an action charging defendant with patent infringement. Defendant has counterclaimed for invalidity, unenforceability and non-infringement.

---

1. "A typical privilege log should describe each document as to which privilege is claimed by (1) document production number and date; (2) author and author's address; (3) addressees and recipients of the document (direct and by copy) and addresses of addressees and recipients; (4) the nature of the document (letter, memorandum, etc.) and the number of its pages; (5) the matters discussed in the document; and as to such matters about which privilege is claimed (6) the nature of the privilege that is invoked." Alvin K. Hellerstein, *A Comprehensive Survey of the Attorney–Client Privilege and Work Product Doctrine*, 540 PLI/Lit 589, 876 (1996).

I. Motion to Compel Production.

Since filing of the complaint in this action, both parties have engaged in substantial discovery through interrogatories, depositions and requests for production of documents. The present motion to compel production concerns 255 documents which plaintiff claims are protected by attorney-client privilege or work product immunity. Defendant alleges that any protection which might attach to the documents in question is vitiated by fraud or waiver. In support of its allegations of fraud, defendant has presented to this Court a large number of documentary exhibits. The withheld documents were produced to the Court for in camera inspection, together with a copy of the file wrapper of the Adamek application and copies of certain produced documents which defendant claims constitute a waiver of privilege.

For the most part, the disputed documents are communications between Hercules patent department attorneys and members of the Hercules operating divisions or research department or between patent department attorneys and outside counsel. Some communications were also sent to house counsel in Hercules Legal Department. Claims of attorney-client privilege or work product are also made as to certain internal memoranda, drafts and communications of the Patent Department attorneys or of outside counsel. As the documents embrace a wide range of subject matter, they have been classified into the following categories:

I. Documents relating to the prosecution of the application for the patent in suit.

II. Documents relating to *Adamek, et al. v. Tarney*, Interference No. 93,018.

III. Documents relating to *Hercules v. Copolymer*, Civil Action No. 76–25, in the Eastern District of Louisiana.

IV. Documents relating to the present action.

V. Licenses and agreements relating to the patent in suit.

VI. Documents relating to the scope of the Adamek application.

VII. Documents relating to infringement of the Adamek patent.

VIII. Miscellaneous withheld documents.

Plaintiff has submitted a schedule listing the identification of each document and its recipients, and the grounds supporting the claims of attorney-client privilege or work product immunity.

As with any claim of privilege made in connection with patent matters, the problem of classification into protected and non-protected communications is troublesome. Patent attorneys, particularly those employed in corporate patent departments, often serve dual functions— as legal advisers and as business advisers. Communications between those attorneys and members of operating or research departments often concern technical information which may or may not be relevant to particular legal advice requested from the attorney. As to much of that information, the attorney may be acting merely as a conduit, to relay the data to the Patent Office as part of an *ex parte* patent application. There is a legitimate public interest in insuring that the applicant is not able to circumvent his duty of full disclosure to the Patent Office merely by channeling information into the hands of an attorney. Defendant's allegations of fraud and waiver add further complications. Documents which otherwise satisfy the criteria for attorney-client or work product protection may be discoverable if made in furtherance of a fraud on the Patent Office or if the protection has been waived. The Court has, therefore, examined the documents individually at two levels: to determine first whether the document falls within the scope of the claimed protection; and, second, whether that protection has been vitiated by fraud or waived.

Although defendant attempts to resuscitate the question of the applicability of attorney-client and work product protection to patent matters, that dispute appears now to be well settled. Almost every court which has considered the problem in recent years, including the Third Circuit, has found that communications with respect to patent prosecution or litigation matters may be protected, regardless of whether the attorney is outside counsel, "house" counsel or patent department counsel.

"The court is not impressed with defendant's argument to the effect that those privileges [attorney-client privilege and work product immunity], if existing at all, are deprived of real significance where patents are the subject of the communication. The argument is based in the main upon Judge Fechy's (sic) order in *Zenith Radio Corp. v. Radio Corp. of America*, 121 F. Supp. 792 (D. Del. 1954) and *Georgia-Pacific Plywood Co. v. United States Plywood Corp.*, 18 F.R.D. 463 (S.D. N.Y. 1956). The rationale of those cases seems to be that the information which patent attorneys utilize in preparing their opinions or advising their clients is in the public domain, not confidential, so no privilege can attach. A second basis for these decisions is that in evaluating the merits of the patent, the attorney acts, not as an attorney, but as a technician.

More recent cases convince this court that those cases have lost much of their vitality. Work product and attorney-client privileges exist in the field of patent law and must be respected by the court in regulating discovery. *Collins and Aikman Corp. v. J. P. Stevens & Co.*, 51 F.R.D. 219, 220 (D.S.C. 1971).

"We hold that in a particular situation both attorney-client and work product immunity may be available to the solicitation of a party's own patent. We reject the absolute rule urged by appellant. We deem it wise that flexibility be maintained and that sound judicial discretion be exercised on a case by case basis." *In re Natta*, 410 F.2d 187 (3d Cir. 1969).

Not all communications relevant to patent matters between attorney and client or between attorneys are protected under attorney-client privilege or work product immunity. The scope of protection can be determined only on a case-by-case basis, bearing in mind the purposes of the protection and the need for "flexibility and sound judicial discretion". The desire to protect the confidentiality of the attorney-client relationship and to preserve the integrity of the adversarial process must be balanced against the public interest in full and frank disclosure to the Patent Office and the liberal spirit of the discovery rules. Defendant's request for disclosure and plaintiff's claim of privilege as to each document can only be assessed in light of those competing considerations.

A.   *Attorney–Client Privilege.*

The attorney-client privilege is designed to promote full disclosure by the client to his attorney by protecting the confidentiality of communications between the client and the attorney. Only if the client is assured that the information he relays in confidence, when seeking legal advice, will be immune from discovery will he be encouraged to disclose fully all relevant information to his attorney.

The often-quoted language of Judge Wyzanski in *United States v. United Shoe Machinery Corp.*, 89 F. Supp. 357 (D. Mass. 1950), sets out the conditions which must be satisfied:

> The privilege applies only if (1) the asserted holder of the privilege is or sought to become a client; (2) the person to whom the communication was made (a) is a member of the bar of a court, or his subordinate and (b) in connection with this communication is acting as a lawyer; (3) the communication relates to a fact of which the attorney was informed (a) by his client (b) without the presence of strangers (c) for the purpose of securing primarily either (i) an opinion on law or (ii) legal services or (iii) assistance in some legal proceeding, and not (d) for the purpose of committing a crime or tort; and (4) the privilege has been (a) claimed and (b) not waived by the client.

89 F. Supp. at 358–59.

It is essential that the communications between client and attorney concern legal assistance and advice in order to be privileged. It is not essential, however, that the request for advice be express. Client communications intended to keep the attorney apprised of continuing business developments, with an implied request for legal advice based thereon, or self-initiated attorney communications intended to keep the client posted on legal developments and implications may also be protected. The privilege also extends to the attorney's legal advice and opinions which encompass the thoughts and confidences of the client. On the other hand, communications made in the routine course of business, such as transmittal letters or acknowledgment of receipt letters, which disclose no privileged matters and which are devoid of legal advice or requests for such advice are not protected.

The application of the attorney-client privilege to communications made in connection with patent prosecution or enforcement raises some difficult line-drawing problems. Is an employee who is not necessarily a member of a control group, but who develops and communicates information to the attorney at the direction of a "control group" member, a "client" for the purposes of the privilege? When is the communication between client and attorney concerned primarily with legal advice and when does it involve primarily business advice? When is technical information (such as results of research, tests and experiments), which is communicated to the attorney, unprotected because of the duty of full disclosure to the Patent Office?

Since a corporation acts only through its representatives the Court must distinguish between those employees who act as representatives of the corporation and those who do not. Only the former qualify as "clients" for the purpose of the privilege. In making that determination, the Court has considered all the relevant circumstances, including the nature and content of the communications, the extent of the disclosure within the corporation, the relationship of the employees involved to the communication and to the corporation, and the purpose of the attorney-client privilege.

Plaintiff has submitted an uncontroverted affidavit listing the titles and responsibilities of each employee of Hercules who sent or received any of the disputed documents. *See* Affidavit of Edwin H. Dafter, Jr., Esquire. The Court is satisfied that all of those employees fall within the scope of the attorney-client privilege. Most of the named employees, outside of the Legal and Patent Departments, occupy positions of executive responsibility in the operating divisions or Research Department of Hercules. The documents reflect that they were kept apprised, on a continuing basis, of specific and general legal developments relevant to the area of their responsibilities, and that they had authority to control or substantially participate in decisions to be taken on the advice of the lawyer. Consequently, those employees can be considered members of the corporate "control group." *City of Philadelphia v. Westinghouse*, 210 F. Supp. 483 (E.D. Pa. 1962).

It is not as clear that Keim and Vandenberg, senior chemists in the Research Department, and Christman, Lukach and Amberg, research chemists in the Research Department, were members of the control group. Although each of them had some input into the decision-making process, their major contribution was in performing experiments and relaying technical information upon request to attorneys in the Patent Department. Those chemists were operating, however, at the express or implied direction of control group members to supply the attorneys with the necessary technical information and expertise pursuant to a request for legal advice. The Court must consider that, at least with respect to patent matters, members of the control group often will not have personal access to the required technical information. The policy of full disclosure underlying the attorney-client privilege requires the preservation of the confidentiality of that information when it is communicated at the direction of a member of the control group, for the purpose of soliciting legal advice. In *Duplan Corporation v. Deering Milliken, Inc., supra*, the court considered this problem in the context of the day-to-day workings of a corporation:

> Thus, the main consideration is whether the particular representative of the client, to whom or from whom the communication is made, is involved in rendering information necessary to the decisionmaking process concerning a problem on which legal advice is sought. One can envision that in some situations, the attorney has to go far down the ranks; in other instances, the attorney can obtain the necessary information close to the top. The extent of the attorney-client privilege will vary with the individual situation; the climates are seldom identical.

397 F. Supp. at 1165. It is apparent, from the affidavits presented and the documents themselves that much of the necessary technical information could be obtained only from the chemists in the Research Department. Consequently, all doubts about applicability of the privilege to communications to or from Keim, Vandenberg, Christman, Lukach and Amberg have been resolved in favor of the plaintiff.

With respect to the attorneys who received or sent communications, there is a question only about Whitson, who is listed as a patent agent in the Hercules Patent Department. There is authority for the proposition that no communications between client and a patent agent are subject to the attorney-client privilege. Most of the cases deal, however, with communications between the client and an outside patent agent who handles patent matters on an independent basis. In certain circumstances, a patent agent employed in the Patent Department of a corporation may qualify as a "subordinate" of an attorney if he is working at the direction of and under the supervision of an attorney.

Only one document, Number 61, was sent to or received by Mr. Whitson. That document concerns a request for legal research to be performed by the agent, for the benefit of the attorney. The Court can see no difference between this request and one made to a junior associate in a law firm. In both cases, the work would be performed under the direct supervision of the attorney, to be used in the rendering of legal advice. Accordingly, protection will not be denied to Document Number 61 on the basis that it was communicated to a patent agent.

The determination of when an attorney is "acting as a lawyer" is particularly difficult in patent matters. Since the Supreme Court indicated in *Sperry v. State of Florida*, 373 U.S. 379 (1963) that the preparation and prosecution of patent applications are "hallmark activities of a lawyer," courts have consistently held that confidential communications between attorney and client for the purpose of securing legal advice concerning preparation or prosecution of a patent application are protected, whether the attorney is employed as outside counsel, house counsel, or as a member of the Patent Department. The holding of early cases such as *Zenith Radio Corp. v. Radio Corp. of America*, 121 F. Supp.

792 (D. Del. 1954); and *American Cyanamid Co. v. Hercules Powder Co.*, 211 F. Supp. 85 (D. Del. 1962) that an attorney was not acting as a lawyer when making initial office preparatory determinations of patentability drafting or comparing patent specifications and claims; preparing the application for letters patent or amendments thereto and prosecuting patents or handling interferences is consequently of little weight. *See, Collins & Aikman Corp. v. J. P. Stevens & Co., supra; Chore–Time Equipment, Inc. v. Big Dutchman, Inc.*, 255 F. Supp. 1020 (W.D. Mich. 1966); *Ledex, Inc. v. U.S.*, 172 USPQ 538 (Ct. Cl. 1972).

The problem remains, however, of separating out business from legal advice. An important responsibility of most patent attorneys, especially those employed by corporate patent departments, is to assess the business implications of the company's patent position. Many of the communications between the patent attorney and non-legal personnel of the corporation would therefore predominately reflect business concerns, such as the competitive position of the company, marketing strategy, licensing policy, etc. The Court recognizes that business and legal advice may often be inextricably interwoven. A single proposed course of conduct such as patenting and licensing of an invention will have both legal and business ramifications, and the lawyer may advise as to both in a single communication. As was pointed out in *Jack Winter, Inc. v. Koratron, Inc., supra*, it is necessary to separate out the two, in the interest of preserving the integrity of the privilege itself:

> As is not infrequently the case in patent matters, the problem of classification here was particularly troublesome as the attorneys for Koratron performed virtually every task incident to filing for and obtaining a patent or trademark registration. They were so closely associated with the activities of Koratron that picking out from the mass of documents presented to the court those which involved non-legal transactions not soliciting or offering legal advice, and the separating of these from documents which did involve the exercise of the attorney's art, became at times an arduous and complex exercise. Yet we have sought to not lose sight of the importance of the distinction, for it is important that the attorney-client privilege not be down-graded in the interests of expedient results.

If the primary purpose of a communication is to solicit or render advice on non-legal matters, the communication is not within the scope of the attorney-client privilege. Only if the attorney is "acting as a lawyer"— giving advice with respect to the legal implications of a proposed course of conduct—may the privilege be properly invoked. In addition, if a communication is made primarily for the purpose of soliciting legal advice, an incidental request for business advice does not vitiate the attorney-client privilege.

The attorney-client privilege does not protect technical information such as the results of research, tests, and experiments communicated to the attorney, not calling for a legal opinion or interpretation, but meant primarily for aid in completing a patent application. The attorney serves merely as a conduit for such information to the Patent Office. The fact that a communication contains technical information, however, does not automatically preclude application of the privilege. If the primary purpose of the document is to solicit legal advice based on that information, the privilege applies. The procedure employed by Judge Doyle in *Jack Winter, Inc. v. Koratron Co., Inc., supra*, is instructive:

> A number of documents have been ruled to fall outside the boundaries of the attorney-client privilege. This has been done only after most careful consideration of the actual contents of each document. The determinations have been particularly difficult in instances of communications primarily factual in nature. Generally, when factual information was communicated so that the attorney could disclose it in a patent or trademark application, the communication was viewed as non-privileged. On the other hand, documents containing considerable technical factual information but which were nonetheless primarily concerned with giving legal guidance to the client were classified as privileged. In other words, doubts have been resolved in favor of the privilege.

B. Work Product.

Plaintiff's claim of work product immunity must be considered as separate and apart from claims of attorney-client privilege, as the two protections are distinct:

> While the work product doctrine is closely related to the attorney-client privilege because the work product represents efforts expended by the attorney during the course of the attorney-client relationship (citation omitted), the two concepts are treated quite differently and, in the eyes of the law, are independent legal concepts reflecting different policy considerations.

Kearney & Trecker Corp. v. Giddings & Lewis, Inc., 296 F. Supp. 979 (E.D. Wis. 1969). The Court in *Scourtes v. Fred W. Albrecht Grocery Co.*, 15 F.R.D. 55, 58 (N.D. Ohio 1953), outlined the difference between the policies behind the two doctrines:

> The purpose of the attorney-client privilege is to encourage full disclosure of information between an attorney and his client by guaranteeing the inviolability of their confidential communications. The 'work product of the attorney', on the other hand, is accorded protection for the purpose of preserving our adversary system of litigation by assuring an attorney that his private files shall, except in unusual circumstances, remain free from the encroachments of opposing counsel.

The work product protection is a limited immunity of comparatively recent origin. In *Hickman v. Taylor*, 329 U.S. 495 (1947), the Supreme Court carved out a limited exception to the broad scope of discovery under the Federal Rules:

> Here is simply an attempt, without purported necessity or justification, to secure written statements, private memoranda and personal recollections prepared or formed by an adverse party's counsel in the course of his legal duties. As such, it falls outside the arena of

discovery and contravenes the public policy underlying the orderly prosecution and defense of legal claims. Not even the most liberal of discovery theories can justify unwarranted inquiries into the files and the mental impressions of an attorney.

The doctrine has since been codified in Fed. R. Civ. P. 26(b)(3):

> Subject to the provisions of subdivision (b)(4) of this rule, a party may obtain discovery of documents and tangible things otherwise discoverable under subdivision (b)(1) of this rule and prepared in anticipation of litigation or for trial by or for another party or by or for that other party's representative ... only upon a showing that the party seeking discovery has substantial need of the materials in the preparation of his case and that he is unable without undue hardship to obtain the substantial equivalent of the materials by other means. In ordering discovery of such materials when the required showing has been made, the court shall protect against disclosure of the mental impressions, conclusions, opinions, or legal theories of an attorney or other representative of a party concerning the litigation.

In general, the doctrine protects memoranda, recorded mental impressions, synopses of witness statements, drafts of documents, etc., prepared by an attorney "with an eye to litigation", unless substantial good cause can be shown for its production.

The work product rule is the result of a balancing between the policy of full disclosure behind the federal discovery rules and "the desire to promote the effectiveness of the adversary system by safeguarding the vigorous representation of a client's cause from the possible debilitative effects of susceptibility to discovery." *Developments in the Law—Discovery, supra*, 74 Harv. L. Rev. at 1028. The policy behind the rule is not to protect all recorded opinions, observations and impressions of an attorney made in connection with any legal problem, but to protect the integrity of the adversary process.

> This work product immunity is the embodiment of a policy that a lawyer doing a lawyer's work in preparation of a case for trial should not be hampered by the knowledge that he might be called upon at any time to hand over the results of his work to an opponent.

Duplan Corp. v. Moulinage et Retorderie de Chavanoz, 487 F.2d 480 (4th Cir. 1973).

The rationale is restricted to "in anticipation of litigation" on the theory that an attorney who does not envision litigation (except as a remote contingency of any legal action) will not anticipate discovery requests, and therefore the fear of disclosure will not deter full and adequate consideration of the client's problem.

The fact that litigation may still be a contingency at the time the document is prepared has not been held to render the privilege inapplicable, if the prospect of litigation is identifiable because of specific claims that have already arisen. The test to be applied is whether, in light of the nature of the documents and the factual situation in this particular case, the document can fairly be said to have been prepared or obtained because of the prospect of litigation. Courts have held work product immunity applicable to preliminary drafts of legal documents, license agreements and/or assignments, opinion letters and background memoranda with respect to the scope and validity of patents and patent applications, attorney's analysis or assessments of a party's position with respect to other parties in an ongoing interference, and intra-office or file notes and memoranda containing summaries of conferences, legal research and comments on technical information, prepared by outside patent counsel or patent department attorneys in connection with an interference.

Nor is the immunity limited to proceedings in a court of record. The work product rule applies equally to documents prepared in anticipation of proceedings before the Board of Patent Interferences. Consequently, those documents in Category II which were prepared by attorney in anticipation of the *Adamek, et al. v. Tarney* Interference and which reflect the mental impressions, observations and/or opinions of the attorney are protected.

In this District, work product has been held applicable to documents generated in anticipation of *ex parte* proceedings in the Patent Office, as well as documents prepared in anticipation of interference proceedings. Judge Layton, in *In re Natta*, 48 F.R.D. 319, 321 (D. Del. 1969), interpreted the language of the Third Circuit in *In re Natta*, 410 F.2d 187 (3d Cir. 1969), as follows:

> But I am further convinced that the Third Circuit, in effect, went further and disapproved the distinction therein discussed between *ex parte* proceedings and interference proceedings and stated the law to be that documentary material relating both to ex parte applications for a patent, as well as patent interference proceedings, was subject to a claim of privilege.

The scope of that privilege is still limited, however, by the requirement that the document be prepared "with an eye toward litigation". The prosecution of an application before the Patent Office is not an adversary, but an *ex parte* proceeding. Although the process involves preparation and defense of legal claims in a quasi-adjudicatory forum, the give-and-take of an adversary proceeding is by and large absent. In addition, implicit in the applicant's duty of full disclosure to the Patent Office is the attorney's responsibility to make a complete investigation of the merits of the applicant's claim. A blanket rule permitting claims of work product as to any documents generated in anticipation of a patent prosecution is therefore unnecessary to provide additional incentive for the attorney to investigate and prepare the application fully.

On the other hand, a responsible patent attorney always anticipates the possibility of future litigation involving the patent. It is possible that, during the *ex parte* prosecution, certain memoranda or recordings, etc. prepared by the attorney may reflect concerns more relevant to future litigation than to the ongoing prosecution. If the primary concern of the attorney is with claims which would potentially arise in future litigation, the work product immunity applies; if the attorney's primary concern is claims which have arisen or will arise during the *ex parte* prosecution of the application, however, the work product rule does not apply.

Several of the documents which plaintiff claims are protected by work product were prepared in anticipation of litigation between plaintiff and a third party, Copolymer Rubber & Chemical Corporation. Although some courts have held that documents prepared for one case are freely discoverable in a different case, this Court accepts the "sounder view" that the documents prepared for one case have the same protection in a second case where the two cases are closely related in parties or subject matter. Plaintiff in the instant case was also plaintiff in the *Hercules v. Copolymer* litigation. The joint venture agreement which gave rise to the causes of action in *Hercules v. Copolymer* concerned joint production of EPT rubber under the Adamek patent. Consequently, many of the issues were related to the one involved here. Under those circumstances, the protection applicable in those proceedings extends to the instant proceeding. Defendant has not made any showing of substantial need or undue hardship in obtaining the substantial equivalent of the materials by other means. The Court recognizes the difficulty of making such a showing without having access to the documents themselves. However, the Court sees no reason why the defendant would not be able to obtain relevant information contained in those documents through other discovery means, such as depositions and interrogatories. Accordingly, production will be denied.

C. Fraud.

In opposition to plaintiff's claims, defendant relies primarily on a showing of alleged fraud to vitiate any privilege or immunity. Defendant avers that, during the prosecution of the Adamek patent, representatives of Hercules intentionally misrepresented or withheld facts relevant to the scope of prior art and concealed or only partially represented the results of relevant *ex parte* tests, and that accordingly protection should be denied as to all disputed documents.

Allegedly, these misrepresentations and failures to reveal were motivated by a desire to obtain "broadened" claims which would cover terpolymers made with a bridged-ring compound having an exocyclic double bond such as those then being manufactured by Exxon. In the original specification to the Adamek, et al. application, the examples use a bridged-ring compound with two double bonds inside the rings, such as DCP. In November, 1964, attorneys for Adamek filed amended claims which specified that the bridged-ring hydrocarbon contain at least two double bonds. That amendment was rejected as overly broad and failing to point out and distinctly claim the invention on the ground, *inter alia*, that the claims read on compounds wherein the double bonds may be either in the ring or in a straight-chain, side substituent (*i.e.*, containing an exocyclic double bond), or both. The Examiner remarked that the claims could be placed in allowable condition by limiting the bridged-ring compounds to those containing only two double bonds, which double bonds are both inside the rings. Plaintiff maintained, at the time and in argument on the present motions, that the invention is broad enough to cover both types of compounds—those with both bonds inside the rings and those with one double bond inside the ring and one on an exocyclic side chain. In support of its position before the Patent Office, plaintiff presented to the Examiner a number of affidavits and arguments with respect to the operability and usefulness of compounds with an exocyclic double bond. Defendant urges that in those affidavits and arguments, plaintiff made certain fraudulent misrepresentations and omissions which were material to the Examiner's decision to grant the Adamek patent.

Specifically, defendant contends that plaintiff fraudulently misrepresented the state of prior art, in that plaintiff failed to inform the Patent Office of three relevant prior art patents: (1) U.S. Patent No. 2,933,480 to Gresham, which disclosed an EPT rubber using a straight-chain diene as the third monomer; (2) Belgian Patent No. 546,150, assigned to Montecatini, which disclosed the use of cyclopentadiene as a termonomer for alpha-olefins; and (3) Belgian Patent No. 543,292, assigned to Goodrich–Gulf, which discloses the use of cyclic dienes as termonomers for alpha-olefins. Plaintiff admits that during prosecution of the Adamek patent, it had knowledge of the Gresham and Goodrich–Gulf Belgian patents, but points out that none of the patents in question disclosed the use of bridged-ring hydrocarbons as the third monomer. According to plaintiff, the Gresham and Goodrich–Gulf references were felt to be irrelevant to the Adamek prosecution, since the novelty of the Adamek invention lay in the use of the bridged-ring compounds, which were allegedly significantly different from the cyclic or straight-chain compounds used by others.

Defendant further alleges that an affidavit of Dr. Woodhams, one of the inventors of the patent in suit, which was presented to the Patent Office in connection with the November, 1964 amendments, is misleading and incomplete. The Woodhams' affidavit was apparently prepared in response to the Examiner's expressed concern that the use of a bridged-ring compound with an exocyclic double bond might produce an inoperative copolymer. Keim and Christman repeated one of the examples of the Adamek application, using such a bridged-ring compound, 5–vinyl–2–norbornene, and sent the resulting product to Woodhams for testing. Woodhams reported that the product was operative, that is, that it did vulcanize with sulfur. Defendant alleges that those tests and subsequent tests which were not reported to the Patent Office, showed "poor" or "indifferent" results, but that later plaintiff made representations to the Patent Office on the basis of those results to the effect that a commercially attractive terpolymer could be produced from 5–vinyl–2–norbornene in accordance with Adamek, et al. In response, plaintiff contends that defendant has illegitimately juxtaposed representations made in several different affidavits presented to the Patent Office. According to plaintiff, the Woodhams' affidavit correctly reported the test results, and those results were intended only to determine whether or not vinyl norbornene terpolymers could be sulfur-cured, not whether the product had optimal physical properties. Later representations as to the usefulness and commercial attractiveness of such terpolymers were made by Dr. Spurlin, Technical Assistant in the Hercules Research Center, allegedly on the basis of later, more extensive work by Hoechst, a German company affiliated with Hercules, and others.

Communications between attorney and client, otherwise protected, which are made in furtherance of a crime or fraud are not protected by attorney-client privilege or work product immunity. On a discovery motion, the moving party bears the burden of showing, first, a *prima facie* case of fraud:

> We begin with the observation that while a *prima facie* showing need not be such as to actually prove the disputed fact, it must be such as to subject the opposing party to the risk of non-persuasion if the evidence as to the disputed fact is left unrebutted. (footnotes and citations omitted).

Duplan Corp. v. Deering Milliken, Inc., 540 F.2d 1215 (4th Cir. 1976). Second, defendant must show that the communications were made in furtherance of the fraud. Communications made before the fact of or during the commission of a fraud are not protected, since to allow protection to attach to such communications would permit an attorney to be a principal or accessory to a fraud without fear of discovery and would permit the client to commit fraud with the aid of legal advice beforehand. Communications after the fact are still protected, however, since one of the primary purposes of the attorney-client privilege is to allow consultation in the interest of establishing a legal defense. In *W. R. Grace & Co. v. P. Ballantine & Sons, Inc., supra,* for instance, the court held that any documents dated later than the date of the issuance of the patent in suit would not lose protection on the grounds of fraud, since the documents were not prepared until after completion of the alleged fraud.

At this point, the Court does not find it necessary to decide whether a *prima facie* case of fraud has been made out by defendant. Even assuming *arguendo* that defendant had shown a *prima facie* case of fraud, none of the protected documents could be said to have been prepared in furtherance of that fraud.[17] Many of the documents are dated later than October 12, 1965, the date of issuance of the Adamek patent. Defendant urges that nevertheless some of those documents may contain information relevant to the fraud, and therefore should be discoverable.

---

17. Since counsel for defendant has not had an opportunity to see any of the disputed documents, it is obviously difficult for counsel to demonstrate that particular documents were generated in furtherance of fraud. Presumably, if the documents had been made available, counsel would have argued strenuously in favor of the discoverability of certain of those documents. In the absence of such an opportunity, the Court has examined with particular care all the documents which would otherwise be protected by attorney-client privilege or work product immunity for subject matter and content, in light of the documentary evidence presented by defendant.

The fraud exception is a narrow one. If the documents were prepared subsequent to completion of the alleged fraud, they could not be "in furtherance" of the fraud. In any event, none of the documents, including those prepared subsequent to the issuance of the patent, relate to the alleged instances of fraud or reflect information, opinion or advice relevant to the issues of scienter or intent. The bulk of the documents were prepared in connection with proceedings other than the *ex parte* prosecution of the patent, and reflect rather the immediate concerns of the attorney and client with respect to distinct and separate issues. Those documents which deal directly with the *ex parte* prosecution do not contain information or advice which could be construed as "furthering" the alleged fraud. Accordingly, none of the protected documents are discoverable on the grounds of fraud. The Court does not reach, however, the merits of defendant's showing.

D. Waiver.

Finally, defendant contends that plaintiff has waived any privilege or immunity it might otherwise assert. Plaintiff has produced 31 documents, previously identified as privileged, without reservation as to waiver of privilege. Eighteen of those documents were apparently produced "inadvertently." In general, the voluntary waiver by a client, without limitation, of one or more privileged documents passing between a certain attorney and the client discussing a certain subject waives the privilege as to all communications between the same attorney and the same client on the same subject. Similarly, an attorney may be held to have waived work product immunity by voluntarily producing certain documents which otherwise would be protected under the work product doctrine. Since the attorney-client privilege is a client's privilege, while work product immunity may be invoked only by an attorney, waiver of attorney-client privilege does not necessarily also waive work product immunity, as to an attorney's memoranda on the same subject.

This qualification to the rule of attorney-client or work product protection can only be applied with reference both to the objectives of the protection and of the qualification. The underlying rationale is one of fairness. A party cannot disclose only those facts beneficial to its case and refuse to disclose, on the grounds of privilege, related facts adverse to its position:

> When a client voluntarily waives the privilege as to some documents that the client considers not damaging and asserts the privilege as to other documents that the client considers damaging, the rule compelling production of all documents becomes applicable. The reason behind the rule is one of basic fairness.

Duplan Corp. v. Deering Milliken, Inc., 397 F. Supp. at 1161–2. Even if certain facts or documents were disclosed inadvertently, the protection may be waived.

Defendant's argument with respect to the expansiveness of the waiver exception is unfounded in the law. The waiver exception has been narrowly construed. The privilege or immunity has been found to be waived only if facts relevant to a particular, narrow subject matter have been disclosed in circumstances in which it would be unfair to deny the other party an opportunity to discover other relevant facts with respect to that subject matter. In *International Business Machines v. Sperry Rand Corp., supra,* the Court held the privilege waived only "to the limited extent that it dealt with the defects in the BINAC which Sperry believed Northrop had excused." In *International Paper Co. v. Fibreboard Corp.,* 63 F.R.D. 88 (D. Del. 1974), defendant made certain factual assertions in an affidavit with respect to a specific meeting between the Patent Examiner and defendant's counsel. The Court then permitted plaintiff the opportunity to discover other relevant factual details leading up to and including that meeting that were not mentioned in the affidavit. Judge Latchum, in *Lee National Corp. v. Deramus,* 313 F. Supp. 224 (D. Del. 1970), required the defendant to identify certain occasions on which particular subjects relating to by-law and charter amendments were discussed with counsel. In that case, the defendant had freely and voluntarily revealed that the particular subject matter had been discussed on several other specific occasions. Significantly, the Court refused to extend the privilege beyond that limited waiver.

After a careful comparison of the disputed documents with those which have been produced by plaintiff, the Court finds that there has been no waiver either of the attorney-client privilege or of work product immunity with respect to any of the documents. For the most part, the subject matter of the produced documents does not overlap with that of the protected documents. A few documents do overlap to some extent, but only very generally, as being broadly concerned with the progress of the application, licensing policy, etc. The Court found no document which would unfairly deprive defendant of access to facts relevant to particular subject matter disclosed in already produced documents.

Notes

1. The *Hercules* court was presented with a Motion to Compel the Production of Documents where the plaintiff claimed the documents were protected by both attorney-client privilege and work product immunity. The court explained that where the communication is primarily concerned with technical information, and the attorney is merely acting as a conduit for technical information to the Patent Office, there is no privilege. This result centers on the public interest in making sure that an applicant cannot circumvent the duty of full disclosure simply by channeling information through the attorney and labeling it protectable under an assertion of privilege. What happens where the technical information is intertwined with legal advice? Should there be a recommended format for communications between attorney and client where the technical facts are always separated from the advice? Is this practical?

2. To be protectable, it is essential that the communication involve some legal assistance, advice or legal interpretation. Standard transmittal letters kept in the routine course of business, are not covered by the attorney/client privilege or work product doctrine.

3. Work product immunity is an independent concept from the attorney-client privilege. The attorney client privilege doctrine is designed to encourage honest and complete communications between the attorney and client. The work product immunity doctrine offers protection of the adversarial system by assuring that an attorney's private files shall generally remain private. Should the work product doctrine apply to proceedings before the Board of Patent Appeals and Interferences? Does it make a difference that the adversarial proceeding is before an administrative agency rather than a court?

4. An exception to the attorney/client privilege and work product immunity doctrine occurs where the communication is made in furtherance of a crime or fraud. In the case of assertion of fraud, the moving party bears the burden of establishing a *prima facie* case. Once a *prima facie* case of fraud has been made out, the privilege will be pierced and the withheld documents will be produced.

5. A voluntary waiver by a client of the attorney client privilege, without limitation as to a particular subject area, waives the privilege as to all documents regarding that subject. Because of the prejudicial impact such a waiver may have, courts tend to narrowly construe such a waiver.

6. With respect to patent prosecution, the *Hercules* court listed the following items as protectable under the work product immunity doctrine: preliminary drafts of legal documents; license agreements; assignments; opinion letters and background memoranda; analysis in respect of a position in an ongoing interference; intra office memos on legal research; comments on technical information; and documents prepared in anticipation of proceedings before the Board of Patent Appeals and Interferences. If a prior art study identifies references, they should be disclosed, but the study itself could be privileged. Patentability and infringement opinions are privileged.

D. THE USE OF PROTECTIVE ORDERS IN PATENT LITIGATION

A protective order is an effective judicial tool most often used for ensuring efficiency and fairness in the discovery process. Issuance of a protective order during discovery can promote orderly compliance with discovery requests and minimize or eliminate procedural maneuvering. Protective orders are provided for under Rule 26(c) of the Federal Rules of Civil Procedure, which specifies eight applicable categories:

FEDERAL RULES OF CIVIL PROCEDURE—RULE 26(c):

General Provisions Governing Discovery; Duty of Disclosure

(c) Protective Orders. Upon motion by a party or by the person from whom discovery is sought, accompanied by a certification that the movant has in good faith conferred or attempted to confer with other affected parties in an effort to resolve the dispute without court action, and for good cause shown, the court in which the action is pending or alternatively, on matters relating to a deposition, the court in the district where the deposition is to be taken may make any order which justice requires to protect a party or person from annoyance, embarrassment, oppression, or undue burden or expense, including one or more of the following:

(1) that the disclosure or discovery not be had;

(2) that the disclosure or discovery may be had only on specified terms and conditions, including a designation of the time or place;

(3) that the discovery may be had only by a method of discovery other than that selected by the party seeking discovery;

(4) that certain matters not be inquired into, or that the scope of the disclosure or discovery be limited to certain matters;

(5) that discovery be conducted with no one present except persons designated by the court;

(6) that a deposition, after being sealed, be opened only by order of the court;

(7) that a trade secret or other confidential research, development, or commercial information not be revealed or be revealed only in a designated way; and

(8) that the parties simultaneously file specified documents or information enclosed in sealed envelopes to be opened as directed by the court.

If the motion for a protective order is denied in whole or in part, the court may, on such terms and conditions as are just, order that any party or other person provide or permit discovery. The provisions of Rule 37(a)(4) apply to the award of expenses incurred in relation to the motion.

As is obvious from a reading of the rule, its scope and breadth give the court wide discretion including granting relief different from that requested by the parties.

Any number of situations in a patent litigation can cause the filing of a motion for a protective order under this rule. For example, a motion may be filed to limit the number of discovery requests or interrogatories that need to be responded to; to prevent disclosure of business proprietary information such as design documents or financial information; to limit the time and place for a deposition; or to prevent the disclosure of attorney-client communications. These situations can occur where the parties are unable to resolve the specific dispute.

There are situations where the parties may readily agree to abide by a protective order. In such instances, the parties may join in the filing of a motion for protective order asking the court to grant a stipulated protective order. For example, stipulated confidentiality orders are commonly used to protect against dissemination of trade secrets and proprietary information of both parties.

As the rule itself indicates, there are a few preliminary and important steps to take before filing a motion for a protective order. The first is to make sure your client's position is sound. This is embodied in the "good cause" requirement of the rule. A motion should never appear to be purely tactical. Thus, the attorney must fairly assess whether or not the opponent's discovery request is improper as a predicate to any decision to pursue relief with the court. In so doing, an attorney should go beyond the question of whether the request itself is improper, but also assess what would be the proper scope for the request if it were worded correctly. Perhaps there is a compromise position that can be reached if the attorney offers to answer the request if so amended.

Second, Rule 26(c) requires a good faith attempt to resolve the dispute before filing a motion. Of course, it is always a matter of effective advocacy to approach one's opponent before filing any motion to ascertain whether the matter can be resolved amicably. Many local court rules of the U.S. federal district courts also require that the parties "meet and confer" prior to filing any discovery motion. Thus, if counsel has a problem with an opponent's discovery requests, there should be an attempt to resolve the issue with the opponent prior to filing any motion. For example, if a document request is regarded as burdensome or ambiguous since it calls for "all documents related to" a particular subject, with no limitation as to time, an attempt must be made to resolve the matter prior to filing a motion for a protective order. In this instance, the answering attorney could offer to satisfy the opponent's request by supplying representative documents from a more specific area for a given period of time. The opponent might accept such a proposal and obviate the need for a motion battle. Similarly, suggestions on how to re-word pending interrogatories to obviate their perceived improper breadth may also prove fruitful. Indeed, each of the eight categories is subject to possible compromises between opponents acting in good faith.

Another pre-filing consideration is the timing of filing the motion. Last minute filing is dangerous especially if it is perceived as purely tactical, where the court may deny the motion as not showing good cause. *See Nestle Foods Corp. v. Aetna Casualty & Surety Co.*, 129 F.R.D. 483, 486 (D.N.J. 1990) (motion for a protective order should be denied because the defendants failed to avail themselves of the opportunity to negotiate or move for a protective order in a timely manner). This is particularly true if the attempt to meet and confer is just as tardy. True attempts to amicably resolve conflicts require leaving adequate time to consider proposals and counter-proposals, and to effectuate the compromise reached.

There is also the question as to whether the filing of the motion is premature in the absence of a motion to compel. Should the motion be filed on its own, or in response to a motion to compel answered by a cross motion for a protective order? For example, when the scope of permissible inquiry at a deposition is at the center of a discovery dispute, counsel might want to consider whether it is best to file prior to the deposition or after it to see if protection is actually necessary. Many times, the feared improper questioning does not occur. And when it does, the potential conflict is often resolved during the deposition. On the other hand, in situations where problems are inevitable, all parties are put on notice as to the disputed boundaries before the deposition begins by filing a motion for protective order prior to the deposition. The court's resolution prior to the deposition will certainly make the deposition run more smoothly.

Often, the disputed scope occurs during the deposition and cannot be foreseen. An example is an inadvertent statement by the witness that crosses into the area of attorney-client privilege. The questioner declares that a waiver has occurred and wants to further explore the topic. The defending attorney instructs the witness not to answer the question. The matter is left for later briefing and resolution by the court. Following the deposition, the defending counsel may need to resort to the filing of a motion for a protective order. On the other hand, the attorney taking the deposition may file a motion to compel testimony, to which the defending attorney will oppose and may cross-move for a protective order.

1. PROTECTING PRIVILEGE AND WORK PRODUCT

As noted in the *Hercules* case, attorney-client privileged and attorney work product information is protectable. Nevertheless, scope of protection issues are ones that always maximize the litigator's stress level. The dispute often arises in patent cases in the context of reliance on advice of counsel to defend against an allegation of willful infringement. In these situations, the defendant has indicated that it relies on pre-suit opinions of counsel relating to non-infringement and/or invalidity to show its state of mind as a defense against an allegation of willful infringement. Under such circumstances, the defendant must produce all opinions of counsel. Often however, the lines are blurred as to what is properly required for production and what lies outside the scope of the waiver. For example, pre-suit memoranda are often attorney work product in contemplation of litigation. Yet, that very same material may arguably contain opinions of counsel regarding the infringement and validity issues. Similarly, post-filing memoranda, written during the litigation called attorney work product, may arguably reflect opinion of counsel. In such instances, the defendant may respond to a motion to compel production of the documents by opposing the motion and filing a cross motion for a protective order.

2. BUSINESS CONFIDENTIAL INFORMATION AND TRADE SECRETS

A common area for a protective order concerns business proprietary information. The drafters of the Federal Rules and the courts were aware of the need to protect business confidential and trade secret information. Rule 26(c)(7) specifically provides for its protection. A party may choose to continue the discovery process and concurrently request a protective order to shield business confidential and trade secret material.

In considering whether to grant or deny a motion for a protective order regarding this type of information, a three step analysis is applied. The court first asks whether the subject matter at issue is a trade secret or other confidential research, development, or commercial information. A trade secret is traditionally defined by state law. However, many states have adopted the Restatement of Torts § 757 which provides that the following factors should be examined to determine if the information is a trade secret: (1) the extent to which the information is known outside of the business; (2) the extent to which the information is known to those involved in the business; (3) the extent of measures taken to guard the secrecy of the information; (4) the value of the information to the business and its competitors; (5) the amount of effort or money expended by the owner developing the information; and (6) the ease or difficulty with which the information could be properly acquired or duplicated by others. *See* RESTATEMENT OF TORTS § 757 cmt. b (1939). In assessing whether any subject matter is a trade secret or other confidential business information, courts have concluded that a wide variety of business information falls under this umbrella including design information, drawings, blueprints, and other proprietary documentation illustrating design and material changes. Second, the court inquires into whether disclosure of the information would result in "cognizable harm." *See Zenith Radio Corp. v. Matsushita Elec. Indus. Co.,* 529 F. Supp. 866, 889–90 (E.D. Pa. 1981) ("Cognizable harm" includes annoyance, oppression, embarrassment, and competitive disadvantage.). Finally, the court analyzes whether the movant has demonstrated "good cause" by demonstrating "clearly defined and serious injury." Where a party requests that discovery be eliminated rather than just limited, the courts apply the first two steps, and if both are properly demonstrated, the burden shifts to the party seeking discovery to demonstrate that the discovery is "necessary and relevant."

Generally, "there is no absolute privilege for trade secrets and similar confidential information." *Heat & Control, Inc. v. Hester Indus., Inc.,* 785 F.2d 1017, 1025, 228 USPQ 926, 932 (Fed. Cir. 1986) (quoting *Centurion Indus., Inc. v. Warren Steurer & Associates,* 665 F.2d 323, 325–26, 213 USPQ 36 (10th Cir. 1981)). Alleging competitive harm, therefore, is not a guarantee of issuance of a protective order, even when the movant can illustrate specific examples of harmful documents. The movant must demonstrate clear injury to its business. Corporate competitors have a greater chance at clearly defining serious injury to their business than non-competitors because disclosure of trade secrets and other confidential material can have a direct impact on the "well-being of the business". Courts typically recognize that a protective order can be an effective tool for minimizing the risk of harm that a competitor will acquire Rule 26(c)(7) information and use it for its own purposes. *See American Standard Inc. v. Pfizer.,* 828 F.2d 734, 740–41, 3 USPQ2d 1817, 1821 (Fed. Cir. 1987) (disclosure by one party of their research and development materials would place the giving party at a competitive disadvantage.); *see also Duracell Inc. v. SW Consultants, Inc.,* 126 F.R.D. 576, 578–80 (N.D. Ga. 1989) ("[d]isclosure of . . . marketing information to a large competitor could put Power Plus at a serious competitive disadvantage"). Because courts comprehend the potential risks that are involved when confidential information or trade secrets are revealed to a competitor, a movant who can demonstrate that information sought will be revealed to a competitor stands a good chance of prevailing on a motion for a protective order. Courts will engage in a balancing test, weighing the potential competitive harm against the need for disclosure. *See American Standard*, 828 F.2d at 738, 3 USPQ2d at 1819 (granting the movant protective order because disclosure of the information to a competitor would cause irreparable harm); *Coca-Cola Bottling Co. v. Coca–Cola Co.*, 107 F.R.D. 288, 292, 227 USPQ 18, 21 (D. Del. 1985) (denying a protective order to the movant because the adversary was not a competitor). Where the harm outweighs the need, the movant will prevail.

As for burdensome and oppressive discovery, the plaintiff may file a motion to compel, and the defendant may oppose and cross move for a protective order. The basis for the cross motion will also be Federal Rule 26(c). Here again, the underlying facts must clearly demonstrate the burdensome or oppressive nature of the requested discovery. Certainly, document requests that are not limited to either the issues of the litigation or to the time period relevant to the will usually support a motion for a protective order.

E.   SAMPLE DOCUMENT REQUEST

IN THE UNITED STATES DISTRICT COURT
FOR THE NORTHERN DISTRICT OF CALIFORNIA

MIKE'S FISHING, INC.	)	
	)	
Plaintiff,	)	Civil Action No. 99
	)	
v.	)	
	)	
MARK'S BOATS, INC.	)	
	)	
Defendant.	)	

MARK'S BOATS, INC.'S FIRST SET OF REQUESTS FOR PRODUCTION OF DOCUMENTS TO MIKE'S FISHING, INC.

Pursuant to Rule 34 of the Federal Rules of Civil Procedure, defendant Mark's Boats, Inc. ("Mark's Boats") requests that plaintiff, Mike's Fishing, Inc., ("Mike's Fishing"), produce and make available the following documents and things for inspection and copying at the offices of Moore Michel & Lupo, within thirty (30) days after service hereof.

I.   DEFINITIONS

Unless the context indicates otherwise, the following words and phrases are defined and used herein as follows:

1.　The term "document" means all written or graphic matter, however produced or reproduced, in your actual or constructive possession, custody, care or control, including, but not limited to, originals (or copies where originals are unavailable) of correspondence, E-mail, computer storage media, computer software needed to produce in human-readable form data from said computer storage media, instructions for using said computer software, telegrams, notes or sound recordings of any type of personal or telephone conversations, or of meetings or conferences, minutes of directors or committee meetings, memoranda, inter-office communications, studies, analysis, reports, engineering drawings, results of investigations, catalogs, contracts, licenses, agreements, working papers, statistical records, ledgers, books of account, vouchers, invoices, charge slips, freight bills, time sheets or logs, stenographers' notebooks, diaries, or papers similar to any of the foregoing, however, denominated. "Document" shall also mean (1) any copy which is not identical to the original or to any other copy, and (2) any tangible things that is called for by or identified in response to an interrogatory.

2.　The term "you" or "your" means plaintiff, Mike's Fishing, Inc. and each of its subsidiaries, parents, subsidiaries of subsidiaries, divisions, affiliates in which it owns a majority or a controlling interest, and other organizational or operating units, each of their respective predecessors and successors, and each of their respective employees, officers, directors, attorneys, agents, representatives, and all persons acting or purporting to act on their behalf.

3.　The term "Mark's Boats" means defendant Mark's Boat's, Inc., and its employees, officers, attorneys, agents or representatives, and all persons acting or purporting to act on its behalf.

4.　The term "person" means any individual, individuals, business entity, or entities, including, but not limited to, corporations, partnerships, associations, or business trusts, any federal, state, or local government or governmental agency, and any foreign government or foreign government agency.

5.　The term "respecting" means comprising, constituting, reflecting, relating to, concerning, referring to, stating, describing, recording, noting, embodying, containing, mentioning, studying, analyzing, discussing or evaluating.

6.　The terms " '835 Patent" or the "Patent-In-Suit" mean U.S. Patent No. 5,551,835, entitled "Trolling Motor," including any continuations, continuation-in-part, reissues, or reexaminations of the '835 Patent, and any applications which led to the issuance of the '835 Patent.

7.　The term "Foreign Equivalent Patent" means any patent application filed in, or any patent issued by, any country other than the United States that is based in whole or in part upon the invention claimed in the '835 Patent or any application thereto (including any continuations, continuations-in-part, reissues, or reexaminations thereof).

8. The term "date" means the exact day, month, and year, if ascertainable, or if not, the best approximation thereof.

9. The term "Complaint" means the complaint filed by Mike's Fishing, Inc. against Mark's Boat's Inc. in this case.

II. GENERAL INSTRUCTIONS

1. Unless otherwise stated herein, the time period covered by these document requests is January 1, 1990 to the date of production of documents in response thereto. Documents originating before the specified time period but relating to or referring thereto should be included in such production. Documents respecting conception, reduction to practice, prior art, prior public use, prior invention, and any other documents relating to the validity or enforceability of the '835 Patent are unrestricted as to date.

2. There shall be a continuing duty on you to furnish additional documents in response to this document request in accordance with Rule 26(e) of the Federal Rules of Civil Procedure.

3. As used herein, the singular form of a noun or pronoun shall be considered to include within its meaning the plural form of a noun or pronoun so used, and vice versa; the use of the masculine form of a pronoun shall be considered to include also within its meaning the feminine form of the pronoun so used, and vice versa; the use of any tense of any verb shall be considered to include within its meaning all other tenses of the verb so used; and the use of the word "and" shall also include within its meaning the word "or," and vice versa.

4. All documents must be produced in a form that renders them susceptible to copying. Each document should be segregated and identified by the request to which it is primarily responsive.

5. If you are unable to comply fully with any request herein, comply to the extent possible and provide a detailed explanation as to why full compliance is not possible.

6. All requests herein are directed to those documents within your possession, custody, or control, or within the possession, custody or control of your agents, servants and employees, and your attorneys. They also are directed to those firms, corporations, partnerships, or trusts that you control, and to documents in the possession, custody, or control of employees, agents and representatives of such entities.

7. If any document called for is not available or accessible, is no longer in existence, or is withheld under a claim, privilege, or protection against discovery, give the following information for that document:

a. the name and title of the authors(s);

b. the name and title of each person to whom the document was addressed;

c. the name and title of each person to whom a copy of the document was sent, directed, circulated or distributed;

d.   the date of the document;

e.   the number of pages;

f.   a brief description of the nature and subject matter of the document;

g.   the paragraph(s) of the request to which the document is responsive;

h.   the name of each person now in possession of the document or any identical or non-identical copy;

i.   the basis of the claim, privilege or protection against discovery (if applicable);

j.   the reasons why the document is not available or accessible (if applicable); and

k.   the reasons why the document is no longer in existence (if applicable).

III.   DOCUMENT REQUESTS

REQUEST NO. 1

All documents respecting the Easy Troller sent to, received from, or that refer or relate to, Mark's Boats, or any other person.

REQUEST NO. 2

All documents respecting the earliest date on which you first notified Mark's Boats of your rights in the alleged invention claimed in the '835 Patent (including any notification to Mark's Boats of your efforts to obtain patent protection on any alleged invention claimed in the '835 Patent prior to the date on which that patent was issued).

REQUEST NO. 3

All documents respecting any ownership, title, license, assignment, or transfer of the '835 Patent or the alleged invention claimed therein.

REQUEST NO. 4

Mike's Fishings' financial statements from April 1, 1995 to the present date, including all monthly financial statements, balance sheets, cash flow statements and accounting notes, whether audited or unaudited, and all supporting schedules thereto.

REQUEST NO. 5

All reports respecting summaries of your sales of any products which you believe or contend are covered by any of the claims of the '835 Patent, including all monthly, quarterly, and yearly sales summaries of such products, and any documents analyzing such sales.

REQUEST NO. 6

All documents respecting royalty rates and royalty bases which you contend should apply to any sales of products found to infringe the '835 Patent, including any license agreements, royalty reports, negotiations, offers or proposals of licenses, licensing policies, agreements, or settlements respecting trolling motor devices.

REQUEST NO. 7

All documents respecting any lost profits or lost sales that you contend have resulted, or which you believe will result, from Mark's Boats's alleged infringement of the '835 Patent.

REQUEST NO. 8

All documents respecting the identity of customers of any device that uses, embodies, or incorporates the alleged invention claimed in the '835 Patent, and all documents respecting amounts those respective customers have spent in purchasing products covered by the '835 Patent.

REQUEST NO. 9

All documents respecting advertising, promotional literature, or any other efforts by you to promote the use or sales of any product that uses, embodies, or incorporates the alleged invention claimed in the '835 Patent.

REQUEST NO. 10

All documents respecting the design of any product that you believe or contend infringes any claim of the '835 Patent (including Mark's Boats's products, as well as any products made, used, or sold by any third party).

REQUEST NO. 11

All documents respecting the validity or infringement of the '835 Patent, including but not limited to, all prior art, prior art searches, search results, official actions, opinion, patents, publications, public uses, sales or offers for sale, and any other matter that constitutes "prior art" to the alleged invention claimed in the '835 Patent.

REQUEST NO. 12

All documents provided to or received from any expert witness respecting any of your claims or contentions alleged in this lawsuit.

REQUEST NO. 13

All documents respecting your first knowledge or belief that Mark's Boats committed each of the respective acts of infringement, induced infringement, and contributory infringement of the '835 Patent.

REQUEST NO. 14

All documents respecting communications or correspondence between you and other person or entity (including, but not limited to, customers, prospective customers, and government agencies) relating to the '835 Patent, Mark's Boats, the accused infringing product, or your belief that Mark's Boats has infringed, contributorily infringed, or induced infringement of the '835 Patent.

REQUEST NO. 15

All documents respecting the conception and reduction to practice of the invention claimed in the '835 Patent.

REQUEST NO. 16

All documents respecting each of the following: the first sale, first offer for sale, first public use, and first manufacture of any device or apparatus that embodies, incorporates, or practices the invention claimed in the '835 Patent.

REQUEST NO. 17

All documents respecting the first description in a printed publication of the invention claimed in the '835 Patent.

REQUEST NO. 18

All documents respecting any description of the invention claimed in the '835 Patent, including, but not limited to, all invention disclosures, invention records, inventors' notebooks, and specifications.

REQUEST NO. 19

All documents respecting the design, development, manufacture, and production of any product that you believe, allege, or contend embodies or incorporates the invention claimed in the '835 Patent.

REQUEST NO. 20

All documents respecting your allegations in paragraphs 12–14 of the Complaint that Mark's Boats has infringed, willfully infringed, induced others to infringe, and contributed to the infringement of, the '835 Patent.

REQUEST NO. 21

All documents respecting your allegation that Mike's Fishing has been harmed by any action of Mark's Boats, as alleged in paragraph 9 of the Complaint.

REQUEST NO. 22

All documents respecting any of the secondary considerations of nonobviousness of the '835 Patent, including, but not limited to, all documents (if any) respecting commercial success, long felt need, attempts by others, failures by others, commercial acquiescence, licensing, professional approval, copying, or laudatory statements by others regarding the invention claimed in the '835 Patent.

REQUEST NO. 23

All documents respecting the scope and content of the prior art to the '835 Patent, the level of ordinary skill in the art, and any differences between the prior art and the invention claimed in the '835 Patent.

REQUEST NO. 24

All documents sufficient to identify your officers, directors, managers, and any employees with personal knowledge of the design, manufacture, marketing and/or sales of trolling motor devices.

REQUEST NO. 25

All documents respecting efforts to obtain patent protection on the invention claimed in the '835 Patent in the United States and anywhere else in the world, including patent applications, draft patent applications, amendments, remarks, claims, correspondence, and complete copies of all U.S. and foreign file histories.

REQUEST NO. 26

All documents identified in your responses to Mark's Boats's First Set of Interrogatories to Mike's Fishing, served concurrently herewith.
DATE

SAMPLE INTERROGATORIES

IN THE UNITED STATES DISTRICT COURT
FOR THE NORTHERN DISTRICT OF CALIFORNIA

MIKE'S FISHING, INC.	)	
	)	
	)	
Plaintiff,	)	Civil Action No. 99
	)	
v.	)	
	)	
MARK'S BOATS, INC.	)	
	)	
Defendant.	)	
	)	

MARK'S BOATS, INC.'S FIRST SET OF
INTERROGATORIES TO MIKE'S FISHING, INC.

Defendant, Mark's Boats, Inc., ("Mark's Boats"), by its undersigned attorneys, pursuant to Rule 33 of the Federal Rules of Civil Procedure, requests that plaintiff Mike's Fishing, Inc. ("Mike's Fishing") answer the following interrogatories under oath and in writing within 30 days of service hereof.

DEFINITIONS

Unless the context indicates otherwise, the following words and phrases are defined and used herein as follows:

1. The term "document" means all written or graphic matter, however produced or reproduced, in your actual or constructive possession, custody, care or control, including, but not limited to, originals (or copies where originals are unavailable) of correspondence, E-mail, computer storage media, computer software needed to produce in human-readable form data from said computer storage media, instructions for using said computer software, telegrams, notes or sound recordings of any type of personal or telephone conversations, or of meetings or conferences, minutes of directors or committee meetings, memoranda, inter-office communications, studies analyses, reports, engineering drawings, results of investigations, catalogs, contracts, licenses, agreements, working papers, statistical records, ledgers, books of account, vouchers, invoices, charge slips, freight bills, time sheets or logs, stenographers' notebooks, diaries, or papers similar to any of the foregoing, however, denominated. "Document" shall also mean (1) any copy which is not identical to the original or to any other copy, and (2) any tangible thing that is called for by or identified in response to an interrogatory.

2. The term "you" or "your" means plaintiff Mike's Fishing, Inc. and each of its subsidiaries, parents, subsidiaries of subsidiaries, divisions, affiliates in which it owns a majority or a controlling interest, and other organizational or operating units, each of their respective predecessors and successors, and each of their respective employees, officers, directors, attorneys, agents, representatives, and all persons acting or purporting to act on their behalf.

3. The term "Mark's Boats" means defendant Mark's Boats, Inc., and its employees, officers, attorneys, agents or representatives, and all persons acting or purporting to act on its behalf for any purpose whatsoever.

4. The term "person" means any individual, individuals, business entity, or entities, including, but not limited to, corporations, partnerships, associations, or business trusts.

5. The term "respecting" means comprising, constituting, reflecting, relating to, concerning, referring to, stating, describing, recording, noting, embodying, containing, mentioning, studying, analyzing, discussing or evaluating.

6. The terms " '835 Patent" or the "Patent–In–Suit" means U.S. Patent No. 5,551,835, entitled "Trolling Motor," including any continuations, continuation-in-part, reissues, or reexaminations.

7. The term "Foreign Equivalent Patent" means any patent application filed in, or any patent issued by, any country other than the United States that is based in whole or in part upon the invention claimed in the '835 Patent (including any continuations, continuations-in-part, reissues, or reexaminations thereof).

8. The term "date" means the exact day, month, and year, if ascertainable, or if not, the best approximation thereof.

9. The term "Complaint" means the complaint filed by Mike's Fishing, Inc. against Mark's Boats, Inc. in this case.

II. GENERAL INSTRUCTIONS

1. There shall be a continuing duty on you to furnish supplemental responses to these interrogatories in accordance with Rule 26(e) of the Federal Rules of Civil Procedure.

2. As used herein, the singular form of a noun or pronoun shall be considered to include within its meaning the plural form of a noun or pronoun so used, and vice versa; the use of the masculine form of a pronoun shall be considered to include also within its meaning the feminine form of the pronoun so used, and vice versa; the use of any tense of any verb shall be considered to include within its meaning all other tenses of the verb so used; and the use of the word "and" shall also include within its meaning the word "or," and vice versa.

3. Whenever there is a request in these interrogatories to identify a document, please state as to each such document the following information:

   a. the date;

   b. its title and/or all identifying numbers or other identifying categorizing designations and/or a brief description thereof (such as letter, memorandum, manuscript notes, etc.);

   c. the name, title and address of each author, signatory or person preparing the document;

   d. the name, titles and address of addressee and of each other person receiving a copy thereof;

   e. its present location and the name and address of its present custodian;

   f. if the document is not an original, the name and address of the original custodian; and

   g. any other designation necessary to sufficiently identify the document so that a copy thereof may be ordered or obtained from the custodian thereof.

4. Whenever there is a request in these interrogatories to identify a person or party, please provide as to each such person or party the following information:

   a. name;

b.   present or last known residence address;

c.   present or last known business address and telephone number; and

d.   the relationships between any such person or party and Mike's Fishing, including any employer-employee relationship, principal-agent relationship, or licenser-licensee relationship, and the dates any such relationship existed.

5.   Whenever there is a request in these interrogatories to identify a communication, if such a communication was written, please provide all the information requested in subparagraphs (a) through (g) of paragraph 4 of these General Instructions; if such communications were oral, provide the following information;

a.   the date of such communication;

b.   the name, titles and address of each party to such communication;

c.   the name, titles and address of each person hearing such communication or having personal knowledge thereof;

d.   whether such communication occurred by telephone or by direct personal confrontation; and

e.   the place where such communication took place.

6.   Whenever there is a request in these interrogatories to "describe" or "state" facts, provide the following information:

a.   describe or state fully the underlying facts rather than any ultimate facts or conclusions of fact or law;

b.   particularize as to time, place, manner, identity of persons involved and amounts; and

c.   where documents are involved, describe the subject matter or contents thereof.

7.   If you assert either the attorney-client privilege or work product immunity, or both, as to any document for which identification is requested by any of the interrogatories, provide the following information:

a.   the nature of the document;

b.   the author, sender, recipient of the original and each recipient of a copy;

c.   the date of the document;

d.   the names appearing on any circulation list associated with such document;

e.   a summary of the subject matter of such document in sufficient detail to permit the Court to reach a determination in the event of a motion under Rule 37 of the Federal Rules of Civil Procedure; and

f. an indication of the basis for assertion of privilege or work product immunity.

8. If you assert either the attorney-client privilege or work product immunity, or both, as to any non-documentary information called for by these interrogatories, provide the following.

a. a summary statement of such information in sufficient detail to permit the Court to reach a determination in the event of a motion under Rule 37 of the Federal Rules of Civil Procedure; and

b. an indication of the basis for assertion of privilege or work product immunity.

9. If a particular interrogatory or part thereof cannot be answered:

a. answer to the extent possible and specify the reasons for your inability to answer the remainder thereof;

b. identify any documents which might contain material relevant to the answer sought; and

c. identify the person who might have knowledge of material relevant to the answer sought.

10. If you cannot state the finality of your response to an interrogatory until after service of your responses to this set of interrogatories, please so indicate and respond to such interrogatory to the best of your ability in view of the present state of your discovery.

III.   INTERROGATORIES

INTERROGATORY NO. 1

Describe fully the circumstances surrounding your first notification to Mark's Boats that you had applied for, or that you had already received, patent protection on the alleged invention disclosed and claimed in the '835 Patent. Identify all documents respecting your first such notification to Mark's Boats.

INTERROGATORY NO. 2

Identify each claim of the '835 Patent which you assert is infringed by Mark's Boats, and with respect to each such claim: (a) identify each accused trolling motor which is asserted by you to be an infringement of the '835 Patent; and (b) describe fully how each limitation of each such claim is met by each of Mark's Boats's accused devices, including in your response a detailed claim chart showing an element-by-element analysis of each allegedly infringed claim, and the corresponding elements that you contend exist in any of Mark's Boats's accused products or processes.

INTERROGATORY NO. 3

Identify all witnesses whom you believe are knowledgeable about the substance of, or the factual basis for, your allegations regarding each of the following: (a) infringement of the '835 Patent; (b) conception and reduction to practice of the alleged invention of the '835 Patent; (c) prior art to the invention claimed in the '835 Patent; (d) damages for any of the alleged acts of infringement; and (e) Mark's Boats's alleged willful infringement of the '835 Patent.

INTERROGATORY NO. 4

With respect to the subject matter of the '835 Patent:

(a) For each claim of the '835 Patent, identify the date on which the inventor first conceived of the alleged invention claimed in the '835 Patent, and describe in detail the events and chronology leading to the conception.

(b) Identify the earliest date that the alleged invention claimed in the '835 Patent was reduced to practice in the form of a prototype, drawings, detailed description, or otherwise, and describe in detail the events and chronology leading to said reduction to practice.

(c) Identify each and every prototype, model, drawing and written description of the apparatus and method claimed in the '835 Patent, and the date that each such prototype, model, drawing, and written description was completed.

(d) Identify each and every instance of actual use of the alleged invention claimed in the '835 Patent prior to the filing of the application for the '835 Patent, including the identity of all witnesses to such actual use.

INTERROGATORY NO. 5

Identify each patent application which has been filed by you or on your behalf on the alleged invention claimed in the '835 Patent anywhere in the world.

INTERROGATORY NO. 6

Identify all persons who have made, used, or sold products, or licensed or offered for sale products, which you believe are covered by or practice the alleged invention claimed in the '835 Patent.

INTERROGATORY NO. 7

Identify the earliest publication (including the date and title of that publication) discussing trolling motors as claimed in the '835 Patent, and identify all persons with knowledge of the facts that support your answer.

INTERROGATORY NO. 8

Identify all documents, sales, offers for sale, publications, public uses, or anything else that constitutes "prior art" to the alleged invention claimed in the '835 Patent, including in your response the results of all prior art searches and all known prior art (regardless of whether such prior art was included in any Information Disclosure Statement filed during the course of the prosecution of the '835 Patent).

INTERROGATORY NO. 9

Describe fully the history of the development of the Perch Troller including a detailed chronology of the design, development, manufacturing, testing, and sales of the system. Identify all persons who are knowledgeable as to these facts, and identify all documents (including but not limited to engineering or design drawings, detailed descriptions, software code, and operating manuals) that describe the design, manufacture, and/or use of the Perch Troller.

INTERROGATORY NO. 10

Identify the date and circumstances surrounding each attempt by you to sell, offer for sale, license, or otherwise grant any rights in the alleged invention of the '835 Patent.

INTERROGATORY NO. 11

Explain your contention as to the proper measure of damages caused by Mark's Boats alleged infringement of the '835 Patent in the following manner:

(a) If you contend that you are entitled to an award of lost profits, describe in detail the factual bases on which you predicate that contention, including without limitation, any reasons why you should not be limited to a reasonable royalty.

(b) If you contend that you are entitled to an award of reasonable royalty damages, describe in detail what you believe to be a reasonable royalty to be paid by Mark's Boats under 35 U.S.C. § 284, including the detailed factual bases on which you predicate your calculation of a reasonable royalty.

(c) If you contend that you are entitled to an award of increased damages, describe in detail the factual bases on which you predicate that contention, including without limitation any reasons why Mark's Boats infringement should be deemed willful, or this case deemed extraordinary.

INTERROGATORY NO. 12

Identify all persons, not already identified in your answer to the foregoing interrogatories, having knowledge or information pertinent to the allegations, facts, legal theories, and contentions set forth in your Complaint.

DATE:

_____

Chapter Six

EXPERTS

INTRODUCTION

Like all cases, witness credibility is of paramount importance in a patent case. Patent cases can be dry and technical in nature focusing on technical details and commercial facts. The experts should be able to explain the disputed technology and issues in laymen's terms that the fact finder will understand. All of the witnesses should use the same terminology. It is important to develop a theme in the trial; a compelling story to tell the fact finder why your client should prevail. The expert testimony should be consistent with, and support this theme. Demonstrative exhibits and graphic material often assist in keeping the fact finder interested in the testimony. Such demonstrative exhibits include charts, claim charts, computer-animated videos, one of the patented products, and one of the infringing products. If the witness is going to use demonstrative exhibits, the witness should practice with the exhibits to aid in a smooth presentation before the fact finder.

The order of presenting witnesses at trial depends on the issues in dispute. In a typical patent infringement suit, the patent owner's case-in-chief will address infringement and damages and the patent owner's witnesses will include:

1. The inventor (and/or company representative where the patent rights have been assigned).

2. Technical expert.

3. Patent expert.

4. Damages expert.

Since the defendant has the burden of proof on all invalidity and unenforceability issues, the patent owner should defend on these grounds during her rebuttal rather than in her case-in-chief.

The accused infringer's case-in-chief depends upon the defenses raised, but generally addresses non-infringement defenses, invalidity defenses, unenforceability defenses and damages. The defendant's witnesses at trial will generally include:

1. A company representative with knowledge of the accused product and its market.

2. Technical expert.

3. Patent expert.

4. Damages expert.

A. INVENTORS

The fact finder usually wants to hear the inventor's tale. Providing the inventor's testimony about her struggles to invent, develop, and solve technical problems humanizes the infringement suit. The inventor can be a sympathetic witness and juries hold inventors in higher esteem than the faceless corporations battling over lost profits. If the inventor is a likeable, credible witness, she makes an excellent first witness. The inventor can testify about the state of the art at the time of her invention, her recognition of a problem with the existing technology, the failure of the prior art to solve the problem, and her inventive process (the technical obstacles she faced during development of the invention and its reduction to practice). If the inventor is testifying to establish dates of conception and reduction to practice earlier than the application filing date, such testimony requires corroboration. The corroborative evidence could be documentary (orders for parts, lab notebooks) or the testimony of others (co-workers or assistants who worked on the invention, indirect observers, or in-house or other patent counsel who the inventor contacted (although using an attorney to corroborate dates of invention raises privilege waiver issues which need to be carefully considered)). Inventors should not generally testify on claim construction as such self-serving, after-the-fact testimony is often not favored by the Federal Circuit.

If the inventor is unavailable or would not make a good witness, the technical expert can provide most of the same information. To tell more of a story, the technical expert's testimony can be supplemented with fact witnesses such as an employee of the corporation who was working on the same invention or related projects, other scientists or engineers who tried to solve the same problem but failed, or a person who benefitted from the invention.

B. SELECTION OF EXPERTS

Selection of the proper experts can be determinative in a patent case. Lawyers often select experts they have worked with in the past. The client can also be helpful in selecting a technical expert because they know most people in their field. The first consideration is whether to utilize an employee of the corporation as the technical expert or to hire an unrelated third party in the technical field. The in-house technical expert may face charges of bias from opposing counsel, but is often the most knowledgeable on the technology. In addition, since the in-house expert works for the client, less chance exists that the expert will become entangled in other commitments and be unable to devote the necessary time to the job. It is important to thoroughly research the expert, including her educational background, professional experience, training, prior testimony and writings because the opposing counsel certainly will.

The attorney should select expert witnesses early in the litigation to use them as a sounding board for theories of the case and during discovery and depositions to understand the information being produced and to help formulate the best questions to ask. In fact, attorneys often have their technical expert sit in on the deposition of the opposing technical expert.

When choosing experts, it is important to consider how the judge or jury will receive the person, their credibility, and how well they stand up to cross-examination. Prior witness experience can be helpful. However, too much prior experience turns the expert into a "hired gun" who the jury may perceive as willing to say anything for a price. The importance of having a credible expert who can keep the jury's attention cannot be overstated. Excellent credentials are an asset, but if the jury sleeps through the expert's testimony or cannot follow it because of language differences or the inability of the expert to simplify issues, then the excellent credentials are worthless. Selecting a technical expert with the proper amount of expertise is a difficult task. Everything is obvious to the Nobel Laureate. The ideal technical expert should have good credentials and some experience in the technical industry of the patent. Consider the level of skill in the art and the inventor's background when assessing the type of technical expert to select.

C. TYPES OF EXPERTS

1. TECHNICAL EXPERTS

Each side will normally select one technical expert who will explain the technology to the jury and opine on infringement and validity issues. The technical expert for the patent owner will pay tribute to the invention, explaining the nature and extent of the improvement over the prior art, and opine on the construction of the claims and the defendant's infringement. If the patent owner is alleging infringement under the doctrine of equivalents, the technical expert needs to make a detailed showing of how only insubstantial differences exists between the patented invention and the accused device, giving particularized testimony on function/way/result. The technical expert for the accused infringer will explain why the accused product does not infringe and show that the patented invention is not entitled to protection. For example, technical experts can testify on what is the level of skill in the art, whether the patent specification is enabling, the state of the prior art, and whether the invention is anticipated or obvious. It is imperative that this expert be able to explain the technology and to reduce the complex technical details to manageable elements that the judge and jury can grasp.

The technical expert can be a powerful tool during the claim construction process or Markman hearing. Although the starting point for claim construction is intrinsic evidence (the patent and its prosecution history), recognizing that the judge is almost never one of ordinary skill in the art, the Federal Circuit has repeatedly endorsed the use of experts for providing the judge with background on the technology sufficient to determine what the claim terms mean to one of ordinary skill in the art.

> This court has made strong cautionary statements on the proper use of extrinsic evidence, which might be misread by some members of the bar as restricting a trial court's ability to hear such evidence. We intend no such thing. To the contrary, trial courts generally can hear expert testimony for background and education on the technology implicated by the presented claim construction issues, and trial courts have broad discretion in this regard. Furthermore, a trial court is quite correct in hearing and relying on expert testimony on an ultimate claim construction question in cases in which the intrinsic evidence (i.e., the patent and its file history—the "patent record") does not answer the question.

Key Pharmaceuticals v. Hercon Labs. Corp., 161 F.3d 709, 716, 48 USPQ2d 1911 (Fed. Cir. 1998) (citations omitted). Hence, the technical expert can always assist the court in understanding the technology. Expert testimony is also useful if a claim term is ambiguous. For example, when a claim uses terms of approximation such as "about 4" or "approximately 6–9" a technical expert may be of particular assistance. Means-plus-function clauses are also fertile ground for technical expert testimony.

2. PATENT LAWYERS

In addition to technical experts, patent law experts who have experience with the practices of the Patent and Trademark Office can provide the court with insight into patent prosecution which can be relevant to a variety of issues including: claim construction, inequitable conduct and prosecution history estoppel. This testimony should not be provided by the patent attorney who prosecuted the patent application at issue in the suit. Moreover, the expert chosen to testify should not consult with the attorney who prosecuted the application or be given access to the prosecuting attorney's files regarding the patent application. The patent expert should make an independent determination as to the meaning of the claim terms based on the documentary evidence available to the public including how the claims are limited by the amendments and arguments made during prosecution. Patent lawyers are often called to testify on willful infringement issues as well, opining on the quality of an attorney opinion and the reasonableness of a defendant's reliance thereon.

3. DAMAGES EXPERTS

Damages issues are not generally as interesting for a jury; they are typically number crunching (unless willful infringement is an issue).

Moreover, the damages expert is often the last witness to testify. Therefore, it is important to choose a dynamic damages expert who can keep the jury interested. Demonstrative exhibits are a must to help the jury understand the damages theory. Juries also respond well to experts who come off the stand and create an exhibit to teach the jury. This expert must have good credentials and be believable. It is important that the damages expert understand the numbers and the patent law issues and be able to communicate her testimony to the jury in easy to understand terms.

A damages expert will be either an accountant, an economist, or a company official familiar with the corporate sales and profits. Often the company official will provide the factual testimony and evidence and the economist or accountant will analyze the facts and calculate a damage award. Typically the accounting and economist experts are obtained from consulting firms that specialize in damages calculations for litigations. In addition, the big 6 accounting firms each have departments that offer damages experts for patent litigations. The best way to locate a good damages expert is word of mouth. Search cases within the last 5 years to compile a list of potential damages experts and contact attorneys who have worked with these experts.

The damages expert will testify as to the lost profits and/or reasonable royalties calculation and explain to the jury why they are supported by the evidence. This can include an analysis of the infringer's financial and sales information, the patent owners sales, profits, fixed and variable costs, and analysis of the relevant market. Common areas of testimony for the damages expert includes:

(1) consumer surveys of importance of patented feature to buying decision;

(2) marketing and business plans for importance of patented feature to product positioning;

(3) marketing capacity to sell incremental infringing sales;

(4) pricing segments or tiers in the market and whether there is effective competition goods or services in question, including cross-price elasticity estimation;

(5) direct competition between parties, including distribution, outlets, geographic submarkets, income and other demographic profiles of typical buyers of two products, to show whether the products are the first and second choice of a number of customers;

(6) sales correlations or regression analysis to prove sales increase when inventions are added, and sales decrease with infringement;

(7) estimations of price erosion through statistical analysis on other means;

(8) profitability—the calculation may differ from lost profits to reasonable royalty . . .

(9) royalties in the industry; and

    (10) using hypothetical, analytical, or other approach to reasonable royalty.

James Gould & James Langenfeld, *Antitrust and Intellectual Property: Landing on Patent Avenue in the Game of Monopoly*, 37 IDEA: J.L. & TECH. 449, 487–88 (1997).

    Whether the case requires an economist or an accountant generally depends on its complexity. For the straight forward case, an accountant will be sufficient. The accountant can testify on lost profits or reasonable royalties based on the market data supplied by the fact witnesses. The accountant should have her M.B.A. and/or C.P.A. For more complicated cases where a need exists for market and competition analysis of competing products with different prices and features, a Ph.D. economist can better model and predict the damages entitlements. The economist will have more training in competition and market analysis than an accountant.

    The factual information which the damages expert relies upon should be provided by someone with knowledge of the industry. A company official can testify on the relevant market, the availability of competing products, the demand for the patented product, the ability of the patent owner to satisfy the demand, reasons for price cuts, and provide evidence of any industry practices such as an established royalty rate or expected profit margin.

    Although damages experts can be very costly, it is important to involve them in the case early. If the liability and damages portions of the trial have been bifurcated, there may be some breathing room before you need to hire a damages expert. The damages theories need to be thoroughly analyzed and understood before the trial takes place. The damages expert should talk to the employees of the client who are most familiar with the financial and marketplace issues that the expert will address. This should be done as early as possible; at a minimum, before the damages expert becomes locked into a position by her expert report or deposition. It could be disastrous for the damages expert to commit to a theory of damages and to have the fact witnesses undermine that opinion with contradicting facts. The client's employees can also aid the expert in understanding the client's documents.

D.   DISCOVERY OF EXPERT'S WORK

FEDERAL RULE OF CIVIL PROCEDURE—Rule 26:

(a)(2) Disclosure of Expert Testimony.

    (A) In addition to the disclosures required by paragraph (1), a party shall disclose to other parties the identity of any person who may be used at trial to present evidence under Rules 702, 703, or 705 of the Federal Rules of Evidence.

    (B) Except as otherwise stipulated or directed by the court, this disclosure shall, with respect to a witness who is retained or specially employed to provide expert testimony in the case or whose duties as an employee of the party regularly involve giving expert testimony, be accompanied by a written report prepared and signed by the witness. The report shall contain a complete statement of all opinions to be expressed and the basis and reasons therefor; the data or other information considered by the witness in forming the opinions; any exhibits to be used as a summary of or support for the opinions; the qualifications of the witness, including a list of all publications authored by the witness within the preceding ten years; the compensation to be paid for the study and testimony; and a listing of any other cases in which the witness has testified as an expert at trial or by deposition within the preceding four years.

(C) These disclosures shall be made at the times and in the sequence directed by the court. In the absence of other directions from the court or stipulation by the parties, the disclosures shall be made at least 90 days before the trial date or the date the case is to be ready for trial or, if the evidence is intended solely to contradict or rebut evidence on the same subject matter identified by another party under paragraph (2)(B), within 30 days after the disclosure made by the other party. The parties shall supplement these disclosures when required under subdivision (e)(1).

* * *

(b)(4) Trial Preparation: Experts.

(A) A party may depose any person who has been identified as an expert whose opinions may be presented at trial. If a report from the expert is required under subdivision (a)(2)(B), the deposition shall not be conducted until after the report is provided.

(B) A party may, through interrogatories or by deposition, discover facts known or opinions held by an expert who has been retained or specially employed by another party in anticipation of litigation or preparation for trial and who is not expected to be called as a witness at trial, only as provided in Rule 35(b) or upon a showing of exceptional circumstances under which it is impracticable for the party seeking discovery to obtain facts or opinions on the same subject by other means.

However, be sure to consult your local rules which may modify these requirements. Rule 26(a)(3) permits district courts to opt out of expert disclosures.

1. TESTIFYING VERSUS NON-TESTIFYING EXPERTS

You should assume that any documents used to prepare a testifying expert are discoverable. Therefore, it is important to limit the documents that you show to the expert to avoid waiving privilege with respect to the documents. *See Vaughan Furniture Co. v. Featureline Mfg., Inc.*, 156 F.R.D. 123, 128 (M.D.N.C. 1994) (holding that "when a party names its attorney as an expert witness, the witness must produce all documents considered by him or her in the process of formulating the expert opinion, including documents containing opinions"). In addition, it is important to counsel the expert against taking notes on documents or on conversations with counsel because all of these notes would be discoverable.

Discovery is more limited with respect to non-testifying experts who have been consulted. In fact, a consulting expert who will not testify at trial is practically immune from discovery. The Federal Rules permit identification of such experts only where exceptional circumstances exist. What would qualify as exceptional circumstances? Would the defendant be entitled to discovery on the patent attorney who prosecuted the patent application in the suit if the defendant was alleging inequitable conduct? *See Bio–Rad Lab., Inc. v. Pharmacia, Inc.*, 130 F.R.D. 116, 14 USPQ2d 1924 (C.D. Cal. 1990) (yes). *See also Queen's University at Kingston v. Kinedyne Corp..*, 161 F.R.D. 443, 447, 37 USPQ2d 1398, 1402 (D. Kan. 1995) (exceptional circumstances were not proven where the defendant did not allege the unavailability of other experts and had designated an expert of its own to testify).

Would "expert shopping" be exceptional circumstances? A party would be expert shopping if they consulted several different experts and had each prepare a report, but only chose one to testify. If the patent owner obtained three expert reports that the defendant was not infringing and then one report that the defendant was infringing, are the three non-infringing reports discoverable? If the defendant obtained an infringement opinion from an attorney after receiving notice of the patent and the opinion found that the defendant was likely infringing, but that the patent is invalid, is this entire opinion discoverable? Can the defendant disclose only the portion regarding validity? *See Saint–Gobain/Norton Indus. Ceramics Corp. v. General Elec. Co.*, 884 F. Supp. 31, 33, 34 USPQ2d 1728, 1729 (D. Mass. 1995); *Kelsey-Hayes Co. v. Motor Wheel Co.*, 155 F.R.D. 170, 172 (W.D.Mich. 1991); *Smith v. Alyeska Pipeline Service Co.*, 538 F. Supp. 977, 979 (D. Del. 1982); *Fonar Corp. v. Johnson & Johnson*, 227 USPQ 886, 887 (D. Mass. 1985); *Handgards, Inc. v. Johnson & Johnson*, 413 F. Supp. 926, 929 (N.D. Cal. 1976).

2. REPORTS

Although Rule 26 has detailed disclosure requirements for experts, expert reports, and depositions, some district courts have eliminated the expert disclosure requirements by local rule. The expert disclosure requirements can also be modified by stipulation of the parties or court order. Keep in mind that not exchanging reports means that the opposing side will not know your expert's arguments until she is deposed, however, this also means that you will be in the dark as to their arguments as well.

If you are exchanging expert reports (as is normally the case in patent litigations), you will want to discuss with the expert your expectations regarding written work product. Because opposing counsel has a right to request all draft versions of the expert report and everything the expert "considered" in forming her opinion (not just everything the expert relied upon), most counsel will instruct their experts not to take any notes, not to write on documents, and not to print out drafts of expert reports. Most experts type their report directly into the computer and replace each existing draft with a new draft. During deposition, the expert will be questioned on the documents she considered in forming her opinion and conversations she had with attorneys. The expert will also be questioned regarding how much of the report she drafted and how much the attorney drafted.

Some experts routinely allow the attorney to draft the report. A word of caution, the expert's credibility will be undermined if the expert report is clearly the work of the lawyer and a greater chance exists that the expert will contradict the report while testifying if the words are not their own. In *New York v. Anheuser–Busch*, 811 F. Supp. 848, 869 (E.D. N.Y. 1993), the expert admitted during his testimony that portions of the report had been written by the attorney. Although the court did not exclude the expert testimony, it held that this "seriously damaged" the expert's credibility. *Id.*

Other experts will insist upon drafting their reports themselves so that every word is their own. The attorney should work closely with the technical expert in drafting her report because she may be unaware of the legal tests and standards. For example, the patent owner would not want her technical expert referring to the invention as obvious because this word has legal significance in a patent case of which the expert may be unaware. Patent law experts can and should draft their own reports. In the drafting processes, these experts often discover compelling arguments about why your client should prevail. Regardless of the type of expert, when the expert is drafting her own report, the attorney will want to stay actively involved to make certain the expert is: addressing all of the relevant issues; clear on the legal requirements; consistent with the theme or story; and done with the report by the deadline.

The expert report must meet the requirements of Rule 26. If the expert report does not contain all of the information required by Rule 26 (the data considered by the expert, the compensation received, prior testimony within the preceding four years, etc), the court may bar the expert from testifying altogether. The report must contain a "complete statement of all opinions to be expressed" and the "basis and reasons therefor." A sample expert report appears at the end of this chapter. An expert's testimony is limited to her report. Most courts will not permit an expert to opine on any issue not disclosed in the report. *See Coalition to Save Our Children v. State Bd. of Educ. of State of Del.*, 90 F.3d 752, 775–76 (3d Cir. 1996) (expert testimony excluded on topics not disclosed in an expert report); *Walsh v. McCain Foods Ltd.*, 81 F.3d 722, (7th Cir. 1996) (expert testimony limited to what was disclosed in expert report). Rule 37(c) permits the exclusion of expert testimony on an issue that was not disclosed in an expert report if the information was withheld "without substantial justification."

Although it is important to identify all the issues on which the expert may testify, you need to consider how comprehensive the report should be. Often expert reports are exchanged early in the litigation process. Giving opposing counsel the details of all your arguments too early in the process may put you at a disadvantage. The more comprehensive the expert report is, the more you educate opposing counsel as to your arguments and the more time they have to rebut them. However, you will want to provide fairly comprehensive expert reports not only to assure that you have complied with Rule 26 obligations, but also to convince the other side to settle.

The expert should reserve the right to supplement her report in response to the expert reports proffered by opposing counsel as well as new evidence added during the trial or later in discovery. For example, the patent owner's expert will generate a report on infringement which will be submitted to the court. The defendant's expert will generate a report on non-infringement and invalidity. At this point, the patent owner's expert may want to submit a supplemental report opining on validity.

Rule 26 requires that expert reports be exchanged at least 90 days before trial and supplemental reports rebutting the opposing expert's evidence are due within 30 days after the exchange of initial expert reports. Failure to comply with the deadlines can result in exclusion of your expert. *See, e.g., Congressional Air, Ltd. v. Beech Aircraft Corp.*, 176 F.R.D. 513, 517 (D. Md. 1997) (motion to exclude rebuttal expert testimony granted because of untimely filing of rebuttal expert report). In *Trilogy Communications, Inc. v. Times Fiber Communications, Inc.*, 109 F.3d 739, 744, 42 USPQ2d 1129, 1133 (Fed. Cir. 1997), the Court held:

> Trilogy's expert witness submitted a report within the time period established by the district court. However, the report lacked certain information required under the rule, including the identity of exhibits to be used in summary of or in support of his opinions. The court granted Trilogy an extension of time to supplement the report with the missing information so that the report would be in compliance with the rule. Trilogy thereafter submitted a second expert's report, a rebuttal report, and an affidavit by the expert. These submissions were made after the due date for expert's reports had passed. The documents contained new opinions and information and did not merely supplement the original report. The court ruled that to the extent the supplemental reports contained new opinions not found in the original report, they should be stricken from the record. The court further ruled that the expert's affidavit which incorporated the new opinions should likewise be stricken as inadmissible.

Some firms will hire two experts both of which are prepared to testify and use the testimony of the expert that holds up better in the deposition. Can you exclude the testimony of the expert you decide not to use?

E.   PROPER ROLE OF EXPERT TESTIMONY

Trial courts often give the parties wide latitude in using experts in a patent case. The Federal Rules of Evidence govern the use of expert testimony.

FEDERAL RULE OF EVIDENCE—Rule 702:

Testimony by Experts

If scientific, technical, or other specialized knowledge will assist the trier of fact to understand the evidence or to determine a fact in issue, a witness qualified as an expert by knowledge, skill, experience, training, or education, may testify thereto in the form of an opinion or otherwise.

FEDERAL RULE OF EVIDENCE—Rule 703:

Bases of Opinion Testimony by Experts

The facts or data in the particular case upon which an expert bases an opinion or inference may be those perceived by or made known to the expert at or before the hearing. If of a type reasonably relied upon by experts in the particular field in forming opinions or inferences upon the subject, the facts or data need not be admissible in evidence.

FEDERAL RULE OF EVIDENCE—Rule 704:

Opinion on Ultimate Issue

(a) Except as provided in subdivision (b), testimony in the form of an opinion or inference otherwise admissible is not objectionable because it embraces an ultimate issue to be decided by the trier of fact.

(b) No expert witness testifying with respect to the mental state or condition of a defendant in a criminal case may state an opinion or inference as to whether the defendant did or did not have the mental state or condition constituting an element of the crime charged or of a defense thereto. Such ultimate issues are matters for the trier of fact alone.

FEDERAL RULE OF EVIDENCE—Rule 705:

Disclosure of Facts or Data Underlying Expert Opinion

The expert may testify in terms of opinion or inference and give reasons therefor without first testifying to the underlying facts or data, unless the court requires otherwise. The expert may in any event be required to disclose the underlying facts or data on cross-examination.

Notes

1. **Court Appointed Experts.** In addition to experts selected by the parties (the hired guns), the court will, on occasion, determine that it needs its own expert. Federal Rule of Evidence 706 allows the court to appoint an expert agreed upon by the parties or to select an expert of its own choosing. The court appointed expert is subject to deposition by both parties and can testify at trial subject to cross examination. The parties split the costs of the court appointed expert. The jury can be informed that the expert is court appointed. The existence of a court appointed expert in no way limits the parties. They are still free to select individual experts to testify in their case-in-chief.

2. **Gatekeeper Role of District Judge.** In *Daubert v. Merrell Dow Pharmaceuticals, Inc.*, 509 U.S. 579, 27 USPQ2d 1200 (1993), the Supreme Court held the district court must ensure that any scientific evidence presented at trial is based upon valid scientific reasoning and methods. If

you object to scientific testimony, you should file a motion *in limine* to exclude the evidence.

SAMPLE EXPERT REPORT

IN THE UNITED STATES DISTRICT COURT
FOR THE NORTHERN DISTRICT OF CALIFORNIA

MIKE'S FISHING, INC.	)))	
Plaintiff,	))	Civil Action No. 99
v.	))	
MARK'S BOATS, INC.	))	
Defendant.	))	

EXPERT REPORT OF
PAT SALMON

The following information is provided pursuant to Rule 26(a)(2)(B) and the Pretrial Order entered in this action.

1.   A complete statement of all opinions to be expressed by me at trial and the basis and reasons for all such opinions is attached hereto as **Attachment 1**. The opinions contained herein are based on the analysis done to date. I reserve the right to supplement this report, as appropriate, after reviewing the reports of Mark's Boats expert witnesses and their supporting material.

2.   The information considered by me in forming the opinions noted in paragraph one above is identified in **Attachment 1**.

3.   My background, experience, publications, and other credentials are set forth in my curriculum vitae, which is attached hereto as **Attachment 2.** This curriculum vitae contains a list of all of the publications which I have authored. I have testified as an expert at trial or by deposition once in the preceding four years in *Mike's Fishing v. L.L. Green, Inc.* (Case No. 97) (D. Ma. 1998).

4.   Counsel for Mike's Fishing have asked that I render expert testimony in the above-captioned action. My fee for the time I spend preparing any studies in this matter, as well as testifying (either by deposition or by trial) is $300 per hour.

Dated this 10th day of June 2000.

_____

Pat Salmon

Attachment 1
Pat Salmon

If called to testify in this case, I will express the following opinions at the trial, the basis and reasons for which are set forth below and detailed in the documentation identified below. I will testify so as to instruct the jury in the basic electrical, mechanical, and navigational concepts necessary to understand trolling motors with autopilots like the one disclosed in the '835 patent. I will explain the meaning of the terms used in the claims of the '835 patent as those terms are understood by one of ordinary skill in the art.

Claim 1 of the '835 patent reads:

> 1.   An autopilot coupled to a bow-mounted trolling motor that pulls the boat, the autopilot comprising:
>
> [1]   a steering motor coupled to said trolling motor, said steering motor being disposed to turn said trolling motor left or right in response to input signals;
>
> [2]   a steering circuit electrically coupled to said steering motor, said steering circuit being disposed to generate said input signals;
>
> [3]   a compass electrically coupled to said steering circuit, said compass being disposed to transmit heading signals to said steering circuit when the boat deviates from the target heading by a predetermined amount.

Specifically, I will testify:

CLAIM CONSTRUCTION

1.   A "trolling motor" as used in the patent is the thrust motor. It is the portion of the trolling unit which turns the propeller. This construction is supported by the specification at Col. 2, lines 17–18 ("a bow-mounted trolling motor (thrust motor) that pulls the boat"). The trolling unit is the complete system including the trolling motor, the mounting mechanism, the propeller, the control head, the compass, the steering circuit, the shaft, the steering motor and any associated foot pedal.

2.   The word "coupled" appears in four places in claim 1. In the preamble, the autopilot is coupled to the trolling motor. In [1], the steering motor is coupled to the trolling motor (thrust motor). One of ordinary skill in the art understands the word coupled as interacting or communicating. It can be any form of interaction: mechanical, electrical, or optical. There is no limitation prior to the word coupled which limits it to any particular kind of coupling. It is clear from the claims that when a particular coupling was intended, such a limitation was specified in the claims. For example, in [2] and [3], the claim delineates "electrically coupled" elements.

In [2] and [3] of claim 1, the claim is limited to "electrically coupled," so neither mechanical nor optical coupling would result in literal infringement. In [2], the steering circuit is electrically coupled to the steering motor. In [3], the compass is electrically coupled to the steering circuit. An electrical coupling is any sort of communication or relaying of an electrical signal. For example, a wire, a wire cable, or a radio frequency communication would each be an electrical coupling. It is not limited to a single wire and there does not have to be a direct connection between two devices for them to be electrically coupled. For example, when you have a heading detector which connects to a microprocessor which then connects to a steering circuit, the heading detector and the steering circuit are "electrically coupled" despite the presence of other elements in-between.

3.   The term "compass" means a device used to sense the magnetic field of the earth.

INFRINGEMENT

4.   The Easy Troller infringes the '835 patent under the doctrine of equivalents.

5.   The Easy Troller schematics indicate that it is a bow-mounted trolling motor that pulls the boat.

6.   The Easy Troller schematics indicate that it has an autopilot system which includes a steering motor coupled to the trolling motor (thrust motor). These elements are connected by gears (a mechanical coupling). The steering motor causes the thrust motor to turn left or right in response to input signals.

7.   The Easy Troller schematics indicate that it has an autopilot system which includes a steering circuit which is electrically connected to the steering motor by a wire.

8.   The Easy Troller heading detector is a magnetometer which works just like a compass. They both read the heading of the boat; they detect heading by taking a reading based on the earth's magnetic field and they both communicate this reading to the microprocessor in the steering circuit when the heading changes by a predetermined amount. The Easy Troller transmits heading signals to the steering circuit when the boat deviates from the target heading by 5%. The Easy Troller heading detector is optically connected to the steering circuit. Those of skill in the art know that all forms of coupling (mechanical, optical and electrical) are known to be interchangeable. There are insubstantial differences between the optical coupling of the Easy Troller and the electrical coupling of claim 1.

Basis for the Opinion

The basis and reasoning of this opinion is my education, training, and experience as an electrical engineer, my education, training, and experience in the fishing boat and motor industry, and my review and analysis of:

1. The '835 patent including its claims, written description and drawings. (Exhibit A)

2. File History of the Application for the '835 patent. (Exhibit B)

3. Easy Troller electrical and mechanical schematics. (Exhibit C)

4. Easy Troller "Owner's Instruction Manual." (Exhibit D)

5. The Easy Troller.

In a standard expert report, these exhibits would be attached at the end of the report and the expert's resume would follow.

Problems

Who is this expert working for? Will this expert be permitted to opine on validity issues? Does this report meet the requirements of Rule 26?

Chapter Seven

POST-DISCOVERY STRATEGIES AND PREPARATION FOR TRIAL

Introduction

At the close of discovery, counsel is presented with the formidable task of sifting through all information gathered during the discovery process to present a persuasive case to the judge or jury. After this task is performed, a series of necessary steps follow. First and foremost, the trial lawyer must outline the case that will be presented consistent with the discovered evidence in a way that presents an interesting story. The story must be simple but not so sparsely presented to fail to establish an adequate record for appeal. Of course, this story should have a central theme presented through witnesses, documents, and visual aids. Thus, it is a primary objective of the trial lawyer to present each witness and document in such a way to support this crucial central theme. An interesting dilemma for the trial lawyer is that the story's presentation is complicated by an adversary altering the story as it is told, both through the art of cross-examination and through witnesses who present rebuttal evidence often contradicting the story.

In short, the presentation of the trial is like a play written by two playwrights, each with a different point of view, each seeking a different ending to the play. The product will not be known until both authors have presented their story, and the fact-finder has evaluated it. Thus, to prevail, the actual pretrial preparation must be thorough and all aspects thought out. There is only one presentation of the trial, only one presentation of the play, and the trier of fact will determine the ending.

Prior to the scripting and presentation of trial, there are some preliminary and important steps to be taken. First, from a procedural standpoint, trial counsel must determine whether there are any motions that simplify the trial by eliminating issues which can be decided solely on the basis of law. Similarly, trial counsel must consider whether to file motions to exclude certain evidence that is inappropriate for the finder of fact. This is particularly true where a jury is involved. There is also the need to consider the order of presentation of the trial and whether or not all issues shall be presented at one time or whether the trial should be bifurcated (or trifurcated) into multiple segments for simplification. All of these factors must be thought through prior to the pretrial conference and the submission of the pretrial order.

A. DISPOSITIVE MOTIONS

It is often possible to dispose of an entire case or parts of a case based on motions for summary judgment. Rule 56 sets forth the criteria for summary judgment motions.

FEDERAL RULES OF CIVIL PROCEDURE—Rule 56:

Summary Judgment

(a) For Claimant. A party seeking to recover upon a claim, counterclaim, or cross-claim or to obtain a declaratory judgment may, at any time after the expiration of 20 days from the commencement of the action or after service of a motion for summary judgment by the adverse party, move with or without supporting affidavits for a summary judgment in the party's favor upon all or any part thereof.

(b) For Defending Party. A party against whom a claim, counterclaim, or cross-claim is asserted or a declaratory judgment is sought may, at any time, move with or without supporting affidavits for a summary judgment in the party's favor as to all or any part thereof.

(c) Motion and Proceedings Thereon. The motion shall be served at least 10 days before the time fixed for the hearing. The adverse party prior to the day of hearing may serve opposing affidavits. The judgment sought shall be rendered forthwith if the pleadings, depositions, answers to interrogatories, and admissions on file, together with the affidavits, if any, show that there is no genuine issue as to any material fact and that the moving party is entitled to a judgment as a matter of law. A summary judgment, interlocutory in character, may be rendered on the issue of liability alone although there is a genuine issue as to the amount of damages.

(d) Case Not Fully Adjudicated on Motion. If on motion under this rule judgment is not rendered upon the whole case or for all the relief asked and a trial is necessary, the court at the hearing of the motion, by examining the pleadings and the evidence before it and by interrogating counsel, shall if practicable ascertain what material facts exist without substantial controversy and what material facts are actually and in good faith controverted. It shall thereupon make an order specifying the facts that appear without substantial controversy, including the extent to which the amount of damages or other relief is not in controversy, and directing such further proceedings in the action as are just. Upon the trial of the action the facts so specified shall be deemed established, and the trial shall be conducted accordingly.

(e) Form of Affidavits; Further Testimony; Defense Required. Supporting and opposing affidavits shall be made on personal knowledge, shall set forth such facts as would be admissible in evidence, and shall show affirmatively that the affiant is competent to testify to the matters stated therein. Sworn or certified copies of all papers or parts thereof referred to in an affidavit shall be attached thereto or served therewith. The court may permit affidavits to be supplemented or opposed by depositions, answers to interrogatories, or further affidavits. When a motion for summary judgment is made and supported as provided in this rule, an adverse party may not rest upon the mere allegations or denials of the adverse party's pleading, but the adverse party's response, by affidavits or as otherwise provided in this rule, must set forth specific facts showing that there is a genuine issue for trial. If the adverse party does not so respond, summary judgment, if appropriate, shall be entered against the adverse party.

Rule 56 states that summary judgment motion orders are appropriate where there is "... no genuine issue as to any material fact and ... the moving party is entitled to judgment as a matter of law." Fed. R. Civ. P. 56(c). "Summary judgment procedure is properly regarded not as a disfavored procedural shortcut but rather as an integral part of the Federal Rules as a whole, which are designed 'to secure the just, speedy and inexpensive determination of every action.'" *Celotex Corp. v. Catrett*, 477 U.S. 317, 324 (1986). Summary judgment is as applicable to patent cases as any other type of case. The moving party has the initial burden of proving the absence of a genuine issue of material fact and the responding party, if it chooses to oppose the motion, has the duty of showing that there is a genuine issue of material fact requiring a trial. *Celotex*, 477 U.S. at 321–22; Fed. R. Civ. P. 56(e). Furthermore, when the grounds for summary judgment involve the invalidity or enforceability of a patent, the burden of proof facing the challenger to the patent's validity must be considered. *National Presto Indus., Inc. v. West Bend Co.*, 76 F.3d 1185, 1189, 37 USPQ2d 1685, 1687 (Fed. Cir. 1996). Thus, where the defendant replies with an assertion of invalidity, it must establish its case by clear and convincing evidence. *Checkpoint Sys. v. U.S. Int'l Trade Comm'n*, 54 F.3d 756, 761, 35 USPQ2d 1042, 1046 (Fed. Cir. 1995). Similarly, in a patent case involving a summary judgment on infringement, the standard of proof where the moving party is the plaintiff-patentee is preponderance of evidence. *ZMI Corp. v. Cardiac Resuscitator Corp.*, 844 F.2d 1576, 158, 6 USPQ2d 1557, 1562 (Fed. Cir. 1988).

Summary judgment is an excellent mechanism for paring down the issues in the case. It is also an opportunity to educate the judge.

NATIONAL PRESTO INDUS., INC. v. WEST BEND CO.

76 F.3d 1185, 37 USPQ2d 1685 (Fed. Cir. 1996)

Before NEWMAN, LOURIE, and RADER, Circuit Judges.

NEWMAN, Circuit Judge.

National Presto Industries and The West Bend Company each appeals from the judgment of the United States District Court for the Western District of Wisconsin, concerning Presto's United States Patent

No. 5,089,286 (the '286 patent) for a device that cuts vegetables into spiral curls.

The issues of patent validity and inducement to infringe were decided by summary judgment, and the issues of infringement, willfulness of infringement, and damages were tried to a jury. The district court enhanced the jury's damages award by one half, and denied Presto's request for attorney fees. On appeal by each side of the aspects that were decided adversely to it, we affirm the judgment in all respects.

I

PATENT VALIDITY

On West Bend's motion for summary judgment on the issue of validity, the district court granted judgment in favor of Presto, holding that the '286 patent was not invalid. This summary judgment in favor of the non-moving party is challenged by West Bend, both as to the merits of the decision and with respect to the procedure.

The trial court has authority to dispose of issues summarily when the requirements of Rule 56 are met, provided that the adversely affected party has an adequate opportunity to respond and the summary procedure does not deny due and fair process. In *Celotex Corp. v. Catrett*, 477 U.S. 317, 326, (1986), the Court remarked that "district courts are widely acknowledged to possess the power to enter summary judgment *sua sponte*, so long as the losing party was on notice that she had to come forward with all of her evidence." *See Sawyer v. United States*, 831 F.2d 755, 759 (7th Cir. 1987) (the movant must have opportunity to respond to the non-movant's position before summary judgment may be granted in favor of the non-movant); *Horn v. City of Chicago*, 860 F.2d 700, 703–04 n. 6 (7th Cir. 1988) (a *sua sponte* summary judgment should not be granted when it takes the affected party by surprise).

West Bend in its motion cited two Japanese publications that West Bend stated were closer prior art than the references cited by the patent examiner in granting the '286 patent. Presto in its opposition discussed the relevant prior art including the references that were cited by the examiner. The parties did not dispute the facts of the scope and content of the prior art, the differences between the claimed invention and the prior art, and the level of ordinary skill in the field of the invention. West Bend's motion brought forth extensive materials and argument by both sides on the issue of validity, and West Bend had full opportunity to respond and did respond to Presto's position that the '286 patent was not invalid.

West Bend states that it did not raise all of the grounds of invalidity that it might have raised, particularly with respect to validity based on 35 U.S.C. § 112. Presto responds that West Bend presented the affidavit of its patent expert that he had thoroughly studied the Presto patent and its prosecution history, and that during the entire summary judgment proceeding neither West Bend nor its patent expert mentioned the existence of any basis for challenging validity other than under 35 U.S.C.

§ 103. Moreover, in its opposition to Presto's motion *in limine* to preclude West Bend from presenting invalidity defenses at trial, West Bend made only passing mention and did not proffer any evidence in support of a § 112 invalidity defense. We have not been shown reversible error in the district court's procedure, in view of West Bend's motion, the record, and the entirety of the proceedings directed to the issue of validity.

West Bend points to the district court's recognition that the meaning of certain claim terms, such as the word "frame" and the phrase "configured for reception," were in dispute. West Bend argues that these disputed meanings raise questions of material fact with respect to the issue of validity, thus precluding the grant of summary judgment. However, West Bend did not show that the disputed aspects of the meanings of the challenged terms were material to the issue of validity, and we do not discern an issue of conflicting claim interpretations with respect to the determinations of validity and of infringement. In deciding a motion for summary judgment of invalidity the burden of proof must be considered. *See Anderson v. Liberty Lobby, Inc.*, 477 U.S. 242, 254 (1986) (heightened standard of clear and convincing evidence, which would be party's burden at trial, is to be considered when evaluating sufficiency of evidence on motion for summary judgment). Appellate review is on the same basis. Taking cognizance of the requirement that patent invalidity must be proved by clear and convincing evidence, we affirm the summary judgment that the '286 patent is not invalid.

IV.

INDUCEMENT TO INFRINGE

On cross-appeal Presto argues that West Bend, with knowledge of Presto's commercial device and Presto's patent activities, acted to flood the market with West Bend's "imitation" during the months before the Presto patent issued. Presto states that West Bend, by these actions, actively induced infringement of the Presto patent after patent issuance, in violation of 35 U.S.C. § 271(b) ("Whoever actively induces infringement of a patent shall be liable as an infringer.").

The district court held that as a matter of law there could not be liability for pre-issuance activity leading to post-issuance infringement, and refused to give the question to the jury. Presto contends that this holding is incorrect, and requests remand for trial of the factual issue of inducement.

A

Since the question was decided summarily, as a matter of law, the factual premises as set forth by Presto must be assumed, and disputed facts resolved in favor of Presto for the purpose of determining whether the judgment was correct and the issue properly withheld from the jury. The context is as follows:

Presto commercially introduced its vegetable cutter in April 1991. In June 1991, upon hearing trade rumors that West Bend was developing a similar product, Presto's chairman told West Bend's president that Presto had applied for a patent. West Bend accelerated its activity and increased its production, and the West Bend vegetable cutter was first sold in September 1991. In November 1991, West Bend's president agreed to receive and was sent a copy of Presto's allowed claims. The Presto patent issued on February 18, 1992, and suit was filed that day.

Presto's position is that its damages from West Bend should include recompense for infringing retail sales and use, after patent issuance, of devices that were placed into commerce by West Bend during a reasonable period before Presto's patent issued. Presto cites several cases that have imposed liability for inducement to infringe when articles were placed in commerce with the knowledge and intent that they would be resold or used to infringe the patent, and when compensation for post-issuance infringement would not be readily available from the direct infringers. Presto argues that the criterion for liability under § 271(b) is whether infringement by West Bend's customers was directly, foreseeably, and intentionally caused by West Bend's activities, and that it is not controlling whether these activities occurred before or after Presto's patent was issued. Presto states that the district court erred in holding that there can never be liability for pre-issuance inducement, even in circumstances when the inducer had knowledge that the patent was about to issue and would be directly infringed by resale and use, and when the inducer acted with the intent that this direct infringement would occur.

B

The question now presented is whether remedy under § 271(b) is available, subject to proof, against persons who deliberately place later-infringing items into the chain of commerce before the patent issues.

Thus Presto states that the district court erred, and that Presto should have been permitted to show that West Bend had knowledge of Presto's patent application and the allowed claims, and acted in violation of law to flood the market with the intent that its retailers and their customers would directly infringe the patent. As evidence of West Bend's knowledge and culpable intent Presto points, *inter alia*, to the "hold harmless" undertakings between West Bend and some of its retailers with respect to future liability for infringement. Presto states that at least after West Bend had actual knowledge of Presto's allowed claims, West Bend did not act prudently and in good faith to avoid infringement. Presto states that West Bend fully expected that its shipments to retailers in the weeks before patent issuance would be resold in part after patent issuance, and that the devices were intended to be used after patent issuance.

Presto states that it has an inadequate remedy for the infringing retail sales and uses after patent issuance. "As a practical matter, [the patentee] cannot bring an action against thousands of retailers." *Procter & Gamble*, 604 F. Supp. at 1489, 225 USPQ (BNA) at 932. Presto argues that § 271(b) is not by its terms limited by when the inducement occurred, but only by whether direct infringement ensued. Thus Presto argues that the law does not bar recovery for acts of inducement committed before patent issuance, when the actor not only had the knowledge that a patent application is pending, but also had the intent that as a direct result of its actions there would be direct infringement by others after patent issuance. In *Manville Sales Corp. v. Paramount Systems*, 917 F.2d 544, 553, 16 USPQ2d (BNA) 1587, 1594 (Fed. Cir. 1990) the Federal Circuit explained that "The plaintiff has the burden of showing that the alleged infringer's actions induced infringing acts and that he knew or should have known his actions would induce actual infringements." However, in *Manville* there was no issue of pre-issuance activity.

West Bend, in turn, argues that § 271(b) was not intended to reach pre-issuance activities. West Bend points out that there can be no liability for infringement of a pending patent application, and that the law of inducement is similarly limited. West Bend argues that much can happen to prevent or delay the patent grant, and that there are many opportunities for abuse by patentees. West Bend points out that the "warning" of impending patent issuance, whether by a "patent pending" marking or by direct information from the patentee, imposes no liability but is simply a cautionary notice of a possible future event. West Bend criticizes the recent district court decisions contrary to its position, and points out the general rule that without a patent there can not be infringement.

C

The question is not whether, on the facts of this case, West Bend's action led to infringement by others, at least as a disputed material fact requiring trial. The threshold question is whether the absolute rule of law adopted by the district court is correct. There are cogent arguments of fact, law, and policy on both sides of the issue, as have been thoroughly presented by the parties. We conclude that the district court was correct, and that as a matter of law § 271(b) does not reach actions taken before issuance of the adverse patent.

The summary judgment of the district court, holding as a matter of law that West Bend was not liable for inducement of infringement based on the products made and sold by West Bend before patent issuance, is affirmed.

Notes

1. As can be seen, summary judgment was used here to eliminate two issues, patent invalidity and inducement of infringement from presentation to the jury. Both issues were decided by the Court.

2. **Summary Judgment on Issues of Law v. Issues of Fact.** It is easier to win summary judgment on issues of law than issues of fact. Claim construction is ideal for summary judgment resolution. Equitable issues such as laches and equitable estoppel or invalidity defenses (legal issues) such as best mode, non-enablement, or an on-sale bar, are often ripe for summary

judgment. However, even when an issue is one of law, summary judgment can be difficult where there are underlying fact issues. For example, it is usually difficult for an accused infringer to prove invalidity on a motion for summary judgment (even though invalidity is a question of law), because it is a heavily fact based issue. Certainly, it is easier where the assertion is based on an anticipation defense (involving one reference) as opposed to an obviousness defense where two or more references must be combined.

3. Summary judgment is often appropriate to resolve literal infringement and infringement under the doctrine of equivalents. Once the judge construes the claims, there may be no disputed issues remaining. In *Warner-Jenkinson Co. v. Hilton Davis Chem. Co.*, 117 S.Ct. 1040, 1053 n. 8, 41 USPQ2d 1865 (1997), the Supreme Court offered the following guidance with respect to infringement under the doctrine of equivalents:

> With regard to the concern over unreviewability due to black-box jury verdicts, we offer only guidance, not a specific mandate. Where the evidence is such that no reasonable jury could determine two elements to be equivalent, district courts are obliged to grant partial or complete summary judgment. *See* Fed. Rule Civ. Proc. 56; *Celotex Corp. v. Catrett*, 477 U.S. 317, 322–323 (1986). If there has been a reluctance to do so by some courts due to unfamiliarity with the subject matter, we are confident that the Federal Circuit can remedy the problem. Of course, the various legal limitations on the application of the doctrine of equivalents are to be determined by the court, either on a pretrial motion for partial summary judgment or on a motion for judgment as a matter of law at the close of the evidence and after the jury verdict. Fed. Rule Civ. Proc. 56; Fed. Rule Civ. Proc. 50. Thus, under the particular facts of a case, if prosecution history estoppel would apply or if a theory of equivalence would entirely vitiate a particular claim element, partial or complete judgment should be rendered by the court, as there would be no further material issue for the jury to resolve. Finally, in cases that reach the jury, a special verdict and/or interrogatories on each claim element could be very useful in facilitating review, uniformity, and possibly postverdict judgments as a matter of law. *See* Fed. Rule Civ. Proc. 49; Fed. Rule Civ. Proc. 50. We leave it to the Federal Circuit how best to implement procedural improvements to promote certainty, consistency, and reviewability to this area of the law.

4. There are limits to summary judgment. The court may not make credibility determinations or draw inferences adverse to the movant and no facts may be found unless the reasonable fact finder could not have found them otherwise.

5. **Cross Motions**. When the parties both move for summary judgment on the same issue, such as infringement, it is implicitly conceded that there is no issue of material fact in dispute. *See Beech Aircraft Corp. v. EDO Corp.*, 990 F.2d 1237, 1245, 26 USPQ2d 1572, 1579 (Fed. Cir. 1993).

B. MOTIONS IN LIMINE

Often, a crucial pretrial question involves whether or not certain evidence should be excluded at trial. In the pre-trial stage of the case, these questions are usually initiated by the filing of a motion *in limine*. Motions *in limine* are governed generally by the Federal Rules of Evidence and concern the question of what constitutes competent evidence. Motions *in limine* arise also under Fed. R. Civ. P. 37(c)(1) as a request for sanctions to be imposed by the court for failure to comply with discovery. *See* MOORE'S FEDERAL PRACTICE Ch. 37 and Ch. 26.23[2][a][iii].

More broadly, motions *in limine* on the liability issues are also covered by existing case law. For example, 35 U.S.C. § 102 defines what constitutes prior art. If the asserted prior art to invalidate a patent has on its face a date that would disqualify it from being prior art, then it is a proper subject for a motion *in limine*. Similarly, whether or not a witness is qualified to give technical expert testimony may be decided in response to a motion *in limine* presenting excerpts from depositions showing no basis for expertise in the given technology.

Last minute attempts to change positions or add information not previously produced are opportune areas for the use of motions *in limine*. For example, Rule 26(e) requires that the anticipated areas of testimony for an expert be provided in the expert's report, as well as at the expert's deposition, and that any additions or supplementations that might follow be identified. Where the expert's opinion is offered belatedly, or attempts to add new and untimely bases for the opinion such as new test results, or directly contradicts the opinions stated in the expert's report, it may be precluded based on a motion *in limine*. *See, e.g., Miksis v. Howard*, 106 F.3d 754, 757 (7th Cir. 1997) and *Reliance Insurance Co. v. Louisiana Land & Exploration Co.*, 110 F.3d 253, 257–58 (5th Cir. 1997).

It must be noted, however, that courts are reluctant to exclude testimony as a sanction under Fed. R. Civ. P. 37(c)(1). Courts regard exclusion as a drastic remedy only to be applied in cases where the party's conduct "represents flagrant bad faith and callous disregard of the Federal Rules." *McNerney v. Archer Daniels Midland Co.*, 164 F.R.D. 584, 586 (W.D. N.Y. 1995). Thus, in considering a motion for sanctions under Rule 37(c)(1), courts generally consider:

(1) the importance of the excluded testimony;

(2) the explanation of the party for its failure to comply with the required disclosure;

(3) the potential prejudice that would arise from allowing the testimony; and

(4) the availability of a continuance to cure such prejudice.

Equal Employment Opportunity Comm'n v. General Dynamics Corp., 999 F.2d 113, 115 (5th Cir. 1993).

C. BIFURCATION, TRIFURCATION AND THE ORDER OF TRIAL

FEDERAL RULE OF CIVIL PROCEDURE—*Rule 42:*

Consolidation; Separate Trials

(b) Separate Trials. The court, in furtherance of convenience or to avoid prejudice, or when separate trials will be conducive to expedition and economy, may order a separate trial of any claim, cross-claim, counter-claim, or third-party claim, or of any separate issue or of any number of claims, cross-claims, counterclaims, third-party claims, or issues, always preserving inviolate the right of trial by jury as declared by the Seventh Amendment to the Constitution or as given by a statute of the United States.

LAITRAM CORP. v. HEWLETT–PACKARD CO.

791 F. Supp. 113, 22 USPQ2d 1597 (E.D. La. 1992)

ORDER AND REASONS

FELDMAN, District Judge.

Before the Court is defendant's motion for separate trials on the liability issues in this case and on the questions concerning damages and willful infringement, and for a stay of all discovery on damages and willful infringement. For the reasons that follow defendant's motion is DENIED to the extent that defendant requests separate trials with separate juries and a stay of discovery.

However, it is hereby ORDERED that the trial will proceed in three separate and distinct phases. Liability will first be tried to a verdict, and, if necessary, the trial will proceed immediately thereafter to the damages phase before the same jury. The Court will thereafter discharge the jury and receive evidence regarding willful infringement. Discovery will continue as scheduled on all issues in this case.

I.

Plaintiff, Laitram Corporation, has sued the defendant, Hewlett Packard Company, for patent infringement. Plaintiff contends that calculators the defendant manufactures and sells infringe five Laitram patents (specifically, U.S. patent Nos. 4,547,860; 4,860,234; 4,910,697; 4,924,431; and 4,999,795). The patented inventions are related to calculator technology, and were developed by James P. Lapeyre.

Plaintiff maintains that Mr. Lapeyre disclosed some of the technology related to his patented inventions to defendant, and that defendant initially expressed interest to Mr. Lapeyre. However, plaintiff maintains that defendant later rejected an offer of a license to commercially exploit the inventions. Plaintiff sued after it discovered that defendant was making calculators in violation of Laitram's patents.

Defendant wants the Court to order separate trials on the issues relating to infringement of the patents, and then on the questions concerning damages and willful infringement. Defendant also asks the Court to stay all discovery on damages and willful infringement until after the liability trial.

LAW AND APPLICATION

Federal Rule of Civil Procedure 42(b) authorizes courts to order separate trials on issues in the same case when separation is appropriate. Rule 42(b) directs:

> The court, in furtherance of convenience, or to avoid prejudice, or when separate trials will be conducive to expedition and economy, may order a separate trial of any claim, cross-claim counterclaim, or third party claim, or of any separate issue or of any number of claims, cross-claims, counterclaims, third party claims or issues, always preserving inviolate the right of trial by jury as declared by the Constitution or as given by a statute of the United States.

Contrary to defendant's contentions, it is not now a "well accepted rule in patent litigation" for courts to proceed first with a liability trial, and reach damages and willful infringement issues in a separate and later trial if necessary. Rather, courts have repeatedly emphasized that whether to bifurcate a trial, even a patent trial, is always a question committed to the sound discretion of the trial court, and the court is expected to exercise its discretion on a case-by-case basis.

In patent cases, as in others, separate trials should be the exception, not the rule. But that does not mean that there are not often special considerations in patent controversies which make these cases candidates for some kind of special trial management. *See Swofford v. B & W, Inc.*, 34 F.R.D. 15, 19–20 (S.D. Tex. 1963). Still, courts should not order separate trials "unless such a disposition is clearly necessary." *Wolens v. F.W. Woolworth Co.*, 209 USPQ 569 (N.D. Ill. 1980).

Rule 42(b) expresses three separate justifications for bifurcation. A court may separate issues if (1) it would avoid prejudice, (2) it would be convenient to do so, or (3) it would be economical or would expedite the litigation to do so. However, the Fifth Circuit has correctly cautioned district courts to bear in mind before ordering separate trials in the same case that the "issue to be tried [separately] must be so distinct and separable from the others that a trial of it alone may be had without injustice." *Swofford v. B & W, Inc.*, 336 F.2d 406, 415 (5th Cir. 1964). That is, even if bifurcation might somehow promote judicial economy, courts should not order separate trials when "bifurcation would result in unnecessary delay, additional expense, or some other form of prejudice." *Apollo Computer*, 707 F. Supp. at 1433. Essentially, then, courts must balance the equities in ruling on a motion to bifurcate. It is that counsel which animates the Court's decision.

II.

Defendant asks the Court to order two separate trials and two separate discovery phases. Defendant contends that the first phase of the proceedings should be limited to issues concerning whether it has infringed any valid Laitram patent. Then, only if the jury in the liability trial finds liability, the Court should allow discovery on damages and willful infringement with another trial to thereafter follow on these questions. The Court finds that defendant has not demonstrated that any of Rule 42(b)'s considerations for bifurcation support defendant's proposal.

The Court is mindful of the advantages that bifurcation of the issues in this case could bring. Certainly, some economy in the cost of discovery would be accomplished. But that does not outweigh the significant problems that would arise if the Court were to order two wholly separate trials before two different juries (on the jury issues). Accordingly, the Court holds that there must be a single proceeding in this case, but that the trial should be divided into three separate phases.

The Court will maintain in place the present discovery schedule so that discovery will proceed on all issues. At trial, the parties will first try all issues regarding liability (validity of the patent, enforceability and infringement). The jury will decide whether defendant infringed any valid Laitram patent. If defendant is found to have infringed any Laitram patent, the trial will immediately proceed, before the same jury, to the question of damages (that is, what reasonable royalty does defendant owe plaintiff?). After the jury reaches its damages verdict, the Court will hear the evidence regarding willful infringement, and make a determination whether this is an "exceptional case" in which increased damages and attorney's fees should be assessed under 35 U.S.C. §§ 284 and 285.

A.

Prejudice is the Court's most important consideration in deciding whether to order separate trials under Rule 42(b). The Court must balance two types of competing claims of prejudice. First, those who seek bifurcation of patent cases typically contend, as does the defendant here, that they will be prejudiced because the issues and evidence surrounding infringement and damages in patent cases are complicated and potentially confusing to the jury. Courts have accepted these problems as central concerns in ordering separate trials. *See Mag Instrument, Inc. v. J. Baxter Brinkman International Corp.*, 123 F.R.D. 543, 545 (N.D. Tex. 1988) ("[B]ifurcation will eliminate the need for the jury to listen to complex damages testimony which ultimately would have no bearing on the case."). Trying all the issues at once could clutter the record unnecessarily and make the jury's already challenging task doubly difficult. Also, there is the danger (especially perilous in complicated trials with many separate and distinct issues) that the jury will consider evidence that may be admissible on only one issue to the moving party's prejudice on other issues.

However, those who are contrary-minded contend, as does the plaintiff, that they will be prejudiced by the considerable delay that will result if the Court orders separate trials and separate discovery periods. An unreasonable delay in a case's resolution amounts to prejudice to the one opposing separation. It is clearly not in the public interest.

Defendant has established that the issues in this case are sufficiently complex and so distinct that one trial on all issues could well perplex the jury. It will be difficult enough to educate the jury about the various concepts comprising the validity, enforceability and infringement issues that influence liability.[1] To include at the same time proof of the damages issues could risk needless juror confusion.

In this case, plaintiff claims royalty damages for defendant's use of plaintiff's patented inventions. The royalty inquiry reaches at least fifteen separate factors, only a few of which are even tangentially related to liability. The jury will have to decide the amount of the reasonable royalty for each patented invention it finds was infringed. The amount of the royalty for each infringed product depends upon detailed and complicated financial and accounting data concerning, among other things, the infringing product's commercial success, and how much of that success can be attributed to the infringed invention.

The Court finds that the jury's task in determining liability will be made significantly easier if it is spared this highly technical evidence until the jury is narrowly focused on the specific issues to which the evidence is relevant (the damages inquiry). *See Shepard*, 45 F.R.D. at 537 (trial of validity, infringement and damages together "would only clutter the record and tend to confuse the jury."). Rather than having to present all the evidence concerning plaintiff's alleged damages at once, the parties can wait to see precisely which inventions and HP calculators are involved, and limit their damages proof to them.

Regarding willful infringement, the Court finds that the same considerations require separation of the proceedings regarding willfulness from the damages and liability phases. It is well-settled that the issue of whether a defendant is liable for increased damages because it willfully infringed a patent is determined by the judge and not the jury. *See Swofford*, 336 F.2d at 412. Evidence of willfulness should be presented in an environment that insures the jury will not be influenced by it.

Accordingly, the Court finds that if it were to take evidence on all issues about liability, damages and willful infringement together, there would be a substantial risk of the type of prejudice from jury confusion contemplated by Rule 42(b). However, the Court also believes that separate juries, separate trials, and separate discovery phases would unduly prejudice plaintiff by unreasonably delaying the end of this case. All of defendant's concerns regarding prejudice from jury confusion can be treated by separating the issues for trial within a single proceeding.

---

1. These concepts include the relevant "prior art," the level of skill in the art, "obviousness," keyboard designs, electrical and mechanical engineering concepts, "enablement," "best mode," "indefiniteness," and "lack of support in the specification."

See Joy Technologies, 772 F. Supp. at 849 (unitary trial favored when court can solve problems by bifurcating issues into different phases within the same trial).[2]

B.

Rule 42(b) also permits courts to phase a case into separate trials on distinct issues if it would be convenient to do so. Central to that question is the determination whether the issues would involve many of the same witnesses and documentary evidence. If the proof overlaps substantially, the parties, the witnesses and the court are inconvenienced by requiring the presentation of evidence several times.

The Court's decision to phase the liability, damages, and willful infringement issues within a single trial with one discovery track will make this proceeding more convenient than if the Court bifurcated the case into separate trials, with two discovery phases and two juries. This model also reduces any problem of evidentiary overlap. In the damages phase, the parties will not have to repeat any evidence relevant to liability that also bears on the reasonable royalty owed.

C.

Finally, Rule 42(b) allows a court to bifurcate a case when separation would promote judicial economy or lead to more rapid final resolution of the dispute. These considerations again weigh against the plan defendants offer. Rather, the Court finds that it can promote the goals of judicial economy and quicker resolution of the case if it maintains one discovery track and one trial, but takes liability issues first, and then proceeds, if necessary, to damages.

Defendant temptingly contends that the prospect of early settlement would be enhanced if the Court orders separate trials and discovery periods. Driven by experience rather than rhetoric, the Court disagrees. It is true that if the Court tries liability first and the jury finds for the plaintiff, the defendant will be likely to redouble its efforts to settle the case rather than risk a highly unfavorable damages verdict. However, neither the plaintiff nor the defendant in such a case is likely to enter serious settlement negotiations until they have done substantial discovery regarding damages. Thus, this argument is unconvincing. Any chances for settling this case will depend upon the good faith willingness of the parties, not their tactical constructs.

An order of separate trials before two juries with two discovery periods would serve judicial economy in one last and important way. If

---

2. Defendant also contends that it will be prejudiced if the Court allows discovery to proceed on the willful infringement issue, because it will be required to reveal to plaintiff confidential attorney-client communications that defendant contemplates will be necessary to defend against these charges. The Court does not agree that defendant will be prejudiced if it must reveal this information. Defendant may indeed be required to give plaintiff any privileged information it plans to use in its defense at trial. However, because this information would presumably support defendant's position, it would not be "prejudiced," in a legal sense, if it had to disclose the material to plaintiff. Furthermore, counsel and the Court are perfectly capable of crafting appropriate protective orders.

the Court limits discovery during the first period to liability only, the parties are likely to come to the Court with repeated disputes over how requested material is related to liability, damages, state of mind, or all these issues. The Court will not escalate the paper war that is surely impending in this case.

Accordingly, defendant's motion is DENIED. However, it is hereby ORDERED that the single trial in this case will proceed in three separate and distinct phases. Liability will first be tried to a verdict, and, if necessary, the trial will proceed immediately thereafter to the damages phase before the same jury. The Court will then discharge the jury and hear evidence regarding willfulness. Discovery will continue as scheduled as to all issues.

Notes

1.   The *Laitram* case is an example of a court using an alternative to actual bifurcation to achieve all the goals of Rule 42: avoiding prejudice, maintaining convenience, and achieving judicial economy. The use of trial "phases" is a feasible means of accomplishing judicial efficiency and convenience without unduly prejudicing any party or delaying judicial determination.

2.   Was the court's reluctance to order separate discovery and trials in the *Laitram* case influenced by the defendant's size and its probable ability to better afford the increase in cost that would result from the separate proceedings?

3.   **Bifurcation of Liability and Damages.** Whether to request bifurcation of the trial depends on many factors. Among those are the questions of delay and cost. With respect to delay, a bifurcation of the liability and damage phases of the trial, so that the damages trial occurs only when liability has been found against the defendant, can result in a considerable delay. In some bifurcation situations, discovery does not commence until after the end of the liability phase. This may result in a delay of several months before the damage trial can be held. After this second discovery period ends, there is yet again the normal and costly preparation and presentation of trial. There is also the practical problem of whether the original jury can be re-assembled. Thus, the second trial may be held much later and before a new jury. One way of overcoming this delay is to permit the taking of all discovery during the same period prior to the liability trial. Following a finding of liability against the defendant, the judge can order the same jury to hear the damage case immediately. As you might imagine, bifurcation that results in delay of trial will also result in extra cost to the clients. It is axiomatic that each month of a litigation will result in a higher overall cost. Thus, significant costs will be added in a case in which final judgment is delayed for six months to a year.

4.   **Bifurcation of Willful Infringement Issues.** Bifurcation, however, may be appropriate in some circumstances. This is particularly true in situations where willful infringement is asserted by the plaintiff and the defendant is forced into the decision of having to rely on advice of counsel as a defense to enhanced damages, thereby waiving the attorney-client privilege. The practical consequence of such a decision is to turn over the

attorney opinions on which the client relied. These opinions often disclose the strategies that will be used in the litigation. They also pose the situation where the attorney who authored the opinions becomes a necessary witness and subject to possible disqualification in the presentation of the trial to a jury. To overcome this situation, courts have suggested that bifurcation of the willful infringement question may be an appropriate way to delay the trial on the willful infringement until after a liability trial has been held. However, often the willful infringement evidence is inextricably intertwined with the infringement evidence, making this is an impractical alternative.

5. **Claim Construction**. With the advent of the *Markman* decision from the Supreme Court concerning the need for the trial judge to perform claim interpretation before the jury trial, there is also the possibility of bifurcation (or trifurcation) for consideration of the claim construction issue prior to the liability phase of the trial. The so-called *"Markman* hearing" can be held prior to the trial to give the judge an opportunity to construe the claims so that the parties know going into trial how the court will interpret the claims. (*See* Chapter Eight, *infra.*) Some courts reject this idea as yet another costly expense for the clients with further delay in the disposition of the case and prefer to hear the presentation of all of the evidence at trial and then interpret the claims just prior to instructing the jury.

ELF ATOCHEM N. AM., INC. v. LIBBEY–OWENS–FORD CO.

894 F. Supp. 844, 37 USPQ2d 1065 (D. Del. 1995)

McKELVIE, District Judge.

I.   The Impact of Markman on Trial of Patent Cases

The Federal Circuit's decision in Markman will undoubtedly change the face of patent litigation as it clearly did in this case. A number of procedural issues flow from this decision.

In the normal course of litigation, courts should endeavor to manage cases in such a way that all claims and issues in a civil action are presented for resolution in one trial. Moreover, in accordance with Congress's mandate in the Civil Justice Reform Act, this court schedules cases for trial within one year from the filing date of the complaint and generally schedules trials to last no more than two weeks.

The court's experience with this relatively rigid time frame shows that it promotes more efficient resolution of civil matters. For example, faced with firm and certain trial dates parties are often encouraged to settle rather than proceed to trial. Furthermore, and perhaps more importantly, this time frame assures parties that by a date certain they will have a final resolution of issues facing and affecting them as a result of litigation. Fixed trial time often leads parties to try only the core issues of their case, without wasting the court's and jury's time with issues upon which the party may have little chance of success.

In spite of this general practice, separate trials or staged resolution of issues may be worthwhile in certain circumstances. *See Johns Hop-*

kins Univ. v. CellPro, 160 F.R.D. 30, 33 (D. Del. 1995). As this court noted, Federal Rule of Civil Procedure 42 provides that a court may order separate trials on claims or issues in an action when it is in the interests of efficient judicial administration. In *CellPro*, this court addressed claims for willful infringement and the resulting mischief which has become a consistent problem in patent cases. This court refused to order separate trials of liability, damages, and willful infringement because CellPro failed to satisfy the requirements of Rule 42.

In *Markman*, the Federal Circuit stated, in no uncertain terms, that it would have the final say as to the meaning of words in a claim of a patent, according no deference to decisions by the various United States District Court Judges. 52 F.3d at 979. That is, in spite of a trial judge's ruling on the meaning of disputed words in a claim, should a three-judge panel of the Federal Circuit disagree, the entire case could be remanded for retrial on different claims.

As evidenced by this case and others pending in this court, in view of *Markman*, parties will now routinely move for the early resolution of the claim construction issue either under Federal Rule of Civil Procedure 56 or 12(b)(6). In a bench trial, the court can delay resolution of the claim construction issue until all of the evidence has been presented. However, in a jury trial, delaying resolution of this issue until trial may raise serious practical problems of how to adequately and fairly rule on these often difficult and vitally important issues at the close of the evidence while a jury waits. Moreover, in jury cases, it may be more efficient to put the case in a posture to have the Federal Circuit review the claim interpretation issue before trying the case to a jury, in order to avoid wasting two weeks or more of a citizen's time because the court erroneously instructed the jury on the meaning of a claim term. However, this approach could add significant time and expense to the ultimate resolution of the litigation.

Sensing the importance of claim construction on the outcome of patent cases, parties will likely seek ways to promptly bring the issue before the Federal Circuit. In cases where parties dispute facts surrounding the accused product, once the court resolves the meaning of claim terms the parties will seek an immediate interlocutory appeal to avoid the possibility of dual trials should the Federal Circuit reverse the trial court's claim construction on an appeal from a jury verdict. Where the parties do not dispute the facts surrounding the accused product, they may stipulate to the remaining issues on infringement and appeal to the Federal Circuit from a final order on that issue. In either situation, a case could be appealed to the Federal Circuit only months after the complaint is filed. This would be an unusual procedure for a district court to consistently face in patent cases.

Finally, it remains to be seen what the impact of the court's new role as arbiter of the meaning of disputed words in the claims of patents will have on a party's right to a jury trial on validity issues. For example, it is unclear how the issue of indefiniteness will be presented to a jury

where this court instructs the jury on the meaning of vague words that commonly appear in patent claims, such as "substantially."

Notes

1.   What is the best argument you can make to support a request that the so-called "*Markman* hearing" should be merged into the trial on the merits, and that after hearing the trial and prior to instructing the jury, the judge interprets the claims? What is your best argument against this proposal?

D.   FINAL PRETRIAL CONFERENCE

Federal Rule of Civil Procedure—Rule 16:

Rule 16. Pretrial Conferences; Scheduling; Management

(d) Final Pretrial Conference. Any final pretrial conference shall be held as close to the time of trial as reasonable under the circumstances. The participants at any such conference shall formulate a plan for trial, including a program for facilitating the admission of evidence. The conference shall be attended by at least one of the attorneys who will conduct the trial for each of the parties and by any unrepresented parties.

(e) Pretrial Orders. After any conference held pursuant to this rule, an order shall be entered reciting the action taken. This order shall control the subsequent course of the action unless modified by a subsequent order. The order following a final pretrial conference shall be modified only to prevent manifest injustice.

(f) Sanctions. If a party or party's attorney fails to obey a scheduling or pretrial order, or if no appearance is made on behalf of a party at a scheduling or pretrial conference, or if a party or party's attorney is substantially unprepared to participate in the conference, or if a party or party's attorney fails to participate in good faith, the judge, upon motion or the judge's own initiative, may make such orders with regard thereto as are just, and among others any of the orders provided in Rule 37(b)(2)(B), (C), (D). In lieu of or in addition to any other sanction, the judge shall require the party or the attorney representing the party or both to pay the reasonable expenses incurred because of any noncompliance with this rule, including attorney's fees, unless the judge finds that the noncompliance was substantially justified or that other circumstances make an award of expenses unjust.

The final pretrial conference constitutes a critical juncture in the litigation process. At this time, the trial's course is outlined by the parties and the court. The accompanying pretrial order will identify the issues, witnesses, exhibits, and other matters to be tried and presented. It will also advise the court of any outstanding motions for summary judgment or *in limine* to be decided. It is often a very intricate document of considerable length, complicated by the fact that it must be prepared as a joint effort of the parties. Many district courts have their own local rules governing the preparation of the pretrial order. The significance of the pretrial order is that it provides a roadmap for the conduct of the

trial and the issues to be litigated. Failure to include a matter in a pretrial order can result in the court forbidding its introduction at trial.

C.   VAN DER LELY N.V. v. F. LLI MASCHIO S.N.C.

221 USPQ 34 (S.D. Ohio 1983)

HOLSCHUH, District Judge

The plaintiff, C. Van de Lely N.V. (hereafter Lely) brings this action for patent infringement against defendant F. Lli Maschio S.n.c. (hereafter Maschio). Maschio has counterclaimed under 28 U.S.C. §§ 2201 and 2202 for a declaratory judgment of invalidity and non-infringement of the patents in suit. The jurisdiction of the Court is invoked under 28 U.S.C. § 1338 with respect to the plaintiff's claim of patent infringement, and under 28 U.S.C. § 2201 with respect to defendant's request for declaratory judgments.

The present action was filed on June 22, 1978. After extensive discovery, numerous conferences between the parties and the Court, and the adoption by the Court of a final pretrial order, which was agreed to by the parties, the trial of this action commenced on November 4, 1982, and concluded on January 6, 1983.

During the course of the trial of this action a number of objections were raised upon which this Court reserved rulings. The plaintiff objected to, and this Court reserved rulings on the admissibility into evidence of defense exhibits XX, GGG, III, YYY, FFFF and K. The Court also reserved rulings on the plaintiff's objections to the qualification of Mr. Richard Killworth, Dr. Louis Boehman, and Mr. Nathaniel French as expert witnesses for the defendant, and to the subsequent testimony of those individuals. Defendant has objected to certain portions of the testimony of two of the plaintiff's expert witnesses, Dr. Holmes and Dr. Smith. Finally, the Court reserved ruling on the objection raised by the plaintiff to the attempt by the defendant to assert the defense of anticipation under 35 U.S.C. § 102. This matter is now before the Court for disposition of those objections.

In addition to the issues left unresolved at trial, the parties have filed several post-trial motions in this action, and these motions must be ruled on at this time. Specifically, this order will address and dispose of the plaintiff's motion to strike and/or for a determination that the plaintiff need not respond to certain portions of defendant's brief, and the defendant's motion to amend the record.

IV.   Defendant's Attempt to Raise New Defenses

A.   *Defendant's Assertion of the Anticipation Defense*

In its opening statement, the defendant asserted that one or more of the plaintiff's patents was invalid for anticipation under 35 U.S.C. § 102. Plaintiff immediately objected to defendant's raising the defense of invalidity due to anticipation under 35 U.S.C. § 102. Plaintiff objected because:

Having expressly disclaimed any such defense in response to an express discovery request in that regard, having amended such a defense out of its Answer, having agreed to a Final Pretrial Order which did not include anticipation as a defense, issue or counter-claim, having denied plaintiff discovery in this regard, and by failing to seek any amendment of the pleadings or the Final Pretrial Order prior to trial, defendant has knowingly waived anticipation as a defense in this action. Moreover, plaintiff would be seriously preju-diced if defendant were now permitted to assert and rely upon a such a defense and claim.

This Court directed the parties to file briefs on the question of whether the defendant should be permitted to raise the issue of anticipa-tion at that point in the trial. After reviewing the materials submitted by the parties, this court reversed ruling on this objection.

The facts in the instant case show that defendant Maschio asserted the defense of anticipation in its original answer. (Defendant's Answer, paragraphs a, b, i, j, and k.) Plaintiff Lely propounded a series of interrogatories to defendant Maschio regarding the basis for Maschio's defenses. Interrogatory No. 36 asked the defendant to:

a. State whether defendant contends that any claim in the patents in suit is anticipated under 35 U.S.C. § 102.

b. * * * identify each claim alleged to be anticipated and identify by date, place, person and subject matter the alleged prior art which defendant contends anticipates the claim.

c. * * * explain in detail where defendant claims to find each element alleged to be anticipated.

Defendant Maschio responded to the plaintiff's interrogatories in April 1979 by stating that it had "not completed its research as to the anticipatory prior art" and that a "specific answer [would be provided] as soon as possible."

A specific response to Interrogatory 36 was finally provided by defendant Maschio in August 1979. The defendant's response stated:

Defendant MASCHIO modified its previous partial answer to state that it does not contend claims of the patents in suit are anticipated under 35 U.S.C. § 102.

Defendant Maschio clarified its response to Interrogatory 36 in 1981 by a "further answer" which once again noted that defendant Maschio "does not contend that claims of the patents in suit are anticipated under 35 U.S.C. 102. * * *" Defendant Maschio stated further that its answer "should be construed as meaning no single prior art patent or other printed publication totally anticipates all of the claimed features of any single LELY patent."

In May 1982 defendant Maschio filed an Amended Answer, which omitted the previously asserted paragraphs raising the defense of antici-pation under 35 U.S.C. § 102. On August 6, 1982, a Final Pretrial Order was filed in this case pursuant to Fed. R. Civ. P. 16. This Order was agreed to by both the defendant and the plaintiff. At no point in the Final Pretrial Order did defendant Maschio raise a defense, issue or claim based on anticipation under 35 U.S.C. § 102. On August 13, 1982, defendant Maschio filed a second Amended Answer and Counterclaim, which also made no mention of a defense or claim of invalidity based on anticipation under 35 U.S.C. § 102.

Finally, the record in this case reveals that defendant Maschio has never attempted to seek an amendment to the Final Pretrial Order to raise the issue of anticipation under 35 U.S.C. § 102. The first time this Court was aware that the defendant would attempt to argue invalidity of the plaintiff's patents under 35 U.S.C. § 102 due to anticipation was during the course of the trial of this case when the defendant mentioned the anticipation issue in its opening statement. Plaintiff has represented that the defendant's opening statement was the first anticipation it had that the defendant would attempt to raise the issue of anticipation.

Defendant Maschio does not dispute any of the above facts. The defendant instead argues that the plaintiff cannot claim surprise or prejudice in this case for a number of reasons. First defendant states that "[a]lthough [its] AMENDED ANSWER specifically avers invalidity based upon obviousness, the language of the AMENDED ANSWER closely parallels the statutory language of 35 U.S.C. 102 (a, b, c, d, e, f and g)." Next defendant argues that counsel for Lely was notified of defendant's position as of October 21, 1982, due to a letter which the defendant sent to plaintiff. That letter listed single prior art references allegedly showing every element of certain claims. Thus, defendant Maschio concludes that the plaintiff should have inferred that the defendant would argue anticipation. Finally, the defendant argues there was no surprise when the defendant attempted to assert the 35 U.S.C. § 102 anticipation issue because during the course of the October 29, 1982, deposition of Mr. Nathaniel R. French, expert witness for the defense, Mr. French indicated he thought the claims of one of the Lely patents were invalid under 35 U.S.C. § 102.

Fed. R. Civ. P. 16 states in pertinent part:

In any action, the court may in its discretion direct the attorneys for the parties to appear before it for a conference to consider

(1) The simplification of the issues;

(2) The necessity or desirability of amendments to the pleadings;

(3) The possibility of obtaining admissions of fact and of documents which will avoid unnecessary proof;

(4) The limitation of the number of expert witnesses;

(5) The advisability of a preliminary reference of issues to a master for findings to be used as evidence when the trial is to be by jury;

(6) Such other matters as may aid in the disposition of the action.

The Court shall make an order which recites the action taken at the conference, the amendments allowed to the pleadings, and the agreements made by the parties as to any of the matters considered, and which limits the issues for trial to those not disposed of by admissions or agreements of counsel; and such order when entered controls the subsequent course of the action, unless modified at the trial to prevent manifest injustice.

The importance of pretrial orders has been recognized by numerous courts. These orders

> play a crucial role in implementing the purposes of the Federal Rules of Civil Procedure "to secure the just, speedy, and inexpensive determination of every action." Fed. R. Civ. P. 1. Unless pretrial orders are honored and enforced, the objectives of the pretrial conference to simplify issues and avoid unnecessary proof by obtaining admissions of fact will be jeopardized if not entirely nullified. Accordingly, a party need offer no proof at trial as to matters agreed to in the order, nor may a party offer evidence or advance theories at the trial which are not included in the order or which contradict its terms. Disregard of these principles would bring back the days of trial by ambush and discourage timely preparation by the parties for trial.

"Issues presented at a pre-trial conference, incorporated in a pretrial order supercede the pleadings in the case." *Howard v. Kerr Glass Mfg. Co.*, No. 81–1246, slip op. At 5 (6th Cir. filed Feb. 9, 1983). Federal courts take the position that

> A "definitive pre-trial order reflecting the agreement of the parties, having been entered into after full discovery, must, of course, control the subsequent course of the action. Fed. R. Civ. P. 16(b)." *Case v. Abrams*, 352 F.2d 193, 195 (10th Cir. 1965). When issues are defined by the pretrial order, "they ought to be adhered to in the absence of some good and sufficient reason." *Id.* at 195–96. The trial judge may therefore reject contentions not included in a proper pretrial order. In the Sixth Circuit "[a] party's failure to advance theories of recovery in the pre-trial statement constitutes waiver."

McKinney v. Galvin, No. 81–1472, slip op. at 2 n.3 (6th Cir., filed March 2, 1983).

In the present case, the parties agreed to and submitted to this Court for approval a detailed and definitive Final Pretrial Order. That order was thirty-two pages in length and included numerous exhibits and appendices. At no point in that order is the issue of anticipation mentioned. Instead, the section of the order dealing with contested issues of fact specifically frames the factual issues as being whether the subject matter of the patent was "obvious," a defense or claim of invalidity pursuant to 35 U.S.C. § 103.[5] This specific framing of the

---

5. Section C of Part IV, Agreed Statements and Lists, of the Final Pretrial Order sets out the issues of fact which the parties agree are contested. Contested issues of fact 12 through 16 set out the contested issues of fact which are relevant to the question of

the patents' validity. Each of these contested issues of fact is framed in terms of obviousness. By way of example contested issue of fact 12 states:

> Were the differences between the subject matter sought to be patented in the four

issues by the parties and the failure of the Final Pretrial Order to mention the defense of anticipation pursuant to 35 U.S.C. § 102, when coupled with the defendant's past acts abandoning the defense of anticipation, compels this Court to conclude that the Final Pretrial Order in this case does not even implicitly include the defense or claim of anticipation.

Under rule 16, this Court has authority to modify the Final Pretrial Order in this case if in the Court's discretion modification was determined to be necessary "to prevent manifest injustice." Although the defendant has never formally requested this Court to modify the Final Pretrial Order in this case and, thus, technically may not be entitled to a modification, the Court will treat the defendant's brief filed on November 9, 1982, on the issue of anticipation as a request to modify the Final Pretrial Order.

Before this Court could properly exercise its discretion to modify the Final Pretrial Order, the Court must consider several factors. These factors include:

1. the degree of prejudice to the defendant resulting from failure to modify;
2. the degree of prejudice to plaintiff from a modification;
3. the impact of a modification at this stage of the litigation on the orderly and efficient conduct to the case; and
4. the degree of willfulness, bad faith or inexcusable neglect on the part of the defendant.

If, after considering these factors, this Court finds that a refusal to allow a modification might result in injustice while allowance would cause no substantial injury to the opponent and no more than slight inconvenience to the court, the Court should permit the Final Pretrial Order to be modified. The burden of establishing manifest injustice sufficient to permit a modification of the Final Pretrial Order falls squarely on the moving party.

Initially, this Court notes that the defendant has recognized and argued the interrelationship between the defense or claim of anticipation under 35 U.S.C. § 102 and the defense or claim of "obviousness" under 35 U.S.C. § 103. In simple terms, if a patent claim is invalid due to anticipation under 35 U.S.C. § 102, that claim would also be invalid due to obviousness under 35 U.S.C. § 103, although a claim that is invalid due to obviousness is not necessarily also invalid due to anticipation. Because of this relationship between the anticipation and obviousness defenses, the defendant in the present case cannot argue that it would be greatly prejudiced by this Court's refusal to modify the Final Pretrial

patents in suit, and the prior art such that the subject matter as a whole would have been obvious at the time the inventions claimed by Plaintiff were made to a person having ordinary skill in the art to which the subject matter pertains, based upon another invention which was known or used by others in this country, or patented or described in a printed publication in this or a foreign country, before the invention thereof by the inventors claimed by Plaintiff?

Order to permit the defendant to assert the issue of anticipation. Although the legal analysis and trial preparation would differ, if the defendant had evidence of anticipation that evidence would also be sufficient to prove the defendant's obviousness claim.

In the present case, if a modification of the Final Pretrial Order had been allowed after the commencement of the trial, it is clear that the plaintiff would have been the victim of surprise and would be greatly prejudiced. The actions of the defendant prior to trial all indicate that the defendant had waived any claim or defense based on anticipation under 35 U.S.C. § 102. The defendant had refused to provide the plaintiff with discovery materials on the issue of anticipation based on the defendant's claim that it was dropping any claim or defense based on anticipation. Thus, the plaintiff was not afforded any opportunity prior to trial to prepare to meet a claim or defense of anticipation. To permit the defendant to "ambush" the plaintiff at trial would create the very prejudice which Fed. R. Civ. P. 16 was designed to eliminate.

Additionally, this Court finds that allowing a modification of the Final Pretrial Order in this case after the commencement of the trial or the case would substantially disrupt the orderly and efficient conduct of the case. This Court feels that a modification to allow the assertion of the anticipation issue would require a substantial delay in the conclusion of this case and force the parties to reopen discovery. If anticipation were an issue in this case the plaintiff would be entitled, in this Court's opinion, to an opportunity to present any additional evidence on this issue that discovery might uncover. In short, the record of the protracted two month trial of this case would have to be reopened in order to insure that the anticipation issue has been fairly and adequately addressed.

Finally, the Court does not need to determine whether the defendant acted in bad faith or willfully in failing to assert the anticipation issue prior to trial because the record establishes that at the very least the failure was due to the defendant's inexcusable neglect. Defendant has offered no explanation for its failure to inform the Court or plaintiff's counsel of the defendant's intention to reassert the anticipation issue after having specifically dropped that issue from this case.

Balancing the above-mentioned factors this Court concludes that it should not, in its discretion, modify the Final Pretrial Order in this case to permit the defendant to assert the previously waived issue of anticipation. The Court feels that under the circumstances of this case, the allowance of such a modification after the commencement of the trial would amount to an abuse of discretion.

Notes

1. What if the evidence adduced at trial supports a new claim not identified in the pre-trial order? Does it make a difference in the Court's consideration of a request to modify the pre-trial order that the adduced evidence also supports another claim that is identified in the pre-trial order?

2. What happens if discovery occurs after the "Final Pre-trial Order" and new evidence is adduced which could support a claim for relief not identified in the Final Pre-trial Order? What arguments would you make to support modification of the pre-trial order?

3. Would it make a difference if the new evidence adduced at trial should have been produced by your opponent during the discovery period?

Chapter Eight

CLAIM CONSTRUCTION

The first step in an infringement suit, for the patentee or the alleged defendant, is to understand the scope of the claims. The claims are the metes and bounds of the inventor's property right. How the claims are construed will often determine infringement and validity. The claim construction must be the same for infringement and validity. While it is possible to defend an infringement suit on grounds unrelated to the scope of the claims, such as laches or equitable estoppel, most cases do involve a question of claim interpretation.

Broken down there are three parts of a claim: the preamble, transition and body. The preamble is the beginning portion of the claim which gives the general technical environment for the claimed invention. The transition is the word or words following the preamble and preceding the body of the claim. The most common transition term is *comprising* (a synonym for which is *including*) because it is an open transition meaning that the claim reads on devices that contain the claimed elements plus any other elements. If the transition words are *consisting of*, a closed transition, then the claims read on a device which has the enumerated elements and nothing else. There is a transition in the middle, *consisting essentially of,* which means that the claim reads on an accused device which has the claimed elements and other elements which do not generally affect or interfere with the activity of the disclosed elements. Finally, the body of the claim introduces the claim elements and sets forth their relationship to each other. Identify the preamble, transition and body in the following claim:

1. A utensil for eating, comprising:

    (a) a handle; and

    (b) three prongs attached to said handle at the same end.

Would this claim read on an accused device with a handle and four prongs? How about on a Swiss army knife which includes a three pronged fork with a handle attached to a number of other devices?

Patents are directed to those skilled in the art to which the subject matter pertains. Terms that appear in the patent claims and written description are to be construed as one of ordinary skill in the art would construe them. There is one exception to this rule: the patentee is permitted to be her own lexicographer. This means that the patentee is free to define terms that she uses in her patent claims anyway she wishes, as long as she defines them in the written description. If, however, the patentee has not defined a term in her written description then that term is to be construed as one of ordinary skill in the art would understand it. Claim construction is a task performed exclusively by the judge and is arguably the most important step in a patent infringement suit. Because patent cases often involve complex cutting-edge technology like semiconductor fabrication processes, human growth hormone or computer software, the judge is seldom one of ordinary skill in the art. Therefore, it is important to educate the judge as to how one of ordinary skill in the art would understand the claim terms. This can be accomplished in many different ways which we will explore in this chapter.

A. WHO CONSTRUES PATENT CLAIMS?— A QUESTION OF LAW

MARKMAN v. WESTVIEW INSTRUMENTS, INC.

517 U.S. 370, 38 USPQ2d 1461 (1996)

Justice SOUTER delivered the opinion of the Court.

The question here is whether the interpretation of a so-called patent claim, the portion of the patent document that defines the scope of the patentee's rights, is a matter of law reserved entirely for the court, or subject to a Seventh Amendment guarantee that a jury will determine the meaning of any disputed term of art about which expert testimony is offered. We hold that the construction of a patent, including terms of art within its claim, is exclusively within the province of the court.

I

The Constitution empowers Congress "[t]o promote the Progress of Science and useful Arts, by securing for limited Times to Authors and Inventors the exclusive Right to their respective Writings and Discoveries." U.S. Const., Art. I, § 8, cl. 8. Congress first exercised this authority in 1790, when it provided for the issuance of "letters patent," Act of Apr. 10, 1790, ch. 7, § 1, 1 Stat. 109, which, like their modern counterparts, granted inventors "the right to exclude others from making, using, offering for sale, selling, or importing the patented invention," in exchange for full disclosure of an invention, H. Schwartz, Patent Law and Practice 1, 33 (2d ed. 1995). It has long been understood that a patent must describe the exact scope of an invention and its manufacture to "secure to [the patentee] all to which he is entitled, [and] to apprise the public of what is still open to them." Under the modern American system, these objectives are served by two distinct elements of a patent document. First, it contains a specification describing the invention "in such full, clear, concise, and exact terms as to enable any person skilled in the art ... to make and use the same." 35 U.S.C. § 112. Second, a patent includes one or more "claims," which "particularly poin[t] out and distinctly clai[m] the subject matter which the applicant regards as his invention." 35 U.S.C. § 112. "A claim covers and secures a process, a machine, a manufacture, a composition of matter, or a design, but never the function or result of either, nor the scientific explanation of their operation." 6 Lipscomb § 21:17, at 315–316. The claim "define[s] the scope of a patent grant," and functions to forbid not only exact copies of an invention, but products that go to "the heart of the invention but avoid the literal language of the claim by making a noncritical change." In this opinion, the word "claim" is used only in this sense peculiar to patent law.

Characteristically, patent lawsuits charge what is known as infringement and rest on allegations that the defendant "without authority ma[de], use[d] or [sold the] patented invention, within the United States during the term of the patent therefor...." 35 U.S.C. § 271(a). Victory in an infringement suit requires a finding that the patent claim "covers the alleged infringer's product or process," which in turn necessitates a determination of "what the words in the claim mean."

Petitioner in this infringement suit, Markman, owns United States Reissue Patent No. 33,054 for his "Inventory Control and Reporting System for Drycleaning Stores." The patent describes a system that can monitor and report the status, location, and movement of clothing in a dry-cleaning establishment. The Markman system consists of a keyboard and data processor to generate written records for each transaction, including a bar code readable by optical detectors operated by employees, who log the progress of clothing through the dry-cleaning process. Respondent Westview's product also includes a keyboard and processor, and it lists charges for the dry-cleaning services on bar-coded tickets that can be read by portable optical detectors.

Markman brought an infringement suit against Westview and Althon Enterprises, an operator of dry-cleaning establishments using Westview's products (collectively, Westview). Westview responded that Markman's patent is not infringed by its system because the latter functions merely to record an inventory of receivables by tracking invoices and transaction totals, rather than to record and track an inventory of articles of clothing. Part of the dispute hinged upon the meaning of the word "inventory," a term found in Markman's independent claim 1, which states that Markman's product can "maintain an inventory total" and "detect and localize spurious additions to inventory." The case was tried before a jury, which heard, among others, a witness produced by Markman who testified about the meaning of the claim language.

After the jury compared the patent to Westview's device, it found an infringement of Markman's independent claim 1 and dependent claim 10. The district court nevertheless granted Westview's deferred motion for judgment as a matter of law, one of its reasons being that the term "inventory" in Markman's patent encompasses "both cash inventory and the actual physical inventory of articles of clothing." Under the trial court's construction of the patent, the production, sale, or use of a tracking system for dry cleaners would not infringe Markman's patent unless the product was capable of tracking articles of clothing throughout the cleaning process and generating reports about their status and location. Since Westview's system cannot do these things, the district court directed a verdict on the ground that Westview's device does not have the "means to maintain an inventory total" and thus cannot "detect and localize spurious additions to inventory as well as spurious deletions therefrom," as required by claim 1.

Markman appealed, arguing it was error for the district court to substitute its construction of the disputed claim term 'inventory' for the construction the jury had presumably given it. The United States Court of Appeals for the Federal Circuit affirmed, holding the interpretation of claim terms to be the exclusive province of the court and the Seventh Amendment to be consistent with that conclusion. Markman sought our review on each point, and we granted certiorari. 515 F.3d 967 (1995). We now affirm.

II

The Seventh Amendment provides that "[i]n Suits at common law, where the value in controversy shall exceed twenty dollars, the right of trial by jury shall be preserved...." U.S. Const., Amdt. 7. Since Justice Story's day, *United States v. Wonson*, 28 F. Cas. 745, 750 (No. 16,750) (CC Mass. 1812), we have understood that "[t]he right of trial by jury thus preserved is the right which existed under the English common law when the Amendment was adopted." Baltimore & Carolina Line, Inc. v. Redman, 295 U.S. 654, 657 (1935). In keeping with our long-standing adherence to this "historical test," Wolfram, *The Constitutional History of the Seventh Amendment*, 57 MINN. L. REV. 639, 640–643 (1973), we ask, first, whether we are dealing with a cause of action that either was tried at law at the time of the Founding or is at least analogous to one that was, *see, e.g., Tull v. United States*, 481 U.S. 412, 417 (1987). If the action in question belongs in the law category, we then ask whether the particular trial decision must fall to the jury in order to preserve the substance of the common-law right as it existed in 1791.

A

As to the first issue, going to the character of the cause of action, "[t]he form of our analysis is familiar. 'First we compare the statutory action to 18th-century actions brought in the courts of England prior to the merger of the courts of law and equity.' " *Granfinanciera, S.A. v. Nordberg*, 492 U.S. 33, 42 (1989). Equally familiar is the descent of today's patent infringement action from the infringement actions tried at law in the 18th century, and there is no dispute that infringement cases today must be tried to a jury, as their predecessors were more than two centuries ago.

B

This conclusion raises the second question, whether a particular issue occurring within a jury trial (here the construction of a patent claim) is itself necessarily a jury issue, the guarantee being essential to preserve the right to a jury's resolution of the ultimate dispute. In some instances the answer to this second question may be easy because of clear historical evidence that the very subsidiary question was so regarded under the English practice of leaving the issue for a jury. But when, as here, the old practice provides no clear answer, we are forced to make a judgment about the scope of the Seventh Amendment guarantee without the benefit of any foolproof test.

The Court has repeatedly said that the answer to the second question "must depend on whether the jury must shoulder this responsibility as necessary to preserve the 'substance of the common-law right of trial by jury.'" *Tull v. United States*, *supra*, at 426 (quoting *Colgrove v. Battin*, 413 U.S. 149, 156 (1973)). "'Only those incidents which are regarded as fundamental, as inherent in and of the essence of the system of trial by jury, are placed beyond the reach of the legislature.'" *Tull v. United States*, *supra*, at 426.

The "substance of the common-law right" is, however, a pretty blunt instrument for drawing distinctions. We have tried to sharpen it, to be sure, by reference to the distinction between substance and procedure. We have also spoken of the line as one between issues of fact and law.

But the sounder course, when available, is to classify a mongrel practice (like construing a term of art following receipt of evidence) by using the historical method, much as we do in characterizing the suits and actions within which they arise. Where there is no exact antecedent, the best hope lies in comparing the modern practice to earlier ones whose allocation to court or jury we do know, seeking the best analogy we can draw between an old and the new, *see Tull v. United States*, *supra*, at 420–421 (we must search the English common law for "appropriate analogies" rather than a "precisely analogous common-law cause of action").

C

"Prior to 1790 nothing in the nature of a claim had appeared either in British patent practice or in that of the American states," Lutz, *Evolution of the Claims of U.S. Patents*, 20 J. PAT. OFF. SOC. 134 (1938), and we have accordingly found no direct antecedent of modern claim construction in the historical sources. Claim practice did not achieve statutory recognition until the passage of the Act of 1836, and inclusion of a claim did not become a statutory requirement until 1870. Although, as one historian has observed, as early as 1850 "judges were ... beginning to express more frequently the idea that in seeking to ascertain the invention 'claimed' in a patent the inquiry should be limited to interpreting the summary, or 'claim,'" Lutz, *supra*, at 145, "[t]he idea that the claim is just as important if not more important than the description and drawings did not develop until the Act of 1870 or thereabouts." Deller, *supra*, § 4, at 9.

At the time relevant for Seventh Amendment analogies, in contrast, it was the specification, itself a relatively new development, that represented the key to the patent. Thus, patent litigation in that early period was typified by so-called novelty actions, testing whether "any essential part of [the patent had been] disclosed to the public before," and "enablement" cases, in which juries were asked to determine whether the specification described the invention well enough to allow members of the appropriate trade to reproduce it.

The closest 18th-century analogue of modern claim construction seems, then, to have been the construction of specifications, and as to that function the mere smattering of patent cases that we have from this period[4] shows no established jury practice sufficient to support an argument by analogy that today's construction of a claim should be a guaranteed jury issue. Few of the case reports even touch upon the proper interpretation of disputed terms in the specifications at issue and none demonstrates that the definition of such a term was determined by the jury. This absence of an established practice should not surprise us, given the primitive state of jury patent practice at the end of the 18th century, when juries were still new to the field. Although by 1791 more than a century had passed since the enactment of the Statute of Monopolies, which provided that the validity of any monopoly should be determined in accordance with the common law, patent litigation had remained within the jurisdiction of the Privy Council until 1752 and hence without the option of a jury trial. Indeed, the state of patent law in the common-law courts before 1800 led one historian to observe that "the reported cases are destitute of any decision of importance. . . . At the end of the eighteenth century, therefore, the Common Law Judges were left to pick up the threads of the principles of law without the aid of recent and reliable precedents." Hulme, *On the Consideration of the Patent Grant, Past and Present*, 13 L.Q. REV. 313, 318 (1897). Earlier writers expressed similar discouragement at patent law's amorphous character, and, as late as the 1830's, English commentators were irked by enduring confusion in the field.

Markman seeks to supply what the early case reports lack in so many words by relying on decisions like *Turner v. Winter*, 1 T.R. 602, 99 Eng. Rep. 1274 (K.B. 1787), and *Arkwright v. Nightingale*, Dav. Pat. Cas. 37 (C.P. 1785), to argue that the 18th-century juries must have acted as definers of patent terms just to reach the verdicts we know they rendered in patent cases turning on enablement or novelty. But the conclusion simply does not follow. There is no more reason to infer that juries supplied plenary interpretation of written instruments in patent litigation than in other cases implicating the meaning of documentary terms, and we do know that in other kinds of cases during this period

---

4. Before the turn of the century, "no more than twenty-two cases came before the superior courts of London." H. DUTTON, THE PATENT SYSTEM AND INVENTIVE ACTIVITY DURING THE INDUSTRIAL REVOLUTION, 1750–1852, p. 71 (1984).

judges, not juries, ordinarily construed written documents. The probability that the judges were doing the same thing in the patent litigation of the time is confirmed by the fact that as soon as the English reports did begin to describe the construction of patent documents, they show the judges construing the terms of the specifications. This evidence is in fact buttressed by cases from this Court; when they first reveal actual practice, the practice revealed is of the judge construing the patent. These indications of our patent practice are the more impressive for being all of a piece with what we know about the analogous contemporary practice of interpreting terms within a land patent, where it fell to the judge, not the jury, to construe the words.[8]

D

Losing, then, on the contention that juries generally had interpretive responsibilities during the 18th century, Markman seeks a different anchor for analogy in the more modest contention that even if judges were charged with construing most terms in the patent, the art of defining terms of art employed in a specification fell within the province of the jury. Again, however, Markman has no authority from the period in question, but relies instead on the later case of *Neilson v. Harford*, Webs. Pat. Cas. 328 (Exch. 1841). There, an exchange between the judge and the lawyers indicated that although the construction of a patent was ordinarily for the court, judges should "leav[e] the question of words of art to the jury," *id.*, at 350 (Alderson, B.); see also *id.*, at 370 (judgment of the court). Without, however, in any way disparaging the weight to which Baron Alderson's view is entitled, the most we can say is that an English report more than 70 years after the time that concerns us indicates an exception to what probably had been occurring earlier.[9] In place of Markman's inference that this exceptional practice existed in 1791 there is at best only a possibility that it did, and for anything more than a possibility we have found no scholarly authority.

III

Since evidence of common law practice at the time of the Framing does not entail application of the Seventh Amendment's jury guarantee to the construction of the claim document, we must look elsewhere to characterize this determination of meaning in order to allocate it as

---

8. As we noted in *Brown v. Huger*, 21 How. 305, 318 (1859):

> With regard to the second part of this objection, that which claims for the jury the construction of the patent, we remark that the patent itself must be taken as evidence of its meaning; that, like other written instruments, it must be interpreted as a whole ... and the legal deductions drawn therefrom must be conformable with the scope and purpose of the entire document. This construction and these deductions we hold to be within the exclusive province of the court.

9. In explaining that judges generally construed all terms in a written document at the end of the 18th century, one historian observed that "[i]nterpretation by local usage for example (today the plainest case of legitimate deviation from the normal standard) was still but making its way." 9 Wigmore, Evidence § 2461, at 195. We need not in any event consider here whether our conclusion that the Seventh Amendment does not require terms of art in patent claims to be submitted to the jury supports a similar result in other types of cases.

between court or jury. We accordingly consult existing precedent and consider both the relative interpretive skills of judges and juries and the statutory policies that ought to be furthered by the allocation.

A

The two elements of a simple patent case, construing the patent and determining whether infringement occurred, were characterized by the former patent practitioner, Justice Curtis. "The first is a question of law, to be determined by the court, construing the letters-patent, and the description of the invention and specification of claim annexed to them. The second is a question of fact, to be submitted to a jury." *Winans v. Denmead*, 15 How., at 338.

In arguing for a different allocation of responsibility for the first question, Markman relies primarily on two cases, *Bischoff v. Wethered*, 9 Wall. 812 (1870), and *Tucker v. Spalding*, 13 Wall. 453 (1872). These are said to show that evidence of the meaning of patent terms was offered to 19th-century juries, and thus to imply that the meaning of a documentary term was a jury issue whenever it was subject to evidentiary proof. That is not what Markman's cases show, however.

In order to resolve the Bischoff suit implicating the construction of rival patents, we considered "whether the court below was bound to compare the two specifications, and to instruct the jury, as a matter of law, whether the inventions therein described were, or were not, identical." 9 Wall., at 813 (statement of the case). We said it was not bound to do that, on the ground that investing the court with so dispositive a role would improperly eliminate the jury's function in answering the ultimate question of infringement. On that ultimate issue, expert testimony had been admitted on "the nature of the various mechanisms or manufactures described in the different patents produced, and as to the identity or diversity between them." *Id.* at 814. Although the jury's consideration of that expert testimony in resolving the question of infringement was said to impinge upon the well-established principle "that it is the province of the court, and not the jury, to construe the meaning of documentary evidence," *id.* at 815, we decided that it was not so. We said:

> the specifications ... profess to describe mechanisms and complicated machinery, chemical compositions and other manufactured products, which have their existence in pais, outside of the documents themselves; and which are commonly described by terms of the art or mystery to which they respectively belong; and these descriptions and terms of art often require peculiar knowledge and education to understand them aright.... Indeed, the whole subject-matter of a patent is an embodied conception outside of the patent itself.... This outward embodiment of the terms contained in the patent is the thing invented, and is to be properly sought, like the explanation of all latent ambiguities arising from the description of external things, by evidence in pais.

Bischoff does not then, as Markman contends, hold that the use of expert testimony about the meaning of terms of art requires the judge to submit the question of their construction to the jury. It is instead a case in which the Court drew a line between issues of document interpretation and product identification, and held that expert testimony was properly presented to the jury on the latter, ultimate issue, whether the physical objects produced by the patent were identical. The Court did not see the decision as bearing upon the appropriate treatment of disputed terms. As the opinion emphasized, the Court's "view of the case is not intended to, and does not, trench upon the doctrine that the construction of written instruments is the province of the court alone. It is not the construction of the instrument, but the character of the thing invented, which is sought in questions of identity and diversity of inventions." *Id.*, at 816. Tucker, the second case proffered by Markman, is to the same effect. Its reasoning rested expressly on Bischoff, and it just as clearly noted that in addressing the ultimate issue of mixed fact and law, it was for the court to "lay down to the jury the law which should govern them." Tucker, *supra*, at 455.

If the line drawn in these two opinions is a fine one, it is one that the Court has drawn repeatedly in explaining the respective roles of the jury and judge in patent cases, and one understood by commentators writing in the aftermath of the cases Markman cites. Walker, for example, read Bischoff as holding that the question of novelty is not decided by a construction of the prior patent, "but depends rather upon the outward embodiment of the terms contained in the [prior patent]; and that such outward embodiment is to be properly sought, like the explanation of latent ambiguities arising from the description of external things, by evidence in pais." A. Walker, Patent Laws § 75, p. 68 (3d ed. 1895). He also emphasized in the same treatise that matters of claim construction, even those aided by expert testimony, are questions for the court:

> Questions of construction are questions of law for the judge, not questions of fact for the jury. As it cannot be expected, however, that judges will always possess the requisite knowledge of the meaning of the terms of art or science used in letters patent, it often becomes necessary that they should avail themselves of the light furnished by experts relevant to the significance of such words and phrases. The judges are not, however, obliged to blindly follow such testimony.

Id., § 189, at 173. Virtually the same description of the court's use of evidence in its interpretive role was set out in another contemporary treatise:

> The duty of interpreting letters-patent has been committed to the courts. A patent is a legal instrument, to be construed, like other legal instruments, according to its tenor.... Where technical terms are used, or where the qualities of substances or operations mentioned or any similar data necessary to the comprehension of the language of the patent are unknown to the judge, the testimony of

witnesses may be received upon these subjects, and any other means of information be employed. But in the actual interpretation of the patent the court proceeds upon its own responsibility, as an arbiter of the law, giving to the patent its true and final character and force.

W. Robinson, Law of Patents § 732, pp. 481–483 (1890).

In sum, neither *Bischoff* nor *Tucker* indicates that juries resolved the meaning of terms of art in construing a patent, and neither case undercuts Justice Curtis's authority.

B

Where history and precedent provide no clear answers, functional considerations also play their part in the choice between judge and jury to define terms of art. We said in *Miller v. Fenton*, 474 U.S. 104, 114 (1985), that when an issue "falls somewhere between a pristine legal standard and a simple historical fact, the fact/law distinction at times has turned on a determination that, as a matter of the sound administration of justice, one judicial actor is better positioned than another to decide the issue in question." So it turns out here, for judges, not juries, are the better suited to find the acquired meaning of patent terms.

The construction of written instruments is one of those things that judges often do and are likely to do better than jurors unburdened by training in exegesis. Patent construction in particular "is a special occupation, requiring, like all others, special training and practice. The judge, from his training and discipline, is more likely to give a proper interpretation to such instruments than a jury; and he is, therefore, more likely to be right, in performing such a duty, than a jury can be expected to be." *Parker v. Hulme*, 18 F. Cas. at 1140. Such was the understanding nearly a century and a half ago, and there is no reason to weigh the respective strengths of judge and jury differently in relation to the modern claim; quite the contrary, for "the claims of patents have become highly technical in many respects as the result of special doctrines relating to the proper form and scope of claims that have been developed by the courts and the Patent Office." Woodward, *Definiteness and Particularity in Patent Claims*, 46 Mich. L.Rev. 755, 765 (1948).

Markman would trump these considerations with his argument that a jury should decide a question of meaning peculiar to a trade or profession simply because the question is a subject of testimony requiring credibility determinations, which are the jury's forte. It is, of course, true that credibility judgments have to be made about the experts who testify in patent cases, and in theory there could be a case in which a simple credibility judgment would suffice to choose between experts whose testimony was equally consistent with a patent's internal logic. But our own experience with document construction leaves us doubtful that trial courts will run into many cases like that. In the main, we expect, any credibility determinations will be subsumed within the necessarily sophisticated analysis of the whole document, required by the standard construction rule that a term can be defined only in a way that comports with the instrument as a whole. Thus, in these cases a jury's capabilities to evaluate demeanor, *cf. Miller*, *supra*, at 114, 117, to sense the "mainsprings of human conduct," *Commissioner v. Duberstein*, 363 U.S. 278, 289 (1960), or to reflect community standards, *United States v. McConney*, 728 F.2d 1195, 1204 (9th Cir. 1984) (*en banc*), are much less significant than a trained ability to evaluate the testimony in relation to the overall structure of the patent. The decisionmaker vested with the task of construing the patent is in the better position to ascertain whether an expert's proposed definition fully comports with the specification and claims and so will preserve the patent's internal coherence. We accordingly think there is sufficient reason to treat construction of terms of art like many other responsibilities that we cede to a judge in the normal course of trial, notwithstanding its evidentiary underpinnings.

C

Finally, we see the importance of uniformity in the treatment of a given patent as an independent reason to allocate all issues of construction to the court. As we noted in *General Elec. Co. v. Wabash Appliance Corp.*, 304 U.S. 364, 369 (1938), "[t]he limits of a patent must be known for the protection of the patentee, the encouragement of the inventive genius of others and the assurance that the subject of the patent will be dedicated ultimately to the public." Otherwise, a "zone of uncertainty which enterprise and experimentation may enter only at the risk of infringement claims would discourage invention only a little less than unequivocal foreclosure of the field," *United Carbon Co. v. Binney & Smith Co.*, 317 U.S. 228, 236, 55 USPQ 381 (1942), and "[t]he public [would] be deprived of rights supposed to belong to it, without being clearly told what it is that limits these rights." *Merrill v. Yeomans*, 94 U.S. 568, 573 (1877). It was just for the sake of such desirable uniformity that Congress created the Court of Appeals for the Federal Circuit as an exclusive appellate courts for patent cases, H.R.Rep. No. 97–312, pp. 20–23 (1981), observing that increased uniformity would "strengthen the United States patent system in such a way as to foster technological growth and industrial innovation." *Id.* at 20.

Uniformity would, however, be ill served by submitting issues of document construction to juries. Making them jury issues would not, to be sure, necessarily leave evidentiary questions of meaning wide open in every new court in which a patent might be litigated, for principles of issue preclusion would ordinarily foster uniformity. But whereas issue preclusion could not be asserted against new and independent infringement defendants even within a given jurisdiction, treating interpretive issues as purely legal will promote (though it will not guarantee) intrajurisdictional certainty through the application of stare decisis on those questions not yet subject to interjurisdictional uniformity under the authority of the single appeals court.

Accordingly, we hold that the interpretation of the word "inventory" in this case is an issue for the judge, not the jury, and affirm the decision of the Court of Appeals for the Federal Circuit.

Notes

1. **Procedural Problems for the District Courts.** When Should *Markman* Hearings Occur? In *Elf Atochem North America, Inc. v. Libbey–Owens–Ford Co.*, 894 F. Supp. 844, 37 USPQ2d 1065 (D. Del. 1995), Judge McKelvie discussed when the district court judge could construe patent claims:

> the "obligation" created by the Federal Circuit to instruct the jury on the meaning of the words used by an inventor in a claim basically leaves a district court with three options. The court can attempt to resolve these disputes on the paper record. Second, the court can hold a trial to resolve the disputes. Finally, the court can wait until trial and attempt to resolve claim disputes the evening before the jury must be instructed.

Id. at 850. District courts are experimenting with the timing and manner of conducting claim construction. Some district courts refuse to conduct Markman hearings, instead construing the claims using only the patent and prosecution history for guidance. Others routinely conduct Markman hearings like mini-trials where the parties may argue their interpretations and present evidence and expert witnesses, after which the court determines the claim construction. In *Elf*, the court conducted a two-day bench trial to resolve the dispute over the meaning of claim terms before the jury trial. *Id.* Judge Rader of the Federal Circuit, sitting by designation in a patent trial, conducted a model patent trial which included a two-day evidentiary hearing (a Markman hearing) to receive testimony from qualified experts about the meaning of the patent claims. *See Loral Fairchild Corp. v. Victor Co. of Japan, Ltd.*, 906 F. Supp. 798, 802 (E.D.N.Y. 1995). The court permitted each side to present two expert witnesses. *Id.* Judge Rader counseled that:

> with most aspects of trial hinging on this determination—now "strictly a question of law for the court"—a conscientious court will generally endeavor to make this ruling before trial. A trial court faced with conflicting views of technical terms may prudently enlist the aid of qualified experts to determine the meaning of the claim terms. As in this case, this proceeding to assist the court in ascertaining the law is likely to occur after discovery in which the parties have exchanged information relevant to their understanding of the claims.

Loral Fairchild Corp. v. Victor Co. of Japan, 911 F. Supp. 76, 79 (E.D.N.Y. 1996) (Rader, J., sitting by designation). However, not all district courts will agree to resolve claim construction prior to trial. *See Johns Hopkins Univ. v. Cellpro, Inc.*, 894 F. Supp. 819, 826–27 (D. Del. 1995) (the court informed the parties of its claim construction on the eve of the last day of trial).

Often, the parties will prefer an early *Markman* hearing since claim construction is often dispositive of infringement or validity. A good way to do this is to bring a summary judgment motion of infringement or noninfringement near the close of discovery. Early claim construction also ensures that the jury is presented with only relevant evidence. If the court waits until the end of the trial to proffer a claim construction, the experts who testified for the losing party on claim construction will have little credibility with the jury as the judge would have already instructed the jury that the claims should not be construed as that expert opined. On the other hand, judges dislike the technical nature of the questions presented in patent cases and may prefer to put off the distasteful exercise as long as possible. They may also believe that it is more efficient not to hold a Markman hearing when the same witnesses will be called at trial. When do you think the district court should render a claim construction?

In his dissent in *Cybor Corp. v. FAS Techs., Inc.*, 138 F.3d 1448, 1474–75 n. 12, 46 USPQ2d 1169, 1190 n. 12 (Fed. Cir. 1998) (*in banc*), Judge Rader stated that Markman "dictates many deviations from the normal procedural course for litigation." Judge Rader identified several of the new procedural obstacles below:

The following is an incomplete list of procedural deviations required by Markman I:

1. Multiple trials, problem I: If hearings are necessary to interpret complex claims, the trial court must set aside time in its crowded docket for one proceeding to interpret claims and a second (potentially with a jury) to determine infringement and other issues.

2. Claim interpretation, problem I: Fearing that it may not receive the opportunity to supplement expert reports or reopen discovery after the judge's interpretation, a party often argues alternative claim construction theories from the outset of litigation. This extends the time and expense of the claim interpretation proceedings.

3. Bias toward summary judgments: In practical terms, Markman I directs the proceedings toward summary judgment on the central issue of the litigation at a potentially premature stage of issue development. Prematurely addressing issues, even at the appellate level, can result in expensive repetition of effort. *See CVI/Beta Ventures, Inc. v. Tura LP*, 112 F.3d 1146, 1157–58, 1160 n.7, 42 USPQ2d 1577, 1585, 1587 n.7 (Fed. Cir. 1997) (finding error in a claim construction that had been affirmed in an earlier appeal), *cert. denied*, 118 S. Ct. 1039 (1998).

4. Claim interpretation, problem II: As soon as the trial court issues a claim interpretation, both sides often seek to shift their original claim interpretations to accommodate the judge's views. Thus, the parties seek to revise expert reports or reopen discovery to account for the judge's interpretation. This maneuvering leads to procedural battles over surprise and motions for additional time to prepare for trial. *See Loral Fairchild Corp. v. Victor Co.*, 906 F. Supp. 798 (E.D.N.Y. 1995) (interpreting claims); *Loral Fairchild Corp. v. Victor Co.*, 911 F. Supp. 76, 80–81 (E.D.N.Y. 1996) (preventing plaintiff from changing theory of infringement in response to claim interpretation).

5. The new evidence dilemma: As a result of the new and perhaps somewhat unexpected interpretation, the parties scramble to create and acquire new evidence for their infringement arguments.

6. The learning curve problem: Like all human endeavors, claim interpretation is a learning process. The trial judge makes every effort to state the precise scope of the claims at the close of the initial proceeding, but often, with the additional learning during the infringement trial, realizes that the initial interpretation was too broad or too narrow in some respects. The judge then faces the dilemma of changing the rules in the middle of the game.

7. The judge as a trial issue: With the judge's claim interpretation central to the issues of infringement, trial counsel will try to exploit the judge's stature with the jury to show that the court is on their side.

8. Multiple trials, problem II: In the words of United States District Court Judge Roderick McKelvie: "[I]n spite of a trial judge's ruling on the meaning of disputed words in a claim, should a three-judge panel of the Federal Circuit disagree, the entire case could be remanded for retrial on [a] different [claim interpretation]." *Elf Atochem North Am., Inc. v. Libbey–Owens–Ford Co.*, 894 F. Supp. 844, 857, 37 USPQ2d 1065, 1075 (D. Del. 1995).

Trial judges can often address each of the above with careful case management, but at the cost of expending scarce trial court resources.

2. The Northern District of California Claim Construction Rules. The United States District Court for the Northern District of California has established Local Rules of Practice in Patent Cases. N.D. Cal. Civ. L.R. §§ 16(6)-(11). These local rules specifically address claim construction procedures and hearings in patent cases. The claim construction procedures require each party to serve a Proposed Claim Construction Statement on all other parties. This statement is to include: the identification of any special or uncommon meanings for words or phrases within the claim; material in the specification or prosecution history that describes or explains the elements of the claim; and extrinsic evidence such as expert testimony and inventor testimony that supports the proposed claim construction. Each opposing party must then file a Response to Proposed Claim Construction Statement in which it must identify any disputed terms and explain why its proposed construction is the proper one. Once all parties have served their responses, the parties meet and confer to prepare a Joint Claim Construction Statement. The joint statement must include: the construction of the claim terms on which all parties agree; each parties proposed construction for disputed terms; suggested dates for holding the Claim Construction Hearing; and a list of witnesses to be called at the hearing, along with the subject matter of each witness' testimony and an estimate of the time required for the testimony. Within 30 days of receiving the joint statement, the court will send the parties a notice for the Claim Construction Hearing. Each phase in the claim construction process requires adherence to time limitations specified in the rules, which promotes rapid adjudication once the Complaint has been filed. The local rules were adopted in July 1997. Although no other district courts have adopted their own local rules, at least one other court has used the Northern District's rules as a guide. *See Precision Shooting Equip., Inc. v. High Country Archery*, 1 F. Supp.2d 1041 (D. Ariz. 1998).

3. **What should the standard of review be for claim construction?** Does the Supreme Court opinion in *Markman* resolve the issue of what should be the standard of review on appeal? The Federal Circuit generally applied the *de novo* standard of review following the Supreme Court's decision in *Markman*. In some cases, however, a clearly erroneous standard was applied to findings considered to be factual in nature that are incident to the judge's construction of patent claims. *See Eastman Kodak Co. v. Goodyear Tire & Rubber Co.*, 114 F.3d 1547, 1555–56, 42 USPQ2d 1737, 1742 (Fed. Cir. 1997) (reliance on expert testimony to clarify ambiguous claim term is acceptable and deference is given to the district court's credibility determination); *Serrano v. Telular Corp..*, 111 F.3d 1578, 1586, 42 USPQ2d 1538, 1544 (Fed. Cir. 1997) (Mayer, J., concurring); *Metaullics Sys. Co. v. Cooper,* 100 F.3d 938, 939, 40 USPQ2d 1798, 1799 (Fed. Cir. 1996). In these cases, the court (Chief Judge Mayer and Judge Rader) contended that while the Supreme Court did conclude that claim construction is a matter for the judge, not the jury, it did not hold that claim construction was entirely a matter of law or that *de novo* review should exist on appeal. *See Metaullics*, 100 F.3d at 939, 40 USPQ2d at 1799 ("Even if this court were to disregard the Supreme Court's functional rationale, because claim construction is a mixed question of law and fact, we may be required to defer to a trial court's factual findings. Where a district court makes findings of fact as a part of claim construction, we may not set them aside absent clear error.") (citations omitted). The Federal Circuit resolved this conflict *in banc* when it decided *Cybor Corp. v. FAS Techs., Inc.*, 138 F.3d 1448, 1454, 46 USPQ2d 1169, 1173 (Fed. Cir. 1998) (*in banc*). The Court confirmed its holding in *Markman v. Westview Instruments, Inc.*, 52 F.3d 967, 979, 34 USPQ2d 1321, 1329 (Fed. Cir. 1995) (*in banc*)—that claim construction is a purely legal issue subject to *de novo* review on appeal. Can you think of any circumstances where the district court judge must make factual findings in construing the claims? Where does Judge Mayer's clear error, also known as the clearly erroneous standard of review, come from?

4. **How will the Standard of Review Affect Predictability?** Do you think *de novo* review by the Federal Circuit of claim construction will increase or decrease predictability for the litigants in a patent case? Do you think the number of claim construction reversals by the Federal Circuit will increase or decrease? Should a more deferential standard of review apply? Could a deferential standard of review result in inconsistent claim constructions?

5. **Interlocutory Appeals.** Certification of the claim construction issue for interlocutory appeal pursuant to 28 U.S.C. § 1292(b) (1994) could be a way to obtain a prompt claim construction decision from the Federal Circuit. The district court could interpret the claims and certify that issue for immediate appeal. However, the Federal Circuit has thus far refused to grant interlocutory appeals which are certified for appeal from the district

courts on claim construction issues. In *Flores v. Union Pacific R. R.*, 101 F.3d 715 (Table) (Fed. Cir. 1996), the trial court certified an interlocutory judgment for appeal after a Markman hearing, but the Federal Circuit refused to accept the appeal—on the ground that it was not in the interest of judicial efficiency to do so. What would be the pros and cons of permitting the losing party to immediately appeal the district court's claim construction? *See* John B. Pegram, *Markman and its Implications*, 78 J. Pat. & Trademark Off. Soc'y 560, 567 (1996) (listing five reasons why certification might not become a common practice). Should the parties litigate infringement and validity under the district court's claim construction only to have the construction reversed on appeal or should the losing party on claim construction just stipulate to have judgment entered against her on infringement in order to be able to appeal this issue immediately?

6.   What happens if on appeal the Federal Circuit interprets the claims differently than the parties or the district court during the trial? Should the case be remanded for a new trial on infringement under this new claim construction so that the parties have a chance to proffer evidence on this new construction? *See Exxon Chem. Patents, Inc. v. Lubrizol Corp.*, 64 F.3d 1553, 35 USPQ2d 1801 (Fed. Cir. 1995); *J.T. Eaton & Co. v. Atlantic Paste & Glue Co.*, 106 F.3d 1563, 41 USPQ2d 1641 (Fed. Cir. 1997) (the Federal Circuit did not adopt the claim constructions of the trial court or the interpretations offered by both parties, instead relying on the testimony of a single expert witness to establish the meaning of a patent claim).

7.   Should the Federal Circuit's claim construction be final and binding? Can the Federal Circuit render one claim construction on an appeal from a preliminary injunction hearing and then render a different claim construction when the case is appealed after final judgment? *See CVI/Beta Ventures, Inc. v. Tura LP,* 112 F.3d 1146, 42 USPQ2d 1577 (Fed. Cir. 1997); *CVI/BETA Ventures, Inc. v. Tura LP*, 120 F.3d 1260, 43 USPQ2d 1860 (Fed. Cir. 1997).

VITRONICS CORP. v. CONCEPTRONIC, INC.

90 F.3d 1576, 39 USPQ2d 1573 (Fed. Cir. 1996)

Before MICHEL and LOURIE, Circuit Judges, and FRIEDMAN, Senior Circuit Judge.

MICHEL, Circuit Judge.

Vitronics Corporation ("Vitronics") appeals the September 27, 1995 order of the United States District Court for the District of New Hampshire, entering judgment as a matter of law that Vitronics did not prove that Conceptronic, Inc. ("Conceptronic") infringed claim 1 of U.S. Patent No. 4,654,502 ("the '502 patent").... Because we conclude that the specification of the '502 patent dictates a claim interpretation in accordance with the plaintiff's proposed construction, and that, so construed, the '502 patent may have been infringed, we reverse the trial court's decision and remand for further proceedings.

BACKGROUND

The Patented Invention

Vitronics and Conceptronic both manufacture ovens used in the production of printed circuit boards. The ovens are used to solder electrical devices (such as resistors, capacitors and integrated circuits) to the boards. Several methods of soldering devices to boards have been developed; the '502 patent, assigned to Vitronics, is directed to one of those methods.

Specifically, the '502 patent is directed to a method for the reflow soldering of surface mounted devices to a printed circuit board in which the circuit board is moved by a conveyor through a multizone oven. In this process, a solder paste is placed on the circuit board and the devices to be soldered (with attached connectors) are placed on the paste. The circuit board is then placed on what is basically a conveyor belt running through an oven and passing through several different heating zones. In the final and hottest zone, the solder paste melts and forms a connection between the device and the circuit board. The boards remain in the last heating zone for only a short duration, allowing the solder to reach a temperature high enough to cause the solder to melt and reflow while maintaining the devices themselves below the solder reflow temperature. Due to this temperature differential, the solder flows up the device connectors to form a solid connection.

[At issue is how the phrase "solder reflow temperature" in claim 1 should be construed.]

Proceedings Before the District Court

This action was brought on November 26, 1991 by Vitronics against Conceptronic for infringement of both the '502 patent. At the time the suit was filed, Conceptronic was selling the "Mark series" line of ovens. Conceptronic later discontinued the Mark series and began selling the "HVC series" line of ovens. Prior to trial, the parties stipulated that every limitation of claim 1 of the '502 patent was met by the HVC series of ovens, except the limitation requiring the utilization of "nonfocused infrared panel emitters" and the limitation that the temperature of the devices must be maintained below the "solder reflow temperature."

Vitronics, by way of a request for a jury instruction, asked the court to construe the meaning of the "solder reflow temperature" limitation. The specific instruction sought by Vitronics was as follows:

> In considering the question of whether the '502 method patent has been infringed by the Mark and HVC Series ovens, you have to decide whether, in use, those ovens maintain the temperature of the devices below the solder reflow temperature. The phrase "solder reflow temperature" in the '502 patent means the temperature reached by the solder during the period it is reflowing during the final stages of the soldering process, sometimes referred to as the "peak solder reflow temperature." It does not mean the "liquidus temperature," the temperature at which the solder first begins to

melt. Thus, if the temperature of the devices stays below that of the solder, the '502 method patent is infringed by the Mark and HVC Series ovens.

Thus, Vitronics contended that, as used in the claim, solder reflow temperature means peak reflow temperature, i.e., a temperature approximately 20° C above the liquidus temperature, at which the solder is completely melted and moves freely. Conceptronic, on the other hand, contended that solder reflow temperature means 183° C, i.e., the liquidus temperature of a particular type of solder known as 63/37 (Sn/Pb) solder.

The district court delayed construing the disputed language until the close of testimony, at which time it ruled in favor of Conceptronic and concluded that the term "solder reflow temperature" as used in claim 1 refers to 183° C. Vitronics then conceded that the court was required to grant judgment as a matter of law in favor of Conceptronic, as Vitronics had not presented any evidence of infringement under the court's interpretation of solder reflow temperature. This appeal followed.

Claim Construction Aids Before the District Court

In spite of Vitronics' early request for a jury instruction on the proper claim construction, the district court delayed announcing its claim construction until hearing all the evidence put forth at trial. During trial, and in their briefs to the district court in support of their respective claim constructions, the parties discussed the patent specification, expert testimony, prior testimony and writings of Vitronics and its employees, and technical references. The most pertinent materials are discussed below.

The Patent Specification

Vitronics relied heavily upon the patent itself to support its asserted claim construction. Although Vitronics conceded that the term "solder reflow temperature" may be ambiguous when considered in isolation, it argued that the specification clearly shows that, as used in the claim, solder reflow temperature means peak reflow temperature rather than the liquidus temperature. In particular, Vitronics pointed to that part of the specification that describes a preferred embodiment:

> A preferred embodiment of the invention for reflow soldering of surface mounted devices to printed circuit boards will now be described. The printed circuit boards are typically made of epoxy-glass, such as fire retardant 4(FR-4), or polyamide glass. These boards typically degrade above temperatures of 225° C. The solder may be, for example, 60/40 (Sn/Pb), 63/37 (Sn/Pb), or 62/36/2 (Sn/Pb/Ag), all of which have a liquidus temperature (i.e. begin to melt) of about 190° C and a peak reflow temperature of about 210°–218° C. Thus, to effect reflow soldering without damaging the board, the solder must be allowed to reach a temperature of at least 210° C, but the board cannot reach a temperature of 225° C.

* * *

The board is then sent into a fifth zone 5 to bring the temperature of the board up to a temperature of approximately 210° C, the devices up to approximately 195° C, and the solder up to approximately 210° C for a period of time of from about 10 to about 20 seconds to cause the solder to flow. Because the devices are cooler than the board, the solder flows up the devices.... The board spends approximately 60 seconds in the fifth zone, but only about 10 to 20 seconds at 210° C. Thus, the board is at the solder reflow temperature for only a short period of time and the devices never reach the solder reflow temperature.

Vitronics pointed out that, in the example described as the preferred embodiment, the temperature of the solder is raised to 210° C, the peak reflow temperature, and the temperature of the devices is raised to 195° C, 5° above the 190° C liquidus temperature. Thus, as argued by Vitronics, the term "solder reflow temperature" must be construed so that it refers to the peak reflow temperature because the claim requires that the temperature of the devices be maintained below "said solder reflow temperature"; if solder reflow temperature were construed to refer to liquidus temperature, the preferred embodiment would not be covered by the patent claims.

Expert Testimony

Conceptronic relied heavily on the expert testimony of Dr. Rothe. Dr. Rothe testified that the meaning of the term "solder reflow temperature" in claim 1 is synonymous with liquidus temperature. Dr. Rothe further testified that the solder reflow temperature for 63/37 (Sn/Pb) is 183° C. Dr. Rothe likewise testified at trial that several technical articles written by those skilled in the art supported his view that solder reflow temperature refers to liquidus temperature.

The Testimony of Mr. Hall

Conceptronic also relied on the testimony of Mr. Hall, the Chief Engineer at Vitronics. At trial, Mr. Hall confirmed that during his deposition he had testified that the reflow temperature of solder was 183° C. Mr. Hall also testified that, during his deposition, he had used solder reflow temperature to refer to liquidus temperature. However, at another point in his trial testimony, Hall explained that, while in his earlier deposition testimony he had used solder reflow temperature to refer to liquidus temperature, he did not suggest that was how the term was used in the patent. Rather, Hall testified the patent uses the term to refer to the peak reflow temperature.

In its brief supporting its proposed construction of claim 1, both at the trial court level and here on appeal, Conceptronic relied on a memorandum written by Vitronics which contains the following language: "Tin/lead solders commonly used by the electronic products industry have a 'liquidus' or 'reflow' temperature in the order of 183° C." However, this phrase is in the background section of the memorandum and later in the same memorandum, Vitronics discussed the issue of infringement as being whether the temperature of the devices was maintained below "the temperatures of the leads at which the solder is reflowing."

Without indicating which evidence it relied upon, the district court simply ruled that solder reflow temperature meant 183° C.

ANALYSIS

The Use of Intrinsic and Extrinsic Evidence in Claim Construction

A literal patent infringement analysis involves two steps: the proper construction of the asserted claim and a determination as to whether the accused method or product infringes the asserted claim as properly construed. *Markman v. Westview Instruments, Inc.*, 52 F.3d 967, 976, 34 USPQ2d 1321, 1326 (Fed. Cir. 1995) (*in banc*).... Claim construction is the only step in the infringement analysis at issue in this appeal.

In determining the proper construction of a claim, the court has numerous sources that it may properly utilize for guidance. These sources have been detailed in our previous opinions, as discussed below, and include both intrinsic evidence (e.g., the patent specification and file history) and extrinsic evidence (e.g., expert testimony).

It is well-settled that, in interpreting an asserted claim, the court should look first to the intrinsic evidence of record, i.e., the patent itself, including the claims, the specification and, if in evidence, the prosecution history. Such intrinsic evidence is the most significant source of the legally operative meaning of disputed claim language.

First, we look to the words of the claims themselves, both asserted and nonasserted, to define the scope of the patented invention. Although words in a claim are generally given their ordinary and customary meaning, a patentee may choose to be his own lexicographer and use terms in a manner other than their ordinary meaning, as long as the special definition of the term is clearly stated in the patent specification or file history. *Hoechst Celanese Corp. v. BP Chems. Ltd.*, 78 F.3d 1575, 1578, 38 USPQ2d 1126, 1129 (Fed. Cir. 1996) ("A technical term used in a patent document is interpreted as having the meaning that it would be given by persons experienced in the field of the invention, unless it is apparent from the patent and the prosecution history that the inventor used the term with a different meaning."); *Hormone*, 904 F.2d at 1563, 15 USPQ2d at 1043 ("It is a well-established axiom in patent law that a patentee is free to be his or her own lexicographer and thus may use terms in a manner contrary to or inconsistent with one or more of their ordinary meanings.").

Thus, second, it is always necessary to review the specification to determine whether the inventor has used any terms in a manner inconsistent with their ordinary meaning. The specification acts as a dictionary when it expressly defines terms used in the claims or when it defines terms by implication. As we have repeatedly stated, "[c]laims must be read in view of the specification, of which they are a part." The specification contains a written description of the invention which must be clear and complete enough to enable those of ordinary skill in the art to make and use it. Thus, the specification is always highly relevant to the claim construction analysis. Usually, it is dispositive; it is the single best guide to the meaning of a disputed term.

Third, the court may also consider the prosecution history of the patent, if in evidence. This history contains the complete record of all the proceedings before the Patent and Trademark Office, including any express representations made by the applicant regarding the scope of the claims. As such, the record before the Patent and Trademark Office is often of critical significance in determining the meaning of the claims. *See Markman*, 52 F.3d at 980, 34 USPQ2d at 1330; *Southwall Tech., Inc. v. Cardinal IG Co.*, 54 F.3d 1570, 1576, 34 USPQ2d 1673, 1676 (Fed. Cir. 1995) ("The prosecution history limits the interpretation of claim terms so as to exclude any interpretation that was disclaimed during prosecution."). Included within an analysis of the file history may be an examination of the prior art cited therein. *Autogiro Co. of Am. v. United States*, 181 Cl. Ct. 55, 384 F.2d 391, 399, 155 USPQ 697, 704 (1967) ("In its broader use as source material, the prior art cited in the file wrapper gives clues as to what the claims do not cover.").

In most situations, an analysis of the intrinsic evidence alone will resolve any ambiguity in a disputed claim term. In such circumstances, it is improper to rely on extrinsic evidence. *See, e.g., Pall Corp. v. Micron Separations, Inc.*, 66 F.3d 1211, 1216, 36 USPQ2d 1225, 1228 (Fed. Cir. 1995) ("In construing the claims we look to the language of the claims, the specification, and the prosecution history. Extrinsic evidence may also be considered, if needed to assist in determining the meaning or scope of technical terms in the claims."); *Hormone*, 904 F.2d at 1562, 15 USPQ2d at 1043 ("Claim interpretation involves a review of the specification, the prosecution history, the claims (including unasserted as well as asserted claims), and, if necessary, other extrinsic evidence, such as expert testimony."). In those cases where the public record unambiguously describes the scope of the patented invention, reliance on any extrinsic evidence is improper. The claims, specification, and file history, rather than extrinsic evidence, constitute the public record of the patentee's claim, a record on which the public is entitled to rely. In other words, competitors are entitled to review the public record, apply the established rules of claim construction, ascertain the scope of the patentee's claimed invention and, thus, design around the claimed invention. Allowing the public record to be altered or changed by extrinsic evidence introduced at trial, such as expert testimony, would make this right meaningless. The same holds true whether it is the patentee or the alleged infringer who seeks to alter the scope of the claims.

The Proper Construction of the Claim Term "Solder Reflow Temperature"

As can be readily seen from those portions of the specification set forth above, the meaning of the disputed term "solder reflow temperature" in claim 1 of the '502 patent is clear from a reading of the claim itself and the patent specification. The "peak reflow temperature" and "liquidus temperature" are clearly defined in the specification as having distinctly different meanings. Specifically, for the solders described in the specification, liquidus temperature is about 190° C and the peak reflow temperature is about 210° to 218° C. Moreover, in the preferred embodiment described in the patent, the solder is heated to a temperature of 210° C but the temperature of the devices is maintained at approximately 195° C, i.e., below the peak reflow temperature (210° C) but above the liquidus temperature (190° C). Therefore, in order to be consistent with the specification and preferred embodiment described therein, claim 1 must be construed such that the term "solder reflow temperature" means the peak reflow temperature, rather than the liquidus temperature. Indeed, if "solder reflow temperature" were defined to mean liquidus temperature, a preferred (and indeed only) embodiment in the specification would not fall within the scope of the patent claim. Such an interpretation is rarely, if ever, correct and would require highly persuasive evidentiary support, which is wholly absent in this case. *See Modine Mfg. Co. v. United States Int'l Trade Comm'n*, 75 F.3d 1545, 1550, 37 USPQ2d 1609, 1612 (Fed. Cir. 1996); *see also Hoechst*, 78 F.3d at 1581, 38 USPQ2d at 1130 ("We share the district court's view that it is unlikely that an inventor would define the invention in a way that excluded the preferred embodiment, or that persons of skill in this field would read the specification in such a way.").

The District Court's Reliance on Extrinsic Evidence

Since the claim, read in light of the patent specification, clearly uses the term "solder reflow temperature" to mean the peak reflow temperature, rather than the liquidus temperature, that should have been the end of the trial court's analysis. Only if there were still some genuine ambiguity in the claims, after consideration of all available intrinsic evidence, should the trial court have resorted to extrinsic evidence, such as expert testimony, in order to construe claim 1. Moreover, even if the judge permissibly decided to hear all the possible evidence before construing the claim, the expert testimony, which was inconsistent with the specification and file history, should have been accorded no weight.

Here, the trial judge considered not only the specification, but also expert testimony and other extrinsic evidence, such as the paper written by the former Vitronics employee. No doubt there will be instances in which intrinsic evidence is insufficient to enable the court to determine the meaning of the asserted claims, and in those instances, extrinsic evidence, such as that relied on by the district court, may also properly be relied on to understand the technology and to construe the claims. Extrinsic evidence is that evidence which is external to the patent and file history, such as expert testimony, inventor testimony, dictionaries, and technical treatises and articles.[6] However, as we have recently re-

---

6. Although technical treatises and dictionaries fall within the category of extrinsic evidence, as they do not form a part of an integrated patent document, they are worthy of special note. Judges are free to consult such resources at any time in order to better understand the underlying technology and may also rely on dictionary defi-

emphasized, extrinsic evidence in general, and expert testimony in particular, may be used only to help the court come to the proper understanding of the claims; it may not be used to vary or contradict the claim language. Nor may it contradict the import of other parts of the specification. Indeed, where the patent documents are unambiguous, expert testimony regarding the meaning of a claim is entitled to no weight. "Any other rule would be unfair to competitors who must be able to rely on the patent documents themselves, without consideration of expert opinion that then does not even exist, in ascertaining the scope of a patentee's right to exclude." Nor may the inventor's subjective intent as to claim scope, when unexpressed in the patent documents, have any effect. Such testimony cannot guide the court to a proper interpretation when the patent documents themselves do so clearly.

In addition, a court in its discretion may admit and rely on prior art proffered by one of the parties, whether or not cited in the specification or the file history. This prior art can often help to demonstrate how a disputed term is used by those skilled in the art. Such art may make it unnecessary to rely on expert testimony and may save much trial time. As compared to expert testimony, which often only indicates what a particular expert believes a term means, prior art references may also be more indicative of what all those skilled in the art generally believe a certain term means. Once again, however, reliance on such evidence is unnecessary, and indeed improper, when the disputed terms can be understood from a careful reading of the public record. Nor may it be used to vary claim terms from how they are defined, even implicitly, in the specification or file history.

Unfortunately, here the trial judge did use the extrinsic evidence to vary or contradict the manifest meaning of the claims. The trial judge was presented with expert testimony and other evidence that some of those skilled in the relevant art, including certain Vitronics employees, sometimes used the term "solder reflow temperature" and "liquidus temperature" interchangeably. He apparently relied on this testimony in reaching his conclusion that, as used in claim 1, solder reflow temperature meant 183° C.[7] However, regardless of how those skilled in the art would interpret a term in other situations, where those of ordinary skill, on a reading of the patent documents, would conclude that the documents preclude the term being given the meaning propounded by the expert witnesses, we must give it the meaning indicated by the patentee in the patent claim, specification and file history. Thus, expert testimony tending to show that those skilled in the art would, in certain circumstances, understand "solder reflow temperature" to mean the solder liquidus temperature is entitled to no weight in light of the clear

nitions when construing claim terms, so long as the dictionary definition does not contradict any definition found in or ascertained by a reading of the patent documents.

7. Although the trial judge's reasoning does not appear in the record, he must have relied on the testimony presented by Conceptronic that "solder reflow temperature" and "liquidus temperature" were synonymous and the undisputed testimony that the liquidus temperature of 63/37 (Sn/Pb) solder is 183° C.

contrary meaning shown in the specification. Because the specification clearly and unambiguously defined the disputed term in the claim, reliance on this extrinsic evidence was unnecessary and, hence, legally incorrect.

Had the district court relied on the expert testimony and other extrinsic evidence solely to help it understand the underlying technology, we could not say the district court was in error. But testimony on the technology is far different from other expert testimony, whether it be of an attorney, a technical expert, or the inventor, on the proper construction of a disputed claim term, relied on by the district court in this case. The latter kind of testimony may only be relied upon if the patent documents, taken as a whole, are insufficient to enable the court to construe disputed claim terms. Such instances will rarely, if ever, occur.

Notes

1. **Hierarchy of Evidence.** Clearly a hierarchy of evidence has arisen for judges to use in construing claims. In construing the claims in a patent, courts look to three main sources: (1) the claim language, (2) the specification, and (3) the prosecution history. *Markman v. Westview Instruments, Inc.*, 52 F.3d 967, 979, 34 USPQ2d 1321, 1329 (Fed. Cir. 1995), *aff'd*, 517 U.S. 370 (1996). The court may also consider extrinsic evidence when helpful, such as expert testimony, learned treatises, and even sales literature. *Markman*, 52 F.3d at 979–980, 34 USPQ2d at 1329–30.

> Extrinsic evidence consists of all evidence external to the patent and prosecution history, including expert and inventor testimony, dictionaries, and learned treatises. This evidence may be helpful to explain scientific principles, the meaning of technical terms, and terms of art that appear in the patent and prosecution history. Extrinsic evidence may demonstrate the state of the prior art at the time of the invention.

Id. at 980, 34 USPQ2d at 1330.

2. **Who should testify in a Markman hearing?** Although in *Vitronics*, the Federal Circuit held that the district court improperly relied on expert testimony to alter the plain meaning of the claim, that does not mean that expert testimony should never be presented. Expert testimony is often necessary to explain the technology to the judge. A court may receive testimony from experts to aid the court in coming to a correct conclusion as to the meaning of claim terms or to understand the technology. Hence, even if the claims can be construed solely be reference to the intrinsic evidence, it is not unusual for the district court to receive extrinsic evidence such as expert testimony as background information and to explain the technology. In *Mantech Environmental Corp. v. Hudson Environmental Services, Inc.*, 152 F.3d 1368, 1373, 47 USPQ2d 1732, 1737 (Fed. Cir. 1998), the Court held:

> In this case, the district court was legally correct both in admitting and accepting the testimony of the parties' expert witnesses "for the purpose of background in the technical area at issue," CleanOX, slip op. at 5, and then basing its claim construction solely upon

intrinsic evidence. Although this information always may be admitted by the trial court to educate itself about the patent and the relevant technology, the claims and the written description remain the primary and more authoritative sources of claim construction. Thus, they always must be considered and where clear must be followed. In this case, the claims and written descriptions are dispositive, for they clearly define a "well" more narrowly than the extrinsic evidence. Therefore, it was not legal error as Mantech proposes for the district court to refuse to rely on the expert testimony for anything more than background.

The experts can be technical experts testifying as to how one of ordinary skill in the art would interpret a term or patent experts. The patent experts are frequently practitioners, former Commissioners of Patents, Patent Office Officials or law professors with experience interpreting claims and familiarity with patent office practice. While the inventor may testify as to how one of ordinary skill in the art would interpret the patent claims, the inventor may not testify as to what he meant in the patent claim. *Markman v. Westview Instruments, Inc.*, 52 F.3d 967, 985–86, 34 USPQ2d 1321, 1334–35 (Fed. Cir. 1995) (*in banc*) ("No inquiry as to the subjective intent of the applicant or P.T.O. is appropriate or even possible in the context of a patent infringement suit. The intent of the inventor when he used a particular term is of little or no probative weight in determining the scope of a claim (except as documented in the prosecution history)."). There are also several limits regarding the introduction of testimony by the examiner who examined the patent application. That testimony can only be introduced through deposition and is limited to factual matters and cannot probe the mental process of the examiner. *See Green v. Rich Iron Co.*, 944 F.2d 852, 853, 20 USPQ2d 1075, 1076 (Fed. Cir. 1991). The focus of claim construction is on the objective test of how one of ordinary skill in the art would construe the claim term, not the subjective intent of the parties.

3. **One of Ordinary Skill in the Art.** "As a general rule, the construing court interprets words in a claim as one of skill in the art at the time of invention would understand them. Therefore, the testimony of one skilled in the art about the meaning of claim terms at the time of the invention will almost always qualify as relevant evidence." *Eastman Kodak Co. v. Goodyear Tire & Rubber Co.*, 114 F.3d 1547, 1555, 42 USPQ2d 1737, 1742 (Fed. Cir. 1997) (citations omitted). Some dispute can arise over whether the expert is one of ordinary skill in the art. Factors to determine the level of ordinary skill in the art include: the educational level of the inventor, the educational level of those who work in the industry, types of problems encountered in the art, prior art solutions to the problems, how quickly advances are made, and the sophistication of the technology.

4. **Ambiguous Words in a Claim**. Using imprecise language in claim terms can be tricky. Such terms include: "about," "approximately," "essentially," "close to," "substantially," or "relatively." Although imprecise, these terms are generally not found legally indefinite. As long as the patent disclosure gives one skilled in the art sufficient guidance to enable him to ascertain the scope of the claim with reasonable certainty and provided the terms in question adequately distinguish the claimed subject matter from

the prior art. In *Andrew Corp. v. Gabriel Elec.*, 847 F.2d 819, 821, 6 USPQ2d 2010, 2012 (Fed. Cir. 1988), the Federal Circuit explained:

> The district court held the Knop patent claims invalid, stating that terms in the claims such as "approach each other", "close to", "substantially equal", and "closely approximate", with reference to the E-plane and H-plane RPEs, were too vague to satisfy the requirement of definiteness stated in 35 U.S.C. § 112. One or more of these terms appears in each of the claims ... The criticized words are ubiquitous in patent claims. Such usages, when serving reasonably to describe the claimed subject matter to those of skill in the field of the invention, and to distinguish the claimed subject matter from the prior art, have been accepted in patent examination and upheld by the courts. As this court put it in *Rosemount, Inc. v. Beckman Instruments, Inc.*, 727 F.2d 1540, 1546–47, 221 USPQ 1, 7 (Fed. Cir. 1984):
>
>> Beckman attacks the claims as indefinite, primarily because "close proximity" is not specifically or precisely defined. As stated in the district court's Memorandum Decision, "to accept Beckman's contention would turn the construction of a patent into a mere semantic quibble that serves no useful purpose."
>
> In *Rosemount* the district court found that " 'close proximity' is as precise as the subject matter permits."

See also Peter G. Dilworth, *About "About" and other Imprecise Claim Terms*, 78 JPTOS 423 (1996); Richard G. Berkley, *Some Practical Aspects of Amendment Practice in the Electromechanical Arts*, 464 PLI/Pat 157, 199–200 (1996).

B. CANONS OF CLAIM INTERPRETATION

Like canons of statutory construction, canons or rules for claim construction have been developing.

> The task of claim construction requires us to examine all the relevant sources of meaning in the patent record with great care, the better to guarantee that we determine the claim's true meaning. As we have often noted, these sources include the patent's claims, specification, and, if in evidence, its prosecution history. In addition, a number of canons, such as the doctrine of claim differentiation, guide our construction of all patent claims.

Athletic Alternatives, Inc. v. Prince Mfg., Inc., 73 F.3d 1573, 1578, 37 USPQ2d 1365, 1370 (Fed. Cir. 1996) (citations omitted). These canons of claim construction are tools to be employed in claim construction methodology, they provide guideposts, but no one is always dispositive or absolute in its application. The next section of this chapter discusses many of the canons of claim construction which have been established by the Federal Circuit.

1. CLAIMS SHOULD BE INTERPRETED SUCH THAT THE PREFERRED EMBODIMENT FALLS WITHIN THEIR SCOPE

As the Federal Circuit held in *Vitronics*, an interpretation of a claim which would not include the preferred embodiment disclosed in the specification is "rarely, if ever, correct." 90 F.3d at 1583. *See also Gentry Gallery, Inc. v. Berkline Corp.*, 134 F.3d 1473, 1477, 45 USPQ2d 1498, 1501 (Fed. Cir. 1998); *Abtox, Inc. v. Exitron Corp.*, 131 F.3d 1009, 1010 (Fed. Cir. 1997); *Modine Mfg. Co. v. United States Int'l Trade Comm'n*, 75 F.3d 1545, 1550, 37 USPQ2d 1609, 1612 (Fed. Cir. 1996); *Hoechst Celanese Corp. v. BP Chems. Ltd.*, 78 F.3d 1575, 1581, 38 USPQ2d 1126, 1130 (Fed. Cir. 1996).

2. A PATENT CLAIM IS NOT NECESSARILY LIMITED TO THE PREFERRED EMBODIMENT/LIMITATIONS FROM THE WRITTEN DESCRIPTION SHOULD NOT BE READ INTO THE CLAIMS

Limitations from the specification and the preferred embodiment disclosed therein should not be read into the claims. *See Cybor Corp. v. FAS Tech. Inc.*, 138 F.3d 1448, 1471, 46 USPQ2d 1169, 1187 (Fed. Cir. 1998). A patent claim is not necessarily limited to the preferred embodiment. *See Transmatic*, 53 F.3d at 1277; *Laitram Corp. v. Cambridge Wire Cloth Co.*, 863 F.2d 855, 865, 9 USPQ2d 1289, 1299 (Fed. Cir. 1988) ("References to a preferred embodiment, such as those often present in a specification, are not claim limitations."); *Texas Instruments, Inc. v. United States Int'l Trade Comm'n*, 805 F.2d 1558, 1563, 231 USPQ 833, 835 (Fed. Cir. 1986) ("This court has cautioned against limiting the claimed invention to preferred embodiments or specific examples in the specification."). "Ordinarily a claim element that is claimed in general descriptive words, when a numerical range appears in the specification and in other claims, is not limited to the numbers in the specification or the other claims." *Modine Mfg. Co. v. United States Int'l Trade Comm'n*, 75 F.3d 1545, 1551, 37 USPQ2d 1609, 1612 (Fed. Cir. 1996). While a limitation from the specification should not be read into a broadly written claim, a claim interpretation must be supported by the specification otherwise there is a potential written description problem under § 112. *See Gentry Gallery, Inc. v. Berkline Corp.*, 134 F.3d 1473, 1479–80, 45 USPQ2d 1498, 1502–03 (Fed. Cir. 1998).

3. TWO CLAIMS IN THE SAME PATENT SHOULD BE INTERPRETED AS HAVING DIFFERENT SCOPE—THE DOCTRINE OF CLAIM DIFFERENTIATION

Under the doctrine of claim differentiation one should presume that there is a difference in scope among the claims of a patent. *See D.M.I., Inc. v. Deere & Co.*, 755 F.2d 1570, 225 USPQ 236 (Fed. Cir. 1985). "When a limitation is included in several claims but is stated in terms of apparently different scope, there is a presumption that a difference in scope is intended and is real. Such a presumption can be overcome, but the evidence must be clear and persuasive." *Modine Mfg. Co. v. United States Int'l Trade Comm'n,* 75 F.3d 1545, 1551, 37 USPQ2d 1609, 1612 (Fed. Cir. 1996). When some claims are broad and others claims are narrow, the narrow limitations cannot be read into the broad claims. *See D.M.I.,* 755 F.2d at 1574, 225 USPQ at 239. For example, in *Transmatic, Inc. v. Gulton Indus.,* 53 F.3d 1270, 35 USPQ2d 1035 (Fed. Cir. 1995), claim 1 included a "light housing" for a public transit vehicle. Claim 3, which was dependant on claim 1, required that the "light housing" have "a horizontal wall with an inward securement formation" for attachment to a vehicle. The Federal Circuit held that the doctrine of claim differentiation prevented the court from reading the structural limitation of claim 3 into claim 1. 53 F.3d at 1277–78, 35 USPQ2d at 1041.

In *Autogiro Co. of Am. v. United States,* 384 F.2d 391, 404, 155 USPQ 697, 708 (Ct. Cl. 1967), the court ruled:

> The concept of claim differentiation ... states that claims should be presumed to cover different inventions. This means that an interpretation of a claim should be avoided if it would make the claim read like another one. Claim differentiation is a guide, not a rigid rule. If a claim will bear only one interpretation, similarity will have to be tolerated.

The doctrine of claim differentiation cannot, however, broaden claims beyond their correct scope as determined in light of the specification and prosecution history. *See Multiform Desiccants, Inc. v. Medzam, Ltd.,* 133 F.3d 1473, 45 USPQ2d 1429 (Fed. Cir. 1998). This means that claims which are written differently may ultimately cover the same subject matter. *See Moleculon Research Corp. v. CBS, Inc.,* 793 F.2d 1261, 1269, 229 USPQ 805, 810 (Fed. Cir. 1986) (affirming claim construction even though it rendered a dependant claim redundant). Consider this excerpt from *Tandon Corp. v. United States Int'l Trade Comm'n,* 831 F.2d 1017, 1023, 4 USPQ2d 1283, 1288 (Fed. Cir. 1987):

> There is presumed to be a difference in meaning and scope when different words or phrases are used in separate claims. To the extent that the absence of such difference in meaning and scope would make a claim superfluous, the doctrine of claim differentiation states the presumption that the difference between claims is significant. At the same time, practice has long recognized that "claims may be multiplied ... to define the metes and bounds of the invention in a variety of different ways." Thus two claims which read differently can cover the same subject matter. Further, as this court stated in *D.M.I.,* 755 F.2d at 1574 n. 2, 225 USPQ at 238 n. 2, "[c]laims are always interpretable in light of the specification that led to the patent." *See also Autogiro,* 384 F.2d at 397, 155 USPQ at 702 ("No matter how clear a claim appears to be, lurking in the background are documents that may completely disrupt initial views on its meaning").... Whether or not claims differ from each other, one can not interpret a claim to be broader than what is contained in the specification and claims as filed.

4. CLAIMS SHOULD BE INTERPRETED SO AS TO PRESERVE THEIR VALIDITY

"When claims are amenable to more than one construction, they should when reasonably possible be interpreted so as to preserve their validity." *Modine Mfg. Co. v. United States Int'l Trade Comm'n,* 75 F.3d 1545, 1557, 37 USPQ2d 1609, 1617 (Fed. Cir. 1996). *See also Texas Instruments, Inc. v. United States Int'l Trade Comm'n*, 871 F.2d 1054, 1065, 10 USPQ2d 1257, 1265 (Fed. Cir. 1989) ("Ambiguous claims, whenever possible, should be construed so as to preserve their validity."); *ACS Hosp. Sys., Inc. v. Montefiore Hosp.*, 732 F.2d 1572, 1577, 221 USPQ 929, 932 (Fed. Cir. 1984). However, this rule of construction does not justify reading a limitation into a claim which the patentee expressly deleted during prosecution. *See Texas Instruments*, 871 F.2d at 1065, 10 USPQ2d at 1265.

This canon of construction is often employed by the alleged infringer who will argue that if the patent is construed in the manner suggested by the patentee, the patent will be invalid for failure to enable or obviousness or some other invalidity grounds. The claim construction determination provides an ideal time to introduce the judge to invalidity concepts and the prior art of record. The alleged infringer must take care to preserve her affirmative invalidity defenses separately as well so that if the judge rules in favor of the patentee, she can still present an invalidity case at trial. When interpreting claims should all prior art be considered or only prior art of record?

5. WHEN THERE IS AN EQUAL CHOICE BETWEEN A BROAD AND A NARROW CLAIM CONSTRUCTION, THE NARROW ONE SHOULD ALWAYS BE ADOPTED

In *Athletic Alternatives, Inc. v. Prince Mfg., Inc.*, 73 F.3d 1573, 37 USPQ2d 1365 (Fed. Cir. 1996), the Federal Circuit held that when a claim is subject to two possible constructions, the narrower construction should be adopted as a penalty for the patentee's ambiguity. In *Athletic Alternatives*, the claim term at issue recited a pattern of splay for a tennis racket where the offset distance of the string splay "varies between" minimum distances and maximum distances. The issue was whether "varies between" means that the distance of string splay must change (any accused product which had two different distances, a minimum and a maximum would infringe) or whether "varies between" means that the offset distance must take on at least three values, the minimum, the maximum and an intermediate value. The tennis racket accused of infringing in this case had only two different string splay distances. The specification offered no guidance and the prosecution history supported both interpretations. The Court held that both proposed claim constructions were equally plausible meanings and because under § 112 the patentee is required to particularly point out and distinctly claim the patented invention, the narrower construction should be adopted.

6. A TERM USED REPEATEDLY IN THE PATENT CLAIMS SHOULD BE CONSTRUED CONSISTENTLY

If a claim term appears in more than one claim, it should be construed the same in each. *See CVI/Beta Ventures, Inc. v. Tura LP*, 112 F.3d 1146, 1159, 42 USPQ2d 1577, 1586 (Fed. Cir. 1997). In general, a claim term that appears in both a parent and a continuation application will have the same meaning. *Sanders Brine Shrimp Co. v. Bonneville Artemia Int'l, Inc.*, 970 F. Supp. 892, 899–900 (D. Utah 1997).

7. A PREAMBLE IS A LIMITATION WHEN IT BREATHES LIFE AND MEANING INTO THE CLAIMS

The purpose of a preamble is to set forth the general nature of the invention being claimed. In general, the preamble is not a claim limitation. Therefore, it need not normally be present in an infringing device in order for infringement to exist. However, the preamble acts as an additional claim limitation in two circumstances: (1) if a claim term gets its significance or meaning from the preamble; or (2) if the preamble is essential to particularly point out the invention defined by the claims. What do these terms mean?

The most common way to determine if a claim term gets its meaning from the preamble is if the preamble actually defines the element first and the claim refers back. For example, in *Bell Communications Research, Inc. v. Vitalink Communications Corp.*, 55 F.3d 615, 620, 34 USPQ2d 1816, 1820 (Fed. Cir. 1995), the court held that where the claim body expressly refers back to the preamble, it will be a limitation. In *Bell Communications*, the court held, "[t]hese two steps of the claimed method, by referring to *'said* packet,' expressly incorporate by reference the preamble phrase 'said packet including a source address and a destination address." 55 F.3d at 621, 34 USPQ2d at 1820.

The introductory phrase is essential to point out the invention defined by the claims, if it is necessary to give life and meaning to the claims. "When the claim drafter chooses to use both the preamble and the body to define the subject matter of the claimed invention, the invention so defined, and not some other, is the one the patent protects." *Bell Communications Research, Inc. v. Vitalink Communications Corp.*, 55 F.3d 615, 620, 34 USPQ2d 1816, 1820 (Fed. Cir. 1995). For example, when the patentee uses the claim preamble to recite structural limitations of his claimed invention, the preamble is a claim limitation. *See In re Paulsen*, 30 F.3d 1475, 1479, 31 USPQ2d 1671, 1673 (Fed. Cir. 1994) ("[T]erms appearing in a preamble may be deemed limitations of a claim when they give meaning to the claim and properly define the invention.") (internal quotation omitted); *London v. Carson Pirie Scott & Co.*, 946 F.2d 1534, 1539, 20 USPQ2d 1456, 1459 (Fed. Cir. 1991) ("The shank is defined in the preamble as that portion of the hanger 'between the supporting hook for the hanger and the support for the garment.' This is not merely a suggested use or 'clarifying language,' as London argues, but rather a limitation supported by structure which must be satisfied by Samsonite's clamp, either literally or equivalently[,] if infringement is to be found."); *Loctite Corp. v. Ultraseal Ltd.*, 781 F.2d 861, 866, 228 USPQ 90, 92 (Fed. Cir. 1985) ("Although it appears in the preambles of the '012 patent claims, the term 'anaerobic' breathes life and meaning into the claims and, hence, is a necessary limitation to them."); *Perkin-Elmer Corp. v. Computervision Corp.*, 732 F.2d 888, 896, 221 USPQ 669, 675 (Fed. Cir. 1984) ("The system of claim 1 is one of unity magnification and is image forming. Those limitations appear in the preamble, but are necessary to give meaning to the claim and properly define the invention."). Also keep in mind that the specification and the prosecution history inform your analysis as to whether or not the preamble is a claim limitation. Was the preamble added in response to a rejection by the examiner? This would also be an indicator that the preamble constitutes a limitation.

Another clue as to whether the preamble constitutes a legal limitation is whether it has been consistently applied throughout the entire set of claims. For example, if a patent read:

1.   A trolling motor, comprising:

   (a) a handle;

   (b) a thrust motor connected to said handle; and

   (c) a means for securing said thrust motor to a boat.

2.   A bow-mounted trolling motor, comprising:

   (a) a handle;

   (b) a thrust motor connected to said handle;

   (c) a means for securing said thrust motor to a boat; and

   (d) a propeller attached to said thrust motor.

In this example, it is likely that the phrase "bow-mounted trolling motor" will be construed as a legal limitation.

The preamble should not be treated as a limitation where the claim apart from the introductory clause completely defines the subject matter of the invention, and the preamble merely stated a purpose or intended use of that subject matter. In the following example, the terms "motor for trolling" is not likely to be construed as a legal limitation, it is more likely just a statement of purpose or intended use for the claimed invention.

1.   A motor for trolling, comprising:

   (a) a handle;

   (b) a thrust motor connected to said handle; and

   (c) a means for securing said thrust motor to a boat.

Remember our example at the beginning of the chapter, the claim for a fork:

1.   A utensil for eating, comprising:

   (a) a handle; and

(b) three prongs attached to said handle at the same location.

Does this preamble constitute a claim limitation? If not, could this claim then be asserted against every farmer using a pitch fork to bail hay?

Whether a preamble breathes life and meaning into a claim is a difficult issue. There is certainly not a black letter rule. There are cases going each way which seem almost indistinguishable from one another. Consequently there is a lot of room for dispute and argument when an infringement case involves a question of whether the preamble constitutes a limitation. Finally, when a Jepson claim is involved, the preamble always constitutes a limitation. A Jepson claim is a claim to an improvement where the preamble recites the prior art and the body recites the improvement.

8. A PATENTEE CAN BE HIS OWN LEXICOGRAPHER

An inventor is free to define words used in a claim. However, where the inventor chooses to redefine words she must clearly indicate the new definition in the patent or prosecution history and she must use it consistently in the specification. Where the inventor fails to clearly indicate she has adopted an uncommon or new definition to a word used in a claim, the common meaning to one of ordinary skill in the art controls. *See Markman v. Westview Instruments, Inc.,* 52 F.3d 967, 980, 34 USPQ2d 1321, 1330 (Fed. Cir. 1995) (*in banc*), *aff'd,* 517 U.S. 370 (1996) ("[A] patentee is free to be his own lexicographer. The caveat is that any special definition given to a word must be clearly defined in the specification.") (citations omitted). The specification should be considered a dictionary for construing the claims.

In *Desper Products Inc. v. QSound Labs Inc.,* 157 F.3d 1325, 48 USPQ2d 1088 (Fed. Cir. 1998), the Court held that based on the prosecution history, the claim term "prior to" should be construed to mean following despite the plain meaning of the words.

Prosecution history is an important source of intrinsic evidence in interpreting claims because it is a contemporaneous exchange between the applicant and the examiner.... During the prosecution of claim 7 of the '462 patent, QSound treated claim 1 and claim 7 (then claim 8) together even though one used "following" language and the other used "prior to" language. In successfully overcoming the prior art rejection based on the British patent, QSound argued that "claims 1 and 8 have been amended hereby to make it more clear that the first channel signal is always maintained separate and apart from the second channel signal following the step of altering the amplitude and shifting the phase in at least one of those signals." (Emphasis added). Thus, even though only claim 1 included the "following" language, QSound itself considered the scope of claims 1 and 8 commensurate in this regard.

Because the public has the right to rely on the applicants' remarks in seeking allowance of their claims, we agree with the district court that "prior to" should be construed to mean after the altering of the amplitude and shifting of the phase has begun.

Id. at 1336–37, 48 USPQ2d at 1096–97 (citations omitted). Is this going too far?

There is a tension between using the specification to interpret a claim term and impermissibly reading a limitation which appears in the specification into the claims. Limitations should not be read from the specification into a claim in which they do not appear. In *Renishaw v. Marposs Societe per Azioni*, 158 F.3d 1243, 48 USPQ2d 1117 (Fed. Cir. 1998), the Court addressed this very tension. The claim required that the probe generate a trigger signal "when said sensing tip contacts an object." Renishaw argued that the term "when" should be given its broad dictionary definitions such as "at or after" or "in the event that." If the term was given one of these broad definitions, then the claim would read on a device that does not generate a signal until after contact and deflection. The court acknowledged that the claim language itself precluded signal generation at the precise moment of contact, and that some deflection would occur before signaling. However, the court held that the specification indicates that the patentee wanted to generate the signal as soon as possible after contact and that this provides insight into the interpretation of "when." Therefore, the claim covers probes which generate signals within a non-appreciable period of time after contact (the delay in generating the signal must be insignificant). The court differentiated between reading a limitation into the claim from the written description and using the written description to interpret a term that appears in the claim. Do you agree with this conclusion by the court?

9. CLAIM CONSTRUCTION ESTOPPEL

The prosecution history informs the claim construction analysis. The doctrine of prosecution history estoppel applies to limit the range of equivalents that a claim is entitled to under the doctrine of equivalents. It is not generally correct to refer to prosecution history estoppel in the context of claim construction and literal infringement. However, we know that the prosecution history affects how the claim terms are to be construed for all purposes, not just the doctrine of equivalents.

Problems

Below you will find a fictional U.S. patent for an electronic autopilot system for a trolling motor.[8] You represent either Mike's Fishing, the '835 patent assignee, or Mark's Boats.

Mark's Boats manufactures and sells a bow-mounted trolling motor, The Easy Troller, with an electronic autopilot system. Mike's Fishing has accused Mark's Boats of infringing the '835 patent. Upon an examination of The Easy Troller and its sales literature you discover that it has an autopilot coupled to a trolling motor. It has a heading detector which is essential just

---

8. This fictitious patent is based on a United States Patent No. 5,202,835 issued to Steven J. Knight and assigned to John-son Fishing Inc. It is used in this book with their permission.

like the heading detector of the '835 patent except that it uses a magnetometer instead of a compass to determine the heading. When the motor deviates from the target heading by 5% the heading detector sends a heading signal to the microprocessor in the steering circuit. The heading detector and the steering circuit are optically coupled. The steering circuit is connected by a wire to the steering motor and it tells the steering motor whether to turn right or left. The steering motor is connected by gears to the lower motor. You are not certain whether the Easy Troller has a manual override switch. You meet with one of Mark's boat mechanics, Bobby, who says:

> I don't think The Easy Troller infringes because the trolling motor does not turn in response to input signals from the steering motor. Everyone in the industry refers to the trolling motor as everything that comes in the box. If you go to Target to buy one of these things the boxes are marked trolling motors. The whole machine is the trolling motor. Here look, even the sales literature from Mike's Fishing, the assignee, refers to the trolling motor as the whole package. The way I read the claim, the trolling motor has to turn left or right in response to signals from the steering motor. Well, the whole Easy Troller does not turn left or right. The only parts that turn are the steering motor, the shaft, and the lower motor which produces the thrust.

Bobby is 22 and has been working with boats since he was 10 years old. He says he plans on going to college in a few years. He wants to become a mechanical engineer.

1. Is there any additional information you would like to obtain before you advise your client? Have you performed a sufficient pre-filing investigation under Rule 11 to file a complaint?

2. You consult Mr. Salmon who has been working in the fishing boat and motor industry for 30 years. Mr. Salmon has two patents of his own on fishing motors. You tell Mr. Salmon about Bobby's comments. Mr. Salmon scratches his head and says, "The kid is right. When we talk about a trolling motor we are talking about the whole package." Mr. Salmon is willing to testify.

3. You contact Michael Perch, the inventor, who says that he did not intend to limit the invention to a compass, that is why the claim says heading detector. He also tells you that he did not intend to require that the whole machine rotate. He points out that on the product that he designed, and that Mike's Fishing sells, all the parts do not rotate.

4. Based on the information you currently have prepare a claim chart and be prepared to argue for your client's claim construction in an upcoming *Markman* hearing.

5. Prepare a list of witnesses that you intend to call and the substance of their testimony.

6. You discover that Mark's Boats is about to begin manufacturing The Easy Troller 2 which is identical to The Easy Troller 1 except that it is a stern-mounted motor that pulls the boat through the water (so the boat is actually moving through the water stern first) and it does not have a manual override feature. Will this infringe the '835 patent?

United States Patent [19]

Perch

[11] Patent Number: **5,551,835**

[45] Date of Patent: **Apr. 1, 1995**

[54] **Trolling Motor**

[75] Inventors: **Michael J. Perch**, Naperville, IL

[73] Assignee: Mike's Fishing

[21] Appl. No.: 920, 200

[22] Filed: January 8, 1994

References Cited

U.S. PATENT DOCUMENTS

3,927,635	Masuzawa, et al.	12/04/75
2,450,904	Kramer	9/10/85
2,913,056	Kramer	1/15/86
2,419,451	Keller	4/22/87
4,403,676	Kulpa	8/15/91
4,848,003	Chalupny, et al.	3/01/92

[57] **ABSTRACT**

A trolling unit with autopilot coupled to the trolling motor and producing a thrust to pull a boat is disclosed. The system contains a bow-mounted trolling motor and a steering motor connected to the bow-mounted motor. The current heading of the boat is detected by the heading detector. The current heading and the target heading are compared by a steering circuit and used to generate input signals to the steering motor.

4 Claims, 2 drawings

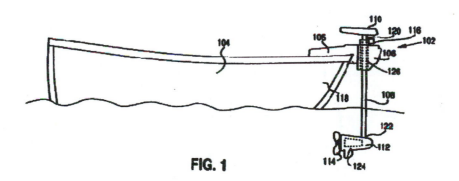

FIG. 1

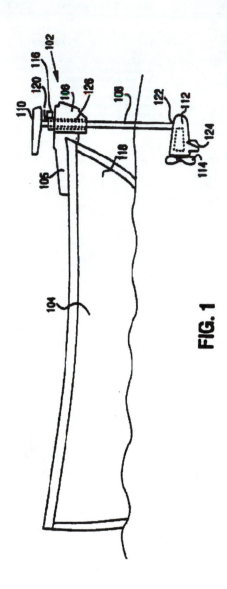

FIG. 1

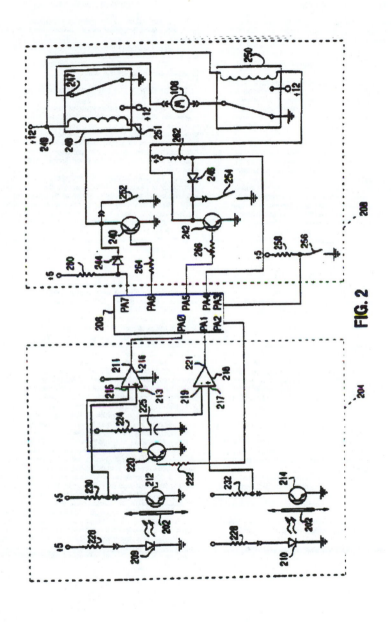

FIG. 2

1
TROLLING MOTOR

FIELD OF THE INVENTION

This invention relates generally to a trolling motor with an autopilot used to maintain a target heading of a boat, and in particular to a bow-mounted trolling motor with an autopilot used on a fishing boat.

BACKGROUND OF THE INVENTION

The trolling motor is a motor placed on a boat, generally a fishing boat which propels or pulls the boat at approximately 5 miles per hour. Use of electronic autopilot systems in boats has become very popular. Such systems are used to maintain a target heading of a boat without requiring a person to steer the boat. Such systems allow the user to troll on a preset course giving the user two free hands in order to fish.

The basic function of any electronic autopilot system of a boat is to establish and maintain a predetermined or target heading of the boat. Electronic steering systems generally operate by adjusting the current heading of the boat whenever the boat deviates from the target heading.

The only known electronic steering systems for fishing boats are used with stern-mounted motors. A common problem with stern-mounted electronic steering systems is that they overshoot their target heading. Electronic steering systems used with stern-mounted motors require two sensors: one to sense the current heading of the boat and one to sense the direction of the thrust motor. Two sensors are required in order to avoid overshooting the target heading, a common problem with motors that push rather than pull the boat. In addition, the hardware and software for stern-mounted motor steering systems must be capable of determining the magnitude of the steering correction in order to adjust the difference between the current heading of the boat and the heading of the thrust motor as the boat approaches the target heading. The use of two sensors and hardware and software capable of changing the magnitude of correction increases the cost of the electronic autopilot system.

SUMMARY OF THE INVENTION

The electronic autopilot system of the present invention is to be used on a bow-mounted motor and it requires only one sensor. The hardware and software of the present invention do not need to determine the magnitude of the correction. The electronic autopilot system of the present invention is designed for a bow-mounted motor that pulls the boat. Since the bow-mounted motor pulls rather than pushes the boat like a stern-mounted motor, it avoids the overshooting problem. To maintain the target heading the electronic steering system on a bow-mounted motor need only adjust the current heading of the thrust motor in the exact direction of the target heading and the boat will be brought back on course. The electronic autopilot system of the present invention is easy to use and includes a manual override feature. Finally the present invention is less complicated and less expensive than known electronic autopilot systems for stern-mounted motors.

An important object of the electronic autopilot system of the present invention is that it is designed for use with a bow-mounted motor.

A further object of the invention is to advantageously require only a single direction sensor.

Another object of the invention is that the hardware and software does not need to determine the magnitude of the steering correction.

Another object of the invention is that it includes a

2

manual override feature.

DESCRIPTION OF THE FIGURES

Other objects of the invention will appear in the specification and will be apparent from the accompanying drawings in which.

Fig. 1 is an illustration of a boat employing the present invention.

Fig. 2 is an electronic schematic of the electronic autopilot system of the preferred embodiment.

DESCRIPTION OF THE PREFERRED EMBODIMENT

The electronic autopilot system of the present invention is to be used with a thrust motor that pulls the boat. Examples of motors on which this invention will function include: a bow-mounted trolling motor (thrust motor) that pulls the boat and a stern-mounted motor which pulls the boat in a direction opposite to that normally traveled. A boat with a thrust motor will eventually follow the thrust motor and travel in the direction of the thrust motor.

To use the electronic autopilot system of the present invention, the user manually steers the boat in the desired direction and turns the electronic autopilot system on by flipping the on switch. The electronic autopilot system stores the heading to which the user manually steered the boat as the target heading and continuously monitors the heading of the thrust motor. If the heading of the thrust motor deviates from the target heading by more than 2%, the electronic autopilot system steers the thrust motor to the target heading. For example, if the boat drifts to the left, the electronic autopilot system steers the thrust motor to the right to bring it back on course.

FIG 1 is an illustration of a boat using the present invention. Trolling unit 102 includes a base assembly 105 which is mounted in a permanent fixed position to the bow 118 of a fishing boat 104 using bolts. Trolling unit 102 includes a control head 110, a shaft 108, a steering motor 106, a motor housing 124, a trolling motor (thrust motor) 112, and a propeller 114. When shaft 108 rotates, the motor housing 124 also rotates.

FIG 2 is an electronic schematic of the electronic autopilot system of the preferred embodiment. Since boat 104 follows the trolling unit 102, a compass 202 can be placed in the control head 110 to determine the current heading of the boat.

The heading detector 204 includes: the compass 202, the microprocessor 206, and the other related circuitry in 204. The sensor portion of the heading detector 204 can be a compass or a magnetometer or a potentiometer. Each of which are capable of detecting the heading of the thrust motor. The advantage of using a compass is that in addition to detecting heading, it can communicate the boat's course tot he user (north, south, east, west). The microprocessor 206 and other related circuitry 204 then compare the heading to the target heading which is stored in microprocessor 206. When the trolling unit deviates from the target heading by more than 2%, the heading detector generates a heading signal which is transmitted to the steering circuit.

The steering circuit 208 includes: the microprocessor 206 and the related circuitry in 208 which receives the heading signal from the heading detector 204 and generates an input signal for the steering motor 106 instructing it to turn left or right.

The steering circuit 208 includes a manual override switch 252 which allows the user to select a new target heading. The manual override switch 252 in the preferred embodiment is a foot pedal which is electrically coupled to the rest of the steering circuit 208. Foot pedal 252 is like a break pedal on a car, when it is depressed the electronic autopilot system turns off. The user can

3

then use the foot pedal to steer the boat. If the foot pedal is pushed to the right, the thrust motor will turn right. If the foot pedal is pushed to the left, the thrust motor will turn left. When the foot pedal is released the electronic autopilot system is turned back on and it locks on to the heading at that moment as the new target heading. Using a foot pedal is advantageous because it keeps the users hands free to fish as they redirect the boat.

        The steering motor 106 receives the input signal from the steering circuit 208 and turns the trolling motor right or left as required.

        Although the preferred construction has been described in detail, it should be regarded as an illustration or example of the structure and not as a limitation or restriction thereof, as many other constructions, combinations, and arrangements of the parts may be made without departing from the spirit and scope of the invention.

I claim:

1.   An autopilot coupled to a bow-mounted trolling motor that pulls a boat, the autopilot comprising:

        a steering motor coupled to said trolling motor, said steering motor being disposed to turn said trolling motor left or right in response to input signals;

        a steering circuit electrically coupled to said steering motor, said steering circuit being disposed to generate said input signals;

        a compass electrically coupled to said steering circuit, said compass being disposed to transmit heading signals to said steering circuit when the boat deviates from the target heading by a predetermined amount.

2.   The autopilot of claim 1 wherein said steering circuit comprises a microprocessor.

3.   The autopilot of claim 1 wherein the steering circuit includes a means for manually overriding the autopilot.

4.   An autopilot for a trolling motor comprising: a steering circuit which includes a means for manually overriding the autopilot.

Chapter Nine

PROVING INFRINGEMENT

INTRODUCTION

Under 35 U.S.C. § 271, the patentee can bring suit against anyone who makes, uses, offers to sell, or sells the patented invention—this amounts to infringement of the patent. Suit can also be brought against those who actively induce or contribute to infringement. A patentee will usually charge an alleged infringer with literal infringement and infringement under the doctrine of equivalents. For literal infringement, the patentee must demonstrate that every element in the patent claim is identically present in the accused device. For infringement under the doctrine of equivalents, the patentee must prove that every element or its equivalent is present in the accused device. Both inquiries must be proven on an element-by-element basis. The patentee will generally want to assert every possible claim that she believes is being infringed, not just the broadest claim. Asserting all the claims that the patentee believes are being infringed will protect her infringement case in the event that some of the broader claims are determined to be invalid.

Because most judges and juries are not familiar with patents and their contents, the patent owner's case-in-chief should often begin with a witness who can explain the invention, the inventive process, and the state of the art at the time of the invention to the fact-finder. If the patentee can testify in a persuasive manner, she is an excellent first witness for this purpose. Many believe that fact-finders are particularly sympathetic to inventors, so it is often advantageous to humanize the suit by introducing the jury to the inventor at the outset. The patentee should tell her complete invention story. She should explain the problem she recognized, the state of the prior art at that time (for example, the level of skill in the art at the time and the ways that others tried to overcome the problem if they were aware of it) and the solution she invented. The inventor may also be able to show the similarities between her invention and the accused device. You will usually want to prepare a claim chart which breaks down the claim into elements and compares the claim limitations and the accused device. This claim chart will be useful for the judge during claim construction and it can be blown up and used during examination of the witnesses who will be comparing the patent claim to the accused device before the jury. In advance of trial, the patentee will want to simplify the infringement case for the jury by limiting it to only the issues in dispute.

The patentee has the burden of proving infringement by a preponderance of the evidence. Proof of infringement requires two steps: first, the court must construe the claim limitations that are at issue, and second, the fact-finder must compare the properly construed claims to the accused device. The Court should not determine infringement by comparing the accused device to the patentee's commercial embodiment. The accused device must be compared to the patent claims, not the patentee's product. Chapter Eight addressed the first step in the infringement analysis, this chapter explores the second step, comparing the claims to the accused device.

A.   LITERAL INFRINGEMENT

Literal infringement is usually a straight-forward issue. Once the claims are construed by the court, the fact-finder must determine whether the accused device performs each of the claim limitations identically. The patentee should try to crystalize the infringement issues for trial by getting the defendant to stipulate to the claim limitations which are present in the accused device, leaving the fact-finder to determine whether the disputed limitations are present. Where parties do not dispute any relevant facts regarding an accused product, but disagree over possible claim interpretations, the question of literal infringement collapses into claim construction and is amenable to summary judgment. *See General Mills, Inc. v. Hunt–Wesson, Inc.*, 103 F.3d 978, 41 USPQ2d 1440 (Fed. Cir. 1997).

A method claim can be literally infringed even if the process is performed in a different order unless there is limiting language in the claim which indicates that the steps were meant to be performed in a particular order. For example, language such as "first," "second," or "spreading peanut butter on bread" followed by "spreading jelly on peanut butter can be limiting." Such language may be construed as a limitation that the jelly must be spread first in order for the peanut butter to be spread on the jelly. *See, e.g., Mantech Environmental Corp. v. Hudson Environmental Services, Inc.*, 152 F.3d 1368, 1376, 47 USPQ2d 1732, 1739 (Fed. Cir. 1998).

B.   DOCTRINE OF EQUIVALENTS

Even if no literal infringement exists, the patent may still be infringed under the doctrine of equivalents if there are only insubstantial differences between the patent claims and the accused device.

WARNER-JENKINSON CO. v. HILTON DAVIS CHEM. CO.

520 U.S. 17, 41 USPQ2d 1865 (1997)

Justice THOMAS delivered the opinion of the Court.

Nearly 50 years ago, this Court in *Graver Tank & Mfg. Co. v. Linde Air Products Co.*, 339 U.S. 605 (1950), set out the modern contours of what is known in patent law as the "doctrine of equivalents." Under this doctrine, a product or process that does not literally infringe upon the express terms of a patent claim may nonetheless be found to infringe if there is "equivalence" between the elements of the accused product or process and the claimed elements of the patented invention. *Id.*, at 609. Petitioner, which was found to have infringed upon respondent's patent under the doctrine of equivalents, invites us to speak the death of that doctrine. We decline that invitation. The significant disagreement within the Court of Appeals for the Federal Circuit concerning the application of *Graver Tank* suggests, however, that the doctrine is not free from confusion. We therefore will endeavor to clarify the proper scope of the doctrine.

I

The essential facts of this case are few. Petitioner Warner–Jenkinson Co. and respondent Hilton Davis Chemical Co. manufacture dyes. Impurities in those dyes must be removed. Hilton Davis holds United States Patent No. 4,560,746 ('746 patent), which discloses an improved purification process involving "ultrafiltration." The '746 process filters impure dye through a porous membrane at certain pressures and pH levels, resulting in a high purity dye product.

The '746 patent issued in 1985. As relevant to this case, the patent claims as its invention an improvement in the ultrafiltration process as follows:

> In a process for the purification of a dye ... the improvement which comprises: subjecting an aqueous solution ... to ultrafiltration through a membrane having a nominal pore diameter of 5–15 Angstroms under a hydrostatic pressure of approximately 200 to 400 p.s.i.g., at a pH from approximately 6.0 to 9.0, to thereby cause separation of said impurities from said dye....

The inventors added the phrase "at a pH from approximately 6.0 to 9.0" during patent prosecution. At a minimum, this phrase was added to distinguish a previous patent (the "Booth" patent) that disclosed an ultrafiltration process operating at a pH above 9.0. The parties disagree as to why the low-end pH limit of 6.0 was included as part of the claim.[2]

---

2. Petitioner contends that the lower limit was added because below a pH of 6.0 the patented process created "foaming" problems in the plant and because the pro-

cess was not shown to work below that pH level. Respondent counters that the process was successfully tested to pH levels as low as 2.2 with no effect on the process because

In 1986, Warner–Jenkinson developed an ultrafiltration process that operated with membrane pore diameters assumed to be 5–15 Angstroms, at pressures of 200 to nearly 500 p.s.i.g., and at a pH of 5.0. Warner–Jenkinson did not learn of the '746 patent until after it had begun commercial use of its ultrafiltration process. Hilton Davis eventually learned of Warner–Jenkinson's use of ultrafiltration and, in 1991, sued Warner–Jenkinson for patent infringement.

As trial approached, Hilton Davis conceded that there was no literal infringement, and relied solely on the doctrine of equivalents. Over Warner-Jenkinson's objection that the doctrine of equivalents was an equitable doctrine to be applied by the court, the issue of equivalence was included among those sent to the jury. The jury found that the '746 patent was not invalid and that Warner–Jenkinson infringed upon the patent under the doctrine of equivalents. The jury also found, however, that Warner–Jenkinson had not intentionally infringed, and therefore awarded only 20% of the damages sought by Hilton Davis. The District Court denied Warner–Jenkinson's post-trial motions, and entered a permanent injunction prohibiting Warner–Jenkinson from practicing ultrafiltration below 500 p.s.i.g. and below 9.01 pH. A fractured en banc Court of Appeals for the Federal Circuit affirmed.

The majority below held that the doctrine of equivalents continues to exist and that its touchstone is whether substantial differences exist between the accused process and the patented process. The court also held that the question of equivalence is for the jury to decide and that the jury in this case had substantial evidence from which it could conclude that the Warner–Jenkinson process was not substantially different from the ultrafiltration process disclosed in the '746 patent.

There were three separate dissents, commanding a total of 5 of 12 judges. Four of the five dissenting judges viewed the doctrine of equivalents as allowing an improper expansion of claim scope, contrary to this Court's numerous holdings that it is the claim that defines the invention and gives notice to the public of the limits of the patent monopoly. *Id.*, at 1537–1538 (Plager, J., dissenting). The fifth dissenter, the late Judge Nies, was able to reconcile the prohibition against enlarging the scope of claims and the doctrine of equivalents by applying the doctrine to each element of a claim, rather than to the accused product or process "overall." *Id.*, at 1574 (Nies, J., dissenting). As she explained it, "[t]he 'scope' is not enlarged if courts do not go beyond the substitution of equivalent elements." All of the dissenters, however, would have found that a much narrowed doctrine of equivalents may be applied in whole or in part by the court.

II

In *Graver Tank* we considered the application of the doctrine of equivalents to an accused chemical composition for use in welding that

of foaming, but offers no particular explanation as to why the lower level of 6.0 pH was selected.

differed from the patented welding material by the substitution of one chemical element. 339 U.S. at 610. The substituted element did not fall within the literal terms of the patent claim, but the Court nonetheless found that the "question which thus emerges is whether the substitution [of one element for the other] ... is a change of such substance as to make the doctrine of equivalents inapplicable; or conversely, whether under the circumstances the change was so insubstantial that the trial court's invocation of the doctrine of equivalents was justified." *Id.* The Court also described some of the considerations that go into applying the doctrine of equivalents:

> What constitutes equivalency must be determined against the context of the patent, the prior art, and the particular circumstances of the case. Equivalence, in the patent law, is not the prisoner of a formula and is not an absolute to be considered in a vacuum. It does not require complete identity for every purpose and in every respect. In determining equivalents, things equal to the same thing may not be equal to each other and, by the same token, things for most purposes different may sometimes be equivalents. Consideration must be given to the purpose for which an ingredient is used in a patent, the qualities it has when combined with the other ingredients, and the function which it is intended to perform. An important factor is whether persons reasonably skilled in the art would have known of the interchangeability of an ingredient not contained in the patent with one that was.

Id., at 609.

Considering those factors, the Court viewed the difference between the chemical element claimed in the patent and the substitute element to be "colorable only," and concluded that the trial court's judgment of infringement under the doctrine of equivalents was proper. *Id.*, at 612.

A

Petitioner's primary argument in this Court is that the doctrine of equivalents, as set out in *Graver Tank* in 1950, did not survive the 1952 revision of the Patent Act, 35 U.S.C. § 100 et seq., because it is inconsistent with several aspects of that Act. In particular, petitioner argues: (1) the doctrine of equivalents is inconsistent with the statutory requirement that a patentee specifically "claim" the invention covered by a patent, 35 U.S.C. § 112; (2) the doctrine circumvents the patent reissue process—designed to correct mistakes in drafting or the like—and avoids the express limitations on that process, 35 U.S.C. §§ 251–252; (3) the doctrine is inconsistent with the primacy of the Patent and Trademark Office (PTO) in setting the scope of a patent through the patent prosecution process; and (4) the doctrine was implicitly rejected as a general matter by Congress' specific and limited inclusion of the doctrine in one section regarding "means" claiming, 35 U.S.C. § 112, ¶ 6. All but one of these arguments were made in *Graver Tank* in the context of the 1870 Patent Act, and failed to command a majority.[3]

---

3. *Graver Tank* was decided over a vigorous dissent. In that dissent, Justice Black   raised the first three of petitioner's four arguments against the doctrine of equiva-

The 1952 Patent Act is not materially different from the 1870 Act with regard to claiming, reissue, and the role of the PTO. Compare, e.g., 35 U.S.C. § 112 ("The specification shall conclude with one or more claims particularly pointing out and distinctly claiming the subject matter which the applicant regards as his invention") with The Consolidated Patent Act of 1870, ch. 230, § 26, 16 Stat. 198, 201 (the applicant "shall particularly point out and distinctly claim the part, improvement, or combination which he claims as his invention or discovery"). Such minor differences as exist between those provisions in the 1870 and the 1952 Acts have no bearing on the result reached in *Graver Tank*, and thus provide no basis for our overruling it. In the context of infringement, we have already held that pre–1952 precedent survived the passage of the 1952 Act. We see no reason to reach a different result here.

Petitioner's fourth argument for an implied congressional negation of the doctrine of equivalents turns on the reference to "equivalents" in the "means" claiming provision of the 1952 Act. Section 112, ¶ 6, a provision not contained in the 1870 Act, states:

> An element in a claim for a combination may be expressed as a means or step for performing a specified function without the recital of structure, material, or acts in support thereof, and such claim shall be construed to cover the corresponding structure, material, or acts described in the specification and equivalents thereof.

Thus, under this new provision, an applicant can describe an element of his invention by the result accomplished or the function served, rather than describing the item or element to be used (e.g., "a means of connecting Part A to Part B," rather than "a two-penny nail"). Congress enacted § 112, ¶ 6 in response to *Halliburton Oil Well Cementing Co. v. Walker*, which rejected claims that "do not describe the invention but use 'conveniently functional language at the exact point of novelty,'" 329 U.S. 1, 8 (1946) (citation omitted). *See In re Donaldson Co.*, 16 F.3d 1189, 1194 (Fed. Cir. 1994) (Congress enacted predecessor of § 112, ¶ 6 in response to *Halliburton*). Section 112, ¶ 6 now expressly allows so-called "means" claims, with the proviso that application of the broad literal language of such claims must be limited to only those means that are "equivalent" to the actual means shown in the patent specification. This is an application of the doctrine of equivalents in a restrictive role, narrowing the application of broad literal claim elements. We recognized

lents. *See* 339 U.S., at 613–614 (doctrine inconsistent with statutory requirement to "distinctly claim" the invention); *id.*, at 614–615 (patent reissue process available to correct mistakes); *id.*, at 615, n. 3 (duty lies with the Patent Office to examine claims and to conform them to the scope of the invention; inventors may appeal Patent Office determinations if they disagree with result).

Indeed, petitioner's first argument was not new even in 1950. Nearly 100 years before *Graver Tank*, this Court approved of the doctrine of equivalents in *Winans v. Denmead*, 15 How. 330 (1854). The dissent in *Winans* unsuccessfully argued that the majority result was inconsistent with the requirement in the 1836 Patent Act that the applicant "particularly 'specify and point' out what he claims as his invention," and that the patent protected nothing more. *Id.*, 15 How. at 347 (Campbell, J., dissenting).

this type of role for the doctrine of equivalents in *Graver Tank* itself. 339 U.S., at 608–609. The added provision, however, is silent on the doctrine of equivalents as applied where there is no literal infringement.

Because § 112, ¶ 6 was enacted as a targeted cure to a specific problem, and because the reference in that provision to "equivalents" appears to be no more than a prophylactic against potential side effects of that cure, such limited congressional action should not be overread for negative implications. Congress in 1952 could easily have responded to *Graver Tank* as it did to the *Halliburton* decision. But it did not. Absent something more compelling than the dubious negative inference offered by petitioner, the lengthy history of the doctrine of equivalents strongly supports adherence to our refusal in *Graver Tank* to find that the Patent Act conflicts with that doctrine. Congress can legislate the doctrine of equivalents out of existence any time it chooses. The various policy arguments now made by both sides are thus best addressed to Congress, not this Court.

B

We do, however, share the concern of the dissenters below that the doctrine of equivalents, as it has come to be applied since Graver Tank, has taken on a life of its own, unbounded by the patent claims. There can be no denying that the doctrine of equivalents, when applied broadly, conflicts with the definitional and public-notice functions of the statutory claiming requirement. Judge Nies identified one means of avoiding this conflict:

> [A] distinction can be drawn that is not too esoteric between substitution of an equivalent for a component in an invention and enlarging the metes and bounds of the invention beyond what is claimed.

> . . . . .

> Where a claim to an invention is expressed as a combination of elements, as here, 'equivalents' in the sobriquet 'Doctrine of Equivalents' refers to the equivalency of an element or part of the invention with one that is substituted in the accused product or process.

> . . . . .

> This view that the accused device or process must be more than 'equivalent' overall reconciles the Supreme Court's position on infringement by equivalents with its concurrent statements that 'the courts have no right to enlarge a patent beyond the scope of its claims as allowed by the Patent Office.' The 'scope' is not enlarged if courts do not go beyond the substitution of equivalent elements.

We concur with this apt reconciliation of our two lines of precedent. Each element contained in a patent claim is deemed material to defining the scope of the patented invention , and thus the doctrine of equivalents must be applied to individual elements of the claim, not to the invention as a whole. It is important to ensure that the application of the doctrine, even as to an individual element, is not allowed such broad play as to effectively eliminate that element in its entirety. So long as the doctrine of equivalents does not encroach beyond the limits just described, or beyond related limits to be discussed *infra*, we are confident that the doctrine will not vitiate the central functions of the patent claims themselves.

III

A

Petitioner first argues that Graver Tank never purported to supersede a well-established limit on non-literal infringement, known variously as "prosecution history estoppel" and "file wrapper estoppel." According to petitioner, any surrender of subject matter during patent prosecution, regardless of the reason for such surrender, precludes recapturing any part of that subject matter, even if it is equivalent to the matter expressly claimed. Because, during patent prosecution, respondent limited the pH element of its claim to pH levels between 6.0 and 9.0, petitioner would have those limits form bright lines beyond which no equivalents may be claimed. Any inquiry into the reasons for a surrender, petitioner claims, would undermine the public's right to clear notice of the scope of the patent as embodied in the patent file.

We can readily agree with petitioner that *Graver Tank* did not dispose of prosecution history estoppel as a legal limitation on the doctrine of equivalents. But petitioner reaches too far in arguing that the reason for an amendment during patent prosecution is irrelevant to any subsequent estoppel. In each of our cases cited by petitioner and by the dissent below, prosecution history estoppel was tied to amendments made to avoid the prior art, or otherwise to address a specific concern—such as obviousness—that arguably would have rendered the claimed subject matter unpatentable.

It is telling that in each case this Court probed the reasoning behind the Patent Office's insistence upon a change in the claims. In each instance, a change was demanded because the claim as otherwise written was viewed as not describing a patentable invention at all—typically because what it described was encompassed within the prior art. But, as the United States informs us, there are a variety of other reasons why the PTO may request a change in claim language. And if the PTO has been requesting changes in claim language without the intent to limit equivalents or, indeed, with the expectation that language it required would in many cases allow for a range of equivalents, we should be extremely reluctant to upset the basic assumptions of the PTO without substantial reason for doing so. Our prior cases have consistently applied prosecution history estoppel only where claims have been amended for a limited set of reasons, and we see no substantial cause for requiring a more rigid rule invoking an estoppel regardless of the reasons for a change.

In this case, the patent examiner objected to the patent claim due to a perceived overlap with the Booth patent, which revealed an ultrafiltration process operating at a pH above 9.0. In response to this objection, the phrase "at a pH from approximately 6.0 to 9.0" was added to the claim. While it is undisputed that the upper limit of 9.0 was added in order to distinguish the Booth patent, the reason for adding the lower limit of 6.0 is unclear. The lower limit certainly did not serve to distinguish the Booth patent, which said nothing about pH levels below 6.0. Thus, while a lower limit of 6.0, by its mere inclusion, became a material element of the claim, that did not necessarily preclude the application of the doctrine of equivalents as to that element. Where the reason for the change was not related to avoiding the prior art, the change may introduce a new element, but it does not necessarily preclude infringement by equivalents of that element.

We are left with the problem, however, of what to do in a case like the one at bar, where the record seems not to reveal the reason for including the lower pH limit of 6.0. In our view, holding that certain reasons for a claim amendment may avoid the application of prosecution history estoppel is not tantamount to holding that the absence of a reason for an amendment may similarly avoid such an estoppel. Mindful that claims do indeed serve both a definitional and a notice function, we think the better rule is to place the burden on the patent-holder to establish the reason for an amendment required during patent prosecution. The court then would decide whether that reason is sufficient to overcome prosecution history estoppel as a bar to application of the doctrine of equivalents to the element added by that amendment. Where no explanation is established, however, the court should presume that the PTO had a substantial reason related to patentability for including the limiting element added by amendment. In those circumstances, prosecution history estoppel would bar the application of the doctrine equivalents as to that element. The presumption we have described, one subject to rebuttal if an appropriate reason for a required amendment is established, gives proper deference to the role of claims in defining an invention and providing public notice, and to the primacy of the PTO in ensuring that the claims allowed cover only subject matter that is properly patentable in a proffered patent application. Applied in this fashion, prosecution history estoppel places reasonable limits on the doctrine of equivalents, and further insulates the doctrine from any feared conflict with the Patent Act.

Because respondent has not proffered in this Court a reason for the addition of a lower pH limit, it is impossible to tell whether the reason for that addition could properly avoid an estoppel. Whether a reason in fact exists, but simply was not adequately developed, we cannot say. On remand, the Federal Circuit can consider whether reasons for that portion of the amendment were offered or not and whether further opportunity to establish such reasons would be proper.

B

Relying on *Graver Tank's* references to the problem of an "unscrupulous copyist" and "piracy," petitioner [next argued that infringement under the doctrine of equivalents requires a showing of intent. The Court held that the doctrine is intent-neutral.]

If the essential predicate of the doctrine of equivalents is the notion of identity between a patented invention and its equivalent, there is no basis for treating an infringing equivalent any differently than a device that infringes the express terms of the patent. Application of the doctrine of equivalents, therefore, is akin to determining literal infringement, and neither requires proof of intent.

Petitioner also points to *Graver Tank*'s seeming reliance on the absence of independent experimentation by the alleged infringer as supporting an equitable defense to the doctrine of equivalents. The Federal Circuit explained this factor by suggesting that an alleged infringer's behavior, be it copying, designing around a patent, or independent experimentation, indirectly reflects the substantiality of the differences between the patented invention and the accused device or process. According to the Federal Circuit, a person aiming to copy or aiming to avoid a patent is imagined to be at least marginally skilled at copying or avoidance, and thus intentional copying raises an inference—rebuttable by proof of independent development—of having only insubstantial differences, and intentionally designing around a patent claim raises an inference of substantial differences. This explanation leaves much to be desired. At a minimum, one wonders how ever to distinguish between the intentional copyist making minor changes to lower the risk of legal action, and the incremental innovator designing around the claims, yet seeking to capture as much as is permissible of the patented advance.

But another explanation is available that does not require a divergence from generally objective principles of patent infringement. In both instances in *Graver Tank* where we referred to independent research or experiments, we were discussing the known interchangeability between the chemical compound claimed in the patent and the compound substituted by the alleged infringer. The need for independent experimentation thus could reflect knowledge—or lack thereof—of interchangeability possessed by one presumably skilled in the art. The known interchangeability of substitutes for an element of a patent is one of the express objective factors noted by *Graver Tank* as bearing upon whether the accused device is substantially the same as the patented invention. Independent experimentation by the alleged infringer would not always reflect upon the objective question whether a person skilled in the art would have known of the interchangeability between two elements, but in many cases it would likely be probative of such knowledge.

Although *Graver Tank* certainly leaves room for petitioner's suggested inclusion of intent-based elements in the doctrine of equivalents, we do not read it as requiring them. The better view, and the one consistent with Graver Tank's predecessors and the objective approach to infringement, is that intent plays no role in the application of the doctrine of equivalents.

C

Finally, petitioner proposes that in order to minimize conflict with the notice function of patent claims, the doctrine of equivalents should be limited to equivalents that are disclosed within the patent itself. A milder version of this argument, which found favor with the dissenters below, is that the doctrine should be limited to equivalents that were known at the time the patent was issued, and should not extend to after-arising equivalents.

As we have noted, with regard to the objective nature of the doctrine, a skilled practitioner's knowledge of the interchangeability between claimed and accused elements is not relevant for its own sake, but rather for what it tells the fact-finder about the similarities or differences between those elements. Much as the perspective of the hypothetical "reasonable person" gives content to concepts such as "negligent" behavior, the perspective of a skilled practitioner provides content to, and limits on, the concept of "equivalence." Insofar as the question under the doctrine of equivalents is whether an accused element is equivalent to a claimed element, the proper time for evaluating equivalency—and thus knowledge of interchangeability between elements—is at the time of infringement, not at the time the patent was issued. And rejecting the milder version of petitioner's argument necessarily rejects the more severe proposition that equivalents must not only be known, but must also be actually disclosed in the patent in order for such equivalents to infringe upon the patent.

IV

The various opinions below, respondents, and amici devote considerable attention to whether application of the doctrine of equivalents is a task for the judge or for the jury. However, despite petitioner's argument below that the doctrine should be applied by the judge, in this Court petitioner makes only passing reference to this issue.

Petitioner's comments go more to the alleged inconsistency between the doctrine of equivalents and the claiming requirement than to the role of the jury in applying the doctrine as properly understood. Because resolution of whether, or how much of, the application of the doctrine of equivalents can be resolved by the court is not necessary for us to answer the question presented, we decline to take it up. The Federal Circuit held that it was for the jury to decide whether the accused process was equivalent to the claimed process. There was ample support in our prior cases for that holding. Nothing in our recent *Markman* decision necessitates a different result than that reached by the Federal Circuit. Whether, if the issue were squarely presented to us, we would reach a different conclusion than did the Federal Circuit is not a question we need decide today.[8]

---

8. With regard to the concern over unreviewability due to black-box jury verdicts, we offer only guidance, not a specific mandate. Where the evidence is such that no reasonable jury could determine two elements to be equivalent, district courts are

V

All that remains is to address the debate regarding the linguistic framework under which "equivalence" is determined. Both the parties and the Federal Circuit spend considerable time arguing whether the so-called "triple identity" test—focusing on the function served by a particular claim element, the way that element serves that function, and the result thus obtained by that element—is a suitable method for determining equivalence, or whether an "insubstantial differences" approach is better. There seems to be substantial agreement that, while the triple identity test may be suitable for analyzing mechanical devices, it often provides a poor framework for analyzing other products or processes. On the other hand, the insubstantial differences test offers little additional guidance as to what might render any given difference "insubstantial."

In our view, the particular linguistic framework used is less important than whether the test is probative of the essential inquiry: Does the accused product or process contain elements identical or equivalent to each claimed element of the patented invention? Different linguistic frameworks may be more suitable to different cases, depending on their particular facts. A focus on individual elements and a special vigilance against allowing the concept of equivalence to eliminate completely any such elements should reduce considerably the imprecision of whatever language is used. An analysis of the role played by each element in the context of the specific patent claim will thus inform the inquiry as to whether a substitute element matches the function, way, and result of the claimed element, or whether the substitute element plays a role substantially different from the claimed element. With these limiting principles as a backdrop, we see no purpose in going further and micromanaging the Federal Circuit's particular word-choice for analyzing equivalence. We expect that the Federal Circuit will refine the formulation of the test for equivalence in the orderly course of case-by-case determinations, and we leave such refinement to that court's sound judgment in this area of its special expertise.

VI

Today we adhere to the doctrine of equivalents. The determination of equivalence should be applied as an objective inquiry on an element-

obliged to grant partial or complete summary judgment. If there has been a reluctance to do so by some courts due to unfamiliarity with the subject matter, we are confident that the Federal Circuit can remedy the problem. Of course, the various legal limitations on the application of the doctrine of equivalents are to be determined by the court, either on a pretrial motion for partial summary judgment or on a motion for judgment as a matter of law at the close of the evidence and after the jury verdict. Thus, under the particular facts of a case, if prosecution history estoppel would apply or if a theory of equivalence would entirely vitiate a particular claim element, partial or complete judgment should be rendered by the court, as there would be no further material issue for the jury to resolve. Finally, in cases that reach the jury, a special verdict and/or interrogatories on each claim element could be very useful in facilitating review, uniformity, and possibly postverdict judgments as a matter of law. We leave it to the Federal Circuit how best to implement procedural improvements to promote certainty, consistency, and reviewability to this area of the law.

by-element basis. Prosecution history estoppel continues to be available as a defense to infringement, but if the patent-holder demonstrates that an amendment required during prosecution had a purpose unrelated to patentability, a court must consider that purpose in order to decide whether an estoppel is precluded. Where the patent holder is unable to establish such a purpose, a court should presume that the purpose behind the required amendment is such that prosecution history estoppel would apply. Because the Court of Appeals for the Federal Circuit did not consider all of the requirements as described by us today, particularly as related to prosecution history estoppel and the preservation of some meaning for each element in a claim, we reverse and remand for further proceedings consistent with this opinion.

Justice GINSBURG, with whom Justice KENNEDY joins, concurring.

I join the opinion of the Court and write separately to add a cautionary note on the rebuttable presumption the Court announces regarding prosecution history estoppel. I address in particular the application of the presumption in this case and others in which patent prosecution has already been completed. The new presumption, if applied woodenly, might in some instances unfairly discount the expectations of a patentee who had no notice at the time of patent prosecution that such a presumption would apply. Such a patentee would have had little incentive to insist that the reasons for all modifications be memorialized in the file wrapper as they were made. Years after the fact, the patentee may find it difficult to establish an evidentiary basis that would overcome the new presumption. The Court's opinion is sensitive to this problem, noting that "the PTO may have relied upon a flexible rule of estoppel when deciding whether to ask for a change" during patent prosecution.

Because respondent has not presented to this Court any explanation for the addition of the lower pH limit, I concur in the decision to remand the matter to the Federal Circuit. On remand, that court can determine—bearing in mind the prior absence of clear rules of the game—whether suitable reasons for including the lower pH limit were earlier offered or, if not, whether they can now be established.

Notes

1. **At the Time of Infringement.** Do you agree with the Supreme Court's holding that equivalents should be determined at the time of infringement? Should the patentee be entitled to claim that the use of a later developed equivalent which she did not disclose in her patent still results in infringement?

2. **The Federal Circuit Remand.** On remand, the Federal Circuit declined to clarify the procedure for implementing the new prosecution history estoppel presumption stating:

We hesitate to specify the procedures that the district court can employ to answer the question posed by the newly created presumption of prosecution history estoppel. The better course is to allow the district court to use its discretion to decide whether hearings are necessary or whether the issue can adequately be determined on a written record. If the district court determines that a reason not related to patentability prompted an amendment, the court must then decide if that reason is sufficient to overcome estoppel. In conducting the inquiry, the Supreme Court has cautioned the courts to consider carefully the importance of public notice and reliance on the prosecution history, as well as the need for fairness to the patentee.

Hilton Davis Chem. Co. v. Warner–Jenkinson Co., 114 F.3d 1161, 1163, 43 USPQ2d 1152, 1154 (Fed. Cir. 1997).

How should the patentee be allowed to prove the reason for claim limitation changes? Should the patentee be limited to using record evidence, namely the patent and prosecution history, or should she be permitted to offer evidence outside of the public record to substantiate a reason for the claim change? How about testimony by the inventor or patent attorney? What about documentary evidence such as written correspondence between the patent attorney and the patentee regarding the claim changes or the patent attorney's notes? Should the court hold a *Hilton Davis* hearing (like a *Markman* hearing) to determine the reason for the claim change? At what stage in the proceedings should these issues be resolved?

3. **A Reason Related to Patentability**. What did the Supreme Court mean when it held that a presumption of prosecution history estoppel would attach unless the patentee could prove that the amendment was made for "a purpose unrelated to patentability." *Warner-Jenkinson*, 117 S. Ct. at 1044. If the amendment was made to overcome a prior art reference, this certainly would be related to patentability. What about an amendment made to satisfy the enablement requirement or overcome an indefiniteness problem? This issue is explored in more detail in the next chapter.

4. **Relevant Time Period**. Should there be different treatment for those patents that were prosecuted prior to the *Warner-Jenkinson* decision and those that come after?

5. **The Function/Way/Result Test**. After *Warner–Jenkinson*, the Federal Circuit has continued to use the function/way/result test to determine whether there is infringement under the doctrine of equivalents. *See Vehicular Tech. Corp. v. Titan Wheel Intern., Inc.*, 141 F.3d 1084, 1089, 46 USPQ2d 1257, 1261 (Fed. Cir. 1998) ("In its brief and at oral argument, Tractech emphasizes that its captured plug can be a substantial equivalent, for doctrine of equivalents purposes, of the claimed captured inner spring limitation, only if the plug performs the same or substantially the same functions of the inner spring in substantially the same way, to produce substantially the same result. In this respect, Tractech correctly states the law, and PowerTrax speaks not to the contrary.").

The patentee has the burden of proving infringement under the doctrine of equivalents by a preponderance of the evidence. To prove infringement under the doctrine the patentee would generally use the testimony of one of ordinary skill in the art. The patentee would enter evidence that one of ordinary skill in the art knows that two elements are interchangeable or that one of ordinary skill in the art believes that the two elements perform substantially the same function in substantially the same way to achieve the same result. The patentee must offer particularized testimony and linking argument as to the function, way and result of each element of the accused device; it is insufficient for the expert to testify merely that the accused device and the claim element are equivalent. *See, e.g., Dawn Equipment Co. v. Kentucky Farms Inc.*, 140 F.3d 1009, 46 USPQ2d 1109 (Fed. Cir. 1998) (holding that expert testimony that the Kentucky Farms device was equivalent to the claim because they both had pins and that the sliding verses rotating motion of the pins was a common alternative was insufficient especially in light of the contrary statements in the patent specification); *Texas Instruments Inc. v. Cypress Semiconductor Corp.*, 90 F.3d 1558, 39 USPQ2d 1492 (Fed. Cir. 1996) (holding that conclusory expert testimony that the accused processes met the function-way-result test is insufficient without a particularized discussion of the way the die pad in the accused device operates similar to the patent claim and an explanation as to why the function and result are the same).

6. **Limitations on the Doctrine of Equivalents.** A determination of the scope of equivalents to which a patentee is entitled requires resort to many doctrines and limitations which have been established by the Federal Circuit including: (1) the all elements rules discussed in *Warner-Jenkinson*; (2) the doctrine of prosecution history estoppel and the new presumption established in *Warner-Jenkinson*; (3) the all advantages rule; (4) prior art; and (5) disclosures in the specification. Finally, the scope of equivalents also depends on how new the invention is. If the invention is in a crowded field, the range of equivalents would be narrow whereas pioneering inventions should be given a broader range. These limitations are discussed in detail in the next chapter.

C. MEANS–PLUS–FUNCTION CLAIMS

Statutory Provision—35 U.S.C. § 112 ¶ 6:

An element in a claim for a combination may be expressed as a means or step for performing a specified function without the recital of structure, material, or acts in support thereof, and such claim shall be construed to cover the corresponding structure, material or acts described in the specification and equivalents thereof.

A patentee can describe her invention in terms of what it does; she can use functional language. For example, a claim could describe a "means for holding two pieces of wood together." This is means-plus-function language or functional claim language. It uses the words *means for* followed by the function, holding two pieces of wood together. To interpret this claim element, you look to the written description portion of the specification which should detail the structure for performing this function. For example, the written description might discuss "using a nail to join two pieces of wood." The claim would thus cover a nail or equivalent thereof which holds two pieces of wood together.

How do you know when a claim is using functional language? Generally, it is quite simple. When a claim uses the term *means* or *means for* it usually invokes § 112 ¶ 6 and when a claim does not employ the word *means* it usually does not going to invoke § 112 ¶ 6. This rule is not absolute as some of the notes prove, but it is a good rule of thumb for claim construction.

For literal infringement of a means-plus-function claim limitation, the accused device must have an equivalent structure which performs an identical function. For infringement under the doctrine of equivalents, the accused device must have an equivalent structure that performs an equivalent function.

CHIUMINATTA CONCRETE CONCEPTS, INC. v. CARDINAL INDUS., INC.

145 F.3d 1303, 46 USPQ2d 1752 (Fed. Cir. 1998)

Before MICHEL, PLAGER, and LOURIE, *Circuit Judges*.

LOURIE, *Circuit Judge*.

Cardinal Industries, Inc. and Green Machine Corporation (collectively Cardinal) appeal from the decision of the United States District Court for the Central District of California granting Chiuminatta Concrete Concepts, Inc., Edward Chiuminatta, and Alan Chiuminatta's (collectively Chiuminatta's) motion for partial summary judgment of infringement of two of Chiuminatta's patents.

The district court found that Cardinal infringed claim 11, an apparatus claim, of U.S. Patent B1 5,056,499 and infringed claims 1, 2, and 3, all method claims, of U.S. Patent B1 4,889,675. Because the district court erroneously construed a means-plus-function limitation of the apparatus claims, we reverse the summary judgment of infringement of that patent. We affirm the decision in all other respects.

BACKGROUND

Chiuminatta owns two patents, the '499 patent and the '675 patent relating to an apparatus and method, respectively, for cutting concrete before it has completely cured to a hardened condition. The apparatus claims are directed to a rotary saw that has two significant features. First, the leading edge of the saw rotates in an upward direction so as to prevent the accumulation of displaced wet concrete in the groove created behind the saw. Second, a support surface applies downward pressure at the point where the saw blade emerges from the concrete in order to prevent the upwardly rotating blade from damaging the concrete (commonly referred to as raveling, chipping, spalling, or cracking).

Claim 11 of the '499 patent (the sole apparatus claim on appeal) reads, with emphasis added, as follows:

A saw for cutting concrete even before the concrete has hardened to its typical, rock-like hardness, comprising:

a circular concrete cutting blade having sides and a leading cutting edge;

a motor connected to rotate the concrete cutting blade in an up-cut rotation;

means connected to the saw *for supporting the surface of the concrete* adjacent the leading edge of the cutting blade to inhibit chipping, spalling, or cracking of the concrete surface during cutting;

wheel means for movably supporting the saw on the surface of the concrete during cutting.

As illustrated in the following figure adapted from the patent, the only structure disclosed for supporting the surface of the concrete is a skid plate.

An Embodiment of the Invention   **The Accused Device**

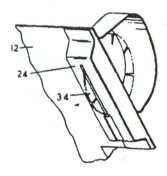
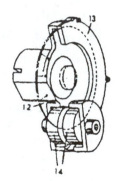

The written description summarizes the invention, stating:

An apparatus is provided for cutting a groove in soft concrete. The apparatus can cut the concrete anytime after the concrete is finished and before the concrete attains its rock like hardness. . . .

The soft concrete saw has a base plate [12] on which are mounted two wheels and a skid plate [24], each of which contacts the concrete to provide three point support on the concrete. . . . The saw blade [34] extends through a . . . slot in the skid plate, in order to project into and cut the concrete below the skid plate.

The dimensions of the slot in the skid plate are selected to support the concrete immediately adjacent the saw blade so as to prevent cracking of the concrete as it is cut.

Cardinal manufactures and sells the accused device, the Green Machine® saw. It, too, uses a rotary blade that rotates upward at its leading edge. Additionally, as illustrated above, the accused device has two small wheels [14] mounted adjacent to the leading edge of the saw blade [12]. Cardinal concedes that these wheels support the surface of the concrete in order to prevent chipping, spalling, or cracking.

It is undisputed that the wheels in the accused device meet the "supporting the surface" step of the claimed method.

Upon cross motions for summary judgment, the district court ruled in favor of Chiuminatta. It held that (1) Cardinal's manufacture and sale of the accused device infringed claim 11 of the '499 patent.... The district court then granted Chiuminatta's motion for a permanent injunction and released Chiuminatta's preliminary injunction bond. Cardinal appeals each of the rulings to this court.

Discussion

A.   *The '499 Patent*

1.   Literal Infringement

Cardinal asserts that the district court erred by granting Chiuminatta's motion for summary judgment of infringement of claim 11 of the '499 patent and that the court erroneously construed the means limitation in that claim to include every conceivable support surface. Cardinal concedes that the accused device meets every claim limitation except the "means ... for supporting the surface of the concrete." However, Cardinal argues that under a proper analysis, that means limitation should be construed as corresponding only to the disclosed skid plate and to structures that are equivalent to that skid plate. An equivalent structure, argues Cardinal, is one that includes the essential structural components of the disclosed apparatus. Cardinal identifies in its brief the key essential structural component as a "hard plate fixedly mounted to the base of the saw," although Cardinal concedes that the particular shape of the plate and its means for attachment are not essential.

Chiuminatta responds that the district court correctly construed the means-plus-function limitation and properly concluded as a matter of law that the limitation reads on the accused device. Specifically, Chiuminatta argues that the limitation was properly construed as being broader than the disclosed skid plate to encompass any "support surface." Chiuminatta asserts that the court correctly premised its infringement finding on the observation that "both [the structure in the patent and the wheels of the accused device] consist of flat planes on either side of the saw blade which hold the concrete in place."

We must determine whether the district court erred in concluding that the means limitation reads on the accused device as a matter of law. Neither party argues that there are disputed fact questions regarding the accused device. Both parties agree that the means-plus-function clause is the only limitation in dispute and that all other limitations are met by the accused device. What they dispute is whether the scope of the means clause is broad enough to encompass wheels such as those on the accused device.

A means-plus-function limitation contemplated by 35 U.S.C. § 112, ¶ 6 (1994) recites a function to be performed rather than definite structure or materials for performing that function. Such a limitation must be construed "to cover the corresponding structure, material, or acts described in the specification and equivalents thereof." *Id.* "To determine whether a claim limitation is met literally, where expressed as a means for performing a stated function, the court must compare the accused structure *with the disclosed structure*, and must find equivalent *structure* as well as *identity* of claimed *function* for that structure." *Pennwalt Corp. v. Durand–Wayland, Inc.*, 833 F.2d 931, 934, 4 USPQ2d 1737, 1739 (Fed. Cir. 1987) (*in banc*) (emphasis in original). A determination of the claimed function, being a matter of construction of specific terms in the claim, is a question of law, reviewed *de novo. See Cybor Corp. v. FAS Techs., Inc.*, 138 F.3d 1448, 46 USPQ2d 1169 (Fed. Cir. 1998) (in banc); *Markman v. Westview Instruments, Inc.*, 52 F.3d 967, 979, 34 USPQ2d 1321, 1329 (Fed. Cir. 1995) (in banc), *aff'd*, 517 U.S. 370, 38 USPQ2d 1461 (1996). Likewise, the "means" term in a means-plus-function limitation is essentially a generic reference for the corresponding structure disclosed in the specification. Accordingly, a determination of corresponding structure is a determination of the meaning of the "means" term in the claim and is thus also a matter of claim construction. *See B. Braun Med., Inc. v. Abbott Lab.*, 124 F.3d 1419, 1424–25, 43 USPQ2d 1896, 1899–1900 (Fed. Cir. 1997) (determining *de novo* which structures disclosed in the specification corresponded to the means limitation); *cf. Markman*, 52 F.3d at 977 n.8, 34 USPQ2d at 1327 n.8 (reserving only the question whether a determination of equivalence under § 112, ¶ 6 is a question of law or fact). Cardinal argues that the district court erroneously identified as the disclosed structure broad functional language in the specification rather than physical structure. Chiuminatta responds that the passage identified by the district court, a "support surface or plate . . . in movable contact with the surface of the concrete," is indeed structure. We agree with Cardinal that the court misidentified the corresponding structure. The function recited in the means clause of claim 11 is "supporting the surface of the concrete adjacent to the leading edge of the cutting blade to inhibit chipping, spalling, or cracking of the concrete surface during cutting."

The specification clearly identifies the structure performing that function as the skid plate, which is the only embodiment of the "support surface" disclosed in the specification:

> A support surface or plate is in movable contact with the surface of the concrete 13 in order to support the surface of the concrete immediately adjacent the groove being cut in the concrete 13. In the illustrated embodiment, this surface takes the form of a skid plate 24 which depends from the base plate 12 in the direction of the concrete 13.

The structure of the skid plate is broadly described in the specification of the '499 patent as follows:

> a generally rectangular strip of metal having rounded ends 26 and 28 between which is a flat piece 30. The flat piece 30 is generally parallel to the base plate 12. . . .

'499 patent, col. 5, ll. 5–19. The text continues,

the saw blade 34 extends ... through an aperture such as slot 38 (FIG. 3) in the skid plate 24.... The slot 38 is also generally rectangular in shape, and is placed on the flat piece 30 of skid plate 24.

The specification of the '499 patent elaborates on the details of the preferred skid plate, more particularly defining the structure in ways unrelated to the recited function. These additional structural aspects are not what the statute contemplates as structure *corresponding* to the recited function. For example, in the preferred embodiment, the skid plate runs beyond the leading edge and continues down the entire length of the saw blade in order to reduce wobbling of the cutting blade. Additionally, the skid plate of the preferred embodiment is sized such that it helps support the weight of the saw. These structural aspects are thus not the means by which the saw "supports the surface of the concrete" and accordingly are not to be read as limiting the scope of the means clause. The corresponding disclosed physical structure is the skid plate, a generally flat hard plate that straddles the leading edge of the cutting blade. The district court's conclusion that the term "support surface" sufficiently identifies the structure is therefore erroneous.

Having identified the corresponding structure of the recited means, the next question is whether the wheels of the accused device are equivalent to that structure. "[S]ection 112, paragraph 6, rules out the possibility that any and every means which performs the function specified in the claim *literally* satisfies that limitation." *Pennwalt Corp.*, 833 F.2d at 934, 4 USPQ2d at 1739. The proper test is whether the differences between the structure in the accused device and any disclosed in the specification are insubstantial. *See Valmont Indus., Inc. v. Reinke Mfg. Co.*, 983 F.2d 1039, 1043, 25 USPQ2d 1451, 1455 (Fed. Cir. 1993) ("In the context of section 112, however, an equivalent results from an insubstantial change which adds nothing of significance to the structure, material, or acts disclosed in the patent specification."); *Alpex Computer Corp. v. Nintendo Co.*, 102 F.3d 1214, 1222, 40 USPQ2d 1667, 1673 (Fed. Cir. 1996) (noting that equivalents under § 112, ¶ 6, and under the doctrine of equivalents both relate to insubstantial changes), *cert. denied*, 117 S. Ct. 2480 (1997).

Cardinal argues to us that the question whether a particular accused structure is equivalent to the disclosed structure is a question of law. The district court did not expressly decide this issue and on the facts of this case it is unnecessary for us to resolve it as well. Because, as discussed below, in any event, no reasonable jury could have found that the accused device has an equivalent to the disclosed structure, we need not resolve the question expressly left open by our in banc court in *Markman*, "whether a determination of equivalents under § 112, para. 6 is a question of law or fact." *Markman*, 52 F.3d at 977 n.8, 34 USPQ2d at 1327 n.8.

Cardinal argues that the wheels of its device are not equivalent to the disclosed skid plate because they are rotatably mounted. It asserts that for a structure to be equivalent to a skid plate, it must include substantially all of the structural features of a skid plate, and thus must be hard, flat, and fixedly attached to the saw. Chiuminatta responds that the district court properly held the wheels of the accused device to be within the scope of the claims. Chiuminatta asserts that the differences between the skid plate and wheels are insubstantial, and that an equivalent structure need not be flat or fixedly attached. Chiuminatta argues that the wheels of the accused device are equivalent because "in use, the [accused] wheels compress to form flattened planes on each side of the saw blade, coinciding with the structure of a skid plate."

The fundamental flaw in Chiuminatta's argument is that "flattened planes" are not structure. The undisputed structure that produces the concededly identical function of supporting the concrete consists of soft round wheels that are rotatably mounted onto the saw. The assertedly equivalent structures are wheels, and the differences between the wheels and the skid plate are not insubstantial. The former support the surface of the concrete by rolling over the concrete while the latter skids. The former are soft, compressible, and round; the latter is hard and predominantly flat (albeit with rounded edges to prevent gouging of the concrete). Additionally, the wheels rotate as opposed to skid as the saw moves across the concrete and thus have a different impact on the concrete. Since the wheels and the skid plate are substantially different from each other, they cannot be equivalent, and no reasonable jury could so find.

Chiuminatta also argues that the wheels are equivalent to the skid plate because they are interchangeable; the alleged infringer's saw may be outfitted with a skid plate and the patentee's saw may be outfitted with the accused wheels. This argument is not persuasive. Almost by definition, two structures that perform the same function may be substituted for one another. The question of known interchangeability is not whether both structures serve the same function, but whether it was known that one structure was an equivalent of another. Moreover, a finding of known interchangeability, while an important factor in determining equivalence, is certainly not dispositive. Such evidence does not obviate the statutory mandate to compare the accused structure to the corresponding structure. Moreover, Chiuminatta has not alleged that those of ordinary skill in the art recognized the interchangeability of metal plates with wheels for supporting the surface of concrete. Significantly, the patent discusses the use of wheels in the context of supporting and stabilizing the saw, but never once suggests that wheels could perform the function of the skid plate. Notwithstanding the discussion in the specification regarding the inherent drawbacks of a skid plate, including potential gouging of the concrete and increased drag against the concrete, there is no hint in the specification that the skid plate could be replaced by small wheels adjacent to the blade for supporting the concrete.

Because the wheels of the accused device are not equivalent to the skid plate disclosed in the '499 patent, the accused structure is not within the scope of the claim. Accordingly, the district court erred by granting Chiuminatta's motion for summary judgment of literal infringement.

2. *Doctrine of Equivalents Infringement*

Chiuminatta argues that, should we rule against it on the question of literal infringement, we may affirm the district court under the doctrine of equivalents. Although the district court did not reach the issue because it found literal infringement, Chiuminatta argues that the undisputed evidence of record conclusively establishes that the wheels of the accused device differ from the patented invention only insubstantially. Such an assertion cannot succeed given our determination regarding literal infringement under § 112, ¶ 6.

Although an equivalence analysis under § 112, ¶ 6, and the doctrine of equivalents are not coextensive (for example, § 112, ¶ 6, requires identical, not equivalent function) and have different origins and purposes, their tests for equivalence are closely related. *Warner-Jenkinson Co. v. Hilton Davis Chem. Co.*, 117 S. Ct. 1040, 1048, 41 USPQ2d 1865, 1870–71 (1997) ("[Equivalents under § 112] is an application of the doctrine of equivalents in a restrictive role, narrowing the application of broad literal claim elements. We recognized this type of role for the doctrine of equivalents in *Graver Tank* itself."). Both § 112, ¶ 6, and the doctrine of equivalents protect the substance of a patentee's right to exclude by preventing mere colorable differences or slight improvements from escaping infringement, the former, by incorporating equivalents of disclosed structures into the literal scope of a functional claim limitation, and the latter, by holding as infringements equivalents that are beyond the literal scope of the claim. They do so by applying similar analysis of insubstantiality of the differences. Thus, a finding of a lack of literal infringement for lack of equivalent structure under a means-plus-function limitation may preclude a finding of equivalence under the doctrine of equivalents.

There is an important difference, however, between the doctrine of equivalents and § 112, ¶ 6. The doctrine of equivalents is necessary because one cannot predict the future. Due to technological advances, a variant of an invention may be developed after the patent is granted, and that variant may constitute so insubstantial a change from what is claimed in the patent that it should be held to be an infringement. Such a variant, based on after-developed technology, could not have been disclosed in the patent. Even if such an element is found not to be a § 112, ¶ 6, equivalent because it is not equivalent to the structure disclosed in the patent, this analysis should not foreclose it from being an equivalent under the doctrine of equivalents.

That is not the case here, where the equivalence issue does not involve later-developed technologies, but rather involves technology that predates the invention itself. In such a case, a finding of non-equivalence for § 112, ¶ 6, purposes should preclude a contrary finding under the doctrine of equivalents. This is because, as we have already determined, the structure of the accused device differs substantially from the disclosed structure, and given the prior knowledge of the technology asserted to be equivalent, it could readily have been disclosed in the patent. There is no policy-based reason why a patentee should get two bites at the apple. If he or she could have included in the patent what is now alleged to be equivalent, and did not, leading to a conclusion that an accused device lacks an equivalent to the disclosed structure, why should the issue of equivalence have to be litigated a second time? As indicated, this consideration does not necessarily apply regarding variants of the invention based on after-developed technologies.

Our case law clearly provides that equivalence under the doctrine of equivalents requires that each claim limitation be met by an equivalent element in the accused device. Because this requirement is not met for § 112, ¶ 6, purposes with respect to one limitation, it is therefore not met in this case for doctrine of equivalents purposes. An element of a device cannot be "not equivalent" and equivalent to the same structure. *See, e.g., Dawn Equip. Co. v. Kentucky Farms Inc.*, 140 F.3d 1009, 1017–22, 46 USPQ2d 1109, 1115–18 (Fed. Cir. 1998) (Plager, J., additional views).

In this case there can also be no doctrine of equivalents infringement because, as we have explained, the structure in the accused device, the wheels, operates in a substantially different way compared with the structure of the claimed device, the skid plate. The former support the surface of the concrete by rolling over the concrete while the latter skids. The former are soft, compressible, and round; the latter is hard and predominantly flat (albeit with rounded edges to prevent gouging of the concrete). Additionally, the wheels rotate as opposed to skid as the saw moves across the concrete and thus have a different impact on the concrete. The wheels flatten slightly, applying more localized pressure against the concrete than that produced by a hard flat skid plate. Accordingly, for this additional reason, it cannot be an equivalent under the doctrine of equivalents and the district court is directed to enter summary judgment of non-infringement.

AFFIRMED-IN–PART AND REVERSED–IN–PART

Another interesting means-plus-function language case follows. In this case, the Court applied the doctrine of equivalents to a means-plus-function claim term.

DAWN EQUIPMENT CO. v. KENTUCKY FARMS INC.

140 F.3d 1009, 46 USPQ2d 1109 (Fed. Cir. 1998)

Before NEWMAN, MICHEL, and PLAGER, *Circuit Judges*.

PLAGER, Circuit Judge.

In this patent infringement case, the jury determined that the accused device, although not literally infringing, infringed under the doctrine of equivalents. The trial judge gave judgment accordingly, and denied defendant's motion for judgment as a matter of law ("JMOL"). Because on these facts no reasonable jury could have found infringement, we reverse the denial of defendant's motion for JMOL and order judgment for the defendant.

BACKGROUND

Plaintiff Dawn Equipment Company ("Dawn Equipment") sued defendant Kentucky Farms Incorporated ("Kentucky Farms") for infringement of U.S. Patent No. 5,129,282 ("'282 patent"), entitled "Mechanism for Selectively Repositioning a Farm Implement." Shortly before holding a jury trial, the trial judge held a Markman hearing to construe the only asserted patent claim. The trial judge instructed the jury on his claim construction and thereafter submitted the issues of literal infringement and infringement under the doctrine of equivalents to the jury. The issues were submitted by way of two special interrogatories that asked the jury to answer with a simple yes or no whether there was literal infringement and whether there was infringement under the doctrine of equivalents. The jury returned its verdict, answering "no" to literal infringement and "yes" to infringement under the doctrine of equivalents. Kentucky Farms filed a motion for JMOL on the doctrine of equivalents infringement verdict. The trial judge denied the motion, and this appeal followed.

The '282 patent discloses a device for adjusting the height of a farm implement such as a row cleaning device. A row cleaning device, which frequently consists of a pair of wheels having sharp teeth, is often attached to a planter to clear residue from the planter's path. In pointing out problems in the prior art, the '282 patent describes prior art "multi-hole pinned height adjustment" mechanisms. The patent explains that raising or lowering such prior art mechanisms can be very time-consuming, tedious, and repetitive. Adjusting the height of such mechanisms requires the operator to manually elevate and shift the farm implement to align holes and insert pins. The patent also explains that the loose pins used in the prior art mechanisms are easily lost. Moreover, when adjusting the height of such a prior art mechanism, the operator is required to place himself beneath the farm implement, which increases the risk of accidents and injuries.

The '282 patent explains that these problems are avoided by using an improved mechanism, illustrated in Figures 1 and 2 of the patent, reproduced below. Figure 1 shows the height adjusting mechanism in the lowered position; Figure 2 shows the same device in the raised position. The device includes a control/locking means 46 for alternating the implement between the raised and lowered positions. The control/locking means includes a handle 48, cylindrical rods 50 and 56, a cylindrical shaft 52, and a transverse pin 54 carried on the cylindrical shaft 52. A spring 68 biases the mechanism in the raised position, as shown in Figure 2. In the lowered position, the pin 54 is engaged in the slot 72, against the bias of the spring 68. To move the implement from the lowered position to the raised position, the operator presses down on and turns the handle 48 to rotate the pin 54 out of the slot 72. The spring 68 then overcomes the weight of the farm implement and pushes the implement into the raised position. The patent explains that this operation can be performed safely and quickly from above the farm implement.

The accused Kentucky Farms device, illustrated below, includes a connecting bar 10, which telescopes within a rectangular sleeve 12. A row cleaning device, or other farm implement, is attached to the connecting bar 10 at a pair of axes 14. The sleeve 12 is bolted onto a mounting bracket 16, which is attached to a planter. The connecting bar 10 is inserted in sleeve 12, and a bolt 20 is inserted in the uppermost opening in the connecting bar 10, to prevent the connecting bar from slipping down through the sleeve 12. A spring 22, attached at its upper end to the sleeve 12, and at its lower end to the connecting bar 10, supports a portion of the weight of the connecting bar and attached row cleaning device.

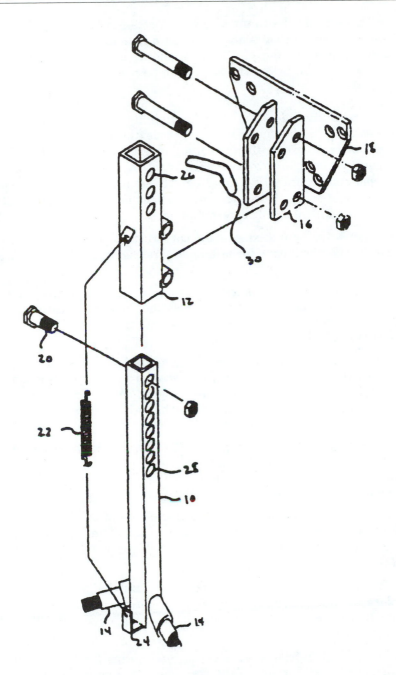

The Kentucky Farms device has a multiple-hole, pinned height adjustment mechanism. In that mechanism, a removable angled pin 30 is used to secure the connecting bar 10 within the sleeve 12 at a desired height, thereby setting the height of the attached row cleaning device. In particular, the connecting bar 10 is adjusted to the desired height, and then the pin 30 is inserted through one set of holes 26 in the sleeve and one set of holes 28 in the connecting bar. A retaining clip (not shown in the above diagram) is then placed through a hole in the straight end of the pin 30, to prevent the pin 30 from sliding out. The retaining clip must first be removed before the height can be readjusted.

DISCUSSION

2.   It is standard doctrine that determining infringement is a two-step process. First, the court must construe the asserted claims as a matter of law to ascertain their meaning and scope. Second, the claims as construed are compared to the allegedly infringing device. To infringe a claim, each claim limitation must be present in the accused product, literally or equivalently. Thus, the construction of each claim limitation is crucial to the infringement determination.

We begin with the first step, claim construction. The pertinent claim limitation here is the means for locking and releasing, recited specifically as:

> means for locking the connecting means in one of the first and second positions and for selectively releasing the connecting means to allow the connecting means to be slid into the other of the first and second positions therefor;

Section 112, ¶ 6 specifies that such limitations "shall be construed to cover the corresponding structure . . . described in the specification and equivalents thereof." Here, the most closely corresponding structure described in the specification (that is, in the written description) is the control/locking means 46, described as:

> A control/locking means 46 for selectively raising and lowering the implement/tool 8 includes an external handle 48, a first cylindrical rod 50, a cylindrical base portion 52 including a transverse pin 54, and a second cylindrical rod 56 coaxial with the rod 50.

The patent goes on to explain that "the handle 48 of the locking means 46 is used to selectively rotate the . . . pin 54 into and out of [the] slot 72." The patent illustrates this structure in Figures 1 and 2 (included above).

As a matter of claim construction, the trial judge identified the rotatable shaft 52, the pin 54, and the slot 72 as the structure corresponding to the means for locking and releasing, and accordingly instructed the jury:

> The second [claim clause at issue] is [the] means for locking the connecting [means] in one of the first and second positions and for selectively releasing the connecting means to allow the connecting means to be slid into the other of the first and second positions therefor. The court has determined that the structure described in the patent for performing this function is the rotatable shaft 52, the pin 54, and the slot 72 with which the pin is moved in and out of engagement, the slot being in the bracket 24 to lock the movable connecting stem assembly 30 to the fixed guide bracket 24 in the

raised or lowered position. This structure is shown in Figures 1, 2, and 3 of the '282 patent.

As we shall now explain, even construing the corresponding structure as including only the rotatable shaft, pin and slot, Kentucky Farms' device does not infringe because, under this claim construction, Kentucky Farms' device, though it performs the specified locking and releasing function, does not include equivalent structure.

Under the function-way-result test, one considers whether the element of the accused device at issue performs substantially the same function, in substantially the same way, to achieve substantially the same result, as the limitation at issue in the claim. In *Warner-Jenkinson* the Supreme Court observed that this test "may be suitable for analyzing mechanical inventions." 117 S. Ct. at 1054, 41 USPQ2d (BNA) at 1875. We have such an invention here, and the jury was instructed on this test as well as the insubstantial differences test.

With the legal background set, we now consider the issue presented by the parties: does Kentucky Farms' device include an equivalent to the claimed locking and releasing means, such that Kentucky Farms satisfies the means-plus-function limitation under the doctrine of equivalents? Dawn Equipment in essence asserts that the multiple-hole, pinned height-adjustment mechanism in Kentucky Farms' device is equivalent to the structure set forth in the patent. As already described, the multiple-hole, pinned height-adjustment mechanism in Kentucky Farms' device includes a loose angled pin 30 and two sets of holes 26 and 28. Thus, based on the above claim construction, the issue of infringement under the doctrine of equivalents is, in the vernacular of the function-way-result test, whether the loose pin and holes combination in Kentucky Farms' device performs substantially the same function, in substantially the same way, to achieve substantially the same result as the rotatable shaft, pin and slot mechanism shown in Figures 1 and 2 of the '282 patent. We reach the obvious conclusion that, applying this test, no reasonable jury could have found infringement under the doctrine of equivalents.

While the functions of the two mechanisms are the same (i.e., locking and releasing a connecting member), the way and result are not substantially the same. The mechanisms are structurally quite different, and operate quite differently. In the patented device, the pin 54 is permanently fixed to the rotatable shaft 52 and is locked into and released from engagement with the slot 72 by rotating the shaft 52. In sharp contrast, in Kentucky Farms' device, the pin 30 is not attached to anything and is inserted in and removed from the holes 26 and 28 by hand.

There is damning evidence within the text of the '282 patent itself that the two mechanisms do not operate in substantially the same way. Specifically, the patent strongly suggests, if not teaches, that they are not equivalent. The '282 patent, in its Background of the Invention section, describes the problems with prior art "multi-hole pinned height adjustment" mechanisms. The patent teaches that such mechanisms are time-consuming to adjust and are prone to misadjustment by inserting the pin in the wrong holes, and furthermore the loose pins in such mechanisms are easily lost. Kentucky Farms' multiple-hole, pinned height-adjustment mechanism is such a mechanism and shares these same problems. In contrast, the '282 patent teaches that the mechanism provided by the patented invention is directed at solving these problems. These statements in the patent alone strongly suggest, if not mandate, judgment in Kentucky Farms' favor.

Furthermore, consistent with these statements in the patent, Dawn Equipment was unable to provide sufficient evidence that the Kentucky Farms' loose pin and holes mechanism operates in substantially the same way as the rotatable shaft, pin and slot mechanism disclosed in the patent. Indeed, while Dawn Equipment presented substantial expert testimony on infringement, the experts, in testifying with regard to these two mechanisms, merely compared the pins in the two mechanisms. The experts testified that the mechanisms were similar because they both had pins, and opined that the sliding versus rotating motions of the pins in the two mechanisms were simply common alternatives. Most notably, the experts made no reference to the rotatable shaft 52 in the mechanism disclosed in the '282 patent. In essence, the experts opined that the two mechanisms were equivalent because they both used pins and because sliding versus rotating the respective pins was, in their opinions, a common alternative.

Mere comparison of the pins is insufficient to establish that the devices operate in substantially the same way. As the jury was instructed, the relevant structure disclosed in the '282 patent included at least the rotatable shaft, pin and slot—not merely a pin. The testimony by Dawn Equipment's experts fails to establish that Kentucky Farm's loose pin and holes combination is equivalent to the rotatable shaft, pin and slot mechanism, particularly in view of the contrary statements in the '282 patent.

With regard to the result, Kentucky Farms' loose pin and holes combination does not accomplish substantially the same results provided by the rotatable shaft, pin and slot mechanism disclosed in the '282 patent. In particular, the patent touts that the invention reduces adjustment time, prevents misadjustment and eliminates the problem of easily lost pins. The disclosed shaft, pin and slot mechanism plays a major role in achieving these results. Because the mechanism is easy and quick to operate, adjustment time is reduced, and because the mechanism only allows for two positions (lowered and raised), misadjustment is prevented. Furthermore, because the pin is fixed to the rotatable shaft, the pin cannot be lost. In sharp contrast, Kentucky Farms' loose pin and holes combination accomplishes none of these touted results. As the patent describes, a loose pin and holes mechanism is time consuming to adjust, is prone to misadjustment because of the multiple holes, and the loose pin is easily lost.

Accordingly, viewing the record as a whole, the jury's verdict of infringement under the doctrine of equivalents is not supported by substantial evidence. No reasonable jury could have found infringement under the doctrine of equivalents.

CONCLUSION

The judgment denying the defendant's motion for JMOL is reversed; judgment for the defendant is ordered.

Notes

1. **When does § 112 ¶ 6 apply?** The rule of thumb is that if the claim uses the term *means* it is a means-plus-function limitation, if it does not use the word *means* then it does not invoke § 112 ¶ 6. In *Greenberg v. Ethicon Endo–Surgery, Inc.*, 91 F.3d 1580, 1583–84, 39 USPQ2d 1783, 1785–87 (Fed. Cir. 1996) (citations omitted), the Federal Circuit discussed when a claim term invokes § 112 ¶ 6:

> The question whether a claim element triggers section 112(6) is ordinarily not a difficult one. Claim drafters conventionally use the preface "means for" (or "step for") when they intend to invoke section 112(6), and there is therefore seldom any confusion about whether section 112(6) applies to a particular element.... We disagree with the district court's conclusions. In our view, the factors on which the district court relied do not justify treating the claim language at issue in this case as falling within the purview of section 112(6).

> First, the fact that a particular mechanism—here "detent mechanism"—is defined in functional terms is not sufficient to convert a claim element containing that term into a "means for performing a specified function" within the meaning of section 112(6). Many devices take their names from the functions they perform. The examples are innumerable, such as "filter," "brake," "clamp," "screwdriver," or "lock." Indeed, several of the devices at issue in this case have names that describe their functions, such as "graspers," "cutters," and "suture applicators." ... It is true that the term "detent" does not call to mind a single well-defined structure, but the same could be said of other commonplace structural terms such as "clamp" or "container." What is important is not simply that a "detent" or "detent mechanism" is defined in terms of what it does, but that the term, as the name for structure, has a reasonably well understood meaning in the art.

> Second, we do not agree with the district court that the term "detent mechanism" in the '501 patent should be treated as synonymous with the term "detent means" simply because the patent uses the term "detent means" in place of "detent mechanism" on two occasions in the "summary of the invention" portion of the specification. The drafter of the application that matured into the '501 patent appears to have been enamored of the word "means," as the word is used repeatedly in the summary of the invention. A close reading of the specification reveals, however, that

the term is used in that portion of the patent simply as a shorthand way of referring to each of the key structural elements of the invention. Each of those elements is subsequently described in detail, without the use of the term "means," in the "description of the invention" portion of the specification, and each is subsequently claimed, again without the use of the term "means," in claim 1 of the patent.

Finally, we disagree with the district court that the decision in *Interspiro USA Inc. v. Figgie Int'l Inc.*, 815 F. Supp. 1488, 27 USPQ2d 1321 (D. Del. 1993), *aff'd*, 18 F.3d 927, 30 USPQ2d 1070 (Fed. Cir. 1994), is directly on point here. One of the elements in that case claimed "detent means . . . for moving and maintaining [the] movable member" in a breathing regulator for a fireman's mask. The district court in *Interspiro* characterized that element as containing means-plus-function language and therefore invoked section 112(6), a characterization with which this court concurred on appeal. While the language in the *Interspiro* case was in classic "means-plus-function" format, the language in Dr. Greenberg's patent was not. Section 112(6) provides that an element in a claim for a combination "may be expressed" as a means for performing a function, which indicates that the patentee is afforded the option of using the means-plus-function format. The question then is whether, in the selection of claim language, the patentee must be taken to have exercised that option.

In the *Interspiro* case, the patentee's choice of "means-plus-function" language made it clear that the patentee had elected to invoke section 112(6). In this case, by contrast, the element in question did not use conventional "means-plus-function" language, no other element of the claim was in means-plus-function form, and nothing cited to us from the prosecution history or elsewhere suggests that the patentee intended to claim in that fashion. There is therefore no reason to read the claim language in this case as reciting a means for performing a function, within the meaning of section 112(6).

We do not mean to suggest that section 112(6) is triggered only if the claim uses the word "means." The Patent and Trademark Office has rejected the argument that only the term "means" will invoke section 112(6) and we agree. Nonetheless, the use of the term "means" has come to be so closely associated with "means-plus-function" claiming that it is fair to say that the use of the term "means" (particularly as used in the phrase "means for") generally invokes section 112(6) and that the use of a different formulation generally does not. In this case, because we have found no reason to depart from that general principle, we conclude that the phrase "cooperating detent mechanism defining the conjoint rotation of said shafts in predetermined intervals" was not intended to invoke section 112(6) and should not be construed to do so.

In *Sage Products, Inc. v. Devon Industries, Inc.*, 126 F.3d 1420, 1427, 44 USPQ2d 1103 (Fed. Cir. 1997), the court reiterated that the use of "means" gave rise to a presumption of falling within the statute, but noted that the presumption is not conclusive. The presumption can be overcome when a claim uses the word "means," but does not recite a corresponding function for the means. *See York Products, Inc. v. Central Tractor Farm & Family Center*, 99 F.3d 1568, 1574, 40 USPQ2d 1619, 1624 (Fed. Cir. 1996) (holding that § 112 ¶ 6 did not apply despite the use of the word means in the claim because the claim language did not "link the term 'means' to a function," but instead "recit[ed] structure").

The presumption can also be overcome when the claim does recite a function, but then goes on to elaborate sufficient structure within the claim itself to perform entirely the recited function. *See Cole v. Kimberly–Clark Corp.*, 102 F.3d 524, 527, 41 USPQ2d 1001, 1003 (Fed. Cir. 1996) (holding that the limitation "perforation means . . . for tearing" did not fall within § 112 ¶ 6 because the term "perforation" gave it "definite structure"). *But see Unidynamics Corp. v. Automatic Products Int'l Ltd.*, 157 F.3d 1311, 48 USPQ2d 1099 (Fed. Cir. 1998) (holding that the limitation "spring means tending to keep the door closed" did fall within the ambit of § 112 ¶ 6 despite the structural term "spring"). Interestingly both *Cole* and *Unidynamics* were written by Judge Rich. Judge Rich distinguished *Cole* because in that case the claim not only described the structure (perforations) that performed the claimed function (tearing), but also described the location and extent of the structure. It appears that Judge Rich may be backpeddling from *Cole* and limiting its application.

The Court also stated that when a claim uses the term means multiple times, the claim should be scrutinized more carefully to determine if they are all really means-plus-function limitations. *See, e.g., Cole v. Kimberly–Clark Corp.*, 102 F.3d 524, 530, 41 USPQ2d 1001, 1006 (Fed. Cir. 1996) (holding "perforation means" not to invoke § 112 ¶ 6 the court stated: "[t]he drafter of claim 1 in the '239 patent was clearly enamored of the word 'means': six of the seven elements in that claim include the words 'means,' which occurs in the claim fourteen times").

There are also times when a claim contains a means-plus-function clause despite the absence of the magic *means for* language. *See Mas–Hamilton Group v. LaGard Inc.,* 156 F.3d 1206, 48 USPQ2d 1010 (Fed. Cir. 1998) (holding the term "lever moving element" should be construed under § 112 ¶ 6 despite the absence of any "means" language because this claim term is described in terms of its function, not in terms of its mechanical structure); *Raytheon Co. v. Roper Corp..,* 724 F.2d 951, 957, 220 USPQ 592, 597 (Fed. Cir. 1983) (construing functional language introduced by "so that" to be equivalent to "means for" claim language).

Wouldn't a black letter rule be better?

2. **The Structure Disclosed in the Specification.** The patent must identify a structure that performs the function in the means-plus-function clause. A structure disclosed in the specification is the corresponding structure if the specification or prosecution history clearly links or associates that structure to the function recited in the claim. *See Kahn v. General Motors Corp.*, 135 F.3d 1472, 1476, 45 USPQ2d 1608, 1611 (Fed. Cir. 1998); *B. Braun Med., Inc. v. Abbott Lab.*, 124 F.3d 1419, 1424, 43 USPQ2d 1896, 1900 (Fed. Cir. 1997). The duty to link or associate structure with the function is

the *quid pro quo* for the convenience of employing § 112 ¶ 6. *B. Braun Med.*, 124 F.3d at 1424, 43 USPQ2d at 1900 (citing *O.I. Corp. v. Tekmar Co.*, 115 F.3d 1576, 1583, 42 USPQ2d 1777, 1782 (Fed. Cir. 1997)).

What happens if the structure is not clearly identified and linked to the function? The alleged infringer should challenge the validity of the patent for failing to particularly point out and distinctly claim the invention as required by § 112 ¶ 2. This is known as the definiteness requirement. *See In re Donaldson Co.*, 16 F.3d 1189, 1195, 29 USPQ2d 1845, 1850 (Fed. Cir. 1994) (*in banc*) (holding that if the patentee fails to set forth an adequate disclosure in the specification of the structure that corresponds to the means-plus-function element, the patent fails to particularly point out and distinctly claim the invention); *In re Dossel*, 115 F.3d 942, 945–47, 42 USPQ2d 1881, 1884–85 (Fed. Cir. 1997) (same).

3. **Where Can the Structure Be Found?** Section 112 ¶ 6 says that a means-plus-function element covers the corresponding structure described in the specification. What is the specification? If there is a structure in the drawings, is that sufficient? What if the structure is in the Background of the Invention section of the patent? *See Vas–Cath, Inc. v. Mahurkar*, 935 F.2d 1555, 1565, 19 USPQ2d 1111, 1118 (Fed. Cir. 1991) ("under proper circumstances, drawings . . . may provide a 'written description' of an invention as required by § 112"); *Storer v. Hayes Microcomputer Products, Inc.*, 995 F. Supp. 185, 46 USPQ2d 1083 (D. Mass. 1998) (a prior art reference in the specification can supply the missing structure in a means-plus-function claim).

4. **How Many Structures Must Be Disclosed?** For example, a patent claims as one of its elements, "a means for designating a number for each call," and the specification states, "a designation unit can create a sequential or random number for each call." However, the only structure disclosed in the specification is a random number generator. Does this means claim cover a sequential number generator? *See Fonar Corp. v. General Elec. Co.*, 107 F.3d 1543, 1551–52, 41 USPQ2d 1801, 1807 (Fed. Cir. 1997) (explaining that although the specification states that other wave forms may be used, it fails to specifically identify those wave forms and thus the § 112, ¶ 6 claim is limited to the generic gradient wave form actually disclosed). If multiple structures are disclosed in the specification for performing a function, the means-plus-function clause covers all of these structures and their equivalents. *See Serrano v. Telular Corp.*, 111 F.3d 1578, 1582, 42 USPQ2d 1538, 1541 (Fed. Cir. 1997).

5. **Is the Equivalents Determination under § 112 ¶ 6 A Question of Law or Fact?** Under § 112 ¶ 6, when the patentee uses means-plus-function language, the scope of the claim is the structure defined in the specification for performing the claimed function and equivalents thereof. The Federal Circuit has left open the question of whether the determination of equivalents under § 112 ¶ 6 is a question of law for the judge or a question of fact for the fact-finder. Do you think the § 112 ¶ 6 equivalents determination is a question of fact like equivalents under the doctrine of equivalents or a question for the judge like claim construction? Is the determination of structural equivalents, pursuant to § 112 ¶ 6, a part of the claim construction process and therefore a matter for the judge? Prior to

Markman, equivalents for purposes of § 112 ¶ 6 was treated as a question of fact for the factfinder. *See In re Hayes Microcomputer Products, Inc. Patent Litigation*, 982 F.2d 1527, 1541, 25 USPQ2d 1241, 1251 (Fed. Cir. 1992); *Palumbo v. Don–Joy Co.*, 762 F.2d 969, 226 USPQ 5 (Fed. Cir. 1985). However, in *Markman*, the Federal Circuit explicitly left open the question of whether equivalents for means-plus-function clause structures is a question of law or fact. *See Markman v. Westview Instruments, Inc.*., 52 F.3d 967, 977 n. 8, 34 USPQ2d 1321, 1337 n. 8 (Fed. Cir. 1995) ("we express no opinion on the issue of whether a determination of equivalents under § 112, para. 6 is a question of law or fact"). Who would you prefer to have determining the equivalents to the structure disclosed in the specification for the means-plus-function clause, the judge or the jury?

6. **Should There Be a Doctrine of Equivalents for Means–Plus–Function Claim Limitations?** In *Dawn Equipment Co. v. Kentucky Farms Inc.*, 140 F.3d 1009, 46 USPQ2d 1109 (Fed. Cir. 1998), the Federal Circuit considered whether there should be a doctrine of equivalents for means-plus-function claims. The majority opinion stated: "because neither party addresses the point, we shall assume that it is legally proper to apply the doctrine of equivalents to a claim drafted in means-plus-function form." *Dawn Equipment*, 140 F.3d at 1015 n.2, 46 USPQ2d at 1119. However, all three judges addressed this issue in additional opinions. Judge Plager opined that insubstantial differences test and the way and result portion of the function/way/result test (the tests for determining equivalents under the doctrine) should also apply to equivalents under § 112 ¶ 6. Since there is no difference between the tests, Judge Plager concluded that the doctrine should have no application to those aspects of claim limitations drawn in means-plus-function form. *Id.* at 1022, 46 USPQ2d at 1118. Judge Michel questioned whether affording the patentee additional protection under the doctrine of equivalents for means-plus-function limitations conflicts with the language and intent of § 112 ¶ 6. *Id.* at 1023, 46 USPQ2d at 1119. What do you think?

7. **When Is Equivalents Under § 112, ¶ 6 Determined?** In *Chiuminatta Concrete*, the Federal Circuit held that one difference between the doctrine of equivalents and equivalents under § 112 ¶ 6 is that under the doctrine of equivalents a later-developed technology can be an equivalent even though it did not exist at the time of the patent filing. The Supreme Court clearly established the rule for determining equivalents at the time of infringement in *Warner-Jenkinson*. Although the Court never explicitly stated when you determine equivalents under § 112 ¶ 6, if it is not at the time of infringement, when is it? When do you determine whether the patent meets the other § 112 requirements such as best mode and enablement?

8. **Step-plus-function claims.** Although the statute clearly provides for step-plus-function claims, few cases have addressed this issue. Step-plus-function claims would be method claims that use language such as *step for* and then recite a function. In *O.I. Corp. v. Tekmar Co.*, 115 F.3d 1576, 42 USPQ2d 1777 (Fed. Cir. 1997), the Federal Circuit considered whether a method claim invoked § 112 ¶ 6:

> Here, the language in question is "the step[s] of . . . passing the analyte slug through a passage." The district court considered the

statement which appears in the preamble, "removing water vapor from an analyte slug," as a function which invokes application of section 112, ¶ 6. We do not agree. The preamble statement of the purpose of the overall process does not constitute an associated function for the two "passing" steps of claim 9. Performing a series of steps inherently produces a result, in this case the removal of water vapor from the analyte slug, but a statement in a preamble of a result that necessarily follows from performing a series of steps does not convert each of those steps into step-plus-function clauses. The steps of "passing" are not individually associated in the claim with functions performed by the steps of passing.

Id. at 1583. The Court concluded that step-plus-function claims exist only when the claim articulates a step for performing a function without specifying the acts. *Id.* If the claim term had been drafted as a "step for removing water vapor from the analyte slug" without any acts, then it would have implicated § 112 ¶ 6 and the specification would have had to explain the acts, namely passing the analyte slug through a heated passage to remove water vapor. What is the difference between a function and an act?

Problems

Mike's Fishing has identified additional motor manufacturers which it believes may be infringing the '835 patent and it would like your opinion. Referring to the '835 patent in Chapter Eight, consider whether any of the following infringe the '835 patent literally or under the doctrine of equivalents.

1. **The Easy Troller 1.** Remember that the Easy Troller 1 is a bow-mounted trolling motor with an electronic autopilot system. It has a heading detector which is essential just like the heading detector of the '835 patent except that it uses a magnetometer instead of a compass to determine the heading. When the motor deviates from the target heading by 5% the heading detector sends a heading signal to the microprocessor in the steering circuit. The heading detector and the steering circuit are optically coupled. The steering circuit is connected by a wire to the steering motor and it tells the steering motor whether to turn right or left. The steering motor is connected by gears to the lower motor. Mr. Salmon, your technical expert, tells you that a magnetometer works just like a compass. They both read the heading of the boat; they detect heading by taking a reading based on the earth's magnetic field and they both communicate this reading to the microprocessor in the steering circuit. Mr. Salmon also tells you that each form of coupling (mechanical, optical and electrical) are known to be interchangeable. Does the Easy Troller infringe any of the patent claims?

You also discover that The Easy Troller has a handle attached to the top of the trolling motor which resembles a handle on a bicycle with a brake. When you depress the brake portion of the handle the autopilot system is disengaged. Holding on to the brake, the user can manually turn the motor. When the handle is released the auto-pilot re-engages. Does the Easy Troller infringe the patent claims literally or under the doctrine of equivalents?

2. **The Easy Troller 2.** The Easy Troller 2 is identical to The Easy Troller 1 except that it is a stern-mounted motor that pulls the boat through the water (so the boat is actually moving through the water stern first) and it does not have a manual override feature. Does the Easy Troller 2 infringe any of the patent claims?

3. **The Cutter.** The Cutter is a bow-mounted trolling motor with an autopilot system. The Cutter has a heading detector which uses a sensometer instead of a compass to detect heading. Your expert tells you that sensometers, which were invented in 1999, are interchangeable with a compass. The Cutter has a heading detector and a steering circuit. The steering circuit uses a microprocessor. The heading detector and the steering circuit are optically connected. Which claims does the Cutter infringe?

Chapter Ten

PROVING NON–INFRINGEMENT

INTRODUCTION—LIMITATIONS ON INFRINGEMENT

The accused infringer should carefully review the patent at issue, the prosecution history and the prior art to prepare a defense to the patentee's claims of infringement. The alleged infringer will often argue that her product does not infringe. Do not let the name of this chapter, Proving Non-Infringement, confuse you. The patentee has the burden of proving infringement by a preponderance of the evidence. However, once the patentee makes out a prima facie showing of infringement, the accused infringer will want to counter by narrowing the claims or demonstrating that the accused device does not contain all of the elements of the claim. There are several limitations to infringement that have evolved in the case law including: (1) the all elements rule; (2) prosecution history estoppel; (3) prior art; (4) unclaimed disclosures in the specification; and (5) the all advantages rule. These limitations can serve as the basis for a motion for summary judgment of noninfringement by the alleged infringer. Often these issues, like prosecution history estoppel, should be argued during claim construction, as they will affect the way the claim is construed for both literal infringement and infringement under the doctrine of equivalents. These limitations will be discussed in detail in this chapter.

A. THE ALL ELEMENTS/LIMITATIONS RULE

PENNWALT CORP. v. DURAND–WAYLAND, INC.

833 F.2d 931, 4 USPQ2d 1737 (Fed. Cir. 1987)

BISSELL, Circuit Judge.

The district court found that Durand–Wayland's accused devices do not infringe any claim, literally or under the doctrine of equivalents. Unable to view that finding as clearly erroneous under Fed. R. Civ. P. 52(a), we affirm the judgment of noninfringement.

BACKGROUND

Pennwalt sued Durand–Wayland for infringing claims 1, 2, 10 and 18 (claims-at-issue) of its U.S. Patent No. 4,106,628 (the '628 patent) on an invention of Aaron J. Warkentin and George A. Mills, entitled "Sorter for Fruit and the Like." Following a nonjury trial on the issues of patent infringement and validity, the district court, on March 22, 1984, issued an opinion concluding that ... the accused devices did not infringe any of the claims-at-issue, either literally or under the doctrine of equivalents.

OPINION

The '628 patent claims a sorter. The principal object of the invention is to provide a rapid means for sorting items, such as fruit, by color, weight, or a combination of these two characteristics. The sorter recited in claims 1 and 2 conveys items along a track having an electronic-weighing device that produces an electrical signal proportional to the weight of the item, along with signal comparison means, clock means, position indicating means, and discharge means, each of which performs specified functions. The specification describes the details of a "hard-wired" network consisting of discrete electrical components which perform each step of the claims, e.g., by comparing the signals from the weighing device to reference signals and sending an appropriate signal at the proper time to discharge the item into the container corresponding to its weight. The combined sorter of claims 10 and 18 is a multifunctional apparatus whereby the item is conveyed across the weighing device and also carried past an optical scanner that produces an electrical signal proportional to the color of the item. The signals from the weighing device and color sensor are combined and an appropriate signal is sent at the proper time to discharge the item into the container corresponding to its color and weight.

Durand–Wayland manufactures and sells two different types of sorting machines. The first accused device, the "Microsizer," sorts by weight only and employs software labeled either Version 2 or Version 5. The second accused device employs software labeled Version 6 and sorts by both color and weight through the use of the "Microsizer" in conjunction with a color detection apparatus called a "Microsorter."

II.

INFRINGEMENT UNDER THE DOCTRINE OF EQUIVALENTS

Under the doctrine of equivalents, infringement may be found (but not necessarily) if an accused device performs substantially the same overall function or work, in substantially the same way, to obtain substantially the same overall result as the claimed invention. That formulation, however, does not mean one can ignore claim limitations. As this court recently stated in *Perkin-Elmer Corp. v. Westinghouse Elec. Corp.*, 822 F.2d 1528, 3 USPQ2d 1321 (Fed. Cir. 1987):

> One must start with the claim, and though a "non-pioneer" invention may be entitled to some range of equivalents, a court may not, under the guise of applying the doctrine of equivalents, erase a plethora of meaningful structural and functional limitations of the claim on which the public is entitled to rely in avoiding infringe-

ment.... Though the doctrine of equivalents is designed to do equity, and to relieve an inventor from a semantic strait jacket when equity requires, it is not designed to permit wholesale redrafting of a claim to cover non-equivalent devices, i.e., to permit a claim expansion that would encompass more than an insubstantial change.

[I]n applying the doctrine of equivalents, each limitation must be viewed in the context of the entire claim.... "It is ... well settled that each element of a claim is material and essential, and that in order for a court to find infringement, the plaintiff must show the presence of every element or its substantial equivalent in the accused device." *Lemelson v. United States*, 752 F.2d 1538, 1551, 224 USPQ 526, 533 (Fed. Cir. 1985). To be a "substantial equivalent," the element substituted in the accused device for the element set forth in the claim must not be such as would substantially change the way in which the function of the claimed invention is performed.

After a full trial, the district court made findings that certain functions of the claimed inventions were "missing" from the accused devices and those which were performed were "substantially different." The district court observed that "because the 'Microsizer' uses different elements and different operations (on the elements it does use) than the elements and operations disclosed in the patent-in-suit to achieve the desired results, infringement can only be found if the different elements and operations are the legal equivalents of those disclosed in the patent-in-suit." It is clear from this that the district court correctly relied on an element-by-element comparison to conclude that there was no infringement under the doctrine of equivalents, because the accused devices did not perform substantially the same functions as the Pennwalt invention. For example, the district court found in part:

The machine described in the patent-in-suit uses shift registers that respond to "clock pulses" in order to indicate the various positions of the items to be sorted before each item is discharged. The "Microsizer" does not have any "indicating means" to determine positions of the items to be sorted since the microprocessor stores weight and color data, not the positions of the items to be sorted. After a piece of fruit has been analyzed by the "Microsorter" and while it is in transit from the optical detection means to the weight scale, the color value determined by the "Microsorter" is sorted in a color value queue. A color value queue pointer (which changes in value) points to the location of the data corresponding to the next piece of fruit to reach the weight scale. A weight value queue pointer (which also changes in value) is used to correspond to the number of cups between the weight scale and the drop location. The microprocessor software utilizes a random access memory that stores the digital numbers which resulted from the conversion of the analog signals generated by the "Microsorter" and the weight scale, and the queue pointers (under clock control) point to the memory location that has the data about a piece of fruit. The data is never "shifted" around, but rather is just stored in memory until the software routines call for data to be utilized in subsequent portions of the program(s). Thus, the "Microsizer" has neither a "first position indicating means" nor a "second position indicating means." The machine described in the patent-in-suit produces signals that indicate where the fruit is, i.e. track the progression of each cup. The "Microsizer" does not.

With respect to the scope of equivalent functions, the court correctly limited the claims, based upon review of the prosecution history, stating that "the claims of the patent should be read in light of the careful phraseology [of functions] chosen by the inventors" because "the machine disclosed in the patent-in-suit was carefully described so that it did not read on the prior art." As the court correctly noted, the invention was not a pioneer, but an improvement in a crowded art. The claims are "broad" with respect to what type of product can be sorted, i.e., "items" and, thus, sorters of all types of "items" fall within the relevant prior art. The claims are narrow, however, with respect to how the claimed sorter operates. Originally, the claims contained no position indicating means element with its associated functional limitations. The addition of that element was crucial to patentability. A device that does not satisfy this limitation at least equivalently does not function in substantially the same way as the claimed invention.

The trial court found that the accused devices do not have any position indicating means to determine positions of the items to be sorted. Specifically with respect to claims 10 and 18, the court correctly held that "the microprocessor stores weight and color data, not the positions of the items to be sorted." Since each of the claims-at-issue requires a position indicating means and the same analysis applies to each, we set forth only the relevant language of claim 10:

> first position indicating means responsive to a signal from said clock means and said signal from said second comparison means for continuously indicating the position of an item to be sorted while the item is in transit between said optical detection means and said electronic weighing means,

> second position indicating means responsive to the signal from said clock means, the signal from said first comparison means and said first position indicating means for generating a signal continuously indicative of the position of an item to be sorted after said item has been weighed.

The testimony of Dr. Alford, Durand–Wayland's expert, was that the accused machine had no component which satisfied either of the above limitations defining position indicating means, and Pennwalt has admitted that the accused machines do not sort by keeping track of the physical location of an item in transit, continuously or otherwise, as required by each of these limitations.

Pennwalt argues that there is a way to find out where an item is physically located on the track in the accused machine. Its witness, Dr.

Moore, testified "you could find the location of a particular fruit as it moves from the scale to the drop by counting the distance from the stored value for that fruit back to the place the pointer is indicating at the start of the queue." Dr. Alford, Durand-Wayland's expert, admitted this was possible. Thus, Pennwalt asserts that the accused devices have "position indicating means."

One need not explain the technology to understand the inadequacy of Dr. Moore's testimony. As Dr. Moore himself indicates, the accused machine simply does not do what he explains "could" be done. It is admitted that the physical tracking of fruit is not part of the way in which the Durand-Wayland sorter works, in contrast to the claimed sorter which requires some means for "continuously indicating the position of an item to be sorted." While a microprocessor theoretically could be programmed to perform that function, the evidence led the court to a finding that the Durand-Wayland machines performed a substantially different function from that which each of the claims requires.

With respect to the other limitations of claim 10, Pennwalt admits that the asserted "position indicating means" of Durand–Wayland does not meet the limitation that the means must be "responsive to . . . said signal from said second comparison means" because no comparison is made on the Durand–Wayland machine before the discharge point. However, Pennwalt contends that Durand–Wayland "has merely changed the position of an operable element, but the operation and results achieved are the same as those claimed." Pennwalt's analysis is flawed in significant respects.

First, the claim requires that the "position indicating means" must be responsive to certain specified signals. Thus, finding some combination of components in the accused device that might also be labeled a "position indicating means" is a meaningless exercise when such combination is not responsive to the specified signal. As stated in *Panduit Corp. v. Dennison Mfg. Co.*, 810 F.2d 1561, 1576, 1 USPQ2d 1593, 1603 (Fed. Cir. 1987):

> In interpreting the claims, the district court committed fundamental legal error when it analyzed each by a single word description of one part of the claimed tie. In patent law, a word ("teeth"; "hinge"; "ledge") means nothing outside the claim and the description in the specification. A disregard of claim limitations, as here, would render claim examination in the PTO meaningless. If, without basis in the record, courts may so rewrite claims, the entire statutory-regulatory structure that governs the drafting, submission, examination, allowance, and enforceability of claims would crumble.

Second, the district court correctly rejected Pennwalt's assertion that the memory component of the Durand–Wayland sorter which stores information as to weight and color of an item performed substantially the same functions as claimed for the position indicating means. The district court found that a memory function is not the same or substantially the same as the function of "continuously indicating" where an item is physically located in a sorter. On this point the record is indisputable that before the words "continuously indicating" were added as an additional limitation, the claim was unpatentable in view of prior art which, like the accused machines, stores the information with respect to sorting criteria in memories, but did not "continuously" track the location.

Thus, the facts here do not involve later-developed computer technology which should be deemed within the scope of the claims to avoid the pirating of an invention. On the contrary, the inventors could not obtain a patent with claims in which the functions were described more broadly. Having secured claims only by including very specific functional limitations, Pennwalt now seeks to avoid those very limitations under the doctrine of equivalents. This it cannot do. Simply put, the memory components of the Durand–Wayland sorter were not programmed to perform the same or an equivalent function of physically tracking the items to be sorted from the scanner to the scale or from the scale to its appropriate discharge point as required by the claims.

Contrary to Pennwalt's arguments, the district court did not disregard the need to consider a range of equivalent functions under the doctrine of equivalents. Rather, upon evaluation of the evidence, the court concluded, as a fact, that no component in the Durand–Wayland devices performed a function within the permissible range of equivalents for the function of the first position indicating means. That function is required by all of the claims-at-issue. No means in the accused devices performs that function and thus there could be no literal infringement. No means with an equivalent function was substituted in the accused devices and thus there can be no infringement under the doctrine of equivalents. The district court's finding of no infringement is not clearly erroneous.

BENNETT, Senior Circuit Judge, dissenting in part, with whom COWEN, Senior Circuit Judge, and EDWARD S. SMITH and PAULINE NEWMAN, Circuit Judges, join.

The majority opinion contravenes Supreme Court precedents, which do not leave the majority free to rewrite the doctrine of equivalents without regard for *stare decisis* principles. In so doing, the majority has made shortsighted policy choices. The majority has contrived an analytical framework for the doctrine of equivalents that is little more than a redundant literal infringement inquiry, which renders the doctrine of equivalents so unduly restrictive and inflexible as to end its usefulness as judicial doctrine. As this court is confronted in the future with different factual settings in the varied and increasingly complex technologies that comprise this court's patent cases, the court will be forced to admit (or ignore) the full extent of the ties with which it has bound itself today.

The majority facially retains the historical test set forth in *Graver Tank & Mfg. Co. v. Linde Air Prods. Co.*, 339 U.S. 605, 85 USPQ 328

(1950), for infringement under the doctrine of equivalents by stating that infringement in such instances may be found if an accused device performs substantially the same overall function or work, in substantially the same way, to obtain substantially the same overall result as the claimed invention. But in practical effect, the majority has eviscerated the underlying rationale of the Graver Tank test by requiring, under the doctrine of equivalents, an exact equivalent for each element of the claimed invention. The majority in fact commends the district court for undertaking the proper doctrine of equivalents determination, which the majority describes as an element-by-element comparison of the accused device and the patent-in-suit. However, the purported "element-by-element comparison" was never the extent of the doctrine of equivalents analysis under our here-ignored precedents which also required that the analysis be undertaken in light of the entirety of the accused device and entirety of the patent-in-suit.

Even the district court in this case recognized that our precedents require more. Unlike the limited analysis attributed to it by the majority, once the district court determined that all the elements in the patent-in-suit or equivalents of those elements (as determined under 35 U.S.C. § 112–6) were not present in the accused device, it attempted to go beyond the element-by-element comparison to determine whether the "different elements and operations" used in the accused device were "the legal equivalents of those disclosed in the patent-in-suit." Although in my opinion the district court did not completely understand the significance of the requirement to view the "claimed invention as a whole" and therefore erred in making the proper inquiry, the district court nevertheless was attempting to comply with our precedents that undeniably required application of the doctrine of equivalents to the invention as a whole. This required the fact finder to decide by viewing the accused device as a whole whether it and the claimed invention operate in substantially the same way and have substantially the same function and result as the claimed invention.

The application of the doctrine of equivalents to "the claimed invention as a whole" as expressed by this court in *Hughes Aircraft Co. v. United States*, 717 F.2d 1351, 1364, 219 USPQ 473, 482, is inherent in the policy expressed in *Graver Tank*. In order to determine equivalency in light of "the purpose for which an ingredient is used in a patent" and "the qualities it has when combined with the other ingredients" as mandated by the Supreme Court, it is indeed necessary to view the entire claim as a whole, and not merely to conduct an element by element comparison. It is only after such an analysis that the fact finder can determine, in light of the entire claim and all of its limitations, whether the changes or substitutions made alter substantially the way that the accused device works when compared to the claimed invention as a whole.

Thus, the proper inquiry was and should remain whether the devices considered as a whole satisfy the tripartite test of *Graver Tank*. That question has yet to be properly and completely considered by the trial court in this case. I would vacate the district court's decision of noninfringement under the doctrine of equivalents, and remand for a proper consideration of that question in light of the law set out in our prior precedents and this opinion. The question of infringement, whether literal or by equivalents, is a question of fact. It is a question for the district court to decide while properly applying the applicable law. Because the district court's factual findings were made under a misapplication of the law of the doctrine of equivalents, remand for completion of the fact-findings relating to the issue of infringement under the doctrine is the only proper course of action.

NIES, Circuit Judge, additional views.

It is also axiomatic that infringement requires that the claim "read on" the accused device. That means that the patent owner must show structure in the accused device that satisfies the limitations chosen by the inventor to define his invention. An infringement analysis, thus, requires that the courts look at each element of the claim, that is, proceed through the claim element-by-element, and look for correspondence in the allegedly infringing device. If an accused device does not contain at least an equivalent for each limitation of the claim, there is no infringement because a required part of the claimed invention is missing. Indeed, this hoary principle has long been known as the "All Elements" rule.

Notes

1. The all elements rule was affirmed by the Supreme Court in *Warner-Jenkinson* where the Court held that the doctrine of equivalents must be applied element-by-element, not just to the invention as a whole.

2. **What is an Element?** In *Corning Glass Works v. Sumitomo Electric USA., Inc.*, 868 F.2d 1251, 9 USPQ2d 1962 (Fed. Cir. 1989), the Federal Circuit rejected Sumitomo's argument that every term in the claim was an element for purposes of the all elements rule:

> Sumitomo's analysis illustrates the confusion sometimes encountered because of misunderstanding or misleading uses of the term "element" in discussing claims. "Element" may be used to mean a single limitation, but it has also been used to mean a series of limitations which, taken together, make up a component of the claimed invention. In the All Elements rule, "element" is used in the sense of a limitation of a claim.

Compare this with the Court's ruling in *Hoganas AB v. Dresser Indus., Inc.*, 9 F.3d 948, 954, 28 USPQ2d 1936, 1942 (Fed. Cir. 1993).

> In further support of our conclusion, we note that Hoganas' invention is only a modest advance over Matheny, and thus is not entitled to pioneering status or the broad range of equivalents which normally accompanies that status. Moreover, Hoganas is not entitled to a range of equivalents which would erase "meaningful structural and functional limitations of the claim on which the public is entitled to rely in avoiding infringement." *Perkin-Elmer Corp. v.*

Westinghouse Elec. Corp., 822 F.2d 1528, 1532, 3 USPQ2d 1321, 1324 (Fed. Cir. 1987). But that would be the effect of concluding that the accused product infringes under the doctrine of equivalents. As we noted earlier in this opinion, the phrase "straw-shaped" means that the claimed elements are hollow, while the accused fiber is solid. A conclusion that a solid fiber is equivalent to a hollow "straw-shaped" element would eviscerate the plain meaning of that phrase.

The dispute over what constitutes an element for purposes of the doctrine of equivalents can greatly affect the range of equivalents. Will the accused infringer prefer to have several limitations constitute one element or have every limitation considered a separate element?

3. **The Dolly Rule.** In *Dolly, Inc. v. Spalding & Evenflo Cos.*, 16 F.3d 394, 29 USPQ2d 1767 (Fed. Cir. 1994), the Court held that the patentee cannot argue that her claim covers a structure that is specifically excluded by the claims under the doctrine of equivalents. In *Dolly*, the claim recited a portable, adjustable child's play chair with a stable, rigid frame, a seat panel, and a back panel. The Court held that the accused device which had a seat and a back panel which fit together to form a stable rigid frame was not equivalent. "A stable rigid frame assembled from the seat and back panels is not the equivalent of a separate stable rigid frame which the claim language specifically [requires]." *Id.* at 400, 29 USPQ2d at 1771. Hence when the claim "specifically excludes" the argued equivalent there is no infringement. Does this exception threaten to swallow the rule (doctrine of equivalents)?

4. **Pioneering Inventions**. When a small advance is made in a crowded art, the patentee is generally only entitled to a narrow range of equivalents. When the invention is pioneering, like the transistor, the patentee would be entitled to a broader range of equivalents. Consider the following comments from *Texas Instruments, Inc. v. United States Int'l Trade Comm'n*, 846 F.2d 1369, 1370, 6 USPQ2d 1886, 7 USPQ2d 1414, (Fed. Cir. 1988) (citations and footnotes omitted):

> Texas Instruments ("TI") again asserts that because its Patent No. 3,819,921 describes a "pioneer" invention the claims should be given an enhanced breadth of interpretation . . .

> The Supreme Court in *Westinghouse v. Boyden Power–Brake Co.*, 170 U.S. 537, 562 (1898), characterized a pioneering invention as "a distinct step in the progress of the art, distinguished from a mere improvement or perfection of what had gone before." Courts early recognized that patented inventions vary in their technological or industrial significance. Indeed, inventions vary as greatly as human imagination permits.

> There is not a discontinuous transition from "mere improvement" to "pioneer." History shows that the rules of law governing infringement determinations are amenable to consistent application despite the variety of contexts that arise. The judicially "liberal" view of both claim interpretation and equivalency accorded a "pioneer" invention, is not a manifestation of a different legal standard based on an abstract legal concept denominated "pioneer." Rather,

the "liberal" view flows directly from the relative sparseness of prior art in nascent fields of technology.

In the case of the claimed "pocket-size" calculator, we do not share the Commission's denigration of TI's contribution. However, even its "pioneer" status does not change the way infringement is determined. The patentee's disclosure, the prosecution history, and the prior art still provide the background against which the scope of claims is determined.

What effect does the pioneering status of an invention have on infringement? How do you prove that an invention is pioneering? With some inventions you just "know it when you see it." With others, evidence of commercial success and industry impact will help.

The next case has had a long history. Hughes brought this suit against the government for infringing its spacecraft patent in 1973. As you can see, the following opinion is the fourteenth one to be generated in this case. Sometimes, the resolution of an issue is more important than the outcome.

HUGHES AIRCRAFT CO. v. UNITED STATES

140 F.3d 1470, 46 USPQ2d 1285 (Fed. Cir. 1998)

Before RADER, Circuit Judge, ARCHER, Senior Circuit Judge, and BRYSON, Circuit Judge.

ARCHER, Senior Circuit Judge.

This case returns to this court after the Supreme Court's vacatur and remand of *Hughes Aircraft Co. v. United States*, 86 F.3d 1566, 39 USPQ2d 1065 (Fed. Cir. 1996) (Hughes XIII), in light of the Court's decision in *Warner-Jenkinson Co. v. Hilton Davis Chemical Co.*, 520 U.S. 17 (1997). Because *Hughes Aircraft Co. v. United States*, 717 F.2d 1351, 219 USPQ 473 (Fed. Cir. 1983) (Hughes VII) satisfies the legal requirements announced in Warner–Jenkinson, we affirm.

BACKGROUND

The Williams patent relates to an apparatus for control over the orientation, or attitude, of a spacecraft using commands from a ground control station. The relevant limitations of claim 1 of the Williams patent read:

(e) means disposed on said body for providing an ***indication to a location external to said body of the instantaneous spin angle position*** of said body about said axis and the orientation of said axis with reference to a fixed external coordinate system;

(f) and means disposed on said body ***for receiving from said location control signals synchronized*** with said indication;

(g) said valve being coupled to said last-named means and responsive to said control signals for applying fluid to said fluid expulsion means ***in synchronism therewith*** for precessing said body to orient said axis into a predetermined desired relationship with said fixed external coordinate system.

(Emphasis added). In order to correct the attitude of the spacecraft, the ground crew must be able to calculate the instantaneous spin angle (ISA) position. The ISA position is the angle between two specific planes. The first plane, the rotating plane, is defined by the location of the precessing jet and the satellite's axis of rotation. The second plane, the reference plane, is defined by a fixed reference point in an external coordinate system (such as the sun or another star) and the spin axis. The angle between these planes at a given moment in time is the ISA position with reference to a fixed external coordinate system. Thus, the ISA position generally measures the location of the precessing jet in its rotational cycle relative to the reference plane.

Two pieces of information are needed to calculate the ISA position: the spin rate of the satellite and the instant in time at which the rotating plane passes by the fixed point in the fixed external coordinate system and at which the jet is closest to the fixed reference point. The invention uses onboard sensors to collect this data and then transmits this information to Earth to allow the ground crew to determine the satellite's existing and desired orientations. After making the necessary calculations, the ground crew pulses the attitude jet by radio signal commands to precess, or tip, the spin axis of the satellite to the desired position.

In the accused "store and execute" (S/E) craft, the satellite retrieves the same raw data but calculates the ISA position onboard. The spin rate and information to determine the orientation of the satellite is transmitted to the ground. In most of the S/E craft, the satellite does not provide information sufficient to calculate the ISA position.[1] After receiving the spin rate, the ground crew performs the necessary calculations to adjust the attitude of the craft. This information is then sent to and stored in the satellite. The precession does not occur, however, until the ground crew sends an execute command to the satellite.

In 1982, the then-Court of Claims originally determined, inter alia, that the accused S/E devices did not infringe the patent literally or under the doctrine of equivalents. (Hughes VI). On appeal, this court reversed the noninfringement judgment, holding that the S/E devices infringe under the doctrine of equivalents, and remanded for a determination of just compensation. After the decision by the Court of Federal Claims on remand, Hughes appealed, challenging the assessment of damages, and the government cross-appealed, again challenging the liability determination of Hughes VII in light of this court's in banc decision in *Pennwalt Corp. v. Durand–Wayland, Inc.*, 833 F.2d 931, 4 USPQ2d 1737 (Fed. Cir. 1987) (*in banc*). This court affirmed the damages determination and

---

1. Even for the craft that do supply sufficient data, however, the ground crew does not rely on the information to precess the satellite because the information is re-tained on board the satellite. Instead, this information appears to be transmitted for research purposes.

refused, under the doctrine of law of the case, to reconsider the Hughes VII decision. The Supreme Court, however, granted *certiorari*, vacated the judgment, and remanded the case (GVR order) to this court for reconsideration in light of its decision in *Warner-Jenkinson*.

Turning to the merits, we first address the effect of the "all-elements" rule (sometimes referred to as the "all-limitations" rule) enunciated in *Warner-Jenkinson* on the *Hughes VII* decision. The Supreme Court clarified the doctrine of equivalents by noting that:

> [e]ach element contained in a patent claim is deemed material to defining the scope of the patented invention, and thus the doctrine of equivalents must be applied to individual elements of the claim, not to the invention as a whole. It is important to ensure that the application of the doctrine, even as to an individual element, is not allowed such broad play as to effectively eliminate that element in its entirety.

Thus, the test for equivalence is to be applied to the individual claim limitations:

> An analysis of the role played by each element in the context of the specific patent claim will thus inform the inquiry as to whether a substitute element matches the function, way, and result of the claimed element, or whether the substitute element plays a role substantially different from the claimed element.

117 S. Ct. at 1054; *see Pennwalt*, 833 F.2d at 935, 4 USPQ2d at 1740 (" '[T]he plaintiff must show the presence of every element or its substantial equivalent in the accused device.' To be a 'substantial equivalent,' the element substituted in the accused device for the element set forth in the claim must not be such as would substantially change the way in which the function of the claimed invention is performed." (citations omitted)).

The government argues that the all-elements rule demands that we depart from the reasoning in *Hughes VII*, in which the court stated that the trial court erred in not "apply[ing] the doctrine of equivalents to the claimed invention as a whole." *Hughes VII*, 717 F.2d at 1364, 219 USPQ at 482. According to the government, to conclude that the claim limitations in paragraphs (e), (f), and (g) are met equivalently by elements in the accused devices would vitiate those claim limitations. The government additionally urges that the arguably corresponding elements of the S/E system differ substantially from the claim limitations by storing the ISA position value onboard in lieu of transmitting an indication of the ISA position to the ground, by not acting in synchronism with the control signals, and by not firing the precession jet within a fixed period of time after receiving the command signal.

Hughes responds that there is no reason to depart from the conclusion reached in Hughes VII because Warner–Jenkinson did not significantly alter the all-elements rule as stated in Pennwalt. Moreover, the *Hughes VII* court, in Hughes' opinion, did perform the required element-by-element analysis mandated by *Warner-Jenkinson*.

We conclude that the analysis performed in *Hughes VII* satisfies the all-elements rule as stated in *Warner-Jenkinson*. Regarding claim paragraph (e), the court in *Hughes VII* concluded that the transmission to the ground crew of the spin rate and information sufficient to calculate the sun angle in the S/E vehicles "is the modern day equivalent to providing an indication of the ISA to the ground...." This information, while insufficient to calculate the ISA position, was sufficient to enable the ground crew to control the satellite, which is substantially the same function performed and the identical result achieved by transmitting the indication of the ISA position to the ground.

Furthermore, although the information sent is insufficient to calculate the ISA position, this does not demonstrate a substantial difference in the way the element functions. This is a case in which a "subsequent change in the state of the art, such as later-developed technology, obfuscated the significance of [the] limitation at the time of its incorporation into the claim." *Sage Prods., Inc. v. Devon Indus., Inc.*, 126 F.3d 1420, 1425, 44 USPQ2d 1103, 1107 (Fed. Cir. 1997); *cf. Warner–Jenkinson*, 117 S. Ct. at 1053 ("Insofar as the question under the doctrine of equivalents is whether an accused element is equivalent to a claimed element, the proper time for evaluating equivalency ... is at the time of infringement, not at the time the patent was issued."); *Pennwalt*, 833 F.2d at 938, 4 USPQ2d at 1742 ("[T]he facts here do not involve later developed computer technology which should be deemed within the scope of the claims to avoid the pirating of an invention."). The court in *Hughes VII* determined that the change in the S/E devices was the result of a technological advance not available until after the patent issued. Relying on testimony of one of skill in the art at the time of infringement, the court in *Hughes VII* concluded that this advance resulted in an insubstantial change in the way the element performed its function. See id. (citing testimony that an engineer would realize that transmission of the ISA position was no longer necessary as a result of the change in technology).

The court in *Hughes VII* also concluded that the "synchronism" limitations in paragraphs (f) and (g) were also equivalently met by the accused devices. Again, as a result of an advance in technology, the satellite system was able at the time of infringement to store the precession information and to wait to precess the satellite until receipt of the execute command. Thus, the synchronism in the accused device is coordinated by the computer instead of by real-time execution of the command from the ground. As recognized in *Hughes VII*, "[t]he difference between operation by retention and operation by sending is achieved by relocating the function, making no change in the function performed, or in the basic manner of operation, or in the result obtained." The court in *Hughes VII* correctly performed an analysis of the function, way, and result of the individual elements in the accused devices and concluded that these elements equivalently met the claim limitations at issue.

Accordingly, we conclude that *Warner-Jenkinson* provides no basis to alter the decision in *Hughes VII* because the court properly applied the all-elements rule.

Notes

1. **Later Developed Technologies**. Notice how the Federal Circuit deals with the difficult task of applying the all elements rule and determining equivalence at the time of infringement. Ultimately the court concluded that the later developed technologies "obfuscate[d] the significance of [the] limitations." Does this mean the all elements rule can be ignored when after-developed technologies no longer need to include one of the claim limitations in order to practice the invention?

B. PROSECUTION HISTORY ESTOPPEL

LITTON SYS., INC. v. HONEYWELL, INC.

140 F.3d 1449, 46 USPQ2d 1321 (Fed. Cir. 1998)

RADER, Circuit Judge.

The United States Supreme Court vacated the judgment in *Litton Systems, Inc. v. Honeywell, Inc.*, 87 F.3d 1559, 39 USPQ2d 1321 (Fed. Cir. 1996) (*Litton I*), and remanded to this court for further consideration in light of *Warner-Jenkinson Co. v. Hilton Davis Chemical Co.*, 117 S. Ct. 1040 (1997).

In *Litton I*, this court reversed the trial court's grant of JMOL. This court determined that:

(1) substantial evidence supported the jury's findings that Honeywell's hollow cathode and RF processes infringed the '849 reissue; . . .

Litton's patents claim a method for coating a substrate with multiple layers of optical materials. The method uses an ion beam from a Kaufman-type ion beam source to sputter deposit the optical materials on the substrate. The result is an almost perfectly reflective mirror, an essential component for ring-laser gyroscopes (RLGs). RLGs control navigation in aircraft. Honeywell's alleged infringing methods for making these mirrors use ion beams from hollow cathode and RF ion beam sources.

Claim Construction

In this case, the question of infringement turns primarily on the interpretation of the phrase "Kaufman-type ion beam source" in claim 1 of the '849 reissue. Litton contends that the appropriate interpretation of "Kaufman-type ion beam source" encompasses any broad-beam, multi-apertured, gridded ion beam source. Litton's proposed construction, however, is inconsistent with the prosecution history of the '849 reissue.

In the course of prosecuting the '849 reissue, Litton argued that the term "ion beam source" in its original claims could not "properly be construed to refer to any other ion beam gun but the Kaufman gun."

Paper No. 15 at 8. Moreover, a declaration accompanying Litton's remarks plainly stated: "Those skilled in the coating arts ... would reasonably construe these claims to refer ... only to the Kaufman-type ion-beam guns referred to in the specification of this application." Paper No. 16 at 7. Thus, Litton defined "ion beam source" to mean only the Kaufman-type gun. This definition acquires even more credibility when Litton later amended its claims to cover a "Kaufman-type ion beam source." If, as Litton insisted, one of skill could only construe the broad term to mean a Kaufman-type gun, certainly the specific term encompasses nothing more.

At column 4, lines 44–57, the reissue's specification describes a Kaufman-type ion beam source:

> The ion beam gu[n] 4 is a commercially available ion [e]mitting ap[p]aratus generally known in the art as a Kauffman [sic] type ion beam gun. The gun's cathode 6 is a therm[i]onic emitter, i.e., it emits electrons by passing an electric current through it which heats the wire. The cathode 6 emits electrons which are accelerated towards the anode 8. The electrons being accelerated from the cathode to the anode strike argon atoms and in so doing dislodge electrons from the argon. The results are positively charged argon ions which are accelerated away from the anode and towards the grids 12 and 14. Permanent bar magnets 10 attached to the anode introduce a magnetic field into the area between the cathode and the anode.

Thus, this court interprets the phrase "Kaufman-type ion beam source" to include a thermionic (hot-wire) cathode, an anode, grids, and magnets.

This court detects no legally significant distinction between the phrases, "Kaufman-type ion beam source" and "Kaufman-type ion beam gun." During the prosecution of the reissue, Litton used the terms "gun" and "source" interchangeably. For example, in response to one of the examiner's rejections, Litton stated: "Applicants need not add the words 'Kaufman gun' or 'Kaufman source' to claim 1 because claim 1 cannot properly be construed to refer to any other ion beam gun but the Kaufman gun."

In sum, after consideration of the primary sources for construing patent claim meaning, this court interprets the phrase "Kaufman-type ion beam source" to encompass any ion beam gun with the four stated components: a hot-wire cathode, an anode, grids, and magnets.

LITERAL INFRINGEMENT

Literal infringement requires that the accused device contain each limitation of the claim exactly; any deviation from the claim precludes a finding of literal infringement. Because Honeywell's hollow cathode process does not employ a hot-wire cathode and its RF ion beam process does not use a cathode at all, this court affirms the trial court's grant of JMOL that the accused hollow cathode and RF ion beam processes do not literally infringe the asserted claims of the '849 reissue.

INFRINGEMENT UNDER THE DOCTRINE OF EQUIVALENTS

Because Honeywell's processes do not literally infringe Litton's claimed method, this court now considers the issue of infringement under the doctrine of equivalents. Litton asserts that Honeywell's hollow cathode and RF ion beam sources are equivalents of the "Kaufman-type ion beam source" in claim 1. Honeywell contends that they are not equivalents, and, more importantly, that Litton's admissions and amendments during patent prosecution estop it from asserting any equivalents to the "Kaufman-type ion beam source."

As discussed above, the "Kaufman-type ion beam source" phrase means a source with a hot-wire cathode, an anode, grids, and magnets. . . . The district court adopted an interpretation of the "Kaufman-type ion beam source" identical to that which this court has adopted. In denying infringement under the doctrine of equivalents, the district court reasoned—despite evidence of interchangeability and insubstantial differences—that the "Kaufman-type ion beam source" limitation could not embrace a range of equivalents that extended to a source that worked in a substantially different way.

In light of the additional clarification supplied by case law in the intervening period, this court vacates the district court's grant of JMOL to allow it to consider other rationales for judgment as a matter of law—for both the hollow cathode and RF processes. Specifically, this court provides the district court an opportunity to consider: (1) whether, as outlined below, prosecution history estoppel precludes infringement under the doctrine of equivalents, (2) whether prior art precludes infringement under the doctrine of equivalents, *Wilson Sporting Goods Co. v. David Geoffrey & Assocs.*, 904 F.2d 677, 684, 14 USPQ2d 1942, 1948 (Fed. Cir. 1990), and (3) whether, under the reasoning of *Warner-Jenkinson*, application of the doctrine of equivalents would "effectively eliminate [an] element in its entirety," *Warner-Jenkinson*, 117 S. Ct. at 1049, 41 USPQ2d at 1871. In sum, this court remands to permit examination of the application of the doctrine of equivalents.

PROSECUTION HISTORY ESTOPPEL

In *Warner-Jenkinson*, the Supreme Court changed some aspects of the law of prosecution history estoppel. However, the extent of this change was limited. Honeywell argues that *Warner-Jenkinson* held that if a claim element has been added by amendment for reasons of patentability, prosecution history estoppel automatically bars all equivalents for that element, regardless of whether the administrative record before the Patent and Trademark Office (PTO) shows that the applicant surrendered all coverage beyond the literal claim scope. Honeywell's position, however, would both bar after-arising equivalents expressly approved by the Supreme Court and bar any equivalents whatsoever to the vast majority of claim limitations amended during patent prosecution.

This court determines in this opinion that the Supreme Court did not in fact effect such a sweeping change. Instead the Supreme Court adhered to the longstanding doctrine that an estoppel only bars recapture of that subject matter actually surrendered during prosecution. The common practice of amending a claim during prosecution, even amending to overcome prior art, does not necessarily surrender all subject matter beyond the literal scope of the amended claim limitation.

In *Warner-Jenkinson*, the Supreme Court ... discussed the "well-established limit on non-literal infringement, known variously as 'prosecution history estoppel' and 'file wrapper estoppel.'" *Id.* at 1049, 41 USPQ2d at 1871. The Court noted: "In each of our cases ... prosecution history estoppel was tied to amendments made to avoid the prior art, or otherwise to address a specific concern—such as obviousness...." *Id.* Thus, the Court reaffirmed that the reason for claim amendments remains relevant to application of an estoppel. A claim amendment to avoid prior art prevents recapture of subject matter the applicant surrendered to obtain patent protection. "Where the reason for the [claim] change was not related to avoiding the prior art ... [the prosecution history] does not necessarily preclude infringement by equivalents...." *Id.* at 1050–51, 41 USPQ2d at 1872. The Supreme Court thus noted that an amendment during prosecution does not foreclose all application of the doctrine of equivalents. Rather a court must inquire into the reasons for an amendment before invoking an estoppel.

In *Warner-Jenkinson*, however, the patent prosecution record disclosed no reason for Hilton Davis's claim amendments. In this context, the Court established a presumption that when an applicant narrows a claim element during prosecution, a trial court should presume that the applicant did so for a reason related to patentability. Consequently, where a patent owner cannot show a reason fo[r] the amendment other than patentability, "a court should presume that the purpose behind the ... amendment is such that prosecution history estoppel would apply." *Id.* at 1054, 41 USPQ2d at 1876. Thus, the Supreme Court articulated an additional rule to trigger, in applicable circumstances, prosecution history estoppel. But that is all the Supreme Court articulated. Although *Warner-Jenkinson* supplied new guidance about when prosecution history estoppel might apply, the Court did not change the scope or effect of the estoppel.

In accord with the Supreme Court's understanding, this court has repeatedly stated that application of prosecution history estoppel does not necessarily limit a patentee to the literal language of the amended element—even when an amendment has been made to overcome the prior art. Thus, an amendment to claim language in response to prior art "may have a limiting effect within a spectrum ranging from great to small to zero. The effect may or may not be fatal to application of a range of equivalents broad enough to encompass a particular accused product. It is not fatal to application of the doctrine itself." *Hughes Aircraft Co. v. United States*, 717 F.2d 1351, 1363, 219 USPQ 473, 481 (Fed. Cir. 1983).

Despite the Supreme Court's overall reasoning, Honeywell argues that *Warner-Jenkinson* eliminated any scope for prosecution history estoppel. In other words, according to Honeywell, any claim language amended during prosecution for reasons related to patentability has no range of equivalents. To support its transformation of infringement rules, Honeywell points to the following language:

> Where no explanation is established, however, the court should presume that the PTO had a substantial reason related to patentability for including the limiting element added by amendment. In those circumstances, *prosecution history estoppel would bar the application of the doctrine [sic] equivalents as to that element.*

Warner-Jenkinson, 117 S. Ct. at 1051, 41 USPQ2d at 1873 (emphasis added).

Read in context, this passage does not effect the sweeping change advocated by Honeywell. As noted above, the entire context of the *Warner-Jenkinson* opinion shows that the Supreme Court approved the PTO's practice of requesting amendments with the understanding that the doctrine of equivalents would still apply to the amended language. As noted above, this court had repeatedly articulated that rule. In that context, it is telling that the Supreme Court was careful to avoid disturbing basic rules and assumptions. Footnotes 6 and 7 further evince an intent "[t]o [not] change so substantially the rules of the game." *Warner-Jenkinson*, 117 S. Ct. at 1050 n. 6, 41 USPQ2d at 1876 n.6. Footnote 6 appears to explain further the Court's rejection of the petitioner's proposed any-type-of-amendment, no-equivalents rule. Footnote 7 explains that "where a change is made to overcome an objection based on the prior art," a court should explore "the reason (right or wrong) for the objection and the manner in which the amendment addressed and avoided the objection." *Id.* at 1051 n.7, 41 USPQ2d at 1876 n.7. These footnotes evince the Court's intent to change as little as possible.

The Supreme Court began its discussion of prosecution history estoppel by acknowledging that in each of its cases estoppel "was tied to amendments made to avoid the prior art, or otherwise to address a specific concern—such as obviousness—that arguably would have rendered the claimed subject matter unpatentable." *Warner-Jenkinson*, 117 S. Ct. at 1049, 41 USPQ at 1872. Thus, from the outset, the Court recognized that the *Warner-Jenkinson* standard "related to patentability" encompassed amendments "made to avoid the prior art." The Court then observed:

> It is telling that in each case this Court probed the reasoning behind the Patent Office's insistence upon a change in the claims. In each instance, a change was demanded because the claim as otherwise written was viewed as not describing a patentable invention at all— typically because what it described was encompassed within the prior art.

Id. at 1050, 41 USPQ2d at 1872.

The Supreme Court then proceeded to recognize that "there are a variety of other reasons why the PTO may request a change in claim language." *Id*. For this proposition, the Court cited the United States' amicus brief, which refers to amendments made to overcome indefiniteness and nonenablement rejections. Thus, the Court concluded, "[o]ur prior cases have consistently applied prosecution history estoppel only where claims have been amended for a limited set of reasons, and we see no substantial cause for requiring a more rigid rule invoking an estoppel regardless of the reasons for a change." *Warner-Jenkinson*, 117 S. Ct. at 1050, 41 USPQ2d at 1872.

Although not automatically erecting an estoppel, an amendment made for reasons other than patentability may still give rise to an estoppel. This court has acknowledged that even arguments made during prosecution without amendments to claim language—if sufficient to evince a clear and unmistakable surrender of subject matter—may estop an applicant from recapturing that surrendered matter under the doctrine of equivalents. Estoppel by clear and unmistakable surrender without claim amendments may arise even when the arguments to the examiner were not necessary to distinguish prior art. This principle presupposes that the applicant has made the surrender unmistakable enough that the public may reasonably rely on it. By logical extension, if an applicant makes an amendment unrelated to patentability which evinces an unmistakable surrender, that action will preclude recapture of the surrendered subject matter under the doctrine of equivalents.

PROSECUTION HISTORY OF THE '849 REISSUE

Turning to application of the doctrine of prosecution history estoppel in this case, this court first recognizes that Litton amended its claims. The applicant amended claim 1 to add language about the "Kaufman-type ion beam source." Thus, this court must examine whether that amendment occurred for a reason related to patentability. The applicant filed the '849 reissue on July 2, 1985. At that time, independent claim 1 read as follows:

> 1. A method of fabricating multiple layer optical films, said multiple layer optical films comprising optical layers having different indices of refraction comprising:
>
> bombarding targets obliquely with *an ion beam* in a vacuum chamber to sputter deposit a plurality of optical film layers on a base;
>
> controlling the atmosphere inside the vacuum chamber to provide sufficient gas to sustain the ion beam and the proper amount of oxygen to accomplish proper stoichiometry of the thin films; and
>
> depositing multiple layers of different materials on said base by varying the targets being bombarded by the ion beam; and
>
> continuously rotating said base during the deposition of said multiple optical layers.

(Emphasis added.) In the next month, August 1985, Litton submitted a patentability report citing eighty-two references. Litton took pains to separately list and distinguish each of these references. Often Litton explained that a given reference "does not disclose Applicant's [Litton's] claimed ion beam sputtering techniques."

In December 1985, ... the examiner rejected all the claims as obvious under section 103. In addition to extensive reliance on the Laznovsky article, the examiner rejected the claims "under 35 U.S.C. 103 as ... unpatentable over the combination of admitted prior art contained in [the] 'Patentability Report.' "

In its June 1986 response, Litton acknowledged that all the prior art in the patentability report, as well as the Laznovsky article, occasioned the obviousness rejection. Indeed Litton again a second time listed by number each of the eighty-two references previously cited along with the Laznovsky article and expressly distinguished its claims from each piece of prior art. Beyond the express reference-by-reference distinctions, Litton further distinguished the invention from these eighty-three references as follows:

> What is novel and unobvious about Applicants' invention is the use of ion-beam sputtering techniques, *and particularly the use of Kaufman gun ion beam techniques*, to form multiple-layer optical films on a base with optical layers having different indices of refraction....

(emphasis added). At this point, Litton also included for the first time its "Kaufman-type" limitation in several dependent claims.

Nonetheless, the examiner issued a final rejection again under section 103 on July 3, 1986. The examiner focused on one ion beam source in the prior art—the duoplasmatron source of the Bernard patent. The rejection highlighted the discontinuity between the claims' general requirement for an "ion beam source" and Litton's arguments directed to a more narrow "Kaufman-type ion beam source":

> As for applicants' arguments based upon an alleged unexpected result obtained by use of a Kauffman [sic] type ion gun rather than a duoplasmatron type ion gun, it is noted that most of the claims are not limited to any particular type of ion gun; thus applicants are arguing a limitation not in the claims. Moreover, Kauffman [sic] type ion sources are standard in the art; their use in ion beam sputtering apparatus constitutes nothing unobivous [sic]. *See e.g.* Laznovsky at page 47, column 1. Lastly, applicants merely allege an unexpected result; no comparative data are supplied.

In conclusion, the examiner again a second time rejected Litton's claims "over the combination of references as made in the first Office action." In rejecting again over all eighty-three references, the examiner pointed out as noted above that Litton had not limited its claims "to any particular type of ion gun."

In December 1986, Litton replied: "Contrary to the contentions in Paper No. 11, Applicants' claims relate only to Kaufman-type ion-beam sputtering because duoplasmatron sources are today, and were in 1978, devices that no one of ordinary skill in the art would use for forming multiple layer optical coatings." Litton argued that the examiner had read claim 1 broadly to include duoplasmatron ion beam sources when it "[could not] properly be construed to refer to any other ion beam gun but the Kaufman gun."

In addition, Litton submitted three declarations under 37 C.F.R. § 1.132 supporting its nonobviousness contentions. These declarations highlighted the unexpected results from the Kaufman-type guns and the slow deposition rates of the duoplasmatron. In particular, the Baumeister declaration contended:

> Those skilled in the coating arts, in reading claims 1 and 3–10 of this application for reissue, knowing that duoplasmatron sources are unworkable for making multiple layer optical coatings of any kind, let alone the multiple layer optical coatings referred to in claims 1 and 3–10, would reasonably construe these claims to refer not to duoplasmatron sputtering sources, but only to the Kaufman-type ion-beam guns referred to in the specification of this application.

Recognizing that the examiner had rejected over all eighty-three references, however, Litton again a third time cited and individually distinguished each of the cited references. Indeed for emphasis, Baumeister also resubmitted all eighty-three references with his declaration as evidence that he had considered and distinguished the relevant prior art.

Apparently, the declarations persuaded the examiner. After a January 1987 telephone communication, he made the following notes:

> The examiner initiated the interview to inform applicant's attorney that allowance of the application was possible if all the claims were limited to Kaufman gun sources being used in the claimed process. Unless the claims were so limited, the examiner indicated that a 35 U.S.C. 112 Par 2 rejection [,] on the basis that applicants were not claiming what they regarded as their invention in view of their argument contained in paper no. 15 filed 12/16/86 [,] would be made in the next office action on the merits. The paper #15 overcomes the other previously made objections.

Thus, at this point, the examiner conditioned allowance of the claims on an amendment limiting the invention to Kaufman gun sources.

In its March 1987 response, Litton treated the examiner's threat as a formal section 112 rejection. Litton incorporated the Kaufman-type ion beam source limitation into claim 1 (the "Kaufman-type amendment"), stating that the amendment was made "to overcome the rejections of these claims under 35 USC § 112, second paragraph." With this action, Litton submitted for still a fourth time all eighty-three references and a number-by-number explanation of the distinctions between its invention and each of those references.

The examiner allowed the amended claims and closed prosecution on the merits on June 26, 1987.... Claim 1 is representative of the other claims; wherever the phrase "an ion beam" had appeared, Litton substituted "an ion beam produced by or derived from a Kaufman-type ion beam source."

Even this action, however, did not complete the prosecution history. After another technical examiner interview in April 1987, Litton submitted again the entire list of the eighty-three references complete with distinctions from its invention. This final June 1987 submission was the fifth time (sixth counting the Baumeister declaration) that Litton had raised and expressly distinguished its invention from each of the eighty-three references.

Effect of the Kaufman-type Amendment

In view of the foregoing prosecution history, this court now considers whether the Kaufman-type amendment was related to patentability. Litton argues that the amendment came after the applicants had "overcome the other previously made [obviousness] rejections." Litton characterizes its amendment as a response to a rejection under 35 U.S.C. § 112, ¶ 2 because the "applicants were not claiming what they regarded as their invention." Litton cites *Warner–Jenkinson* for the proposition that amendments in response to section 112 rejections are not related to patentability. Because its amendment responded to a section 112 rejection, Litton argues that its amendment was not "related to patentability" and this court should not presume that the amendment created an estoppel.

Although amendments made in response to indefiniteness and enablement rejections are generally not made "in response to the prior art," the amendment made in response to the section 112 rejection at issue here, a "regards as his invention" rejection, was related to patentability. Without evidence to the contrary, an examiner generally should presume that a claim recites what the applicant regards as his invention. Moreover, "some material submitted by [the] applicant, other than his specification" must warrant this type of section 112 rejection. Thus, an examiner generally makes a "regards as his invention" rejection only as an applicant's position becomes clear over the course of prosecution. In other words, this rejection almost always follows some other rejection of the inventive material set forth in the claim.

Consequently, this court cannot ignore the rejections which preceded this "regards as his invention" rejection. This particular "regards as his invention" rejection followed a series of obviousness rejections. In effect, the examiner threatened to reject again for obviousness unless the applicant restated its claim to match the scope of its narrow arguments for patentability. In this context, the section 112 rejection carried the same message as the prior obviousness rejection. An obviousness rejection is of course made in response to prior art. Consequently, this court determines that Litton made its amendment for reasons related to patentability.

Scope of the Estoppel

Because Litton's amendment was made for reasons related to patentability, prosecution history estoppel applies to the phrase "Kaufman-type ion beam source." As previously indicated, however, estoppel does not bar Litton from invoking the doctrine of equivalents altogether with respect to the "Kaufman-type ion beam source" limitation. Accordingly, this court now considers the scope of what Litton actually surrendered.

As a basic proposition, the standard for determining whether subject matter has been relinquished is whether one of ordinary skill in the art would objectively conclude from the prosecution history that an applicant surrendered it. *See Mark I Mktg. Corp. v. R.R. Donnelly & Sons Co.*, 66 F.3d 285, 291, 36 USPQ2d 1095, 1100 (Fed. Cir. 1995). As noted earlier, either amendments or arguments made by an applicant may be the basis for this conclusion.

When prosecution history estops a patentee, the court ascertains the scope of the estoppel in several ways. First, "a patentee is estopped from recovering through equivalency that which was deemed unpatentable in view of the prior art." *Pall Corp. v. Micron Separations, Inc.*, 66 F.3d 1211, 1219, 36 USPQ2d 1225, 1230. In other words, when an applicant, in response to an examiner's prior art rejection, amends a claim by substituting one limitation for another, the applicant cannot later assert that the original limitation is an equivalent of the substituted limitation. Thus, the doctrine prevents the applicant from completely recapturing the subject matter rejected by the examiner.

In addition, when an applicant narrows a claim element in the face of an examiner's rejection based on the prior art, the doctrine estops the applicant from later asserting that the claim covers, through the doctrine of equivalents, features that the applicant amended his claim to avoid. A patentee is also estopped to assert equivalence to "trivial" variations of such prior art features. Depending on the facts of the case, an amendment may also limit the patentee to its literal claim scope.

In addition, as noted earlier, an applicant's arguments may constitute a clear and unmistakable surrender of subject matter. Such arguments preclude recapture of that subject matter. As noted above, this type of estoppel can arise regardless of the *Warner-Jenkinson* presumptions. Of course, applicants commonly make arguments in combination with an amendment, as in this case. In such circumstances, the scope of estoppel is a product of the effects of both factors working in concert.*

According to these principles, Litton's conduct clearly estops it from asserting that a duoplasmatron source is equivalent to a "Kaufman-type" source. This estoppel falls within one of the categories mentioned above—an amendment which narrows a claim element to avoid prior art. Duoplasmatron sources were in the prior art specifically cited by the examiner in his rejection of claim 1. In response, Litton narrowed its claim language "ion beam source" to "Kaufman-type ion beam source" by making an amendment this court has determined to be "related to

---

* Contrary to the suggestions in the dissenting opinion, it is not necessary that a reference be specifically cited by the examiner as the reason for a rejection in order for it to give rise to an estoppel. Arguments made by an applicant in an information disclosure statement or otherwise during prosecution may form the basis of an estoppel without regard to whether the argument was made in response to a rejection or the prior art was cited by the examiner.

patentability." This record suffices to exclude duoplasmatron sources from the permissible range of equivalents.

Determining whether Litton's conduct estops it from claiming that either Honeywell's hollow cathode or its RF ion beam source is an equivalent presents a more complicated inquiry. The examiner did not cite a hollow cathode ion beam source nor an RF ion beam source. Therefore, Litton did not amend its claim to avoid these sources. However, this alone does not preclude estoppel.

Presented with section 103 rejections to all its claims based upon the many references which Litton repeatedly cited and expressly distinguished, Litton demonstrated patentability over the prior art by submitting declarations attesting to the unexpected results obtained from the Kaufman-type source. *See* Paper Nos. 16 at 5 (Baumeister declaration) and 16A at 3 (declaration of Dr. Samuel Lu). Moreover, Litton argued in unmistakable terms that the phrase "ion beam source" referred only to a "Kaufman-type ion beam source." The record shows Litton made that argument in the face of at least five other types of ion beam sources among the eighty-three references and the Harper chapter. These included a hollow cathode source discussed in the Harper chapter and an RF ion beam source described in the Lane article (Reference No. 73 among Litton's oft-cited references).

On the unique facts of this case—Litton's unmistakable arguments that its claims encompassed only the "Kaufman-type ion beam source," the five (or six) unambiguous declarations by Litton and its affiants expressly distancing its invention from the references before the examiner, and Litton's amendment—one of ordinary skill in the art would reasonably conclude that Litton surrendered the other ion beam sources disclosed in the references before the examiner. Contrary to what the dissent suggests, these references were central to the course of the prosecution. Moreover, this result does not automatically, without more, mandate that in every case an estoppel arises based on any reference before an examiner. Rather, in this unique case, Litton repeatedly referred expressly to the many references it presented to the examiner, distinguished each reference by number over and over, and then further insisted that its claims encompassed only processes with Kaufman-type sources. To confirm that its invention was different from these references, Litton further amended its claim—in the face of its knowledge of all the ion beam sources disclosed in these references—in response to the examiner's rejection. Under these telling circumstances, the administrative record estops Litton from asserting the equivalence of any ion beam source before the examiner.

In view of Honeywell's accused devices, the hollow cathode source disclosed in the Harper chapter and the RF source disclosed in the Lane article are particularly relevant to the inquiry of estoppel here.

Other sources before the examiner may be relevant. However, the trial court made no findings about the relationship, if any, between any of the sources before the examiner and the sources in Honeywell's accused processes. For example, if the pertinent differences between either (1) the Harper source and Honeywell's hollow cathode source or (2) the Lane source and Honeywell's RF source are trivial, then the surrender of each disclosed source necessarily includes a surrender of its corresponding accused source. Alternatively, if the differences between either (1) the Harper source and Honeywell's hollow cathode sources or (2) the Lane source and Honeywell's RF sources are not trivial, then Litton did not surrender the accused source by surrendering the corresponding disclosed source.

Yet whether Honeywell's hollow cathode and RF ion beam sources constitute trivial variations of the Harper and Lane sources, respectively, are factual determinations that the district court never addressed. The same is true for any other sources before the examiner. Because the trial record is silent on these issues, this court cannot conclude as a matter of law whether the record estops Litton from asserting that the accused hollow cathode and RF sources are equivalents of the Kaufman-type limitation.

Accordingly, this court remands for a determination of the factual issues underlying prosecution history estoppel: namely, whether the accused hollow cathode source or the accused RF source constitutes a trivial variation of any of the sources before the examiner. If the district court determines that the variations are trivial for either of the accused sources, it should enter judgment as a matter of law that the process using that accused source does not infringe under the doctrine of equivalents. However, if the district court concludes that there is no estoppel, then it should proceed with the factual determination of infringement under the doctrine of equivalents.

NEWMAN, Circuit Judge, concurring in part, dissenting in part.

I concur in the judgment insofar as it remands the case to the district court for redetermination of infringement in terms of the doctrine of equivalents. The jury's claim construction was the subject of sharply conflicting expert testimony at trial, and there was substantial evidence on which a reasonable jury could have reached its claim construction, which in turn supported its verdicts of infringement. However, applying *Markman v. Westview Instruments, Inc.*, 517 U.S. 370, 38 USPQ2d 1461 (1996), and construing the claims *de novo*, I agree with the court that the "Kaufman-type" ion beam source was incorrectly construed. The correct construction of "Kaufman-type" precludes a finding of literal infringement by these two beam sources, and provides a fresh basis for determination of the question of equivalency. Since that was not the basis at trial, I concur in remanding for that purpose.

Since the correct construction of "Kaufman-type" relies heavily on the prosecution history, I agree that guidance to the trial court is warranted. However, I do not agree with the panel majority that a search report, filed in compliance with the duty of disclosure, produces prosecution history estoppel as to the complete and detailed content of all of the references listed in that report. References not cited by and not relied on by the examiner, but filed and explained by the applicant in accordance with Rule 56 and its implementing rules, do not generate prosecution history estoppel. The role of the prosecution history in generating an estoppel is different from its role in construing the claims. Thus I must, respectfully, dissent from the panel majority's change in the law of prosecution history estoppel.

A. THE PATENTABILITY REPORT

Litton filed a Patentability Report listing eighty-two references: forty-two scientific articles and forty United States and foreign patents. Litton also filed a document containing concise explanations of the relevance of each listed reference. The Report is a collection of the major scientific and technical literature on optical film production by ion beam sputtering, and includes not only references on the Kaufman-type ion beam source but also the duoplasmatron, hollow cathode, radio frequency, and most or all other sources of ion beams, as well as the technology of producing laser mirrors. The examiner cited the entire Report, without analysis of its contents, as "admitted prior art." Indeed, these eighty-two (later enlarged to eighty-three) references span the field of optical films formed by ion beams.

The report was filed in compliance with 37 C.F.R. § 1.56, in accordance with § 1.97(a). As a means of complying with the duty of disclosure set forth in § 1.56, applicants are encouraged to file an information disclosure statement. For each of the eighty-two references Litton provided a statement of the subject matter and its relevance, as required by 37 C.F.R. § 1.98(a)(2):

> § 1.98(a) (1985) Any disclosure statement filed . . . shall include . . .

> (2) a concise explanation of the relevance of each listed item.

Thus for each reference Litton provided a one-sentence summary, of which the following are typical:

> The Spenser et al article discloses ion beam-deposited polycrystalline diamond-like films, but does not disclose Applicants' claimed ion beam sputtering methods.

> The Prival et al article discloses ion beam sputtering apparatus and techniques, but does not disclose or suggest Applicants' claimed ion beam sputtering techniques.

In examining the original patent the examiner had cited four patents and two articles. In examining the reissue application the examiner cited the Patentability Report as "admitted prior art" and two references: the Bernard patent and the Laznovsky article. The examiner explained that the admitted prior art showed these laser mirrors broadly, and cited Bernard and Laznovsky for specific aspects of the invention. The entire text of the examiner's rejection is as follows:

> Claims 1 and 3–15 are rejected under U.S.C. § 103 as being unpatentable over the combination of admitted prior art contained in "Patentability Report" filed by applicants on August 30, 1985 and Laznovsky.

The prior art cited by applicants and mentioned in the "Background of the Invention" section of the original patent amply establishes that laser mirrors comprising quarter wave stacks of layers of materials of different refractive indices materials were known prior to the instant invention. Laznovsky teaches, commencing at page 52 thereof, that ion beam sputtering using a rotating substrate may yield uniform films. Moreover, Laznovsky at page 54 teaches that ion beam sputtering of certain oxidic targets results in loss of oxygen, which must be compensated for by addition of oxygen background gas to the atmosphere inside the vacuum chamber. The features recited in instant claims 3 and 8 are also disclosed by Laznovsky.

[The Bernard patent] cited by applicants ... is cited and ... teaches that multiple layer coatings comprising different materials sputtered from different targets may be formed by ion-beam sputtering (Bernard, Col. 1, lines 38–51; col. 4, lines 1–18). It thus would have been obvious, at the time the invention was made, to fabricate the known multi-layer laser mirror stacks using the apparatus and techniques of Laznovsky (including stoichiometry control of deposited films by oxygen addition to the background gas, substrate rotation, pre-sputter cleaning of the targets by ion bombardment, and target cooling), in view of the clear teachings of Bernard pertaining to the use of multi-targeted ion-beam sputtering apparatus for depositing multilayered films of differing composition. Choice of suitable layer materials of higher and lower refractive index clearly follows from the prior art and does not constitute unobvious modification of the references.

Of the references listed in the Patentability Report only the Bernard patent was cited by the examiner. None of the eighty-one other references was mentioned by the examiner, throughout the lengthy prosecution. The examiner referred to the "admitted prior art" as "establish[ing] that laser mirrors comprising quarter wave stacks ... were known prior to the instant invention."

Litton responded by distinguishing its invention from the prior art mirrors and from the teachings in the Laznovsky and Bernard references, and from the "admitted prior art" as follows:

The remaining references that fall within the category that the Examiner has denominated 'admitted prior art' are, in Applicants' opinion, of marginal relevance. Please see Applicants' Reissue Declaration and Power of Attorney accompanying this amendment for a discussion of the patentable distinctions between the claims on file and the disclosures of these references.

In the referenced Reissue Declaration Litton grouped all of the references listed in the Patentability Report, in general statements of which the following is typical:

Claims 1 and 13 also patentably distinguish over items 1–15, 17–19, 21, 23 and 24, 26–41, and 44, 45, 48 and 49 above, because none of these references discloses an ion-beam sputtering method to make any product, let alone the multiple-layer optical films comprising optical layers having different indices of refraction referred to in claims 1 and 13.

It is incorrect to hold that by these statements Litton generated prosecution history estoppel as to the complete content of each and every one of the eighty-one uncited references. These broad and non-specific distinctions of groups of uncited references do not eliminate recourse to equivalency as to the entire subject matter of every uncited reference. The examiner is required, by the rules of patent examination, specifically to identify the references on which he is relying and to state the reasons for any rejection. Manual of Patent Exam. Proc. § 707.07(d). That was done as to Bernard and Laznovsky, the references that were "central to the course of the prosecution," in the words of the panel majority. It is simply incorrect to assign "centrality" and thus estoppel to the eighty-one references on the list, none of which the examiner or Litton identified as grounds of unpatentability.

Over the course of the prosecution Litton made several resubmissions of the Patentability Report and the explanation of relevance. All of the documents that the majority characterizes as Litton's "repeated references" to the eighty-three items are the filing or refiling of these same documents. Thus, after their initial filing, the Patentability Report and the explanation of relevance were again filed, attached to a declaration of Joel Nathanson, an officer of Litton, accompanied by discussion of the Bernard and Laznovsky references and the issues raised by a third-party protester to the reissue. In a subsequent declaration of Dr. Baumeister he also attached the Patentability Report, and specifically argued Bernard and Laznovsky in the context of the state of this art as shown in the Report.

These documents were again filed when the examiner required a new Reissue Oath, wherein Litton again broadly and briefly distinguished the listed references by categories. . . .

These are the six "over and over" submissions stressed by the panel majority. It is incorrect to describe these resubmissions of the same documents as "repeated references" that transform into prosecution history estoppel the entire content of every reference on the Patentability Report. Further, Litton did not "acknowledge" that each reference on the Report was of prior art status, as the panel majority states. Litton simply repeated the examiner's words, in the conventional form of an applicant's Response:

> Remaining for consideration is the Examiner's rejection of claims 1, 3–10, 12 and 13 under 35 USC § 103 as allegedly unpatentable over the combination of what the Examiner calls the "admitted prior art" contained in the patentability report in view of Laznovsky or over French Patent 2,129,996 [the Bernard patent] in view of Laznovsky.

This was not an admission that the eighty-one references in addition to Bernard and Laznovsky were grounds of estoppel.

The use of an applicant's search report to create an estoppel as to references not specifically cited by the examiner and not a basis of rejection, is a major change in the law of prosecution history estoppel. Applicants often submit lengthy lists of references in compliance with Rule 56, lest they be charged with inequitable conduct for whatever they leave out. The filing of a list of references in accordance with Rule 97, and their description under Rule 98(a)(2), does not create an estoppel as to the full technical content of every reference on the list. Estoppel arises from an examiner's rejection based on a specific reference and an applicant's position taken to avoid that specific reference. It does not arise from the applicant's exposition of his invention and its place in the field of technology. Such an exposition may be relevant to claim interpretation; it does not, however, produce prosecution history estoppel as to uncited references.

The mischievous consequence of this new rule is to convert into estoppel the information provided in accordance with the duty of disclosure. The history of Rule 56 shows the many uncertainties and pitfalls surrounding an applicant's provision of information to the Patent Office. The court today adopts a draconian rule of estoppel flowing from an applicant's compliance with the disclosure rules, for it is notorious that the applicant will be criticized wherever he draws the line in disclosing references known to him. This new rule can only deter the broad disclosure that has shielded applicants from the "plague" of inequitable conduct charges that the disclosure requirements have spawned. *Cf.* Notice of Final Rulemaking [Duty of Disclosure], 57 Fed. Reg.2021, 2022 (1992) ("It is in the best interest of the Office and the public to permit and encourage individuals to cite information to the Office without fear of making an admission against interest.") This new pitfall in an already uncertain practice diminishes the utility of the patent system, thereby disserving the national interest in innovation, new products, and industrial growth.

This new rule seriously erodes the doctrine of equivalents, with the anomalous result that the more fully the patent applicant complies with the duty of disclosure, the greater the range of equivalents he stands to lose to prosecution history estoppel. The inappropriate consequences of this ruling are revealed in today's result whereby the trial court must base prosecution history estoppel on two references that neither the applicant, the examiner, the protestor, nor the trial judge, considered relevant. From this rule, and its application in this case, I must dissent.

Notes

1. *Litton Sys., Inc. v. Honeywell, Inc.* has an interesting history. Litton and Honeywell are the largest manufacturers of inertial navigation systems for commercial planes. After a three and a half month trial and three weeks of deliberations by the jury, a verdict was returned that Litton's patents were valid and infringed under the doctrine of equivalents. The jury awarded Litton $1.2 billion in damages. The district court on JMOL overturned the verdict holding the patent invalid and unenforceable. In 1997, the Federal

Circuit reversed, reinstating the jury finding of infringement under the doctrine of equivalents, but vacating the $1.2 billion damage award and remanding for a new trial on damages. The Supreme Court granted *certiorari* and vacated the Federal Circuit decision ordering the Federal Circuit to reconsider its decision in light of *Warner-Jenkinson*. The preceding opinion written by Judge Rader is the Federal Circuit's reconsideration of the Litton case. On June 18, the Federal Circuit denied a request for *en banc* review of the Litton decision. Three judges, Clevenger, Plager and Gajarsa dissented. Judge Clevenger and Gajarsa both argued that the Litton decision contradicts the Supreme Court's *Warner-Jenkinson* decision which held that the doctrine of equivalents is not available for an amended limitation when the amendment was made for patentability reasons. Judge Gajarsa cited the following Supreme Court language from *Warner-Jenkinson*:

> Where no explanation is established, however, the court should presume that the PTO had a substantial reason related to patentability for including the limiting element added by amendment. In those circumstances, prosecution history estoppel would bar the application of the doctrine [of] equivalents as to that element.

Do you agree? Do you think the Federal Circuit's holding that a limiting claim amendment or argument made during prosecution history does *not* mean that the applicant is automatically entitled to no range of equivalents for that element is a good result? Will this interpretation increase predictability? Would a bright line test that once an amendment is made for patentability reasons the doctrine of equivalents is inapplicable be better?

2.   Was there any need for this confusing new rule of law? In this case, Litton argued that its ion beam source was limited to only Kaufman type ion beam sources: Claim 1 cannot "properly be construed to refer to any other ion beam gun but the Kaufman gun." This statement by the applicant is a clear relinquishment of anything other than a Kaufman type ion beam source. A better holding by the court might have been:

> Generally, a claim amendment made during prosecution to overcome prior art does not bar all equivalents. It only bars what was disclosed in those prior art references. However, in this case, the claim amendments were accompanied by arguments explicitly limiting the claim to *only Kaufman type ion beam sources*. This amounted to a clear and unmistakeable surrender of subject matter beyond the Kaufman type ion beam. Therefore, in this case there is no range of equivalents for this claim limitation.

3.   Do you agree that the prosecution history estoppel should apply to all of the 83 references disclosed by the applicant? What effect is this going to have on patent prosecution?

4.   **Does the Reason for the Amendment Matter?** *Warner-Jenkinson* warns that those who prosecute patents should take care to be clear in the prosecution and explain the reason for any amendments. What reasons for claim amendments would not be related to patentability? If the patentee amended his claim to overcome an enablement rejection or an indefiniteness rejection, are these amendments made for patentability reasons? *See Pall Corp. v. Micron Separations, Inc.*, 66 F.3d 1211, 1219–20, 36 USPQ2d 1225,

1230–31 (Fed. Cir. 1995) Would a rule that all amendments act as an estoppel be better?

5. **When Does Prosecution History Estoppel Occur?** Do you think that arguments as well as amendments should trigger prosecution history estoppel? Do you think that statements about prior art in an Information Disclosure Statement (IDS) can trigger prosecution history estoppel even when there is no rejection? *See Ekchian v. Home Depot, Inc.*, 104 F.3d 1299, 1303–4, 41 USPQ2d 1364, 1368–69 (Fed. Cir. 1997). Generally, listing references in an IDS does not amount to an admission that they are prior art or that they are material to patentability. *See C & F Packing Co. v. IBP, Inc.*, 1998 WL 101543, *5 (N.D. Ill. 1998). Do you think that canceling a claim during prosecution should trigger an estoppel?

6. **No range of equivalents when the *Warner-Jenkinson* presumption applies.** In *Sextant Avionique v. Analog Devices, Inc.*, ___ F.3d ___, 49 USPQ2d 1865 (Fed. Cir. 1999), the first case to apply the *Warner-Jenkinson* presumption of prosecution history estoppel, the Federal Circuit held that when the presumption applies the patent holder gets no range of equivalents (i.e prosecution history estoppel acts as an absolute bar). In *Sextant*, the patentee added a "metallization" limitation to the capacitor plates claim element. The Court held that although this limitation was not necessary to overcome the prior art cited by the examiner, no other reason for its addition was disclosed. Therefore, the Court presumed that the amendment was made for a reason related to patentability. The Court next addressed what the scope of the estoppel should be, namely whether there should be an absolute bar of all equivalents when the presumption applies or whether the patentee should still be entitled to some range of equivalents (as in *Litton*). The Court held that "in circumstances in which the *Warner-Jenkinson* presumption is applicable, i.e., where the reason for an amendment is unclear from an analysis of the prosecution history record, and unrebutted by the patentee, the prosecution history estoppel arising therefrom is total and completely "bars" the application of the doctrine of equivalents as to the amended limitation." *Id.* at 1875. The Court reasoned that this outcome is consistent with *Warner-Jenkinson* and strengthened by the "public notice" function of claims and pragmatic considerations that when the reason for the amendment is unclear from the prosecution history there is no way for a reasonable competitor to determine the scope of the estoppel. *Id.* at 1873–75.

7. **Reasonable Competitor Test.** The test for applying prosecution history estoppel does not turn on the subjective intent of the applicant or what the applicant believed or intended to give up to the public. The test for determining what subject matter was surrendered is objective and depends on what a competitor, reading the prosecution history, would reasonably conclude was given up by the applicant. *See Insituform Tech, Inc. v. Cat Contracting, Inc.*, 99 F.3d 1098, 1107, 40 USPQ2d 1602 (Fed. Cir. 1996); *Mark I Mktg. Corp. v. R.R. Donnelley & Sons*, 66 F.3d 285, 291, 36 USPQ2d 1095, 1100 (Fed. Cir. 1995).

8. **A Question of Law.** The application of prosecution history estoppel is a question of law which makes it ideal for resolution on summary judgment. *See Mark I*, 66 F.3d at 291, 36 USPQ2d at 1100.

9. **Does Prosecution History Estoppel Pass from Parent to Child?** Should an amendment made in a parent application pass to a continuation application? *See Mark I Mktg. Corp. v. R.R. Donnelley & Sons Co.*, 66 F.3d 285, 291, 36 USPQ2d 1095, 1100 (Fed. Cir. 1995) (the prosecution history of the parent and grandparent applications are relevant to determining the scope of a claim in a continuation application); *Jonsson v. Stanley Works*, 903 F.2d 812, 14 USPQ2d 1863 (Fed. Cir. 1990) (holding that prosecution history of parent application is relevant to understanding scope of claims issuing in a continuation-in-part application). When faced with a final rejection by the examiner, it is not uncommon for an applicant to file a continuation application rather than appeal to the Board. Consider how the Court in *Mark I*, used the prosecution history of the parent applications against the continuation:

> The prosecution history of the '241 patent indicates that the grandparent '668 application broadly claimed a process for reproducing color images by printing with two printing plates and two inks. The claims were rejected over prior art that suggested replicating a color image using two printing plates and two inks. Instead of responding to the rejection, Mark I filed the '815 continuation-in-part application with new claims. Mark I then narrowed the '815 claims to require that the first printing plate be made by sequentially interposing filters. Subsequently, in its Petition to Make Special, Mark I argued that the sequential interposition of filters distinguished the claimed invention from the prior art. The '815 application claims were then rejected over a combination of references which, in the PTO's view, suggested using supplemental film exposures in a two-color printing process. Rather than respond to the rejection, Mark I again chose to file a continuation-in-part application with new claims. The claims in the '659 application were even narrower than the '815 claims, and required that both plates be made by sequentially interposing colored filters.

> Donnelley argues that the prosecution history of the '241 patent shows that Mark I surrendered claim coverage for a process not involving sequential interposition of colored filters. We agree. The prosecution history demonstrates that Mark I was unsuccessful in obtaining allowance of the claims until they were narrowed to require that both the first and the second printing plates be made by sequentially interposing particular combinations of colored filters. Moreover, during prosecution Mark I asserted that the claims were patentably distinguishable over the prior art based on these process steps. Thus, in our view a competitor reviewing the prosecution history of the '241 patent reasonably would conclude that, in order to procure issuance of the patent, Mark I surrendered claim coverage to a process not involving sequential interposition of filters.

Mark I, 66 F.3d at 291–292, 36 USPQ2d at 1100. However, should amendments or arguments made in the parent always estop the continuation? As discussed above it is common practice when facing a final rejection to permit the allowed claims to issue and file a continuation to continue the battle over the rejected claims. Consider the following scenario. The applicant amends parent claims 1–10 to overcome a prior art rejection by the examiner (based on the Smith patent), and argues that claims 1–10 are now patentable over the Smith prior art. However, the applicant does not amend claims 11–20 to include the new limitation. The examiner allows claims 1–10 and finally rejects claims 11–20 stating that no new arguments have been made as to claims 11–20. The applicant then files a continuation application with claims 11–20 and the claims are ultimately allowed. The examiner never rejects the claims based on Smith and the applicant makes no arguments regarding Smith. Should prosecution history estoppel apply to the continuation application? Should an amendment made to overcome prior art in a continuation reach back to a parent?

10.   Prosecution history estoppel applies whether the examiner's rejection was correct or not. Hence a defense that prosecution history estoppel does not apply because the examiner's rejection was not based on prior art would not succeed. *See Exhibit Supply Co. v. Ace Patents Corp.*, 315 U.S. 126, 137, 52 USPQ 275 (1942).

C.   PRACTICING THE PRIOR ART

WILSON SPORTING GOODS CO. v. DAVID GEOFFREY & ASSOCS.

904 F.2d 677, 14 USPQ2d 1942 (Fed. Cir. 1990)

RICH, Circuit Judge.

These appeals, consolidated by agreement, are from judgments of the United States District Court for the District of South Carolina in two actions brought by Wilson Sporting Goods Co. (Wilson) for infringement of United States Patent 4,560,168 ('168), entitled "Golf Ball." Trial was before a United States Magistrate by consent.... [T]he magistrate entered judgment of liability against Dunlop Slazenger Corporation (Dunlop) upon jury verdicts of patent validity and willful infringement.... We reverse in part and vacate in part each judgment.

BACKGROUND

A.   The Proceedings

Wilson is a full-line sporting goods company and is one of about six major competitors in the golf ball business. Among its well-known balls are the ProStaff and Ultra. Dunlop is also a major player in the golf ball business. It competes head-to-head with Wilson by selling the Maxfli Tour Limited and Slazenger balls. It sells the Maxfli Tour Limited ball to numerous distributors, but sells the Slazenger ball only to DGA, which distributes the ball to U.S. customers.

On August 2, 1988, Wilson separately sued Dunlop and DGA for patent infringement in the United States District Court for the District of South Carolina.

B.   The Technology

For more than a century, golfers have been searching for a "longer" ball. As one of the parties put it, "distance sells." Inventors have experimented with numerous aspects of ball design over the years, but as United States Golf Association (U.S.G.A.) rules began to strictly control ball size, weight, and other parameters, inventors focused their efforts on the "dimples" in the ball's surface. According to one witness, new dimple designs provide the only real opportunity for increasing distance within the confines of U.S.G.A. rules.

Dimples create surface turbulence around a flying ball, lessening drag and increasing lift. In lay terms, they make the ball fly higher and farther. While this much is clear, "dimple science" is otherwise quite complicated and inexact: dimples can be numerous or few, and can vary as to shape, width, depth, location, and more.

Wilson's '168 patent claims a certain configuration of dimples on a golf ball cover. The shape and width of the dimples in the '168 patent is for the most part immaterial. What is critical is their location on the ball. The goal is to create a more symmetrical distribution of dimples.

Generally speaking, the dimples in the patent are arranged by dividing the cover of a spherical golf ball into 80 imaginary spherical triangles and then placing the dimples (typically several hundred) into strategic locations in the triangles. The triangles are constructed as follows. First, the ball is divided into an imaginary "icosahedron," as shown in Figure 1. An icosahedral golf ball is completely covered by 20 imaginary equilateral triangles, 5 of which cover each pole of the ball and ten of which surround its equator. Second, the midpoints of each of the sides of each of the 20 icosahedral triangles are located, as shown in Figure 2. Third, the midpoints are joined, thus subdividing each icosahedral triangle into four smaller triangles.

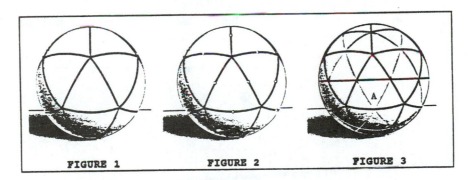

FIGURE 1   **FIGURE 2**   **FIGURE 3**

The resulting 80 imaginary triangles are shown in Figure 3. Critically important are the light lines which join the midpoints. As can be seen from Figure 3, they form the arcs of circles which pass completely around the widest part of the ball. There are six such circles, referred to in the patent as "great circles."

All of the claims of the '168 patent require this basic golf ball having eighty sub-triangles and six great circles. Particular claims require variations on the placement of dimples in the triangles, with one common theme—the dimples must be arranged on the surface of the ball so that no dimple intersects any great circle. Equivalently stated, the dimples must be arranged on the surface of the ball so that no dimple intersects the side of any central triangle. *See* Figure 4, below. When the dimples are arranged in this manner, the ball has six axes of symmetry, compared to prior balls which had only one axis of symmetry.

C. *Patent and Trademark Office (PTO) Proceedings*

Wilson employee Steven Aoyama filed his patent application on April 27, 1984. Twenty seven claims were presented. All were allowed on the first action without comment by the examiner. The patent issued on December 24, 1985, to Wilson as assignee of Aoyama.

Claim 1, the only independent claim, reads:

1. A golf ball having a spherical surface with a plurality of dimples formed therein and six great circle paths which do not intersect any di[m]ples, the dimples being arranged by dividing the spherical surface into twenty spherical triangles corresponding to the faces of a regular icosahedron, each of the twenty triangles being subdivided into four smaller triangles consisting of a central triangle and three apical triangles by connecting the midpoints [of the sides] of each of said twenty triangles along great circle paths, said dimples being arranged so that the dimples do not intersect the sides of any of the central triangles. [Bracketed insertions ours.]

The remaining 26 claims are dependent upon claim 1. They contain further limitations as to the number and location of dimples in the subtriangles. Claim 7, for example, requires that all "central triangles [have] the same number of dimples." Other dependent claims locate dimples on the perimeter of the apical triangles, so that dimples are shared by adjacent apical triangles. *See* Figure 5.

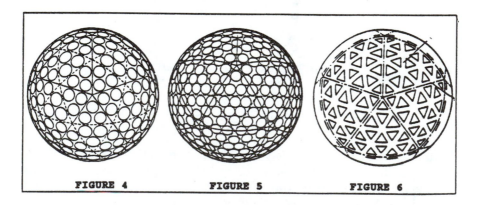

FIGURE 4   FIGURE 5   FIGURE 6

D. *The Prior Art*

The most pertinent prior art is a 1932 British patent to Pugh, which was cited by the examiner. Pugh teaches that a golf ball can be divided into any regular polyhedron, including an icosahedron. Pugh also discloses sub-dividing each of the twenty icosahedral triangles into smaller triangles. As an example, shown in Figure 6, Pugh divides each icosahedral triangle into sixteen sub-triangles, in contrast to the four sub-triangles required by the '168 patent. (The dimples in Pugh are triangular.) Nonetheless, Figure 6 (which is Figure 3 of the Pugh patent) makes clear that Pugh's sixteen sub-triangles are merely further divisions of four larger sub-triangles. Claim 3 of Pugh explains his invention (our emphasis):

> 3. A method of distributing a pattern with substantial uniformity over the surface of a sphere, such as a golf ball, which consists in ... form[ing] equilateral triangles in the case of the ... icosahedron ... , dividing the sides of the triangles so found into the same number of equal or substantially equal parts and finally *joining corresponding points in each pair of sides of each triangle by a series of arcs of great circles*, substantially as described.

The prior art also includes several patents to Uniroyal and a Uniroyal golf ball sold in the 1970's. The Uniroyal ball is an icosahedral ball having six great circles with 30 or more dimples intersecting the great circles by about 12–15 thousandths of an inch. We discuss it extensively below.

E. The Accused Balls

There are four accused products, all of which the jury found to infringe. The following table summarizes the characteristics of each accused ball:

BALL	DIMPLES	COVER	INFRINGER
Maxfli Tour Limited MD	432	Surlyn	Dunlop
Maxfli Tour Limited HT	432	Balata	Dunlop
Slazenger Interlock 480 (S)	480	Surlyn	Dunlop & DGA
Slazenger Interlock 480 (B)	480	Balata	Dunlop & DGA

The accused balls (collectively "Dunlop's balls") have dimples which are arranged in an icosahedral pattern having six great circles, but the six great circles are not dimple-free as the claims literally require. The number of dimples which intersect great circles and the extent of their intersection were disputed by the parties, but the evidence most favorable to appellee Wilson can be summarized as follows (units of last two columns are 0.001"):

BALL	DIMPLES	DIMPLES INTERSECTED	DIMPLE RADIUS	EXTENT OF INTERSECTION
MD	432	60	60–80	7.5
HT	432	60	60–80	8.7
Interlock (S)	480	60	60–80	4.0
Interlock (B)	480	60	60–80	4.0

OPINION

1. Dunlop's Argument

The only theory of liability presented to the jury by Wilson was infringement under the doctrine of equivalents. Dunlop's argument for reversal is straightforward. It contends that there is no principled difference between the balls which the jury found to infringe and the prior art Uniroyal ball; thus to allow the patent to reach Dunlop's balls under the doctrine of equivalents would improperly ensnare the prior art Uniroyal ball as well.

2. Independent Claim 1

Infringement may be found under the doctrine of equivalents if an accused product "performs substantially the same overall function or work, in substantially the same way, to obtain substantially the same overall result as the claimed invention." *Pennwalt Corp. v. Durand–Wayland, Inc.*, 833 F.2d 931, 934, 4 USPQ2d 1737, 1739 (Fed. Cir. 1987) (en banc). Even if this test is met, however, there can be no infringement if the asserted scope of equivalency of what is literally claimed would encompass the prior art. This issue—whether an asserted range of equivalents would cover what is already in the public domain—is one of law, which we review de novo, but we presume that the jury resolved underlying evidentiary conflicts in Wilson's favor.

This court on occasion has characterized claims as being "expanded" or "broadened" under the doctrine of equivalents. Precisely speaking, these characterizations are inaccurate. To say that the doctrine of equivalents extends or enlarges the claims is a contradiction in terms. The claims—i.e., the scope of patent protection as defined by the claims—remain the same and application of the doctrine expands the right to exclude to "equivalents" of what is claimed. The doctrine of equivalents, by definition, involves going beyond any permissible interpretation of the claim language; i.e., it involves determining whether the accused product is "equivalent" to what is described by the claim language.

This distinction raises an interesting question: If the doctrine of equivalents does not involve expanding the claims, why should the prior art be a limitation on the range of permissible equivalents? It is not because we construe claims narrowly if necessary to sustain their validity. As we have said, the doctrine of equivalents does not involve expansion of the claims. Nor is it because to hold otherwise would allow the patentee to preempt a product that was in the public domain prior to the invention. The accused products here, as in most infringement cases, were never "in the public domain." They were developed long after the invention and differ in several respects from the prior art.

The answer is that a patentee should not be able to obtain, under the doctrine of equivalents, coverage which he could not lawfully have obtained from the PTO by literal claims. The doctrine of equivalents exists to prevent a fraud on a patent, not to give a patentee something which he could not lawfully have obtained from the PTO had he tried. Thus, since prior art always limits what an inventor could have claimed, it limits the range of permissible equivalents of a claim.

Whether prior art restricts the range of equivalents of what is literally claimed can be a difficult question to answer. To simplify analysis and bring the issue onto familiar turf, it may be helpful to conceptualize the limitation on the scope of equivalents by visualizing a hypothetical patent claim, sufficient in scope to literally cover the accused product. The pertinent question then becomes whether that hypothetical claim could have been allowed by the PTO over the prior art. If not, then it would be improper to permit the patentee to obtain that coverage in an infringement suit under the doctrine of equivalents. If the hypothetical claim could have been allowed, then prior art is not a bar to infringement under the doctrine of equivalents.

Viewing the issue in this manner allows use of traditional patentability rules and permits a more precise analysis than determining whether an accused product (which has no claim limitations on which to focus) would have been obvious in view of the prior art. In fact, the utility of this hypothetical broader claim may explain why "expanded claim" phraseology, which we now abandon, had crept into our jurisprudence. Finally, it reminds us that Wilson is seeking patent coverage beyond the limits considered by the PTO examiner.

In this context it is important to remember that the burden is on Wilson to prove that the range of equivalents which it seeks would not ensnare the prior art Uniroyal ball. The patent owner has always borne the burden of proving infringement, and there is no logical reason why that burden should shift to the accused infringer simply because infringement in this context might require an inquiry into the patentability of a hypothetical claim. Any other approach would ignore the realities of what happens in the PTO and violate established patent law. Leaving this burden on Wilson does not, of course, in any way undermine the presumed validity of Wilson's actual patent claims. In the present situation, Wilson's claims will remain valid whether or not Wilson persuades us that it is entitled to the range of equivalents sought here.

The specific question before us, then, is whether Wilson has proved that a hypothetical claim, similar to claim 1 but broad enough to literally cover Dunlop's balls, could have been patentable. As we have explained above, Dunlop's balls are icosahedral balls with six great circles, five of which are intersected by dimples. The balls contain 432 to 480 dimples, 60 of which intersect great circles in amounts from 4 to 9 thousandths of an inch. In order for a hypothetical claim to cover Dunlop's balls, its limitations must permit 60 dimples to intersect the great circles by at least 9 thousandths of an inch. Thus, the issue is whether a hypothetical claim directed to an icosahedral ball having six great circles intersected by 60 dimples in amounts up to 9 thousandths of an inch could have been patentable in view of the prior art Uniroyal ball.

On the Uniroyal ball, the extent to which the dimples intersect the great circles is from 12 to 15 thousandths of an inch. Stated as a percentage of dimple radius, the intersection permitted in the hypothetical claim is 13% or less, and the dimples on the Uniroyal ball intersect by 17% to 21%. The number of dimples which intersect the great circles is also similar for the hypothetical claim and the prior art Uniroyal ball. The pertinent hypothetical claim limitation reads on any ball having 60 or less intersecting dimples. This limitation reads on the prior art Uniroyal ball, which has 30 intersecting dimples. If viewed in relative terms, the hypothetical claim limitation reads on any ball which has less than 14% of its dimples intersecting great circles. Roughly 12% of the dimples on the Uniroyal ball intersect great circles.

We hold that these differences are so slight and relatively minor that the hypothetical claim—which permits twice as many intersecting dimples, but with slightly smaller intersections—viewed as a whole would have been obvious in view of the Uniroyal ball. As Dunlop puts it, there is simply "no principled difference" between the hypothetical claim and the prior art Uniroyal ball. Accordingly, Wilson's claim 1 cannot be given a range of equivalents broad enough to encompass the accused Dunlop balls.

3.   Dependent Claims

Before separately analyzing the asserted dependent claims, we should first explain why we are bothering to do so. This court has stated: "It is axiomatic that dependent claims cannot be found infringed unless the claims from which they depend have been found to have been infringed." *Wahpeton Canvas Co. v. Frontier, Inc.*, 870 F.2d 1546, 1553 & n. 9, 10 USPQ2d 1201, 1208 & n.9 (Fed. Cir. 1989). While this proposition is no doubt generally correct, it does not apply in the circumstances of this case.

Here, we have reversed the judgment of infringement of independent claim 1 solely because the asserted range of equivalents of the claim limitations would encompass the prior art Uniroyal ball. The dependent claims, of course, are narrower than claim 1; therefore, it does not automatically follow that the ranges of equivalents of these narrower claims would encompass the prior art, because of their added limitations.

We have considered each asserted dependent claim and conclude that none could be given a range of equivalents broad enough to encompass Dunlop's balls because that would extend Wilson's patent protection beyond hypothetical claims it could lawfully have obtained from the PTO.

Notes

1.   **The Hypothetical Claim**. Use of hypothetical claim practice did not materialize to any large degree after *Wilson Sporting Goods*. Indeed, the Wilson Sporting Goods hypothetical claim has been criticized by some members of the patent bar. *See* Albert B. Kimball Jr., *Hilton Davis: Practical Implications and Emerging Issues*, 507 PLI/Pat 845, 860 (1998) ("The

hypothetical claim test, although admirably precise as a brightline approach to the issue, seems impractical and cumbersome to apply, both at the trial and appellate level."); Henrik D. Parker, *Doctrine of Equivalents Analysis after Wilson Sporting Goods: The Hypothetical Claim Hydra*, 18 AIPLA Q. J. 262 (1990) (the hypothetical claim analysis set forth in *Wilson Sporting Goods* "will inject an excessive amount of confusion and complication into the presentation and consideration of evidence at trial"). Having the patentee prove validity of a hypothetical claim is time-consuming, expensive and confusing to the fact finder. The following passage illustrates some of the difficulty with the hypothetical claim in a jury trial:

> The problems resulting from its attempted use in a jury trial should be self-evident. First, as previously noted, it tends to blend together the hitherto separate issues of infringement and patentability, at least in the eyes of a jury, no matter how precisely worded the jury charge might be. The hypothetical claim covering the accused product must be evaluated to see if it would have been allowable.
>
> Second, precisely worded jury charges tend to be long and cumbersome. It is difficult to envision a simply jury instruction about the hypothetical claim analysis for a case involving equivalents. Its use to determine whether or not prior art placed a limit on the doctrine of equivalents would need to be explained.
>
> Next, based on the jury instruction, would the judge or jury be asked to hypothesize a claim? If so, how could the reviewing court know what the claim was? If not, how can it be determined that there was a properly defined limit of the reach of equivalents?
>
> Failing these, there is no certainty whether or not there could be a proper finding of identity in function, way and result. The hypothetical claim technique is a very sophisticated concept. It is difficult to see how it could be succinctly explained with reasonable clarity as a part of a jury charge.
>
> Third, and even more telling, is that the hypothetical claim approach in effect thrusts the trial judge into the position of having to rule, separate from the validity analysis required as a part of its trial efforts, on the patentability of what is by definition a "hypothetical" situation. Most judges are busy enough with real problems in litigation. Asking the Court to evaluate patentability in what is termed a hypothetical context may be hard to sell to the court.

Albert B. Kimball Jr., *Hilton Davis: Practical Implications and Emerging Issues*, 507 PLI/Pat 845, 861–62 (1998).

2. **The Federal Circuit Retreat**. The Federal Circuit itself has stepped back from application of the *Wilson Sporting Goods* hypothetical claim analysis. In *International Visual Corp. v. Crown Metal Mfg. Co.*, 991 F.2d 768, 772, 26 USPQ2d 1588, 1591 (Fed. Cir. 1993) (citations omitted) the court held:

> Hypothetical claim analysis is an optional way of evaluating whether prior art limits the application of the doctrine of equivalents. It is simply a way of expressing the well-established principle "that a

patentee should not be able to obtain, under the doctrine of equivalents, coverage which he could not lawfully have obtained from the PTO by literal claims." If utilized, this approach requires a court to visualize a hypothetical claim that enlarges the scope of an issued claim so that it literally covers an accused device and to determine whether that hypothetical claim would have been patentable over the prior art.

With a 40% reversal of district court claim constructions by the Federal Circuit, district courts may not be eager to construct a hypothetical claim, construe it and determine its patentability. In *Key Mfg. Group, Inc. v. Microdot, Inc.*, 925 F.2d 1444, 17 USPQ2d 1806 (Fed. Cir. 1991) (citations omitted), the Federal Circuit reversed a finding of infringement under the doctrine of equivalents because the trial court improperly interpreted a hypothetical claim:

> The Microdot structure also does not infringe under the doctrine of equivalents. Rather Microdot's structure is described in the prior art, specifically in the Chaivre, Allmanna, and Erdmann patents.

> While not obligatory in every doctrine of equivalents determination, the hypothetical claim rationale of *Wilson Sporting Goods Co. v. David Geoffrey & Assocs.*, 904 F.2d 677, 14 USPQ2d 1942 (Fed. Cir. 1990) helps define the limits imposed by prior art on the range of equivalents. The Wilson hypothetical claim analysis does not envision application of a full-blown patentability analysis to a hypothetical claim. Wilson simply acknowledges that prior art limits the coverage available under the doctrine of equivalents. A range of equivalents may not embrace inventions already disclosed by prior art.

> A hypothetical claim drawn to cover literally the Microdot nut would not be patentable over the prior art. The Chaivre, Allmanna, and Erdmann patents would make the Microdot nut obvious. Contrary to Key's assertion, no single prior art reference need include each element of the hypothetical claim. The question under Wilson is whether the hypothetical claim "could have been allowed by the PTO over the prior art." Because the Microdot nuts and, thus the hypothetical claim, are obvious in light of these three prior art references, the doctrine of equivalents does not reach the accused nuts.

However, the teachings of *Wilson Sporting Goods*, that a patentee cannot capture through the doctrine of equivalents what he could not have patented because of the prior art remains a time honored principle. In practice, it is more common for the defendant to argue that he is *practicing the prior art*. The defendant will contend that his accused device is similar to the prior art, not the patented invention. For example, in *General Am. Transp. Corp. v. Cryo–Trans, Inc.*, 93 F.3d 766, 771–72, 39 USPQ2d 1801, 1804 (Fed. Cir. 1996), the court applied the *Wilson* teachings without constructing any hypothetical claims:

Furthermore, the district court's finding of infringement under the doctrine of equivalents was also clearly erroneous, for two reasons. First, the finding violated the principle that the doctrine may not be used to expand the scope of the patentee's right to exclude so as to encompass the prior art. Here, the AFFX 2002 railcar had all the elements of claim 1 except that its compartment for holding CO_2 snow had openings adjacent to only one side wall and it had no openings adjacent to the end walls. This design was known to be deficient because "hot spots" (areas of thawing) tended to form in the cargo area opposite the side where the CO_2 gas was introduced. Clearly those of ordinary skill in the art would have known that insufficient CO_2 gas was reaching this area. Thus, it would have been obvious to more uniformly cool the entire cargo area by providing openings along both side walls. The Kurth patent, in fact, disclosed a cryogenic railcar in which the compartment for holding the solid CO_2 had openings adjacent to both side walls. The AFFX 2002 and Kurth railcars were in the same field of endeavor as the claimed invention and were properly combinable prior art. The Kurth patent was not before the PTO during the prosecution of the '876 patent.

We are therefore convinced that the prior art fairly suggested a cryogenic railcar having the combination of features present in GATC's railcar, including a compartment having openings adjacent to both of the car's side walls. Thus, since allowing the claims to encompass GATC's car would cause the claims to cover subject matter obvious over the prior art, the car cannot be held to infringe the '876 patent under the doctrine of equivalents.

3. **Burden of Proof.** According to *Wilson*, the patentee has the burden of proving the patentability of hypothetical claims. The patentee has the burden of proving that the range of equivalents that it seeks will not ensnare the prior art. However, in *National Presto Indus., Inc. v. West Bend Co.*, 76 F.3d 1185, 1192, 37 USPQ2d 1685, 1689 (Fed. Cir. 1996) (citations omitted), the Court suggested that the infringer has the burden of proving that the accused device is in the prior art:

> The trial court need not create a hypothetical claim and determine its hypothetical patentability before the jury can find the facts of equivalency vel non. When the patentee has made a prima facie case of infringement under the doctrine of equivalents, the burden of coming forward with evidence to show that the accused device is in the prior art is upon the accused infringer, not the trial judge. West Bend did not offer such evidence. Indeed, West Bend does not reconcile the asserted unpatentability of a hypothetical claim that covers its device with its argument that its device is itself patented. We discern no error in the absence of a "hypothetical claim" analysis.

D. DISCLOSURE IN SPECIFICATION IS DEDICATED TO THE PUBLIC IF NOT CLAIMED

MAXWELL v. J. BAKER, INC.

86 F.3d 1098, 39 USPQ2d 1001 (Fed. Cir. 1996)

Before LOURIE, Circuit Judge, SKELTON, Senior Circuit Judge, and SCHALL, Circuit Judge.

LOURIE, Circuit Judge.

J. Baker, Inc. appeals from the final judgment of the United States District Court for the District of Minnesota in which the court denied J. Baker's motion for judgment as a matter of law after a jury verdict of infringement of claims 1, 2, and 3 of U.S. Patent 4,624,060, owned by the inventor, Susan M. Maxwell. Because the court erred when it denied J. Baker's motion for judgment as a matter of law on the issue of infringement, but did not err otherwise, we affirm-in-part, reverse-in-part, vacate-in-part, and remand.

BACKGROUND

In retail shoe stores, pairs of shoes must be kept together to prevent them from becoming disorganized and mismatched. Typically, manufacturers connect pairs of shoes using plastic filaments threaded through each shoe's eyelets. However, some shoes do not have eyelets and cannot be connected in this manner. Thus, manufacturers have resorted to other methods of keeping the shoes together such as making a hole in the side of each shoe and threading a filament through these holes. This method creates problems for retailers and manufacturers because the shoes are damaged by the process.

Maxwell, an employee at a Target retail store, recognized this problem and invented a system for connecting shoes that do not have eyelets. She secured tabs along the inside of each shoe and connected the shoes with a filament threaded through a loop or hole in each tab. By securing the tabs inside the shoe, she preserved the integrity and appearance of the shoes.

Maxwell filed a patent application entitled "System for Attaching Mated Pairs of Shoes Together," which issued as the '060 patent on November 25, 1986. Figure 2 of the patent illustrates the preferred embodiment of the invention and is shown below.

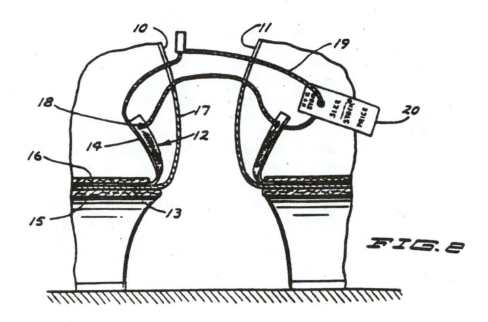

Claim 1, with reference numbers to figure 2 added, is representative of the claims at issue:

1.   A system for attaching together mated pairs of shoes, which comprises in combination:

(A) a pair of shoes, each of which has an inner sole [16] and an outer sole [15], each shoe also having a shoe upper with an inside surface [17] and a top edge, each of said shoes further having a fastening tab [12] and means for securing said tab between said inner and outer soles,

(1) said fastening tab [12] being an integral sheet with two parts,(2) the first of said parts [13] comprising one end of the elongated tab [12] extending horizontally between the inside surfaces of the outer sole [15] and inner sole [16] of the shoe and firmly secured thereto with said securing means,

(3) the second of said parts [14] comprising the opposite end of the elongated tab [12] extending from one edge of the inner sole [16] and vertically upward along but spaced from the inside surface of the shoe upper [17] and extending so that said opposite end remains beneath the top edge of said shoe upper,

(4) the second of said parts [14] having an aperture in the form of a loop formed by doubling the fastening tab [12] over on itself, and

(B) a filamentary fastening element [19] extending through the apertures of each of said fastening tabs [12], the ends of the filamentary element [19] being joined together in a closed loop;

whereby said pair of shoes is attached together by said fastening element [19] passing through the aperture in each of said tabs [12] so that on removal of said fastening element [19], said shoes separate and said tabs [12] are not visible outside said shoe uppers.

J. Baker sells and distributes shoes through leased footwear departments in retail stores. Under a typical leasing arrangement, a retail store provides J. Baker with the exclusive right to operate a shoe department within the store. J. Baker selects the merchandise, stocks the shelves at the stores, and serves the customers. In exchange, the retail store receives a portion of the sales receipts.

J. Baker purchases the shoes it sells from independent manufacturers. Between the mid-1980's and 1990, J. Baker instructed its manufacturers to connect shoes together for sale using a fabric loop inserted under a shoe's sock lining (the "under the sock lining" version) as shown below.

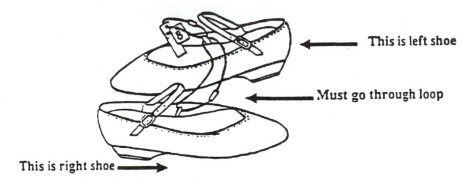

In June 1990, Maxwell informed J. Baker's in-house counsel that she believed that J. Baker infringed the '060 patent. In response, J. Baker designed two alternate shoe connection systems. In the "counter pocket" version, shown below, a tab was stitched into the counter pocket of the shoe between the sole and the top of the shoe.

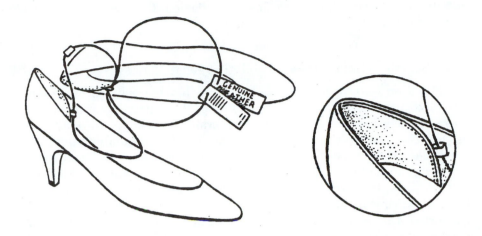

In the "top line" version, shown below, a tab was stitched into the top lining seam of the shoe.

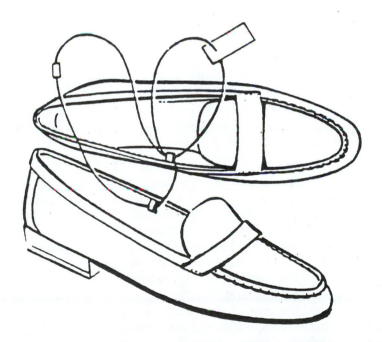

Maxwell sued J. Baker on December 12, 1990, alleging infringement of the '060 patent. After a month long trial, a jury returned a special verdict finding that the '060 patent was valid; J. Baker infringed claims 1, 2, and 3 of the patent.

J. Baker filed a motion for judgment as a matter of law and a motion for a new trial arguing, inter alia, that J. Baker did not infringe either literally or by equivalence ... The court denied J. Baker's motions. J. Baker appeals.

DISCUSSION

3.   J. Baker's "Counter Pocket" and "Top Line" Versions

Based on its proper claim construction that the claimed "fastening tab" does not include a shoe's inner lining, the district court held that no reasonable jury could have found literal infringement in J. Baker's use of the "counter pocket" and "top line" fastening systems. In particular, the court found that these versions did not secure the fastening tabs between the inner and outer soles of the shoes as required by the claims. However, the court denied J. Baker's JMOL motion on the issue of infringement because it determined that substantial evidence supported the jury's finding of infringement under the doctrine of equivalents.

J. Baker argues that the district court erred in sustaining the jury's verdict, asserting that Maxwell dedicated to the public the use of a fastening tab attached to a shoe lining by disclosing that alternate system in the specification, but failing to claim it. In particular, J. Baker relies on Maxwell's disclosure in the specification that "[a]lternatively, the tabs may be stitched into a lining seam of the shoes at the sides or back of the shoes," col. 2, 11. 41–43, asserting that this language describes the accused shoes. Maxwell counters, relying on the Supreme Court's decision in *Graver Tank & Manufacturing Co. v. Linde Air Products Co.*, 339 U.S. 605, 85 USPQ 328 (1950), that the inclusion of the alternative description in the specification actually supports a finding of equivalence. We agree with J. Baker.

In *Unique Concepts, Inc. v. Brown*, 939 F.2d 1558, 19 USPQ2d 1500 (Fed. Cir. 1991), we reiterated the well-established rule that "subject matter disclosed but not claimed in a patent application is dedicated to the public." 939 F.2d at 1562–63, 19 USPQ2d at 1504. We have frequently applied this rule to prohibit a finding of literal infringement when an accused infringer practices disclosed but unclaimed subject matter. This rule, however, applies equally to prevent a finding of infringement under the doctrine of equivalents. A patentee may not narrowly claim his invention and then, in the course of an infringement suit, argue that the doctrine of equivalents should permit a finding of infringement because the specification discloses the equivalents. Such a result would merely encourage a patent applicant to present a broad disclosure in the specification of the application and file narrow claims, avoiding examination of broader claims that the applicant could have filed consistent with the specification. This is clearly contrary to 35 U.S.C. § 112, which requires that a patent applicant "particularly point[ ] out and distinctly claim[ ] the subject matter which the applicant regards as his invention." 35 U.S.C. § 112 (1994). It is also contrary to our system of patent examination, in which a patent is granted following careful examination of that which an applicant claims as her invention.

Thus, we agree with J. Baker that subject matter disclosed in the specification, but not claimed, is dedicated to the public.[2]

Here, Maxwell limited her claims to fastening tabs attached between the inner and outer soles. She disclosed in the specification, without claiming them, alternatives in which the fastening tabs could be "stitched into the lining seam of the shoes." Col. 2, l. 42. By failing to claim these alternatives, the Patent and Trademark Office was deprived of the opportunity to consider whether these alternatives were patentable. A person of ordinary skill in the shoe industry, reading the specification and prosecution history, and interpreting the claims, would conclude that Maxwell, by failing to claim the alternate shoe attachment systems in which the tabs were attached to the inside shoe lining, dedicated the use of such systems to the public. As a matter of law, J. Baker could not infringe by using an alternate shoe attachment system that Maxwell dedicated to the public. Therefore, we reverse the district court's decision denying J. Baker's JMOL motion that its "counter pocket" and "top line" systems did not infringe under the doctrine of equivalents.

Notes

1. **How does this rule affect prosecution?** If the patentee could get equivalent coverage for everything disclosed in the specification, would it file broader or narrower claims? How will this rule affect the way that specifications are written? Patent prosecutors should review the written description carefully to ensure that *all* disclosed embodiments are encompassed within the literal scope of at least one claim.

2. **Dedication to the Public Rule.** In *YBM Magnex, Inc. v. International Trade Comm'n*, 145 F.3d 1317, 46 USPQ2d 1843 (Fed. Cir. 1998), the Federal Circuit appears to have narrowed *Maxwell* claiming that *Maxwell* did not create a new rule that all subject matter disclosed in a patent specification is dedicated to the public. The Court held that such a rule would be inconsistent with Supreme Court precedent, namely *Graver Tank*. The Court also cited the Supreme Court decision in *Warner-Jenkinson* as supporting its decision although it is difficult to find any direct support for the Court's holding in this case. In *YBM Magnex*, the patent claimed a permanent magnet alloy consisting of "30 to 36 of at least one rare earth element, 60 to 66 iron, **6,000 to 35,000 ppm oxygen and balance boron**." Although not specifically claimed, permanent alloy magnets having an oxygen content between 5,450 and 6,000 ppm were disclosed in the patent's written description. YBM charged that the importation of permanent magnet alloys having an oxygen content between 5,450 and 6,000 infringed the patent claim under the doctrine of equivalents. In *YBM Magnex*, the Court did not contend that the panel erred in deciding *Maxwell*, rather it limited *Maxwell* to its facts. Hence when a patent discloses and fully describes two distinct alternative embodiments of the invention but claims only one of them the other continues to be dedicated to the public.

---

2. Of course, within two years from the grant of the original patent, a patentee may seek reissuance of the patent and attempt to enlarge the scope of the claims to include the disclosed but previously unclaimed subject matter. 35 U.S.C. § 251 (1994).

Should YBM Magnex be able to claim that alloys with an oxygen content outside of the claimed range infringe under the doctrine of equivalents when such a range is mentioned in the written description?

4. Does this rule apply to equivalents under § 112, ¶ 6?

E. THE ALL ADVANTAGES RULE

VEHICULAR TECH. CORP. v. TITAN WHEEL INT'L, INC.

141 F.3d 1084, 46 USPQ2d 1257 (Fed. Cir. 1998)

Before NEWMAN, PLAGER, and CLEVENGER, Circuit Judges.

CLEVENGER, Circuit Judge.

In this patent infringement action relating to automotive locking differentials, the United States District Court for the Central District of California granted a preliminary injunction to Vehicular Technologies Corporation (PowerTrax). The court's order, based on infringement under the doctrine of equivalents, enjoined Titan Wheel International, Inc., Dyneer Corp., Transamerica Auto Parts Co., and Leon Rosser Auto Service, Inc. (collectively Tractech), from making, using, or selling allegedly infringing differentials, and ordered a recall of all differentials in the possession of Tractech's distributors. Having previously stayed the preliminary injunction pending appeal, we now decide that the district court erred in concluding that PowerTrax had a reasonable likelihood of success in establishing infringement under the doctrine of equivalents. We therefore vacate the grant of a preliminary injunction and remand.

I

PowerTrax is the assignee of U.S. Patent No. 5,413,015 (the '015 patent). PowerTrax and Tractech compete in the market for automatic locking differentials for use in automotive vehicles. An automotive axle is typically split into two half-axles with a differential located between the two half-axles. The differential allows the wheels on opposite sides of the vehicle to spin at different rates (for example, while the vehicle is rounding a corner). A normal open differential applies equal torque to each wheel, which can create a problem when a wheel encounters icy conditions. Because the wheel on ice needs very little torque before it spins, that same low torque is delivered to the other wheel. Even if the other wheel has traction, it may not receive enough force to move the vehicle, and the vehicle will be stuck, requiring engine revving, rocking, pushing, or towing to get moving.

A locking differential is one type of device that addresses this torque transfer problem. When one wheel slips, a locking differential shifts all of the available drive force to the wheel that has traction. A locking differential accomplishes this feat with two sets of toothed rotating clutch plates: a set of drive plates and a set of driven plates. An exploded view of a locking differential that is representative of the prior art, as depicted by consent of the parties in Exhibit C at page A1134 of the appellate joint appendix, is pictured below:

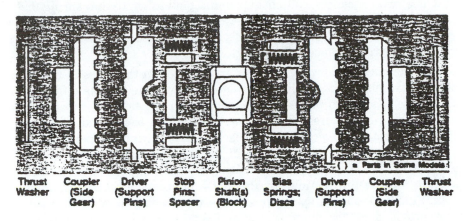

| Thrust Washer | Coupler (Side Gear) | Driver (Support Pins) | Stop Pins; Spacer | Pinion Shaft(s) (Block) | Bias Springs; Discs | Driver (Support Pins) | Coupler (Side Gear) | Thrust Washer |

In this locking differential, the drive plates (referred to as "Drivers" in the figure) are mounted back-to-back with their toothed surfaces facing outward. Under the force from multiple bias springs, the drive plates push away from each other and against the toothed surfaces of the driven plates (referred to as "Couplers" in the figure), which are attached to each half-axle of the vehicle. In the prior art, as pictured, each bias spring had one end fitted into a hole (not shown) in the back of a drive plate and an opposite end in contact with a thin disk (referred to as a "Disc" in the figure). The disk in turn contacted a stop pin inserted in a corresponding hole (not shown) in the back of the other drive plate. The holes held the spring and pin in place, and the disk helped the spring to rest properly against the end of the pin. Thus, multiple spring-disk-pin assemblies located between the drive plates and near the plates' edges coupled the opposing inner surfaces of the drive plates to each other and provided a biasing force which pushed the drive plates apart.

The spring-disk-pin design of the prior art created special installation problems. Many locking differentials are designed as after-market add-ons whose parts can be installed into an existing differential by a do-it-yourself backyard mechanic. However, there is very little space inside a differential to install all the parts. With the spring-disk-pin design, each small part had to be carefully inserted in the tight space between the drive plates and then repositioned, often using a prying tool and a hacksaw blade to hold the parts in place and the spring in a compressed position. The disks were particularly troublesome because they slid around on the end of the spring and often fell off or were lost during installation.

The '015 patent is directed toward an improved locking differential whose parts are easier to manufacture, install, and maintain than those of prior art locking differentials. The application for the '015 patent, filed June 28, 1993, and listing John Zentmyer (Zentmyer) as the inventor, focused on three main improvements: (1) window openings in the outside rims of the drive plates, (2) newly designed spring assemblies that use two concentric coil springs and a pin rather than a spring-disk-pin grouping, and (3) spring passageways with oblong cross-sections. The focus of this appeal is on the patent's replacement of the spring-disk-pin grouping with two concentric springs.

In the patented device, the pins are inserted in the holes in the back of the drive plates before the drive plates are mounted in the differential case. After the drive plates are in place, the pins are slid into position and a spring is compressed and inserted through each window opening into the spring hole at the end of each pin. The windows permit easier installation, and the substitution of an inner spring for the old disk eliminates the problem of lost disks. The inner spring also creates a surface for the pin to ride on, thereby functioning like the eliminated disk. Finally, the inner spring produces extra biasing force in addition to that provided by the outer spring and serves as a backup if the outer spring should break.

PowerTrax introduced the new design in 1993 as the Lock–Rite locking differential, two years before the '015 patent issued. Tractech reverse-engineered the Lock–Rite and copied the design into a product known as the E–Z Locker. At an October 1995 industry trade show where Tractech introduced the E–Z Locker, PowerTrax first notified Tractech of the '015 patent and its belief that the E–Z Locker infringed the patent. Tractech's Director of Engineering, working from the trade show and with assistance from Tractech's patent counsel, immediately developed two modifications of the E–Z Locker. First, he replaced the inner spring of the two spring assembly with a single spring and a plug stuck in one end of the spring. Second, he eliminated small holes around the periphery of the drive plates that led to the pin passageways.

The spring assemblies of the prior art, Fig. 5 of the '015 patent, and the accused E–Z Locker device . . . are shown below:

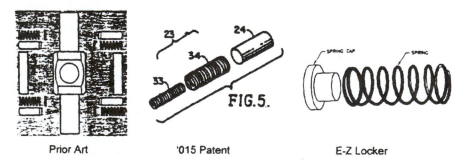

Prior Art   '015 Patent   E-Z Locker

On March 1, 1996, PowerTrax sued Tractech for patent infringement, trade dress infringement, misappropriation of trade secrets, breach of contract, and promissory estoppel. PowerTrax filed a motion for a preliminary injunction on all of its claims, but restricted its infringement argument to infringement under the doctrine of equivalents. Limiting its ruling to the patent infringement claim, the district court granted PowerTrax's motion and issued a preliminary injunction.

II

An infringement analysis involves two steps. The claim scope is first determined, and then the properly construed claim is compared with the accused device to determine whether all of the claim limitations are present either literally or by a substantial equivalent. Claim construction begins, as it must, with the words of the claims. In this case, claim 1 is representative (emphasis added):

1.   A differential mechanism comprising:

output means;

driving means in spaced relationship to said output means;

driven means operably responsive to said driving means for powering said output means;

said driving means having a pair of clutch driving members coaxially disposed with respect to each other and having opposing spaced-apart surface faces;

biasing means interposed between said driving surface faces comprising at least a pin in alignment with a spring assembly consisting of two concentric springs bearing against one end of said pin;

said springs and said pin in axial alignment disposed in an elongated passageway jointly provided in each of said pair of clutch drive members;

each of said clutch drive members has inspection and access openings communicating with said passageway so as to expose said springs and said pins respectively; and

said spring passageway is of oblong configuration in transverse cross-section.

Claims 2–4, the remaining claims, differ slightly from claim 1, but all require the claim limitation: "a spring assembly consisting of two concentric springs bearing against one end of said pin."

We focus on the "spring assembly" limitation because if that limitation cannot be found in the E–Z Locker locking differentials, either literally or by equivalence, as a matter of law there can be no infringement. *See Pennwalt Corp. v. Durand–Wayland Inc.,* 833 F.2d 931, 935, 4 USPQ2d 1737, 1739 (Fed. Cir. 1987) *(in banc).* For purposes of its motion for preliminary injunction, PowerTrax admitted that the limitation is not literally met by the E–Z Locker locking differential because the E–Z Locker employs a spring and a plug, rather than two concentric springs as the claims require. PowerTrax nonetheless argued before the district court, and argues again on appeal, that the plug in the E–Z Locker is an equivalent to the inner spring claimed in the '015 patent.

III

Before the district court, the parties fundamentally disagreed on how the court should address and resolve the equivalents issue. Tractech argued that the claim language itself, properly understood, generally informs and, in this case, limits the range of equivalents available to the spring assembly limitation. According to Tractech, the pertinent claim limitation can be met under the doctrine of equivalents only by structure equivalent to two concentric springs, and that Tractech's plug—a simple improvement of the prior art pesky disk—is not the equivalent of the second spring added to the prior art by the '015 patent.

[T]he district court kept its focus on the claim language, reading in the claim "a new type of spring assembly designed to be installed through the window and eliminate certain loose or unattended 'disks' in the original Lock–Right product." Because the claimed structure performs certain functions, the district court, in considering the doctrine of equivalents, correctly sought to ascertain the functions identified with the claimed two spring assembly. More specifically, for purposes of its doctrine of equivalents analysis, the district court held that the patent claims a:

> spring assembly [that] includes an outer spring and a captured inner-spring. The functions of the spring assembly in the patented invention are: (i) the provision of biasing force to engage the driver and coupler; (ii) through the windows installation; and (iii) the elimination of the loose disks in the original Lock–Right product.

Turning its focus to the accused device, the district court noted that Tractech substitutes a "captured inner plug" for the captured inner spring claimed in the patent, and concluded that Tractech's spring assembly (spring-plus-plug) "accomplishes the same functions, in substantially the same way, with the same result, as the Lock–Right assembly." Consequently, on August 30, 1996, the district court entered its preliminary injunction against Tractech, from which a timely appeal was taken to this court.

IV

In its brief and at oral argument, Tractech emphasizes that its captured plug can be a substantial equivalent, for doctrine of equivalents purposes, of the claimed captured inner spring limitation, only if the plug performs the same or substantially the same functions of the inner spring in substantially the same way, to produce substantially the same result. In this respect, Tractech correctly states the law, and PowerTrax speaks not to the contrary. As the Supreme Court recently stated: "Each element contained in a patent claim is deemed material to defining the scope of the patented invention, and thus the doctrine of equivalents must be applied to individual elements of the claim, not to the invention as a whole." *Warner-Jenkinson Co. v. Hilton Davis Chem. Co.*, 117 S. Ct. 1040, 1049, 41 USPQ2d 1865, 1871 (1997). Consequently, a claim is infringed only if each limitation in the claim is found in the accused device, either literally or by a substantial equivalent. The focus in this case is on the question of whether the captured plug in the accused device can be a substantial equivalent to the claimed inner spring.

To answer that question, we follow the guidance given by the Supreme Court in *Warner-Jenkinson*:

> An analysis of the role played by each element in the context of the specific patent claim will thus inform the inquiry as to whether a substitute element matches the function, way and result of the claimed element, or whether the substitute element plays a role substantially different from the claimed element.

117 S. Ct. at 1054, 41 USPQ2d at 1875. In other words, if a claim limitation must play a role in the context of the specific claim language, then an accused device which cannot play that role, or which plays a substantially different role, cannot infringe under the doctrine of equivalents. The question of whether an explicit function has been identified with a claim limitation entails an examination of the claim and the explanation of it found in the written description of the patent. *See Applied Materials, Inc. v. Advanced Semiconductor Materials Am., Inc.*, 98 F.3d 1563, 1574, 40 USPQ2d 1481, 1489–90 (Fed. Cir. 1996) (examining written description to ascertain functions identified with a claim limitation); *cf., Vitronics Corp. v. Conceptronic, Inc.*, 90 F.3d 1576, 1582, 39 USPQ2d 1573, 1577 (Fed. Cir. 1996) (stating that the written description is "always highly relevant" in construing a claim, and that "it is the single best guide to the meaning of a disputed term").

In some cases, the patent's prosecution history also may reveal the identification of a specific function relating to claimed structure.

V

In this case, the written description makes clear a function of the spring assembly that was not addressed by the district court when it considered PowerTrax's preliminary injunction motion. Only two pages long, the written description emphasizes repeatedly the capacity of the inner spring to serve as a back-up, or replacement, or redundancy for the outer spring in the event of the outer spring's failure, as a significant betterment over the prior art. For example, in the Brief Description of the Prior Art in the BACKGROUND OF THE INVENTION, the patent states:

> [P]roblems and difficulties have been encountered with the above conventional construction [i.e., prior art] which stems largely from the fact that the use of conventional single spring interfacing means and pin interconnection between clutch members is difficult and cumbersome to manufacture, install and maintain. This stems largely from the fact that the single compression spring construction sometimes fails and it is difficult to replace or repair broken or damaged springs.

Col. 1, lines 31–39. In the SUMMARY OF THE INVENTION, the patent notes that the dual spring feature increases both the strength and the reliability of the biasing means, col. 2, lines 14–20, and states that "[a]nother object of the present invention resides in the replacement of the single spring arrangement in the conventional differential mechanisms with an assembly composed of two oppositely-wound concentric springs," col. 2, lines 26–29. The statements continue in the DESCRIPTION OF THE PREFERRED EMBODIMENT:

> Referring to FIG. 5, it can be seen that the resilient means takes the form of a pair of springs 33 and 34 which are concentric with respect to one another since the spring of smaller diameter, represented by number 33, is inserted into the hollow of the spring 34. Therefore, should one spring break or become weakened, the mechanism will continue to function as the second spring will bear the load and prevent the broken spring from exiting the assembly.

Col. 4, lines 21–29.

The statements just quoted indicate that the concentric spring assembly is characterized by its ability to stay centered on the end of the pin and to continue functioning when the outer spring breaks (i.e., it performs a back-up function). The statements clearly inform a reader of the patent about the role played by the inner spring and the scope the patentee intended his patent to cover. They affect the interpretation of the patent given by the patent examiner in determining whether the claims are patentable over the prior art and by competitors attempting to avoid infringement; likewise, they must affect the range of equivalents allowed by the court. As we have previously held, "[o]ther players in the marketplace are entitled to rely on the record made in the Patent Office in determining the meaning and scope of the patent." *Lemelson v. General Mills, Inc.*, 968 F.2d 1202, 1208, 23 USPQ2d 1284, 1289 (Fed. Cir. 1992). The spring-plug structure of the accused E–Z Locker product is entirely incapable of performing the key backup function, thus strongly suggesting that the spring-plug structure is more than insubstantially different from the claimed spring assembly. Furthermore, the capacity of the inner spring to create a surface for the pin to ride on, a function stressed by PowerTrax on appeal, is performed in a different way by the accused spring-plug structure. Similarly, the accused spring-plug structure eliminates the pesky disk problem, another recited function for the inner spring, in a different way. Thus, on the record before us, there exists a substantial likelihood that the spring-plug structure is substantially different than the claimed spring assembly. Consequently, we conclude that the district court committed reversible error in determining that PowerTrax had a reasonable likelihood of success on the merits of proving that Tractech infringes under the doctrine of equivalents.

In an echo of its arguments in the trial court, PowerTrax argues that reaching such a conclusion requires the application of linguistic chicanery that rends the heart from Zentmyer's true invention and permits Tractech to escape infringement by the simple substitution of a plug for a spring. This is not a case, however, in which the true invention as claimed is overwhelmed by unnecessary semantic literalism. Rather, multiple statements in the written description itself speak to the role of the spring assembly limitation. The patent announces a function desired by the patentee, namely spring back-up. It touts the benefit of the dual spring assembly claimed in the patent as compared to assemblies with only one spring. As for the purported ease with which Tractech may have designed around this patent, that result was invited by the language used by the patentee to define his claim.

Furthermore, our emphasis on the statements made in the written description does not result in the fabrication, from the preferred embodiment, of a limitation not otherwise in the claim. *See Constant v. Advanced Micro–Devices Inc.*, 848 F.2d 1560, 1571, 7 USPQ2d 1057, 1064 (Fed. Cir. 1988) ("Although the specification may aid the court in interpreting the meaning of disputed language in the claims, particular embodiments and examples appearing in the specification will not generally be read into the claims."). Instead, the claims specifically require that an infringing device consist of two springs (either literally or equivalently). Thus, the question here is whether the plug of the accused devices is insubstantially different than the captured inner spring in the claimed device. Here, the "spring assembly" claim limitation itself has functions which it performs, and those functions are stated in the written description. A doctrine of equivalents inquiry requires "[a]n analysis of the role played by each element in the context of the specific patent claim," *Warner–Jenkinson*, 117 S. Ct. at 1054, 41 USPQ2d at 1875; otherwise, the inquiry could easily result in a wholesale vitiation of a recited claim limitation.

CONCLUSION

The district court's finding on the likelihood of success is wrong because it was based on error concerning the functions performed by a claim limitation, and it thus misapprehended the possible range of equivalents available to the patentee. Tractech's E–Z Locker and the spring assembly claimed in the '015 patent are two separate branches of a tree that is rooted in the prior art pin-disk-spring assembly, and the question is whether those two branches are insubstantially separated. The claims as understood in light of the written description are directed toward structures that perform explicit functions. When considering those functions and the lack of one key function in the accused devices, we conclude that PowerTrax does not have a reasonable likelihood of establishing, on the present record, the insubstantiality of that difference. We therefore vacate the grant of the preliminary injunction and remand.

NEWMAN, Circuit Judge, dissenting.

This appeal is from the grant of a preliminary injunction. Although my colleagues on this panel, having vacated the injunction, remand the case to the district court, they also have pre-judged the issue on remand. By imposing a new rule of law that overrides the facts of equivalency, the panel majority bars liability for infringement by an equivalent device if the equivalent does not possess the unclaimed advantages or functions described in the specification. This new rule of law is contrary to the law of claim interpretation and it is contrary to the precedent of equivalency.

It greatly narrows the scope of potential equivalents, and limits the findings available to be made by the trier of fact.

In seeking optimum judicial administration of a judgemade doctrine whose purpose is to prevent fraud upon the patent, this new rule weighs heavily against patentees whose inventions have been copied. Whether continuing judicial withdrawal of the availability of the doctrine of equivalents is in the national interest is a complex question of economic policy and property theory. In Warner–Jenkinson, however, the Court reaffirmed the viability of the doctrine. Now it is time for this court to lay to rest the tensions that have been resolved, and implement the law as it has been entrusted to us.

A.   The "All–Advantages" Rule

The panel majority holds that the advantages mentioned in the specification, although not included in the claims, must be possessed by the accused device before there can be a finding of infringement by equivalency. This is neither a correct nor a useful rule of law. It directly contradicts the rule of claim construction that bars the importing of limitations into the claims from the specification. It renders the technologic facts of equivalency irrelevant, for it precludes a finding of equivalency whenever the accused device does not possess the unclaimed advantages described in the patent, whatever the actual significance of these unclaimed aspects.

It is entirely contrary to precedent to create this new rule of law that makes irrelevant the evidentiary bases of technologic equivalency. Precedent has established a carefully wrought balance between, on the one hand, providing an adequate incentive to innovation and fair protection to the inventor's property, and on the other hand allowing others to build upon the inventor's contribution. Precedent implements this balance through the facts found upon comparing function/way/result and the substantiality of the changes. It is incorrect to delimit these findings by imposing new barriers to consideration of the relevant evidence.

B.   No "Separate Body of Case Law" Supports the Incorrect "All–Advantages" Rule

The purpose of the doctrine of equivalents is to prevent a form of fraud, as the Supreme Court called it in *Graver Tank*. Its purpose is to protect inventors from those who would take the invention and by insubstantial change avoid the letter of the claims. Precedent contains a wealth of illustration of the balance of the tension between the notice function of claims and the goal of securing to inventors the earned benefits of their technological contributions. The cases that the panel majority states support its new theory, in fact simply illustrate various classical applications of the doctrine of equivalents. I do not share the majority's characterization of this precedent as supporting its new rule of law.

C.   The Zentmyer Invention

All of the elements of the '015 patent claim were conceded to be literally present in the Tractech device except for the biasing means, which is set forth in clause [5] of Claim 1:

1.   A differential mechanism comprising:

[1]   output means;

[2]   driving means in spaced relationship to said output means;

[3]   driven means operably responsive to said driving means for powering said output means;

[4]   said driving means having a pair of clutch driving members coaxially disposed with respect to each other and having opposing spaced-apart surface faces;

[5]   biasing means interposed between said driving member surface faces comprising at least a pin in alignment with a spring assembly consisting of two concentric springs bearing against one end of said pin;

[6]   said springs and said pin in axial alignment disposed in an elongated passageway jointly provided in each of said pair of clutch drive members;

[7]   each of said clutch drive members has inspection and access openings communicating with said passageway so as to expose said springs and said pins respectively; and

[8]   said spring passageway is of oblong configuration in transverse cross-section.

(Spacing and numbering added.)

The biasing means as claimed comprises a pin aligned with a spring assembly consisting of two concentric springs bearing against the pin. The biasing means of the accused (Powertrax) device also comprises a pin and a spring assembly bearing against the pin. The accused spring assembly, however, instead of having concentric (outer and inner) springs, consists of an outer spring and an inner plug. It was conceded, at least at the preliminary injunction hearing, that the spring/plug assembly performed the same biasing function in the same way as the concentric spring assembly and achieved the same result. There was proffered deposition testimony of witnesses for both sides to the effect that the claimed and the accused spring assemblies were fully interchangeable.

Tractech's Director of Engineering testified that the inner plug served the same role as the inner spring. To the question, "What were the functions of the inner springs, as you viewed them?," he answered:

There's only two possible functions. Number one is to fill up a hole, that was my judgment is the reason that it was in. So that pin that was adjacent to the spring would bear against a nice, full flat surface, and the only other possible reason would be to give you more spring force, and I didn't feel that we needed additional spring force.

He did not mention what the majority now calls the "key back-up function." Both sides agreed that the "backup" function (the patent does not use this term) of the inner spring was of minor significance. The claims do not include this function. Nonetheless, my colleagues now hold, as a matter of law, that this unclaimed function must be literally present in the accused device, in order to find equivalency.

This new and absolute rule is presented by the majority as rendering irrelevant any evidence of insubstantiality of the differences, or sameness of function/way/result, with reference to the function described in claim clause [5]. This is a marked departure from precedent—a departure with no redeeming benefit if equivalency is to be fairly adjudicated. The importance of a property mentioned in the specification is a fact to be found and weighed. It is improper to foreclose such evidence by ruling that every unclaimed advantage must be present, whatever its relative significance in practice.

The Zentmyer patent describes six "objects" of his invention. The "primary object" is to "provide a means of assembly which simplifies both manufacture and installation of component parts in said differential mechanism." This object and advantage, it is agreed, is met by the accused device. The other objects are to increase strength and reliability of the joinder of the clutch parts, to permit ready installation without special tools, to provide an access opening in the clutch members and their housing, to impinge the spring assembly directly on the pins instead of on a connecting medium, and to provide an oblong passageway. All of these objects and advantages are realized in the accused device.

In describing the preferred embodiment Zentmyer discusses the advantage of the redundancy of the second spring, although that is not the primary purpose described for the spring assembly. The primary purpose is to interact with the pin and to eliminate the previously-used loose disk; this is fully achieved by the accused spring assembly. The equivalency of the change in the biasing means, whereby the concentric spring structure is replaced with an outer spring/inner plug, must be found on the evidence.

It is not a fair reading of the specification or prosecution history to hold that the patentee made a "specific exclusion" of all spring assemblies lacking the potential redundancy of this preferred embodiment. The patent, in the description of the preferred embodiment, states that should one spring break, "the second spring will bear the load and prevent the broken spring from exiting the assembly." As I have mentioned, this function was viewed by even the accused infringer as unnecessary. The Tractech Director of Engineering who produced both the initial exact copies of the PowerTrax differential and the later spring/plug modification (after the patent issued) stated that the spring/plug version was just as durable as the concentric spring version. This again contravenes the majority's insistence that spring backup was a "key" function whose absence negated any possibility of equivalency. This is a factual issue to be weighed, not a legal imperative.

The majority recognizes that this invention is directed to overcoming the problems with the prior art structure containing a separate disk, and the associated difficulties of installation, failure, and replacement. These are the problems that were overcome by Zentmyer in the device described in the '015 patent. It was not disputed, at the preliminary injunction hearing, that the accused Tractech device overcame the same problems, by using an almost identical structure. By requiring literal presence of the unclaimed backup potential in the substituted assembly the panel majority distorts and pre-judges its remand for findings on the question of equivalency. It is improper to create a new "imprisoning formula," *see Graver Tank & Mfg. Co. v. Linde Air Prods. Co.*, 339 U.S. 605, 609, 85 USPQ 328, 332 (1950), whereby absence of a single unclaimed advantage described in the specification is deemed fatal, as a matter of law, to a finding of infringement under the doctrine of equivalents.

It is the claims that define the invention. *See* 35 U.S.C. § 112/2 ("The specification shall conclude with one or more claims particularly pointing out and distinctly claiming the subject matter which the applicant regards as his invention.").... Advantages described in the body of the specification, if not included in the claims, are not per se limitations to the claimed invention. *See Applied Materials*, 98 F.3d at 1574, 40 USPQ2d at 1489 (only when the inventor's purpose is included in the claims does the purpose serve as "a limitation of the claimed invention [that] should be met either literally or equivalently in order to satisfy the criteria of infringement").

Information in the specification may of course be relevant when finding the facts of equivalency; but the panel majority has posited its "all-advantages" rule as a threshold rule of law. Since it is incorrect to read into the claims any unclaimed advantages described in the specification, it is equally incorrect to hold that any potential equivalent must, as a matter of law, possess these unclaimed advantages. This is directly contrary to the guidance provided in *Warner-Jenkinson*:

> An analysis of the role played by each element in the context of the specific patent claim will thus inform the inquiry as to whether a substitute element matches the function, way and result of the claimed element, or whether the substitute element plays a role substantially different from the claimed element.

117 S. Ct. at 1054, 41 USPQ2d at 1875.

The Supreme Court recognized that infringement by equivalency arises only when the accused subject matter is outside the literal reading of the patent claims. Thus the panel majority errs both in reading all of the advantages of the preferred embodiment into the claims, and in requiring that all advantages, whatever their substance, must be literally present in the accused device before the accused device can be deemed equivalent to what is claimed. . . .

Thus I must, respectfully, dissent.

Notes

1. In this case, the advantage was disclosed in the specification, but the court states that advantages in the prosecution history would warrant a similar result. Hence the crafty accused infringer can often scour the specification and the prosecution history to discover some function accomplished by the patented invention which is not accomplished by her accused device.

2. Do you think that the majority in *Vehicular Tech.* is improperly reading a claim limitation from the written description portion of the specification into the claims? In determining whether two items are equivalents should the court look to the possible functions or ways or results disclosed in the specification? Must the accused element equivalently perform each function in order to be an equivalent?

3. Do you think that the all advantages rule should apply to equivalents under § 112 ¶ 6?

Problems

You represent Mike's Fishing. Mike has identified another company that he believes is infringing his '835 patent. He wants your opinion on whether to sue.

1. Wayne's Motors sells a stern-mounted trolling motor with an electronic steering system that pulls the boat. The motor is mounted on the stern and it pulls the boat in the direction opposite of normal travel (the boat proceeds through the water stern first). Should Mike sue Wayne for infringement?

Prosecution History of '835 Patent

You obtain a copy of the prosecution history of the '835 patent which discloses the following information:

Applicant originally filed claim 1 as follows:

1. An autopilot coupled to a trolling motor, the autopilot comprising:

> a steering motor coupled to said trolling motor, said steering motor being disposed to turn said trolling motor left or right in response to input signals;
>
> a steering circuit coupled to said steering motor, said steering circuit being disposed to generate said input signals;
>
> a compass coupled to said steering circuit, said compass being disposed to transmit heading signals to said steering circuit when the boat deviates from the target heading by a predetermined amount.

In his First Office Action, the Examiner rejected claim 1:

Claim 1 is rejected under § 103 as being unpatentable over Kulpa in view of Chalupny. In regard to claim 1, Kulpa clearly discloses an autopilot system for a trolling motor with a heading detector, steering circuit, steering motor, and thrust motor as claimed. Kulpa does not disclose the use of a compass as a heading detector, but does disclose a magnetometer. Chalupny discloses an autopilot system that follows a set direction using a compass. One of ordinary skill in the art would have found it obvious to use the teachings of Chalupny in Kulpa.

The applicant filed an amendment and response. He amended the claims as follows:

    1. An autopilot coupled to a *bow-mounted* trolling motor *that pulls the boat*, the autopilot comprising:

        a steering motor coupled to said trolling motor, said steering motor being disposed to turn said trolling motor left or right in response to input signals;

        a steering circuit *electrically* coupled to said steering motor, said steering circuit being disposed to generate said input signals;

        a compass *electrically* coupled to said steering circuit, said compass being disposed to transmit heading signals to said steering circuit when the boat deviates from the target heading by a predetermined amount.

In his response, the applicant argued:

The applicant respectfully asserts that the substitution of the Chalupny compass for the Kulpa magnetometer would not render obvious the present invention as now claimed. Both Chalupny and Kulpa are typical stern-mounted autopilot system. Stern-mounted autopilot systems push the boat resulting in overshoot problems with the autopilot system. The autopilot system of the present invention is for a thrust motor which pulls the boat. Unlike systems which use motors that push the boat, this system does not require the calculation of steering magnitude and it does not require two directional sensors.

The Examiner then allowed the claims to issue.

Armed with a copy of the prosecution history, you realize that you need to rethink the advice you are going to give Mike's Fishing.

    1. Does the Easy Troller 1 with its heading detector and steering circuit optically connected, and its magnetometer, infringe the '835 patent? Would your analysis change if you knew that Mark's Boats has a patent on its autopilot system?

    2. Does the Easy Troller 2, a stern-mounted trolling motor which pulls the boat, infringe?

Chapter Eleven

PROVING INVALIDITY

INTRODUCTION

When accused of patent infringement, it is a common defense for the defendant to challenge the validity of the patent that is allegedly being infringed. If the patent is proven invalid then the infringer can practice the invention.

The party attacking validity faces an uphill battle, especially where a jury is involved. Juries tend to respect patents, entrepreneurial inventors, and the PTO. Jurors tend to be reluctant to substitute their opinions for those of the PTO Examiner who they assume is an expert in the field and who determined that this patent with its blue ribbon (which you can expect the patentee to wave repeatedly in front of the jury) should be issued. In addition, when an infringer challenges the patent's validity, it often sounds like an after-the-fact excuse for why the infringer should not be penalized for stealing or copying the patentee's invention. Remember, the accused infringer does not put on his case on invalidity until after the jury has already heard the patentee's case-in-chief on infringement, which undoubtedly makes it look like the infringer stole the patentee's invention.

To prove invalidity the accused infringer should simplify the evidence and focus on establishing a theme that the patentee, not the accused infringer, is the bad guy. The theme could be that the patentee claimed more than he had a right to claim, or that he was attempting to monopolize something that was in the public domain and should have been freely available for everyone to use, or that the patentee withheld important information from the public to gain some sort of commercial advantage—"the patentee wants to have his cake and eat it too defense" or that the patentee did not uphold his end of the bargain and provide a disclosure that teaches people how to make or use the invention. If the patentee is successfully portrayed as a bad guy, the jury will feel justified in taking away the patent. The accused infringer may also want to demonstrate his efforts at independent invention and attempts to design around the patent, to avoid appearing like an unscrupulous copyist.

A. OVERCOMING THE PRESUMPTION OF VALIDITY

STATUTORY PROVISION—35 U.S.C. § 282:

Presumption of validity; defenses

A patent shall be presumed valid. Each claim of a patent (whether in independent, dependent, or multiple dependent form) shall be presumed valid independently of the validity of other claims; dependent or multiple dependent claims shall be presumed valid even though dependent upon an invalid claim. . . . The burden of establishing invalidity of a patent or any claim thereof shall rest on the party asserting such invalidity.

Patents granted by the PTO are presumed valid. Accused infringers who challenge the validity of a patent have the burden of overcoming this presumption by clear and convincing evidence. Each claim in a patent is an individual invention; therefore, each claim must be separately proven invalid. For example, a dependant claim can be valid even though it is dependent on an invalid claim. The presumption of validity reflects the deference accorded to the PTO's decision to grant a patent in light of its technical and legal expertise in determining patentability.

When attacking the validity of a patent, the alleged infringer will fair better by producing prior art not previously considered by the PTO. *See American Hoist & Derrick Co. v. Sowa & Sons*, 725 F.2d 1350, 1360, 220 USPQ 763, 770 (Fed. Cir. 1984). Presenting the jury with prior art that was not considered by the PTO Examiner makes it easier for the jury to conclude that the patent was invalid and that, if the Examiner had all the prior art, she would have surely concluded that the patent should not issue. In this way the alleged infringer is not asking the jury to conclude that the examiner made a mistake in issuing the patent.

There are four basic requirements for patentability:

1. the invention must fall within the class of statutory subject matter delineated in 35 U.S.C. § 101;

2. the invention must be useful under 35 U.S.C. § 101;

3. the invention must be novel under 35 U.S.C. § 102; and

4. the invention must be nonobvious under 35 U.S.C. § 103.

The alleged infringer can base an invalidity claim on any of these grounds. In addition, there are several formal requirements which the patent must comply with to be valid (35 U.S.C. § 112):

1. the specification must include a disclosure of the best mode known to the inventor at the time the patent was filed (the best mode requirement);

2. the specification must enable a person skilled in the art to practice the invention (the enablement requirement); and

3. the specification must fully disclose every claimed element to demonstrate that the inventor had possession of the

invention at the time of the patent filing (the written description requirement).

The alleged infringer may attack the validity of the patent on these grounds as well. This chapter explores how the accused infringer can prove that the patent is invalid.

B. IDENTIFYING PRIOR ART

How does an accused infringer begin to formulate an invalidity defense? She begins by obtaining possible prior art to use for anticipation or obviousness. There are several ways to identify prior art that may render a patent invalid. The patent itself and the prosecution history of the patent at issue provide an excellent start to the search. These sources contain all of the prior art disclosed by the patentee to the Examiner and considered by the Examiner in deciding to issue the patent. In addition, the alleged infringer should look at the references cited in the prior art disclosed in the patent. Patent Examiners in the art group to which the patent pertains can also point the accused infringer to pertinent prior art. The next step is often to contact a professional patent search firm to help identify possible prior art, including US patents, European or Japanese patents, and technical literature in the field.

The accused infringer will want to identify a technical expert early in the case. See Chapter Six. This expert, who is skilled in the technical art to which the patent pertains and should be able to identify relevant technical journals and other literature and people in the field working on the same technology. Your client will also have employees who can point you to sources of relevant prior art: technical journals, literature, and competitors. These competitors may be willing to provide you with additional prior art in the form of publications, public uses, commercial activity, or prior invention. If the third parties refuse to assist you, you have the option of using a third party subpoena (a risky proposition because an unwilling third party may actually end up supporting the validity of the patent). Finally, the patentee should be asked in discovery (usually by document request or interrogatory) about possible prior art that has come to his attention. Often this is prior art cited to the patentee by prospective licensees during licensing negotiations. The patentee should also be asked about other suits involving the patent which could reveal other prior art.

Once you identify relevant prior art, you may want to contact the authors of the publications or the inventors named on a patent. These individuals can often direct you to additional prior art, including public uses and commercial activity. Public use and sale information is valuable because the patent Examiner is usually unaware of it.

C.   FAILURE TO CLAIM PATENTABLE SUBJECT MATTER—§ 101

Statutory Provision—35 U.S.C. § 101:

Inventions Patentable

Whoever invents or discovers any new and useful process, machine, manufacture, or composition of matter, or any new and useful improvement thereof, may obtain a patent therefore, subject to the conditions and requirements of this title.

One method of attack on a patent is to examine if what has been patented is patentable subject matter. This is seldom successful because statutory subject matter includes almost anything under the sun made by man. *See Diamond v. Chakrabarty*, 447 U.S. 303, 309, 206 USPQ 193 (1980). However, § 101 does have some limits. Laws of nature, physical phenomena, and abstract ideas are not patentable. Likewise, failure to claim patentable subject matter can be a viable challenge to validity in software cases because mathematical algorithms are not patentable. Of course, simply drafting the software claims to employ means-plus-function language may avoid a possible § 101 rejection. Consider the following case that addresses the patentability of software and business methods (once considered unpatentable).

STATE STREET BANK & TRUST CO. v. SIGNATURE FINANCIAL GROUP, INC.

149 F.3d 1368, 47 USPQ2d 1596 (Fed. Cir. 1998)

Before RICH, PLAGER, and BRYSON, Circuit Judges.

RICH, Circuit Judge.

Signature Financial Group, Inc. (Signature) appeals from the decision of the United States District Court for the District of Massachusetts granting a motion for summary judgment in favor of State Street Bank & Trust Co. (State Street), finding U.S. Patent No. 5,193,056 (the '056 patent) invalid on the ground that the claimed subject matter is not encompassed by 35 U.S.C. § 101 (1994). We reverse and remand because we conclude that the patent claims are directed to statutory subject matter.

BACKGROUND

Signature is the assignee of the '056 patent which is entitled "Data Processing System for Hub and Spoke Financial Services Configuration." The '056 patent issued to Signature on 9 March 1993, naming R. Todd Boes as the inventor. The '056 patent is generally directed to a data processing system (the system) for implementing an investment structure which was developed for use in Signature's business as an administrator and accounting agent for mutual funds. In essence, the system, identified by the proprietary name Hub and Spoke®, facilitates a structure whereby mutual funds (Spokes) pool their assets in an investment portfolio (Hub) organized as a partnership. This investment configuration provides the administrator of a mutual fund with the advantageous combination of economies of scale in administering investments coupled with the tax advantages of a partnership.

State Street and Signature are both in the business of acting as custodians and accounting agents for multi-tiered partnership fund financial services. State Street negotiated with Signature for a license to use its patented data processing system described and claimed in the '056 patent. When negotiations broke down, State Street brought a declaratory judgment action asserting invalidity, unenforceability, and noninfringement in Massachusetts district court, and then filed a motion for partial summary judgment of patent invalidity for failure to claim statutory subject matter under § 101. The motion was granted and this appeal followed.

Discussion

We hold that declaratory judgment plaintiff State Street was not entitled to the grant of summary judgment of invalidity of the '056 patent under § 101 as a matter of law, because the patent claims are directed to statutory subject matter.

The following facts pertinent to the statutory subject matter issue are either undisputed or represent the version alleged by the nonmovant. The patented invention relates generally to a system that allows an administrator to monitor and record the financial information flow and make all calculations necessary for maintaining a partner fund financial services configuration. As previously mentioned, a partner fund financial services configuration essentially allows several mutual funds, or "Spokes," to pool their investment funds into a single portfolio, or "Hub," allowing for consolidation of, inter alia, the costs of administering the fund combined with the tax advantages of a partnership. In particular, this system provides means for a daily allocation of assets for two or more Spokes that are invested in the same Hub. The system determines the percentage share that each Spoke maintains in the Hub, while taking into consideration daily changes both in the value of the Hub's investment securities and in the concomitant amount of each Spoke's assets.

In determining daily changes, the system also allows for the allocation among the Spokes of the Hub's daily income, expenses, and net realized and unrealized gain or loss, calculating each day's total investments based on the concept of a book capital account. This enables the determination of a true asset value of each Spoke and accurate calculation of allocation ratios between or among the Spokes. The system additionally tracks all the relevant data determined on a daily basis for the Hub and each Spoke, so that aggregate year end income, expenses, and capital gain or loss can be determined for accounting and for tax purposes for the Hub and, as a result, for each publicly traded Spoke.

It is essential that these calculations are quickly and accurately performed. In large part this is required because each Spoke sells shares to the public and the price of those shares is substantially based on the Spoke's percentage interest in the portfolio. In some instances, a mutual fund administrator is required to calculate the value of the shares to the nearest penny within as little as an hour and a half after the market closes. Given the complexity of the calculations, a computer or equivalent device is a virtual necessity to perform the task.

The '056 patent application was filed 11 March 1991. It initially contained six "machine" claims, which incorporated means-plus-function clauses, and six method claims. According to Signature, during prosecution the examiner contemplated a § 101 rejection for failure to claim statutory subject matter. However, upon cancellation of the six method claims, the examiner issued a notice of allowance for the remaining present six claims on appeal. Only claim 1 is an independent claim.

The district court began its analysis by construing the claims to be directed to a process, with each "means" clause merely representing a step in that process. However, "machine" claims having "means" clauses may only be reasonably viewed as process claims if there is no supporting structure in the written description that corresponds to the claimed "means" elements. *See In re Alappat*, 33 F.3d 1526, 1540–41, 31 USPQ2d 1545, 1554 (Fed. Cir. 1994) (*in banc*). This is not the case now before us.

When independent claim 1 is properly construed in accordance with § 112, ¶ 6, it is directed to a machine, as demonstrated below, where representative claim 1 is set forth, the subject matter in brackets stating the structure the written description discloses as corresponding to the respective "means" recited in the claims.

   1.   A data processing system for managing a financial services configuration of a portfolio established as a partnership, each partner being one of a plurality of funds, comprising:

(a) computer processor means [a personal computer including a CPU] for processing data;

(b) storage means [a data disk] for storing data on a storage medium;

(c) first means [an arithmetic logic circuit configured to prepare the data disk to magnetically store selected data] for initializing the storage medium;

(d) second means [an arithmetic logic circuit configured to retrieve information from a specific file, calculate incremental increases or decreases based on specific input, allocate the results on a percentage basis, and store the output in a separate file] for processing data regarding assets in the portfolio and each of the funds from a previous day and data regarding increases or decreases in each of the funds, [sic, funds'] assets and for allocating the percentage share that each fund holds in the portfolio;

(e) third means [an arithmetic logic circuit configured to retrieve information from a specific file, calculate incremental increases and decreases based on specific input, allocate the results on a percentage basis and store the output in a separate file] for processing data regarding daily incremental income, expenses, and net realized gain or loss for the portfolio and for allocating such data among each fund;

(f) fourth means [an arithmetic logic circuit configured to retrieve information from a specific file, calculate incremental increases and decreases based on specific input, allocate the results on a percentage basis and store the output in a separate file] for processing data regarding daily net unrealized gain or loss for the portfolio and for allocating such data among each fund; and

(g) fifth means [an arithmetic logic circuit configured to retrieve information from specific files, calculate that information on an aggregate basis and store the output in a separate file] for processing data regarding aggregate year-end income, expenses, and capital gain or loss for the portfolio and each of the funds.

Each claim component, recited as a "means" plus its function, is to be read, of course, pursuant to § 112, ¶ 6, as inclusive of the "equivalents" of the structures disclosed in the written description portion of the specification. Thus, claim 1, properly construed, claims a machine, namely, a data processing system for managing a financial services configuration of a portfolio established as a partnership, which machine is made up of, at the very least, the specific structures disclosed in the written description and corresponding to the means-plus-function elements (a)-(g) recited in the claim. A "machine" is proper statutory subject matter under § 101. We note that, for the purposes of a § 101 analysis, it is of little relevance whether claim 1 is directed to a "machine" or a "process," as long as it falls within at least one of the four enumerated categories of patentable subject matter, "machine" and "process" being such categories.

This does not end our analysis, however, because the court concluded that the claimed subject matter fell into one of two alternative judicially-created exceptions to statutory subject matter. The court refers to the first exception as the "mathematical algorithm" exception and the second exception as the "business method" exception. Section 101 reads:

> Whoever invents or discovers any new and useful process, machine, manufacture, or composition of matter, or any new and useful improvement thereof, may obtain a patent therefor, subject to the conditions and requirements of this title.

The plain and unambiguous meaning of § 101 is that any invention falling within one of the four stated categories of statutory subject matter may be patented, provided it meets the other requirements for patentability set forth in Title 35, i.e., those found in §§ 102, 103, and 112, ¶ 2.

The repetitive use of the expansive term "any" in § 101 shows Congress's intent not to place any restrictions on the subject matter for which a patent may be obtained beyond those specifically recited in § 101. Indeed, the Supreme Court has acknowledged that Congress intended § 101 to extend to "anything under the sun that is made by man." *Diamond v. Chakrabarty*, 447 U.S. 303, 309 (1980); *see also Diamond v. Diehr*, 450 U.S. 175, 182 (1981). Thus, it is improper to read limitations into § 101 on the subject matter that may be patented where the legislative history indicates that Congress clearly did not intend such limitations. *See Chakrabarty*, 447 U.S. at 308 ("We have also cautioned that courts 'should not read into the patent laws limitations and conditions which the legislature has not expressed.' " (citations omitted)).

The "Mathematical Algorithm" Exception

The Supreme Court has identified three categories of subject matter that are unpatentable, namely "laws of nature, natural phenomena, and abstract ideas." *Diehr*, 450 U.S. at 185. Of particular relevance to this case, the Court has held that mathematical algorithms are not patentable subject matter to the extent that they are merely abstract ideas. *See Diehr*, 450 U.S. 175, *passim*; *Parker v. Flook*, 437 U.S. 584 (1978); *Gottschalk v. Benson*, 409 U.S. 63 (1972). In *Diehr*, the Court explained that certain types of mathematical subject matter, standing alone, represent nothing more than abstract ideas until reduced to some type of practical application, i.e., "a useful, concrete and tangible result." *Alappat*, 33 F.3d at 1544, 31 USPQ2d at 1557.[4]

Unpatentable mathematical algorithms are identifiable by showing they are merely abstract ideas constituting disembodied concepts or truths that are not "useful." From a practical standpoint, this means that to be patentable an algorithm must be applied in a "useful" way. In *Alappat*, we held that data, transformed by a machine through a series of mathematical calculations to produce a smooth waveform display on a rasterizer monitor, constituted a practical application of an abstract idea (a mathematical algorithm, formula, or calculation), because it produced "a useful, concrete and tangible result"—the smooth waveform.

Similarly, in *Arrhythmia Research Technology, Inc. v. Corazonix Corp.*, 958 F.2d 1053, 22 USPQ2d 1033 (Fed. Cir. 1992), we held that the transformation of electrocardiograph signals from a patient's heartbeat by a machine through a series of mathematical calculations constituted a practical application of an abstract idea (a mathematical algorithm, formula, or calculation), because it corresponded to a useful, concrete or tangible thing—the condition of a patient's heart.

Today, we hold that the transformation of data, representing discrete dollar amounts, by a machine through a series of mathematical calculations into a final share price, constitutes a practical application of

---

4. This has come to be known as the mathematical algorithm exception. This designation has led to some confusion, especially given the Freeman–Walter–Abele analysis. By keeping in mind that the mathematical algorithm is unpatentable only to the extent that it represents an abstract idea, this confusion may be ameliorated.

a mathematical algorithm, formula, or calculation, because it produces "a useful, concrete and tangible result"—a final share price momentarily fixed for recording and reporting purposes and even accepted and relied upon by regulatory authorities and in subsequent trades.

The district court erred by applying the Freeman–Walter–Abele test to determine whether the claimed subject matter was an unpatentable abstract idea. The Freeman–Walter–Abele test was designed by the Court of Customs and Patent Appeals, and subsequently adopted by this court, to extract and identify unpatentable mathematical algorithms in the aftermath of *Benson* and *Flook*. *See In re Freeman*, 573 F.2d 1237, 197 USPQ 464 (CCPA 1978) as modified by *In re Walter*, 618 F.2d 758, 205 USPQ 397 (CCPA 1980). The test has been thus articulated:

> First, the claim is analyzed to determine whether a mathematical algorithm is directly or indirectly recited. Next, if a mathematical algorithm is found, the claim as a whole is further analyzed to determine whether the algorithm is "applied in any manner to physical elements or process steps," and, if it is, it "passes muster under § 101."

In re Pardo, 684 F.2d 912, 915, 214 USPQ 673, 675–76 (CCPA 1982) (citing *In re Abele*, 684 F.2d 902, 214 USPQ 682 (CCPA 1982)).

After *Diehr* and *Chakrabarty*, the Freeman–Walter–Abele test has little, if any, applicability to determining the presence of statutory subject matter. As we pointed out in *Alappat*, 33 F.3d at 1543, 31 USPQ2d at 1557, application of the test could be misleading, because a process, machine, manufacture, or composition of matter employing a law of nature, natural phenomenon, or abstract idea is patentable subject matter even though a law of nature, natural phenomenon, or abstract idea would not, by itself, be entitled to such protection.[6] The test determines the presence of, for example, an algorithm. Under *Benson*, this may have been a sufficient indicium of nonstatutory subject matter. However, after *Diehr* and *Alappat*, the mere fact that a claimed

---

6. *See e.g. Parker v. Flook*, 437 U.S. 584, 590 (1978) ("[A] process is not unpatentable simply because it contains a law of nature or a mathematical algorithm."); *Funk Bros. Seed Co. v. Kalo Inoculant Co.*, 333 U.S. 127, 130 (1948) ("He who discovers a hitherto unknown phenomenon of nature has no claim to a monopoly of it which the law recognizes. If there is to be invention from such a discovery, it must come from the application of the law to a new and useful end."); *Mackay Radio & Tel. Co. v. Radio Corp. of Am.*, 306 U.S. 86, 94 (1939) ("While a scientific truth, or the mathematical expression of it, is not a patentable invention, a novel and useful structure created with the aid of knowledge of scientific truth may be.").

[W]hen a claim containing a mathematical formula implements or applies that formula in a structure or process which, when considered as a whole, is performing a function which the patent laws were designed to protect (e.g., transforming or reducing an article to a different state or thing), then the claim satisfies the requirements of § 101.

Diehr, 450 U.S. at 192; *see also In re Iwahashi*, 888 F.2d 1370, 1375, 12 USPQ2d 1908, 1911 (Fed. Cir. 1989); *Taner*, 681 F.2d at 789, 214 USPQ at 680. The dispositive inquiry is whether the claim as a whole is directed to statutory subject matter. It is irrelevant that a claim may contain, as part of the whole, subject matter which would not be patentable by itself. "A claim drawn to subject matter otherwise statutory does not become nonstatutory simply because it uses a mathematical formula, computer program or digital computer." *Diehr*, 450 U.S. at 187.

invention involves inputting numbers, calculating numbers, outputting numbers, and storing numbers, in and of itself, would not render it nonstatutory subject matter, unless, of course, its operation does not produce a "useful, concrete and tangible result." *Alappat*, 33 F.3d at 1544, 31 USPQ2d at 1557. After all, as we have repeatedly stated,

> every step-by-step process, be it electronic or chemical or mechanical, involves an algorithm in the broad sense of the term. Since § 101 expressly includes processes as a category of inventions which may be patented and § 100(b) further defines the word "process" as meaning "process, art or method, and includes a new use of a known process, machine, manufacture, composition of matter, or material," it follows that it is no ground for holding a claim is directed to nonstatutory subject matter to say it includes or is directed to an algorithm. This is why the proscription against patenting has been limited to *mathematical* algorithms....

In re Iwahashi, 888 F.2d 1370, 1374, 12 USPQ2d 1908, 1911 (Fed. Cir. 1989) (emphasis in the original).

The question of whether a claim encompasses statutory subject matter should not focus on *which* of the four categories of subject matter a claim is directed to—process, machine, manufacture, or composition of matter—but rather on the essential characteristics of the subject matter, in particular, its practical utility. Section 101 specifies that statutory subject matter must also satisfy the other "conditions and requirements" of Title 35, including novelty, nonobviousness, and adequacy of disclosure and notice. For purpose of our analysis, as noted above, claim 1 is directed to a machine programmed with the Hub and Spoke software and admittedly produces a "useful, concrete, and tangible result." *Alappat*, 33 F.3d at 1544, 31 USPQ2d at 1557. This renders it statutory subject matter, even if the useful result is expressed in numbers, such as price, profit, percentage, cost, or loss.

The Business Method Exception

As an alternative ground for invalidating the '056 patent under § 101, the court relied on the judicially-created, so-called "business method" exception to statutory subject matter. We take this opportunity to lay this ill-conceived exception to rest. Since its inception, the "business method" exception has merely represented the application of some general, but no longer applicable legal principle, perhaps arising out of the "requirement for invention"—which was eliminated by § 103. Since the 1952 Patent Act, business methods have been, and should have been, subject to the same legal requirements for patentability as applied to any other process or method.[10]

---

10. As Judge Newman has previously stated,

> [The business method exception] is ... an unwarranted encumbrance to the definition of statutory subject matter in section 101, that [should] be discarded as

error-prone, redundant, and obsolete. It merits retirement from the glossary of section 101.... All of the "doing business" cases could have been decided using the clearer concepts of Title 35. Patentability does not turn on whether the

The business method exception has never been invoked by this court, or the CCPA, to deem an invention unpatentable. Application of this particular exception has always been preceded by a ruling based on some clearer concept of Title 35 or, more commonly, application of the abstract idea exception based on finding a mathematical algorithm.

Similarly, *In re Schrader*, 22 F.3d 290, 30 USPQ2d 1455 (Fed. Cir. 1994), while making reference to the business method exception, turned on the fact that the claims implicitly recited an abstract idea in the form of a mathematical algorithm and there was no "transformation or conversion of subject matter representative of or constituting physical activity or objects." 22 F.3d at 294, 30 USPQ2d at 1459 (emphasis omitted).

State Street argues that we acknowledged the validity of the business method exception in *Alappat* when we discussed *Maucorps* and *Meyer*:

> *Maucorps* dealt with a business methodology for deciding how salesmen should best handle respective customers and *Meyer* involved a 'system' for aiding a neurologist in diagnosing patients. Clearly, neither of the alleged 'inventions' in those cases falls within any § 101 category.

Alappat, 33 F.3d at 1541, 31 USPQ2d at 1555. However, closer scrutiny of these cases reveals that the claimed inventions in both *Maucorps* and *Meyer* were rejected as abstract ideas under the mathematical algorithm exception, not the business method exception. *See In re Maucorps*, 609 F.2d 481, 484, 203 USPQ 812, 816 (CCPA 1979); *In re Meyer*, 688 F.2d 789, 796, 215 USPQ 193, 199 (CCPA 1982).

Even the case frequently cited as establishing the business method exception to statutory subject matter, *Hotel Security Checking Co. v. Lorraine Co.*, 160 F. 467 (2d Cir. 1908), did not rely on the exception to strike the patent. In that case, the patent was found invalid for lack of novelty and "invention," not because it was improper subject matter for a patent. The court stated "the fundamental principle of the system is as old as the art of bookkeeping, i.e., charging the goods of the employer to the agent who takes them." *Id.* at 469. "If at the time of [the patent] application, there had been no system of bookkeeping of any kind in restaurants, we would be confronted with the question whether a new and useful system of cash registering and account checking is such an art as is patentable under the statute." *Id.* at 472.

This case is no exception. The district court announced the precepts of the business method exception as set forth in several treatises, but

claimed method does "business" instead of something else, but on whether the method, viewed as a whole, meets the requirements of patentability as set forth in Sections 102, 103, and 112 of the Patent Act.

In re Schrader, 22 F.3d 290, 298, 30 USPQ2d 1455, 1462 (Fed. Cir. 1994) (Newman, J., dissenting).

noted as its primary reason for finding the patent invalid under the business method exception as follows:

> If Signature's invention were patentable, any financial institution desirous of implementing a multi-tiered funding complex modelled (sic) on a Hub and Spoke configuration would be required to seek Signature's permission before embarking on such a project. *This is so because the '056 Patent is claimed [sic] sufficiently broadly to foreclose virtually any computer-implemented accounting method necessary to manage this type of financial structure.*

Whether the patent's claims are too broad to be patentable is not to be judged under § 101, but rather under §§ 102, 103 and 112. Assuming the above statement to be correct, it has nothing to do with whether what is claimed is statutory subject matter.

In view of this background, it comes as no surprise that in the most recent edition of the Manual of Patent Examining Procedures (MPEP) (1996), a paragraph of § 706.03(a) was deleted. In past editions it read:

> Though seemingly within the category of process or method, a method of doing business can be rejected as not being within the statutory classes. *See Hotel Security Checking Co. v. Lorraine Co.,* 160 F. 467 (2d Cir. 1908) and *In re Wait,* 24 USPQ 88, 22 CCPA 822 (1934).

MPEP § 706.03(a) (1994). This acknowledgment is buttressed by the U.S. Patent and Trademark 1996 Examination Guidelines for Computer Related Inventions which now read:

> Office personnel have had difficulty in properly treating claims directed to methods of doing business. Claims should not be categorized as methods of doing business. Instead such claims should be treated like any other process claims.

Examination Guidelines, 61 Fed. Reg. 7478, 7479 (1996). We agree that this is precisely the manner in which this type of claim should be treated. Whether the claims are directed to subject matter within § 101 should not turn on whether the claimed subject matter does "business" instead of something else.

Notes

1. As the preceding case demonstrates, there are some limits upon what may be patented. What would be examples of unpatentable subject matter? Should human genes be patentable? Should medical procedures or life saving drugs be patentable? Should sports moves such as a new tennis swing or dunk shot be patentable?

2. **Utility.** In addition to defining statutory subject matter, § 101 requires that an invention be useful before it can be patented. A patent's utility is rarely challenged by accused infringers because the patented invention need not be superior to prior inventions; rather it only needs to have some use. As you can imagine, an inventor is not likely (due to the expense) to seek patent protection for an invention that is not useful. While the issue of utility is unlikely to arise in an electrical or mechanical

invention, whose uses are readily apparent, it can arise in chemical and biotech inventions. Chemical researchers often develop compounds without knowing how they could be used. Should these compounds be patentable before a use is established? Similarly, gene fragments can be sequenced and produced without knowledge of the uses of these sequences. Should the sequence nonetheless be patented where the claimed utility is that the gene is useful in furthering scientific research?

The chemical and biological arts are unpredictable. Minor changes in chemical compounds can radically alter their properties and effects. Accordingly, in these arts greater proof of utility is required. *See generally Brenner v. Manson*, 383 U.S. 519, 148 USPQ 689 (1966); *In re Brana*, 51 F.3d 1560, 34 USPQ2d 1436 (Fed. Cir. 1995). Evidence that two compounds are structurally similar and that one has a proven utility is insufficient proof that the other will have the same utility. *See* Patent Office Utility Guidelines, 60 Fed. Reg. 36263 (July 14, 1995). What kind of evidence is sufficient to satisfy the utility requirement in these cases?

D. ANTICIPATION—§ 102

Statutory Provision—35 U.S.C. § 102:

Conditions for Patentability, novelty and loss of right to patent.

A person shall be entitled to a patent unless–

(a) the invention was known or used by others in this country, or patented or described in a printed publication in this or a foreign country, before the invention thereof by the applicant for patent, or

(b) the invention was patented or described in a printed publication in this or a foreign country or in public use or on sale in this country, more than one year prior to the date of the application for patent in the United States,

The accused infringer will frequently argue that the patent is anticipated. To succeed on a claim of anticipation under § 102(a), the accused infringer must prove that the prior art contains every element of the patent claim. Anticipation is a question of fact that the jury should resolve. Under § 102(a), a patent is anticipated (lacks novelty) if the invention was *publicly* known or used by others in this country before the applicant's date of invention. Initially, the date the application was filed is treated as the patentee's date of invention. Hence, an alleged infringer makes out a *prima facie* case of invalidity if he proves by clear and convincing evidence that the invention was publicly known or used by others before the application date. However, the patentee can rebut this case by proving an earlier date of invention. Hence, it is important for the party challenging validity to pin down the inventor's dates of inventive activity as soon as possible (and before you are required by a discovery request to reveal your prior art). This can be accomplished through interrogatories or by deposing the inventor. Once you have the inventor on record as to his dates of conception and actual reduction to practice then you can better assess the prior art you are aware of to determine its applicability to the invention date and determine if further searching is necessary for prior art before this date. If you can find prior art which predates the inventor's date of invention, then you can avoid arguing over corroboration.

1. § 102(a)—KNOWN OR USED BY OTHERS

An invention is known or used by others under § 102(a) if it is publicly know or used by others in this country. *See Carella v. Starlight Archery & Pro Line Co.*, 804 F.2d 135, 139, 231 USPQ 644, 646 (Fed. Cir. 1986). Factors to consider in determining whether a public use amounts to being known or used by others include:

1. the number of observers;

2. the intent of the inventor;

3. the number of uses of the invention; and

4. the extent to which the observers understand the disclosed technology.

The best evidence to prove a § 102(a) known or used claim is physical evidence combined or supplemented with oral testimony. For example, the alleged infringer could find a prior inventor of the claimed invention who contends that he used it in public prior to the patentee's date of invention. The defendant should ideally present this witness and physical evidence substantiating his claims. Physical evidence could include notes, letters, invoices, notebooks, sketches, drawings, photographs, or models. Detailed proof is required to meet the clear and convincing evidentiary standard that the alleged infringer faces when charging invalidity.

PATENTEE'S REBUTTAL EVIDENCE—CORROBORATION IS REQUIRED

The Federal Circuit has held that claims of prior public knowledge or use under § 102(a) based on oral evidence such as an individual claiming he publicly used the invention prior to the patentee's date of invention must be corroborated. *See Woodland Trust v. Flowertree Nursery, Inc.*, 148 F.3d 1368, 1371, 47 USPQ2d 1363, 1367 (Fed. Cir. 1998). In *Woodland Trust*, the patentee sued Flowertree Nursery for infringement of a patent for a method of protecting foliage from freezing. Flowertree argued that the patent was invalid under § 102(a) because the owner of Flowertree, Hawkins, used the system thirty years earlier but then abandoned it after ten years. Hawkins' claims of prior public use were corroborated by four witnesses, all friends and family. The court held this evidence insufficient to prove prior public use by clear and convincing evidence. The court held that the party challenging validity of a patent has a heavy burden when the only evidence is the oral testimony of interested persons and their friends and family, particularly as to long past events.

In evaluating the sufficiency of the corroboration in *Woodland Trust,* 138 F.3d at 1371, 47 USPQ2d at 1367, the Federal Circuit held that a number of factors should be considered under a "rule of reason" approach including:

(1) the relationship between the corroborating witness and the alleged prior user;

(2) the time period between the event and trial;

(3) the interest of the corroborating witness in the subject matter in suit;

(4) contradiction or impeachment of the witness' testimony;

(5) the extent and details of the corroborating testimony;

(6) the witness' familiarity with the subject matter of the patented invention and the prior use;

(7) the probability that a prior use could occur considering the state of the art at the time; and

(8) the impact of the invention on the industry, and the commercial value of its practice.

2. § 102(a) or § 102(b)—OTHER PATENTS OR PRINTED PUBLICATIONS

The accused infringer can prove lack of novelty by showing that the invention was patented or described in a printed publication either before the applicant's invention (§ 102(a)) or more than a year prior to the filing date of the application (§ 102(b)).

Any patent (foreign or domestic) is prior art for what it claims at the time it issues, regardless of whether it was publicly accessible. A patent may also be a printed publication if it is made publicly available. In many foreign countries patent applications are published 18 months after they are filed. In the U.S. patent applications are published when they issue. These published applications or patents are "printed publications" under the statute for all that they disclose, not just what they claim.

A prior art document is a printed publication when it is *publicly accessible*. A printed publication is not necessarily publicly accessible as of the date on its cover. Often publications are not placed in the hands of subscribers until months after the date on the cover. Hence an article is a printed publication under the statute when it is received by the relevant public.

Scholarly papers such as a thesis or paper become publicly accessible, and therefore a "printed publication," when they are cataloged and indexed in a meaningful way. A thesis is not a printed publication on the date it is turned in, but rather on the day that the public has access to it. A single thesis deposited in a college library can be a printed publication rendering a patent invalid as long as it is cataloged in a way so that those of skill in the art can gain access to it. *See In re Hall*, 781 F.2d 897, 228 USPQ 453 (Fed. Cir. 1986). Generally, the cataloging must be by subject matter to be meaningful cataloging by author's last name would not be sufficient.

Notes

1. **Inherency.** A reference must identically disclose every element in a claim in order to anticipate under § 102(a). However, if an element is not disclosed, but is inherent from what is disclosed (*i.e*, it naturally always follows from what is disclosed), then there is § 102(a) anticipation even though one of the claimed elements is not actually disclosed. It is not enough for § 102(a) that an undisclosed element is obvious to one of ordinary skill in the art. In *Continental Can Co. USA, Inc. v. Monsanto Co.*, 948 F.2d 1264, 20 USPQ2d 1746 (Fed. Cir. 1991) (citations omitted), the Federal Circuit summarized the law of inherency:

> To serve as an anticipation when the reference is silent about the asserted inherent characteristic, such gap in the reference may be filled with recourse to extrinsic evidence. Such evidence must make clear that the missing descriptive matter is necessarily present in the thing described in the reference, and that it would be so recognized by persons of ordinary skill. "Inherency, however, may not be established by probabilities or possibilities. The mere fact that a certain thing may result from a given set of circumstances is not sufficient." If, however, the disclosure is sufficient to show that the natural result flowing from the operation as taught would result in the performance of the questioned function, it seems to be well settled that the disclosure should be regarded as sufficient.

2. **Enablement Required**. To anticipate, in addition to disclosing all of the claimed elements, the reference must enable one skilled in the art to practice the invention. *See Key Pharm., Inc. v. Hercon Lab. Corp.*, 981 F. Supp. 299, 310–11 (D. Del. 1997). For example, if the patentee claimed a method of making a chemical compound, it is not enough if the reference merely discloses the chemical compound without enabling one skilled in the art to make it.

3. **Genus/Species**. A prior art species anticipates a later claimed genus that includes the species. However, a prior art genus does not anticipate a later claimed species if the species has significant and unpredictable advantages over the other members of the genus.

PATENTEE'S REBUTTAL EVIDENCE—ANTEDATING A REFERENCE

The patentee can rebut a prima facie case of invalidity under § 102(a) (but not § 102(b)) by proving an earlier date of invention. This requires the patentee to prove either conception or an actual reduction to practice antedating the reference. Conception is the formation in the mind of the inventor of a definite and permanent idea of the complete invention. Reduction to practice is when there is a physical embodiment of the invention which has been sufficiently tested to prove that it works for its intended purposes (testing has verified operability).

A claim to an earlier invention date by the patentee requires corroboration. The patentee may corroborate an invention date with witnesses, lab notebooks signed and dated by others, invoices demonstrating that the parts to build the invention were ordered or received, or sending by registered mail to himself or others a disclosure of the invention.

3. ON SALE/PUBLIC USE BARS—§ 102(b)

Under § 102(b), once an invention is offered for sale or used in public, the inventor has one year in which to file for a patent. Unlike § 102(a), § 102(b) does not require precise identity between the claim and the invention that was used in public or offered for sale. It is enough if the claim would have been obvious in light of what was offered for sale. If the invention was in public use or on sale more than one year prior to the filing date, the patent is invalid. Notice the date that the inventor invented (conceived or reduced to practice) is irrelevant under § 102(b).

The following case considers the statutory meaning of public use.

EGBERT v. LIPPMANN
104 U.S. 333 (1881)

J. WOODS delivered the opinion of the court.

This suit was brought for an alleged infringement of the complainant's reissued letters-patent, No. 5216, dated Jan. 7, 1873, for an improvement in corset-springs.

The specification for the reissue declares:—

This invention consists in forming the springs of corsets of two or more metallic plates, placed one upon another, and so connected as to prevent them from sliding off each other laterally or edgewise, and at the same time admit of their playing or sliding upon each other, in the direction of their length or longitudinally, whereby their flexibility and elasticity are greatly increased, while at the same time much strength is obtained.

The second claim is as follows:—

A pair of corset-springs, each member of the pair being composed of two or more metallic plates, placed on another, and fastened together at their centres, and so connected at or near each end that they can move or play on each other in the direction of their length.

The bill alleges that Barnes was the original and first inventor of the improvement covered by the reissued letters-patent, and that it had not, at the time of his application for the original letters, been for more than two years in public use or on sale, with his consent or allowance.

The answer takes issue on this averment and also denies infringement. On a final hearing the court dismissed the bill, and the complainant appealed.

We have, therefore, to consider whether the defense that the patented invention had, with the consent of the inventor, been publicly used for more than two years prior to his application for the original letters, is sustained by the testimony in the record.

The sixth, seventh, and fifteenth sections of the act of July 4, 1836, c. 357 (5 Stat. 117), as qualified by the seventh section of the act of March 8, 1839, c. 88 (*Id*. 353), were in force at the date of his application. Their effect is to render letters-patent invalid if the invention which they cover was in public use, with the consent and allowance of the inventor, for more than two years prior to his application. Since the passage of the act of 1839 it has been strenuously contended that the public use of an invention for more than two years before such application, even without his consent and allowance, renders the letters-patent therefore void.

It is unnecessary in this case to decide this question, for the alleged use of the invention covered by the letters-patent to Barnes is conceded to have been with his express consent.

The evidence on which the defendants rely to establish a prior public use of the invention consists mainly of the testimony of the complainant.

She testifies that Barnes invented the improvement covered by his patent between January and May, 1855; that between the dates named the witness and her friend Miss Cugier were complaining of the breaking of their corset-steels. Barnes, who was present, and was an intimate friend of the witness, said he thought he could make her a pair that would not break. At their next interview he presented her with a pair of corset-steels which he himself had made. The witness wore these steels a long time. In 1858 Barnes made and presented to her another pair, which she also wore a long time. When the corsets in which these steels were used wore out, the witness ripped them open and took out the steels and put them in new corsets. This was done several times.

It is admitted, and, in fact, is asserted, by complainant, that these steels embodied the invention afterwards patented by Barnes and covered by the reissued letters-patent on which this suit is brought.

Joseph H. Sturgis, another witness for complainant, testifies that in 1863 Barnes spoke to him about two inventions made by himself, one of which was a corset-steel, and that he went to the house of Barnes to see them. Before this time, and after the transactions testified to by the complainant, Barnes and she had intermarried. Barnes said his wife had a pair of steels made according to his invention in the corsets which she was then wearing, and if she would take them off he would show them to witness. Mrs. Barnes went out, and returned with a pair of corsets and a pair of scissors, and ripped the corsets open and took out the steels. Barnes then explained to witness how they were made and used.

The question for our decision is, whether this testimony shows a public use within the meaning of the statute.

We observe, in the first place, that to constitute the public use of an invention it is not necessary that more than one of the patented articles should be publicly used. The use of a great number may tend to strengthen the proof, but one well-defined case of such use is just as effectual to annul the patent as many. For instance, if the inventor of a mower, a printing-press, or a railway-car makes and sells only one of the articles invented by him, and allows the vendee to use it for two years, without restriction or limitation, the use is just as public as if he had sold and allowed the use of a great number.

We remark, secondly, that whether the use of an invention is public or private does not necessarily depend upon the number of persons to whom its use is know. If an inventor, having made his device, gives or sells it to another, to be used by the donee or vendee, without limitation or restriction, or injunction of secrecy, and it is so used, such use is public, even though the use and knowledge of the use may be confined to one person.

We say, thirdly, that some inventions are by their very character only capable of being used where they cannot be seen or observed by the public eye. An invention may consist of a lever or spring, hidden in the running gear of a watch, or of a rachet, shaft, or cog-wheel covered from view in the recesses of a machine for spinning or weaving. Nevertheless, if its inventor sells a machine of which his invention forms a part, and allows it to be used without restriction of any kind, the use is a public one. So, on the other hand, a use necessarily open to public view, if made in good faith solely to test the qualities of the invention, and for the purpose of experiment, is not a public use within the meaning of the statute. *Elizabeth v. Pavement Company*, 97 U.S. 126.

Tested by these principles, we think the evidence of the complainant herself shows that for more than two years before the application for the original letters there was, by the consent and allowance of Barnes, a public use of the invention, covered by them. He made and gave to her two pairs of corset-steels, constructed according to his device, one in 1855 and one in 1858. They were presented to her for use. He imposed no obligation of secrecy, nor any condition or restriction whatever. They were not presented for the purpose of experiment, nor to test their qualities. No such claim is set up in her testimony. The invention was at the time complete, and there is no evidence that it was afterwards changed or improved. The donee of the steels used them for years for the purpose and in the manner designed by the inventor. They were not capable of any other use. She might have exhibited them to any person, or made other steels of the same kind, and used or sold them without violating any condition or restriction imposed on her by the inventor.

According to the testimony of the complainant, the invention was completed and put into use in 1855. The inventor slept on his rights for eleven years. Letters-patent were not applied for till March, 1866. In the mean time, the invention had found its way into general, and almost universal, use. A great part of the record is taken up with the testimony of the manufacturers and venders of corset-steels, showing that before he applied for letters the principle of his device was almost universally used in the manufacture of corset-steels. It is fair to presume that having learned from this general use that there was some value in his invention, he attempted to resume, by his application, what by his acts he had clearly dedicated to the public.

> An abandonment of an invention to the public may be evinced by the conduct of the inventor at any time, even within the two years named in the law. The effect of the law is that no such consequence will necessarily follow from the invention being in public use or on sale, with the inventor's consent and allowance, at any time within the two years before his application; but that, if the invention is in public use or on sale prior to that time, it will be conclusive evidence of abandonment, and the patent will be void.

Elizabeth v. Pavement Company, supra.

We are of opinion that the defense of two years' public use, by the consent and allowance of the inventor, before he made application for letters-patent, is satisfactorily established by the evidence.

J. MILLER dissenting.

The word public is, therefore, an important member of the sentence. A private use with consent, which could lead to no copy or reproduction of the machine, which taught the nature of the invention to no one but the party to whom such consent was given, which left the public at large as ignorant of this as it was before the author's discovery, was no abandonment to the public, and did not defeat his claim for a patent. If the little steep spring inserted in a single pair of corsets, and used by only one woman, covered by her outer-clothing, and in a position always withheld from public observation, is a public use of that piece of steel, I am at a loss to know the line between a private and public use.

The opinion argues that the use was public, because, with the consent of the inventor to its use, no limitation was imposed in regard to its use in public. It may be well imagined that a prohibition to the party so permitted against exposing her use of the steel spring to public observation would have been supposed to be a piece of irony. An objection quite the opposite of this suggested by the opinion is, that the invention was incapable of a public use. That is to say, that while the statute says the right to the patent can only be defeated by a use which is public, it is equally fatal to the claim, when it is permitted to be used at all, that the article can never be used in public.

I cannot on such reasoning as this eliminate from the statute the word public, and disregard its obvious importance in connection with the remainder of the act, for the purpose of defeating a patent otherwise meritorious.

W.L. GORE & ASSOC., INC. v. GARLOCK, INC.

721 F.2d 1540, 220 USPQ 303 (Fed. Cir. 1983)

Before MARKEY, Chief Judge, and DAVIS and MILLER, Circuit Judges.

MARKEY, Chief Judge.

Appeal from a judgment of the District Court for the Northern District of Ohio holding U.S. Patents 3,953,566 ('566) and 4,187,390 ('390) invalid.

BACKGROUND

Tape of unsintered polytetrafluorethylene (PTFE) (known by the trademark TEFLON of E.I. du Pont de Nemours, Inc.) had been stretched in small increments. W.L. Gore & Associates, Inc. (Gore), assignee of the patents in suit, experienced a tape breakage problem in the operation of its "401" tape stretching machine. Dr. Robert Gore, Vice President of Gore, developed the invention disclosed and claimed in the '566 and '390 patents in the course of his effort to solve that problem. The 401 machine was disclosed and claimed in Gore's U.S. Patent 3,664,915 ('915) and was the invention of Wilbert L. Gore, Dr. Gore's father. PTFE tape had been sold as thread seal tape, i.e., tape used to keep pipe joints from leaking.

Dr. Gore experimented with heating and stretching of highly crystalline PTFE rods. Despite slow, careful stretching, the rods broke when stretched a relatively small amount. Conventional wisdom in the art taught that breakage could be avoided only by slowing the stretch rate or by decreasing the crystallinity. In late October, 1969, Dr. Gore discovered, contrary to that teaching, that stretching the rods as fast as possible enabled him to stretch them to more than ten times their original length with no breakage. Further, though the rod was thus greatly lengthened, its diameter remained virtually unchanged throughout its length. The rapid stretching also transformed the hard, shiny rods into rods of a soft, flexible material.

Gore developed several PTFE products by rapidly stretching highly crystalline PTFE, including: (1) porous film for filters and laminates; (2) fabric laminates of PTFE film bonded to fabric to produce a remarkable material having the contradictory properties of impermeability to liquid water and permeability to water vapor, the material being used to make "breathable" rainwear and filters; (3) porous yarn for weaving or braiding into other products, like space suits and pump packing; (4) tubes used as replacements for human arteries and veins; and (5) insulation for high performance electric cables.

On May 21, 1970, Gore filed the patent application that resulted in the patents in suit. The '566 patent has 24 claims directed to processes for stretching highly crystalline, unsintered, PTFE. The processes, inter alia, include the steps of stretching PTFE at a rate above 10% per second and at a temperature between about 35° C and the crystalline melt point of PTFE. The '390 patent has 77 claims directed to various products obtained by processes of the '566 patent.

PROCEEDINGS

On Nov. 2, 1979, Gore sued Garlock for infringement of process claims 3 and 19 of the '566 patent, and sought injunctive relief, damages, and attorney fees. Garlock counterclaimed on Dec. 18, 1979, for a declaratory judgment of patent invalidity, non-infringement, fraudulent solicitation, and entitlement to attorney fees. On Feb. 7, 1980, Gore filed a second suit for infringement of product claims 14, 18, 36, 43, 67 and 77 of the '390 patent. In light of a stipulation, the district court consolidated the two suits for trial.

The district court, in a thorough memorandum accompanying its judgment, and in respect of the '566 patent declared all claims of the patent invalid under 102(b) because the invention had been in public use and on sale more than one year before Gore's patent application, as evidenced by Budd's use of the Cropper machine.

35 U.S.C. § 102(b) provides:

A person shall be entitled to a patent unless—

(b) the invention was patented or described in a printed publication in this or a foreign country or in public use or on sale in this country, more than one year prior to the date of the application for patent in the United States, or . . .

§ 102(b) and the Cropper Machine

In 1966 John W. Cropper (Cropper) of New Zealand developed and constructed a machine for producing stretched and unstretched PTFE thread seal tape. In 1967, Cropper sent a letter to a company in Massachusetts, offering to sell his machine, describing its operation, and enclosing a photo. Nothing came of that letter. There is no evidence and no finding that the present inventions thereby became known or used in this country.

In 1968, Cropper sold his machine to Budd, which at some point thereafter used it to produce and sell PTFE thread seal tape. The sales agreement between Cropper and Budd provided:

ARTICLE "E"—PROTECTION OF TRADE SECRETS ETC.

1. BUDD agrees that while this agreement is in force it will not reproduce any copies of the said apparatus without the express written permission of Cropper nor will it divulge to any person or persons other than its own employees or employees of its affiliated corporations any of the said known-how or any details whatsoever relating to the apparatus.

2. BUDD agrees to take all proper steps to ensure that its employees observe the terms of Article "E" 1 and further agrees that whenever it is proper to do so it will take legal action in a Court of

competent jurisdiction to enforce any one or more of the legal or equitable remedies available to a trade secret plaintiff.

Budd told its employees the Cropper machine was confidential and required them to sign confidentiality agreements. Budd otherwise treated the Cropper machine like its other manufacturing equipment.

A former Budd employee said Budd made no effort to keep the secret. That Budd did not keep the machine hidden from employees legally bound to keep their knowledge confidential does not evidence a failure to maintain the secret. Similarly, that du Pont employees were shown the machine to see if they could help increase its speed does not itself establish a breach of the secrecy agreement. There is no evidence of when that viewing occurred. There is no evidence that a viewer of the machine could thereby learn anything of which process, among all possible processes, the machine is being used to practice. As Cropper testified, looking at the machine in operation does not reveal whether it is stretching, and if so, at what speed. Nor does looking disclose whether the crystallinity and temperature elements of the invention set forth in the claims are involved. There is no evidence that Budd's secret use of the Cropper machine made knowledge of the claimed process accessible to the public.

The district court held all claims of the '566 patent invalid under 102(b) because "the invention" was "in public use [and] on sale" by Budd more than one year before Gore's application for patent. Beyond a failure to consider each of the claims independently, and a failure of proof that the claimed inventions as a whole were practiced by Budd before the critical May 21, 1969 date, it was error to hold that Budd's activity with the Cropper machine, as above indicated, was a "public" use of the processes claimed in the '566 patent, that activity having been secret, not public.

Assuming, *arguendo*, that Budd sold tape produced on the Cropper machine before October 1969, and that tape was made by a process set forth in a claim of the '566 patent, the issue under § 102(b) is whether that sale would defeat Dr. Gore's right to a patent on the process inventions set forth in the claims.

If Budd offered and sold anything, it was only tape, not whatever process was used in producing it. Neither party contends, and there was no evidence, that the public could learn the claimed process by examining the tape. If Budd and Cropper commercialized the tape, that could result in a forfeiture of a patent granted them for their process on an application filed by them more than a year later. *D.L. Auld Co. v. Chroma Graphics Corp.*, 714 F.2d 1144, at 1147–48 (Fed. Cir. 1983); *See Metallizing Engineering Co. v. Kenyon Bearing & Auto Parts Co.*, 153 F.2d 516, 68 USPQ 54 (2d Cir. 1946). There is no reason or statutory basis, however, on which Budd's and Cropper's secret commercialization of a process, if established, could be held a bar to the grant of a patent to Gore on that process.

Early public disclosure is a linchpin of the patent system. As between a prior inventor who benefits from a process by selling its product but suppresses, conceals, or otherwise keeps the process from the public, and a later inventor who promptly files a patent application from which the public will gain a disclosure of the process, the law favors the latter. The district court therefore erred as a matter of law in applying the statute and in its determination that Budd's secret use of the Cropper machine and sale of tape rendered all process claims of the '566 patent invalid under § 102(b).

Notes

1. Under § 102(b) what type of use qualifies as a public use/on sale bar?

Use By	Informing Use (PUBLIC)	Non–informing Use (Not Secret)	Secret Use
Applicant	*See Pennock v. Dialogue*, 27 U.S. 1 (1829)	*See Egbert v. Lippmann*, 104 U.S. 333 (1881)	*See Metallizing Eng'g Co. v. Kenyon Bearing & Auto Parts Co.*, 153 F.2d 516, 68 USPQ 54 (2d Cir. 1946)
3rd Party	*See Bedford v. Hunt*, 3 Fed. Cas. 37 (C.C.D. Mass. 1817)	??	*See W.L. Gore & Assocs., Inc. v. Garlock, Inc.*, 721 F.2d 1540, 220 USPQ 303 (Fed. Cir. 1983)

2. **Theft and Disclosure by a Third Party**. A § 102(b) bar exists even if an unscrupulous third party steals the patentee's invention and discloses it to the public. *See Evans Cooling Sys., Inc. v. General Motors Corp.*, 125 F.3d 1448, 1453, 44 USPQ2d 1037, 1041 (Fed. Cir. 1997).

3. **Peer Review Forum is Not a Public Use**. Does sending an article in to a journal for publication constitute a ''public use'' which would start the public use bar clock ticking? In *Xerox Corp. v. 3Com Corp.*, 26 F. Supp.2d 492 (W.D.N.Y. 1998), the court held that a single disclosure of a videotaped demonstration of an invention to an industry conference review board for purposes of determining whether the invention would be presented at the conference did not constitute a public use. The court held that the videotape was submitted for the limited purpose of determining whether it would be presented at the conference and with the expectation that it would be kept confidential. The court found that a holding that disclosures in the peer review forum are public uses would have a chilling effect on future scientific and academic submissions. What if one of the peer reviewers began using the invention after seeing the videotape? Would this use constitute a public use? What remedies would be available to the inventor?

4. The factors that should be considered for determining whether there is an on-sale bar include:

1. the concreteness of the offer (e.g., were prices and delivery dates specified);

2. the inventor's level of satisfaction with the invention (i.e., could this be an experimental use; have there been any post-delivery modifications of the invention);

3. the stage of development of the invention (i.e., reduced to practice, substantially complete);

4. the nature of the invention (e.g., is it a simple mechanical invention such that a reduction to practice is unnecessary); and

5. the policy factors.

Should a patentee be able to extend her monopoly by advertising her product and collecting millions of dollars worth of orders over a period of several years by claiming that the invention was not on sale because all of the pieces were never put together? There are four policy considerations that should be balanced in any on-sale bar analysis:

1. the policy against removing inventions which the public has justifiably come to believe are freely available;

2. the policy favoring prompt disclosure;

3. the policy of preventing an inventor from commercially exploiting his monopoly beyond the statutory time period; and

4. the policy of giving the inventor a reasonable amount of time following sales activity to determine whether a patent is a worthwhile investment.

When is an invention sufficiently reduced to practice to be on sale?

The Federal Circuit has been struggling with whether an invention need be reduced to practice in order to be on sale. Early on-sale bar cases required that the invention be *on hand* for delivery to a purchaser before an offer for sale would be considered a bar under § 102(b). Courts eventually backed off of the on-hand requirement, instead requiring that the invention be reduced to practice (physically built and tested to verify operability) to invoke the on-sale bar. *See, generally e.g., Timely Prods. Corp. v. Arron*, 523 F.2d 288, 187 USPQ 257 (2d Cir. 1975). In *UMC Elec. Co. v. United States*, 816 F.2d 647, 2 USPQ2d 1465 (Fed. Cir. 1987), the Federal Circuit held that reduction to practice is not an absolute requirement of the on-sale bar. Instead the court balanced a number of policy considerations to determine, under the totality of the circumstances, whether the invention was on-sale.

In apparent contradiction to *UMC*, in *Seal-Flex, Inc. v. Athletic Track & Court Const.*, 98 F.3d 1318, 40 USPQ2d 1450 (Fed. Cir. 1996), the Federal Circuit held that the on-sale bar is not triggered unless the patentee has a "complete invention" at the time of the relevant on sale activity—returning to a pre-*UMC* requirement of a complete invention. In the next opinion to address this issue, *Micro Chem., Inc. v. Great Plains Chem. Co.*, 103 F.3d 1538, 41 USPQ2d 1238 (Fed. Cir. 1997), the Federal Circuit held that the criterion for determining whether an invention is on sale is whether the invention is "substantially complete" with "reason to expect that it would work for its intended purpose upon completion."

Then, in the same year in *Pfaff v. Wells Elec., Inc.*, 124 F.3d 1429, 1434, 43 USPQ2d 1928, 1932 (Fed. Cir. 1997), *aff'd*, 119 S. Ct. 304, 48 USPQ2d 1641 (1998), the Federal Circuit held that a patent directed to sockets for testing leadless chip carriers was invalid under the on sale bar because at the time of the alleged offer for sale, the inventor had made "detailed engineering drawings" of the invention and had sent them to a vendor for tooling and production. Hence, the on-sale bar applied even though no sockets had been made nor tested. The Court rejected the inventor's arguments that cycle testing was required before he could be sure that the sockets would perform properly, finding instead that the testing was for fatigue testing rather than functionality testing and that durability was not part of the claimed invention. The Supreme Court granted *certiorari* on the question:

> In view of the longstanding statutory definition that the one-year grace period to an "on sale" bar can start to run only after an invention is fully completed, should the Pfaff patent have been held invalid under 35 U.S.C. § 102(b) when Mr. Pfaff's invention was admittedly not "fully completed" more than one year before he filed his patent application?

The Supreme Court opinion affirmed the Federal Circuit. Do you agree with the test the Supreme Court created? Will it increase certainty and predictability?

PFAFF v. WELLS ELECTRONICS, INC.

119 S. Ct. 304, 48 USPQ2d 1641 (1998)

STEVENS, J., delivered the opinion for a unanimous Court.

Section 102(b) of the Patent Act of 1952 provides that no person is entitled to patent an "invention" that has been "on sale" more than one year before filing a patent application. We granted *certiorari* to determine whether the commercial marketing of a newly invented product may mark the beginning of the 1–year period even though the invention has not yet been reduced to practice.[1]

I

On April 19, 1982, petitioner, Wayne Pfaff, filed an application for a patent on a computer chip socket. Therefore, April 19, 1981, constitutes the critical date for purposes of the on-sale bar of 35 U.S.C. § 102(b); if the 1–year period began to run before that date, Pfaff lost his right to patent his invention.

Pfaff commenced work on the socket in November 1980, when representatives of Texas Instruments asked him to develop a new device for mounting and removing semiconductor chip carriers. In response to this request, he prepared detailed engineering drawings that described the design, the dimensions, and the materials to be used in making the socket. Pfaff sent those drawings to a manufacturer in February or March 1981.

Prior to March 17, 1981, Pfaff showed a sketch of his concept to representatives of Texas Instruments. On April 8, 1981, they provided

---

1. "A process is reduced to practice when it is successfully performed. A machine is reduced to practice when it is assembled adjusted and used. A manufacture is reduced to practice when it is completely manufactured. A composition of matter is reduced to practice when it is completely composed." *Corona Cord Tire Co. v. Dovan Chemical Corp.*, 276 U.S. 358, 383, 48 S. Ct. 380, 387 (1928).

Pfaff with a written confirmation of a previously placed oral purchase order for 30,100 of his new sockets for a total price of $91,155. In accord with his normal practice, Pfaff did not make and test a prototype of the new device before offering to sell it in commercial quantities.[2]

The manufacturer took several months to develop the customized tooling necessary to produce the device, and Pfaff did not fill the order until July 1981. The evidence therefore indicates that Pfaff first reduced his invention to practice in the summer of 1981. The socket achieved substantial commercial success before Patent No. 4,491,377 (the '377 patent) issued to Pfaff on January 1, 1985.[3]

After the patent issued, petitioner brought an infringement action against respondent, Wells Electronics, Inc., the manufacturer of a competing socket. Wells prevailed on the basis of a finding of no infringement.[4] When respondent began to market a modified device, petitioner brought this suit, alleging that the modifications infringed six of the claims in the '377 patent.

After a full evidentiary hearing before a Special Master, the District Court held that two of those claims (1 and 6) were invalid because they had been anticipated in the prior art. Nevertheless, the court concluded that four other claims (7, 10, 11, and 19) were valid and three (7, 10, and 11) were infringed by various models of respondent's sockets. Adopting the Special Master's findings, the District Court rejected respondent's § 102(b) defense because Pfaff had filed the application for the '377 patent less than a year after reducing the invention to practice.

The Court of Appeals reversed, finding all six claims invalid. Four of the claims (1, 6, 7, and 10) described the socket that Pfaff had sold to Texas Instruments prior to April 8, 1981. Because that device had been offered for sale on a commercial basis more than one year before the patent application was filed on April 19, 1982, the court concluded that those claims were invalid under § 102(b). That conclusion rested on the court's view that as long as the invention was "substantially complete at the time of sale," the 1–year period began to run, even though the

---

2. At his deposition, respondent's counsel engaged in the following colloquy with Pfaff:

"Q. Now, at this time [late 1980 or early 1981] did we [sic] have any prototypes developed or anything of that nature, working embodiment?

"A. No.

"Q. It was in a drawing. Is that correct?

"A. Strictly in a drawing. Went from the drawing to the hard tooling. That's the way I do my business.

"Q. 'Boom-boom'?

"A. You got it.

"Q. You are satisfied, obviously, when you come up with some drawings that it is going to go—'it works'?

"A. I know what I'm doing, yes, most of the time."

3. Initial sales of the patented device were:

1981	$350,000
1982	$937,000
1983	$2,800,000
1984	$3,430,000

4. *Pfaff v. Wells Electronics, Inc.,* 9 USPQ2d 1366 (N.D. Ind. 1988). The court found that the Wells device did not literally infringe on Pfaff's '377 patent based on the physicallocation of the sockets' conductive pins.

invention had not yet been reduced to practice. The other two claims (11 and 19) described a feature that had not been included in Pfaff's initial design, but the Court of Appeals concluded as a matter of law that the additional feature was not itself patentable because it was an obvious addition to the prior art. Given the court's § 102(b) holding, the prior art included Pfaff's first four claims.

Because other courts have held or assumed that an invention cannot be "on sale" within the meaning of § 102(b) unless and until it has been reduced to practice, *see, e.g., Timely Products Corp. v. Arron*, 523 F.2d 288, 299–302 (2d Cir. 1975); *Dart Industries, Inc. v. E.I. du Pont De Nemours & Co.*, 489 F.2d 1359, 1365 n. 11 (7th Cir. 1973) and because the text of § 102(b) makes no reference to "substantial completion" of an invention, we granted *certiorari*.

II

The primary meaning of the word "invention" in the Patent Act unquestionably refers to the inventor's conception rather than to a physical embodiment of that idea. The statute does not contain any express requirement that an invention must be reduced to practice before it can be patented. Neither the statutory definition of the term in § 100 nor the basic conditions for obtaining a patent set forth in § 101 make any mention of "reduction to practice." The statute's only specific reference to that term is found in § 102(g), which sets forth the standard for resolving priority contests between two competing claimants to a patent. That subsection provides:

> In determining priority of invention there shall be considered not only the respective dates of conception and reduction to practice of the invention, but also the reasonable diligence of one who was first to conceive and last to reduce to practice, from a time prior to conception by the other.

Thus, assuming diligence on the part of the applicant, it is normally the first inventor to conceive, rather than the first to reduce to practice, who establishes the right to the patent.

It is well settled that an invention may be patented before it is reduced to practice. In 1888, this Court upheld a patent issued to Alexander Graham Bell even though he had filed his application before constructing a working telephone. Chief Justice Waite's reasoning in that case merits quoting at length:

> It is quite true that when Bell applied for his patent he had never actually transmitted telegraphically spoken words so that they could be distinctly heard and understood at the receiving end of his line, but in his specification he did describe accurately and with admirable clearness his process, that is to say, the exact electrical condition that must be created to accomplish his purpose, and he also described, with sufficient precision to enable one of ordinary skill in such matters to make it, a form of apparatus which, if used in the way pointed out, would produce the required effect, receive the words, and carry them to and deliver them at the

appointed place. The particular instrument which he had, and which he used in his experiments, did not, under the circumstances in which it was tried, reproduce the words spoken, so that they could be clearly understood, but the proof is abundant and of the most convincing character, that other instruments, carefully constructed and made exactly in accordance with the specification, without any additions whatever, have operated and will operate successfully. A good mechanic of proper skill in matters of the kind can take the patent and, by following the specification strictly, can, without more, construct an apparatus which, when used in the way pointed out, will do all that it is claimed the method or process will do.

The law does not require that a discoverer or inventor, in order to get a patent for a process, must have succeeded in bringing his art to the highest degree of perfection. It is enough if he describes his method with sufficient clearness and precision to enable those skilled in the matter to understand what the process is, and if he points out some practicable way of putting it into operation.

The Telephone Cases, 126 U.S. 1, 535–536 (1888).

When we apply the reasoning of The Telephone Cases to the facts of the case before us today, it is evident that Pfaff could have obtained a patent on his novel socket when he accepted the purchase order from Texas Instruments for 30,100 units. At that time he provided the manufacturer with a description and drawings that had "sufficient clearness and precision to enable those skilled in the matter" to produce the device. The parties agree that the sockets manufactured to fill that order embody Pfaff's conception as set forth in claims 1, 6, 7, and 10 of the '377 patent. We can find no basis in the text of § 102(b) or in the facts of this case for concluding that Pfaff's invention was not "on sale" within the meaning of the statute until after it had been reduced to practice.

III

Pfaff nevertheless argues that longstanding precedent, buttressed by the strong interest in providing inventors with a clear standard identifying the onset of the 1–year period, justifies a special interpretation of the word "invention" as used in § 102(b). We are persuaded that this nontextual argument should be rejected.

As we have often explained, most recently in *Bonito Boats, Inc. v. Thunder Craft Boats, Inc.*, 489 U.S. 141, 151 (1989), the patent system represents a carefully crafted bargain that encourages both the creation and the public disclosure of new and useful advances in technology, in return for an exclusive monopoly for a limited period of time. The balance between the interest in motivating innovation and enlightenment by rewarding invention with patent protection on the one hand, and the interest in avoiding monopolies that unnecessarily stifle competition on the other, has been a feature of the federal patent laws since their inception. As this Court explained in 1871:

Letters patent are not to be regarded as monopolies ... but as public franchises granted to the inventors of new and useful improvements for the purpose of securing to them, as such inventors, for the limited term therein mentioned, the exclusive right and liberty to make and use and vend to others to be used their own inventions, as tending to promote the progress of science and the useful arts, and as matter of compensation to the inventors for their labor, toil, and expense in making the inventions, and reducing the same to practice for the public benefit, as contemplated by the Constitution and sanctioned by the laws of Congress.

Seymour v. Osborne, 11 Wall. 516, 533–534. Consistent with these ends, § 102 of the Patent Act serves as a limiting provision, both excluding ideas that are in the public domain from patent protection and confining the duration of the monopoly to the statutory term.

We originally held that an inventor loses his right to a patent if he puts his invention into public use before filing a patent application. "His voluntary act or acquiescence in the public sale and use is an abandonment of his right." *Pennock v. Dialogue*, 2 Pet. 1, 24, 7 L. Ed. 327 (1829) (Story, J.). A similar reluctance to allow an inventor to remove existing knowledge from public use undergirds the on-sale bar.

Nevertheless, an inventor who seeks to perfect his discovery may conduct extensive testing without losing his right to obtain a patent for his invention—even if such testing occurs in the public eye. The law has long recognized the distinction between inventions put to experimental use and products sold commercially. In 1878, we explained why patentability may turn on an inventor's use of his product.

It is sometimes said that an inventor acquires an undue advantage over the public by delaying to take out a patent, inasmuch as he thereby preserves the monopoly to himself for a longer period than is allowed by the policy of the law; but this cannot be said with justice when the delay is occasioned by a *bona fide* effort to bring his invention to perfection, or to ascertain whether it will answer the purpose intended. His monopoly only continues for the allotted period, in any event; and it is the interest of the public, as well as himself, that the invention should be perfect and properly tested, before a patent is granted for it. *Any attempt to use it for a profit, and not by way of experiment, for a longer period than two years before the application, would deprive the inventor of his right to a patent.*

Elizabeth v. American Nicholson Pavement Co., 97 U.S. 126, 137 (1877) (emphasis added).

The patent laws therefore seek both to protect the public's right to retain knowledge already in the public domain and the inventor's right to control whether and when he may patent his invention. The Patent Act of 1836, 5 Stat. 117, was the first statute that expressly included an on-sale bar to the issuance of a patent. Like the earlier holding in *Pennock*, that provision precluded patentability if the invention had been placed on sale at any time before the patent application was filed. In

1839, Congress ameliorated that requirement by enacting a 2–year grace period in which the inventor could file an application. 5 Stat. 353.

In *Andrews v. Hovey*, 123 U.S. 267, 274 (1887), we noted that the purpose of that amendment was "to fix a period of limitation which should be certain"; it required the inventor to make sure that a patent application was filed "within two years from the completion of his invention," *Id*. In 1939, Congress reduced the grace period from two years to one year. 53 Stat. 1212.

Petitioner correctly argues that these provisions identify an interest in providing inventors with a definite standard for determining when a patent application must be filed. A rule that makes the timeliness of an application depend on the date when an invention is "substantially complete" seriously undermines the interest in certainty.[5] More-over, such a rule finds no support in the text of the statute. Thus, petitioner's argument calls into question the standard applied by the Court of Appeals, but it does not persuade us that it is necessary to engraft a reduction to practice element into the meaning of the term "invention" as used in § 102(b).

The word "invention" must refer to a concept that is complete, rather than merely one that is "substantially complete." It is true that reduction to practice ordinarily provides the best evidence that an invention is complete. But just because reduction to practice is sufficient evidence of completion, it does not follow that proof of reduction to practice is necessary in every case. Indeed, both the facts of the *Telephone Cases* and the facts of this case demonstrate that one can prove that an invention is complete and ready for patenting before it has actually been reduced to practice.[6]

5. The Federal Circuit has developed a multifactor, "totality of the circumstances" test to determine the trigger for the on-sale bar. *See, e.g., Micro Chemical, Inc. v. Great Plains Chemical Co.*, 103 F.3d 1538, 1544 (Fed. Cir. 1997) (stating that, in determining whether an invention is on sale for purposes of 102(b), " 'all of the circumstances surrounding the sale or offer to sell, including the stage of development of the invention and the nature of the invention, must be considered and weighed against the policies underlying section 102(b)' "); *see also UMC Electronics Co. v. United States*, 816 F.2d 647, 656 (Fed. Cir. 1987) (stating the on-sale bar "does not lend itself to formulation into a set of precise requirements"). As the Federal Circuit itself has noted, this test "has been criticized as unnecessarily vague." *Seal-Flex, Inc. v. Athletic Track & Court Const.*, 98 F.3d 1318, 1323, n.2 (Fed. Cir. 1996).

6. Several of this Court's early decisions stating that an invention is not complete until it has been reduced to practice are best understood as indicating that the in-

vention's reduction to practice demonstrated that the concept was no longer in an experimental phase. *See, e.g., Seymour v. Osborne*, 11 Wall. 516, 552, 20 L. Ed. 33 (1870) ("Crude and imperfect experiments are not sufficient to confer a right to a patent; but in order to constitute an invention, the party must have proceeded so far as to have reduced his idea to practice, and embodied it in some distinct form"); *Clark Thread Co. v. Willimantic Linen Co.*, 140 U.S. 481, 489 (1891) (describing how inventor continued to alter his thread winding machine until July 1858, when "he put it in visible form in the shape of a machine.... It is evident that the invention was not completed until the construction of the machine"); *Corona Cord Tire Co. v. Dovan Chemical Corp.*, 276 U.S., at 382–383 (stating that an invention did not need to be subsequently commercialized to constitute prior art after the inventor had finished his experimentation. "It was the fact that it would work with great activity as an accelerator that was the discovery, and that was all, and the necessary reduction to use is

2 conditions of the on-sale bar

We conclude, therefore, that the on-sale bar applies when two conditions are satisfied before the critical date. First, the product must be the subject of a commercial offer for sale. An inventor can both understand and control the timing of the first commercial marketing of his invention. The experimental use doctrine, for example, has not generated concerns about indefiniteness, and we perceive no reason why unmanageable uncertainty should attend a rule that measures the application of the on-sale bar of § 102(b) against the date when an invention that is ready for patenting is first marketed commercially. In this case the acceptance of the purchase order prior to April 8, 1981, makes it clear that such an offer had been made, and there is no question that the sale was commercial rather than experimental in character.

Second, the invention must be ready for patenting. That condition may be satisfied in at least two ways: by proof of reduction to practice before the critical date; or by proof that prior to the critical date the inventor had prepared drawings or other descriptions of the invention that were sufficiently specific to enable a person skilled in the art to practice the invention.[7] In this case the second condition of the on-sale bar is satisfied because the drawings Pfaff sent to the manufacturer before the critical date fully disclosed the invention.

The evidence in this case thus fulfills the two essential conditions of the on-sale bar. As succinctly stated by Learned Hand: "[I]t is a condition upon an inventor's right to a patent that he shall not exploit his discovery competitively after it is ready for patenting; he must content himself with either secrecy, or legal monopoly." *Metallizing Engineering Co. v. Kenyon Bearing & Auto Parts Co.*, 153 F.2d 516, 520 (2d Cir. 1946).

The judgment of the Court of Appeals finds support not only in the text of the statute but also in the basic policies underlying the statutory scheme, including § 102(b). When Pfaff accepted the purchase order for his new sockets prior to April 8, 1981, his invention was ready for patenting. The fact that the manufacturer was able to produce the socket using his detailed drawings and specifications demonstrates this fact. Furthermore, those sockets contained all the elements of the invention claimed in the '377 patent. Therefore, Pfaff's '377 patent is invalid because the invention had been on sale for more than one year in

shown by instances making clear that it did so work, and was a completed discovery'').

7. The Solicitor General has argued that the rule governing on-sale bar should be phrased somewhat differently. In his opinion, "if the sale or offer in question embodies the invention for which a patent is later sought, a sale or offer to sell that is primarily for commercial purposes and that occurs more than one year before the application renders the invention unpatentable. *Seal-Flex, Inc. v. Athletic Track and Court*

Constr., 98 F.3d 1318, 1325 (Fed. Cir. 1996) (Bryson, J., concurring in part and concurring in the result)." It is true that evidence satisfying this test might be sufficient to prove that the invention was ready for patenting at the time of the sale if it is clear that no aspect of the invention was developed after the critical date. However, the possibility of additional development after the offer for sale in these circumstances counsels against adoption of the rule proposed by the Solicitor General.

this country before he filed his patent application. Accordingly, the judgment of the Court of Appeals is affirmed.

PATENTEE'S REBUTTAL EVIDENCE: EXPERIMENTAL USE

When faced with an attack to a patent's validity based on the on-sale or public use bars, the patentee may defend himself by showing the sale or public use was experimental rather than commercial.

CITY OF ELIZABETH v. AMERICAN NICHOLSON PAVEMENT CO.

97 U.S. 126 (1877)

J. BRADLEY delivered the opinion of the court.

This suit was brought by the American Nicholson Pavement Company against the city of Elizabeth, N.J., George W. Tubbs, and the New Jersey Wood–Paving Company, a corporation of New Jersey, upon a patent issued to Samuel Nicholson, dated Aug. 20, 1867, for a new and improved wooden pavement, being a second reissue of a patent issued to said Nicholson Aug. 8, 1854. The reissued patent was extended in 1868 for a further term of seven years. A copy of it is appended to the bill; and, in the specification, it is declared that the nature and object of the invention consists in providing a process or mode of constructing wooden block pavements upon a foundation along a street or roadway with facility, cheapness, and accuracy, and also in the creation and construction of such a wooden pavement as shall be comparatively permanent and durable, by so uniting and combining all its parts, both superstructure and foundation, as to provide against the slipping of the horses' feet, against noise, against unequal wear, and against rot and consequent sinking away from below. Two plans of making this pavement are specified. Both require a proper foundation on which to lay the blocks, consisting of tarred-paper or hydraulic cement covering the surface of the road-bed to the depth of about two inches, or of a flooring of boards or plank, also covered with tar, or other preventive of moisture. On this foundation, one plan is to set square blocks on end arranged like a checker-board, the alternate rows being shorter than the others, so as to leave narrow grooves or channel-ways to be filled with small broken stone or gravel, and then pouring over the whole melted tar or pitch , whereby the cavities are all filled and cemented together. The other plan is, to arrange the blocks in rows transversely across the street, separated a small space (of about an inch) by strips of board at the bottom, which serve to keep the blocks at a uniform distance apart, and then filling these spaces with the same material as before. The blocks forming the pavement are about eight inches high. The alternate rows of short blocks in the first plan and the strips of board in the second plan should not be higher than four inches.

The bill charges that the defendants infringed this patent by laying down wooden pavements in the city of Elizabeth, N.J., constructed in substantial conformity with the process patented, and prays an account of profits, and an injunction.

[Defendants] also averred that the alleged invention of Nicholson was in public use, with his consent and allowance, for six years before he applied for a patent, on a certain avenue in Boston called the Mill-dam; and contended that said public use worked an abandonment of the pretended invention.

The question to be considered is, whether Nicholson's invention was in public use or on sale, with his consent and allowance, for more than two years prior to his application for a patent, within the meaning of the sixth, seventh, and fifteenth sections of the act of 1836, as qualified by the seventh section of the act of 1839, which were the acts in force in 1854, when he obtained his patent. It is contended by the appellants that the pavement which Nicholson put down by way of experiment, on Mill-dam Avenue in Boston, in 1848, was publicly used for the space of six years before his application for a patent, and that this was a public use within the meaning of the law.

To determine this question, it is necessary to examine the circumstances under which this pavement was put down, and the object and purpose that Nicholson had in view. It is perfectly clear from the evidence that he did not intend to abandon his right to a patent. He had filed a caveat in August, 1847, and he constructed the pavement in question by way of experiment, for the purpose of testing its qualities. The road in which it was put down, though a public road, belonged to the Boston and Roxbury Mill Corporation, which received toll for its use; and Nicholson was a stockholder and treasurer of the corporation. The pavement in question was about seventy-five feet in length, and was laid adjoining to the toll-gate and in front of the toll-house. It was constructed by Nicholson at his own expense, and was placed by him where it was, in order to see the effect upon it of heavily loaded wagons, and a varied and constant use; and also to ascertain its durability, and liability to decay. Joseph L. Lang, who was toll-collector for many years, commencing in 1849, familiar with the road before that time, and with this pavement from the time of its origin, testified as follows:

> Mr. Nicholson was there almost daily, and when he came he would examine the pavement, would often walk over it, cane in hand, striking it with his cane, and making particular examination of its condition. He asked me very often how people liked it, and asked me a great many questions about it. I have heard him say a number of times that this was his first experiment with this pavement, and he thought that it was wearing very well. The circumstances that made this locality desirable for the purpose of obtaining a satisfactory test of the durability and value of the pavement were: that there would be a better chance to lay it there; he would have more room and a better chance than in the city; and, besides, it was a place where most everybody went over it, rich and poor. It was a great thoroughfare out of Boston. It was frequently traveled by teams having a load of five or six tons, and some larger. As these teams usually

stopped at the toll-house, and started again, the stopping and starting would make as severe a trial to the pavement as it could be put to.

This evidence is corroborated by that of several other witnesses in the cause; the result of the whole being that Nicholson merely intended this piece of pavement as an experiment, to test its usefulness and durability. Was this a public use, within the meaning of the law?

An abandonment of an invention to the public may be evinced by the conduct of the inventor at any time, even within the two years named in the law. The effect of the law is, that no such consequence will necessarily follow from the invention being in public use or on sale, with the inventor's consent and allowance, at any time within two years before his application; but that, if the invention is in public use or on sale prior to that time, it will be conclusive evidence of abandonment, and the patent will be void.

But, in this case, it becomes important to inquire what is such a public use as will have the effect referred to. That the use of the pavement in question was public in one sense cannot be disputed. But can it be said that the invention was in public use? The use of an invention by the inventor himself, or of any other person under his direction, by way of experiment, and in order to bring the invention to perfection, has never been regarded as such a use.

Now, the nature of a street pavement is such that it cannot be experimented upon satisfactorily except on a highway, which is always public.

When the subject of invention is a machine, it may be tested and tried in a building, either with or without closed doors. In either case, such use is not a public use, within the meaning of the statute, so long as the inventor is engaged, in good faith, in testing its operation. He may see cause to alter it and improve it, or not. His experiments will reveal the fact whether any and what alterations may be necessary. If durability is one of the qualities to be attained, a long period, perhaps years, may be necessary to enable the inventor to discover whether his purpose is accomplished. And though, during all that period, he may not find that any changes are necessary, yet he may be justly said to be using his machine only by way of experiment; and no one would say that such a use, pursued with a bona fide intent of testing the qualities of the machine, would be a public use, within the meaning of the statute. So long as he does not voluntarily allow others to make it and use it, and so long as it is not on sale for general use, he keeps the invention under his own control, and does not lose his title to a patent.

It would not be necessary, in such a case, that the machine should be put up and used only in the inventor's own shop or premises. He may have it put up and used in the premises of another, and the use may inure to the benefit of the owner of the establishment. Still, if used under the surveillance of the inventor, and for the purpose of enabling him to test the machine, and ascertain whether it will answer the purpose intended, and make such alterations and improvements as experience demonstrates to be necessary, it will still be a mere experimental use, and not a public use, within the meaning of the statute.

Whilst the supposed machine is in such experimental use, the public may be incidentally deriving a benefit from it. If it be a grist-mill, or a carding-machine, customers from the surrounding country may enjoy the use of it by having their grain made into flour, or their wool into rolls, and still it will not be in public use, within the meaning of the law.

But if the inventor allows his machine to be used by other persons generally, either with or without compensation, or if it is, with his consent, put on sale for such use, then it will be in public use and on public sale, within the meaning of the law.

If, now, we apply the same principles to this case, the analogy will be seen at once. Nicholson wished to experiment on his pavement. He believed it to be a good thing, but he was not sure; and the only mode in which he could test it was to place a specimen of it in a public roadway. He did this at his own expense, and with the consent of the owners of the road. Durability was one of the qualities to be attained. He wanted to know whether his pavement would stand, and whether it would resist decay. Its character for durability could not be ascertained without its being subjected to use for a considerable time. He subjected it to such use, in good faith, for the simple purpose of ascertaining whether it was what he claimed it to be. Did he do any thing more than the inventor of the supposed machine might do, in testing his invention? The public had the incidental use of the pavement, it is true; but was the invention in public use, within the meaning of the statute? We think not. The proprietors of the road alone used the invention, and used it at Nicholson's request, by way of experiment. The only way in which they could use it was by allowing the public to pass over the pavement.

Had the city of Boston, or other parties, used the invention, by laying down the pavement in other streets and places, with Nicholson's consent and allowance, then, indeed, the invention itself would have been in public use, within the meaning of the law; but this was not the case. Nicholson did not sell it, nor allow others to use it or sell it. He did not let it go beyond his control. He did nothing that indicated any intent to do so. He kept it under his own eyes, and never for a moment abandoned the intent to obtain a patent for it.

In this connection, it is proper to make another remark. It is not a public knowledge of his invention that precludes the inventor from obtaining a patent for it, but a public use or sale of it. In England, formerly, as well as under our Patent Act of 1793, if an inventor did not keep his invention secret, if a knowledge of it became public before his application for a patent, he could not obtain one. To be patentable, an invention must not have been known or used before the application; but this has not been the law of this country since the passage of the act of 1836, and it has been very much qualified in England. Therefore, if it were true that during the whole period in which the pavement was used, the public knew how it was constructed, it would make no difference in the result.

It is sometimes said that an inventor acquires an undue advantage of the public by delaying to take out a patent, inasmuch as he thereby preserves the monopoly to himself for a longer period than is allowed by the policy of the law; but this cannot be said with justice when the delay is occasioned by a bona fide effort to bring his invention to perfection, or to ascertain whether it will answer the purpose intended. His monopoly only continues for the allotted period, in any event; and it is the interest of the public, as well as himself, that the invention should be perfect and properly tested, before a patent is granted for it. Any attempt to use it for a profit, and not by way of experiment, for a longer period than two years before the application, would deprive the inventor of his right to a patent.

Notes

experimental use factors

1. Experimental use is decided under the totality of the circumstances. Factors to consider in determining if a use is experimental include:

   1. confidential or secrecy agreements with users;
   2. inventor's presence and monitoring;
   3. whether the features being tested are the claim elements;
   4. whether the invention undergoes any modification after the testing;
   5. the number of prototypes;
   6. the number of tests;
   7. the duration of the testing;
   8. whether records were kept concerning the tests;
   9. whether compensation/payment for the invention was received;
   10. the extent of control the investor maintained over the tests;
   11. whether feedback was solicited or received; and
   12. whether there were any attempts to market the invention.

LOUGH v. BRUNSWICK CORP.

86 F.3d 1113, 39 USPQ2d 1100 (Fed. Cir. 1996)

Before PLAGER, LOURIE, and CLEVENGER, Circuit Judges.

LOURIE, Circuit Judge.

In 1986, Steven G. Lough worked as a repairman for a boat dealership in Sarasota, Florida. While repairing Brunswick inboard/outboard boats, he noticed that the upper seal assembly in the stern drives often failed due to corrosion.

Lough determined that the corrosion in the upper seal assembly occurred due to contact between the annular seal and the bell housing aperture. He designed a new upper seal assembly that isolated the annular seal from the aluminum bell housing in order to prevent such corrosion.

After some trial and error with his grandfather's metal lathe, he made six usable prototypes in the spring of 1986. He installed one prototype in his own boat at home. Three months later, he gave a second prototype to a friend who installed it in his boat. He also installed prototypes in the boat of the owner of the marina where he worked and in the boat of a marina customer. He gave the remaining prototypes to longtime friends who were employees at another marina in Sarasota. Lough did not charge anyone for the prototypes. For over a year following the installation of these prototypes, Lough neither asked for nor received any comments about the operability of the prototypes. During this time, Lough did not attempt to sell any seal assemblies.

On June 6, 1988, Lough filed a patent application entitled "Liquid Seal for Marine Stern Drive Gear Shift Shafts," which issued as the '775 patent on July 18, 1989.

Lough sued Brunswick on June 12, 1993, alleging infringement of the '775 patent. Brunswick counterclaimed for a declaratory judgment of patent noninfringement, invalidity, and/or unenforceability. A jury found that Brunswick failed to prove that Lough's invention was in public use before the critical date on June 6, 1987, one year prior to the filing date of the '775 patent. The jury also found that Brunswick infringed claims 1–4 of the '775 patent, both literally and under the doctrine of equivalents. Based on its infringement finding, the jury awarded Lough $1,500,000 in lost profits. After trial, Brunswick filed a Motion for Judgment as a Matter of Law in which it argued, inter alia, that the claimed invention was invalid because it had been in public use before the critical date. The court denied Brunswick's motions without any comment. Brunswick appeals.

DISCUSSION

Brunswick challenges, inter alia, the court's denial of its motion for JMOL on the issue of public use. Brunswick argues that the district court erred in denying its motion for JMOL because the uses of Lough's prototypes prior to the critical date were not experimental. Brunswick asserts that Lough did not control the uses of his prototypes by third parties before the critical date, failed to keep records of the alleged experiments, and did not place the parties to whom the seals were given under any obligation of secrecy. Based on this objective evidence, Brunswick argues that the uses of Lough's prototypes before the critical date were not "experimental." Therefore, Brunswick contends that the jury's verdict was incorrect as a matter of law and that the court erred in denying its JMOL motion.

Lough counters that the test performed with the six prototypes were necessary experiments conducted in the course of completing his invention. He argues that when the totality of circumstances is properly viewed, the evidence supports the jury's conclusion that those uses were experimental. Lough maintains that a number of factors support the jury's experimental use conclusion, including evidence that he received no compensation for the prototypes, he did not place the seal assemblies on sale until after he filed his patent application, and he gave the prototypes only to his friends and personal acquaintances who used them in such a manner that they were unlikely to be seen by the public. He further argues that, to verify operability of the seal assemblies, prototypes had to be installed by mechanics of various levels of skill in boats that were exposed to different conditions. Thus, he asserts that the court did not err in denying Brunswick's JMOL motion. We disagree with Lough.

One is entitled to a patent unless, *inter alia*, "the invention was . . . in public use . . . in this country, more than one year prior to the date of the application for patent in the United States." 35 U.S.C. § 102(b) (1994). We have defined "public use" as including "any use of [the claimed] invention by a person other than the inventor who is under no limitation, restriction or obligation of secrecy to the inventor." *In re Smith*, 714 F.2d 1127, 1134, 218 USPQ 976, 983 (Fed. Cir. 1983). An evaluation of a question of public use depends on "how the totality of the circumstances of the case comports with the policies underlying the public use bar." *Bros v. Sysco Corp.*, 28 F.3d 1192, 1198, 31 USPQ2d 1321, 1324 (Fed. Cir. 1994). These policies include:

> (1) discouraging the removal, from the public domain, of inventions that the public reasonably has come to believe are freely available; (2) favoring the prompt and widespread disclosure of inventions; (3) allowing the inventor a reasonable amount of time following sales activity to determine the potential economic value of a patent; and (4) prohibiting the inventor from commercially exploiting the invention for a period greater than the statutorily prescribed time.

Id. A patentee may negate a showing of public use by coming forward with evidence that its use of the invention was experimental.

Neither party disputes that Lough's prototypes were in use before the critical date. Thus, both parties agree that the issue presented on appeal is whether the jury properly decided that the use of Lough's six prototypes in 1986, prior to the critical date, constituted experimental use so as to negate the conclusion of public use.[4]

"The use of an invention by the inventor himself, or of any other person under his direction, by way of experiment, and in order to bring the invention to perfection, has never been regarded as [a public] use." *City of Elizabeth v. American Nicholson Pavement Co.*, 97 U.S. 126,

---

4. The trial judge instructed the jury as follows:

The law requires that an inventor must file a patent application within one year after his invention is publicly used. Public use means any use of Mr. Lough's invention by any person other than Mr.

Lough who was not limited or restricted in their activities regarding the invention, or not obligated to secrecy by Mr. Lough. Such use, however, does not invalidate Mr. Lough's patent if the use was primarily for *bona fide* experimental purposes.

(1877). This doctrine is based on the underlying policy of providing an inventor time to determine if the invention is suitable for its intended purpose, in effect, to reduce the invention to practice. *See id.* at 137 ("It is sometimes said that an inventor acquires an undue advantage over the public by delaying to take out a patent ... but this cannot be said with justice when the delay is occasioned by a bona fide effort to bring his invention to perfection, or to ascertain whether it will answer the purpose intended."); *see also RCA Corp. v. Data General Corp.*, 887 F.2d 1056, 1061, 12 USPQ2d 1449, 1453 (Fed. Cir. 1989) ("[E]xperimental use, which means perfecting or completing an invention to the point of determining that it will work for its intended purpose, ends with an actual reduction to practice"). If a use is experimental, it is not, as a matter of law, a public use within the meaning of section 102.

To determine whether a use is "experimental," a question of law, the totality of the circumstances must be considered, including various objective indicia of experimentation surrounding the use, such as the number of prototypes and duration of testing, whether records or progress reports were made concerning the testing, the existence of a secrecy agreement between the patentee and the party performing the testing, whether the patentee received compensation for the use of the invention, and the extent of control the inventor maintained over the testing. The last factor of control is critically important, because, if the inventor has no control over the alleged experiments, he is not experimenting. If he does not inquire about the testing or receive reports concerning the results, similarly, he is not experimenting.

In order to justify a determination that legally sufficient experimentation has occurred, there must be present certain minimal indicia. The framework might be quite formal, as may be expected when large corporations conduct experiments, governed by contracts and explicit written obligations. When individual inventors or small business units are involved, however, less formal and seemingly casual experiments can be expected. Such less formal experiments may be deemed legally sufficient to avoid the public use bar, but only if they demonstrate the presence of the same basic elements that are required to validate any experimental program. Our case law sets out these elements. The question framed on this appeal is whether Lough's alleged experiments lacked enough of these required indicia so that his efforts cannot, as a matter of law, be recognized as experimental.

Here, Lough either admits or does not dispute the following facts. In the spring of 1986, he noted that the upper seal assembly in Brunswick inboard/outboard boats was failing due to galvanic corrosion between the annular seal and the aperture provided for the upper seal assembly in the aluminum bell housing. He solved this problem by isolating the annular seal from the aluminum bell housing in order to prevent corrosion. After some trial and error, Lough made six prototypes. He installed the first prototype in his own boat. Lough testified at trial that after the first prototype had been in his boat for three months and he determined that it worked, he provided the other prototypes to friends and acquaintances in order to find out if the upper seal assemblies would work as well in their boats as it had worked in his boat. Lough installed one prototype in the boat of his friend, Tom Nikla. A prototype was also installed in the boat of Jim Yow, co-owner of the dealership where Lough worked. Lough installed a fourth prototype in one of the dealership's customers who had considerable problems with corrosion in his stern drive unit. The final two prototypes were given to friends who were employed at a different marina in Florida. These friends installed one prototype in the boat of Mark Liberman, a local charter guide. They installed the other prototype in a demonstration boat at their marina. Subsequently, this boat was sold. Neither Lough nor his friends knew what happened with either the prototype or the demonstration boat after the boat was sold. After providing the five prototypes to these third parties, Lough did not ask for any comments concerning the operability of these prototypes.

Accepting that the jury found these facts, which either were undisputed or were as asserted by Lough, it cannot be reasonably disputed that Lough's use of the invention was not "experimental" so as to negate a conclusion of public use. It is true that Lough did not receive any compensation for the use of the prototypes. He did not place the seal assembly on sale before applying for a patent. Lough's lack of commercialization, however, is not dispositive of the public use question in view of his failure to present objective evidence of experimentation. Lough kept no records of the alleged testing. Nor did he inspect the seal assemblies after they had been installed by other mechanics. He provided the seal assemblies to friends and acquaintances, but without any provision for follow-up involvement by him in assessment of the events occurring during the alleged experiments, and at least one seal was installed in a boat that was later sold to strangers. Thus, Lough did not maintain any supervision and control over the seals during the alleged testing.

Lough argues that other evidence supports a finding that his uses were experimental, including his own testimony that the prototypes were installed for experimental purposes and the fact that the prototypes were used in such a manner that they were unlikely to be seen by the public. However, "the expression by an inventor of his subjective intent to experiment, particularly after institution of litigation, is generally of minimal value." *TP Laboratories*, 724 F.2d at 972, 220 USPQ at 583. In addition, the fact that the prototypes were unlikely to be seen by the public does not support Lough's position. As the Supreme Court stated in *Egbert v. Lippmann*:

> [S]ome inventions are by their very character only capable of being used where they cannot be seen or observed by the public eye. An invention may consist of a lever or spring, hidden in the running gear of a watch, or of a rachet, shaft, or cog-wheel covered from view in the recesses of a machine for spinning or weaving. Nevertheless, if its inventor sells a machine of which his invention forms

a part, and allows it to be used without restriction of any kind, the use is a public one.

104 U.S. at 336. Moreover, those to whom he gave the prototypes constituted "the public," in the absence of meaningful evidence of experimentation. Thus, we find Lough's reliance on this additional evidence to be of minimal value when viewed in light of the totality of the other circumstances surrounding the alleged experimentation.

We therefore hold that the jury had no legal basis to conclude that the uses of Lough's prototypes were experimental and that the proto-types were not in public use prior to the critical date. Our holding is consistent with the policy underlying the experimental use negation, that of providing an inventor time to determine if the invention is suitable for its intended purpose, i.e., to reduce the invention to practice. Lough's activities clearly were not consistent with that policy. We do not dispute that it may have been desirable in this case for Lough to have had his prototypes installed by mechanics of various levels of skill in boats that were exposed to different conditions. Moreover, Lough was free to test his invention in boats of friends and acquaintances to further verify that his invention worked for its intended purpose; however, Lough was required to maintain some degree of control and feedback over those uses of the prototypes if those tests were to negate public use. Lough's failure to monitor the use of his prototypes by his acquain-tances, in addition to the lack of records or reports from those acquain-tances concerning the operability of the devices, compel the conclusion that, as a matter of law, he did not engage in experimental use. Lough in effect provided the prototype seal assemblies to members of the public for their free and unrestricted use. The law does not waive statutory requirements for inventors of lesser sophistication. When one distributes his invention to members of the public under circumstances that evi-dence a near total disregard for supervision and control concerning its use, the absence of these minimal indicia of experimentation require a conclusion that the invention was in public use.

We conclude that the jury's determination that Lough's use of the invention was experimental so as to defeat the assertion of public use was incorrect as a matter of law. The court thus erred in denying Brunswick's JMOL motion on the validity of claims 1–4 of the '775 patent under § 102(b).

PLAGER, Circuit Judge, dissenting.

I respectfully dissent. As the panel majority correctly notes, the issue is whether, on the totality of the circumstances, Mr. Lough was engaged in "a bona fide effort to bring his invention to perfection, or to ascertain whether it will answer the purpose intended," *City of Elizabeth v. American Nicholson Pavement Co.*, 97 U.S. 126, 137 (1877), or whether he was engaged in selling or, on the facts of this case oddly enough for a working mechanic, giving away his invention to members of the public.

This is not a contest between Evinrude (Outboard Marine Corporation) and Mercury Marine (Brunswick), the two big competitors in this field, to see who can market a better engine. If it were, we could expect the combination of engineering and legal staffs on each side to be punctilious about observing the niceties of our prior opinions on how to conduct experiments so as to avoid any possible running afoul of the public use bar. No, this is a home-made improvement by a man with only a high school education who worked on boats and boat engines, including his own, where he kept encountering the problem with these shaft seals that Mercury Marine had failed to solve. He solved it by trial and error, with an ingenious bushing of his own design, and, on his grandfather's metal lathe, after several tries, fashioned a half-dozen prototype seals that looked like they might do the job.

He put one in his own boat, one in the boat of a close friend, one in the boat of the co-owner of the marine repair shop where he worked, and later put one in the boat of a customer of the shop who was having considerable problems with his stern drive because of the seal difficulty. He gave two to mechanic friends at another marina so they could put them in boats having the same troublesome seal problem, with the understanding they would be used to test the seals in different equipment.

Of course it would have been better for all concerned (except perhaps for Mercury Marine) if Mr. Lough had read our prior opinions before he became an inventor. Then he might have kept detailed lab notes setting out the problem and the possible solutions, and he wisely would have obtained written confidentiality agreements from those allowed to see or use his prototypes. Had he studied our cases first, he no doubt would have developed a detailed questionnaire for the persons to whom he provided the seals, and he would have insisted on periodic written reports. In other words, he would have put in the set of tight controls the majority would have wanted. Instead, he did what seemed appropriate in the setting in which he worked: he waited to hear from his test cases what problems might emerge, and, hearing none, at least none that convinced him he was on the wrong track, he accepted some friendly advice and proceeded to patent his invention.

Yes, he failed to conduct his testing, his experiments, with the careful attention we lawyers, with our clean and dry hands, have come to prefer. But, under all the facts and circumstances, it is more likely than not that he was testing and perfecting his device, rather than simply making it available gratis to members of the general public for what the law calls "public use." The most that can be said for the majority view is that this is a close question under the totality of circumstances. The ultimate question of what is public use under 35 U.S.C. § 102(b) may be a question of law, but in a given case in which the issue is whether in fact the challenged use was experimental (a complete answer to an infringer's defense based on a § 102(b) violation), the issue involves a blend of law and fact. This issue, unlike claim construction, is one in which a jury fully participates. Thus the question before us is not whether, on the facts, we are persuaded Lough retained all the control a well-designed test of the seals would have afforded, but whether a reasonable jury, on all the evidence before it, could have arrived at the conclusion it did. The jury chose to accept Lough's view of the events, and under that view there was more than enough evidence to support a jury finding that he was testing and perfecting his invention during much of the period leading up to the time he applied for his patent.

Notes

1. **How Much Control Must the Patentee Maintain**? The court held that because there was no supervision or control over the seals after they were given away, the use was not experimental. What would be an acceptable level of supervision and control? Would a letter asking that the seal recipients report back in six months suffice?

2. **Sophistication of the Patentee**. Noting that Lough was merely a mechanic without the benefit of legal advice until it was too late, the dissent called for his intent in conducting his testing to be judged by a jury rather than the black letter law. Although this reasoning might have allowed for "justice" in Lough's case, what ramifications would there be for patent policy and all future patent litigation?

4. **Foreign Prior Art—§ 102(d)**

Section 102(d) is very straight-forward. If the patentee filed a foreign patent application more than one year before the U.S. application and the foreign patent issued before the U.S. application was filed, then the patentee is not entitled to a patent in the United States. This is the type of information that is easily ascertained in discovery.

5. **Disclosure in an Earlier Filed US Patent Application— § 102(e)**

If the patentee's invention was disclosed in another patent application that was filed prior to the patentee's invention, then that patent is invalid. If the patentee relies on an invention date earlier than her filing date, her claims will require corroboration.

6. **Derivation—§ 102(f)**

Derivation, a question of fact, requires proof that:

1. the invention was previously conceived by another; and

2. the complete conception was communicated to the patentee.

To succeed in proving derivation, the communication to the patentee must be of the complete invention. The communication must enable one of ordinary skill in the art to make the patented invention: it is not enough that the communication would render the invention obvious. *See generally Gambro Lundia v. Baxter Healthcare Corp.*, 110 F.3d 1573, 42 USPQ2d 1378 (Fed. Cir. 1997).

When deposed, the inventor should be questioned about others who assisted in the development of the invention. In the course of further discovery, the party challenging validity will want to question these individuals to determine their role in the inventive process. An employee who simply builds the invention at the direction of the true inventor has not contributed to its conception and therefore cannot raise a derivation issue.

Patentee's Cure—Correction of Inventorship

Section 256 provides for the correction of inventorship in an issued patent. Under this section, if someone was improperly listed as an inventor (misjoinder) or a proper inventor was not listed (nonjoinder) and there was no deceptive intent on the part of the inventor who was not joined, then the Commissioner may on application of the parties issue a certificate of correction or the court may order correction of the patent. The court only looks at the intent of the nonjoined inventor in determining whether correction should be allowed. *See Stark v. Advanced Magnetics, Inc.*, 29 F.3d 1570, 31 USPQ2d 1290 (Fed. Cir. 1994) ("Congress intended to permit correction of inventorship, without regard to the conduct of the named inventor, as long as there was no deceptive intention on the part of the true inventor."). Hence, as long as the nonjoined inventor had no deceptive intent, then the patent can be corrected to include him. This could avoid a holding of invalidity based on derivation.

7. Priority—§ 102(g)

Statutory Provision—35 U.S.C. § 102(g):

(g) before the applicant's invention thereof the invention was made in this country by another who has not abandoned, suppressed, or concealed it. In determining priority of invention there shall be considered not only the respective dates of conception and reduction to practice of the invention, but also the reasonable diligence of one who is first to conceive and last to reduce to practice, from a time prior to conception by the other.

The alleged infringer will often argue that the patented invention was made by another before the patentee's date of invention. In a § 102(g) priority contest, the one who is first to reduce to practice wins, unless the second to reduce to practice was the first to conceive and acted diligently from a period just prior to the other's conception until their own reduction to practice. Do you think that corroboration should be required for proving conception and reduction to practice? Should it matter whether the claim of prior invention is made by the defendant or an uninvolved third party? *See generally Thomson v. Quixote Corp.*, 166 F.3d 1172, 49 USPQ2d 1530 (Fed. Cir. 1999).

Under section § 104, foreign inventive activity (conception or reduction to practice) can be used for NAFTA countries (Canada and Mexico) after December 8, 1993 and in TRIPS countries (most other countries) after January 1, 1996. This foreign inventive activity can be used to prove prior inventorship under § 102(g). Does it matter that § 102(g) still retains the requirement "in this country?"

E. OBVIOUSNESS—§ 103

The next challenge to patent validity is whether the patentee's claimed invention is obvious in light of the prior art and therefore unpatentable.

Statutory Provision—35 U.S.C. § 103:

Conditions for patentability; non-obvious subject matter

(a) A patent may not be obtained though the invention is not identically disclosed or described as set forth in section 102 of this title, if the differences between the subject matter sought to be patented and the prior art are such that the subject matter as a whole would have been obvious at the time the invention was made to a person having ordinary skill in the art to which said subject matter pertains.

1. DEFENDANT'S PRIMA FACIE CASE

When obviousness is raised as a patent infringement defense, the defendant must prove by clear and convincing evidence that the prior art renders the claimed invention obvious to one skilled in the art. The ultimate question of validity is one of law. The question of obviousness is also a question of law. The underlying factors in the obviousness inquiry are factual questions. Therefore, obviousness is a question of law based on underlying facts. The Federal Circuit has suggested that it is proper to submit the entire question of obviousness to the jury to be resolved. Therefore, the judge can permit the jury to determine whether an invention is obvious or not. On appeal, the Federal Circuit will review a jury's obviousness finding by presuming that the jury found facts in favor of their verdict and then consider *de novo* whether the patent is obvious. A patentee would be wise to request that the jury resolve the obviousness facts by special verdict; this eliminates the presumption regarding the jury's findings. If the district court refused to give special verdicts to the jury, the party that proposed their use should object to preserve the issue for appeal.

Graham v. John Deere, 383 U.S. 1, 148 USPQ 459 (1966) is the seminal case that articulated the test for obviousness. To determine whether a patented invention is obvious the court must determine:

1. the scope and content of the prior art;

2. the differences between the prior art and the claims at issue;

3. the level of ordinary skill in the pertinent art; and

4. the objective or secondary considerations tending to prove obviousness or nonobviousness.

a. *The scope and content of the prior art*

What qualifies as prior art for obviousness?

Everything that qualifies as prior art under § 102 is generally available as a § 103 reference. Section 102, as its title suggests, defines two types of issues: novelty (prior art) and loss of right. All of the prior art defining provisions of § 102 are available references for obviousness purposes. For example, § 102(a) art, a patent or printed publication or something known or used by others, would qualify as prior art for obviousness purposes. Section 102(b) prior art is also available in a § 103 defense, despite the fact that § 103 says "obvious at the time the invention was made" and § 102(b) pertains to references one year before the filing date (which may not be prior to the applicant's date of invention). *See Application of Foster*, 343 F.2d 980, 145 USPQ 166 (CCPA 1965). Sections 102(c) and (d) are loss of right provisions. They define circumstances under which a patentee's actions can cause the loss of his right to a patent. Hence they do not define prior art and are not relevant for an obviousness inquiry. Section 102(e) prior art is also available in an obviousness determination. *See Hazeltine Research, Inc. v. Brenner*, 382 U.S. 252, 147 USPQ 429 (1965) (a previously filed patent application is prior art for obviousness purposes even though it was not publicly known at the time the patent application is filed). Section 102(f) prior art is available in an obviousness determination. *See Oddzon Products, Inc. v. Just Toys, Inc.*, 122 F.3d 1396, 43 USPQ2d 1641 (Fed. Cir. 1997) (§ 102(f) disclosures made to the patentee can render an invention obvious even if they are disclosed confidentially and therefore not publicly known). Section 102(g) prior art can be considered in determining obviousness as it relates to prior inventions of others that are either public or likely to become public (§ 102(g) requires that the invention not be abandoned, suppressed or concealed). *In re Bass*, 474 F.2d 1276, 1290, 177 USPQ 178, 189 (CCPA 1973) (prior invention by another that was not abandoned, suppressed or concealed can be combined with other prior art to support an obviousness determination).

Hindsight is Not Permitted

Most inventions are a combination of old elements. This does not make them obvious. The more references that need to be combined to prove obviousness, the less likely that the invention is obvious. Having to combine a large number of references to render the claim obvious is more like hindsight reconstruction, which is not permitted.

Analogous Arts

A prior art reference is only part of the scope of content of the prior art for obviousness purposes if it is analogous art. Prior art is analogous art if:

1. the reference is from the same field of endeavor; or

2. the reference is reasonably pertinent to the particular problem the inventor was trying to solve.

Whether prior art is analogous is a question of fact. In *In re Clay*, 966 F.2d 656, 659, 23 USPQ2d 1058, 1061 (Fed. Cir. 1992), the Court held:

> A reference is reasonably pertinent if, even though it may be in a different field from that of the inventor's endeavor, it is one which, because of the matter with which it deals, logically would have commended itself to an inventor's attention in considering his problem. Thus, the purposes of both the invention and the prior art are important in determining whether the reference is reasonably pertinent to the problem the invention attempts to solve. If the reference disclosure has the same purpose as the claimed invention,

the reference relates to the same problem, and that fact supports use of that reference in an obviousness [determination].

Hypothetical Person Knows All the Art

The hypothetical person of ordinary skill in the art is presumed to know all of the pertinent prior art. Pretend that the hypothetical person has all of the prior art references taped up on his wall in front of him when he is determining if an invention is obvious. *See In re Winslow*, 365 F.2d 1017, 1020, 151 USPQ 48, 51 (CCPA 1966) ("We think the proper way to apply the 103 obviousness test to a case like this is to first picture the inventor as working in his shop with the prior art references—which he is presumed to know—hanging on the walls around him.").

Patentee's Rebuttal Evidence

Often, the patentee will not agree with the scope and content of the prior art for obviousness as defined by the defendant. Three arguments available to narrow the scope of what can be considered for obviousness are: there is no motivation to combine the suggested references; one or more of the references teaches away from the claimed invention; or the prior art was commonly owned at the time of the invention pursuant to § 103(c).

1. No motivation to combine. The patentee can argue that the references cited by the defendant should not be combined because there is no motivation or suggestion in the art to combine them.

> [When a charge of obviousness] ... depends on a combination of prior art references, there must be some teaching, suggestion, or motivation to combine the references. Although the suggestion to combine references may flow from the nature of the problem, the suggestion more often comes from the teachings of the pertinent references or from the ordinary knowledge of those skilled in the art that certain references are of special importance in a particular field....
>
> To prevent the use of hindsight based on the invention to defeat patentability of the invention, this court requires the examiner to show a motivation to combine the references that create the case of obviousness. In other words, the examiner must show reasons that the skilled artisan, confronted with the same problems as the inventor and with no knowledge of the claimed invention, would select the elements from the cited prior art references for combination in the manner claimed.
>
> This court has identified three possible sources for a motivation to combine references: the nature of the problem to be solved, the teachings of the prior art, and the knowledge of persons of ordinary skill in the art. In this case, the Board relied upon none of these. Rather, just as it relied on the high level of skill in the art to overcome the differences between the claimed invention and the selected elements in the references, it relied upon the high level of skill in the art to provide the necessary motivation. The Board did

not, however, explain what specific understanding or technological principle within the knowledge of one of ordinary skill in the art would have suggested the combination. Instead, the Board merely invoked the high level of skill in the field of art. If such a rote invocation could suffice to supply a motivation to combine, the more sophisticated scientific fields would rarely, if ever, experience a patentable technical advance. Instead, in complex scientific fields, the Board could routinely identify the prior art elements in an application, invoke the lofty level of skill, and rest its case for rejection. To counter this potential weakness in the obviousness construct, the suggestion to combine requirement stands as a critical safeguard against hindsight analysis and rote application of the legal test for obviousness.

In re Rouffet, 149 F.3d 1350, 1357, 47 USPQ2d, 1453, 1458 (Fed. Cir. 1998) (citations omitted).

2. Reference teaches away from the claimed invention.

A reference may be said to teach away when a person of ordinary skill, upon reading the reference, would be discouraged from following the path set out in the reference, or would be led in a direction divergent from the path that was taken by the applicant. The degree of teaching away will of course depend on the particular facts; in general, a reference will teach away if it suggests that the line of development flowing from the reference's disclosure is unlikely to be productive of the result sought by the applicant.

In re Gurley, 27 F.3d 551, 553, 31 USPQ2d 1130, 1131 (Fed. Cir. 1994).

3. Section 103(c).

In 1984, Congress added a provision to § 103, which later became § 103(c), which states:

Subject matter developed by another person, which qualifies as prior art only under subsection (f) or (g) of section 102 of this title, shall not preclude patentability under this section [obviousness] where the subject matter and the claimed invention were, at the time the invention was made, owned by the same person or subject to an obligation of assignment to the same person.

This provision was added to prevent the invalidation of patents under § 103 on the basis of the work of fellow employees engaged in team research. Hence, the patentee can argue that § 102(f) or (g) prior art owned by the same person or corporation at the time of invention is not available as prior art for obviousness purposes. Notice that this section does not apply to § 102(e) prior art.

b. *The differences between the prior art and the claimed invention*

This factor is a relatively straight-forward comparison of the prior art and the claimed invention. It is similar to the comparison that is performed in an infringement analysis, except that, instead of comparing an accused device to the claims, the court compares the prior art to the claims.

c. *The level of ordinary skill in the art*

The patentee will often try to prove that there is a low level of skill in the art whereas the accused infringer will want to prove that the level of skill in the art is high. Why would the accused infringer want the level of skill in the art to be a Nobel laureate? The level of skill in the art is a factual question.

> Factors that may be considered in determining level of ordinary skill in the art include: (1) the educational level of the inventor; (2) type of problems encountered in the art; (3) prior art solutions to those problems; (4) rapidity with which innovations are made; (5) sophistication of the technology; and (6) educational level of active workers in the field. Not all such factors may be present in every case, and one or more of these or other factors may predominate in a particular case. The important consideration lies in the need to adhere to the statute, i.e., to hold that an invention would or would not have been obvious, as a whole, when it was made, to a person of "ordinary skill in the art"—not to the judge, or to a layman, or to those skilled in remote arts, or to geniuses in the art at hand.

Environmental Designs, Ltd. v. Union Oil Co., 713 F.2d 693, 696–97, 218 USPQ 865, 868–69 (Fed. Cir. 1983) (citations omitted).

d. *Objective Evidence of Obviousness*

Although originally referred to as secondary considerations, the Federal Circuit has made it clear that the objective or secondary considerations must be considered as part of every obviousness case. *See Stratoflex, Inc. v. Aeroquip Corp.*, 713 F.2d 1530, 1538–39, 218 USPQ 871, 879 (Fed. Cir. 1983); *Hybritech, Inc. v. Monoclonal Antibodies, Inc.*, 802 F.2d 1367, 1380, 231 USPQ 81, 90 (Fed. Cir. 1986) (secondary considerations are "not merely 'icing on the cake' "). The objective evidence of non-obviousness is generally presented by the patentee to rebut the defendant's contentions that the patented invention was obvious. The objective evidence or secondary considerations of nonobviousness include:

1. commercial success of the invention;

2. long felt need for the invention;

3. failure of others;

4. licenses showing industry respect for the invention;

5. copying of the invention by the accused infringer;

6. unexpected results; and

7. skepticism by others in the field that the invention would work.

For commercial success to be relevant to the obviousness determination, the patentee must demonstrate a nexus between the success and the patented invention. The patentee can use her own sales data and licensees as well as those of the defendant to demonstrate commercial success. The defendant may present evidence that the patentee's invention has not been commercially successful or that if it has been successful, its success was due to something other than the patented invention. For example, the defendant may want to show that the commercial success of the invention was due to advertising and marketing or a feature of the invention other than the patented one.

The following case demonstrates how a patentee can rebut the defendant's obviousness case.

GAMBRO LUNDIA AB v. BAXTER HEALTHCARE CORP.

110 F.3d 1573, 42 USPQ2d 1378 (Fed. Cir. 1997)

Before ARCHER, Chief Judge, LOURIE, and RADER, Circuit Judges.

RADER, Circuit Judge.

In this patent infringement case, Gambro Lundia AB (Gambro) appeals and Baxter Healthcare Corporation (Baxter) cross-appeals a final judgment of the United States District Court for the District of Colorado. The patent at issue, U.S. Patent No. 4,585,552 ('552 patent), claims a "system for the measurement of the difference between two fluid flows in separate ducts." This invention recalibrates sensors during hemodialysis to accurately measure the impurities removed from a patient's blood. Due to error in the district court's analyses of invalidity, unenforceability, and infringement, this court reverses.

BACKGROUND

Hemodialysis, commonly called dialysis, removes contaminants and excess fluid from the patient's blood when the kidneys do not function properly. Hemodialysis works by passing a dialysate solution through a machine, called a dialyzer, which functions as an artificial kidney. In the dialyzer, the dialysate passes on one side of a porous diffusion membrane, while the patient's blood passes on the other side. Because of the pressure differential across the membrane, blood contaminants and excess fluid diffuse through the membrane from the patient's blood into the dialysate. These impurities diffused from the patient's blood are known as ultrafiltrate.

After hemodialysis, the volume of the dialysate is greater. The difference between the initial and end volumes of dialysate can be used to calculate the amount of the ultrafiltrate removed from a patient's blood. This calculation is critical to the success of hemodialysis. Removal of too much or too little ultrafiltrate may lead to severe medical problems or even death.

Repgreen Limited (Repgreen), a British bioengineering company, improved ultrafiltrate calculation. Keith Wittingham, Repgreen's chief designer, introduced the Repgreen monitoring system, the UFM 1000, in late 1977. Wittingham's development relied on the research of Professor Michael Sanderson. The UFM 1000 used two electromagnetic flow sensors to measure the difference between the rate of dialysate flow into and out of the dialyzer. The difference in flow rates indicated the quantity of ultrafiltrate leaving the system. To calibrate the system for an accurate measurement of dialysate flow rates, the operator would direct clean dialysate through both sensors before dialysis. This calibration method, however, could not account for clogging in the outflow sensor during dialysis. Over time, the ultrafiltrate would build up behind the outflow sensor and disrupt the accuracy of the measurements. Experts refer to this increasing inaccuracy as "drift."

In the late 1970s, Gambro sought to improve ultrafiltrate monitoring. During 1979, Wittingham met with Gambro engineers on two occasions to discuss Repgreen's development of an ultrafiltrate monitor for Gambro. In July 1979, after Repgreen went bankrupt, Gambro purchased Repgreen's hemodialysis technology, including the rights to the UFM 1000 monitor. After acquiring Repgreen's technology, Gambro's research team worked for three years on improving ultrafiltration monitors. In June 1982, four Gambro engineers, including Bengt–Ake Gummesson, refined the monitoring system. Their invention ultimately issued as the '552 patent.

Gambro filed its initial patent application in Sweden on September 28, 1982. Gambro followed up with a U.S. application in September 1983. Gunnar Boberg, Repgreen's in-house patent counsel, and Arnold Krumholz, Repgreen's U.S. patent counsel, prosecuted the U.S. application. The examiner rejected claim 1 as anticipated by a German patent application (German '756). In response, Gambro provided the examiner with a German-language copy of German '756, along with arguments prepared by Boberg (who is fluent in German). Based on this submission, the examiner withdrew the rejection. The '552 patent issued on April 29, 1986.

The Gambro invention uses valves to direct clean dialysate around the dialyzer to recalibrate the sensors during dialysis. The invention's valve system can direct clean dialysate through the first flow sensor, around the dialyzer, and through the second flow sensor. To recalibrate, the invention momentarily blocks passage of contaminated dialysate through the outflow sensor. Instead, clean dialysate flows through the outflow sensor and recalibrates the detectors with the same clean dialysate flowing through both intake and outflow sensors. After the brief recalibration, the hemodialysis continues with contaminated dialysate flowing through the second sensor. Claim 1 of the '552 patent reads:

[1] In dialysis equipment including a dialyser, a system for measuring the difference in the rate of flow between first and second fluid streams, said first fluid stream comprising clean dialysis solution flowing to the dialyser and said second fluid stream comprising spent dialysis solution flowing from the dialyser, said system comprising

[2] a first duct for receiving said first fluid stream flowing therethrough,

[3] a second duct for receiving said second fluid stream flowing therethrough,

[4] measuring means for measuring the difference in the rate of flow between said first and second fluid streams within said first and second ducts,

[5] and transferring means for preventing the flow of said second fluid stream through said second duct while flowing said first fluid stream through both said first and second ducts without passing said first fluid stream through the dialyser and without altering said rate of flow of said first fluid stream between said first and second ducts such that said rate of flow of said first fluid stream through said first and second ducts is substantially equal,

[6] whereby the measured difference of the rate of flow of said first fluid stream flowing through said first and second ducts is adaptable as a reference.

In 1984, Baxter acquired the dialysis equipment division of Extracorporeal, Inc. Dissatisfied with the accuracy of the Extracorporeal technology, Baxter developed the Baxter SPS 550 and began marketing the device in December 1987. Gambro filed suit against Baxter in the District Court for the District of Colorado in March 1992 claiming the Baxter SPS 550 infringed the '552 patent. In defense, Baxter asserted the invalidity and unenforceability of the '552 patent.

After a ten-day bench trial on the issues of infringement, validity, and unenforceability, the district court held claim 1 of the Gambro '552 patent invalid for obviousness and derivation, and unenforceable for inequitable conduct. The district court also entered judgment in favor of Baxter on infringement, contributory infringement, inducing infringement, and willful infringement due to the invalidity and unenforceability of the '552 patent. Further, the district court declined to award either party attorney fees or costs.

DISCUSSION

This court reviews the ultimate determination of obviousness de novo. This ultimate determination, however, requires underlying factual findings, which this court examines for clear error.

The district court determined that the prior art embodied each of the elements of claim 1, with the exception of element five—the "transferring means." Specifically, the court found that the prior art, including the UFM 1000, the DM 358, and the German '756 patent, differed from the Gambro invention only in the absence of computer controlled valves to recalibrate the flow sensors during dialysis. The record amply supports these findings.

Thus, the key obviousness question is whether the prior art would teach one of ordinary skill in this art to employ valves for recalibration during dialysis. The district court found that those skilled in the art were clearly aware of the possibility of recalibrating during dialysis, and that substituting a system of computer-controlled valves for the system of hoses in the UFM 1000 and the DM 358 was obvious to those skilled in the art at the time of invention. However, the record must provide a teaching, suggestion, or reason to substitute computer-controlled valves for the system of hoses in the prior art. The absence of such a suggestion to combine is dispositive in an obviousness determination.

The trial judge found that the Gray and Sanderson article, *Precision Differential Fluid Flow Measurement*, "clearly suggests using a valve system to bypass or detour clean dialysate around the dialyzer during the course of a dialysis treatment." The record evidence does not support this finding. Sanderson himself testified that his article did not disclose the use of valves to bypass the dialyzer, but actually taught away from that solution. Rather than recalibration by rerouting the clean dialysate through valves around the dialyzer during dialysis, Sanderson testified that his clinical device rerouted spent dialysate, which has passed through the dialyzer, through both the inflow and outflow sensors. Sanderson testified that this configuration was necessary because it was a medical requirement to maintain the flow of dialysis fluid through the dialyzer. Thus, Sanderson testified that his article taught away from recalibration during dialysis by bypassing the dialyzer.

The Gray and Sanderson article supports this testimony. The article and the clinical trials teach that stopping the fluid flow through the dialyzer for recalibration during dialysis is not possible. The article states: "As it was not possible during dialysis therapy to stop the fluid transfer and thus re-establish the zero base line, a series of valves were inserted around the flowmeter to enable the flow to be changed to a zero differential flow configuration while at the same time maintaining dialysis." Further, the article explains that because it was not possible to bypass the dialyzer during dialysis, "[t]he only solution appeared to lie in the adoption of a differential measurement technique where any signal due to the true differential flow could be effectively isolated from that due to the very much larger common mode signal." Thus, Sanderson's use of the valves to direct spent dialysis through both sensors facilitated a proper baseline for testing the accuracy of the improved sensor. Contrary to the district court's finding, the Gray and Sanderson article teaches away from the use of valves to recalibrate during dialysis by bypassing the dialyzer. Without a suggestion or teaching to combine, Baxter's case of obviousness suffers a significant deficiency.

In addition, the district court did not evaluate fully the fourth prong of the obviousness determination—the objective indicia of nonobviousness. These objective indicia, when present, are invariably relevant to a determination under Section 103. *See Stratoflex, Inc. v. Aeroquip Corp.*, 713 F.2d 1530, 1538, 218 USPQ 871, 879 (Fed. Cir. 1983). These objective indicia "may often be the most probative and cogent evidence [of nonobviousness] in the record." *Id.*

The district court rejected the evidence of long-felt need and declined to address any other consideration. Several objective indicia, however, warrant consideration in this case. For instance, before this litigation, Baxter recognized calibration during dialysis as a significant advance. Baxter touted the advantages of AUTO–ADJUST, as it termed automatic recalibration during dialysis, in the advertising for the allegedly infringing Baxter SPS 550 machines. Baxter's recognition of the importance of this advance is relevant to a determination of nonobviousness.

Additionally, the record contains significant evidence of the commercial success of Gambro's invention. The record shows that Baxter sold over 14,800 dialysis machines allegedly incorporating the Gambro invention since 1987. In fact, Baxter admits that its machines were a commercial success. Of course, the record must show a sufficient nexus between this commercial success and the patented invention. The prominence of the patented technology in Baxter's advertising creates an inference that links the Gambro invention to this success.

Finally, the record also suggests that others in this market had tried to solve the need for improved accuracy of the ultrafiltration monitors. The record reflects that those skilled in the art tried numerous, ultimately unsuccessful, solutions—improving the electronics, improving the flowmeter technology, and recalibrating before dialysis. This objective consideration also supports a conclusion of nonobviousness.

In sum, the record supplies objective evidence of nonobviousness, including Baxter's recognition of the importance of this invention, evidence of commercial success, and evidence of the failure of others to solve the recognized problem. This objective evidence, combined with the lack of a teaching or suggestion to combine, requires a holding of nonobviousness.

Notes

1. **Obviousness for the Jury.** In almost every infringement case, the defendant will charge that the patent is obvious over some combination of the prior art or the prior art and the knowledge in the field. The Federal Circuit has held that even though obviousness is a question of law, the four underlying factors are fact questions, and therefore it is appropriate to submit the issue of obviousness in its entirety to the jury. The patentee ought to request that the jury be given specific interrogatories and special verdict forms with respect to the obviousness factors. *See* Chapter Fifteen.

Problems

Returning again to the '835 patent from Chapter Eight. You discover the following information in a search for prior art:

1. The Fisherman article dated March 1993, which discusses the problems associated with stern-mounted autopilot systems including the overshoot problem. The article suggests that putting autopilot systems on bow-mounted motors may solve this problem and be cheaper to manufacture, but it does not give any detailed description of how to do it.

2. A U.S. patent, the Moore patent, filed December 1, 1991 and issued June 1, 1993 which discloses using a foot pedal manual override switch in a

stern-mounted autopilot system. The patent states: "When the fisher depresses the foot pedal, the auto-pilot system shuts off and the fisher can use the foot pedal to steer the trolling motor." You notice, however, that when the fisher stops depressing the foot pedal, the trolling motor disclosed in the Moore patent turns off.

3. A U.S. patent, the Chalupny patent, issued March 1, 1992, which claims the use of a compass in a stern-mounted auto-pilot system.

During his deposition, the inventor, Perch, reveals that he first had the idea for his invention in January of 1992 at a fishing products trade show in Oregon. He says that the booth on bow-mounted trolling motors was set up right next to the booth on stern-mounted trolling motors and autopilot systems. It occurred to him as he stared at these two booths that a bow-mounted autopilot system would solve the overshoot problem associated with stern-mounted autopilot systems and that putting manual override switch in a foot pedal would free up the fisherman's hands.

When he returned home, he immediately began to construct a prototype of his invention. He ordered the parts right away from the local store; in fact, he may still have the receipts for the parts. While he was in the store he told the owner, Mr. Matthews, about his idea. He was slightly discouraged because Mr. Matthews told him the invention would never work, especially the manual override switch in a foot pedal.

Perch built two prototypes anyway. The prototypes had everything except the manual override feature, which he was still working on. He took one of the prototypes out on Lake Michigan in June of 1992. His friend, Tom Berger, accompanied him. Perch explained how the invention worked to Tom. Perch noticed that the autopilot system generally worked, but not exactly as he intended—it did not seem to turn the motor every time the boat deviated from its target heading. Perch took a few notes on the back of a map regarding what was wrong and how it might be fixed (yes, he still has the map, it is his only map of the Lake).

Tom thought the autopilot was great and asked Perch if he could buy one. Perch sold one of the prototypes to Tom for twice the cost of the parts and asked Tom if he would let him know how it was working. About a month later (July 1992), Tom called Perch and told him that he was fishing with his friend Mike of Mike's Fishing who said he was very interested in purchasing a few of the bow-mounted trolling motors with an autopilot system. Mike offered $100 per motor for 10 motors and asked if they could be delivered by September 1992. In this same conversation Tom told Perch that the prototype did not work properly all the time, it only seemed to keep the boat on track 80% of the time. Perch responded that he still needed to work out a few bugs on the autopilot system and there is no way he could sell them to Mike in September, but Tom should keep up the effective marketing.

Perch fixed the design problem in December 1992. He tested the prototype and the autopilot system worked 100% of the time, but the manual override foot pedal still was not operating properly. He contacted Mike's Fishing and said if the offer still stands, he could have 10 motors ready for Mike in February. Mike said he was no longer interested.

Perch worked on the foot pedal, which he perfected in June 1993. He took the prototypes to Mike's Fishing. Mike bought both prototypes on the spot and offered Tom a job. In November 1993, Tom assigned his patent rights in the autopilot system for the bow-mounted trolling motor to Mike's Fishing. Mike's Fishing has sold thousands of them. They outsell all other trolling motors 2 to 1. Mike's Fishing also licensed 5 trolling manufacturers in other geographic areas to sell the bow-mounted autopilot trolling motor.

What constitutes prior art that can be used in an anticipation or obviousness defense? How would Mark's Boats argue that the patent is invalid in a summary judgment motion? How would Mike's Fishing oppose the summary judgment motion?

F.　THE SPECIFICATION IS INADEQUATE—§ 112

The disclosure of the patent may be attacked for specification flaws. If found, flaws may invalidate a patent.

STATUTORY PROVISION—35 U.S.C. § 112:

The specification shall contain a written description of the invention, and of the manner and process of making and using it, in such full, clear, concise, and exact terms as to enable any person skilled in the art to which it pertains, or with which it is most nearly connected, to make and use the same, and shall set forth the best mode contemplated by the inventor of carrying out his invention.

The specification shall conclude with one or more claims particularly pointing out and distinctly claiming the subject matter which the applicant regards as his invention.

* * *

An element in a claim for a combination may be expressed as a means or step for performing a specified function without the recital of structure, material, or acts in support thereof, and such claim shall be construed to cover the corresponding structure, material, or acts described in the specification and equivalents thereof.

1.　FAILURE TO SET FORTH THE BEST MODE

Section 112, ¶ 1 requires that the best mode for carrying out the invention contemplated by the inventor at the time of application be disclosed in the patent application.

CHEMCAST CORP. v. ARCO INDUS. CORP.
913 F.2d 923, 16 USPQ2d 1033 (Fed. Cir. 1990)

Before ARCHER and MAYER, Circuit Judges, and GEORGE, District Judge.

MAYER, Circuit Judge.

Chemcast Corporation appeals the judgment of the United States District Court for the Eastern District of Michigan that Claim 6 of

United States Patent No. 4,081,879 ('879 patent), the only claim in suit, is invalid because of the inventor's failure to disclose the best mode as required by 35 U.S.C. § 112. We affirm.

Background

The '879 patent claims a sealing member in the form of a grommet or plug button that is designed to seal an opening in, for example, a sheet metal panel. Claim 6, the only claim in suit, depends from Claim 1.

Claim 6: The grommet as defined in claim 1 wherein the material forming said base portion has a durometer hardness reading of less than 60 Shore A and the material forming said locking portion has durometer hardness reading of more than 70 Shore A.[1]

The grommet of Claim 6 is referred to as a dual durometer grommet because it may be composed either of two materials that differ in hardness or of a single material that varies in hardness. In either case, the different hardnesses can be, and for a sufficiently large hardness differential must be, measured with different durometers: Shore A for the softer base portion and Shore D for the harder locking portion. The harder locking portion of the grommet is the focus of this case.

Chemcast and its competitor Arco Industries Corporation are both engaged in the manufacture and sale of sealing members such as grommets, gaskets, and plug buttons. Both sell their products primarily to the automobile industry. Ex–Arco employee Phillip L. Rubright founded Chemcast in 1973 and subsequently conceived of and designed specifically for Oldsmobile, a Chemcast customer, the dual durometer '879 grommet. He filed a patent application together with an assignment of invention to Chemcast in January of 1976; the '879 patent issued in April of 1978.

Chemcast subsequently sued Arco for infringement of Claim 6 of the '879 patent. Arco counterclaimed that the patent was invalid on several grounds, including Rubright's failure to comply with 35 U.S.C. § 112. The district court agreed. It held that, because the '879 patent did not either disclose the best mode contemplated by the inventor of carrying out the invention or particularly point out and distinctly claim

---

1. A device known as a durometer measures the hardness and softness of the materials used in the grommet. The Shore Instrument & Manufacturing Company is a leading manufacturer of durometers used for measuring rubber-like materials. A durometer referred to as a Shore A durometer measures soft, vulcanized rubber and all elastomeric materials, while a Shore D durometer measures rigid materials such as hard rubber and harder grades of plastic. The Shore B and Shore C durometers can be used to measure intermediate hardnesses. There is some overlap in the range of use of the durometers. A conversion chart is published by the Shore Instruments & Manufacturing Co. which shows that the range of 30 to 100 on the scale of a Shore A durometer corresponds to the range of 6 to 58 on a Shore D durometer. The American Society for Testing Materials (ASTM) sets the standards to [sic, with] which the plastics and rubber industry comply [sic, complies] and recommends that hardnesses above 90 on the Shore A scale be measured with a Shore D durometer for greater accuracy.

the subject matter of the invention, Chemcast could not recover on its claim of infringement.

Both parties appealed. We vacated the district court's best mode decision because, in reaching it, the court relied on an incorrect legal standard; reversed the court's holding that Claim 6 did not meet the claim particularity requirements of section 112; and affirmed the judgment on all other issues. We set out the appropriate legal standard for determining compliance with the best mode requirement as follows:

Failure to comply with the best mode requirement amounts to concealing the preferred mode contemplated by the applicant at the time of filing. In order for a district court to conclude that the best mode requirement is not satisfied, the focus must be, and the district court must determine, that the inventor knew of, i.e., "contemplated," and concealed a better mode than he disclosed. The focus for a best mode analysis is not simply on whether the patent discloses the most suitable material for carrying out the claimed invention. Accordingly, we remanded the case to the district court for a redetermination of the best mode issue.

On remand, the court again invalidated the patent for failure to satisfy the best mode requirement. It made 47 factual findings detailing both what, at the time of filing the patent application, Rubright considered to be the best mode of practicing his claimed invention and what the specification as filed disclosed to one of ordinary skill in the art. According to the court, the principal shortcomings of the disclosure were its failure to specify (1) the particular type, (2) the hardness, and (3) the supplier and trade name, of the material used to make the locking portion of the grommet. Therefore, it held that the application as filed failed adequately to disclose the best mode of practicing the invention contemplated by Rubright. Chemcast appeals.

Discussion

A.

The first paragraph of 35 U.S.C. § 112 (1982) provides:

The specification [A] shall contain a written description of the invention, and of the manner and process of making and using it, in such full, clear, concise, and exact terms as to enable any person skilled in the art to which it pertains, or with which it is most nearly connected, to make and use the same, and [B] shall set forth the best mode contemplated by the inventor of carrying out his invention.

We long ago drew and often have focused upon the critical distinction between requirement [A], "enablement," and requirement [B], "best mode." The essence of portion [A] is that a specification shall disclose an invention in such a manner as will enable one skilled in the art to make and utilize it. Separate and distinct from portion [A] is portion [B], the essence of which requires an inventor to disclose the best mode contemplated by him, as of the time he executes the application, of carrying out his invention. Manifestly, the sole purpose of this latter requirement is to restrain inventors from applying for patents while at the same time concealing from the public preferred embodiments of their inventions which they have in fact conceived.

The best mode inquiry focuses on the inventor's state of mind as of the time he filed his application—a subjective, factual question. But this focus is not exclusive. Our statements that "there is no objective standard by which to judge the adequacy of a best mode disclosure," and that "only evidence of concealment (accidental or intentional) is to be considered," *In re Sherwood*, 613 F.2d 809, 816, 204 USPQ 537, 544 (CCPA 1980), assumed that both the level of skill in the art and the scope of the claimed invention were additional, objective metes and bounds of a best mode disclosure.

Of necessity, the disclosure required by section 112 is directed to those skilled in the art. Therefore, one must consider the level of skill in the relevant art in determining whether a specification discloses the best mode. We have consistently recognized that whether a best mode disclosure is adequate, that is, whether the inventor concealed a better mode of practicing his invention than he disclosed, is a function of not only what the inventor knew but also how one skilled in the art would have understood his disclosure.

The other objective limitation on the extent of the disclosure required to comply with the best mode requirement is, of course, the scope of the claimed invention. "It is concealment of the best mode of practicing the claimed invention that section 112 ¶ 1 is designed to prohibit." *Randomex*, 849 F.2d at 588, 7 USPQ2d at 1053. Thus, in *Randomex*, the inventor's deliberate concealment of his cleaning fluid formula did not violate the best mode requirement because his "invention neither added nor claimed to add anything to the prior art respecting cleaning fluid." 849 F.2d at 590, 7 USPQ2d at 1054. Similarly, in *Christianson*, the inventor's failure to disclose information that would have enabled the claimed rifle parts to be interchangeable with all M–16 rifle parts did not invalidate his patents because "the best mode for making and using and carrying out the claimed inventions [did] not entail or involve either the M–16 rifle or interchangeability." Finally, in *DeGeorge* we reversed a finding that an inventor's nondisclosure of unclaimed circuitry with which his claimed circuitry interfaced violated the best mode requirement: "Because the properly construed count does not include a word processor, failure to meet the best mode requirement here should not arise from an absence of information on the word processor." 768 F.2d at 1325, 226 USPQ at 763.

In short, a proper best mode analysis has two components. The first is whether, at the time the inventor filed his patent application, he knew of a mode of practicing his claimed invention that he considered to be better than any other. This part of the inquiry is wholly subjective, and resolves whether the inventor must disclose any facts in addition to those sufficient for enablement. If the inventor in fact contemplated such a preferred mode, the second part of the analysis compares what he knew with what he disclosed—is the disclosure adequate to enable one skilled in the art to practice the best mode or, in other words, has the inventor "concealed" his preferred mode from the "public"? Assessing the adequacy of the disclosure, as opposed to its necessity, is largely an objective inquiry that depends upon the scope of the claimed invention and the level of skill in the art.

Notwithstanding the mixed nature of the best mode inquiry, and perhaps because of our routine focus on its subjective portion, we have consistently treated the question as a whole as factual. "Compliance with the best mode requirement, because it depends on the applicant's state of mind, is a question of fact subject to the clearly erroneous standard of review." *Spectra-Physics*, 827 F.2d at 1535, 3 USPQ2d at 1745. We adhere to that standard here, and review the district court's best mode determination accordingly.

B.

Chemcast alleges that the trial court erred in its best mode analysis by failing to focus, as required, on the claimed invention and on whether the inventor, Rubright, concealed a better mode than he disclosed. Neither allegation has any merit.

Chemcast first argues that, because the '879 patent does not claim any specific material for making the locking portion of the grommet, Rubright's failure to disclose the particular material that he thought worked the best does not violate the best mode requirement. This argument confuses best mode and enablement. A patent applicant must disclose the best mode of carrying out his claimed invention, not merely a mode of making and using what is claimed. A specification can be enabling yet fail to disclose an applicant's contemplated best mode. Indeed, most of the cases in which we have said that the best mode requirement was violated addressed situations where an inventor failed to disclose non-claimed elements that were nevertheless necessary to practice the best mode of carrying out the claimed invention.

Moreover, Chemcast is mistaken in its claim interpretation. While the critical limitation of Claim 6 is a hardness differential of 10 points on the Shore A scale between the grommet base and locking portions, and not a particular material type, some material meeting both this limitation and that of Claim 1, that "said base portion compris[e] an elastomeric material and said locking portion be[ ] more rigid than said base portion," is claimed. That the claim is broad is no reason to excuse noncompliance with the best mode requirement. Here, the information the applicant is accused of concealing is not merely necessary to practice the claimed invention, as in Dana fluoride surface treatment was "necessary to satisfactory performance" of the claimed valve stem seal, it also describes the preferred embodiment of a claimed element, as in *Spectra-Physics* the undisclosed braze cycle was the preferred "means for attaching" and "securing" claimed in the patents at issue.

Chemcast's second argument is equally misplaced. The court devoted no fewer than 13 factual findings to what the inventor Rubright knew as of the filing date of the '879 application. Those findings focus, as did the parties, on the type, hardness, and supplier of the material used to make the locking portion of the grommet.[2] The court found that Rubright selected the material for the locking portion, a rigid polyvinyl chloride (PVC) plastisol composition; knew that the preferred hardness of this material was 75 +/-5 Shore D; and purchased all of the grommet material under the trade name R–4467 from Reynosol Corporation (Reynosol), which had spent 750 man-hours developing the compound specifically for Chemcast. Furthermore, the court found that at the time the '879 application was filed, the only embodiment of the claimed invention known to Rubright was a grommet composed of R–4467, a rigid PVC plastisol composition with a locking portion hardness of 75 +/-5 Shore D.

In light of what Rubright knew, the specification, as issued, was manifestly deficient. It disclosed the following:

> The annular locking portion [ ] of the sealing member [ ] is preferably comprised of a rigid castable material, such as a castable resinous material, either a thermoplastic or thermosetting resin, or any mixtures thereof, for example, polyurethane or polyvinyl chloride. The [locking] portion [ ] also should be made of a material that is sufficiently hard and rigid so that it cannot be radially compressed, such as when it is inserted in the opening [ ] in the panel [ ]. Materials having a durometer hardness reading of 70 Shore A or harder are suitable in this regard.

Col. 4, 11.53–63. The material hardness (75 Shore D) and supplier/trade name (Reynosol compound R–4467) are not explicitly disclosed here or anywhere else in the specification.

Nor, in light of the level of skill in the art, are they implicitly disclosed. Given the specification, one skilled in the art simply could not divine Rubright's preferred material hardness. The court found that "the specification of the open-ended range of materials of '70 Shore A or harder' conceals the best mode 75 Shore D material in part because materials of Shore A and Shore D hardnesses are recognized as different types of materials with different classes of physical properties." As for the specific supplier and trade name designation of the preferred material, the court found that disclosing a list of generic potential materials was "not an adequate disclosure of the best mode PVC Reynosol Compound R–4467."

We agree. That "at least eight other PVC composition suppliers [ ] could have formulated satisfactory materials for the dual durometer grommet," does not, as Chemcast urges, excuse Rubright's concealment

---

2. Prior to and at the time the '879 application was filed, Chemcast used a single type of material from a single supplier for both the base (soft) and locking (hard) portions of the grommet. Since the parties apparently do not dispute that the preferred hardness of the base portion was adequately disclosed, the district court focused, as will we, on the characteristics of the locking portion material.

of his preferred material, and the only one of which he was aware. Again Chemcast confuses enablement and best mode. The question is not whether those skilled in the art could make or use the '879 grommet without knowledge of Reynosol compound R–4467; it is whether they could practice Rubright's contemplated best mode which, the court found, included specifically the Reynosol compound. Rubright knew that Reynosol had developed R–4467 specifically for Chemcast and had expended several months and many hundred man-hours in doing so. Because Chemcast used only R–4467, because certain characteristics of the grommet material were claimed elements of the '879 invention, and because Rubright himself did not know the formula, composition, or method of manufacture of R–4467, section 112 obligated Rubright to disclose the specific supplier and trade name of his preferred material.

Other facts Chemcast points to as obviating the need for Rubright's disclosure of "Reynosol R–4467" are simply irrelevant. That Reynosol considered the formulation of R–4467 a trade secret and that it offered the compound only to Chemcast, do not bear on the state of Rubright's knowledge or the quality of his disclosure. First, it is undisputed that Rubright did not know either the precise formulation or method of manufacture of R–4467; he knew only that it was a rigid PVC plastisol composition denominated "R–4467" by Reynosol. Whatever the scope of Reynosol's asserted trade secret, to the extent it includes information known by Rubright that he considered part of his preferred mode, section 112 requires that he divulge it. Second, whether and to whom Reynosol chooses to sell its products cannot control the extent to which Rubright must disclose his best mode. Were this the law, inventors like Rubright could readily circumvent the best mode requirement by concluding sole-user agreements with the suppliers of their preferred materials.

Nor does the fact that Rubright developed his preferred mode with the requirements of a particular customer in mind excuse its concealment; compliance with section 112 does not turn on why or for whom an inventor develops his invention. An inventor need not disclose manufacturing data or the requirements of a particular customer if that information is not part of the best mode of practicing the claimed invention, but the converse also is true. Whether characterizable as "manufacturing data," "customer requirements," or even "trade secrets," information necessary to practice the best mode simply must be disclosed.

Given the specification and the level of skill or understanding in the art, skilled practitioners could neither have known what Rubright's contemplated best mode was nor have carried it out. Indeed, on these facts, they would not even have known where to look. This is not a case, like *Randomex*, where the inventor indiscriminately disclosed his preferred mode along with other possible modes. Rubright did not disclose his preferred mode at all. His preferred material hardness, 75 Shore D, is three hardness scales removed from the 70 Shore A hardness mentioned in the specification. Neither his preferred source, Reynosol Compound R–4467, nor any other is disclosed.

In this situation and on these facts, where the inventor has failed to disclose the only mode he ever contemplated of carrying out his invention, the best mode requirement is violated.

Notes

1. **Why Do Inventors Not Want to Disclose Their Best Modes?** Inventors have economic incentives to "have their cake and eat it too." If they can obtain a patent monopoly without disclosing the best mode of performing the invention, there is an obvious advantage that continues even after the patent monopoly expires. Even during, the patent monopoly, an undisclosed best mode may hinder competitors efforts to build upon or design around the patent. As patent policy rewards disclosure, it also penalizes less than full disclosure with the threat of patent invalidity should the inventor fail to disclose her best mode.

2. **Hiding or Burying the Best Mode**. The Federal Circuit held that a patentee is allowed to list several possible modes of practicing the invention, one of which is actually the inventor's best mode. *See generally Randomex, Inc. v. Scopus Corp.*, 849 F.2d 585, 7 USPQ2d 1050 (Fed. Cir. 1988). Do you think that the patentee should be allowed to bury his best mode? Is this poor policy?

3. **Later Discovered Better Modes**. The best mode that must be revealed is the one contemplated by the inventor at the time of application. Later discovered modes need not be added to an application in progress or to an issued patent.

4. **Production vs. Manufacturing Details**. The inventor is not required to disclose his best mode for all aspects of an invention's commercial manufacture. In *Wahl Instruments, Inc. v. Acvious, Inc.*, 950 F.2d 1575, 1581–82, 21 USPQ2d 1123, 1128–29 (Fed. Cir. 1991), the Federal Circuit stated:

> Any process of manufacture requires the selection of specific steps and materials over others. The best mode does not necessarily cover each of these selections. To so hold would turn a patent specification into a detailed production schedule, which is not its function. Moreover, a requirement for routine details to be disclosed because they were selected as the "best" for manufacturing or fabrication would lay a trap for patentees whenever a device has been made prior to filing for the patent. The inventor would merely have to be interrogated with increasing specificity as to steps or material selected as "best" to make the device. *A fortiori*, he could hardly say the choice is not what he thought was "best" in some way. Thus, at the point he would testify respecting a step or material or source or detail which is not in the patent, a failure to disclose the best mode would, *ipso facto*, be established. However, the best mode inquiry is not so mechanical. A step or material or source or technique considered "best" in a manufacturing circumstance may have been selected for a non-"best mode" reason, such as the manufacturing equipment was on hand, certain materials were available, prior relationship with supplier was satisfactory, or

other reasons having nothing to do with development of the invention.

* * *

How to mass produce the device is not, however, a best mode of [an] invention or part of what [is] invented.

To overcome the patentee's arguments that what he failed to disclose was merely a production detail, the accused infringer should introduce evidence that the non-disclosed information substantially improves the operation or effectiveness of the claimed invention. Non-disclosed information is not a production detail if it pertains to the quality and nature of the claimed invention; however, it may be if it merely pertains to the quantity or other commercial considerations.

5. **Claims Determine What Must be Disclosed.** The best mode does not require an applicant to disclose a nonclaimed element of the invention when the element is not necessary to the operation of the claimed invention. This is true even when the element is required in order to operate the overall device. *See Applied Med. Resources Corp. v. United States Surgical Corp.*, 147 F.3d 1374, 47 USPQ2d 1289 (Fed. Cir. 1998) (failure to disclose a lubricant which is necessary for operation of a seal is not a best mode violation because it plays no role in the functioning of the patented inventions—the preseal dilator, the seal protector, and the floating seal).

6. **Head in the Sand Tactics: Company is Aware of a Better Mode**. Knowledge will not be imputed to the inventor even if the inventor's company is aware of a better mode. The Federal Circuit held in *Glaxo Inc. v. Novopharm Ltd.*, 52 F.3d 1043, 1049–50, 34 USPQ2d 1565, 1568–70 (Fed. Cir. 1995) that the test for best mode is subjective and based on what the inventor knew at the time of filing the application, not the best mode that the inventor's company contemplated. Knowledge of other employees cannot be imputed to the inventor, even if the company intentionally isolated the inventor from the superior mode of practicing the invention. *Id.* at 1051, 34 USPQ2d at 1570 ("whether Glaxo deliberately walled off the inventor is irrelevant to the issue of failure of his application to disclose the best mode known to him.").

7. **Discovery**. Working for a possible best mode defense, attorneys for the accused infringer will often take very long depositions of the inventor to get her to discuss everything she did in the process of inventing. The attorney will also question the inventor about every embodiment considered and why such embodiments were not disclosed. An inventor will often be eager to explain the importance of every feature of her first commercial embodiment. Inventors are usually well prepared by their counsel not to admit that anything was obvious. If some of these "important" features which are not obvious were not disclosed in the patent specification, you have fertile ground for laying a best mode defense. The patentee should be prepared for a best mode defense when the patentee or her assignee commercially manufactures a mode of the invention that was not disclosed in the patent. This discovery may also fuel an inventorship challenge, especially if the inventor reveals that others assisted in the development of the invention.

2. LACK OF ENABLEMENT

Where the patent does not teach one skilled in the art how to practice the invention claimed, it is not enabling. The enabling instructions in the patent need not explain everything as if to enable one of average intelligence. The inventor is allowed to assume reasonable expertise in the art on the part of the reader as well as requiring some experimentation to reach the result claimed as long as one skilled in the art would know how to do the required experimentation.

IN RE WANDS

858 F.2d 731, 8 USPQ2d 1400 (Fed. Cir. 1988)

Before SMITH, NEWMAN, and BISSELL, Circuit Judges.

EDWARD S. SMITH, Circuit Judge.

This appeal is from the decision of the Patent and Trademark Office (PTO) Board of Patent Appeals and Interferences (board) affirming the rejection of all remaining claims in appellant's application for a patent, serial No. 188,735, entitled "Immunoassay Utilizing Monoclonal High Affinity IgM Antibodies," which was filed September 19, 1980. The rejection under 35 U.S.C. § 112, first paragraph, is based on the grounds that appellant's written specification would not enable a person skilled in the art to make the monoclonal antibodies that are needed to practice the claimed invention without undue experimentation. We reverse.

BACKGROUND

A. The Art.

The claimed invention involves immunoassay methods for the detection of hepatitis B surface antigen by using high-affinity monoclonal antibodies of the IgM isotype. Antibodies are a class of proteins (immunoglobulins) that help defend the body against invaders such as viruses and bacteria. An antibody has the potential to bind tightly to another molecule, which molecule is called an antigen. The body has the ability to make millions of different antibodies that bind to different antigens. However, it is only after exposure to an antigen that a complicated immune response leads to the production of antibodies against that antigen. For example, on the surface of hepatitis B virus particles there is a large protein called hepatitis B surface antigen (HBsAg). As its name implies, it is capable of serving as an antigen. During a hepatitis B infection (or when purified HBsAg is injected experimentally), the body begins to make antibodies that bind tightly and specifically to HBsAg. Such antibodies can be used as regents for sensitive diagnostic tests (e.g., to detect hepatitis B virus in blood and other tissues, a purpose of the claimed invention). A method for detecting or measuring antigens by using antibodies as reagents is called an immunoassay.

Normally, many different antibodies are produced against each antigen. One reason for this diversity is that different antibodies are produced that bind to different regions (determinants) of a large antigen molecule such as HBsAg. In addition, different antibodies may be produced that bind to the same determinant. These usually differ in the tightness with which they bind to the determinant. Affinity is a quantitative measure of the strength of antibody-antigen binding. Usually an antibody with a higher affinity for an antigen will be more useful for immunological diagnostic tests than one with a lower affinity. Another source of heterogeneity is that there are several immunoglobulin classes or isotypes. Immunoglobulin G (IgG) is the most common isotype in serum. Another isotype, immunoglobulin M (IgM), is prominent early in the immune response. IgM molecules are larger than IgG molecules, and have 10 antigen-binding sites instead of the 2 that are present in IgG. Most immunoassay methods use IgG, but the claimed invention uses only IgM antibodies.

For commercial applications there are many disadvantages to using antibodies from serum. Serum contains a complex mixture of antibodies against the antigen of interest within a much larger pool of antibodies directed at other antigens. These are available only in a limited supply that ends when the donor dies. The goal of monoclonal antibody technology is to produce an unlimited supply of a single purified antibody.

The blood cells that make antibodies are lymphocytes. Each lymphocyte makes only one kind of antibody. During an immune response, lymphocytes exposed to their particular antigen divide and mature. Each produces a clone of identical daughter cells, all of which secrete the same antibody. Clones of lymphocytes, all derived from a single lymphocyte, could provide a source of a single homogeneous antibody. However, lymphocytes do not survive for long outside of the body in cell culture.

Hybridoma technology provides a way to obtain large numbers of cells that all produce the same antibody. This method takes advantage of the properties of myeloma cells derived from a tumor of the immune system. The cancerous myeloma cells can divide indefinitely in vitro. They also have the potential ability to secrete antibodies. By appropriate experimental manipulations, a myeloma cell can be made to fuse with a lymphocyte to produce a single hybrid cell (hence, a hybridoma) that contains the genetic material of both cells. The hybridoma secretes the same antibody that was made by its parent lymphocyte, but acquires the capability of the myeloma cell to divide and grow indefinitely in cell culture. Antibodies produced by a clone of hybridoma cells (i.e., by hybridoma cells that are all progeny of a single cell) are called monoclonal antibodies.

B.   The Claimed Invention.

The claimed invention involves methods for the immunoassay of HBsAg by using high-affinity monoclonal IgM antibodies. Jack R. Wands and Vincent R. Zurawski, Jr., two of the three coinventors of the present application, disclosed methods for producing monoclonal antibodies against HBsAg in United States patent No. 4,271,145 (the '145 patent), entitled "Process for Producing Antibodies to Hepatitis Virus and Cell Lines Therefor," which patent issued on June 2, 1981. The '145 patent is incorporated by reference into the application on appeal. The specification of the '145 patent teaches a procedure for immunizing mice against HBsAg, and the use of lymphocytes from these mice to produce hybridomas that secrete monoclonal antibodies specific for HBsAg. The '145 patent discloses that this procedure yields both IgG and IgM antibodies with high-affinity binding to HBsAg. For the stated purpose of complying with the best mode requirement of 35 U.S.C. § 112, first paragraph, a hybridoma cell line that secretes IgM antibodies against HBsAg (the 1F8 cell line) was deposited at the American Type Culture Collection, a recognized cell depository, and became available to the public when the '145 patent issued.

The application on appeal claims methods for immunoassay of HBsAg using monoclonal antibodies such as those described in the '145 patent. Most immunoassay methods have used monoclonal antibodies of the IgG isotype. IgM antibodies were disfavored in the prior art because of their sensitivity to reducing agents and their tendency to self-aggregate and precipitate. Appellants found that their monoclonal IgM antibodies could be used for immunoassay of HbsAg with unexpectedly high sensitivity and specificity. Claims 1, 3, 7, 8, 14, and 15 are drawn to methods for the immunoassay of HBsAg using high-affinity IgM monoclonal antibodies. Claims 19 and 25–27 are for chemically modified (e.g., radioactively labeled) monoclonal IgM antibodies used in the assays. The broadest method claim reads:

> 1. An immunoassay method utilizing an antibody to assay for a substance comprising hepatitis B-surface antigen (HBsAg) determinants which comprises the steps of:
>
> contacting a test sample containing said substance comprising HBsAg determinants with said antibody; and
>
> determining the presence of said substance in said sample;
>
> wherein said antibody is a monoclonal high affinity IgM antibody having a binding affinity constant for said HBsAg determinants of at least 109 M–1.

Certain claims were rejected under 35 U.S.C. § 103; these rejections have not been appealed. Remaining claims 1, 3, 7, 8, 14, 15, 19, and 25–27 were rejected under 35 U.S.C. § 112, first paragraph, on the grounds that the disclosure would not enable a person skilled in the art to make and use the invention without undue experimentation. The rejection is directed solely to whether the specification enables one skilled in the art to make the monoclonal antibodies that are needed to practice the invention. The position of the PTO is that data presented by Wands show that the production of high-affinity IgM anti-HBsAg antibodies is unpredictable and unreliable, so that it would require undue experimentation for one skilled in the art to make the antibodies.

III. ANALYSIS

A. Enablement by Deposit of Microorganisms and Cell Lines.

The first paragraph of 35 U.S.C. § 112 requires that the specification of a patent must enable a person skilled in the art to make and use the claimed invention. "Patents * * * are written to enable those skilled in the art to practice the invention." A patent need not disclose what is well known in art. Although we review underlying facts found by the board under a "clearly erroneous" standard, we review enablement as a question of law.

Where an invention depends on the use of living materials such as microorganisms or cultured cells, it may be impossible to enable the public to make the invention (i.e., to obtain these living materials) solely by means of a written disclosure. One means that has been developed for complying with the enablement requirement is to deposit the living materials in cell depositories which will distribute samples to the public who wish to practice the invention after the patent issues. Administrative guidelines and judicial decisions have clarified the conditions under which a deposit of organisms can satisfy the requirements of section 112. A deposit has been held necessary for enablement where the starting materials (i.e., the living cells used to practice the invention, or cells from which the required cells can be produced) are not readily available to the public. Even when starting materials are available, a deposit has been necessary where it would require undue experimentation to make the cells of the invention from the starting materials.

In addition to satisfying the enablement requirement, deposit of organisms also can be used to establish the filing date of the application as the prima facie date of invention, and to satisfy the requirement under 35 U.S.C. § 114 that the PTO be guaranteed access to the invention during pendency of the application. *In re Lundak*, 773 F.2d at 1222, 227 USPQ at 95–96. Although a deposit may serve these purposes, we recognized, in *In re Lundak*, that these purposes, nevertheless, may be met in ways other than by making a deposit.

A deposit also may satisfy the best mode requirement of section 112, first paragraph, and it is for this reason that the 1F8 hybridoma was deposited in connection with the '145 patent and the current application. Wands does not challenge the statements by the examiner to the effect that, although the deposited 1F8 line enables the public to perform immunoassays with antibodies produced by that single hybridoma, the deposit does not enable the generic claims that are on appeal. The examiner rejected the claims on the grounds that the written disclosure was not enabling and that the deposit was inadequate. Since we hold that the written disclosure fully enables the claimed invention, we need not reach the question of the adequacy of deposits.

B. *Undue Experimentation.*

Although inventions involving microorganisms or other living cells often can be enabled by a deposit, a deposit is not always necessary to satisfy the enablement requirement. No deposit is necessary if the biological organisms can be obtained from readily available sources or derived from readily available starting materials through routine screening that does not require undue experimentation. Whether the specification in an application involving living cells (here, hybridomas) is enabled without a deposit must be decided on the facts of the particular case.

Appellants contend that their written specification fully enables the practice of their claimed invention because the monoclonal antibodies needed to perform the immunoassays can be made from readily available starting materials using methods that are well known in the monoclonal antibody art. Wands states that application of these methods to make high-affinity IgM anti-HBsAg antibodies requires only routine screening, and that does not amount to undue experimentation. There is no challenge to their contention that the starting materials (i.e., mice, HBsAg antigen, and myeloma cells) are available to the public. The PTO concedes that the methods used to prepare hybridomas and to screen them for high-affinity IgM antibodies against HBsAg were either well known in the monoclonal antibody art or adequately disclosed in the '145 patent and in the current application. This is consistent with this court's recognition with respect to another patent application that methods for obtaining and screening monoclonal antibodies were well known in 1980.

The sole issue is whether, in this particular case, it would require undue experimentation to produce high-affinity IgM monoclonal antibodies.

Enablement is not precluded by the necessity for some experimentation such as routine screening. However, experimentation needed to practice the invention must not be undue experimentation. "The key word is 'undue,' not 'experimentation.'"

The determination of what constitutes undue experimentation in a given case requires the application of a standard of reasonableness, having due regard for the nature of the invention and the state of the art. The test is not merely quantitative, since a considerable amount of experimentation is permissible, if it is merely routine, or if the specification in question provides a reasonable amount of guidance with respect to the direction in which the experimentation should proceed.

The term "undue experimentation" does not appear in the statute, but it is well established that enablement requires that the specification teach those in the art to make and use the invention without undue experimentation. Whether undue experimentation is needed is not a single, simple factual determination, but rather is a conclusion reached by weighing many factual considerations. The board concluded that undue experimentation would be needed to practice the invention on the basis of experimental data presented by Wands. These data are not in dispute. However, Wands and the board disagree strongly on the conclusion that should be drawn from that data.

Factors to be considered in determining whether a disclosure would require undue experimentation have been summarized by the board in *In re Forman*, 230 USPQ at 547. They include (1) the quantity of experimentation necessary, (2) the amount of direction or guidance presented, (3) the presence or absence of working examples, (4) the nature of the invention, (5) the state of the prior art, (6) the relative skill of those in the art, (7) the predictability or unpredictability of the art, and (8) the breadth of the claims.

In order to understand whether the rejection was proper, it is necessary to discuss further the methods for making specific monoclonal antibodies. The first step for making monoclonal antibodies is to immunize an animal. The '145 patent provides a detailed description of procedures for immunizing a specific strain of mice against HBsAg. Next the spleen, an organ rich in lymphocytes, is removed and the lymphocytes are separated from the other spleen cells. The lymphocytes are mixed with myeloma cells, and the mixture is treated to cause a few of the cells to fuse with each other. Hybridoma cells that secrete the desired antibodies then must be isolated from the enormous number of other cells in the mixture. This is down through a series of screening procedures.

The first step is to separate the hybridoma cells from unfused lymphocytes and myeloma cells. The cells are cultured in a medium in which all the lymphocytes and myeloma cells die, and only the hybridoma cells survive. The next step is to isolate and clone hybridomas that make antibodies that bind to the antigen of interest. Single hybridoma cells are placed in separate chambers and are allowed to grow and divide. After there are enough cells in the clone to produce sufficient quantities of antibody to analyze, the antibody is assayed to determine whether it binds to the antigen. Generally, antibodies from many clones do not bind the antigen, and these clones are discarded. However, by screening enough clones (often hundreds at a time), hybridomas may be found that secrete antibodies against the antigen of interest.

Wands used a commercially available radio immunoassay kit to screen clones for cells that produce antibodies directed against HBsAg. In this assay the amount of radioactivity bound gives some indication of the strength of the antibody-antigen binding, but does not yield a numerical affinity constant, which must be measured using the more laborious Scatchard analysis. In order to determine which anti-HBsAg antibodies satisfy all of the limitations of appellants' claims, the antibodies require further screening to select those which have an IgM isotype and have a binding affinity constant of at least 109 M–1. The PTO does not question that the screening techniques used by Wands were well known in the monoclonal antibody art.

During prosecution Wands submitted a declaration under 37 C.F.R. § 1.132 providing information about all of the hybridomas that appellants had produced before filing the patent application. The first four fusions were unsuccessful and produced no hybridomas. The next six fusion experiments all produced hybridomas that made antibodies specific for HBsAg. Antibodies that bound at least 10,000 cpm in the commercial radioimmunassay were classified as "high binders." Using this criterion, 143 high-binding hybridomas were obtained. In the declaration, Wands stated that.[27]

---

27. A table in the declaration presented the binding data for antibodies from every cell line. Values ranged from 13,867 to 125,-204 cpm, and a substantial proportion of

It is generally accepted in the art that, among those antibodies which are binders with 50,000 cpm or higher, there is a very high likelihood that high affinity (Ka [greater than] 109 M–1–1) antibodies will be found. However, high affinity antibodies can also be found among high binders of between 10,000 and 50,000, as is clearly demonstrated in the Table.

The PTO has not challenged this statement.

The declaration stated that a few of the high-binding monoclonal antibodies from two fusions were chosen for further screening. The remainder of the antibodies and the hybridomas that produced them were saved by freezing. Only nine antibodies were subjected to further analysis. Four (three from one fusion and one from another fusion) fell within the claims, that is, were IgM antibodies and had a binding affinity constant of at least 109 M–1–1. Of the remaining five antibodies, three were found to be IgG, while the other two were IgM for which the affinity constants were not measured (although both showed binding well above 50,000 cpm).

Apparently none of the frozen cell lines received any further analysis. The declaration explains that after useful high-affinity IgM monoclonal antibodies to HBsAg had been found, it was considered unnecessary to return to the stored antibodies to screen for more IgMs. Wands says that the existence of the stored hybridomas was disclosed to the PTO to comply with the requirement under 37 C.F.R. § 1.56 that applicants fully disclose all of their relevant data, and not just favorable results. How these stored hybridomas are viewed is central to the positions of the parties.

The position of the board emphasizes the fact that since the stored cell lines were not completely tested, there is no proof that any of them are IgM antibodies with a binding affinity constant of at least 109 M–1–1. Thus, only 4 out of 143 hybridomas, or 2.8 percent, were proved to fall within the claims. Furthermore, antibodies that were proved to be high-affinity IgM came from only 2 of 10 fusion experiments. These statistics are viewed by the board as evidence that appellants' methods were not predictable or reproducible. The board concludes that Wands' low rate of demonstrated success shows that a person skilled in the art would have to engage in undue experimentation in order to make antibodies that fall within the claims.

Wands views the data quite differently. Only nine hybridomas were actually analyzed beyond the initial screening for HBsAg binding. Of these, four produced antibodies that fell within the claims, a respectable 44 percent rate of success. (Furthermore, since the two additional IgM antibodies for which the affinity constants were never measured showed binding in excess of 50,000 cpm, it is likely that these also fall within the

the antibodies showed binding greater than 50,000 cpm. In confirmation of Dr. Wand's statement, two antibodies with binding less than 25,000 cpm were found to have affinity constants greater than 109 M–1.

claims.) Wands argues that the remaining 134 unanalyzed, stored cell lines should not be written off as failures. Instead, if anything, they represent partial success. Each of the stored hybridomas had been shown to produce a high-binding antibody specific for HBsAg. Many of these antibodies showed binding above 50,000 cpm and are thus highly likely to have a binding affinity constant of at least 109 M–1–1. Extrapolating from the nine hybridomas that were screened for isotype (and from what is well known in the monoclonal antibody art about isotype frequency), it is reasonable to assume that the stored cells include some that produce IgM. Thus, if the 134 incompletely analyzed cell lines are considered at all, they provide some support (albeit without rigorous proof) to the view that hybridomas falling within the claims are not so rare that undue experimentation would be needed to make them.

The first four fusion attempts were failures, while high-binding antibodies were produced in the next six fusions. Appellants contend that the initial failures occurred because they had not yet learned to fuse cells successfully. Once they became skilled in the art, they invariably obtained numerous hybridomas that made high-binding antibodies against HBsAg and, in each fusion where they determined isotype and binding affinity they obtained hybridomas that fell within the claims.

Wands also submitted a second declaration under 37 C.F.R. § 1.132 stating that after the patent application was submitted they performed an eleventh fusion experiment and obtained another hybridoma that made a high-affinity IgM anti-HBsAg antibody. No information was provided about the number of clones screened in that experiment. The board determined that, because there was no indication as to the number of hybridomas screened, this declaration had very little value. While we agree that it would have been preferable if Wands had included this information, the declaration does show that when appellants repeated their procedures they again obtained a hybridoma that produced an antibody that fit all of the limitations of their claims.

We conclude that the board's interpretation of the data is erroneous. It is strained and unduly harsh to classify the stored cell lines (each of which was proved to make high-binding antibodies against HBsAg) as failures demonstrating that Wands' methods are unpredictable or unreliable.[29] At worst, they prove nothing at all about the probability of success, and merely show that appellants were prudent in not discarding cells that might someday prove useful. At best, they show that high-binding antibodies, the starting materials for IgM screening and Scatchard analysis, can be produced in large numbers. The PTO's position leads to the absurd conclusion that the more hybridomas an applicant makes and saves without testing, the less predictable the applicant's results become. Furthermore, Wands' explanation that the first four attempts at cell fusion failed only because they had not yet learned to

---

29. Even if we were to accept the PTO's 2.8% success rate, we would not be required to reach a conclusion of undue experimentation. Such a determination must be made in view of the circumstances of each case and cannot be made solely by reference to a particular numerical cutoff.

perform fusions properly is reasonable in view of the fact that the next six fusions were all successful. The record indicates that cell fusion is a technique that is well known to those of ordinary skill in the monoclonal antibody art, and there has been no claim that the fusion step should be more difficult or unreliable where the antigen is HBsAg than it would be for other antigens.

When Wands' data is interpreted in a reasonable manner, analysis considering the factors enumerated in *In re Forman* leads to the conclusion that undue experimentation would not be required to practice the invention. Wands' disclosure provides considerable direction and guidance on how to practice their invention and presents working examples. There was a high level of skill in the art at the time when the application was filed, and all of the methods needed to practice the invention were well known.

The nature of monoclonal antibody technology is that it involves screening hybridomas to determine which ones secrete antibody with desired characteristics. Practitioners of this art are prepared to screen negative hybridomas in order to find one that makes the desired antibody. No evidence was presented by either party on how many hybridomas would be viewed by those in the art as requiring undue experimentation to screen. However, it seems unlikely that undue experimentation would be defined in terms of the number of hybridomas that were never screened. Furthermore, in the monoclonal antibody art it appears that an "experiment" is not simply the screening of a single hybridoma, but is rather the entire attempt to make a monoclonal antibody against a particular antigen. This process entails immunizing animals, fusing lymphocytes from the immunized animals with myeloma cells to make hybridomas, cloning the hybridomas, and screening the antibodies produced by the hybridomas for the desired characteristics. Wands carried out this entire procedure three times, and was successful each time in making at least one antibody that satisfied all of the claim limitations. Reasonably interpreted, Wands' record indicates that, in the production of high-affinity IgM antibodies against HBsAG, the amount of effort needed to obtain such antibodies is not excessive. Wands' evidence thus effectively rebuts the examiner's challenge to the enablement of their disclosure.

IV. CONCLUSION

Considering all of the factors, we conclude that it would not require undue experimentation to obtain antibodies needed to practice the claimed invention. Accordingly, the rejection of Wands' claims for lack of enablement under 35 U.S.C. § 112, first paragraph, is reversed.

Notes

1. Lack of enablement issues often arise in cases from high technology areas such as biotech and semiconductors. Why?

2. Evidence that it took those in the art a lot of time to practice the invention strongly suggests "undue experimentation." *See, e.g., Genentech,*

Inc. v. Novo Nordisk, 108 F.3d 1361, 1366, 42 USPQ2d 1001, 1006 (Fed. Cir. 1997) ("If, as Genentech argues, one skilled in the art, armed only with what the patent specification discloses (a DNA sequence encoding a human protein, in this case, hGH, and a single example of an enzyme and its cleavage site), could have used cleavable fusion expression to make a human protein without undue experimentation, it is remarkable that this method was not used to make any human protein for nearly a year or to make hGH for five years." (citations omitted)); *White Consol. Indus., v. Vega Servo–Control, Inc.*, 713 F.2d 788, 790–92, 218 USPQ 961, 962–64 (Fed. Cir. 1983) (a requirement of 18 months to two years of work to practice the patented invention is "undue experimentation"); *In re Ghiron*, 442 F.2d 985, 992, 169 USPQ 723, 727–28 (C.C.P.A. 1971) (a development period of "many months or years … does not bespeak a routine operation but of extensive experimentation and development work").

3. In a recent case, *Genentech, Inc. v. Novo Nordisk*, 108 F.3d 1361, 1366, 42 USPQ2d 1001, 1005 (Fed. Cir. 1997), the Federal Circuit discussed the enablement requirement as follows:

> Patent protection is granted in return for an enabling disclosure of an invention, not for vague intimations of general ideas that may or may not be workable. Tossing out the mere germ of an idea does not constitute enabling disclosure. While every aspect of a generic claim certainly need not have been carried out by an inventor, or exemplified in the specification, reasonable detail must be provided in order to enable members of the public to understand and carry out the invention.

> [A] specification need not disclose what is well known in the art. However, that general, oft-repeated statement is merely a rule of supplementation, not a substitute for a basic enabling disclosure. It means that the omission of minor details does not cause a specification to fail to meet the enablement requirement. However, when there is no disclosure of any specific starting material or of any of the conditions under which a process can be carried out, undue experimentation is required … It is the specification, not the knowledge of one skilled in the art, that must supply the novel aspects of an invention in order to constitute adequate enablement.

(citations omitted). This case was especially interesting because what was appealed was a grant of a preliminary injunction. The Federal Circuit did not, however, limit itself to a reversal of the grant, but rather went on to hold (*sua sponte*) that the claims at issue were not enabled and therefore the patent was invalid. The court justified doing so because the parties had argued during oral argument on appeal that the enablement issue had been "thoroughly ventilated" below at the district court.

4. **A question of law with underlying facts.** Although the question of enablement is one of law, it hinges on several underlying facts, examples of which are given below:

> Enablement, i.e., whether a reference teaches those skilled in the art to make and use the invention without "undue experimentation," is a question of law, which may involve subsidiary questions of fact. In the present case, two primary questions of fact remain

open that prevent this court from deciding the issue. First, who was the person of ordinary skill in the art in the mid-to-early–1970's? Second, what procedures were known by those persons of ordinary skill? Based on these factual determinations, as well as secondary factual considerations, such as the amount of time necessary to conduct experiments in this field and the difficulties encountered in such experimentation, enablement can be resolved.

Abbott Labs. v. Diamedix Corp., 969 F. Supp. 1064, 1069, 43 USPQ2d 1448, 1452 (N.D. Ill. 1997) (citations omitted). Note that enablement must be considered in light of the state of the art as it exists on the date of filing.

3. FAILURE TO SATISFY THE WRITTEN DESCRIPTION REQUIREMENT

To fully identify what is claimed, the patent application is required to include a clear and concise written description. The description may be embodied in attached drawings and diagrams or the original claims. The following case considers the written description requirement in detail.

GENTRY GALLERY, INC. v. BERKLINE CORP.

134 F.3d 1473, 45 USPQ2d 1498 (Fed. Cir. 1998)

LOURIE, Circuit Judge.

The Gentry Gallery appeals from the judgment of the United States District Court for the District of Massachusetts holding that the Berkline Corporation does not infringe U.S. Patent 5,064,244, and declining to award attorney fees for Gentry's defense to Berkline's assertion that the patent was unenforceable. Berkline cross-appeals from the decision that the patent was not shown to be invalid. [B]ecause the court clearly erred in finding that the written description portion of the specification supported certain of the broader claims asserted by Gentry, we reverse the decision that those claims are not invalid under 35 U.S.C. § 112, ¶ 1 (1994).

BACKGROUND

Gentry owns the '244 patent, which is directed to a unit of a sectional sofa in which two independent reclining seats ("recliners") face in the same direction. Sectional sofas are typically organized in an L-shape with "arms" at the exposed ends of the linear sections. According to the patent specification, because recliners usually have had adjustment controls on their arms, sectional sofas were able to contain two recliners only if they were located at the exposed ends of the linear sections. Due to the typical L-shaped configuration of sectional sofas, the recliners therefore faced in different directions. Such an arrangement was "not usually comfortable when the occupants are watching television because one or both occupants must turn their heads to watch the same [television] set. Furthermore, the separation of the two reclining seats at opposite ends of a sectional sofa is not comfortable or conducive to intimate conversation.''

The invention of the patent solved this supposed dilemma by, inter alia, placing a ''console'' between two recliners which face in the same direction. This console ''accommodates the controls for both reclining seats,'' thus eliminating the need to position each recliner at an exposed end of a linear section. Accordingly, both recliners can then be located on the same linear section allowing two people to recline while watching television and facing in the same direction. Claim 1, which is the broadest claim of the patent, reads in relevant part:

> A sectional sofa comprising:
>
> a pair of reclining seats disposed in parallel relationship with one another in a double reclining seat sectional sofa section being without an arm at one end . . .,
>
> each of said reclining seats having a backrest and seat cushions and movable between upright and reclined positions . . .,
>
> a *fixed console* disposed in the double reclining seat sofa section between the pair of reclining seats and with the console and reclining seats together comprising a unitary structure,
>
> said console including an armrest portion for each of the reclining seats; said arm rests remaining fixed when the reclining seats move from one to another of their positions,
>
> and a *pair of control means*, one for each reclining seat; *mounted on the double reclining seat sofa section* . . . .

Claims 9, 10, 12–15, and 19–21 are directed to a sectional sofa in which the control means are specifically located on the console.

In 1991, Gentry filed suit in the District Court for the District of Massachusetts alleging that Berkline infringed the patent by manufacturing and selling sectional sofas having two recliners facing in the same direction. In the allegedly infringing sofas, the recliners were separated by a seat which has a back cushion that may be pivoted down onto the seat, so that the seat back may serve as a tabletop between the recliners. The district court granted Berkline's motion for summary judgment of non-infringement, but denied its motions for summary judgment of invalidity and unenforceability. In construing the language ''fixed console,'' the court relied on, inter alia, a statement made by the inventor named in the patent, James Sproule, in a Petition to Make Special (PTMS). *See* 37 C.F.R. § 1.102 (1997). Sproule had attempted to distinguish his invention from a prior art reference by arguing that that reference, U.S. Patent 3,877,747 to Brennan et al. (''Brennan''), ''shows a complete center seat with a tray in its back.'' Based on Sproule's argument, the court concluded that, as a matter of law, Berkline's sofas ''contain[ ] a drop-down tray identical to the one employed by the Brennan product'' and therefore did not have a ''fixed console'' and did not literally infringe the patent.

Gentry then requested that final judgment be entered so that it could immediately appeal the non-infringement decision. Berkline requested that its invalidity and unenforceability counterclaims proceed to trial on the authority of *Cardinal Chemical Co. v. Morton International, Inc.*, 508 U.S. 83, 26 USPQ2d 1721 (1993). The court agreed with Berkline, stating "that further proceedings will be necessary on the issues of invalidity and inequitable conduct." After a bench trial, the court held that the patent was not invalid under 35 U.S.C. §§ 102 or 103 (1994), and that the claims in which the location of the controls is not limited to the console (claims 1–8, 11, and 16–18) are not invalid under 35 U.S.C. § 112, ¶ 1 (1994)....

DISCUSSION

Berkline ... argues that claims 1–8, 11, and 16–18 are invalid because they are directed to sectional sofas in which the location of the recliner controls is not limited to the console. According to Berkline, because the patent only describes sofas having controls on the console and an object of the invention is to provide a sectional sofa "with a console ... that accommodates the controls for both the reclining seats," '244 patent, col. 1, ll. 35–37, the claimed sofas are not described within the meaning of § 112, ¶ 1. Berkline also relies on Sproule's testimony that "locating the controls on the console is definitely the way we solved it [the problem of building sectional sofa with parallel recliners] on the original group [of sofas]." Gentry responds that the disclosure represents only Sproule's preferred embodiment, in which the controls are on the console, and therefore supports claims directed to a sofa in which the controls may be located elsewhere. Gentry relies on *Ethicon Endo–Surgery, Inc. v. United States Surgical Corp.*, 93 F.3d 1572, 1582 n. 7, 40 USPQ2d 1019, 1027 n. 7 (Fed. Cir. 1996), and *In re Rasmussen*, 650 F.2d 1212, 1214, 211 USPQ 323, 326 (C.C.P.A. 1981), for the proposition that an applicant need not describe more than one embodiment of a broad claim to adequately support that claim.

We agree with Berkline that the patent's disclosure does not support claims in which the location of the recliner controls is other than on the console. Whether a specification complies with the written description requirement of § 112, ¶ 1, is a question of fact, which we review for clear error on appeal from a bench trial. To fulfill the written description requirement, the patent specification "must clearly allow persons of ordinary skill in the art to recognize that [the inventor] invented what is claimed." An applicant complies with the written description requirement "by describing the invention, with all its claimed limitations." *Lockwood v. American Airlines, Inc.*, 107 F.3d 1565, 1572, 41 USPQ2d 1961, 1966 (Fed. Cir. 1997).

It is a truism that a claim need not be limited to a preferred embodiment. However, in a given case, the scope of the right to exclude may be limited by a narrow disclosure. For example, as we have recently held, a disclosure of a television set with a keypad, connected to a central computer with a video disk player did not support claims directed to "an individual terminal containing a video disk player." *See id.* (stating that claims directed to a "distinct invention from that disclosed in the specification" do not satisfy the written description requirement); *see also Regents of the Univ. of Cal. v. Eli Lilly & Co.*, 119 F.3d 1559, 1568, 43 USPQ2d 1398, 1405 (Fed. Cir. 1997) (stating that the case law does "not compel the conclusion that a description of a species always constitutes a description of a genus of which it is a part").

In this case, the original disclosure clearly identifies the console as the only possible location for the controls. It provides for only the most minor variation in the location of the controls, noting that the control "may be mounted on top or side surfaces of the console rather than on the front wall ... without departing from this invention." No similar variation beyond the console is even suggested. Additionally, the only discernible purpose for the console is to house the controls. As the disclosure states, identifying the only purpose relevant to the console, "[a]nother object of the present invention is to provide ... a console positioned between [the reclining seats] that accommodates the controls for both of the reclining seats." Thus, locating the controls anywhere but on the console is outside the stated purpose of the invention. Moreover, consistent with this disclosure, Sproule's broadest original claim was directed to a sofa comprising, inter alia, "control means located upon the center console to enable each of the pair of reclining seats to move separately between the reclined and upright positions." Finally, although not dispositive, because one can add claims to a pending application directed to adequately described subject matter, Sproule admitted at trial that he did not consider placing the controls outside the console until he became aware that some of Gentry's competitors were so locating the recliner controls. Accordingly, when viewed in its entirety, the disclosure is limited to sofas in which the recliner control is located on the console.

Gentry's reliance on *Ethicon* is misplaced. It is true, as Gentry observes, that we noted that "an applicant ... is generally allowed claims, when the art permits, which cover more than the specific embodiment shown." However, we were also careful to point out in that opinion that the applicant "was free to draft claim[s] broadly (within the limits imposed by the prior art) to exclude the lockout's exact location as a limitation of the claimed invention" only because he "did not consider the precise location of the lockout to be an element of his invention." Here, as indicated above, it is clear that Sproule considered the location of the recliner controls on the console to be an essential element of his invention. Accordingly, his original disclosure serves to limit the permissible breadth of his later-drafted claims.

Similarly, *In re Rasmussen* does not support Gentry's position. In that case, our predecessor court restated the uncontroversial proposition that "a claim may be broader than the specific embodiment disclosed in a specification." However, the court also made clear that "[a]n applicant is entitled to claims as broad as the prior art and his disclosure will allow." 650 F.2d 1212, 211 USPQ at 326. The claims at issue in *Rasmussen*, which were limited to the generic step of "adheringly applying" one layer to an adjacent layer, satisfied the written description requirement only because "one skilled in the art who read [the] specification would understand that it is unimportant how the layers are adhered, so long as they are adhered." Here, on the contrary, one skilled in the art would clearly understand that it was not only important, but essential to Sproule's invention, for the controls to be on the console.

In sum, the cases on which Gentry relies do not stand for the proposition that an applicant can broaden his claims to the extent that they are effectively bounded only by the prior art. Rather, they make clear that claims may be no broader than the supporting disclosure, and therefore that a narrow disclosure will limit claim breadth. Here, Sproule's disclosure unambiguously limited the location of the controls to the console. Accordingly, the district court clearly erred in finding that he was entitled to claims in which the recliner controls are not located on the console. We therefore reverse the judgment that claims 1–8, 11, and 16–18, were not shown to be invalid.

Notes

1.   Many believe that the *Gentry Gallery* case dramatically expanded the scope of the written description requirement when it held a genus claim for a simple mechanical invention was invalid for failure to disclose each possible species in the original specification. *See, e.g.,* Laurence H. Pretty, *The Recline and Fall of Mechanical Genus Claim Scope under the "Written Description" in the Sofa Case,* 80 J. Pat. & Trademark Off. Soc'y 469 (1998); Janice M. Mueller, *The Evolving Application of the Written Description Requirement to Biotechnological Inventions,* 13 Berkeley Tech. L.J. 615 (1998). Should the "written description" requirement be more lenient for predictable arts (such as mechanical and electrical inventions) and stricter for unpredictable arts (such as chemical and biotech inventions)?

2.   Judges, juries, and practitioners often confuse the enablement requirement and the written description requirement. The written description and enablement requirement are independent requirements. Satisfying the enablement requirement does not necessarily satisfy the written description requirement. Keep in mind that for enablement, the patent need not disclose things that one of skill in the art would already know. The same is not true for written description. To satisfy the written description requirement, the patent disclosure must support the claims to demonstrate that the inventor possessed the invention at the time the patent application was filed. The written description requirement serves as a benchmark for what was within the scope of the patentee's inventive contribution as of his filing date.

3.   The Federal Circuit held that the written description requirement may be satisfied by a drawing. *See Vas–Cath Inc. v. Mahurkar,* 935 F.2d 1555, 1565, 19 USPQ2d 1111, 1118 (Fed. Cir. 1991). Does this fit within the literal statutory language of § 112? Is the drawing part of the specification under § 112? Are the claims part of the specification under § 112? The written description requirement can also be satisfied by the originally filed claims because they are a part of the original filing, but not by any amended claims. Claims amended or added after the original filing date cannot satisfy the written description requirement because they would constitute new

matter. *See In re Benno*, 768 F.2d 1340, 1346, 226 USPQ 683, 686–87 (Fed. Cir. 1985). Note that in *Gentry Gallery* the claims of the '244 patent, which were held to be invalid because there was no disclosure in the original specification for location of the controls anywhere but on the console, were added after the original filing date. The patentee amended the patent claims during prosecution to broaden them so that they would cover control locations other than the console, after he saw a competitor's product that located the controls elsewhere. If these claims had been present in the originally filed application, would the patent still be invalid for failure to satisfy the written description requirement?

4. **A Question of Fact.** Note that whether a patent specification complies with the written description requirement is a question of fact. The primary considerations have traditionally been the nature of the invention (predictable or unpredictable) and the amount of knowledge imparted to those skilled in the art by the disclosure.

Problems

1. Are the claims of the '835 patent in Chapter Eight supported by the written description?

2. Ms. Liz Horn invents a new type of chain for use on a bicycle. Her claims are to a bicycle with two wheels, the new chain, pedals, a seat and handle bars. In her specification, she discloses as her preferred embodiment, the use of the chain on a bicycle. About 1 year after her patent issues, she discovers that a competitor, Novelty Bikes, is selling tricycles, unicycles, and tandem bikes using her patented chain. How would you advise Ms. Horn?

3. Robert Pace designed a new videophone while working for BIG Electronic Company. BIG is the assignee of the '000 patent claiming the videophone. The patent application was filed on December 1, 1997 and issued January 1, 1999. The patent claims are broadly drafted to cover the use of any imaging chip in the videophone. The specification disclosed only the RC imaging chip in the preferred embodiment.

You represent RC Electronics. BIG has sued RC for patent infringement arguing that RC's videophone which uses the RC imaging chip infringes the '000 patent.

In response to a document request, you receive a memo dated June 15, 1997, from Ms. Linda to the company president, informing her that the videophone would work better with a DAX BIG imaging chip rather than the RC imaging chip Pace currently uses. The memo cc'd Pace. There was a second memo dated June 16, 1997, from the company president to Ms. Linda instructing her not to communicate any of her conclusions to Pace and to start working on a commercial prototype using the superior DAX BIG chip right away. At this point, Pace was walled off from the videophone progress. Test results performed at BIG during September 1997 confirmed that the DAX BIG chip improved the videophone's performance. BIG had the product ready for mass production by December 1998 (in time for the Christmas season).

During Pace's deposition, he says that he received the memo from Ms. Linda, but he disagreed with her claim that the DAX BIG chip would work better. He told the company president that he would need to test the DAX BIG chip to determine whether Linda was correct. The company president responded by assigning him to a new engineering team and a new project, essentially walling him off from any further work on the videophone. Pace tells you that he was not sure the DAX BIG chip would work at all and that he thought it would require a massive redesign of his videophone to employ the chip. As of June 1997, the only chip Pace knew would work was the RC chip. After seeing BIG's commercial product using the DAX BIG chip, Pace agrees that it is superior to the RC chip.

Do you have any possible 112 defenses?

Chapter Twelve

PROVING UNENFORCEABILITY

INTRODUCTION

In addition to challenging the validity of the patent, the accused infringer may want to bring a defense that the patent is unenforceable. Unenforceability is distinctly different from a holding of invalidity although the result may be the same—the patentee cannot enforce his patent. Whether the patent is permanently unenforceable against all infringers, unenforceable against this defendant or unenforceable only for a period of time depends on the action by the patentee which gives rise to the unenforceability. Unenforceability of a patent is an equitable matter which the judge must decide. However, many judges will permit juries to hear the inequitable conduct case and render a special verdict in an advisory role. Ultimately, the judge must determine whether inequitable conduct has occurred. There are several grounds upon which a patent may be held unenforceable including: inequitable conduct, laches, equitable estoppel, patent misuse or shop rights. This chapter will explore the defense of unenforceability.

A. INEQUITABLE CONDUCT— THE BALANCING TEST

RULE 56: Duty To Disclose Information Material To Patentability[1]

REGULATORY PROVISION—37 C.F.R. § 1.56

(a) A duty of candor and good faith toward the Patent and Trademark Office rests on the inventor, on each attorney or agent who prepares or prosecutes the application and on every other individual who is substantively involved in the preparation or prosecution of the application.... All such individuals have a duty to disclose to the Office information they are aware of which is material to the examination of the application. Such information is material where there is a substantial likelihood that a reasonable examiner would consider it important in deciding whether to allow the application to issue as a patent.

---

1. *See* Note 2, *infra*.

Inequitable conduct was originally called "fraud on the patent office." Inequitable conduct is a defense to an infringement charge. In fact, the patentee's competitors (those accused of infringement) are the best watchdogs on the integrity of the disclosures made to the PTO. If the patentee acted inequitably towards the PTO, such action may be uncovered during discovery. To succeed on a charge of inequitable conduct the accused infringer must prove that the patentee withheld material information from the PTO during prosecution of the patent with an intent to deceive. Hence there are two elements to an inequitable conduct charge:

(1) materiality; and

(2) intent.

Both of these elements must be proven by a preponderance of the evidence. If the accused infringer meets this burden and makes a threshold showing of each, the court will balance the factors to determine if inequitable conduct has occurred. If the accused infringer has made a very strong showing of materiality, then less evidence of intent need be established and *vice versa*. If the accused infringer is successful in proving inequitable conduct the patent will be held unenforceable. The patent is unenforceable against all infringers and the unenforceability is permanent; it is not curable.

Under Rule 56, the inventor, the patent attorney who prepares the application, and any other person who participates in the preparation of the application are all bound by the duty of candor to the PTO. This means that if the patent attorney is aware of a material reference, it must be disclosed, even if the inventor is not aware of it.

A word of caution. Inequitable conduct should not be routinely pled in every infringement action.

1. MATERIALITY

MOLINS PLC v. TEXTRON, INC.

48 F.3d 1172, 33 USPQ2d 1823 (Fed. Cir. 1995)

Before LOURIE, NIES and NEWMAN, Circuit Judges.

LOURIE, Circuit Judge.

Molins PLC and John Coventry Smith, Jr. appeal from a judgment of the United States District Court for the District of Delaware holding U.S. Patents 4,369,563 and 4,621,410 unenforceable due to inequitable conduct and awarding attorney fees, costs, and expenses against Molins and Smith, jointly and severally. We affirm-in-part, vacate-in-part, and remand.

BACKGROUND

In 1965, Molins' Research Director, Dr. David Williamson, developed a method for improving batch machining involving a plurality of machine tools arranged to accommodate the manual transport of pallet-mounted workpieces to and from the machine tools (the "batch process"). Molins filed a British patent application for the batch process in the fall of 1965 and filed counterpart applications in a number of countries, including the United States.

In 1966, Williamson invented a fully automated machining system that allows several related families of parts to be machined simultaneously (the "system 24"). Molins filed patent applications for the system 24 in the United Kingdom, the United States, and in other countries during 1966–67. In 1967, the U.S. batch process application was combined with the U.S. system 24 application in a continuation-in-part. The '563 patent later matured from a continuation-in-part of the combined U.S. application. Before the patent issued in January of 1983, however, the batch process claims were canceled and only claims drawn to the system 24 apparatus issued. The '410 patent issued from a divisional application and is directed to the system 24 method of machining.

The '563 patent discloses a system of complementary, numerically-controlled machine tools. Materials to be machined, or "workpieces," are subjected to selected machining operations on selected machine tools in a selected order by the delivery of common form pallets loaded with the workpieces. Transporters deliver pallets between the machine tools, a storage rack, and work stations where the workpieces are automatically delivered in bins from a bin store and are loaded on the pallets. Tool magazines are delivered between a rack and the machine tools by a transporter. A computer controls transport and machining operations, and receives signals from monitors indicating the location of pallets, tool magazines, and bins.

Dennis Whitson began working for Molins in 1967 as one of several British chartered patent agents working in Molins' in-house patent department. He managed Molins' patent department from 1974 through 1981 and was responsible for the prosecution of all of Molins' patent applications directed to the batch process and system 24 inventions. When Whitson retired in 1981, Ivan Hirsh, employed by Molins since 1968, assumed the responsibilities as manager of Molins' patent department. After becoming manager, Hirsh assumed responsibility for prosecuting the applications relating to the patents in suit and for conducting the litigation involving Molins' patents.

Smith served as the primary United States counsel to Molins, representing Molins at the United States Patent and Trademark Office from 1966 through the relevant time period in this case. Beginning in 1967, Smith prosecuted the patent applications leading to the issuance of the '563 and '410 patents. In January of 1980, Molins assigned a one-half interest in the patent applications to Smith in exchange for Smith's agreement to undertake further prosecution at his own expense. In July of 1988, Smith reassigned his interest in the patents to Molins. Smith remained entitled to one-half of all royalty income received by Molins from licenses under the patents entered into prior to July 1, 1988.

Between the fall of 1967 and April 1968, while the relevant U.S. patent applications were pending, Molins' patent department, and specifically Whitson, became aware of prior art referred to here as the "Wagenseil reference." Upon evaluating the Wagenseil reference, Whitson concluded that it fully anticipated the "batch process" claims that Molins initially filed in the United Kingdom and in many other countries including the United States. Accordingly, in 1968 and 1969, Whitson abandoned all the foreign patent applications to the batch process. However, Whitson decided not to abandon the pending U.S. application because it contained both batch process and system 24 claims.

Prosecution of the U.S. and foreign system 24 applications continued. Wagenseil was cited to and by several foreign patent offices, but was not cited by Molins to the PTO. In 1975, Whitson told Smith that there were oppositions to the German system 24 patent application, but he did not inform Smith of the art cited in Germany, which included the Wagenseil reference. Eventually, Molins abandoned all foreign system 24 applications. In the United States, the '563 patent issued in January of 1983, after Molins prevailed in an interference with two other parties.

Later in 1983, Hirsh reviewed the files of the foreign system 24 applications, all of which had been abandoned in the late 1970s. Hirsh found the references that had been cited in the foreign patent prosecution, but not the PTO, including the Wagenseil reference. Hirsh also found Whitson's correspondence relating to the references and to their citation to and by foreign patent offices. Hirsh then informed Smith of the foreign citations. Together, they consulted with outside counsel and, on September 21, 1984, although the '563 patent had already issued, filed a lengthy prior art statement under 37 C.F.R. § 1.501 (Rule 501) on behalf of Molins, listing the Wagenseil reference together with all other prior art references that had been cited during the foreign prosecution.

In October of 1984, Cross & Trecker, Incorporated, the parent corporation of defendant Kearney & Trecker Corporation, filed a request for reexamination of the '563 patent in view of several IBM references. Cross & Trecker filed a Form PTO–1449 listing Wagenseil, which was initialed by the examiner as having been considered in June of 1985. During the reexamination, Molins referred the examiner to the Rule 501 prior art statement previously filed in the '563 patent file. The examiner indicated that, in order to make the prior art of record, Molins was required to submit English language translations of the foreign language references. Accordingly, Molins filed the translations and a brief statement of the relevance of the cited art. The examiner initialed each reference Molins had listed, indicating that he had considered it. The examiner's final office action in the reexamination stated that he had considered all of the cited references. No claims were rejected based on Wagenseil during the reexamination. Re–Examination Certificate B1 4,369,563 was issued on May 13, 1986.

Late in 1986, Molins and Smith filed suit against Textron, Incorporated, Kearney & Trecker, and Avco Corporation (collectively "Textron"), alleging infringement of the '563 and '410 patents. In February of 1989, after approximately three years of discovery, Textron filed a summary judgment motion asserting that the patents were unenforceable due to inequitable conduct in connection with the prosecution of the '563 patent, in particular, concealment of Wagenseil and other information from the PTO. The motion was denied. After more discovery, in June of 1990, Textron again moved for summary judgment, adding new allegations of inequitable conduct relating to Smith's failure to disclose to the PTO allegedly material information regarding a co-pending patent application in the name of Jerome Lemelson, whom Smith also represented. Again, the court denied summary judgment. The court severed the issue of inequitable conduct, and held a bench trial.

On November 24, 1992, the court held that both patents were unenforceable due to inequitable conduct.

DISCUSSION

Inequitable Conduct

Applicants for patents are required to prosecute patent applications in the PTO with candor, good faith, and honesty. This duty extends also to the applicant's representatives. *See FMC Corp. v. Manitowoc Co.*, 835 F.2d 1411, 1415 n. 8, 5 USPQ2d 1112, 1115 n. 8 (Fed. Cir. 1987) (the knowledge and actions of an applicant's representative are chargeable to the applicant). A breach of this duty constitutes inequitable conduct.

Inequitable conduct includes affirmative misrepresentation of a material fact, failure to disclose material information, or submission of false material information, coupled with an intent to deceive. One who alleges inequitable conduct arising from a failure to disclose prior art must offer clear and convincing proof of the materiality of the prior art, knowledge chargeable to the applicant of that prior art and of its materiality, and the applicant's failure to disclose the prior art, coupled with an intent to mislead the PTO.

The withholding of information must meet thresholds of both materiality and intent. Once threshold findings of materiality and intent are established, the court must weigh them to determine whether the equities warrant a conclusion that inequitable conduct occurred. In light of all the circumstances, an equitable judgment must be made concerning whether the applicant's conduct is so culpable that the patent should not be enforced.

1. Whitson's Nondisclosure of Wagenseil During Original Prosecution

Calling this case "the exceptional case among exceptional cases," the district court concluded that Whitson, Molins' in-house patent agent, had engaged in inequitable conduct in the procurement of the '563 patent because he failed to disclose Wagenseil to the PTO, even though he knew it was highly material. The court stated that "[a]lthough

[Textron has] not produced direct evidence of Whitson's intent to deceive, i.e. there are no 'smoking memos' implicating bad faith on the part of Whitson, the overwhelming circumstantial evidence presented in this case leaves little doubt that Whitson intentionally concealed the Wagenseil reference from the U.S. PTO knowing that it was highly material to the U.S. applications."

Although Molins concedes that Wagenseil is highly material to the batch process invention, Molins asserts that the court erred in finding that Wagenseil was material to the '563 patent claims, which relate only to the system 24 invention. Molins points out that, although Wagenseil was cited to and considered by the examiner during reexamination of the '563 patent and during examination of the divisional '410 patent, Wagenseil was not relied upon by the examiner to reject pending claims. According to Molins, Wagenseil was *ipso facto* not material.

Information is "material" when there is a substantial likelihood that a reasonable examiner would have considered the information important in deciding whether to allow the application to issue as a patent. If the information allegedly withheld is not as pertinent as that considered by the examiner, or is merely cumulative to that considered by the examiner, such information is not material.

We have held that the result of a PTO proceeding that assesses patentability in light of information not originally disclosed can be of strong probative value in determining whether the undisclosed information was material. However, the standard to be applied in determining whether a reference is "material" is not whether the particular examiner of the application at issue considered the reference to be important; rather, it is that of a "reasonable examiner." Nor is a reference immaterial simply because the claims are eventually deemed by an examiner to be patentable thereover. Thus, the fact that the examiner did not rely on Wagenseil to reject the claims under reexamination or the '410 method claims is not conclusive concerning whether the reference was material.

The court found that Wagenseil was material because, among other things, it showed a storage and retrieval system in combination with a transfer system, a combination for which the examiner had relied upon two separate references to reject the '563 patent application claims. Moreover, the court found that Wagenseil disclosed relevant features beyond that shown in the prior art; in particular, Wagenseil disclosed a capability for workpieces to recirculate into a machining system and for workpieces to bypass certain machine tools within the system. None of the other prior art systems taught the "recirculate" and "bypass" features taught by Wagenseil.

The court further based its finding of materiality on extensive evidence showing that Whitson indicated during foreign prosecution that Wagenseil was the most relevant prior art to the corresponding foreign system 24 applications of which he was aware. Also, the evidence showed that patent examiners in several foreign countries considered Wagenseil material to the system 24 claims and that Whitson had amended and distinguished system 24 claims in foreign patent offices over Wagenseil. In this regard, the court was mindful of the risk in relying on foreign patent prosecution in light of differences in disclosure requirements, claim practice, form of application, and standard of patentability. On the evidence presented, even that independent of the admissions in the foreign prosecution, we cannot say that the court clearly erred in finding that a reasonable examiner would have considered Wagenseil important in deciding the patentability of the pending system 24 claims in the U.S. application.

3. Whitson's and Smith's Nondisclosure of the Lemelson Patents

During the prosecution of the claims that ultimately issued in the '563 patent, the principal references cited by the examiner against certain of the claims included patents issued in the name of Jerome Lemelson. These patents described an automatic storage system (U.S. Patent 3,049,247) and an automatic production apparatus (U.S. Patent 3,313,014 and its Reissue 26,770). The '014 patent was cited by the examiner in an office action in 1969. Subsequently, the examiner cited the '770 and '247 patents. The court determined that Whitson and Smith engaged in inequitable conduct because they knew of the Lemelson '247, '014, and '770 patents, which were highly material, and they did not disclose those patents to the PTO. Molins and Smith assert that the court erred when it concluded that Whitson and Smith engaged in inequitable conduct in failing to cite the Lemelson patents because the patents were actually cited by the PTO and considered during the '563 patent prosecution, were used to reject pending claims, and were overcome prior to issuance of the '563 patent.

"When a reference was before the examiner, whether through the examiner's search or the applicant's disclosure, it cannot be deemed to have been withheld from the examiner." *Orthopedic Equipment Co. v. All Orthopedic Appliances, Inc.*, 707 F.2d 1376, 1383, 217 USPQ 1281, 1286 (Fed. Cir. 1983) (nondisclosure not material because the examiner independently ascertained the existence of the undisclosed prior art). The Lemelson patents were indeed of record in the '563 patent application. We agree with Molins and Smith that the court's finding that the Lemelson patents were withheld was clearly erroneous. Thus, the failure of Hirsh and Smith to cite these references to the PTO did not constitute inequitable conduct.

4. Smith's Nondisclosure of the Lemelson Application

During the time that the '563 patent was being prosecuted, Smith was also prosecuting a machine tool application, serial number 107,357, that named Lemelson as inventor. At trial, Textron argued that Lemelson claim 11 and Williamson claim 160 defined the same patentable invention, and that Smith violated his duty of candor by not disclosing the Lemelson application to the patent examiner responsible for the Williamson application. *See* MPEP § 2001.06(b) (4th ed., rev. 8, Oct. 1981) (duty to disclose material information includes "duty to bring to the attention of the examiner ... information within [applicant's] knowledge as to other co-pending United States applications which are 'material to the examination' of the application in question."). The court found that Smith's failure to disclose the copending application of Lemelson constituted inequitable conduct because the court found that claim 11 of the Lemelson application was material to the patentability of claim 160 of the '563 application, and because the court inferred an intent to deceive the PTO from the fact of Smith's dual representation of Molins and Lemelson. Smith asserts that the court erred in finding that information regarding the Lemelson application would have been material to the examiner of the '563 patent and that Smith intended to deceive the examiner by not disclosing such information.

The position in which Smith placed himself was one fraught with possible conflict of interest because Smith's dual representation of two clients seeking patents in closely related technologies created a risk of sacrificing the interest of one client for that of the other and of failing to discharge his duty of candor to the PTO with respect to each client. Whether or not there was a conflict of interest, however, is not before us, and we express no opinion thereon. Nor do we express any opinion regarding the apparent conflict between an attorney's obligations to the PTO and the attorney's obligation to clients.

However, regarding Smith's obligation to the PTO, which is before us, we agree with Smith that Textron failed to establish by clear and convincing evidence that inequitable conduct occurred in the nondisclosure of claim 11 of the Lemelson application. Lemelson claim 11 was not material to the patentability of the '563 claims because it was cumulative to art already made of record during prosecution of the '563 patent. A reference that is cumulative to other references of record does not meet the threshold of materiality needed to prove inequitable conduct. Claim 11 was no more pertinent to Williamson claim 160 than was claim 26 of the Lemelson '770 patent, which was already of record in the '563 patent prosecution. Thus the court's finding that the Lemelson claim 11 was material was clearly erroneous and the court's determination of inequitable conduct based on that finding was an abuse of discretion.

CONCLUSION

The judgment of the district court holding U.S. Patents 4,369,563 and 4,621,410 unenforceable due to inequitable conduct is affirmed on the basis that Molins' attorney Whitson intentionally withheld a material reference from the PTO.

Notes

1. **Affidavits are Always Material**. In *Refac Int'l v. Lotus Dev.*, 81 F.3d 1576, 38 USPQ2d 1665 (Fed. Cir. 1996), the Court held that affidavits are inherently material even if they are cumulative. In *Refac Int'l*, in response to an examiner's rejection that the disclosure was inadequate, the applicant had submitted affidavits from three people of varying levels of skill, all of whom said the disclosure was sufficient. Neither the applicant nor the affiant Jones revealed the fact that Jones had worked for the

applicant. In fact, his affidavit listed in meticulous detail all of the places that Jones had been employed, except for the applicant. Refac argued that it did not matter because the Jones affidavit was cumulative of the other two. The Court held that an affidavit is inherently material and held the patent unenforceable for inequitable conduct.

2. **"New" Rule 56.** In 1992, a new rule 56 defining materiality was promulgated; however, because it only applies prospectively, it has not yet been applied by the Federal Circuit.

THE NEW RULE 56: Duty To Disclose Information Material To Patentability

REGULATORY PROVISION—37 C.F.R. § 1.56

(a) A patent by its very nature is affected with a public interest. The public interest is best served, and the most effective patent examination occurs when, at the time an application is being examined, the Office is aware of and evaluates the teachings of all information material to patentability. Each individual associated with the filing and prosecution of a patent application has a duty of candor and good faith in dealing with the Office, which includes a duty to disclose to the Office all information known to that individual to be material to patentability as defined in this section. The duty to disclose information exists with respect to each pending claim until the claim is canceled or withdrawn from consideration, or the application becomes abandoned....

(b) Under this section, information is material to patentability when it is not cumulative to information already of record or being made of record in the application, and

> (1) It establishes, by itself or in combination with other information, a *prima facie* case of unpatentability of a claim; or

> (2) It refutes, or is inconsistent with, a position the applicant takes in:

> (i) Opposing an argument of unpatentability relied on by the Office, or

> (ii) Asserting an argument of patentability.

A *prima facie* case of unpatentability is established when the information compels a conclusion that a claim is unpatentable under the preponderance of evidence, burden-of-proof standard, giving each term in the claim its broadest reasonable construction consistent with the specification, and before any consideration is given to evidence which may be submitted in an attempt to establish a contrary conclusion of patentability.

The Federal Circuit stated the following about the new rule:

> The duty to disclose information material to patentability has been codified in 37 C.F.R. § 1.56 (Rule 56), which was promulgated pursuant to 35 U.S.C. §§ 6 and 131. From 1977 to 1992, Rule 56 defined information as "material" when "there is a substantial likelihood that a reasonable examiner would consider it important

in deciding whether to allow the application to issue as a patent.'' We have adopted this standard as the threshold standard of materiality. In 1992, the PTO changed Rule 56 . . . "[A]dministrative rules will not be construed to have retroactive effect unless their language requires this result." *Bowen v. Georgetown Univ. Hosp.*, 488 U.S. 204, 208 (1988); *see also* 57 Fed.Reg. 2021 (Jan. 17, 1992) (PTO notice of final rulemaking stating that new Rule 56 will be applicable to all applicants and reexamination proceedings pending or filed after March 16, 1992). We thus make no comment regarding the meaning of new Rule 56.

Molins PLC v. Textron, Inc., 48 F.3d 1172, 1179 n. 8, 33 USPQ2d 1823, 1834 n. 8 (Fed. Cir. 1995) (citations omitted). How do you think this new rule will change the law?

3. **Materiality.** A reference does not have to render the claimed invention unpatentable or invalid to be material. *See Merck v. Danbury Pharmacal*, 873 F.2d 1418, 10 USPQ2d 1682 (Fed. Cir. 1989) (withheld information was material even though it would not have rendered the claimed invention obvious). Under new Rule 56, a reference is material if it is *not cumulative* and:

(1) it creates a *prima facie* case of unpatentability;

(2) it supports a position taken by the PTO which the applicant disputes; or

(3) it is inconsistent with a position taken by the applicant.

PATENTEE'S REBUTTAL EVIDENCE: Reference Is Cumulative

A patentee need not cite a reference to the PTO if it is cumulative of other references that were before the examiner or not as material as other references. *Scripps Clinic & Research Found. v. Genentech, Inc.*, 927 F.2d 1565, 1582, 18 USPQ2d 1001, 1014–15 (Fed. Cir. 1991) ("reference that is simply cumulative to other references does not meet the threshold of materiality that is predicate to a holding of inequitable conduct").

2. INTENT

KINGSDOWN MED. CONSULTANTS, LTD. v. HOLLISTER INC.

863 F.2d 867, 9 USPQ2d 1384 (Fed. Cir. 1988)

Before MARKEY, Chief Judge, SMITH and ARCHER, Circuit Judges.

MARKEY, Chief Judge.

Kingsdown Medical Consultants, Ltd. and E.R. Squibb & Sons, Inc., (Kingsdown) appeal from a judgment of the United States District Court for the Northern District of Illinois holding U.S. Patent No. 4,460,363 ('363) unenforceable because of inequitable conduct before the United States Patent and Trademark Office (PTO). We reverse and remand.

Kingsdown sued Hollister Incorporated (Hollister) for infringement of claims 2, 4, 5, 9, 10, 12, 13, 14, 16, 17, 18, 27, 28, and 29 of Kingsdown's '363 patent. The district court held the patent unenforceable because of Kingsdown's conduct in respect of claim 9 and reached no other issue.

The invention claimed in the '363 patent is a two-piece ostomy appliance for use by patients with openings in their abdominal walls for release of waste.

The two pieces of the appliance are a pad and a detachable pouch. The pad is secured to the patient's body encircling the abdominal wall opening. Matching coupling rings are attached to the pad and to the pouch. When engaged, the rings provide a water tight seal. Disengaging the rings allows for removal of the pouch.

A. The Prosecution History

Kingsdown filed its original patent application in February 1978. The '363 patent issued July 17, 1984. The intervening period of more than six-and-a-half years saw a complex prosecution, involving the submission, rejection, amendment, re-numbering, etc., of 118 claims, a continuation application, an appeal, a petition to make special, and citation and discussion of 44 references.

After a series of office actions and amendments, Kingsdown submitted claim 50. With our emphasis on the language of interest here, claim 50 read:

> A coupling for an ostomy appliance comprising a pad or dressing having a generally circular aperture for passage of the stoma, said *pad or dressing aperture encircled by a coupling member* and an ostomy bag also having a generally circular aperture for passage of the stoma, said *bag aperture encircled by a second coupling member*, one of said coupling members being two opposed walls of closed looped annular channel form and the other coupling member of closed loop form having a rib or projection dimensioned to be gripped between the mutaully (sic) opposed channel walls when said coupling members are connected, said rib or projection having a thin resilient deflectible seal strip extending therefrom, which, when said rib or projection is disposed between said walls, springs away therefrom to sealingly engage one of said walls, and in which each coupling member is formed of resilient synthetic plastics material.

The examiner found that claim 50 contained allowable subject matter, but rejected the claim for indefiniteness under 35 U.S.C. § 112, second paragraph, objecting to "encircled," because the coupling ring could not, in the examiner's view, "encircle" the aperture in the pad, the ring and aperture not being "coplanar." The examiner had not in earlier actions objected to "encircled" to describe similar relationships in other claims. Nor had the examiner found the identical "encircled" language indefinite in original claims 1 and 6 which were combined to form claim 50.

To render claim 50 definite, and thereby overcome the § 112 rejection, Kingsdown amended the claim. With our emphasis on the changed language, amended claim 50 read:

> A coupling for an ostomy appliance comprising a pad or dressing having *a body contacting surface and an outer surface with* a generally circular aperture for passage of the stoma extending through said pad or dressing, a coupling member *extending outwardly from said outer pad or dressing surface and encircling the intersection of said aperture and said outer pad or dressing surface*, and an ostomy bag also having a generally circular aperture *in one bag wall* for passage of the stoma with a second coupling member *affixed to said bag wall around the periphery of said bag wall aperture and extending outwardly from said bag wall*, one of said coupling members being two opposed walls of closed looped annular channel form and the other coupling member of closed loop form having a rib or projection dimensioned to be gripped between the mutually opposed channel walls when said coupling members are connected, said rib or projection having a thin resilient deflectible seal strip extending therefrom, which, when said rib or projection is disposed between said walls, springs away therefrom to sealingly engage one of said walls, and in which each coupling member is formed of resilient synthetic plastic material.

To avoid the § 112 rejection, Kingsdown had thus added the pad's two surfaces, replaced "aperture encircled," first occurrence, with "encircling the intersection of said aperture and said outer pad or dressing surface," and deleted "encircled," second occurrence. In an advisory action, the examiner said the changes in claim language overcame the § 112 rejection and that amended claim 50 would be allowable.

While Kingsdown's appeal of other rejected claims was pending, Kingsdown's patent attorney saw a two-piece ostomy appliance manufactured by Hollister. Kingsdown engaged an outside counsel to file a continuation application and withdrew the appeal.

Thirty-four claims were filed with the continuation application, including new and never-before-examined claims and 22 claims indicated as corresponding to claims allowed in the parent application. In prosecuting the continuation, a total of 44 references, including 14 new references, were cited and 29 claims were substituted for the 34 earlier filed, making a total of 63 claims presented. Kingsdown submitted a two-column list, one column containing the claim numbers of 22 previously allowed claims, the other column containing the claim numbers of the 21 claims in the continuation application that corresponded to those previously allowed claims. That list indicated, incorrectly, that claim 43 in the continuation application corresponded to allowed claim 50 in the parent application. Claim 43 actually corresponded to the unamended claim 50 that had been rejected for indefiniteness under § 112. Claim 43 was renumbered as the present claim 9 in the '363 patent.

There was another claim 43. It was in the parent application and was combined with claim 55 of the parent application to form claim 61 in the continuation. Claim 55 contained the language of amended claim 50 relating to "encircled." It was allowed as submitted and was not involved in any discussion of indefiniteness. Claim 61 became claim 27 of the patent.

B. The District Court

Having examined the prosecution history, the district court found that the examiner could have relied on the representation that claim 43 corresponded to allowable claim 50 and rejected Kingsdown's suggestion that the examiner must have made an independent examination of claim 43, because: (1) in the Notice of Allowance, the examiner said the claims were allowed "in view of applicant's communication of 2 July 83"; (2) there was no evidence that the examiner had compared the language of amended claim 50 with that of claim 43; and (3) the examiner could justifiably rely on the representation because of an applicant's duty of candor.

The district court found the materiality element of inequitable conduct, because allowability of claim 50 turned on the amendment overcoming the § 112 rejection in the parent application. Kingsdown's knowledge of materiality was inferred from claim 50 having been deemed allowable in the parent application only after the change in claim language.

The court found the deceitful intent element of inequitable conduct, because Kingsdown was grossly negligent in not noticing the error, or, in the alternative, because Kingsdown's acts indicated an intent to deceive the PTO.

The court found that Kingsdown's patent attorney was grossly negligent in not catching the misrepresentation because a mere ministerial review of the language of amended claim 50 in the parent application and of claim 43 in the continuing application would have uncovered the error, and because Kingsdown's patent attorney had had several opportunities to make that review.

The district court stated that the narrower language of amended claim 50 gave Hollister a possible defense, i.e., that Hollister's coupling member does not encircle the intersection of the aperture and the pad surface because it has an intervening "floating flange" member. The court inferred motive to deceive the PTO because Kingsdown's patent attorney viewed the Hollister appliance after he had amended claim 50 and before the continuation application was filed. The court expressly declined to make any finding on whether the accused device would or would not infringe any claims, but stated that Kingsdown's patent attorney must have perceived that Hollister would have a defense against infringement of the amended version of claim 50 that it would not have against the unamended version.

The district court rejected Kingsdown's argument that unamended claim 50, which became claim 43 and then claim 9 of the '363 patent, satisfied the requirements of § 112 but did not expressly or unequivocally decide that question.

ISSUE

Whether the district court's finding of intent to deceive was clearly erroneous, rendering its determination that inequitable conduct occurred an abuse of discretion.

OPINION

We confront a case of first impression, in which inequitable conduct has been held to reside in an incorrect inclusion in a continuation application of a claim that contained allowable subject matter, but had been rejected as indefinite in the parent application.

Inequitable conduct resides in failure to disclose material information, or submission of false material information, with an intent to deceive, and those two elements, materiality and intent, must be proven by clear and convincing evidence. The findings on materiality and intent are subject to the clearly erroneous standard of Rule 52(a) Fed.R.Civ.P. and are not to be disturbed unless this court has a definite and firm conviction that a mistake has been committed.

"To be guilty of inequitable conduct, one must have intended to act inequitably." *FMC Corp. v. Manitowoc Co., Inc.*, 835 F.2d 1411, 1415, 5 USPQ2d 1112, 1115 (Fed. Cir. 1987). Kingsdown's attorney testified that he was not aware of the error until Hollister mentioned it in March 1987, and the experts for both parties testified that they saw no evidence of deceptive intent. As above indicated, the district court's finding of Kingsdown's intent to mislead is based on the alternative grounds of: (a) gross negligence; and (b) acts indicating an intent to deceive. Neither ground, however, supports a finding of intent in this case.

a. Negligence

The district court inferred intent based on what it perceived to be Kingsdown's gross negligence. Whether the intent element of inequitable conduct is present cannot always be inferred from a pattern of conduct that may be described as gross negligence. That conduct must be sufficient to require a finding of deceitful intent in the light of all the circumstances. We are not convinced that deceitful intent was present in Kingsdown's negligent filing of its continuation application or, in fact, that its conduct even rises to a level that would warrant the description "gross negligence."

It is well to be reminded of what actually occurred in this case—a ministerial act involving two claims, which, because both claims contained allowable subject matter, did not result in the patenting of anything anticipated or rendered obvious by anything in the prior art and thus took nothing from the public domain. In preparing and filing the continuation application, a newly-hired counsel for Kingsdown had two versions of "claim 50" in the parent application, an unamended rejected version and an amended allowed version. As is common, counsel renumbered and transferred into the continuation all (here, 22) claims "previously allowed". In filing its claim 43, it copied the "wrong", i.e., the rejected, version of claim 50. That error led to the incorrect listing of claim 43 as corresponding to allowed claim 50 and to incorporation of claim 43 as claim 9 in the patent. In approving the continuation for filing, Kingsdown's regular attorney did not, as the district court said, "catch" the mistake.

In view of the relative ease with which others also overlooked the differences in the claims, Kingsdown's failure to notice that claim 43 did not correspond to the amended and allowed version of claim 50 is insufficient to warrant a finding of an intent to deceive the PTO. Undisputed facts indicating that relative ease are: (1) the similarity in language of the two claims; (2) the use of the same claim number, 50, for the amended and unamended claims; (3) the multiplicity of claims involved in the prosecution of both applications; (4) the examiner's failure to reject claims using "encircled" in the parent application's first and second office actions, making its presence in claim 43 something less than a glaring error; (5) the two-year interval between the rejection/amendment of claim 50 and the filing of the continuation; (6) failure of the examiner to reject claim 43 under § 112 or to notice the differences between claim 43 and amended claim 50 during what must be presumed, absent contrary evidence, to have been an examination of the continuation; and (7) the failure of Hollister to notice the lack of correspondence between claim 43 and the amended version of claim 50 during three years of discovery and until after it had carefully and critically reviewed the file history 10 to 15 times with an eye toward litigation. That Kingsdown did not notice its mistake during more than one opportunity of doing so, does not in this case, and in view of Hollister's frequent and focused opportunities, establish that Kingsdown intended to deceive the PTO.

We do not, of course, condone inattention to the duty of care owed by one preparing and filing a continuation application. Kingsdown's counsel may have been careless, but it was clearly erroneous to base a finding of intent to deceive on that fact alone.

Hollister argues that the district court correctly determined that the examiner failed to examine the claims in the continuation application. What the district court "determined" was that there was no evidence that examination occurred. No finding on whether examination occurred was made by the district court, and, of course, none may be made by us. In view, however, of certain uncontested facts: (1) the absence of direct evidence that examination did not occur; (2) the presumption of correctness that attaches to administrative action; (3) Manual of Patent Examining Procedure, section 201.07 (requiring further examination of continuation applications); (4) 35 U.S.C. § 131 (requiring examination of each application); (5) the examiner's search notes; (6) the examiner's initialing of the prior art statement; (7) the presence of seven never-before-examined claims; (8) the examiner's "see parent" notation; and (9) the submission of numerous old and newly-cited prior art references requiring comparison with all the claims, we decline to presume, as part of the intent analysis in this case, a failure of the examiner to perform his duty to examine the claims of Kingsdown's continuation application.

Thus the first basis for the district court's finding of deceitful intent (what it viewed as "gross negligence") cannot stand.

b. Acts

The district court also based its finding of deceitful intent on the separate and alternative inferences it drew from Kingsdown's acts in viewing the Hollister device, in desiring to obtain a patent that would "cover" that device, and in failing to disclaim or reissue after Hollister charged it with inequitable conduct. The district court limited its analysis here to claim 9 and amended claim 50.

It should be made clear at the outset of the present discussion that there is nothing improper, illegal or inequitable in filing a patent application for the purpose of obtaining a right to exclude a known competitor's product from the market; nor is it in any manner improper to amend or insert claims intended to cover a competitor's product the applicant's attorney has learned about during the prosecution of a patent application. Any such amendment or insertion must comply with all statutes and regulations, of course, but, if it does, its genesis in the marketplace is simply irrelevant and cannot of itself evidence deceitful intent.

The district court appears to have dealt with claim 9 in isolation because of Hollister's correct statement that when inequitable conduct occurs in relation to one claim the entire patent is unenforceable. But Hollister leapfrogs from that correct proposition to one that is incorrect, i.e., that courts may not look outside the involved claim in determining, in the first place, whether inequitable conduct did in fact occur at all. Claims are not born, and do not live, in isolation. Each is related to other claims, to the specification and drawings, to the prior art, to an attorney's remarks, to co-pending and continuing applications, and often, as here, to earlier or later versions of itself in light of amendments made to it. The district court accepted Hollister's argument that Kingsdown included claim 43 (unamended claim 50) in its continuing application because its chances of proving infringement of claim 43 were greater than would have been its chances of proving infringement of amended claim 50, in view of Hollister's "floating flange" argument against infringement of the latter. Neither the court nor Hollister tells us how Kingsdown could have known in July 1982 what Hollister's defense would be years later, when suit was filed.

Faced with Hollister's assertion that an experienced patent attorney would knowingly and intentionally transfer into a continuing application a claim earlier rejected for indefiniteness, without rearguing that the claim was not indefinite, the district court stated that "how an experienced patent attorney could allow such conduct to take place" gave it "the greatest difficulty." A knowing failure to disclose and knowingly false statements are always difficult to understand. However, a transfer of numerous claims *en masse* from a parent to a continuing application, as the district court stated, is a ministerial act. As such, it is more vulnerable to errors which by definition result from inattention, and is less likely to result from the scienter involved in the more egregious acts of omission and commission that have been seen as reflecting the deceitful intent element of inequitable conduct in our cases.

More importantly, however, the district court's focus on claim 9 caused it to disregard the effect of other claims. In addition to claim 9 and its dependent claims, Kingsdown claimed infringement of claims 2, 4, 5, and 27. The first three of those claims were each broader in some respects than claim 9. The first portion of claim 27, *supra*, corresponded precisely with the amended language of claim 50 on which the district court focused. Claim 27 was allowed, when presented and without amendment, as claim 55 in the parent application. The district court expressly stated that it "did not decide the issue of infringement." Because there has been no decision on whether any of claims 2, 4, 5, and 27 are infringed by Hollister's product, or on whether Kingsdown could have reasonably believed they are, it cannot at this stage be said that Kingsdown needed claim 9 to properly bring suit for infringement. If it did not, the district court's implication of sinister motivation and the court's inference of deceptive intent from Kingsdown's acts would collapse.

The district court, in finding intent, made a passing reference to Kingsdown's continuation of its suit after Hollister charged inequitable conduct. Hollister vigorously argues before us that Kingsdown's continuing its suit while failing to disclaim or reissue is proof of bad faith. A failure to disclaim or reissue in 1987, however, would not establish that Kingsdown acted in bad faith when it filed its continuation application in 1982. Moreover, a suggestion that patentees should abandon their suits, or disclaim or reissue, in response to every charge of inequitable conduct raised by an alleged infringer would be nothing short of ridiculous. The right of patentees to resist such charges must not be chilled to extinction by fear that a failure to disclaim or reissue will be used against them as evidence that their original intent was deceitful. Nor is there in the record any basis for expecting that any such disclaimer or reissue would cause Hollister to drop its inequitable conduct defense or refrain from reliance on such remedial action as support for that defense. Kingsdown's belief in its innocence meant that a court test of the inequitable conduct charge was inevitable and appropriate. A requirement for disclaimer or reissue to avoid adverse inferences would merely encourage the present proliferation of inequitable conduct charges.

We are forced to the definite and firm conviction that a mistake has been committed, amounting to an abuse of discretion. The district court's finding of deceitful intent was clearly erroneous.

RESOLUTION OF CONFLICTING PRECEDENT[16]

"Gross Negligence" and the Intent Element of Inequitable Conduct

Some of our opinions have suggested that a finding of gross negligence compels a finding of an intent to deceive. Others have indicated that gross negligence alone does not mandate a finding of intent to deceive.

"Gross negligence" has been used as a label for various patterns of conduct. It is definable, however, only in terms of a particular act or acts viewed in light of all the circumstances. We adopt the view that a finding that particular conduct amounts to "gross negligence" does not of itself justify an inference of intent to deceive; the involved conduct, viewed in light of all the evidence, including evidence indicative of good faith, must indicate sufficient culpability to require a finding of intent to deceive.

Nature of Question

Some of our opinions have indicated that whether inequitable conduct occurred is a question of law. In *Gardco Mfg. Inc. v. Herst Lighting Co.*, 820 F.2d 1209, 1212, 2 USPQ2d 2015, 2018 (Fed. Cir. 1987), the court indicated that the inequitable conduct question is equitable in nature. We adopt the latter view, i.e., that the ultimate question of whether inequitable conduct occurred is equitable in nature.

Standard of Review

As an equitable issue, inequitable conduct is committed to the discretion of the trial court and is reviewed by this court under an abuse of discretion standard. We, accordingly, will not simply substitute our judgment for that of the trial court in relation to inequitable conduct. "To overturn a discretionary ruling of a district court, the appellant must establish that the ruling is based upon clearly erroneous findings of fact or a misapplication or misinterpretation of applicable law or that the ruling evidences a clear error of judgment on the part of the district court." *PPG Indus. v. Celanese Polymer Specialities Co.*, 840 F.2d 1565, 1572, 6 USPQ2d 1010, 1016 (Fed. Cir. 1988) (Bissell, J., additional views).

EFFECT OF INEQUITABLE CONDUCT

When a court has finally determined that inequitable conduct occurred in relation to one or more claims during prosecution of the patent application, the entire patent is rendered unenforceable. We, in banc, reaffirm that rule as set forth in *J.P. Stevens & Co. v. Lex Tex Ltd.*, 747 F.2d 1553, 1561, 223 USPQ 1089, 1093–94 (Fed. Cir. 1984).

CONCLUSION

Having determined that the district court's finding of intent is clearly erroneous, the panel reverses the judgment based on a conclusion

---

16. Because precedent may not be changed by a panel, *South Corp. v. United States*, 690 F.2d 1368, 1370 n. 2 (Fed. Cir. 1982) (in banc), this section has been considered and decided by an in banc court formed of MARKEY, Chief Judge, RICH, SMITH, NIES, BISSELL, ARCHER, MAYER, and MICHEL, Circuit Judges.

of inequitable conduct before the PTO and remands the case for such further proceedings as the district court may deem appropriate.

Notes

1. **What is Inequitable Conduct.** Failure to cite a reference to the PTO in an IDS or during prosecution is the most common example of inequitable conduct. Others include: failing to disclose a possible public use or on-sale bar activity, providing false affidavits regarding dates of invention, or representing falsified data regarding testing or embodiment examples. Can you think of any others?

2. **How do you prove intent?** You do not need a "smoking gun" to prove intent to deceive. Circumstantial evidence can satisfy the intent requirement. However, it is not enough that the patentee simply did not disclose a prior art reference. There has to be some evidence from which to at least infer an intent to deceive. *See, e.g., Lumenyte Int'l Corp. v. Cable Lite Corp.*, 92 F.3d 1206 (Fed. Cir. 1996), ("the deceptive intent element, in this case, seems properly inferred from the documentary evidence ... [which was] properly regarded as providing clear and convincing evidence that Lumenyte intentionally abandoned the parent application when its officers thought that there was little chance for issuance, but revived it after Fiber Lite introduced its competing product and Lumenyte obtained different patent counsel."). Intent to deceive has also been found where an attorney prosecuting a U.S. application failed to disclose a reference that he had disclosed in foreign applications.

3. **It is Not Inequitable Conduct for** ...

It is not inequitable conduct for the applicant to argue to the examiner that a particular reference is distinguishable from the claimed invention, even if it is not distinguishable because as long as the reference is before the examiner she can make an independent evaluation of it. Therefore, attorney argument regarding how to interpret a reference (even if it is incorrect) is usually not inequitable conduct. *See Haworth, Inc. v. Steelcase, Inc.*, 685 F. Supp. 1422, 1452–53, 8 USPQ2d 1001, 1025 (W.D. Mich. 1988) (citing *Akzo N.V. v. U.S. Int'l Trade Comm'n*, 808 F.2d 1471, 1482, 1 USPQ2d 1241, 1247 (Fed. Cir. 1986)).

It is not inequitable conduct when the applicant does not disclose a reference as long as the examiner discovers it herself. As long as the reference is before the examiner it does not matter whether the examiner found it or the applicant disclosed it. *See Molins PLC v. Textron, Inc.*, 48 F.3d 1172, 1185, 33 USPQ2d 1823,1832 (Fed. Cir. 1995). *But see Molins*, 48 F.3d at 1189 n.7, 33 USPQ2d at 1839 n.7 (Nies, J., dissenting) (citing *A.B. Dick Co. v. Burroughs Corp.*, 798 F.2d 1392, 230 USPQ 849 (Fed. Cir. 1986)).

4. **Burying a Reference**. Do you think it is inequitable conduct for an inventor to bury a particularly material prior art reference among many references in an IDS? In *Molins*, 48 F.3d at 1183–84, 33 USPQ2d at 1831–32, the Federal Circuit held that burying a reference does not amount to inequitable conduct. In *Molins*, a particularly material reference was buried in a disclosure statement that was 11 pages long with 23 U.S. patents, 27

foreign patents, and 44 U.S. and foreign publications. This was held not to be inequitable conduct even though the IDS did not discuss the relevance of any of the references or even provide translations for most of the foreign documents. In a 2–1 decision, the Federal Circuit held that burying a reference could be probative of bad faith, but that it was not inequitable conduct in this case because the examiner had initialed each reference including the material one. His initials indicated that he had read the reference. The law in this area is that when the examiner initials references claiming to have reviewed them, it is presumed that the examiner did consider the references. In addition, it says on the form that the examiner's check means that the reference has been considered. It is presumed that trained public officials do their assigned jobs. Is this an appropriate outcome when an examiner has only a matter of hours to review each application? Is it reasonable to assume that he has read every reference under these circumstances?

5. **Doctrine of Unclean Hands.** In *Consolidated Aluminum Corp. v. Foseco Int'l Ltd.*, 910 F.2d 804, 15 USPQ2d 1481 (Fed. Cir. 1990), the Federal Circuit held that the district court did not abuse its discretion in holding that inequitable conduct in procuring one of the patents-in-suit required a holding that other related patents-in-suit (continuations) were unenforceable. In *Consolidated Aluminum*, the patent applicant intentionally concealed the best mode of practicing the invention and instead disclosed a fictitious inoperable mode. The applicant disclosed the best mode in the later filed continuations which were the related patents-in-suit. The Court discussed this issue as follows:

> The inequitable conduct of failing to disclose the best mode in the 917 patent also significantly affected the 212 and 303 patents, continuations of the 081 patent and improvements on the 917 patent. The withheld best mode of the 917 patent, patented in the 363 patent, was included in the 212 and 303 patents. In fact, the withheld best mode of the 917 patent was incorporated in the 081 patent which was filed on the same day as the 363 patent application, clearly to avoid the 363 patent application being cited as prior art with respect to the 081 patent. Moreover, as noted above, the fact that the slurry was previously withheld in the prior art was not disclosed to the patent examiner in any of these later applications.

> This appeal presents the first instance in which this court is required to consider the equitable maxim "he who comes into equity must come with clean hands" in determining whether inequitable conduct in procuring one patent-in-suit requires a holding that other patents-in-suit are unenforceable ... [In *Keystone Driller*,] the Court stated that "courts of equity do not make quality of suitors the test. They apply the maxim requiring clean hands only where some unconscionable act of one coming for relief has immediate and necessary relation to the equity that he seeks in respect of the matter in litigation."

* * *

Consolidated argues that application of inequitable conduct considerations to the '081, '212, and '303 patents was an abuse of discretion because mere relatedness of subject matter is not a proper basis for such application. In the present case, however, there is more than mere relatedness of subject matter; the prosecution histories of the patents-in-suit establish that Consolidated's inequitable conduct in prosecuting the '917 patent had "immediate and necessary relation", to the equity Consolidated seeks, namely enforcement of the '081, '212 and '303 patents.

See also Keystone Driller Co. v. General Excavator Co., 290 U.S. 240, 245–46, 19 USPQ 228, 230 (1933) (related patents held unenforceable for unclean hands where patentee paid a witness in an earlier suit concerning three of the patents to suppress evidence relating to a prior use of the invention claimed in one); Precision Instrument Mfg. Co. v. Automotive Maintenance Machinery Co., 324 U.S. 806, 815, 65 USPQ 133, 138 (1945) (related patents held unenforceable for unclean hands where patentee submitted a false affidavit concerning dates of invention in an interference proceeding before the PTO and the company discovered the fraud and then settled the interference without informing the PTO of the inequitable conduct). Hence, if multiple patents are being asserted against a defendant and there is an issue of inequitable conduct with respect to one of the patents, the defendant should examine the others to determine if there is an "immediate and necessary relationship." What kind of relationship must there be between the patents in order for the doctrine of unclean hands to render all unenforceable? In Baxter Int'l Inc. v. McGaw, Inc., 149 F.3d 1321, 47 USPQ2d 1225 (Fed. Cir. 1998), the Court held that unenforceability should not be extended to a third patent which issued from a divisional patent application directed to the same invention where the issued claims of the third patent have no relation to the omitted prior art.

PATENTEE'S REBUTTAL EVIDENCE: Good Faith Defense

Evidence that the patentee acted in good faith in prosecuting the patent application must be weighed in determining whether her conduct amounted to inequitable conduct; however, good faith is not dispositive of the issue. Consider the following excerpt from Baxter Int'l, Inc. v. McGaw, Inc., 149 F.3d 1321, 47 USPQ2d 1225 (Fed. Cir. 1998):

Finally, Baxter argues that the district court clearly erred in finding an absence of good faith on the part of the inventors. It is true that evidence of good faith must be considered in determining whether inequitable conduct has been shown by clear and convincing evidence. However, good faith is only one factor to be considered along with the totality of the evidence. The district court considered Baxter's proffered evidence of good faith and found it lacking. Baxter argues on appeal that its efforts to point out relevant prior art to the PTO demonstrates its good faith in prosecuting the '234 and '648 patents. However, as we have stated above, the Borla Device was clearly relevant and the inventors were clearly aware of its existence. Moreover, given the degree to which the patented inventions were based upon the Borla Device, an inference that the inventors were aware of its importance is justified. On balance we cannot say that the district court abused its discretion in determining that the inventors' conduct, in its entirety, warrants a determination that the '234 and '648 patents are unenforceable due to inequitable conduct.

What would be sufficient evidence of good faith? In *Nordberg, Inc. v. Telsmith, Inc.*, 82 F.3d 394, 38 USPQ2d 1593 (Fed. Cir. 1996), the Court held that failure to disclose a use of the invention which was ultimately determined to be a "public use" was not inequitable conduct where the employees had a good faith belief that the field testing occurred under a confidentiality agreement and thus was not material prior art. However, mere assertions by the inventor or the attorney who prosecuted the application that they acted in "good faith" are not sufficient. Specific facts tending to demonstrate a good faith mistake in the law or facts is required.

PROBLEMS

Suppose a company, Evil Chemical, owns three patents on a chemical compound: a patent on the compound itself (the '002 patent), a patent on the method of manufacturing the compound (the '001 patent) and a patent on its use (the '003 patent). Evil sues your company, Innocent Drugs, for infringement of all three patents. You know you are infringing. During the deposition of the inventor, Dr. Smith, you discover that he was aware of a better mode of making the chemical compound which he did not disclose at the request of his company who wanted to be able to manufacture the drug quicker and cheaper than competitors. He tells you that the company did not want to lose its competitive edge by disclosing how to produce the drug. The inventor tells you that the method of manufacture which he did not disclose does not affect the quality of the drug, but it allows you to produce twice as much as the method of manufacture disclosed in the patent. Your excitement quickly vanishes when you realize that even if you can get the method patent held invalid and unenforceable, Evil can get the same damage award because of your infringement of the '002 and '003 patents. Prepare to argue to the judge why the '001 method patent should be held invalid and unenforceable. What arguments can you make regarding the '002 and '003 patents?

B.   PATENT MISUSE

STATUTORY PROVISION—35 U.S.C. § 271 (d):

No patent owner otherwise entitled to relief for infringement or contributory infringement of a patent shall be denied relief or deemed guilty of misuse or illegal extension of the patent right by reason of his having done one or more of the following:

(1) derived revenue from acts which if performed by another without his consent would constitute contributory infringement of the patent;

(2) licensed or authorized another to perform acts which if performed without his consent would constitute contributory infringement of the patent;

(3) sought to enforce his patent rights against infringement or contributory infringement;

(4) refused to license or use any rights to the patent; or

(5) conditioned the license of any rights to the patent or the sale of the patented product on the acquisition of a license to rights in another patent or purchase of a separate product,

unless, in view of the circumstances, the patent owner has market power in the relevant market for the patent or patented product on which the license or sale is conditioned.

Notice that the patent misuse section is written in the negative. Instead of defining what type of conduct is patent misuse, it defines what kind of conduct is *not* patent misuse. Section 271 (1)-(3) was added to the patent code in 1952 to respond to an increasing trend in the courts to eliminate the contributory infringement doctrine by holding most charges of contributory infringement to be patent misuse. Hence, this provision was drafted to address the type of conduct which should not be considered patent misuse.

Patent misuse is an affirmative defense to a patent infringement charge. It must be proven by clear and convincing evidence. To succeed in proving patent misuse, the accused infringer must prove that "the patentee has impermissively broadened the 'physical or temporal scope' of the patent grant with anticompetitive effects." *Windsurfing Int'l, Inc. v. AMF, Inc.*, 782 F.2d 995, 1001, 228 USPQ 562, 566 (Fed. Cir. 1986) (quoting *Blonder-Tongue Lab., Inc. v. University of Ill. Found.*, 402 U.S. 313, 343 (1971)). Whether misuse has occurred should be determined under the rule of reason test.

The purpose behind the defense of patent misuse was discussed by the Court as follows:

The defense of patent misuse arises from the equitable doctrine of unclean hands, and relates generally to the use of patent rights to obtain or to coerce an unfair commercial advantage. Patent misuse relates primarily to a patentee's actions that affect competition in unpatented goods or that otherwise extend the economic effect beyond the scope of the patent grant. *See Mallinckrodt, Inc. v. Medipart, Inc.*, 976 F.2d 700, 703–04, 24 USPQ2d 1173, 1176 (Fed. Cir. 1992) ("The concept of patent misuse arose to restrain practices that did not in themselves violate any law, but that draw anticompetitive strength from the patent right, and thus were deemed to be contrary to public policy.").

Patent misuse is viewed as a broader wrong than antitrust violation because of the economic power that may be derived from the patentee's right to exclude. Thus misuse may arise when the conditions of antitrust violation are not met. The key inquiry is whether, by imposing conditions that derive their force from the patent, the patentee has impermissibly broadened the scope of the patent grant with anticompetitive effect. . . .

The jury instruction on patent misuse was focused primarily on the charge that Bard was attempting to enforce the patents against goods known not to be infringing, the court explaining that antitrust violation is not necessary to find misuse if patents have been used "wrongfully" to exclude competitors: A patent is unenforceable for misuse if the patent owner attempts to exclude products from the marketplace which do not infringe the claims of the patent and the patent owner has actual knowledge that those products do not infringe any claim of the patents. The patent is also unenforceable for misuse when a patent owner attempts to use the patent to exclude competitors from their marketplace knowing that the patent was invalid or unenforceable. A patent will not be rendered unenforceable for misuse if the patent owner has enforced the patent in the good faith belief that the accused products infringed the patent's claims. You may consider all aspects of the conduct of the patent owner in deciding whether a patent has been misused. In order to find misuse, you may not determine that—you need not determine that an antitrust violation has been proved. Even if an antitrust violation has not been proven, you may still find that the patents have been misused if you conclude that the patents have been used wrongfully. This instruction calls to mind the view expressed in *USM Corp. v. SPS Techs., Inc.*, 694 F.2d 505, 510, 216 USPQ 959, 963 (7th Cir. 1982) that the misuse doctrine is "too vague a formulation to be useful." Although the defense of patent misuse indeed evolved to protect against "wrongful" use of patents, the catalog of practices labeled "patent misuse" does not include a general notion of "wrongful" use.

C.R. Bard, Inc. v. M3 Systems, Inc., 157 F.3d 1340, 48 USPQ2d 1225 (Fed. Cir. 1998).

B. BRAUN MED., INC. v. ABBOTT LABS.

124 F.3d 1419, 43 USPQ2d 1896 (Fed. Cir. 1997)

Before MICHEL, PLAGER, and CLEVENGER, Circuit Judges.

CLEVENGER, Circuit Judge.

B. Braun Medical, Inc. (Braun) appeals from the district court's judgment, following a jury trial, that Braun misused its patent, was equitably estopped from asserting its patent, and that, in any event, the accused devices did not infringe the asserted claims of Braun's patent. Abbott Laboratories (Abbott) cross-appeals, seeking attorney fees and damages for Braun's patent misuse. We conclude that the district court erred with respect to its treatment of equitable estoppel and patent misuse. Accordingly, we affirm-in-part, reverse-in-part, vacate-in-part, and remand for further proceedings.

I

The patent in suit, U.S. Patent No. 4,683,916 (the '916 patent), is generally directed to a reflux valve that attaches to an intravenous (IV) line and permits injection or aspiration of fluids by means of a needleless syringe. This type of valve provides safety benefits to health care professionals by reducing the risk of needlestick injuries, which might transmit blood-borne pathogens. Since 1987, Braun has sold an embodiment of the patented reflux valve under the commercial name SafSite ®. The '916 patent contains drawings, reproduced below, that correspond to the SafSite ® valve:

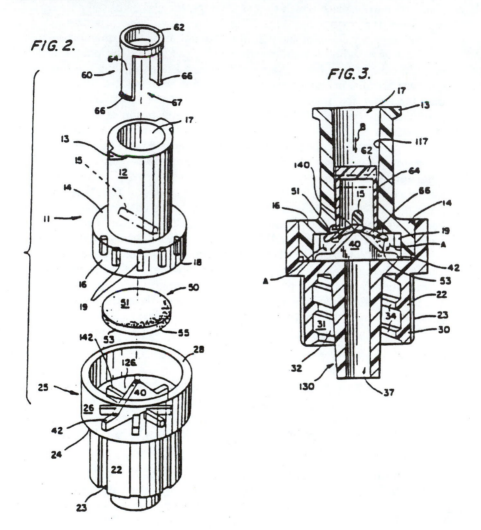

As these drawings show, the valve is formed of a resilient disc 50 sandwiched between two body elements 11 and 25 that fit together. Body element 25 includes a triangular member 40, which supports the center of the resilient disc 50. Body element 11 includes member 60, which, when engaged by a syringe, presses down on the resilient disc 50 to open the normally closed valve.

Beginning in early 1991, Braun and Abbott representatives discussed the purchase by Abbott of the patented SafSite ® valves. Braun informed Abbott that although it was willing to sell SafSite ® valves to Abbott for use on Abbott's primary line and piggyback sets, it would not sell those valves for use on an extension set. In a letter dated October 23,

1991, Randy Prozeller, Abbott's General Manager of Fluid Systems, agreed that his company would abide by these restrictions: "We will honor your company's demand that we not use the valve in question for list numbers other than our primary and primary piggyback sets." Pursuant to this arrangement, Abbott purchased approximately 536,000 SafSite ® valves.

Meanwhile, negotiations continued between Abbott and Braun for purchase of the SafSite ® valves for use with Abbott's extension sets. Because the parties could not reach agreement on these terms, Abbott requested that NP Medical, Inc. (NP Medical) develop a substitute valve. After extensive development, NP Medical developed the accused product: the NP Medical Luer Activated Valve (LAV). The novel aspects of this new valve were claimed in U.S. Patent No. 5,190,067 to Paradis and Kotsifas.

On July 20, 1993, Braun sued Abbott and NP Medical, alleging that the NP Medical LAV infringed claims 1 and 2 of the '916 patent.

The defendants denied infringement, challenged validity and asserted the equitable defenses of patent misuse, estoppel and implied license.... In November 1994, the jury determined that the '916 patent was not invalid and not infringed by the accused NP Medical LAV.... The jury also determined that Braun was estopped from charging the defendants with infringement, and that Braun had misused the '916 patent.

On the basis of the patent misuse finding, Abbott sought damages pursuant to its declaratory judgment counterclaim. Following an additional eight-day trial on this issue, the jury decided that Braun's alleged patent misuse had not caused any damages to Abbott.

[The Court affirmed the district court's finding of noninfringement and reversed the district court's finding that Braun was equitably estopped from suing Abbott for infringement.]

V

The jury also found Braun guilty of patent misuse based on the following instruction from the district court (emphasis added):

> [A] patent holder is not allowed to place restrictions on customers which prohibit resale of the patented product, or allow the customer to resell the patented product only in connection with certain products.... If you find, by a preponderance of the evidence, that Braun placed such restrictions on its customers, including Abbott, you *must* find that Braun is guilty of patent misuse.

Braun contends that this jury instruction is legally erroneous because it essentially creates *per se* liability for any conditions that Braun placed on its sales. We agree.

The resolution of this issue is governed by our precedent in *Mallinckrodt, Inc. v. Medipart, Inc.*, 976 F.2d 700, 24 USPQ2d 1173 (Fed. Cir. 1992). In that case, we canvassed precedent concerning the legality of restrictions placed upon the post-sale use of patented goods. As a general matter, we explained that an unconditional sale of a patented device exhausts the patentee's right to control the purchaser's use of the device thereafter. The theory behind this rule is that in such a transaction, the patentee has bargained for, and received, an amount equal to the full value of the goods. This exhaustion doctrine, however, does not apply to an expressly conditional sale or license. In such a transaction, it is more reasonable to infer that the parties negotiated a price that reflects only the value of the "use" rights conferred by the patentee. As a result, express conditions accompanying the sale or license of a patented product are generally upheld. Such express conditions, however, are contractual in nature and are subject to antitrust, patent, contract, and any other applicable law, as well as equitable considerations such as patent misuse. Accordingly, conditions that violate some law or equitable consideration are unenforceable. On the other hand, violation of valid conditions entitles the patentee to a remedy for either patent infringement or breach of contract. This, then, is the general framework.

In *Mallinckrodt*, we also outlined the framework for evaluating whether an express condition on the post-sale use of a patented product constitutes patent misuse. The patent misuse doctrine, born from the equitable doctrine of unclean hands, is a method of limiting abuse of patent rights separate from the antitrust laws. The key inquiry under this fact-intensive doctrine is whether, by imposing the condition, the patentee has "impermissibly broadened the 'physical or temporal scope' of the patent grant with anticompetitive effect." *Windsurfing Int'l, Inc. v. AMF, Inc.*, 782 F.2d 995, 1001–02, 228 USPQ 562, 566 (Fed. Cir. 1986). Two common examples of such impermissible broadening are using a patent which enjoys market power in the relevant market, *see* 35 U.S.C. § 271(d)(5) (1994), to restrain competition in an unpatented product or employing the patent beyond its 17–year term. In contrast, field of use restrictions (such as those at issue in the present case) are generally upheld and any anticompetitive effects they may cause are reviewed in accordance with the rule of reason.

Because the district court improperly instructed the jury that it must find Braun guilty of patent misuse if Braun placed any use restrictions on its sales of the SafSite ® valves, rather than instructing the jury pursuant to the *Mallinckrodt* framework, we remand the case for further proceedings. On remand, the district court must first determine whether Braun's restriction exceeds the scope of the patent grant. If it does not, then Braun cannot be guilty of patent misuse. If it does, the restriction must be evaluated under the rule of reason. Abbott relies upon an earlier district court decision in *Baldwin-Lima–Hamilton Corp. v. Tatnall Measuring Systems Co.*, 169 F. Supp. 1, 120 USPQ 34 (E.D. Pa. 1958), for the proposition that Braun's actions constitute a per se antitrust violation. That case does not control here. The result in *Baldwin* was driven by the court's belief that any condition placed on a sale constituted patent misuse. As we have explained, however, that reasoning was rejected in *Mallinckrodt*. In addition, the court in *Baldwin* viewed the conduct of the patentee in that case as being akin to a tie-in, which is not alleged in the present case.

VI

After the jury returned a verdict of patent misuse, the district court held a separate eight-day jury trial to determine whether Braun's patent misuse had caused any damages to Abbott. The district court specifically based this trial on the Declaratory Judgment Act, which gives the trial court discretion to grant "further necessary or proper relief based on a declaratory judgment ... after reasonable notice and hearing, against any adverse party whose rights have been determined by such judgment." At the conclusion of this separate trial, the jury found that Abbott had failed to prove that Braun's actions caused it any damages. Subsequently, the district court denied Abbott's motion for a new trial on that issue.

Abbott appeals the district court's decision, arguing that the district court abused its discretion by failing to provide this new trial. Braun responds that Abbott is not entitled to damages, as a matter of law, because patent misuse is simply an affirmative defense that results in the patent being unenforceable; it does not entitle the accused infringer to compensatory damages.

As we have mentioned, the patent misuse doctrine is an extension of the equitable doctrine of unclean hands, whereby a court of equity will not lend its support to enforcement of a patent that has been misused. Patent misuse arose, as an equitable defense available to the accused infringer, from the desire "to restrain practices that did not in themselves violate any law, but that drew anticompetitive strength from the patent right, and thus were deemed to be contrary to public policy." When used successfully, this defense results in rendering the patent unenforceable until the misuse is purged. It does not, however, result in an award of damages to the accused infringer.

The district court held the damages trial based not on the defense of patent misuse, but based instead on Abbott's counterclaim for declaratory judgment. In its counterclaim, Abbott stated that "[t]his is a claim for a declaratory judgment of patent invalidity, unenforceability and non-infringement." After repeating all of the allegations contained in its affirmative defenses, Abbott prayed for the following relief:

1. a dismissal of the complaint,

2. a declaration that Abbott and NP Medical have not infringed Braun's patent,

3. a declaration that the '916 patent is invalid and unenforceable,

4. costs and attorney fees,

5. a declaration that Abbott and NP Medical have an implied license to use the '916 patent,

6. a declaration that Braun is estopped from asserting its patent against Abbott and NP Medical,

7. a declaration that Braun is not entitled to damages for alleged infringement that occurred before the date of Braun's complaint, and

8. "such other and further relief as [the court] deems just and proper."

Relying on 28 U.S.C. § 2202, the district court held that "the Declaratory Judgment Act allows monetary damages to be awarded under a declaratory judgment counterclaim based on patent misuse."

The Declaratory Judgment Act neither expands a court's jurisdiction nor creates new substantive rights. Instead, the Act is a procedural device that provides a new, noncoercive remedy (a declaratory judgment) in cases involving an actual controversy that has not reached the stage at which either party may seek a coercive remedy (such as an injunction or damages award) and in cases in which a party who could sue for coercive relief has not yet done so. Given that the Act merely provides a new noncoercive remedy, it should come as no surprise that the practice in declaratory judgment actions is, "on almost every point, the same as in any civil action."

In order that the court not be unduly limited, the Act also states that once a court properly has jurisdiction to enter a declaratory judgment, it may also grant "[f]urther necessary or proper relief based on a declaratory judgment ... after reasonable notice and hearing." *See* 28 U.S.C. § 2202. This provision allows a court to award coercive relief, in the form of damages or an injunction, as needed based on the circumstances of the case; it was not designed, however, to allow a declaratory judgment plaintiff to avoid the requirements imposed by the substantive law as a predicate to obtaining such relief. Accordingly, § 2202 requires a hearing at which the declaratory judgment plaintiff must state its substantive claim for further relief.

In the present case, if the district court enters a declaratory judgment that the patent is unenforceable due to misuse, it could then exercise its discretion to hold a hearing to allow Abbott to state a substantive claim upon which it is entitled to recover damages. In this regard, contrary to the district court's opinion, monetary damages may not be awarded "under a declaratory judgment counterclaim based on patent misuse," because patent misuse simply renders the patent unenforceable. In other words, the defense of patent misuse may not be converted to an affirmative claim for damages simply by restyling it as a declaratory judgment counterclaim.

Although the district court has the power to entertain a hearing for damages as outlined above, we disagree with Abbott's argument that it is entitled to a new trial on the facts of the present case. As the district court explained, Abbott bore the burden of proving the amount of harm it had suffered, if any, as a result of Braun's actions. Based on the inconsistencies in the testimony of Abbott's witnesses, and based on the lack of contemporaneous documentation concerning damage to Abbott, the jury likely determined that Abbott had failed to meet its burden of proof. Therefore, the district court did not abuse its discretion in denying Abbott's motion for a new trial on damages.

VIII

[T]he district court erred by instructing the jury that it must find patent misuse if Braun placed any post-sale restrictions on use of the SafSite ® valves it sold to Abbott. This issue instead should have been analyzed under the framework established in *Mallinckrodt*, and we remand for that purpose. Finally, the district court did not abuse its discretion in denying Abbott a new trial on damages resulting from Braun's allegedly anticompetitive actions.

Notes

1. **Examples of Patent Misuse**. The courts have identified certain practices as constituting *per se* patent misuse including tying and requiring the payment of post-patent-term royalties. Tying occurs when the patentee conditions a sale under the patent on the purchase of a separate, non-patented, staple good. *See Morton Salt Co. v. G.S. Suppiger Co.*, 314 U.S. 488, 491, 52 USPQ 30 (1942) (conditioning the leasing of patented salt tablet dispensing machines on the purchase of *only* the patentee's unpatented salt tablets was patent misuse). To constitute misuse, the patentee who is requiring the tying arrangement must also have market power.

Post patent-term royalties payments, another type of patent misuse, are when the patentee attempts to extend the term of the patent by requiring the payment of royalties after the patent's expiration. *See Brulotte v. Thys Co.*, 379 U.S. 29, 143 USPQ 264 (1964) (requiring the licensee to pay royalties to the patent holder after the term of the patent had expired was held to be invalid)).

Other examples of patent misuse include: mandatory package licensing (insisting that a licensee pay license fees on two patents to get a license on either one), price restraints, covenants not to deal, and royalties based on total sales (see *Zenith Radio Corp. v. Hazeltine Research, Inc.*, 395 U.S. 100, 161 USPQ 577 (1969) (conditioning the granting of a license based upon the licensee's total sales regardless of the actual use of the patented process or item is misuse)).

2. In *Virginia Panel Corp. v. MAC Panel Co.*, 133 F.3d 860, 869, 45 USPQ2d 1225 (Fed. Cir. 1997), the Court discussed the process of determining whether an activity amounts to patent misuse as follows:

> When a practice alleged to constitute patent misuse is neither per se patent misuse nor specifically excluded from a misuse analysis by § 271(d), a court must determine if that practice is "reasonably within the patent grant, i.e., that it relates to subject matter within the scope of the patent claims." If so, the practice does not have the effect of broadening the scope of the patent claims and thus cannot constitute patent misuse. If, on the other hand, the practice has the effect of extending the patentee's statutory rights and does so with

an anti-competitive effect, that practice must then be analyzed in accordance with the "rule of reason." Under the rule of reason, "the finder of fact must decide whether the questioned practice imposes an unreasonable restraint on competition, taking into account a variety of factors, including specific information about the relevant business, its condition before and after the restraint was imposed, and the restraint's history, nature, and effect."

3. **Curing Patent Misuse.** A holding of patent misuse renders the patent unenforceable for the period of time during which the patent was misused. The patentee can cure the misuse by terminating the offending conduct. When the patentee cures the misuse, the patent is enforceable again. *See BIC Leisure Prods., Inc. v. Windsurfing Int'l, Inc.*, 613 F. Supp. 933, 952, 227 USPQ 927, 942 (S.D. N.Y. 1985).

4. How do you prove that the patentee has the requisite market power? The first step is obviously to define the market. Each side will have its own ideas of what the relevant market should be. After the relevant market is defined, how should the defendant prove that the patentee has market power? What percentage of the market do you think the patentee must possess to prove market power? 90%? 75%? 50%? 40%? What other factors may form the inquiry into whether the patentee has market power? Do you think that high prices and high profits alone prove market power? Other factors include market characteristic considerations:

1. number and strength of competitors;

2. the potential for entry (whether there are high barriers to entry);

3. consumer sensitivity to price changes;

4. market innovations;

5. whether defendant is a multimarket firm;

6. concentration of market;

7. consumer demand;

8. the historic intensity of competition; and

9. the impact of the legal or natural environment.

Should a patent establish a presumption of market power?

C. ANTITRUST COUNTERCLAIMS

NOBELPHARMA AB v. IMPLANT INNOVATIONS, INC.

141 F.3d 1059, 46 USPQ2d 1097 (Fed. Cir. 1998)

Before RICH, PLAGER, and LOURIE, Circuit Judges.

LOURIE, Circuit Judge.

Nobelpharma AB and Nobelpharma USA, Inc. (collectively, NP) appeal from the judgment of the United States District Court for the Northern District of Illinois holding that ... (3) NP was not entitled to

JMOL or, in the alternative, a new trial following the jury verdict in favor of [Implant Innovations, Inc.] [3I] on its antitrust counterclaim against NP, Dr. Per–Ingvar Branemark, and the Institute for Applied Biotechnology. We conclude that the district court did not err in ... denying NP's motion for JMOL or a new trial on the antitrust counterclaim. Accordingly, the decision of the district court is affirmed.

BACKGROUND

Drs. Branemark and Bo–Thuresson af Ekenstam are the named inventors on the '891 patent, the application for which was filed in 1980 and claimed priority from a Swedish patent application that was filed in 1979. The patent claims "an element intended for implantation into bone tissue." This "element," when used as part of a dental implant, is placed directly into the jawbone where it acts as a tooth root substitute. The implants described and claimed in the patent are preferably made of titanium and have a network of particularly-sized and particularly-spaced "micropits." These micropits, which have diameters in the range of about 10 to 1000 nanometers or, preferably, 10 to 300 nanometers, allow a secure connection to form between the implant and growing bone tissue through a process called "osseointegration."

Branemark is also one of the authors of a book published in 1977, entitled "Osseointegrated Implants in the Treatment of the Edentulous Jaw Experienced from a 10–Year Period" (hereinafter "the 1977 Book"). As its title suggests, this book describes a decade-long clinical evaluation of patients who had received dental implants. The 1977 Book includes a single page containing four scanning electron micrographs (SEMs) of titanium implants that exhibit micropits. The caption describing these SEMs reads, in part: "Irregularities are produced during manufacturing in order to increase the retention of the implants within the mineralized tissue." 3I determined, based on measurements and calculations that it presented to the trial court, that the micropits shown in the 1977 Book have diameters within the range claimed in the '891 patent. However, the 1977 Book does not specifically refer to "micropits."

In preparing to file the Swedish patent application, af Ekenstam submitted a draft written description of the invention to the inventors' Swedish patent agent, Mr. Barnieske. This draft referred to the 1977 Book in the following translated passage:

> In ten years of material pertaining to titanium jaw implants in man, Branemark et al. [in the 1977 Book] have shown that a very high frequency of healing, as stated above, can be achieved by utilizing a carefully developed surgical technique and adequately produced implants.

However, Barnieske deleted all reference to the 1977 Book from the patent application that was ultimately filed in Sweden. Similarly, the 1977 Book is not mentioned in the U.S. patent application filed by Barnieske on behalf of Branemark and af Ekenstam.

In June 1980, while the U.S. patent application was pending, Branemark entered into an exclusive license agreement with NP covering the claimed technology. Barnieske kept NP informed of the prosecution of the U.S. patent application and received assistance from NP's U.S. patent agent. The '891 patent issued in 1982; NP has since asserted it in at least three patent infringement suits.

In July 1991, while Branemark was a member of NP's Board of Directors, NP brought this suit alleging that certain of 3I's dental implants infringed the '891 patent. 3I defended on the grounds of invalidity, unenforceability, and non-infringement. 3I also brought an antitrust counterclaim, based in part on the assertion that NP attempted to enforce a patent that it knew was invalid and unenforceable. Specifically, 3I alleged that when NP brought suit, NP was aware that the inventors' intentional failure to disclose the 1977 Book to the U.S. Patent and Trademark Office (PTO) would render the '891 patent unenforceable.

During its case-in-chief, NP introduced portions of a deposition of Branemark that apparently was conducted several years before this trial began in connection with a lawsuit involving neither NP nor 3I. NP also introduced into evidence portions of that deposition that were counter-designated for introduction by 3I. Branemark's deposition testimony included his admissions that one "could consider" the procedure used to manufacture the micropitted surface a trade secret, and "it might be" that there are details "important to making" the micropitted surface that are not disclosed in the patent. At the close of NP's case-in-chief, the district court granted 3I's motion for JMOL of invalidity and non-infringement. The court held that the patent was invalid under § 112, ¶ 1, for failure to disclose the best mode and that NP had failed to prove infringement. The court then denied NP's motion for JMOL on 3I's antitrust counterclaim, proceeded to inform the jury that the court had held the patent invalid, and allowed 3I to present the counterclaim to the jury.

After trial limited to the antitrust issue, the jury found in special verdicts, *inter alia*, that 3I had proven that (1) "the inventors or their agents or attorneys obtained the '891 patent through fraud," (2) NP "had knowledge that the '891 patent was obtained by fraud at the time this action was commenced against 3I," and (3) NP "brought this lawsuit against 3I knowing that the '891 patent was either invalid or unenforceable and with the intent of interfering directly with 3I's ability to compete in the relevant market." The jury awarded 3I approximately $3.3 million in compensatory damages, an amount the court trebled pursuant to section 4 of the Clayton Act, 15 U.S.C. § 15 (1994). The court declined to rule on whether the patent was unenforceable for inequitable conduct, concluding that its judgment of invalidity rendered the issue of enforceability moot.

DISCUSSION

B. Antitrust Liability

I.

After the jury returned its verdict in favor of 3I on its counterclaim that NP violated the antitrust laws by bringing suit against 3I, the court denied NP's motion for JMOL or, in the alternative, for a new trial under Fed.R.Civ.P. 50(b). In denying NP's motion, the district court held that the verdict was supported, *inter alia*, by the jury's factual findings that the patent was obtained through "NP's knowing fraud upon, or intentional misrepresentations to, the [PTO]" and that "NP maintained and enforced the patent with knowledge of the patent's fraudulent derivation" and with the intent of interfering directly with 3I's ability to compete in the relevant market. The court further held, based on these findings, that the jury need not have considered whether NP's suit was "objectively baseless."

In support of its position that the court erred in denying its renewed motion for JMOL, NP argues that there was a lack of substantial evidence to support the jury's findings that the patent was obtained through "fraud" and that NP was aware of that conduct when it brought suit against 3I. NP also argues that these findings, even if supported by substantial evidence, do not provide a legal basis for the imposition of antitrust liability. Finally, NP argues that it is entitled to a new trial because the court failed to instruct the jury that bringing a lawsuit cannot be the basis for antitrust liability if that suit is not "objectively baseless."

3I responds that the jury's explicit findings that the patent was procured through fraudulent conduct and that NP knew of that conduct when it brought suit were supported by substantial evidence, and that these findings provide a sound basis for imposing antitrust liability on NP. Responding to NP's arguments for a new trial, 3I argues that an "objectively reasonable" or "objectively baseless" jury instruction was not necessary because the district court required that 3I prove that NP had actual knowledge of the fraud when it brought suit and that even if such an instruction had been necessary, NP waived this argument by failing to propose a jury instruction relating to an "objectively baseless" standard. We agree with 3I that the court did not err in denying NP's motion for JMOL because substantial evidence supports the jury's findings that the patent was fraudulently obtained and that NP sought to enforce the patent with knowledge of its fraudulent origin. Similarly, the court did not err in denying NP's motion for a new trial because NP was not prejudiced by any legally erroneous jury instruction.

II.

As a general proposition, when reviewing a district court's judgment involving federal antitrust law, we are guided by the law of the regional circuit in which that district court sits. *See Loctite Corp. v. Ultraseal Ltd.*, 781 F.2d 861, 875, 228 USPQ 90, 99 (Fed. Cir. 1985) ("We must approach a federal antitrust claim as would a court of appeals in the circuit of the district court whose judgment we review."). However, we apply our own law, not regional circuit law, to resolve issues that clearly involve our exclusive jurisdiction. *See Pro–Mold & Tool Co. v. Great Lakes Plastics, Inc.*, 75 F.3d 1568, 1574–75, 37 USPQ2d 1626, 1631 (Fed. Cir. 1996) (holding as a matter of Federal Circuit law that an allegation of inequitable conduct in the prosecution of a patent application cannot support a federal unfair competition claim).

Whether conduct in the prosecution of a patent is sufficient to strip a patentee of its immunity from the antitrust laws is one of those issues that clearly involves our exclusive jurisdiction over patent cases. It follows that whether a patent infringement suit is based on a fraudulently procured patent impacts our exclusive jurisdiction.

Moreover, an antitrust claim premised on stripping a patentee of its immunity from the antitrust laws is typically raised as a counterclaim by a defendant in a patent infringement suit. *See Argus Chem. Corp. v. Fibre Glass–Evercoat Co.*, 812 F.2d 1381, 1383, 1 USPQ2d 1971, 1973 (Fed. Cir. 1987) ("*Walker Process*, like the present case, was a patent infringement suit in which an accused infringer filed an antitrust counterclaim."). Because most cases involving these issues will therefore be appealed to this court, we conclude that we should decide these issues as a matter of Federal Circuit law, rather than rely on various regional precedents. We arrive at this conclusion because we are in the best position to create a uniform body of federal law on this subject and thereby avoid the "danger of confusion [that] might be enhanced if this court were to embark on an effort to interpret the laws" of the regional circuits. Accordingly, we hereby change our precedent and hold that whether conduct in procuring or enforcing a patent is sufficient to strip a patentee of its immunity from the antitrust laws is to be decided as a question of Federal Circuit law.[5] This conclusion applies equally to all antitrust claims premised on the bringing of a patent infringement suit. Therefore, *Cygnus*, 92 F.3d at 1161, 39 USPQ2d at 1672, *Loctite*, 781 F.2d at 875, 228 USPQ at 99, and *Atari*, 747 F.2d at 1438–40, 223 USPQ at 1086–87, are expressly overruled to the extent they hold otherwise. However, we will continue to apply the law of the appropriate regional circuit to issues involving other elements of antitrust law such as relevant market, market power, damages, etc., as those issues are not unique to patent law, which is subject to our exclusive jurisdiction.

III.

A patentee who brings an infringement suit may be subject to antitrust liability for the anti-competitive effects of that suit if the alleged infringer (the antitrust plaintiff) proves (1) that the asserted patent was obtained through knowing and willful fraud within the meaning of *Walker Process Equipment, Inc. v. Food Machinery & Chem. Corp.*, 382 U.S. 172, 177, 147 USPQ 404, 407 (1965), or (2) that the infringement suit was "a mere sham to cover what is actually nothing more than an attempt to interfere directly with the business relation-

---

5. Because precedent may not be changed by a panel, *see South Corp. v. United States*, 690 F.2d 1368, 1370 n. 2, 215 USPQ 657, 658 n. 2 (Fed. Cir. 1982) (*in banc*), the issue of "choice of circuit" law set forth in this Section B.II. has been considered and decided unanimously by an *in banc* court consisting of MAYER, Chief Judge, RICH, NEWMAN, MICHEL, PLAGER, LOURIE, CLEVENGER, RADER, SCHALL, BRYSON, and GAJARSA, Circuit Judges.

ships of a competitor," *Eastern R.R. Presidents Conference v. Noerr Motor Freight, Inc.*, 365 U.S. 127, 144 (1961).

In *Walker Process*, the Supreme Court held that in order "to strip [a patentee] of its exemption from the antitrust laws" because of its attempting to enforce its patent monopoly, an antitrust plaintiff is first required to prove that the patentee "obtained the patent by knowingly and willfully misrepresenting facts[6] to the [PTO]." 382 U.S. at 177, 147 USPQ at 407. The plaintiff in the patent infringement suit must also have been aware of the fraud when bringing suit.

Justice Harlan, in a concurring opinion, emphasized that to "achiev[e] a suitable accommodation in this area between the differing policies of the patent and antitrust laws," a distinction must be maintained between patents procured by "deliberate fraud" and those rendered invalid or unenforceable for other reasons. He then stated:

> [T]o hold, as we do not, that private antitrust suits might also reach monopolies practiced under patents that for one reason or another may turn out to be voidable under one or more of the numerous technicalities attending the issuance of a patent, might well chill the disclosure of inventions through the obtaining of a patent because of fear of the vexations or punitive consequences of treble-damage suits. Hence, this private antitrust remedy should not be deemed available to reach [Sherman Act] § 2 monopolies carried on under a nonfraudulently procured patent.

Id. at 180, 147 USPQ at 408.

Consistent with the Supreme Court's analysis in *Walker Process*, as well as Justice Harlan's concurring opinion, we have distinguished "inequitable conduct" from *Walker Process* fraud, noting that inequitable conduct is a broader, more inclusive concept than the common law fraud needed to support a Walker Process counterclaim. Inequitable conduct in fact is a lesser offense than common law fraud, and includes types of conduct less serious than "knowing and willful" fraud.

In *Norton v. Curtiss*, 57 C.C.P.A. 1384, 433 F.2d 779, 792–94 & n. 12, 167 USPQ 532, 543–45 & n. 12 (1970), our predecessor court explicitly distinguished inequitable conduct from "fraud," as that term was used by the Supreme Court in *Walker Process*. The court noted that

> the concept of "fraud" has most often been used by the courts, in general, to refer to a type of conduct so reprehensible that it could alone form the basis of an actionable wrong (e.g., the common law action for deceit.) . . . . Because severe penalties are usually meted out to the party found guilty of such conduct, technical fraud is generally held not to exist unless the following indispensable ele-

---

6. The alleged misrepresentation in that case involved the patentee's sworn statement "that it neither knew nor believed that its invention had been in public use in the United States more than one year prior to filing its patent application when, in fact, [it] was a party to prior use within such time." *Walker Process*, 382 U.S. at 174, 147 USPQ at 406. The PTO does not currently require inventors to file a sworn statement regarding such knowledge or belief. *See* 35 U.S.C § 115 (1994); 37 C.F.R. § 1.63 (1996).

ments are found to be present: (1) a representation of a material fact, (2) the falsity of that representation, (3) the intent to deceive or, at least, a state of mind so reckless as to the consequences that it is held to be the equivalent of intent (scienter), (4) a justifiable reliance upon the misrepresentation by the party deceived which induces him to act thereon, and (5) injury to the party deceived as a result of his reliance on the misrepresentation.

Id. at 792–93, 57 C.C.P.A. 1384, 167 USPQ at 543. The court then contrasted such independently actionable common law fraud with lesser misconduct, including what we now refer to as inequitable conduct, which "fail[s], for one reason or another, to satisfy all the elements of the technical offense." *Norton*, 433 F.2d at 793, 167 USPQ at 543. Regarding such misconduct, "the courts appear to look at the equities of the particular case and determine whether the conduct before them … was still so reprehensible as to justify the court's refusing to enforce the rights of the party guilty of such conduct." *Id.*

Inequitable conduct is thus an equitable defense in a patent infringement action and serves as a shield, while a more serious finding of fraud potentially exposes a patentee to antitrust liability and thus serves as a sword. Antitrust liability can include treble damages. *See* 15 U.S.C. § 15(a) (1994). In contrast, the remedies for inequitable conduct, while serious enough, only include unenforceability of the affected patent or patents and possible attorney fees. *See* 35 U.S.C. §§ 282, 285 (1994). Simply put, *Walker Process* fraud is a more serious offense than inequitable conduct.

In this case, the jury was instructed that a finding of fraud could be premised on "a knowing, willful and intentional act, misrepresentation or omission before the [PTO]." This instruction was not inconsistent with various opinions of the courts stating that omissions, as well as misrepresentations, may in limited circumstances support a finding of *Walker Process* fraud. We agree that if the evidence shows that the asserted patent was acquired by means of either a fraudulent misrepresentation or a fraudulent omission and that the party asserting the patent was aware of the fraud when bringing suit, such conduct can expose a patentee to liability under the antitrust laws. We arrive at this conclusion because a fraudulent omission can be just as reprehensible as a fraudulent misrepresentation. In addition, of course, in order to find liability, the necessary additional elements of a violation of the antitrust laws must be established.

Such a misrepresentation or omission must evidence a clear intent to deceive the examiner and thereby cause the PTO to grant an invalid patent. In contrast, a conclusion of inequitable conduct may be based on evidence of a lesser misrepresentation or an omission, such as omission of a reference that would merely have been considered important to the patentability of a claim by a reasonable examiner. A finding of *Walker Process* fraud requires higher threshold showings of both intent and materiality than does a finding of inequitable conduct. Moreover, unlike a finding of inequitable conduct, a finding of *Walker Process* fraud may not be based upon an equitable balancing of lesser degrees of materiality and intent. Rather, it must be based on independent and clear evidence of deceptive intent together with a clear showing of reliance, i.e., that the patent would not have issued but for the misrepresentation or omission. Therefore, for an omission such as a failure to cite a piece of prior art to support a finding of *Walker Process* fraud, the withholding of the reference must show evidence of fraudulent intent. A mere failure to cite a reference to the PTO will not suffice.

IV.

The district court observed that the Supreme Court, in footnote six of its *PRE* opinion, "left unresolved the issue of how '*Noerr* applies to the *ex parte* application process,' and in particular, how it applies to the *Walker Process* claim." The court also accurately pointed out that we have twice declined to resolve this issue. Therefore, after reviewing three opinions from the Ninth and District of Columbia Circuit Courts of Appeals, the district court made its own determination that *PRE*'s two-part test for a sham is inapplicable to an antitrust claim based on the assertion of a patent obtained by knowing and willful fraud. We do not agree with that determination. *PRE* and *Walker Process* provide alternative legal grounds on which a patentee may be stripped of its immunity from the antitrust laws; both legal theories may be applied to the same conduct. Moreover, we need not find a way to merge these decisions. Each provides its own basis for depriving a patent owner of immunity from the antitrust laws; either or both may be applicable to a particular party's conduct in obtaining and enforcing a patent. The Supreme Court saw no need to merge these separate lines of cases and neither do we.

Consequently, if the above-described elements of *Walker Process* fraud, as well as the other criteria for antitrust liability, are met, such liability can be imposed without the additional sham inquiry required under *PRE.* That is because *Walker Process* antitrust liability is based on the knowing assertion of a patent procured by fraud on the PTO, very specific conduct that is clearly reprehensible. On the other hand, irrespective of the patent applicant's conduct before the PTO, an antitrust claim can also be based on a *PRE* allegation that a suit is baseless; in order to prove that a suit was within *Noerr*'s "sham" exception to immunity, an antitrust plaintiff must prove that the suit was both objectively baseless and subjectively motivated by a desire to impose collateral, anti-competitive injury rather than to obtain a justifiable legal remedy. As the Supreme Court stated:

> First, the lawsuit must be objectively baseless in the sense that no reasonable litigant could realistically expect success on the merits. If an objective litigant could conclude that the suit is reasonably calculated to elicit a favorable outcome, the suit is immunized under *Noerr*, and an antitrust claim premised on the sham exception must fail. Only if challenged litigation is objectively meritless may a court examine the litigant's subjective motivation. Under this second part of our definition of sham, the court should focus on whether the baseless lawsuit conceals "an attempt to interfere directly with the

business relationships of a competitor," through the "use [of] the governmental process—as opposed to the outcome of that process—as an anticompetitive weapon." ... Of course, even a plaintiff who defeats the defendant's claim to *Noerr* immunity by demonstrating both the objective and the subjective components of a sham must still prove a substantive antitrust violation. Proof of a sham merely deprives the defendant of immunity; it does not relieve the plaintiff of the obligation to establish all other elements of his claim.

Thus, under *PRE*, a sham suit must be both subjectively brought in bad faith and based on a theory of either infringement or validity that is objectively baseless. Accordingly, if a suit is not objectively baseless, an antitrust defendant's subjective motivation is immaterial. In contrast with a *Walker Process* claim, a patentee's activities in procuring the patent are not necessarily at issue. It is the bringing of the lawsuit that is subjectively and objectively baseless that must be proved.

V.

As for the present case, we conclude that there exists substantial evidence upon which a reasonable fact finder could strip NP of its immunity from antitrust liability. In particular, there exists substantial evidence that the 1977 Book was fraudulently kept from the PTO during patent prosecution. The jury could reasonably have found that the 1977 Book was fraudulently withheld and that it disclosed the claimed invention. First, the jury could reasonably have concluded that Branemark, through his Swedish patent agent, Barnieske, withheld the 1977 Book with the requisite intent to defraud the PTO. The initial disclosure to Barnieske, provided by Branemark's co-inventor, af Ekenstam, indicated that the studies described in the 1977 Book verified the utility of the claimed invention. While Barnieske did testify that he did not recall his thoughts during the prosecution of the patent and that he would have submitted the 1977 Book to the PTO if he had considered it relevant, the jury was free to disbelieve him. Barnieske could not explain, even in retrospect, why he deleted all reference to the 1977 Book. Importantly, the 1977 Book was thought by at least one inventor to be relevant, as evidenced by the initial disclosure to the patent agent, but it was inexplicably not later disclosed to the PTO. Also, as the author of the 1977 Book and an inventor, Branemark presumably knew of the book's relevance to the invention and could have directed Barnieske not to disclose the book to the PTO. Thus, the jury could properly have inferred that Branemark had the requisite intent to defraud the PTO based on his failure to disclose the reference to the PTO. Such a scheme to defraud is the type of conduct contemplated by *Walker Process*.

Second, substantial evidence upon which a reasonable jury could have relied also indicates that the 1977 Book was sufficiently material to justify a finding of fraud. 3I's expert witness, Dr. Donald Brunette, testified that the SEMs of the 1977 Book depict dental implants having all the elements of the claims asserted by NP. Specifically, he explained how he had determined that the SEMs depict a "biologically flawless material" suitable for use as a dental implant. He also explained how he determined that the depicted micropits have diameters within the claimed range of approximately 10 to 1000 nanometers. Even Branemark, in his deposition testimony, conceded that it would not have been difficult to calculate the size of the micropits depicted in the 1977 Book, given the magnification factors provided in the captions to the SEMs. Accordingly, a reasonable jury could have found, based on the unambiguous claim language, that the 1977 Book anticipated the patent and that the examiner would not have granted the patent if he had been aware of the 1977 Book.

Third, the record indicates that a reasonable jury could have found that NP brought suit against 3I with knowledge of the applicants' fraud. A reasonable jury could have found that two of NP's then-officers, Dr. Ralph Green, Jr. and Mr. Mats Nilsson, were aware of the fraud based on Green's testimony that Nilsson told him: "[I]f the Patent Office did not receive a copy of [the 1977 Book], and if that were true, then we would have a larger problem and that was fraud." Green's testimony also indicates that NP was aware that the 1977 Book was highly material and, in fact, likely rendered the patent invalid. Green testified that he, Nilsson, and Mr. George Vande Sande obtained a legal opinion from NP's attorney, Mr. David Lindley, who indicated that if "we were to sue anyone on the patent we would lose in the first round.... [T]here was prior art, not the least of which was this textbook [the 1977 Book] that would invalidate the patent."

Regarding NP's motion for a new trial, we have concluded that the court's instructions to the jury regarding fraud, to which NP did not object, substantially comport with the law. Specifically, the court emphasized to the jury that to strip NP of its immunity from the antitrust laws, 3I "must prove that the '891 patent was fraudulently ... obtained by clear and convincing evidence." The court also pointed out that only "knowing, willful and intentional acts, misrepresentations or omission" may support a finding of fraud and that the jury should approach such a finding with "great care." As to reliance, the court instructed the jury that "[m]ateriality is shown if but for the misrepresentation or omission the '891 patent would not have been issued." These instructions were not legally erroneous.

Because we conclude that the finding of *Walker Process* fraud was supported by substantial evidence and was based upon a jury instruction that was not legally erroneous or prejudicial, we affirm the denial of NP's motion for JMOL. NP was properly deprived of its immunity from the antitrust laws under *Walker Process*, and it could not have benefitted from additional jury instructions regarding *PRE* or *Noerr*. The court's refusal to so instruct the jury therefore does not require a new trial.

Notes

1. **Antitrust Counterclaims**. As stated in *Nobelpharma AB v. Implant Innovations, Inc.*, 141 F.3d 1059, 1070, 46 USPQ2d 1097, 1106 (Fed. Cir. 1998) "inequitable conduct is ... an equitable defense in a patent infringement action and serves as a shield, while a more serious finding of

fraud potentially exposes a patentee to antitrust liability and thus serves as a sword.'' An alleged infringer with evidence of fraud on the part of the patentee may be awarded treble damages in a successful antitrust counter-claim.

2. **Tension Between Antitrust Laws and Patent Laws**. *Nobelpharma* can be seen as illustrating two competing areas of law. On the one hand, patent law which provides a limited duration monopoly to the patent holder; on the other, antitrust legislation is designed to prevent anticompetitive activity. The tension between these two areas of law stems from different policy considerations. Antitrust legislation is intended to benefit society by fostering legitimate competitive activities. However, patent law, while also ultimately intended to benefit society attempts to achieve this goal by providing incentives to inventors—namely a limited duration monopoly. A patent holder is immune from antitrust liability unless, as demonstrated by *Nobelpharma*, 141 F.3d at 1067, 46 USPQ2d at 1104, the patent holder is stripped of the immunity by fraudulently procuring the patent.

3. *Nobelpharma*, has an interesting procedural history. The Federal Circuit initially decided the antitrust issue in favor of the patent holder. *Nobelpharma AB v. Implant Innovations, Inc.*, 129 F.3d 1463 (Fed. Cir. 1997). However, upon reconsideration and after submitting the ''choice of circuits'' law issue to an *in banc* court, the opinion was withdrawn and the trial court was affirmed.

4. Can refusal to license your patented technology be an antitrust violation? What if your refusal effectively extends your monopoly into an unpatented market? Should a company be permitted to charge exorbitant prices for patented replacement parts to effectively keep competitors out of the market for servicing their products? For example, if a company had a patent on a computer and patents on several of the parts, should it be permitted to charge an exorbitant price for replacement parts in order to keep others out of the business of servicing the computer when it breaks. *See In re Independent Services Organizations Antitrust Litigation*, 964 F. Supp. 1479, (D. Kan. 1997) (''Although a patent holder perhaps extends his 'economic power' by this conduct, he has not expanded the scope of the patented 'invention.' Indeed, the patent statute states that the unilateral refusal to license or use a patent shall not constitute misuse and shall not be deemed an 'illegal extension of the patent right.' 35 U.S.C. § 271(d)(4). The fact that Xerox has attempted to secure the full benefit of its 'patent monopoly' by entering more than one market does not raise any antitrust concerns which have not already been considered and balanced by Congress in enacting the patent statute.'').

D.   LACHES AND EQUITABLE ESTOPPEL

Laches and equitable estoppel are equitable issues that must be decided by the judge. The accused infringer must prove them by a preponderance of the evidence to succeed. The following case examines both doctrines and the differences between them.

A.C. AUKERMAN CO. v. R.L. CHAIDES CONSTRUCTION CO.

960 F.2d 1020, 22 USPQ2d 1321 (Fed. Cir. 1992)

Before NIES, Chief Judge, RICH, NEWMAN, ARCHER, MAYER, PLAGER, LOURIE, CLEVENGER, and RADER, Circuit Judges.

NIES, Chief Judge.

This court reheard Appeal No. 90–1137 in banc to reconsider the principles of laches and equitable estoppel applicable in a patent infringement suit. A.C. Aukerman Co. sued R.L. Chaides Construction Co. in the United States District Court for the Northern District of California for infringement of Aukerman's patents, U.S. Patent Nos. 3,793,133 ('133) and 4,014,633 ('633). The district court held on summary judgment that Aukerman was barred under principles of laches and equitable estoppel from maintaining the suit and Aukerman appeals. We conclude that the correct standards, which we have clarified herein, were not applied in the district court's grant of summary judgment. Moreover, upon application of the correct law, genuine issues of material fact arise with respect to the issues of laches and equitable estoppel. Accordingly, we reverse the court's ruling on the motion for summary judgment and remand for proceedings consistent with this opinion.

I.

Background

The following facts are not disputed. Aukerman is the assignee of the '133 and '633 patents, relating to, respectively, a method and device for forming concrete highway barriers capable of separating highway surfaces of different elevations. The device allows a contractor to slip-form an asymmetrical barrier as the mold is moved down the highway, i.e., to pour the barriers directly onto the highway without having to construct a mold. In settlement of litigation with Gomaco Corporation, a manufacturer of slip-forms which may be used to form regular or variable height barriers, Aukerman entered into an agreement in 1977 which made Gomaco a licensee under the patents and required Gomaco to notify Aukerman of all those who purchased Gomaco's adjustable slip-forms.

Upon notification that Chaides had purchased a slip-form from Gomaco, counsel for Aukerman advised Chaides by letter dated February 13, 1979, that use of the device raised "a question of infringement with respect to one or more of (Aukerman's patents-in-suit)," and offered Chaides a license. Follow-on letters were sent by Aukerman's counsel to Chaides on March 16 and April 12, 1979. Chaides replied by telephone on April 17, 1979 but was unable to speak with counsel for Aukerman. By letter of April 24, 1979, Aukerman's counsel advised Chaides that Aukerman was seeking to enforce its patents against all infringers and that, even though Chaides might be among the smaller contractors, it had the same need for a license as larger firms. He advised further that Aukerman would waive liability for past infringement and infringement under existing contracts if Chaides took a license by June 1, 1979. Chaides responded in late April with a note handwritten on Aukerman's last letter stating that he felt any responsibility was Gomaco's and that, if Aukerman wished to sue Chaides "for $200–$300 a year," Aukerman should do so. There was no further correspondence or contact between the parties for more than eight years. In the interim, Chaides increased its business of forming asymmetrical highway barrier walls. Sometime in the mid–80's, Chaides made a second adjustable mold for pouring step wall which Aukerman alleges is an infringement.

Apparently in 1987, one of Aukerman's licensees, Baumgartner, Inc., advised Aukerman that Chaides was a substantial competitor for pouring asymmetrical wall in California. This advice prompted Aukerman's new counsel to send a letter to Chaides on October 22, 1987, referencing the earlier correspondence, advising that litigation against another company had been resolved, and threatening litigation unless Chaides executed the licenses previously sent within two weeks. Another period of silence followed. On August 2, 1988, Aukerman's counsel again wrote Chaides explaining more fully Aukerman's licensing proposal. When no reply was received, on October 26, 1988, Aukerman filed suit charging Chaides with infringing its '133 and '633 patents.

The district court granted summary judgment in favor of Chaides, holding that the doctrines of laches and estoppel barred Aukerman's claims for relief. The court, citing *Jamesbury Corp. v. Litton Indus. Prods.*, 839 F.2d 1544, 5 USPQ2d 1779 (Fed. Cir. 1988), ruled that Aukerman's delay of more than six years in suing Chaides shifted the burden to Aukerman to prove that its delay was reasonable and was not prejudicial to Chaides. The court rejected Aukerman's proffered excuse that it was engaged in other litigation because such litigation did not cover the period from February 22, 1979, to July 31, 1980, after it first contacted Chaides, and in any event, Aukerman gave no notice to Chaides of any litigation during the period of delay up to October 1987. The court rejected Aukerman's further argument that the delay in suit was attributable to Chaides' representation of de minimis infringement. The court held that the evidence showed prejudice to Chaides in that (1) Chaides would have to pay a license fee on projects it had bid on without having allowed for this normal cost and (2) Chaides might have gone into bankruptcy had it known of its liability for past infringement. The court also held that Chaides' ability to defend itself would be prejudiced because necessary witnesses for Chaides' defense, including the inventor named in the subject patents, were unavailable and that memories of other witnesses, such as Mr. Aukerman's, had faded.

Respecting equitable estoppel, the court placed the burden on Chaides to establish this defense. The court then held that Aukerman's silence for nearly ten years after making an initial protest was sufficiently misleading to constitute bad faith and that Aukerman should have notified Chaides of the effect of the otherwise ambiguous June 1, 1979 deadline. The court went on to determine that Chaides had detrimentally relied on Aukerman's silence in deciding to forego bankruptcy and to bid low on highway contracts.

The court also found the defenses of laches and equitable estoppel were not defeated by reason of Chaides' "unclean hands." In particular, Aukerman had pointed to Chaides having made a copy of the Gomaco slip-form. The court stated Aukerman presented no evidence on "how the copy infringed the patent." Finally, it held that by the mid–80s, when this device was in use, Aukerman had already affirmatively misled Chaides.

For these reasons, the district court entered judgment for Chaides.

II.

SUMMARY

The court has taken this case in banc to clarify and apply principles of laches and equitable estoppel which have been raised as defenses in this patent infringement suit. In summary, for reasons to be more fully discussed, we hold with respect to laches:

    1. Laches is cognizable under 35 U.S.C. § 282 (1988) as an equitable defense to a claim for patent infringement.

    2. Where the defense of laches is established, the patentee's claim for damages prior to suit may be barred.

    3. Two elements underlie the defense of laches: (a) the patentee's delay in bringing suit was unreasonable and inexcusable, and (b) the alleged infringer suffered material prejudice attributable to the delay. The district court should consider these factors and all of the evidence and other circumstances to determine whether equity should intercede to bar pre-filing damages.

    4. A presumption of laches arises where a patentee delays bringing suit for more than six years after the date the patentee knew or should have known of the alleged infringer's activity.

    5. A presumption has the effect of shifting the burden of going forward with evidence, not the burden of persuasion.

With respect to equitable estoppel against a patent infringement claim, we hold that:

    1. Equitable estoppel is cognizable under 35 U.S.C. § 282 as an equitable defense to a claim for patent infringement.

    2. Where an alleged infringer establishes the defense of equitable estoppel, the patentee's claim may be entirely barred.

    3. Three elements must be established to bar a patentee's suit by reason of equitable estoppel:

        a. The patentee, through misleading conduct, leads the alleged infringer to reasonably infer that the patentee does not intend to enforce its patent against the alleged infringer. "Conduct" may include specific statements, action, inaction, or silence where there was an obligation to speak.

 b. The alleged infringer relies on that conduct.

 c. Due to its reliance, the alleged infringer will be materially prejudiced if the patentee is allowed to proceed with its claim.

4. No presumption is applicable to the defense of equitable estoppel.

As equitable defenses, laches and equitable estoppel are matters committed to the sound discretion of the trial judge and the trial judge's decision is reviewed by this court under the abuse of discretion standard. We appreciate that the district court, in deciding the instant case, did not have the benefit of these statements of legal principles which differ in some respects from our precedent. We have no alternative, however, but to rule that, when these principles are applied to the record before us, the district court erred in granting summary judgment in favor of Chaides.

III.

LACHES

A. Viability of Laches Defense

The Supreme Court has long recognized the defense of laches to a patent infringement action brought in equity. Laches may be defined generally as "slackness or carelessness toward duty or opportunity." Webster's Third New International Dictionary (1969). In a legal context, laches may be defined as the neglect or delay in bringing suit to remedy an alleged wrong, which taken together with lapse of time and other circumstances, causes prejudice to the adverse party and operates as an equitable bar. "[Laches] exacts of the plaintiff no more than fair dealing with his adversary." 5 J.N. POMEROY, EQUITY JURISPRUDENCE § 21, at 43 (Equitable Remedies Supp. 1905). In refusing to enforce a patentee's claim of infringement, the Supreme Court invoked the maxim: "Courts of equity, it has often been said, will not assist one who has slept upon his rights, and shows no excuse for his laches in asserting them." *Lane & Bodley*, 150 U.S. at 201.

Extended to suits at law as well, laches became "part of the general body of rules governing relief in the federal court system." Id. at 478. As a defense to a claim of patent infringement, laches was well established at the time of recodification of the patent laws in 1952. The commentary of one of the drafters of the revised patent statute confirms the intention to retain the defense of laches, specifically by 35 U.S.C. § 282:

> The defenses which may be raised in an action involving the validity or infringement of a patent are[:].... 'Noninfringement, absence of liability for infringement, or unenforceability' [35 U.S.C. § 282][;] ... this would include ... equitable defenses such as laches, estoppel and unclean hands.

P.J. Federico, Commentary on the New Patent Law, 35 U.S.C.A. 1, 55 (West 1954). In *J.P. Stevens & Co. v. Lex Tex Ltd. Inc.*, 747 F.2d 1553, 1561, 223 USPQ 1089, 1093 (Fed. Cir. 1984), this court so interpreted section 282 stating: Paragraph (1) [of Section 282] includes "equitable defenses such as laches, estoppel and unclean hands."

Aukerman argues, nevertheless, that the defense of laches is inapplicable, as a matter of law, against a claim for damages in patent infringement suits. For this proposition, Aukerman first argues that recognition of laches as a defense conflicts with 35 U.S.C. § 286 (1988), which provides:

> Except as otherwise provided by law, no recovery shall be had for any infringement committed more than six years prior to the filing of the complaint or counterclaim for infringement in the action.

Per Aukerman, this provision is comparable to a statute of limitations which effectively preempts the laches defense.

Aukerman's argument is doubly flawed. First, Aukerman is in error in its position that, where an express statute of limitations applies against a claim, laches cannot apply within the limitation period. In other areas of our jurisdiction, laches is routinely applied within the prescribed statute of limitations period for bringing the claim.

Second, with respect to section 286 specifically, a six-year limitation on damages, virtually identical to section 286, has been in the patent statute since 1897. As explained in *Standard Oil Co. v. Nippon Shokubai Kagaku Kogyo Co.*, 754 F.2d 345, 347–48, 224 USPQ 863, 865–66 (Fed. Cir. 1985), section 286 is not a statute of limitations in the sense of barring a suit for infringement. Assuming a finding of liability, the effect of section 286 is to limit recovery to damages for infringing acts committed within six years of the date of the filing of the infringement action. One counts backwards from the date of the complaint to limit pre-filing damages arbitrarily. . . .

We are unpersuaded that section 286 should be interpreted to preclude the defense of laches and provide, in effect, a guarantee of six years damages regardless of equitable considerations arising from delay in assertion of one's rights. Without exception, all circuits recognized laches as a defense to a charge of patent infringement despite the reenactment of the damages limitation in the 1952 statute. This is not remarkable inasmuch as the statutory language of section 286 was virtually identical to a predecessor provision under which laches was also recognized.

Aukerman also argues that laches, by reason of being an equitable defense, may be applied only to monetary awards resulting from an equitable accounting, not to legal claims for damages. Inasmuch as the patent statute was amended in 1946 to eliminate the remedy of an equitable accounting, per Aukerman, this change also eliminated the basis for a laches defense. We disagree. . . .

[T]he right to interpose the equitable defense of laches in a civil action is specifically recognized in Fed.R.Civ.P. 8(c). Hence, we are unpersuaded that the technical distinction between application of laches against legal damages and an equitable accounting which Aukerman asks us to draw should be made.

Finally, Aukerman asserts that it is improper to utilize laches as a defense to completely bar recovery of prefiling damages flowing from a continuing tort, such as patent infringement. We understand Aukerman to be arguing that, because each act of infringement is deemed a separate claim, the laches defense, like a statute of limitations, must be established separately with respect to each such act.

Aukerman's theory conflicts with the precedent of the Supreme Court in which laches has been applied against continuing torts as in *Lane & Bodley*, 150 U.S. 193 (patent infringement) and *Menendez v. Holt*, 128 U.S. 514 (1888) (trademark infringement). In those cases, as well as in our precedent and that of other circuits, laches has been viewed as a single defense to a continuing tort up to the time of suit, not a series of individual defenses which must be proved as to each act of infringement, at least with respect to infringing acts of the same nature. To that extent, continuing tortious acts may be deemed to constitute a unitary claim.

In any event, Aukerman's argument, which focuses on acts of the defendant, distorts the basic concept of laches. Laches focuses on the dilatory conduct of the patentee and the prejudice which the patentee's delay has caused. As stated in *Holmberg v. Armbrecht*, 327 U.S. 392, 396 (1946), "a federal court ... may dismiss a suit where the plaintiffs' 'lack of diligence is wholly unexcused; and both the nature of the claim and the situation of the parties was such as to call for diligence.'" (quoting *Benedict v. City of New York*, 250 U.S. 321, 328 (1919)).

Thus, we reaffirm the ruling in *Leinoff v. Louis Milona & Sons*, 726 F.2d 734, 220 USPQ 845 (Fed. Cir. 1984) and our subsequent precedent that laches is available as a defense to a suit for patent infringement. As explained in *Leinoff*, "since there is no statute from which to determine the timeliness of an infringement action, vis-a-vis the patentee's first knowledge of infringement, courts use the equitable doctrine of laches." 726 F.2d at 741, 220 USPQ at 850.

B. Laches Factors

The application of the defense of laches is committed to the sound discretion of the district court. With its origins in equity, a determination of laches is not made upon the application of "mechanical rules." *Holmberg*, 327 U.S. at 396. The defense, being personal to the particular party and equitable in nature, must have flexibility in its application. A court must look at all of the particular facts and circumstances of each case and weigh the equities of the parties.

It is, however, well settled that, to invoke the laches defense, a defendant has the burden to prove two factors:

1. the plaintiff delayed filing suit for an unreasonable and inexcusable length of time from the time the plaintiff knew or reasonably should have known of its claim against the defendant, and

2. the delay operated to the prejudice or injury of the defendant.

The length of time which may be deemed unreasonable has no fixed boundaries but rather depends on the circumstances. The period of delay is measured from the time the plaintiff knew or reasonably should have known of the defendant's alleged infringing activities to the date of suit. However, the period does not begin prior to issuance of the patent.

Material prejudice to adverse parties resulting from the plaintiff's delay is essential to the laches defense. Such prejudice may be either economic or evidentiary. Evidentiary, or "defense" prejudice, may arise by reason of a defendant's inability to present a full and fair defense on the merits due to the loss of records, the death of a witness, or the unreliability of memories of long past events, thereby undermining the court's ability to judge the facts.

Economic prejudice may arise where a defendant and possibly others will suffer the loss of monetary investments or incur damages which likely would have been prevented by earlier suit. Such damages or monetary losses are not merely those attributable to a finding of liability for infringement. Economic prejudice would then arise in every suit. The courts must look for a change in the economic position of the alleged infringer during the period of delay. On the other hand, this does not mean that a patentee may intentionally lie silently in wait watching damages escalate, particularly where an infringer, if he had had notice, could have switched to a noninfringing product. Indeed, economic prejudice is not a simple concept but rather is likely to be a slippery issue to resolve.

A court must also consider and weigh any justification offered by the plaintiff for its delay. Excuses which have been recognized in some instances, and we do not mean this list to be exhaustive, include: other litigation; negotiations with the accused; possibly poverty and illness under limited circumstances; wartime conditions; extent of infringement; and dispute over ownership of the patent. The equities may or may not require that the plaintiff communicate its reasons for delay to the defendant.

A patentee may also defeat a laches defense if the infringer "has engaged in particularly egregious conduct which would change the equities significantly in plaintiff's favor." *Bott*, 807 F.2d at 1576, 1 USPQ2d at 1216–17. Conscious copying may be such a factor weighing against the defendant, whereas ignorance or a good faith belief in the merits of a defense may tilt matters in its favor.

In the simplest or purest form of laches, there need be no direct contact between the plaintiff and the defendant from the time the plaintiff becomes aware of its claim until the suit. *See Safeway Stores v. Safeway Quality Foods*, 433 F.2d 99, 103, 166 USPQ 112, 115 (7th Cir. 1970) ("For sixteen years [plaintiff] did nothing to put the defendants upon notice of its claims.") In other instances, the plaintiff may make an objection to the defendant and then do nothing more for years. In *Lane & Bodley*, laches was found where the plaintiff gave no notice of infringement and delayed suit in order to continue receiving a salary from the defendant. Where there has been contact or a relationship between the parties during the delay period which may give rise to an inference that the plaintiff has abandoned its claim against the defendant, the facts may lend themselves to analysis under principles of equitable estoppel, as well as laches (*see* Section IV *infra*). However, the two defenses are not the same. As we have indicated, laches focuses on the reasonableness of the plaintiff's delay in suit. As will become evident, equitable estoppel focuses on what the defendant has been led to reasonably believe from the plaintiff's conduct. Thus, for laches, the length of delay, the seriousness of prejudice, the reasonableness of excuses, and the defendant's conduct or culpability must be weighed to determine whether the patentee dealt unfairly with the alleged infringer by not promptly bringing suit. In sum, a district court must weigh all pertinent facts and equities in making a decision on the laches defense.

C. Presumption of Laches

As this court explained in *Panduit Corp. v. All States Plastic Mfg. Co.*, 744 F.2d 1564, 1581, 223 USPQ 465, 476 (Fed. Cir. 1984), presumptions, whether created by statute or by judicial ruling, "arise out of considerations of fairness, public policy, and probability."

Courts faced with patent infringement actions "borrowed" the six-year damage limitation period in the patent statute now set out in section 286, as the time period for giving rise to a rebuttable presumption of laches. The six years in the statute, as indicated, begins with the date of suit and counts backward. The six years for laches begins with a patentee's knowledge of infringement and counts forward. Thus, the two periods in real time may be completely unrelated. They have in common only the same number of years. . . .

The presumption of laches arising from a more than six-year delay in filing suit is consonant with the mainstream of the law. The length of the time period—six years—is reasonable compared to the presumptions respecting laches in other situations, which may be as short as one year. Also the presumption provides a yardstick for reaching comparable results in comparable circumstances rather than leaving the matter without any guidelines to a district court's exercise of discretion. In any event, this court adopted a laches presumption seven years ago in *Leinoff*, 726 F.2d at 741–42, 220 USPQ at 850, agreeing with our sister circuits that the presumption represents an equitable balancing of the interests of the parties.

Aukerman asks that we discard the presumption of laches in patent cases and require an alleged infringer to prove each of the underlying factual elements thereby presumed. It argues that the presumption of laches is as unfair in patent litigation as the presumption of prejudice eliminated by our decision in *Cornetta v. United States*, 851 F.2d 1372 (Fed. Cir. 1988), which had previously been afforded the government by reason of an unreasonable delay in bringing a military pay case.

To support this change in the law, Aukerman asserts that prejudice from time delay in patent litigation is "overblown." It argues that patent defenses rest primarily on documentary evidence, not eyewitness accounts, and that, if witnesses forget information, it is likely they have done so long before the six-year period of the presumption. It also notes that an infringer could file a declaratory judgment action. However, our experience, which appellant invokes, has been that testimonial evidence is frequently critical to invalidity defenses and almost always so respecting unenforceability. Further, in assessing the propriety of the laches presumption, it cannot be assumed that the patentee generally makes a charge of infringement which would support a declaratory judgment action by the alleged infringer. In the simplest form of laches, as indicated above, no contact between the parties occurs prior to suit. Thus, this argument does not support a rejection of the laches presumption.

Other arguments by Aukerman that the presumption places unreasonable burdens on the patentee are not persuasive as will become apparent in the section of this opinion, infra, explaining the effect of the presumption.

In sum, we conclude that the presumption of laches based on the relevant six-year period, previously adopted in our precedent, should be maintained. Prima facie, the underlying critical factors of laches are presumed upon proof that the patentee delayed filing suit for more than six years after actual or constructive knowledge of the defendant's alleged infringing activity.

It must be emphasized that the establishment of the factors of undue delay and prejudice, whether by actual proof or by the presumption, does not mandate recognition of a laches defense in every case. Laches remains an equitable judgment of the trial court in light of all the circumstances. Laches is not established by undue delay and prejudice. Those factors merely lay the foundation for the trial court's exercise of discretion. Where there is evidence of other factors which would make it inequitable to recognize the defense despite undue delay and prejudice, the defense may be denied.

D.   *Effect of the Laches Presumption*

By reason of the presumption, absent other equitable considerations, a prima facie defense of laches is made out upon proof by the accused infringer that the patentee delayed filing suit for six years after actual or constructive knowledge of the defendant's acts of alleged infringement. Without the presumption, the two facts of unreasonable delay and prejudice might reasonably be inferred from the length of the delay, but not necessarily. With the presumption, these facts must be inferred, absent rebuttal evidence. As explained in 10 Moore's, *supra*, § 301.02, at III–13–14:

> [A] factual conclusion reached by inference is based on a process of reasoning and experience. A presumption, however, is a method of dealing with proof, normally to give it a greater effect than it would have if it were handled solely by the inferential process.

Numerous decisions indicate or suggest that the defendant's establishing a six-year delay shifts the burden of proof, that is, the ultimate burden of persuasion, from the defendant to the patentee. For example, the *Leinoff* decision could be read to take that position. This view of the laches presumption is legally unsound.

Prior to 1975, the effect of a presumption was debatable. Thereafter, such effect was prescribed by Federal Rule of Evidence 301, effective August 1, 1975. That rule reads:

> Rule 301. Presumptions in General Civil Actions and Proceedings.

> In all civil actions and proceedings not otherwise provided for by Act of Congress or by these rules, a presumption imposes on the party against whom it is directed the burden of going forward with evidence to rebut or meet the presumption, but does not shift to such party the burden of proof in the sense of the risk of nonpersuasion, which remains throughout the trial upon the party on whom it was originally cast.

This rule applies "even if the common law presumption had been accorded a greater weight in the past." 10 Moore's, *supra*, § 301.03, at III–18.

As finally adopted after much scholarly debate, Rule 301 embodies what is known as the "bursting bubble" theory of presumptions. Under this theory, a presumption is not merely rebuttable but completely vanishes upon the introduction of evidence sufficient to support a finding of the nonexistence of the presumed fact. In other words, the evidence must be sufficient to put the existence of a presumed fact into genuine dispute. The presumption compels the production of this minimum quantum of evidence from the party against whom it operates, nothing more. In sum, a presumption is not evidence. If the patentee presents a sufficiency of evidence which, if believed, would preclude a directed finding in favor of the infringer, the presumption evaporates and the accused infringer is left to its proof. That is, the accused infringer would then have to satisfy its burden of persuasion with actual evidence.

As an initial response to the defendant's evidence of at least a six-year delay, a patentee may offer proof that the delay has not in fact been six years—that is, that the time it first learned or should have known of the infringement after the patent issued was within six years. If a patentee is successful on this factual issue, no presumption arises.

Once a presumption of laches arises, the patentee may offer proof directed to rebutting the laches factors. Such evidence may be directed to showing either that the patentee's delay was reasonable or that the defendant suffered no prejudice or both. By raising a genuine issue respecting either factual element of a laches defense, the presumption of laches is overcome.

Thus, the presumption of laches may be eliminated by offering evidence to show an excuse for the delay or that the delay was reasonable, even if such evidence may ultimately be rejected as not persuasive. Such evidence need only be sufficient to raise a genuine issue respecting the reasonableness of the delay to overcome the presumption. Evidence, for example, directed to the excuses discussed in section III B, *supra*, will eliminate the laches presumption if sufficient to raise a genuine issue. By destroying the presumption in its entirety upon presentation of evidence which may justify the delay, the patentee is not disadvantaged by having to prove a negative. Moreover, such evidence is within the patentee's knowledge.

A patentee may similarly eliminate the presumption with an offer of evidence sufficient to place the matters of defense prejudice and economic prejudice genuinely in issue. Thus, the patentee may eliminate the presumption by offering proof that no additional prejudice occurred in the six-year time period, i.e., that evidence respecting an alleged infringer's defenses remains available substantially as before the delay and that economic prejudice of the type delineated in section III B, *supra*, has not occurred.

Elimination of the presumption does not mean the patentee precludes the possibility of a laches defense; it does mean, however, that the presumption of laches plays no role in the ultimate decision. The facts of unreasonable delay and prejudice then must be proved and judged on the totality of the evidence presented.

Even if unable to overcome the presumption, a patentee may be able to preclude application of the laches defense with proof that the accused infringer was itself guilty of misdeeds towards the patentee. This flows from the maxim, "He who seeks equity must do equity."

Finally, we reiterate that, at all times, the defendant bears the ultimate burden of persuasion of the affirmative defense of laches. To the extent statements in [other cases] or other precedent may suggest otherwise, they are expressly overruled. The burden of persuasion does not shift by reason of the patentee's six-year delay.

E.   Standard of Review

On appeal the standard of review of the conclusion of laches is abuse of discretion. An appellate court, however, may set aside a discretionary decision if the decision rests on an erroneous interpretation of the law or on clearly erroneous factual underpinnings. If such error is absent, the determination can be overturned only if the trial court's decision represents an unreasonable judgment in weighing relevant factors.

F.   Laches in This Case

Because we conclude that the district court shifted the ultimate burden of persuasion to the patentee to negate the prima facie defense of laches, the district court's grant of summary judgment on the laches defense must be reversed.

The district court stated it placed the "burden" on the patentee "of showing [that its] delay was not unreasonable and inexcusable." This was a greater burden than the patentee had to bear to overcome the presumption. The patentee bears the burden only of coming forward with sufficient evidence to raise a genuine factual issue respecting the reasonableness of its conduct once the defendant shows delay in excess of six years. Here, Aukerman presented evidence that, during part of the delay, it was engaged in other litigation. The district court rejected this excuse because at no time did Aukerman give Chaides notice of such litigation and of its intention to sue Chaides upon its conclusion. However, there can be no rigid requirement in judging a laches defense that such notice must be given. If a defendant is, for example, aware of the litigation from other sources, it would place form over substance to require a specific notice. Where there is prior contact, the overall equities may require appropriate notice, as in *Jamesbury*. However, a notice requirement is not to be rigidly imposed as the district court did in this case.

Similarly, we believe the court erred in resolving the issue of whether the defendant's infringing activities changed sufficiently to disrupt the laches period. It is not disputed that defendant's conduct changed during the laches time frame both by its manufacturing its own slip-forming device and by greatly increasing the amount of asymmetrical wall it poured. It could not be inferred against the patentee that these changed circumstances should have been known to the patentee or were immaterial to the determination of laches. Upon the record before us, summary judgment of laches was improperly granted. The issue of laches must be tried.

G. *Effect of Laches Defense*

[Laches bars relief on a patentee's claim only for damages accrued prior to suit. Only equitable estoppel bars a claim of damages for future infringement.]

The stated difference in the effect of laches and estoppel has served well to emphasize that more is required in the overall equities than simple laches if an alleged infringer seeks to wholly bar a patentee's claim. Probably no better statement of reasons for limiting a laches defense in patent cases to past acts can be found than in *George J. Meyer Mfg. v. Miller Mfg.*, 24 F.2d 505, 507 (7th Cir. 1928):

> There are peculiar and special reasons why the holder of a patent should not be barred from enforcing his right under the patent because of his failure to promptly sue infringers. Frequently the position of the patentee (financial and otherwise) prevents the institution of suits. The patent litigation is often prolonged and expensive. Moreover from the very nature of the thing he cannot be fully cognizant of all infringements that occur throughout the length and breadth of this country. His information may be largely

hearsay. Then, also, the validity of his patent and the infringement thereof may be, as here, disputed. These defenses present mixed questions of fact and law concerning which there is necessarily some doubt and uncertainty. In many cases, if not in most cases, the doubts are serious ones. For an infringer naturally avoids making [an exact] copy of the patent. In a doubtful case the commercial success of the patented art is at times determinative of the issue of validity. This factor cannot be shown save as time establishes it. Moreover, common experience proves that inventions which appear to be revolutionary are often not accepted by the public and never become a commercial success. A patentee is therefore justified in waiting to ascertain whether realizations equal expectations.

We think, therefore, that there is justification in patent suits for withholding damages for infringements committed prior to the commencement of the suit when laches is established, notwithstanding injunctional relief be granted. But, when it can be shown that the holder of the patent in addition to being guilty of laches has, by his conduct, estopped himself from asserting his rights under the patent, all relief should be denied and the bill dismissed.

IV.

EQUITABLE ESTOPPEL

A.   *General Principles*

Equitable estoppel to assert a claim is another defense addressed to the sound discretion of the trial court. Where equitable estoppel is established, all relief on a claim may be barred. Like laches, equitable estoppel is not limited to a particular factual situation nor subject to resolution by simple or hard and fast rules. At most, courts have provided general guidelines based on fact patterns which have been litigated, albeit attempting to provide a unifying set of principles.

The following statement of the underlying factual elements of equitable estoppel which generally are deemed significant reflects a reasonable and fairly complete distillation from the case law:

> An [equitable] estoppel case ... has three important elements. [1] The actor, who usually must have knowledge of the true facts, communicates something in a misleading way, either by words, conduct or silence. [2] The other relies upon that communication. [3] And the other would be harmed materially if the actor is later permitted to assert any claim inconsistent with his earlier conduct.

Remedies § 2.3, at 42. In other authorities, elements [2] and [3] are frequently combined into a single "detrimental reliance" requirement. However, the statement of reliance and detriment as separate factors adds some clarity in this confusing area of the law.

Unlike laches, equitable estoppel does not require the passage of an unreasonable period of time in filing suit ... Delay in filing suit may be evidence which influences the assessment of whether the patentee's conduct is misleading but it is not a requirement of equitable estoppel.

Even where such delay is present, the concepts of equitable estoppel and laches are distinct from one another.

The first element of equitable estoppel concerns the statements or conduct of the patentee which must "communicate something in a misleading way." The "something" with which this case, as well as the vast majority of equitable estoppel cases in the patent field is concerned, is that the accused infringer will not be disturbed by the plaintiff patentee in the activities in which the former is currently engaged. The patentee's conduct must have supported an inference that the patentee did not intend to press an infringement claim against the alleged infringer. It is clear, thus, that for equitable estoppel the alleged infringer cannot be unaware—as is possible under laches—of the patentee and/or its patent. The alleged infringer also must know or reasonably be able to infer that the patentee has known of the former's activities for some time. In the most common situation, the patentee specifically objects to the activities currently asserted as infringement in the suit and then does not follow up for years.... There is ample subsequent precedent that equitable estoppel may arise where, coupled with other factors, a patentee's "misleading conduct" is essentially misleading inaction. However, plaintiff's inaction must be combined with other facts respecting the relationship or contacts between the parties to give rise to the necessary inference that the claim against the defendant is abandoned.

The second element, reliance, is not a requirement of laches but is essential to equitable estoppel. The accused infringer must show that, in fact, it substantially relied on the misleading conduct of the patentee in connection with taking some action. Reliance is not the same as prejudice or harm, although frequently confused. An infringer can build a plant being entirely unaware of the patent. As a result of infringement, the infringer may be unable to use the facility. Although harmed, the infringer could not show reliance on the patentee's conduct. To show reliance, the infringer must have had a relationship or communication with the plaintiff which lulls the infringer into a sense of security in going ahead with building the plant.

Finally, the accused infringer must establish that it would be materially prejudiced if the patentee is now permitted to proceed. As with laches, the prejudice may be a change of economic position or loss of evidence.

Another significant difference from laches is that no presumption adheres to an equitable estoppel defense. Despite a six-year delay in suit being filed, a defendant must prove all of the factual elements of estoppel on which the discretionary power of the court rests. The reasons for this are two-fold. First, the presumed laches factors, that is, unreasonable and inexcusable delay and prejudice resulting therefrom are not elements of estoppel. Second, the relief granted in estoppel is broader than in laches. Because the whole suit may be barred, we conclude that the defendant should carry a burden to establish the defense based on proof, not a presumption.

Finally, the trial court must, even where the three elements of equitable estoppel are established, take into consideration any other evidence and facts respecting the equities of the parties in exercising its discretion and deciding whether to allow the defense of equitable estoppel to bar the suit.

B. Application of Equitable Estoppel Against Aukerman

While equitable estoppel may be determined on summary judgment, we conclude that the district court improvidently granted summary judgment in this case.

The district court concluded that Aukerman's conduct led Chaides to believe Aukerman had abandoned its claim, that Chaides had relied on Aukerman's conduct to its detriment, and that Chaides was not guilty of unclean hands which would bar Chaides from assertion of an equitable defense. We conclude that the elements supporting equitable estoppel were in genuine dispute, that the evidence was not perceived in the light most favorable to Aukerman, that inferences of fact were drawn against Aukerman and that the entire issue must, in any event, be tried in light of the principles adopted here.

The initial dispute is whether the patentee's conduct was misleading in that Chaides reasonably inferred from Aukerman's conduct that it would be unmolested in using Aukerman's invention. Chaides argued that this factor was shown by the last letter from Aukerman in 1979 setting a deadline for taking a license followed by nine plus years of silence. Aukerman argued that Chaides had to prove intentionally misleading silence. The district court properly rejected Aukerman's argument respecting the need to prove intent to mislead on the basis of *Hottel*, 833 F.2d at 1574–75, 4 USPQ2d at 1941–42. How one characterizes a patentee's silence is immaterial. Properly focused, the issue here is whether Aukerman's course of conduct reasonably gave rise to an inference in Chaides that Aukerman was not going to enforce the '133 and '633 patents against Chaides. Moreover, silence alone will not create an estoppel unless there was a clear duty to speak or somehow the patentee's continued silence reenforces the defendant's inference from the plaintiff's known acquiescence that the defendant will be unmolested. Finally, on summary judgment, such inference must be the only possible inference from the evidence.

In view of the Aukerman/Chaides correspondence, Chaides was in a position to infer, following Chaides' reply stating any infringement problem was Gomaco's, that by remaining silent Aukerman abandoned its claim against Chaides. The length of the delay also favors drawing the inference because the longer the delay, the stronger the inference becomes. Aukerman argues that the delay is excused by reason of litigation against others, even though Chaides was not informed of the litigation. However, that argument is off the mark. A party must generally notify an accused infringer about other litigation for it to impact the defense of equitable estoppel. This "requirement" is a matter of logic. Other litigation can not logically enter into whether Chaides reasonably drew an inference that it would not be sued if such facts are not known to Chaides.

While the above factors favor the nonenforcement inference, Chaides' further statement that Aukerman would only recover $200–$300 a year could lead one in Chaides' position to infer that Aukerman did not sue because the amount in issue was de minimis, not that Aukerman was abandoning its claim against Chaides for all time regardless of quantum. At most Aukerman could merely have been waiving an infringement claim for $300.00 per year.

In view of the different inferences which could be drawn from the exchange of correspondence, it is clear that the court drew an unfavorable inference against Aukerman. That is impermissible on summary judgment.

Respecting misdeeds by Chaides, Aukerman argued Chaides was guilty of inequity by building a "copy" of the mold. The court concluded that there was no evidence that the "copy" infringed the patents, an issue on which Aukerman bore the burden of proof. The district court discounted Aukerman's contentions, construing the testimony of Mr. Chaides that he could not remember any differences between the original and the copy except in size as evidence of noninfringement inasmuch as Aukerman produced no evidence demonstrating "how the copy infringed the patents."

We disagree with the court that, in this phase of the litigation, Aukerman had the burden to prove that the copy infringed. The issue before the court was not a motion by Aukerman for summary judgment of infringement but a motion for summary judgment of equitable estoppel by Chaides. Absent Aukerman's concession of noninfringement, clearly not given, Chaides, the movant, had the burden of proof that the device which Chaides built and which all call a "copy" did not infringe. Under this assignment of burdens, Mr. Chaides' testimony concerning the "copy" of the infringing device, if construed in the light most favorable to Aukerman, could amount to an admission, not a denial, of infringement and, at least, raises an issue of fact. In any event, for purposes of summary judgment, Chaides' copying should have been deemed misconduct to be weighed into the court's decision, but it was not.

We conclude that summary judgment, holding that Aukerman was equitably estopped from assertion of infringement against Chaides, was improperly granted and is reversed. The issue is remanded for trial.

V.

QUANTUM OF PROOF

This court has not previously addressed the issue of what evidentiary burden must be met by litigants seeking to prove a laches or an equitable estoppel defense. Because the question of quantum in patent cases arises in every case within this area of our exclusive jurisdiction, we conclude that a uniform Federal Circuit rule should be adopted.

In civil cases litigants are generally required to prove facts by a preponderance of the evidence. "[E]vidence preponderates when it is more convincing to the trier than the opposing evidence." McCormick, *supra*, at 793. The higher standard of "clear and convincing" proof is typically employed where the danger of deception is present (e.g., establishing the terms of a lost will), where a particular claim is disfavored on policy grounds (e.g., reformation or modification of a written contract), or where a particularly important individual interest is at stake such as one's reputation (e.g., fraud or undue influence). The clear and convincing standard has also been imposed in some aspects of patent litigation by reason of the specific statutory provision that a patent is presumed valid. However, neither laches nor estoppel attacks a patent's validity.

The issue of laches concerns delay by one party and harm to another. Neither of these factors implicates the type of special considerations which typically trigger imposition of the clear and convincing quantum of proof. Indeed, to the limited extent courts have touched on this issue, the great weight of authority favors application of the general preponderance of evidence standard. Accordingly, we hold that "preponderance of the evidence" is the appropriate evidentiary standard to establish the facts relating to the laches issue.

In any event, since no special considerations are implicated by the defense of equitable estoppel as we have defined it herein, we adopt the preponderance of evidence standard in connection with the proof of equitable estoppel factors, absent special circumstances, such as fraud or intentional misconduct.

Notes

1. Why did Aukerman delay ten years before suing Chaides? Keep in mind, patent litigation is expensive and at the time he discovered Chaides was infringing, Chaides was a small time infringer and Aukerman was involved in another patent suit.

2. **Laches Factors.** Notice the different factors and the different remedies for laches and equitable estoppel. An accused infringer succeeds on his claim of laches if he proves:

    1. the patentee's delay in bringing suit was *unreasonable* (from when the patentee knew or should have known of the defendant's infringement); and

    2. the defendant suffered *material prejudice* because of the delay.

If successful on his claim of laches, all damages prior to the suit are barred.

3. **Presumption of Laches.** A presumption of laches arises if the patentee waits more than six years after he knew or should have known about the infringing conduct before bringing suit. When the presumption attaches, the burden of proof switches to the patentee to prove a reason for the delay. Possible justification for delay that the patentee might offer include:

1. the patentee was involved in another litigation;

2. negotiations with the accused;

3. poverty or illness;

4. wartime conditions;

5. the extent of infringement;

6. whether there is any dispute over ownership.

Evidence that the defendant copied the patentee's invention would support the patentee. *TWM Mfg. Co. v. Dura Corp.*, 592 F.2d 346, 349, 201 USPQ 433, 435–36 (6th Cir. 1979).

4. **Equitable Estoppel Factors.** An accused infringer succeeds on his claim of equitable estoppel if he proves:

1. *misleading conduct or communication* by the patentee which leads the infringer to reasonably infer that it will not enforce the patent against the infringer;

2. the infringer *relies* on the patentee's conduct; and

3. the infringer would be *materially prejudiced*.

If successful on his claim of inequitable conduct, the patentee can never bring suit against this infringer. The suit is barred. Unlike unenforceability for inequitable conduct, with equitable estoppel the patentee is only estopped from suing this particular infringer. The patentee can still bring an infringement suit against other infringers.

5. **Material Prejudice—Economic or Evidentiary**. There are two ways that the defendant can prove that he has been materially prejudiced by the patentee's delay in bringing suit: evidentiary or economic. The defendant proves evidentiary prejudice by showing a loss of records, prototypes, death of witnesses, or unreliability of memories. The defendant proves economic prejudice by demonstrating loss of investments such as the defendant built a plant. This factor is treated the same for laches or equitable estoppel.

6. **Differences Between Laches and Estoppel.**

1. When laches is established, damages prior to the suit are barred; when equitable estoppel is established the patentee's entire claim is barred as to this infringer.

2. There is no presumption after six years for equitable estoppel.

3. No unreasonably long period of time must pass before equitable estoppel is proven.

4. If the patentee has a reason for the delay, notice of the reason must be conveyed to the potential infringer to avoid equitable estoppel. The patentee is not required to give the potential infringer notice of a reason for the delay to avoid a laches claim.

7. **Actual Knowledge vs Constructive Knowledge: Is there a Duty to Investigate?** In *Wanlass v. General Elec.*, 148 F.3d 1334, 46 USPQ2d 1915 (Fed. Cir. 1998), Wanlass owned a patent for a single-phase run capacitor electric motor. In 1977, Wanlass offered GE a license which they declined responding that his invention was not new. Between 1977 and

1982, Wanlass tested a few GE products and determined that they were not infringing his patent. After 1982, Wanlass did not test another GE product until 1992. The only way to determine if a product infringes is to test the motor and study the waveforms on an oscilloscope. The circuit diagram and electrical schematics of the motor do not provide adequate information. The court found that testing products for infringement is easy and inexpensive. The products only cost two hundred dollars and the tests only take two hours.

In *Wanlass*, the court described the level of knowledge required for laches to attach as follows:

> The period of delay begins at the time the patentee has actual or constructive knowledge of the defendant's potentially infringing activities. The availability of delay based on constructive knowledge of the alleged infringer's activities imposes on patentees the duty to police their rights. "[T]he law is well settled that where the question of laches is in issue the plaintiff is chargeable with such knowledge as he might have obtained upon inquiry, provided the facts already known by him were such as to put upon a man of ordinary intelligence the duty of inquiry." Although laches will not bar a patentee whose ignorance is justifiable, ignorance will not insulate him from constructive knowledge of infringement in appropriate circumstances.

> These circumstances include "pervasive, open, and notorious activities" that a reasonable patentee would suspect were infringing. For example, sales, marketing, publication, or public use of a product similar to or embodying technology similar to the patented invention, or published descriptions of the defendant's potentially infringing activities, give rise to a duty to investigate whether there is infringement.

> Furthermore, constructive knowledge of the infringement may be imputed to the patentee even where he has no actual knowledge of the sales, marketing, publication, public use, or other conspicuous activities of potential infringement if these activities are sufficiently prevalent in the inventor's field of endeavor. The patentee who is negligently or willfully oblivious to these types of activities cannot later claim his lack of knowledge as justification for escaping the application of laches because the law imputes knowledge when opportunity and interest, combined with reasonable care, would necessarily impart it. Not to improve such opportunity, under the stimulus of self-interest, with reasonable diligence, constitutes laches which in equity disables the party who seeks to revive a right which he has allowed to lie unclaimed from enforcing it, to the detriment of those who have, in consequence, been led to act as though it were abandoned.

Wanlass, 148 F.3d at 1338, 46 USPQ2d at 1917–18 (citations omitted).

The Federal Circuit held that Mr. Wanlass's claim was barred by laches since it was unreasonable for him to have conducted no investigations over a 10-year period to identify alleged infringers. The majority opinion was authored by Chief Judge Mayer and joined by Judge Michel. Judge Rader dissented arguing that the majority opinion created a duty for the patent holder to police the market. *Id.* at 1341, 46 USPQ2d at 1920 (Rader, J., dissenting). In challenging the majorities characterization that the General Electric motor was "open and notorious," and that Wanlass had been unreasonable in not policing the market, Judge Rader stated:

> Wanlass tested some General Electric motors between 1977 and 1982 and found no infringement. Wanlass then turned his attention to other potential infringers. General Electric in 1986 changed to an allegedly infringing motor design. Wanlass did not discover the alleged infringement until 1992. He filed suit in 1995. This court upholds, under the strictures of summary judgment, a determination that Wanlass unreasonably delayed bringing suit. To the contrary, Wanlass had no way to detect that General Electric had made infringing changes. Nonetheless, this court imposes on Wanlass—a small businessman and inventor—the costly and unreasonable burden of periodically checking and rechecking every product in this crowded market to detect infringement. Because Wanlass did not recheck General Electric's motors and did not discover the alleged infringement until 1992, this court construes all facts against him and denies him any chance to proceed with his suit.

* * *

> To my eyes, the law does not entitle General Electric to judgment. In 1979, General Electric indicated to Wanlass that it was not interested in licensing his patents. Between 1977 and 1982, Wanlass had tested a number of motors, including some made by General Electric. His tests did not uncover any motors that infringed his patent. In sum, construing disputed facts in Wanlass's favor as required on summary judgment, these early tests and negotiations lulled him into the belief that General Electric was not interested in his technology and would not infringe.

> In 1986, however, General Electric changed its motor design in a way that allegedly infringes Wanlass's patent. General Electric did not inform Wanlass of its changed design. Nonetheless this court determines that Wanlass had a duty to discover the change. The problem with that determination is that the accused motors operate inside air conditioners and refrigerators. To discover a change would require Wanlass to disassemble appliances to access the motor and then dismantle the motor to discover the internal changes. Indeed, Wanlass theorizes that alterations in one internal part of the motors altered its magnetic properties and caused the infringement. (In light of this theory, which is consistent with the teachings of Wanlass's patent, this court's emphasis on the unchanged circuit diagram is misplaced.) In addition to the complexity of discovering a single instance of infringement, the record of this case shows that General Electric is not the only manufacturer of this type of electric motors in the United States. Many companies make many different models of electric motors for a wide variety of applications. Yet this court requires Wanlass to check and recheck

them for infringement, even if he had early indications that a company was not infringing.

Because these undisputed record facts do not establish that Wanlass's failure to discover the alleged infringement before 1989 was unreasonable, this court imposes on Wanlass an affirmative duty to police his patent. This duty allegedly arises from General Electric's "pervasive, open and notorious activities" that a reasonable patentee would suspect were infringing. *Hall v. Aqua Queen Mfg., Inc.*, 93 F.3d 1548, 1553, 39 USPQ2d 1925, 1928 (Fed. Cir. 1996). The *Hall* case, however, is very different from Wanlass's case. In *Hall*, the patentee had knowledge of other open and notorious potential infringements. In *Hall*, the accused devices were also widely advertised in trade journals and advertised at trade shows. Hall himself, the patentee, was the head of a trade organization. He attended many of these shows and spoke with the management of the accused infringers. Indeed, "Hall [was] a prominent figure in the . . . industry throughout the 1970s and 1980s." In light of these facts, this court properly charged Hall with knowledge of the alleged infringing activities.

In contrast, Wanlass had no indications of widespread infringement to raise his suspicions. General Electric's new motor was not described in any trade publication in sufficient detail to place Wanlass on notice of the possible infringement. Indeed, the record does not indicate when, if ever, General Electric's change in its electric motor design became known outside of General Electric. Moreover, unlike Hall, Wanlass had checked once for infringement and had unsuccessfully tried to license various manufacturers of single phase motors. For good reason, therefore, Wanlass had turned his attention to larger three-phase motors used in industrial applications. A number of articles in business publications described him as abandoning the single phase motor field. Unlike Hall, Wanlass can hardly be described as a prominent figure in the electric motor industry. This court must stretch Hall far beyond its facts to apply it to Wanlass.

In order to bridge the gap between *Hall* and the present case, the majority charges Wanlass with constructive knowledge of General Electric's potential infringement. The majority holds that Wanlass should have discovered the alleged infringing motors within two to three years after General Electric started production. This court explains that General Electric's "sales, marketing, publication, public use, or other conspicuous activities of potential infringement [were] sufficiently prevalent in the inventor's field of endeavor." Again, this standard amounts to a duty on Wanlass to check and recheck large potential infringers.

* * *

Because the majority announces new legal rules and offers so little guidance, patentees can only look to the facts of this case. What they will see will be disheartening, as it represents a substantial new burden. Wanlass's patent claimed an improvement to a component used in a wide variety of applications. The component was not the focus of the advertising campaigns for these products, nor would it have been a feature sought by purchasers of the equipment. Indeed, this court does not say why Wanlass, who had tested General Electric products in the past, should have suspected that General Electric had made changes that resulted in infringement of his patent. Instead this court assumed that, because General Electric is a large company with widely distributed products, Wanlass should have known what it was doing. Therefore, this case places upon patentees the duty to test any product that might contain the claimed invention. For inventions, such as Wanlass's, that have broad potential application, this new requirement is a significant burden.

Wanlass, 148 F.3d at 1341–43, 46 USPQ2d at 1920–22 (Rader, J., dissenting) (citations omitted).

Interestingly, ten days later, the Federal Circuit had another occasion to address Mr. Wanlass's failure to promptly sue a different defendant. In this case, *Wanlass v. Fedders Corp. (Wanlass II)*, 145 F.3d 1461, 47 USPQ2d 1097 (Fed. Cir. 1998), with virtually identical facts, the same panel of judges found that the patentee did not have a duty to test the Fedders products. Judge Michel wrote the following majority opinion which was joined by Judge Rader and Chief Judge Mayer dissented.

We hold, however, that the district court erred in applying the presumption of unreasonable and inexcusable delay because the facts as developed for the summary judgment motion are not without genuine disputes on material issues as to whether Wanlass knew or reasonably should have known of Fedders's allegedly infringing activity before the critical date in 1989.

Fedders presented evidence that Wanlass knew prior to its tests in the 1990s that single-phase motors were frequently used in the air-conditioning industry. From that evidence alone, the district court imposed upon Wanlass a duty to police its patent in the air-conditioning industry, and this duty included an unlimited and undefined duty to test any single-phase motor air conditioner. However, on the record presented on summary judgment, Wanlass could not reasonably be required to perform such a duty. First, Wanlass presented evidence that it was not active in the air-conditioning industry or at least in the single-phase, high-efficiency motor portion of the industry. In fact, Mr. Wanlass averred that he "seldom attended any conventions or shows where their [the air conditioning manufacturers'] products were featured, and then only in the early days, i.e., during the 1970's or early 1980's." Moreover, the mere fact that single-phase motors are used in room air conditioners is not enough to suggest infringement because not all single-phase motors infringe. Only those that use high-efficiency, single-phase motors with a capacitor operating with specific characteristics may. Therefore, policing the industry would require testing of an unknown number of models. Imposing a duty upon Wanlass to monitor the air-conditioning industry by periodically testing all others' products, therefore, would be unreasonable. Yet that is what the district court in effect did.

The district court also found that Fedders is a "well-known brand in the industry and has advertised its compressors and motors and has participated in trade shows for many years." And further, Fedders presented evidence that Wanlass knew sometime in the 1980s that Fedders made room air-conditioning units that may have used single-phase motors. From this evidence alone, the district court inferred that Wanlass "was aware of Fedders, and that they manufactured and sold air conditioners that use the single-phase motors covered in his patent." There is little support, however, for the notion that Wanlass had reason to believe the Fedders product infringed. For example, the advertisements relied upon by Fedders were not shown to have described the capacitor of Wanlass's invention.

Furthermore, Mr. Wanlass never admitted in his deposition testimony or in his declaration that he knew the single-phase motors in the Fedders air conditioners infringed or likely infringed the '135 patent. Nor did he state that all single-phase motors infringed the patent. To the contrary, Mr. Wanlass averred that "I did not, prior to filing suit, know of any way to determine if a motor infringed other than to test it." It was specifically shown, for example, that the circuit schematic did not so indicate. Nor did the appearance of the motor after its removal from the unit. Only testing could reveal infringement if any. No test was conducted until 1995.

According to his deposition testimony, Mr. Wanlass's companies could not afford to purchase and dismantle every air-conditioner model on the market and test the single-phase motor found inside. Moreover, Wanlass would have no more reason to believe that Fedders was infringing its patent than was anyone else in the air-conditioning industry. Wanlass presented evidence that neither all high-efficiency nor all single-phase motors infringed, only possibly those high-efficiency, single-phase motors with a capacitor operating with specific characteristics. Yet there is no evidence that Wanlass knew, for example from advertisements, that the Fedders motors had these characteristics. The inference drawn by the district court, that Wanlass knew that the Fedders single-phase motors were covered by the '135 patent, therefore, is impermissible as both wholly unsupported and as adverse to the non-movant in this summary judgment context. Wanlass did not know, and indeed could not have known, that the single-phase motors used in Fedders's air conditioners infringed the claims of the '135 patent until after a Fedders compressor was tested. And Fedders did not establish on the summary judgment record that Wanlass had any particular reason to do so prior to 1995. Moreover, because of contrary evidence here is an inadequate basis for the district court's implicit finding that a program for testing all air-conditioner compressors of all makers was feasible and affordable and otherwise a reasonable burden to impose on the patentee. For example, no notion of how many products per year would have to be tested was given by the court.

As a patentee, however, Mr. Wanlass could not simply ignore any and all evidence of potentially infringing activity, even if neither he nor his company was in fact still active in the industry. Wanlass knew that certain high-efficiency, single-phase motors used in the room air-conditioning industry might infringe the patent. Although Wanlass did not have a duty to police the room air-conditioning industry by testing all questionable products, he could not ignore evidence of potential infringement for most of the life of the patent, and then, during the patent's twilight, decide to aggressively police his rights by suing manufacturers based on testing evidence that it could and should have obtained several years earlier. Wanlass did have a duty to investigate a particular product if and when publicly available information about it should have led Wanlass to suspect that product of infringing. For example, any advertisements for high-efficiency air conditioners using single phase motors and having a capacitor capable of operating with specific characteristics should have alerted Wanlass to the prospect of infringement and therefore of the need to test that specific, advertised product. On the instant record, however, Fedders failed to show that Wanlass should have known that its model C81B compressor had these characteristics.

Consistent with Wanlass's assertions that he had no reason to suspect Fedders, as opposed to any other of the numerous makers of air conditioners, was infringing the '135 patent, the district court found that the only evidence indicating any sort of prior communication between Wanlass and Fedders was the ambiguous 1982 document. . . .

The 1982 document indicates only that someone at Wanlass contacted someone at Fedders, but apparently no one ever followed up on the original contact. In the context of all the evidence presented, the document cannot be used to infer that Wanlass thought Fedders might be selling infringing motors in its compressors, that Wanlass even knew that Fedders sold high-efficiency, single-phase motors with a capacitor operating with specific characteristics, or that Wanlass purchased and tested a Fedders compressor containing an accused motor prior to 1995. Furthermore, when Mr. Wanlass was asked about the 1982 document in his deposition, he asserted he could remember nothing about it. Hence, the district court was correct that the 1982 document could not be used on summary judgment to show knowledge by Wanlass of Fedders's allegedly infringing activity as early as 1982. However, it would be improper for the district court on remand to disregard the 1982 letter simply because its meaning could not be discerned from the summary judgment record. After an evidentiary hearing, the trial court, the fact finder on the equitable doctrine of laches, will be able properly to draw reasonable inferences either in favor of or adverse to Wanlass regarding the 1982 document and in light of Wanlass's denial of any memory of it.

Wanlass II, 145 F.3d at 1464–66, 47 USPQ2d at 1101 (citations omitted).

Chief Judge Mayer dissented arguing that it was unreasonable for the patentee not to investigate or test any potentially infringing products for a ten year period. How can these two opinions be reconciled? The only difference between the two cases seems to be that the communication between Wanlass and General Electric was not present in the Fedders case. In *Wanlass I*, Wanlass was on notice that General Electric thought his patent was invalid and that GE refused to take a license. The court seems to conclude that this evidence should have put Wanlass on notice that GE was a potential infringer and therefore he had a continuing duty to test GE products. There was no such communication in *Wanlass II*. Fedders was just one of many possible competitors. Given that Wanlass was not on notice that Fedders would disregard the patent, he had no more of a duty to test the Fedder products than the products of any other unknown competitor.

8. In a case of first impression, the Eastern District of Virginia held that laches bars a patentee from obtaining an injunction against purchaser's future use of patented products that were made and sold during the laches period. *See Odetics Inc. v. Storage Tech. Corp.*, 14 F. Supp.2d 785, 47 USPQ2d 1573 (E.D. Va. 1998).

9. **How Long of a Delay is Too Long?** How long of a delay is necessary to trigger laches? There is no magic number of days, weeks, or months of delay required to trigger laches. The only requirement is that the delay be unreasonable. *See Odetics Inc. v. Storage Tech. Corp.*, 919 F. Supp. 911, 927, 38 USPQ2d 1873, 1885 (E.D. Va. 1996) (holding that a three year delay was unreasonable because the delay was inexcusable and because defendants suffered prejudice from it); *Naxon Telesign Corp. v. Bunker Ramo Corp.*, 517 F. Supp. 804, 808, 212 USPQ 920, 923 (N.D. Ill. 1981) (holding that a 58–month delay to find an attorney willing to handle the matter on a contingent fee basis, when the company could have afforded the most expensive trial lawyer in Chicago creates an unjustified delay).

PROBLEMS

1. John Spot comes into your office and tells you he just received a cease-and-desist letter from Phil's Toilets. He gives you the cease-and-desist letter which says that Phil's Toilets believes that John Spot may be infringing its '000 patent (the '000 patent is attached to the cease-and-desist letter). You discover that the '000 patent, which was issued last year, discloses a sanitary toilet seat cover and the rolls of clear plastic tubular material that go in it and slide around the toilet seat to make it sanitary.

Patent claim 1 reads:

1. An apparatus for dispensing a sanitary toilet seat cover comprising:

    [1] a toilet seat;

    [2] a tubular material roll located at one end of the toilet seat and a tubular material collector located at the other end of the toilet seat; and

    [3] a means for pulling the tubular material around the toilet seat.

John Spot tells you that many public restrooms use these sanitary toilet seat covers. He says that a public restroom will exhaust one roll of clear plastic every two days and that the plastic CANNOT be reused. As far as he knows only Phil's Toilets sell the sanitary motorized toilet seat cover and Phil's Toilets services these toilets by replacing the used plastic rolls every other day. John has never sold the complete toilet seat and motor because he knew it was patented, but he has been selling rolls of the clear plastic to people who own these sanitary motorized toilet seat covers along with instructions on how to replace the used rolls themselves. Since he started this business he has had more customers than he can handle and he knows of four other companies who have begun selling rolls of plastic covers (many of which have designs on them).

You contact one of John's customers, Airport X, which tells you that they are really happy with the motorized sanitary toilet seat covers which they bought from Phil's Toilet, but it is much cheaper to buy the replacement rolls from John Spot than to have Phil service the toilets. They fax you a copy of the sales contract which requires Airport X to buy all replacement rolls from Phil's Toilets and that only Phil's Toilets can service the motorized sanitary replacement covers.

Can John be sued for patent infringement? What advice would you give John about possible defenses he may have? Is there any advice you would give to Phil's Toilets?

2. You are employed as a patent attorney by the general practice firm of Moore, Michel & Lupo. You are asked to advise a client, Linda Sou, President of GEE Electronics Inc. ("GEE"). GEE is being sued by U.S. Semiconductor Corporation ("USSC") for infringement of U.S. Patent No. 9,999,999. The suit was filed yesterday. Linda gives you a copy of the complaint and the '999 patent. You scan the complaint and discover that USSC alleges that GEE literally infringes the '999 patent under § 271 and infringes under the doctrine of equivalents.

You notice that the patent was filed on June 15, 1985, issued on January 1, 1987, and assigned to USSC. The inventors listed on the patent are Dr. Smith and Dr. Jones. The '999 patent is for a method of manufacturing semiconductors and is entitled "Charged Coupler Device." The specification tells you charged coupler devices (CCDs) are a type of semiconductor chip used in the light-sensing components of videocameras, facsimile machines, and VCRs. You notice that there are only 5 prior art references listed on the patent (all prior U.S. patents) and when you get the prosecution history you confirm that these are the only references the inventors disclosed to the PTO in their information disclosure statement.

Linda explains that GEE manufactures semiconductors, but they do not use the '999 process. She explains that Dr. Green invented the fabrication process for her CCD100 and it works in a different way. You ask Linda if you can speak to Dr. Green, but she tells you he died several years ago. You also ask if GEE has any of Dr. Green's lab notebooks and Linda explains that it is their normal business practice to shred all business documents after five years.

You ask Linda if she was aware of the '999 patent prior to the infringement suit and she tells you that she did receive a letter from USSC several years ago, she gives you a copy of the letter which reads:

January 1, 1988

Dear GEE Electronics:

We have just been issued the attached patent, U.S. Patent No. 9,999,999. We know that you manufacture semiconductor chips, we believe you to be infringing our patent and want to give you a chance to license our revolutionary technology. We are currently willing to license the technology for 20% of the gross sale price. In fact, several other semiconductor manufactures have already taken a license. Please contact us within 10 days regarding this licensing offer or we will be forced to take legal action.

President, USSC

Linda explains that she never responded to the letter because the terms of the license were outrageous. She tells you that she knows that three major semiconductor manufacturers took licenses at 5% of the gross sale price just to avoid an infringement suit. In addition, she believed that her employee, Dr. Green, invented the process that GEE uses before USSC. After the initial letter, Linda never heard from USSC again until she was sued yesterday. Since 1988, GEE tripled their semiconductor production.

Linda also tells you that she remembers attending a conference in May of 1984 in Palo Alto, California where Dr. Smith and Dr. Jones presented a paper detailing the semiconductor fabrication process and gave a demonstration of how the process worked. There were about 500 engineers at this conference.

How would you advise Linda? What if any affirmative defenses can she raise? If she successfully proves these defenses, what would be the outcome of the trial?

Chapter Thirteen

INJUNCTIVE RELIEF

INTRODUCTION

This chapter explores the equitable remedies available to a patentee. As we shall see in the cases that follow, injunctive relief is often more valuable to a patent owner than the monetary damages she can recover from a defendant.

STATUTORY PROVISION—35 U.S.C. § 283:

The several courts having jurisdiction of cases under this title may grant injunctions in accordance with the principles of equity to prevent the violation of any right secured by patent, on such terms as the court deems reasonable.

A. PRELIMINARY INJUNCTIONS

1. PRACTICAL CONSIDERATIONS

Although preliminary injunctions are generally a good way for the patentee to obtain fast relief for infringement, motions for a preliminary injunction are time-consuming and expensive to prepare. Observe the process used by the district court in the next two cases for addressing the patentees' motions for preliminary injunctions. In *H.H. Robertson*, the court conducted a mini-trial on the motion with a four day hearing including testimony, briefing and argument. In *Hybritech*, the court permitted the parties to conduct limited discovery in preparation for a two day hearing with briefing and argument. In some federal district courts, such as the Northern District of California, the preliminary injunction hearing is limited to argument on the briefs, declarations and affidavits; no live testimony is permitted. In other federal district courts, a full evidentiary hearing, like a mini-trial, is permitted. It is important to consult your local rules when deciding whether to file such a motion.

In many cases, the patentee should decide whether to bring a preliminary injunction motion at the time she files her complaint. In fact, whether the patentee will be seeking a preliminary injunction can factor into a decision regarding where to bring the suit in the first place.

Patentees who wish to move for a preliminary injunction should try to do so as quickly as possible after the complaint is filed. Many patentees will file the motion together with the complaint. If the patentee delays between the filing of the complaint and the motion for the preliminary injunction, the court may infer (and the defendant will often point out) that the injunctive relief is not as urgent as the patentee claims. Delaying after filing the complaint also diminishes the element of surprise that the patentee has in her favor at this point in the proceeding.

The patentee will want to gather as much evidence as possible of infringement, validity, irreparable harm, and public interest prior to filing for the preliminary injunction. A thorough gathering of information is crucial to success on the motion. To establish infringement, the patentee will want to buy the accused product and obtain the defendant's brochures, advertisements, and scientific publications. The patentee will also want to prepare a claim chart. To withstand an attack on validity, the patent owner will rely on the inventor, other employees and possibly a technical expert. The patent owner will want to have affidavits from these witnesses, and documentary evidence such as lab notebooks, photographs, and demonstrative exhibits prepared when the motion is filed. It should be easy to compile this information and other relevant evidence such as commercial success and industry acquisition (by showing licensing) prior to bringing suit because all of this information is in the patentee's possession. The only information that the patent owner cannot prepare in advance is responses to invalidity or unenforceability arguments raised by the defendant and unknown prior art references the defendant may present. Although the filing of an early preliminary injunction motion requires a more extensive pre-suit investigation by the patentee, it is more advantageous for the patentee to file the preliminary injunction motion early in the litigation rather than waiting for discovery and losing the element of surprise. Waiting for discovery to obtain the necessary evidence to file a motion can be a lengthy proposition; the defendant will undoubtedly demand a protective order, the drafting of which can substantially slow the discovery process.

2. FACTORS FOR CONSIDERATION

There arc four factors which the patentee must prove by a preponderance of the evidence to succeed on a motion for a preliminary injunction:

1. a reasonable likelihood of success on the merits;

2. irreparable harm if relief is not granted;

3. balance of the hardships tipping in her favor; and

4. the impact of the injunction on the public interest.

Observe what kind of evidence tends to prove each of these factors in the next two cases and how the court weighs these factors.

H.H. ROBERTSON, CO. v. UNITED STEEL DECK, INC.

820 F.2d 384, 2 USPQ2d 1926 (Fed. Cir. 1987)

Before NEWMAN and BISSELL, Circuit Judges, and NEWMAN, Senior Judge.

PAULINE NEWMAN, Circuit Judge.

United Steel Deck, Inc. (USD) and Nicholas J. Bouras, Inc., (Bouras) appeal the Order of Preliminary Injunction of the United States District Court for the District of New Jersey in favor of the H.H. Robertson Company (Robertson). USD and Bouras were enjoined *pendente lite* from making, using, and selling certain structures which were found to infringe United States Patent No. 3,721,051 (the '051 or Fork patent). We affirm.

BACKGROUND

Robertson is the owner of the '051 patent, invention of Frank W. Fork, issued on March 20, 1973 and entitled "Bottomless Sub–Assembly for Producing an Underfloor Electrical Cable Trench". The invention is a concrete deck structure sub-assembly for distributing electrical wiring. A detailed description of the invention and its development appears in *H.H. Robertson Co. v. Bargar Metal Fabricating Co.*, 225 USPQ 1191, 1192–96 (N.D. Ohio 1984).

Robertson charged Bouras and its affiliated manufacturing company USD with infringement (inducing and contributory infringement) of claims 1, 2, 4, 6, 9, 13, and 14 of the Fork patent. In moving for preliminary injunction Robertson alleged that "there is a reasonable probability of eventual success on the patent infringement claim"; that "the Fork patent was held valid, infringed, contributorily infringed and enforceable by the United States District Court for the Northern District of Ohio in . . . *Bargar*"; that the "accused structures of USD and Bouras are the same or substantially the same as those held . . . to infringe in *Bargar*"; that "[w]here, as here, the patent has been held valid and infringed, irreparable harm is presumed . . . and the harm . . . cannot be fully compensated by money damages"; and that the "balance of equities heavily weighs in favor of Robertson."

The district court held a four-day hearing on the motion, during which witnesses including experts testified on the issues of patent validity and infringement. The legal and equitable issues were briefed and argued. The court concluded that Robertson had "established a basis for the relief it seeks," and granted the preliminary injunction.

ANALYSIS

The standards applied to the grant of a preliminary injunction are no more nor less stringent in patent cases than in other areas of the law. The court in *Smith International* discussed the so-called "more severe" rule that has at times weighed against the grant of preliminary injunctions in patent cases, stating: "The basis for the more severe rule appears to be both a distrust of and unfamiliarity with patent issues and a belief that the *ex parte* examination by the Patent and Trademark Office is inherently unreliable." [*Smith International, Inc. v. Hughes Tool Co.*, 718 F.2d 1573,] 1578, 219 USPQ [686,] 690 [(Fed. Cir. 1983)]. *See also Atlas Powder Co. v. Ireco Chemicals*, 773 F.2d 1230, 1233, 227 USPQ 289, 292 (Fed. Cir. 1985) ("burden upon the movant should be no different in a patent case than for other kinds of intellectual property"). The existing standards for relief *pendente lite*, fairly applied, can accommodate any special circumstances that may arise.

The grant or denial of a preliminary injunction is within the discretionary authority of the trial court. Appellate review is on the basis of whether the court "abused its discretion, committed an error of law, or seriously misjudged the evidence." *Smith International*, 718 F.2d at 1579, 219 USPQ at 691.

The district court applied to Robertson's motion the Third Circuit standard:

> An applicant for a preliminary injunction against patent infringement must show:
>
> ... (1) a reasonable probability of eventual success in the litigation and (2) that the movant will be irreparably injured pendente lite if relief is not granted.... Moreover, while the burden rests upon the moving party to make these two requisite showings, the district court "should take into account, when they are relevant, (3) the possibility of harm to other interested persons from the grant or denial of the injunction, and (4) the public interest."

This is substantially the same standard enunciated by this court.

PATENT VALIDITY

The first question before the district court was whether the movant Robertson had demonstrated a reasonable likelihood that USD and Bouras would fail to meet their burden at trial of proving, by clear and convincing evidence, that the Fork patent claims were invalid.

The burden of proving invalidity is with the party attacking validity. The evidence adduced in connection with a motion for preliminary relief must be considered in this light.

Robertson retained the burden of showing a reasonable likelihood that the attack on its patent's validity would fail. Indeed, the district court placed a greater burden on Robertson than was required, referring to our statement in *Atlas Powder*, 773 F.2d at 1233, 227 USPQ at 292, that a patentee seeking a preliminary injunction must " 'clearly show[ ]' that his patent is valid."

This court's statement in *Atlas Powder* does not change the immutable allocation to the challenger of the burden of proving invalidity, but rather reflects the rule that the burden is always on the movant to demonstrate entitlement to preliminary relief. Such entitlement, however, is determined in the context of the presumptions and burdens that would inhere at trial on the merits.

Before the district court, USD and Bouras argued that all of the Fork patent claims at issue were invalid for obviousness in terms of 35 U.S.C. § 103, and that claim 2 was invalid in terms of 35 U.S.C. § 112. The asserted invalidity for obviousness was based on references that had been before the Ohio court in *Bargar*, including references that had been before the patent examiner during prosecution of the Fork patent application, and three references that were newly presented. The patent claims, the details of the references, and the evidence and argument offered by both sides, need not be here repeated.

The district court in its opinion referred to the detailed analysis by the Ohio court and to its decision that the accused infringers in that case had failed to establish the invalidity of the claims. The district court stated that the "finding of validity of the Fork '051 patent in *Bargar* is persuasive evidence of validity" with respect to the references before that court. The district court further held, upon reviewing the three additional references, that "considering them as part of the prior art does not render obvious the Fork bottomless trench invention." *Id.* We discern no error in the court's conclusion that "the finding in *Bargar* and the evidence submitted in the present case lead to the conclusion that there is a reasonable probability that Robertson will ultimately succeed on the issue of obviousness."

The issue of validity of claim 2 under section 112 raised the question of whether the written description was enabling to one skilled in this art. Reviewing the evidence, including expert testimony, the district court held that "the patent requirements of § 112 are met." The court's determination that the disclosure had not been proven not to be enabling has not been shown to be in error.

Bouras accuses the district court of giving undue weight to the Ohio court's decision of validity and infringement against a different defendant. The district court stated that it "did not rely on *Bargar* as evidence of infringement" but only as evidence of validity with respect to the references actually considered by the Ohio court. There was no error in its so doing. Substantial weight may be given to a patent's litigation history in connection with a motion for relief *pendente lite*. Even the "severe rule" against the grant of preliminary injunctions in patent cases was tempered when a patent had been upheld in other forums or its validity had been acquiesced in by others. A prior adjudication upholding patent validity after a fully litigated trial, including similar issues of fact and law, contributes strong support to the grant of a preliminary injunction.

The decision for our review is not a final judgment of patent validity. Rather, we ascertain whether the district court correctly concluded that Robertson had demonstrated a reasonable likelihood that it will prevail on this issue. On the record before us, the court's conclusion is based on factual findings that have not been shown to be clearly erroneous, it was not error to place weight on the Ohio district court's ruling on validity, and no error in law has been shown.

INFRINGEMENT

The accused structures are described by the buildings in which they have been installed: the Maiden Lane, the Daily News, and the Blue Cross–Blue Shield. USD and Bouras argue that their current trench, the Blue Cross–Blue Shield design, is not "truly bottomless", and that the claims must be interpreted as a matter of law to exclude trenches that are only partially bottomless. To the district court USD and Bouras presented expert testimony in support of this position, countered by expert testimony on behalf of Robertson. The witnesses testified at length concerning the prosecution history and its impact on the interpretation and scope of the claims.

The district court's construction of the claims is explained in relation to its holding on infringement, the court stating that the "key portion of the trench remains bottomless, i.e., the portions giving direct access to the cells." We are not persuaded of error in the district court's construction of the term "bottomless" to apply to the "key portion" of the trench, based on the evidence before it.

The accused structures, and the application thereto of the patent claims, were the subject of analysis and explanation by witnesses on both sides, aided by the physical exhibits. Our review shows thorough exposition of the opposing positions. The district court found that the accused subassemblies are "bottomless in that upper surface portions of the cellular units of the metal subfloor in the region between said opposite sides cooperate with the sub-assembly to create an underfloor electrical cable trench, confront the cover plate, and are exposed to view when the cover plate is removed." The court found that "the horizontal metal sections ... and the horizontal metal strip ... serve no function [and the] key portion of the trench remains bottomless."

In its factual application of the claims to the accused devices, the findings of the district court have not been shown to be clearly in error.

The grant of a preliminary injunction does not require that infringement be proved beyond all question, or that there be no evidence supporting the viewpoint of the accused infringer. The grant turns on the likelihood that Robertson will meet its burden at trial of proving infringement. We sustain the district court's conclusion that "there is a reasonable probability that Robertson will eventually establish that Bouras and USD induced infringement of the Fork '051 patent."

EQUITABLE CONSIDERATIONS

The movant for preliminary injunction must show not only a reasonable likelihood of success on the merits, but also the lack of adequate remedy at law or other irreparable harm.

In matters involving patent rights, irreparable harm has been presumed when a clear showing has been made of patent validity and infringement. This presumption derives in part from the finite term of the patent grant, for patent expiration is not suspended during litigation, and the passage of time can work irremediable harm. The opportunity to practice an invention during the notoriously lengthy course of patent litigation may itself tempt infringers.

The nature of the patent grant thus weighs against holding that monetary damages will always suffice to make the patentee whole, for the principal value of a patent is its statutory right to exclude.

The district court held that irreparable injury was presumed because Robertson had established a "strong likelihood of success in establishing validity and infringement." Such presumption of injury was not, however, irrebuttable. *Roper Corp.*, 757 F.2d at 1272, 225 USPQ at 349 (the presumption "is rebuttable by clear evidence"). The parties gave scant attention in their appellate briefs to the issues of irreparable injury and the balance of harms. During oral argument, in response to an inquiry from the bench, USD and Bouras urged that money damages are an adequate remedy. In response, Robertson emphasized the few remaining years of patent life.

Even when irreparable injury is presumed and not rebutted, it is still necessary to consider the balance of hardships. The magnitude of the threatened injury to the patent owner is weighed, in the light of the strength of the showing of likelihood of success on the merits, against the injury to the accused infringer if the preliminary decision is in error. Results of other litigation involving the same patent may be taken into account, and the public interest is considered. No one element controls the result.

When the movant has shown the likelihood that the acts complained of are unlawful, the preliminary injunction "preserves the status quo if it prevents future trespasses but does not undertake to assess the pecuniary or other consequences of past trespasses." *Atlas Powder Co.*, 773 F.2d at 1232, 227 USPQ at 291. The court in *Atlas Powder* thus distinguished between remedies for past infringement, where there is no possibility of other than monetary relief, and prospective infringement, "which may have market effects never fully compensable in money." *Id.* The cautionary corollary is that a preliminary injunction improvidently granted may impart undeserved value to an unworthy patent.

Thus substantial deference is due the district court's equitable judgment. The district court in its opinion referred to the USD/Bouras portrayal of disruption, loss of business, and loss of jobs, and to Robertson's business needs and patent rights. Observing that "[t]his patent does not have many more years to run", the court held "the equities weigh heavily against the wrongdoer." The court stated that the "protection of patents furthers a strong public policy ... advanced by granting preliminary injunctive relief when it appears that, absent such relief, patent rights will be flagrantly violated."

The grant of a preliminary injunction, if not based on legal error or a serious misjudgment of the evidence, is reviewable only to ascertain whether the grant was within a reasonable range of discretion. We have considered all of the arguments of the parties, and the record before us. The district court's conclusion reflects a reasonable consideration and balance of the pertinent factors, evaluated in accordance with the established jurisprudence, and does not exceed the court's discretionary authority.

AFFIRMED.

HYBRITECH INC. v. ABBOTT LAB.

849 F.2d 1446, 7 USPQ2d 1191 (Fed. Cir. 1988)

Before DAVIS and SMITH, Circuit Judges, and BALDWIN, Senior Circuit Judge.

EDWARD S. SMITH, Circuit Judge.

In this patent case, the United States District Court for the Central District of California issued a preliminary injunction order enjoining Abbott Laboratories (Abbott) from manufacturing, using, or selling monoclonal antibody sandwich assays that infringe claims of Hybritech Inc.'s (Hybritech) United States Patent No. 4,376,110 ('110 patent). This injunction was stayed by the district court pending Abbott's appeal to this court. We affirm.

I. Issue

The sole question on appeal is whether the district court abused its discretion in preliminarily enjoining Abbott from continuing to infringe the '110 patent.

II. Background

Hybritech, since 1979, has been in the business of developing diagnostic test kits employing monoclonal antibodies that detect various antigens. By detecting specific antigens, a broad range of conditions such as pregnancy, cancer, growth hormone deficiency, or hepatitis can be identified. Hybritech is the assignee of the '110 patent, which patent issued March 8, 1983. The '110 patent relates to "Immunometric Assays Using Monoclonal Antibodies" and sets forth claims defining a variety of sandwich assays using monoclonal antibodies.

The '110 patent has been the subject of prior litigation before this court in *Hybritech Inc. v. Monoclonal Antibodies, Inc. (MAB)*. In that proceeding, Hybritech, alleging that the manufacture and sale of Monoclonal Antibodies, Inc.'s (Monoclonal) diagnostic test kits infringed claims of the '110 patent, on March 2, 1984, brought action in district court against Monoclonal seeking both monetary and injunctive relief. The United States District Court for the Northern District of California concluded that the claimed subject matter of the '110 patent was anticipated under 35 U.S.C. § 102(g). The district court, in that case, also held the claims of the '110 patent invalid for obviousness under 35 U.S.C. § 103. In addition, the district court also invalidated the patent on various grounds based on 35 U.S.C. § 112, first and second paragraphs. On appeal to this court, we reversed in all respects the judgment of the district court holding the claims of the '110 patent invalid.

Subsequent to receiving favorable results on appeal to this court in its litigation with Monoclonal, Hybritech on November 14, 1986, brought a patent infringement action against Abbott seeking both monetary and injunctive relief on grounds that Abbott manufactured and sold diagnostic test kits that infringed claims of the '110 patent. Abbott responded to Hybritech's complaint by filing a counterclaim seeking a declaratory judgment that claims of the '110 patent were invalid and not infringed by Abbott.

With respect to Hybritech's request for a preliminary injunction, the parties conducted limited discovery and submitted memoranda and appendices to the district court. After briefing on the motion was complete but before the district court rendered a decision on the motion, the United States Patent and Trademark Office, on April 8, 1987, declared an interference as to the '110 patent among Hybritech and La Jolla Research Foundation, both junior parties, and Hoffmann–LaRoche, Inc., the senior party. Abbott filed a motion for a stay of the district court action pending the outcome of the interference proceeding; however, this motion was denied by the district court.

On April 23–24, 1987, the district court heard oral argument on the preliminary injunction motion and, at the conclusion of the hearing, the district court rendered an oral ruling, including both oral findings of facts and conclusions of law, that Hybritech's motion for a preliminary injunction should be granted. At this time, the district court expressed its intent to put its oral findings and conclusions into writing. On June 12, 1987, the district court formally entered the injunctive order. In addition to entering the injunction order, the district court granted Abbott's motion to stay the preliminary injunction pending the outcome of this appeal. Abbott, on July 10, 1987, filed its notice of appeal on the injunctive order with this court. On July 14, 1987, the district court entered its written findings of facts and conclusions of law based on its prior oral findings of facts and conclusions of law issued April 24th.

III. ANALYSIS

Our review of a district court's grant of a preliminary injunction pursuant to 35 U.S.C. § 283 is limited to determining whether, in granting the preliminary injunction, the district court abused its discretion, committed an error of law, or seriously misjudged the evidence. Applying this standard of review to the proceeding before us, we cannot conclude, as urged by Abbott, that the district court abused its discretion by granting Hybritech's motion for a preliminary injunction.

Turning to the merits, to obtain a preliminary injunction, pursuant to 35 U.S.C. § 283, a party must establish a right thereto in light of four factors: (1) reasonable likelihood of success on the merits; (2) irreparable harm; (3) the balance of hardships tipping in its favor; and (4) the impact of the injunction on the public interest.[12]

These factors, taken individually, are not dispositive; rather, the district court must weigh and measure each factor against the other factors and against the form and magnitude of the relief requested. Although the issuance of an injunction is clearly within the discretion of the district court, the district court's discretion is not absolute and must be measured against the standards governing the issuance of an injunction.

A. Reasonable Likelihood of Success on the Merits

The first factor required to be established by a party seeking a preliminary injunction is that it stands to have a reasonable likelihood of success on the merits when the trial court finally adjudicates the dispute. In seeking a preliminary injunction pursuant to section 283, a patent holder must establish a likelihood of success on the merits both with respect to validity of its patent and with respect to infringement of its patent.

1. Likelihood of Success: Validity

Abbott argues that the district court erred by determining that Hybritech established a likelihood of success on the merits on the issue of the validity of the '110 patent, citing Hybritech's involvement in an interference on the '110 patent wherein Hybritech and the La Jolla Cancer Research Foundation were named as the junior parties and Hoffmann–LaRoche was named as the senior party by virtue of a Swiss patent application. As support for its argument, Abbott further cites one commentator's analysis for the proposition that only 25 percent of the junior parties prevail in an interference proceeding. On this basis, Abbott asserts that the possibility Hybritech would be awarded priority in the interference proceeding was small and contends that the district court erred by determining that Hybritech established a reasonable likelihood of success on the merits on the issue of patent validity. We are not persuaded.

---

12. *T.J. Smith & Nephew*, 821 F.2d at 647, 3 USPQ2d at 1317. We note that confusion exists on the issue whether, in view of *Panduit*, Federal Circuit law or regional circuit law provides the standards governing the issuance of an injunction pursuant to § 283. Because the issuance of an injunction pursuant to this section enjoins "the violation of any right secured by a patent, on such terms as the court deems reasonable," a preliminary injunction of this type, although a procedural matter, involves substantive matters unique to patent law and, therefore, is governed by the law of this court. We recognize, however, that purely procedural questions involving the grant of a preliminary injunction are controlled by the law of the appropriate regional circuit. *See, e.g., Chemlawn Servs.*, 823 F.2d at 517, 3 USPQ2d at 1315 (holding that appropriate regional circuit law controls the issue whether the district court, in granting a preliminary injunction, complied with Rule 52(a) of the Federal Rules of Civil Procedure); *Digital Equip. Corp. v. Emulex Corp.*, 805 F.2d 380, 382 & n. 3, 231 USPQ 779, 781 & n. 3 (Fed. Cir. 1986) (recognizing that this court must look to the law of the appropriate regional circuit in reviewing the issue whether the district court, in granting a preliminary injunction, violated either Rule 52(a) or Rule 65 of the Federal Rules of Civil Procedure).

In concluding that Hybritech established a reasonable likelihood of success on the merits concerning the validity of the '110 patent, the district court recognized both that a pending interference proceeding existed wherein Hybritech was named a junior party and that the existence of the interference raised the possibility that Hybritech may have been denied priority by the time this case is finally resolved. However, despite that possibility, the district court concluded that Hybritech was likely to prevail on the issue of validity notwithstanding the existence of the interference proceeding. On the basis of the evidence before it, the district court concluded that Hybritech was likely to establish a January 1979 date of invention, that based on this court's *MAB* opinion, Hybritech's date of invention was before that of the La Jolla Cancer Research Foundation, and that, in view of 35 U.S.C. § 104, it would be difficult for the Swiss inventors named in the Hoffmann–LaRoche application to prove a date of invention in the United States prior to January 1979. We cannot conclude that the district court abused its discretion or seriously misjudged the evidence in finding a probability of success on the merits despite the pending interference.[17]

Abbott argues that the district court's conclusions regarding the validity of the '110 patent were tainted by its decision to afford dispositive weight to this court's resolution of factual issues in *MAB* and, accordingly, that this case must be remanded to the district court with instructions to make independent factual findings on the record before it. Abbott contends that the district court's misunderstanding of the precedential value of the *MAB* opinion deprived Abbott of due process of law. We disagree.

It is well-established that in context of a motion for preliminary injunction against further infringement of a patent, the patent holder may use a prior adjudication of patent validity involving a different defendant as evidence supporting its burden of proving likelihood of success on the merits. This is not to say that the district court is bound, as a matter of law, by the prior adjudication of validity. Rather, the district court as an exercise of its discretion, may give considerable weight to a prior adjudication of validity in determining the likelihood of success on the merits on the issue of validity in the preliminary injunction proceeding before it.

Contrary to Abbott's assertions, the district court did not misunderstand the precedential value of this court's opinion in *MAB*. The district court stated that "Abbott was not a party to those proceedings [in *MAB*] and is not bound by that ruling in the way a prior party would be." Rather, the district court, in a clear exercise of discretion, accepted as evidence of validity, which evidence the district court considered "virtually dispositive," this court's opinion in *MAB*. Abbott has given us no

---

17. On April 6, 1988, the Patent and Trademark Office Board of Patent Appeals and Interferences issued a decision both denying the inventors named in the Hoffmann–LaRoche application the benefit of their Swiss patent application filing date and appointing the inventors named in the Hybritech application to senior party status. *Engvall v. Gallati*, Interference No. 101,769 (Bd. Pat. App. & Int. Apr. 6, 1988).

reason to hold that the district court abused its discretion by relying on the *MAB* opinion as evidence supporting its determination of success on the merits on the issue of patent validity.

Abbott further argues that the district court failed to make any finding with respect to Abbott's allegation that the claims of the '110 patent were invalid, pursuant to section 112, for indefiniteness on grounds that the claims failed to specify a method by which the data needed to calculate affinity is obtained. Abbott asserts that the district court's failure to recognize the force of this issue vitiates its conclusion that Hybritech is likely to be successful in asserting the validity of its patent. This argument is without merit.

This court has repeatedly recognized that compliance with the second paragraph of section 112 is a question of law. On the basis of the record before us, we cannot hold, in view of the requirements of section 112, that the district court erred by concluding that Hybritech demonstrated a reasonable likelihood of success on the issue of validity.

In its written findings of facts and conclusions of law, the district court addressed the issue of enablement and concluded that the specification of the '110 patent was sufficiently enabling to indicate a likelihood of success. In reaching this conclusion, the district court, with respect to the method by which the data needed to calculate affinity is obtained, expressly found that "most everybody used the Scatchard method to determine affinity constants." Although the enablement requirement, pursuant to section 112, first paragraph, is separate and distinct from the definiteness requirement, pursuant to section 112, second paragraph, this finding by the district court supporting its conclusion that the '110 patent meets the enablement requirement also supports the conclusion that the claims of the '110 patent meet the definiteness requirement, both within the likelihood-of-success analysis. Accordingly, we cannot disturb, pursuant to Abbott's section 112, second paragraph, argument, the district court's grant to Hybritech of the preliminary injunction.

2. *Likelihood of Success: Infringement*

With respect to infringement, Abbott further argues that the district court erred in concluding that the '110 patent claims read on Abbott's TESTPACK and HTSH–EIA assays sufficiently to warrant a finding of likelihood of success. Abbott contends that its TESTPACK and HTSH–EIA assays do not employ antibodies with affinities that fall in the range of affinities claimed in the '110 patent. We disagree.

Analysis of literal infringement is a two-step process. First, the district court must determine the scope of the patent claims. Claim interpretation is a legal question and, on appeal, is reviewed for legal correctness. Underlying the district court's legal conclusion on the scope of the claims, however, may be factual determinations that, to be disturbed by us, must be shown to have been clearly erroneous. Second, the district court must determine whether properly interpreted claims encompass the accused structure. The application of the claim to the accused structure is a fact question and, on appeal, is reviewed under the clearly erroneous standard.

Here, the affinity limitation contained in the claims of the '110 patent, both the solid phase and the labeled antibody, requires antibodies with an affinity of "at least about 10^8 liters/mole." In determining the scope of the claims, in view of this limitation, the district court cited two-to three-fold measurement errors inherent in affinity measurements. On the basis of this factual determination, which determination we cannot hold is clearly erroneous, the district court interpreted, as a matter of law, the '110 patent claim language as reciting a range of affinities that encompassed affinities possessed by Abbott's assays. We cannot hold that the district court erred as a matter of law when it construed the claim limitation in this manner.

In determining whether the claims of the '110 patent encompassed Abbott's TESTPACK and HTSH–EIA assays, the district court first was required to choose between affinity measurements submitted by Abbott and affinity measurements submitted by Hybritech. For the TESTPACK assay, the district court adopted Hybritech's measurement of the affinity of the solid phase antibody at 4.7 to 4.8×10^7 liters/mole and adopted Abbott's measurement of the affinity of the labeled antibody at 7.1 to 7.5 $\times 10^7$ liters/mole. For the HTSH–EIA assay, the district court adopted Hybritech's measurement of the affinity of the labeled antibody at 1.2 to 4.5×10^9 liters/mole, one solid phase antibody at 3.9×10^8 liters/mole, and the second solid phase antibody at 1.7×10^9 liters/mole. On the basis of these measurements, and in view of its interpretation of the claim language "at least about 10^8 liters/mole," the district court determined that Abbott's TESTPACK and HTSH–EIA assays fell within the scope of, and thus infringed, claims of the '110 patent. The two measurements less than 1×10^8 liters/mole, i.e., 4.8×10^7 liters/mole and 7.1 to 7.5×10^7 liters/mole, fall within the two-to three-fold range of measurement error that the district court interpreted the claims of the '110 patent as encompassing. Abbott has given us no grounds to disturb these findings. Accordingly, we must hold that the district court did not err by concluding that Hybritech established a reasonable likelihood of success of proving that Abbott literally infringed claims of the '110 patent. Because of this holding on the question of literal infringement, we need not reach Abbott's arguments concerning infringement pursuant to the doctrine of equivalents.

B. Irreparable Harm

The second factor required to be established by a party seeking a preliminary injunction is that it will suffer irreparable harm if the preliminary injunction is not granted. Abbott proffers three arguments to support its assertion that the district court erred in concluding that Hybritech would suffer irreparable harm in the absence of a preliminary injunction. We are not persuaded by any of these arguments.

First, Abbott argues that the district court erred by presuming the existence of irreparable harm, which presumption flows from a strong showing of validity and infringement. Abbott contends that, although the district court expressly stated that it would not afford Hybritech the benefit of a presumption of irreparable harm, the district court's analysis of irreparable harm, in reality, is based upon such a presumption. This argument is without merit.

Although it is true that the district court analyzed the importance of exclusive rights and the importance of the patent system to competitive markets and examined the kind of irreparable harm which can occur when patent rights are ignored in such a market, the district court did not conclude solely on the basis of these patent rights that Hybritech would be irreparably harmed if the preliminary injunction was not granted. Rather, in reaching its conclusion, the district court listed the following factors upon which it based its decision: (1) the field of technology covered by the '110 patent was new; (2) there was a substantial amount of competition in this field; (3) Abbott has a very large presence in this field; (4) this is a field where technology changes fairly quickly; (5) there is a lot of research being done in this field; (6) the '110 patent could help Hybritech establish a market position and create business relationships in the market; (7) by the time the litigation is finished, it is entirely possible that the value of the patent will be gone and that technology might well bypass it; (8) the potential injury is unpredictable; and, (9) in the absence of the injunction, other potential infringers will be encouraged to infringe. In view of these specific grounds enumerated by the district court, we cannot hold that the district court presumed irreparable harm; rather, it is clear from the record that the district court considered a wide range of factors as the basis for its determination.

Second, Abbott argues that a review of these findings relied upon by the district court in reaching its determination of irreparable harm demonstrates that there is nothing in these generalized observations concerning the diagnostic assay field which supports a conclusion of irreparable harm to Hybritech, even assuming that they were all supported by the evidence. Rather, Abbott contends that money damages would be a fully adequate remedy in the event that Hybritech ultimately establishes that any of Abbott's accused assays infringes a valid claim of the '110 patent. We are not persuaded.

It is well-settled that, because the principal value of a patent is its statutory right to exclude, the nature of the patent grant weighs against holding that monetary damages will always suffice to make the patentee whole. The patent statute provides injunctive relief to preserve the legal interests of the parties against future infringement which may have market effects never fully compensable in money. "If monetary relief were the sole relief afforded by the patent statute then injunctions would be unnecessary and infringers could become compulsory licensees for as long as the litigation lasts." We cannot hold that the district court abused its discretion by granting Hybritech's motion for a preliminary injunction, for the period the litigation is pending, notwithstanding the potential availability of compensatory damages, for this period, after the completion of trial on the merits.

Third, Abbott argues that the district court erred, as a matter of law, in entering a preliminary injunction in the face of undisputed evidence of Hybritech's voluntary and prolonged delay in bringing suit against Abbott. We disagree.

The period of delay exercised by a party prior to seeking a preliminary injunction in a case involving intellectual property is but one factor to be considered by a district court in its analysis of irreparable harm. Although a showing of delay may be so significant, in the district court's discretion, as to preclude a determination of irreparable harm, a showing of delay does not preclude, as a matter of law, a determination of irreparable harm. A period of delay is but one circumstance that the district court must consider in the context of the totality of the circumstances.

Here, the district court was not persuaded that Hybritech's delay in seeking a preliminary injunction against Abbott while it litigated with Monoclonal precludes a finding of irreparable harm. The district court concluded that Hybritech established good cause for seeking relief against Monoclonal first, given its particular situation and financial resources. We cannot hold that this determination by the district court was an abuse of its discretion or based on an error of law.

C. The Balance of Hardships

The third factor required to be considered by the district court in its determination whether to award a preliminary injunction is the balance of hardships. The district court must balance the harm that will occur to the moving party from the denial of the preliminary injunction with the harm that the non-moving party will incur if the injunction is granted.

Abbott argues that the district court erred, as a matter of law, by issuing the preliminary injunction despite determining that Hybritech had not established that the balance of hardships tipped in its favor. On this basis, Abbott contends that the district court's grant of the preliminary injunction should be reversed. We disagree.

Although this court has cited "the balance of hardships tipping in favor of the movant" as one of four factors to be considered by a district court in determining whether to issue a preliminary injunction, we never have required, as a prerequisite to awarding preliminary injunctive relief, that the district court expressly find the existence of this factor. Here, the district court considered the balance of hardships between the parties and concluded that "neither party has a clear advantage." We cannot hold that the district court's conclusion on the balance of hardships, after carefully considering the question, provides grounds for us to disturb its grant of preliminary relief.

D. Impact of the Injunction on the Public Interest

The fourth factor that must be considered by the district court in determining whether to issue a preliminary injunction is the impact of the injunction on the public interest. Typically, in a patent infringement case, although there exists a public interest in protecting rights secured by valid patents, the focus of the district court's public interest analysis should be whether there exists some critical public interest that would be injured by the grant of preliminary relief.

Abbott argues that, although the district court recognized the public interest in product availability by specifically excluding Abbott cancer test kits and Abbott hepatitis kits from the preliminary injunction order, the district court erred in failing to find any public interest considerations with respect to the remaining Abbott products. Abbott contends the district court ignored that (1) the diagnostic community relies upon Abbott for millions of dollars worth of assays, (2) switching by the public of vendors of such assays is an expensive and time consuming undertaking, and (3) supply shortages to the public may result because Hybritech allegedly has experienced substantial difficulties in filling orders promptly. On this basis, Abbott argues that the district court's grant of a preliminary injunction should be reversed. We disagree.

Here, the district court found, with respect to most of Abbott's products involved in this proceeding, that the public interest in enforcing valid patents outweighed any other public interest considerations. Accordingly, with respect to these products, the district court concluded that the public interest was in favor of granting the preliminary injunction. However, with respect to both Abbott's cancer test kits and Abbott's hepatitis test kits, the district court determined that the public interest is served best by the availability of these kits. On this basis, the district court did not enjoin Abbott from producing these products. We cannot hold that the district court's public interest analysis provides a basis for us to disturb its grant to Hybritech of preliminary relief.

Conclusion

In view of the foregoing, we hold that the district court did not abuse its discretion in granting Hybritech preliminary relief. Accordingly, we affirm the preliminary injunctive order of the district court.

Notes

1. **Reasonable Likelihood of Success on the Merits.** The patentee must make a showing of reasonable likelihood of success of both infringement and validity.

   a. *Regarding validity*—the patentee does not have to prove that the patent is valid, only that the defendant's attack on the patent will likely fail. Hence the patentee must prove that the defendant will not be able to prove by clear and convincing evidence that the patent is invalid. If the defendant "fails to identify any persuasive evidence of invalidity, the very existence of the patent satisfies the patentee's burden on the validity issue." *Canon Computer Systems, Inc. v. Nu–Kote Int'l, Inc.*, 134 F.3d 1085, 1088, 45 USPQ2d 1355, 1358 (Fed. Cir. 1998). If necessary, the patentee can prove likelihood of success on validity through prior adjudications on the same or similar issues; successful reexamination of the patent; using expert testimony and other direct evidence such as commercial success and licensing activities to show industry acquiescence. In opposition to the preliminary injunction motion, the defendant should offer evidence to rebut prior adjudication by pointing to different prior art references, third party infringers and with expert affidavits.

b. ***Regarding infringement***—the patentee should use claim charts, expert testimony and successful past infringement suits against similar products.

2. **Irreparable Harm (When the presumption arises).** Irreparable harm to the patentee is presumed when a clear showing of likelihood of success on validity and infringement is proven. *Smith Int'l, Inc. v. Hughes Tool Co.* 718 F.2d 1573, 219 USPQ 686 (Fed. Cir. 1983).

a. If the presumption does not arise, the patent owner can prove irreparable harm by offering evidence such as:

- loss of jobs;

- loss of market share;

- the length of the remaining patent term is short (not many years left);

- the infringer will likely not be able to pay damages;

- other potential infringers will be encouraged to enter the market or increase their existing activities;

- the market for the patented product is short-lived, such as for a fad item or the product is in a field of technology which changes quickly (software); and

- the infringer has a big presence in the field.

b. The infringer can rebut the patentee's claim of irreparable harm with evidence that:

- the patent owner delayed in filing suit or in asking for a preliminary injunction (the patent owner will want to rebut the showing of delay by offering an explanation for the delay such as the fact that the delay was caused because she was involved in litigation with other infringers);

- there was (non-exclusive) licensing activity by the patentee that dilutes the need to grant a preliminary injunction;

- the accused infringer does not compete directly with the patentee (lack of commercial activity by the patentee or different geographic markets favor no preliminary injunction);

- the accused infringer has the capacity to pay whatever damages are assessed;

- there are non-infringing substitutes available;

- the patent owner's share of the market is small (so infringement is not that damaging);

- the patent owner actually offered the defendant a license (this shows that money will be enough for the patentee); and
- the defendant has or will soon cease the allegedly infringing activities.

Consider the following discussion of irreparable harm in *Polymer Tech., Inc. v. Bridwell*, 103 F.3d 970, 974–76, 41 USPQ2d 1185, 1189–90 (Fed. Cir. 1996) (citations omitted):

The district court relied on its finding that most of Polymer's losses could not be attributed to Westmark's allegedly infringing activities. Specifically, the district court found that Ed Nolan's sudden death and overall market competition contributed substantially to Polymer's losses. The court relied upon Westmark's evidence that "nearly a dozen other competitors around the nation produce and sell products similar to Crop–Life" and Joanna Nolan's admission, during Polymer's case in rebuttal, that Polymer's losses were not "entirely" due to Bridwell. Ms. Nolan's lack of business experience was also said to be a factor in Polymer's loss of market share.

Polymer argues that, regardless of the lack of causal link between particular infringing activities and some of its losses, the presumption of irreparable harm was not rebutted by evidence of other potential causes of Polymer's lost revenues. We agree with Polymer that the presumption was not rebutted by the evidence on which the district court relied. The court seemed unduly reliant on its belief that "the fact that [Westmark] may have taken some of [Polymer's] business does not entitle [Polymer] to a preliminary injunction." However, the court assumed that the patent was valid and infringed when it granted Polymer the presumption of irreparable harm. Absent a finding clearly negating irreparable harm, such as that future infringement was no longer likely, that the patentee was willing to forgo its right to exclude by licensing the patent, or that the patentee had delayed in bringing suit, there was no basis for finding that the presumption of irreparable harm was overcome. Because of the very nature of a patent, which provides the right to exclude, infringement of a valid patent inherently causes irreparable harm in the absence of the above or similar exceptions.

The fact that other infringers may be in the marketplace does not negate irreparable harm. A patentee does not have to sue all infringers at once. Picking off one infringer at a time is not inconsistent with being irreparably harmed. Being inexperienced in business also does not negate irreparable harm. Even a poor businessperson is entitled to the exclusionary rights of a patent. Thus, contrary to the rationale adopted by the district court, evidence that Westmark was not the principal or the sole cause of Polymer's lost sales does not provide legal support for the finding that Westmark rebutted the presumption of irreparable harm.

The district court also found that because "damages may be finite in this case due to the seemingly limited market and, therefore, may be readily calculable," any harm suffered by Polymer could be "fully compensated by money damages." Polymer argues that the district court erred by mischaracterizing the market as "limited" and by ignoring the principal value of the patent right: the statutory right to exclude. Westmark argues that, in light of its claim that it will be able to compensate Polymer in damages, the district court's ultimate finding that Westmark rebutted the presumption of irreparable harm was not clearly erroneous. . . .

We have stated that, in the context of a potential loss of market share, "there is no presumption that money damages will be inadequate" in connection with a motion for a preliminary injunction. However, merely asserting that it would have sufficient funds to answer for Polymer's future losses similarly does not sustain Westmark's burden to rebut the presumption of irreparable harm. Competitors change the marketplace. Years after infringement has begun, it may be impossible to restore a patentee's (or an exclusive licensee's) exclusive position by an award of damages and a permanent injunction. Customers may have established relationships with infringers. The market is rarely the same when a market of multiple sellers is suddenly converted to one with a single seller by legal fiat. Requiring purchasers to pay higher prices after years of paying lower prices to infringers is not a reliable business option.

3. Balance of the Hardships

The patent owner will want to offer evidence that its company will suffer greater harm if the injunction is not granted than the defendant will suffer if the injunction is granted. Typically both sides will assert that the grant or denial of the preliminary injunction will cause a hardship to their company, its employees and customers. The defendant will argue that if an injunction is granted it will lose business, and will be forced to fire employees and close plants. The hardships will generally favor the smaller company on the theory that it is more likely to be impacted by the injunction. The patentee will offer evidence that it is being harmed by the continued erosion of its market share and that this market share will be totally lost unless the injunction is granted. It will help if the patentee can show that the defendant has only recently started infringing and that the patentee has an established presence in the field. The patentee will argue to the court that it invested heavily in the research and development of the invention and that it should be permitted to exclude the defendant from infringing. Often evidence that the defendant willfully infringes the patent will tip the hardships inquiry in favor of the patentee.

4. Public Interest

Public Interest—The patent owner will argue that the law favors protection of inventions through patents and that the public interest favors enforcing the patentee's exclusive rights which are guaranteed by law. In rare cases, the defendant will argue that the public interest favors denying the injunctive relief where public health, safety, or welfare will be adversely affected by the grant of an injunction. For example, if a potential health hazard would be caused by granting the injunction, or there is a unique product connected to public health, the public interest may require denial of injunctive relief. *See City of Milwaukee v. Activated Sludge,* 69 F.2d 577 (7th Cir. 1934) (no injunction granted where possible health hazards would result if the city was forced to stop using the patented sewage treatment process);

Hybritech, Inc. v. Abbott Labs., 849 F.2d 1446, 7 USPQ2d 1191 (Fed. Cir. 1988) (preliminary injunction denied because of public interest in availability of cancer and hepatitis testing kits). Can you think of other times when a preliminary injunction should not be granted? What if the patent owner cannot fill the demand for a particular product and granting the injunction would cause a shortage?

5. **Does the Court Have to Consider all Four Factors?** Although the Federal Circuit generally prefers that the trial court consider each of the four factors, it will affirm the denial of a preliminary injunction when the trial court concludes that a factor is not proven. *See Polymer Tech., Inc. v. Bridwell*, 103 F.3d 970, 973–74, 41 USPQ2d 1185, 1188 (Fed. Cir. 1996) ("Before denying a motion for preliminary injunction, an analysis of each of the four factors is generally appropriate 'for reasons of judicial economy and [because it] greatly aids appellate review.' Nevertheless, more limited analysis may support a trial court's denial of a preliminary injunction. For example, a trial court need not make findings concerning the third and fourth factors if the moving party fails to establish either of the first two factors." (citations omitted)).

6. **Staying the Preliminary Injunction.** If you lose a preliminary injunction motion, you can always move to have the district court stay the injunction pending the outcome on appeal. Alternatively, the defendant can file a notice of appeal to the Federal Circuit and a motion with the Federal Circuit to stay the preliminary injunction pending the appeal.

7. **Claim Construction During a Preliminary Injunction.** Claim construction performed pursuant to a preliminary injunction motion is by no means the last word. *See Sofamor Danek Group, Inc. v. DePuy–Motech, Inc.*, 74 F.3d 1216, 1221, 37 USPQ2d 1529, 1532 (Fed. Cir. 1996) ("the trial court has no obligation to interpret claim 1 conclusively and finally during a preliminary injunction proceeding"). In fact, in *CVI/Beta Ventures, Inc. v. Tura LP*, 112 F.3d 1146, 42 USPQ2d 1577 (Fed. Cir. 1997), the Federal Circuit construed the claims one way in the appeal from the grant of the preliminary injunction motion and in *CVI/BETA Ventures, Inc. v. Tura LP*, 120 F.3d 1260, 43 USPQ2d 1860 (Fed. Cir. 1997) construed the same terms in an opposite manner in the appeal from the determination of liability. If claim construction is a question of law for the court, should this happen? Although it is true that resolution of a preliminary injunction motion takes place early in the litigation proceedings, often prior to most discovery, and without the benefit of the more complete record that exists during a full blown trial, can the claim construction change if the court has the patent and prosecution history before it when it renders the construction for preliminary injunction purposes? In *CVI Beta*, the court considered the patent and prosecution history when construing the claims to rule on the preliminary injunction motion and had the same evidence before it when rendering the final claim construction during the trial. No additional evidence was entered or considered by the court. Yet two panels of Federal Circuit judges construed the claims in two different ways at different stages of the proceedings. Does this seem appropriate?

8. **Posting bond.** Obtaining a preliminary injunction is an expensive proposition. Federal Rule of Civil Procedure 65(c) requires that the patent

owner post a bond as security for damages to the infringer if the injunction is determined to be wrongfully granted: "No restraining order or preliminary injunction shall issue except upon the giving of security by the applicant, in such sum as the court deems proper, for the payment of such costs and damages as may be incurred or suffered by any party who is found to have been wrongfully enjoined or restrained." Such bonds can easily run in the hundreds of thousands or even millions of dollars. Do you think that the defendant is always entitled to the bond if it ultimately succeeds in proving the patent invalid or not infringed? *See Hupp v. Siroflex of Am., Inc.*, 122 F.3d 1456, 1467, 43 USPQ2d 1887 (Fed. Cir. 1997). What damages can the defendant recover for under the injunctive bond? What factors should the court consider in assessing the amount to require the patent owner to post?

B. PERMANENT INJUNCTIONS

FEDERAL RULE OF CIVIL PROCEDURE-65(d):

Every order granting an injunction and every restraining order shall set forth the reason for its issuance; shall be specific in terms; shall describe in reasonable detail and not by reference to the complaint or other document, the act or acts sought to be restrained; and is binding only on the parties to the action, their officers, agents, servants, employees and lawyers and on those persons in active concert or participation with them who receive actual notice of the order by personal service or otherwise.

A permanent injunction is almost always awarded against a defendant who has been found to infringe a valid patent. A permanent injunction should be granted even if the defendant is no longer making or selling the product found to infringe. *See W.L. Gore & Associates, Inc. v. Garlock, Inc.*, 842 F.2d 1275, 6 USPQ2d 1277 (Fed. Cir. 1988) (directing the district court to enter the injunction even though Garlock stopped making the infringing products noting that there was no evidence that Garlock had sold or dismantled the equipment used to make those products). Only in rare cases where public health and safety will be affected by granting an injunction will the court refuse to grant the patent owner their statutory rights of exclusivity and instead force them to accept a compulsory license. Can you think of a situation where the court would do this?

It is important when crafting any type of injunction (preliminary or permanent) to be as specific as possible. In *Additive Controls & Measurements Sys. v. Flowdata*, 986 F.2d 476, 477, 25 USPQ2d 1798, 1799 (Fed. Cir. 1993), the Federal Circuit reversed the entry of a two sentence injunction which stated:

> Plaintiff is forever barred from infringing Flowdata's patent. This order is made with the oral consent of ADCON's Secretary Treasurer who appeared before this Court in her official capacity.

The Court held:

> The district court's two sentence injunction in this case does not satisfy the requirements of Rule 65. The brief injunction does not

use specific terms or describe in reasonable detail the acts sought to be restrained. The terse order does not state which acts of Adcon constitute infringement of the '318 patent. The order does not limit its prohibition to the manufacture, use, or sale of the specific infringing device, or to infringing devices no more than colorably different from the infringing device.

Id. at 479–80, 25 USPQ at 1801.

Learning its lesson, on remand, the district court issued a more detailed permanent injunction as part of its final judgment:

> Plaintiff and Counterdefendant Additive Controls and Measurement Systems, Inc. ("Adcon"), its officers, agents, servants, employees, attorneys, and those persons in active concert or participation with them who receive actual notice of this Final Judgment by actual service or otherwise, are hereby RESTRAINED and ENJOINED, from and after the date hereof and until March 28, 2006, or until the date that the United States Letters Patent No. 4,815,318 (the "'318 patent") may be canceled by the United States Patent and Trademark Office for failure to pay any maintenance fee, from directly or indirectly infringing any claims of the Letters Patent No. 4,815,318, by making, using, or selling or causing to be made, used or sold the adjudged infringing flowmeter devices as set forth in Flowdata, Inc.'s ("Flowdata") Trial Exhibits 24, 24–A, 24–B, and 24–C of which Flowdata's Trial Exhibits 2–A, 2–B, 2–C, 2–D and 2–E and drawings thereof and Flowdata's Trial Exhibits Nos. 25 and 25–A, of which Flowdata's Trial Exhibits 2–A, 2–B, 2–C, and 2–D and 2–E are also drawings thereof, and that are attached hereto and incorporated herein by reference for all purposes, (and) any colorable differences or imitations thereof, . . .

Additive Controls & Measurement Sys., Inc. v. Flowdata, Inc., 32 USPQ2d 1747, 1748 (S.D. Tex. 1994). A typical permanent injunction in a patent case will recite the enjoined activity "making, using or selling" by reference to the product found to infringe and will also generally include the language "and any other product that is no more than a colorable difference of the product found to infringe."

In *Century Wrecker Corp. v. E.R. Buske Mfg. Co.*, 913 F. Supp. 1256, 1294–95 (N.D. Iowa 1996), the Court entered the following injunction:

> Defendants E.R. Buske Manufacturing Co., Inc., E.R. Buske Distributing Co. and E.R. Buske, their officers, agents, servants, employees, attorneys, and those persons in active concert or participation with them who receive actual notice of this Order by personal service or otherwise, are permanently enjoined and restrained during the life of the '737 and '978 patents from infringing in any way any of claims 1, 2, 3 and 8 of the '978 patent and claims 1–3, 5–8 and 10–14 of the '737 patent by manufacture, use and/or sale of products embodying the elements of those claims, or colorable variations thereof.

An injunction can also limit indirect as well as direct infringement by the defendant, for example in *Allied-Signal, Inc. v. Filmtec Corp.*, 17

USPQ2d 1692, 1696 (S.D. Cal. 1990), the district court fashioned the injunction as follows:

IT IS HEREBY ORDERED:

1. As of the effective date of this Order, defendants, their officers, agents, servants, employees, attorneys and those persons in active concert or participation with them who receive actual notice of this Preliminary Injunction Order by personal service or otherwise are enjoined from making, using or selling, and actively inducing others to make, use or sell, FT–30 membrane, including "TW-", "BW-", and "SW-" designations thereof, in the United States, and from otherwise infringing claim 9 of United States Patent No. 3,744,642;

2. This Order shall be effective as of 12:00 noon on May 29, 1990, and unless stayed, modified, vacated or reversed, this Order shall continue in full force and effect until and including July 10, 1990.

If a permanent injunction is entered, the defendant can seek aid from the court of appeals by independent application for a stay pursuant to Federal Circuit Rule of Appellate Procedure 8. Rule 8 requires that the defendant file a notice of appeal with the trial court and then a motion with the Federal Circuit requesting a stay of the injunction. In determining whether to grant a stay, the Federal Circuit will consider the same factors that a court considers in determining whether to grant a preliminary injunction motion, whether the stay movant has shown: a strong likelihood of success; irreparable harm; balance of the hardships; and public interest. *See Standard Havens, Prods. Inc. v. Gencor Indus., Inc.*, 897 F.2d 511, 13 USPQ2d 2029 (Fed. Cir. 1990) (granting a stay of a permanent injunction where Gencor proved validity was a close question on appeal and that if the injunction was enforced it would be bankrupt).

C. CONTEMPT PROCEEDINGS

It is frequently the case that after a defendant's product has been found to infringe the patent at issue and an injunction is issued, the defendant will modify or redesign the device (in a manner which she thinks will avoid infringement) and begin making, using or selling this modified device. At this juncture the patentee has two options: file a new complaint alleging that this new device infringes her patent or move the court for contempt of the existing injunction. There are advantages and disadvantages of both options.

The advantages of moving for contempt are that the judge who decides the contempt motion is already familiar with the patent and the technology and can determine in a contempt proceeding whether this modified device also infringes. The court that already presided over a trial where the defendant was found to infringe is likely to be a friendly forum for the patent owner. A judge who already awarded the patentee an injunction to prohibit future infringement will not be pleased with a defendant who ignores her court order. In addition, the defendant cannot raise validity or unenforceability as a defense in a contempt proceeding. Because the judge is already familiar with the technology and patent and there are a limited number of defenses that can be brought, a contempt proceeding is generally quicker and significantly less expensive than a second full blown trial. However, in a contempt proceeding the patentee must prove infringement by clear and convincing evidence to show a violation of the injunction, rather than a mere preponderance of the evidence which would be the burden if a separate infringement action is brought.

The following case is the seminal contempt proceeding case from the Federal Circuit.

KSM FASTENING SYSTEMS, INC. v. H.A. JONES CO.

776 F.2d 1522, 227 USPQ 676 (Fed. Cir. 1985)

Before NIES, NEWMAN and BISSELL, Circuit Judges.

NIES, Circuit Judge.

This appeal is from an order of the United States District Court for the District of New Jersey holding H.A. Jones Company, Inc. and Erico Jones Company (hereinafter collectively Jones) in civil contempt of court for violation of the terms of a consent decree entered in a patent infringement suit. On April 30, 1979, a predecessor of KSM Fastening Systems, Inc., brought suit against Jones alleging infringement of U.S. Patent No. 3,738,217, which claims a particular hanger assembly or anchor for securing refractory linings to furnace walls (KSM's INSULT-WIST), by reason of Jones' manufacture and sale of a device of that type (Jones' THERMAL–LOCK device). Pursuant to a settlement agreement between the parties, which was entered as a consent decree on March 6, 1980, Jones acknowledged the validity of the KSM patent, admitted infringement thereof by its THERMAL–LOCK device, and was enjoined from further infringement.

Jones subsequently put out a modified refractory anchor (ULTRA–LOK I) and on September 22, 1981, KSM moved the court to punish Jones for contempt for violation of the injunction. On July 17, 1984, the court found Jones in contempt by reason of Jones' manufacture and sale of the ULTRA–LOK I device and another model, ULTRA–LOK II, which Jones began marketing in late 1983 or early 1984. This appeal followed.

Under the standard we conclude is appropriate, the judgment must be set aside as a matter of law because of the refusal of the district court to consider whether the Jones ULTRA–LOK devices infringed the claims of the '217 patent. Moreover, the question whether contempt proceedings involving the ULTRA–LOK devices are appropriate must also be reexamined. Therefore, upon remand, the district court is directed to reconsider whether, under the standard set forth herein, infringement with respect to the ULTRA–LOK devices should be tested in contempt proceedings.

I.

While the grant of injunctive authority is clearly in discretionary terms, injunctive relief against an infringer is the norm.... Having enjoined the infringer, a patent owner who is confronted with another possible infringement by that party in the form of a modified device will very likely seek to invoke the power of the court to punish the adjudged infringer for contempt in violating the court's injunctive order. While a patent owner, in such circumstances, could institute a separate suit to enjoin the modified device, the advantages of proceeding on a motion to hold his adversary in contempt are substantial. The adjudged infringer is already under the jurisdiction of the court and may be summoned to appear to respond on the merits, the contempt motion being merely part of the original action. Contempt proceedings are generally summary in nature and may be decided by the court on affidavits and exhibits without the formalities of a full trial, although the movant bears the heavy burden of proving violation by clear and convincing evidence. If violation is found, the contemnor may be punished by fine (payable to the patent owner) and imprisonment, even in civil contempt.

A civil contempt proceeding for violation of an injunction issued after patent litigation, while primarily for the benefit of the patent owner, nevertheless, involves also the concept of an affront to the court for failure to obey its order. As explained in *American Foundry & Manufacturing Co. v. Josam Manufacturing Co.*, 79 F.2d 116, 118, 26 USPQ 338, 339 (8th Cir. 1935):

> A decision adjudging infringement necessarily finds the particular accused device to be within the valid boundary of the patent. The decree usually carries a prohibition against further infringement—not as to any and every possible infringement, but as to the particular device found to be infringement and as to all other devices which are merely "colorable" changes of the infringing one or of the patent. This limitation of the effect of such a decree is occasioned somewhat by the indefinite character of the boundaries of a patent, but more by the character of the remedy—summary contempt proceedings—used to enforce such provisions of a decree. This is merely an application to patent injunction contempt proceedings of the general rule as to all civil contempt proceedings. That rule was stated by this Court to be that "when it is doubtful whether a decree of injunction has been violated, a court is not justified in punishing for contempt, either criminal or civil, for the reason that no one can say with any degree of certainty that the authority of the court needs vindication or that the aggrieved party is entitled to remedial punishment."

In view of these and other considerations to be discussed, where the patent owner seeks to enforce an injunction against an enjoined infringer by reason of a manufacture which was not the subject of the original litigation, the courts have been uniform in exercising restraint in affording the patent owner the benefit of contempt proceedings.

In *MAC Corp. of America v. Williams Patent Crusher & Pulverizer Co.*, 767 F.2d 882, 226 USPQ 515 (Fed. Cir. 1985), this court affirmed the denial of proceedings in contempt where the district court found a "fair ground of doubt" that the injunction against infringement had been violated because of differences between the adjudged and accused devices. In so holding, the court followed the Supreme Court's directive in *California Artificial Stone Paving Co. v. Molitor*, 113 U.S. 609, 618 (1885):

> Process of contempt is a severe remedy, and should not be resorted to where there is *fair ground of doubt* as to the wrongfulness of the defendant's conduct. [Emphasis added.]

Thus, not all subsequent infringements by an enjoined party are deemed in contempt of the court, even though an injunction may be written broadly enjoining, as in *California Paving*, further infringements.

While the courts have been uniform in acknowledging that contempt does not embrace all infringements by modified devices, there has not been uniformity in the actual standards for determining (1) when contempt proceedings will be entertained, and (2) when contempt will be found. These are separate questions and the standard for determining the answer to each must be addressed in this appeal.

II.

Contempt authority is provided to the federal courts under 18 U.S.C. § 401 (1982), which reads:

§ 401. Power of court

A court of the United States shall have power to punish by fine or imprisonment, at its discretion, such contempt of its authority, and none other, as—

> (1) Misbehavior of any person in its presence or so near thereto as to obstruct the administration of justice;

> (2) Misbehavior of any of its officers in their official transactions;

> (3) Disobedience or resistance to its lawful writ, process, order, rule, decree, or command.

Thus, in view of the requirement for definiteness and the limitation of contempt enforcement to "lawful" orders, many courts refrain from broadly enjoining "further infringements" and limit the injunction as indicated in the *American Foundry* opinion. *See, e.g., Square Liner 360°, Inc. v. Chisum*, 691 F.2d 362, 378, 216 USPQ 666, 678 (8th Cir. 1982) (injunction against particular device "and any infringing equivalents" set aside for failing to satisfy "the specificity and description requirements of Rule 65(d)").

If the potent weapon of judicial contempt power is to be brought to bear against a party for violation of an order, "one basic principle built into Rule 65 is that those against whom an injunction is issued should receive fair and precisely drawn notice of what the injunction actually prohibits." *Granny Goose Foods, Inc. v. Brotherhood of Teamsters*, 415 U.S. 423, 444 (1974). Merely telling the enjoined party not to violate a statute is routinely condemned. It is apparent, nevertheless, from a review of patent cases dealing with contempt proceedings that injunctions are frequently drafted or approved by the courts in general terms, broadly enjoining "further infringement" of the "patent," despite the language of Rule 65(d), and Supreme Court interpretation.

The unreasonableness of a decree incorporating a vague or broad prohibition against "infringement" of a "patent" is alleviated because of the universal rule, to be addressed *infra*, that contempt proceedings, civil or criminal, are available only with respect to devices previously admitted or adjudged to infringe, and to other devices which are no more than colorably different therefrom and which clearly are infringements of the patent. This limitation is seen as properly balancing the interests of the respective parties. An enjoined party is entitled to design around the claims of a patent without the threat of contempt proceedings with respect to every modified device although he bears the risk that the enjoining court may find changes to be too insubstantial to avoid contempt.

Conversely, where an injunction is written narrowly against a particular infringing device, contempt may, nevertheless, be found on the basis of a modified infringing device. An enjoined party under a narrow decree will not be permitted to escape on a purely "in rem" theory that only a particular device is prohibited, where it is evident that the modifications do not avoid infringement and were made for the purpose of evasion of the court's order. Again, the standard is whether the differences between the two devices are merely colorable.

III.

The injunction entered in the present case was in the following terms:

> 6. The Defendant ... [is] enjoined and restrained from making, using or selling insulation hangers or refractory anchors of the type and nature identified by the Plaintiff in its Complaint against the Defendant for the remainder of the life of U.S. Patent No. 3,738,217 issued June 12, 1973.

Despite the reference to the complaint, contrary to Rule 65(d), Jones has not challenged this error, nor does Jones challenge that the injunction is enforceable against devices other than the specific THERMAL–LOCK device of the original suit. Jones' challenge is to the standards applied by the district court in holding the company in contempt. Jones urges that its ULTRA–LOCK devices do not infringe the claims of '217 and that the differences between the THERMAL–LOCK and ULTRA-LOK devices are so great that KSM should have to bring a separate suit to determine infringement by these devices. KSM, on the other hand, asks us to endorse the standard on contempt proceedings utilized in this case and, of course, to uphold the contempt judgment.

A.

The standard for determining contempt applied in the present case was that set forth in *Interdynamics, Inc. v. Firma Wolf*, 653 F.2d 93, 210 USPQ 868 (3d Cir. 1981) (*Interdynamics I*), and *Interdynamics, Inc. v. Firma Wolf*, 698 F.2d 157, 217 USPQ 117 (3d Cir. 1982) (*Interdynamics II*), as interpreted by the district court. The district court held that, under *Interdynamics I* and *II*, contempt proceedings should be conducted and contempt found where an enjoined device and an accused device were "merely colorably different," and that in order to determine whether two devices are "merely colorably different," the accused device must be compared to the adjudged device under a "doctrine of equivalents":

> [I]f two devices do the same work in substantially the same way, and accomplish substantially the same result, they are the same, even though different in name, form or shape.

In adjudging Jones to be accountable in contempt proceedings and in holding Jones in contempt, the district court refused to consider whether the accused ULTRA–LOK devices infringed the claims of the '217 patent, rejecting as irrelevant Jones' proffered evidence of the patent and its prosecution history by which Jones sought to prove that its modified device did not infringe the patent claims. The court interpreted *Interdynamics I* and *II* as precluding any consideration of the issue of infringement.

B.

Turning first to the question of the judgment of contempt itself, we agree, of course, that the issue in contempt proceedings is violation *vel non* of the injunction, not patent infringement. Nevertheless, devices which could not be enjoined as infringements on a separate complaint cannot possibly be deemed enjoined as infringements under an existing injunction in contempt proceedings. Infringement is the *sine qua non* of violation of an injunction against infringements.

The authorities are uniform that the modified device must be an infringement to find contempt of such an injunction. Indeed, the *Interdynamics I* and *II* decisions of the Third Circuit require infringement, and the standard it adopted, sought to reach only a narrower class of infringing devices in contempt proceedings, as the following statement indicates:

> Even if the new product may infringe the patent, as long as it is more than "colorably different" *the infringement should not amount to a contempt nor should it be tested in contempt proceedings.*

Interdynamics I, 653 F.2d at 99. The difficulty is simply that the modified doctrine of equivalents adopted by the *Interdynamics* court does not assure a proper finding that the modified device infringes the claims.

It may not properly be assumed, as does the Interdynamics standard, that, because the ULTRA–LOK devices, in a sense, are "equivalents" to the enjoined THERMAL–LOCK device, they are also equivalents of the patent claims. As the Supreme Court observed, "[I]n determining equivalents, things equal to the same thing may not be equal to each other." *Graver Tank*, 339 U.S. at 609. So too, things equal to each other may not be equal to the same thing. In any event, if a determination of infringement by the accused ULTRA–LOK devices depends on a finding of equivalency, such finding must be made in accordance with the range of equivalents permitted by *Graver Tank*. The *Interdynamics* standard adopts familiar words from *Graver Tank*, but not its substance. Thus, no correlation between infringement by the accused device and by the adjudged device necessarily exists as a result of their equivalence to each other under the modified standard of *Interdynamics*.

In making a finding that the accused new device is an infringement, the court cannot avoid looking at the claims of the patent. It may, in some cases, only be necessary to determine that the modified device has not been changed from the adjudged device in a way which affects an element of a claim. In such case the new device, though modified, may be treated the same as the device which was admitted or adjudged to infringe.

In litigated cases, the injunction must be interpreted in light of the rulings of the court on the scope of the claims. The patent owner may not, in contempt proceedings, seek to broaden the scope of the claims which were adjudicated and, thereby, catch the modified device.

Lest there be any doubt, we are speaking of infringement only in the sense of falling within the scope of the claims. Whether there is infringement may not be challenged in contempt proceedings on the basis that the patent is invalid. The validity of the patent is the law of the case in such proceedings.

In the instant case, Jones has admitted that its THERMAL–LOCK device infringed the claims of the '217 patent. The record shows that the Jones THERMAL–LOCK device, indisputably, literally embodies the elements of the claim.

On the other hand, Jones asserts that its ULTRA–LOK devices have been modified in a manner which avoids infringement. An element in claim 1, the only independent claim, is a "stud of rectangular cross section having one pair of opposed sides narrower than the other pair." Claim 1 also specifies, "a plurality of opposed notches . . . cut into the narrower sides of the stud."

There is no dispute that Jones ULTRA–LOK I and II studs do not literally infringe claim 1. The ULTRA–LOK studs are made from round stock which is selectively flattened to produce lateral protrusions. Accordingly, ULTRA–LOK studs are not of "rectangular cross-section" and do not have "opposed notches cut into the narrower sides thereof." Thus, the modified devices cannot be deemed to fall within Jones' admission of infringement with respect to its THERMAL–LOCK device contained in the consent degree. Due process requires that the consent decree be construed in accordance with the circumstances under which it was entered. Infringement of the '217 claims by the ULTRA–LOK devices could only be found under the *Graver Tank* doctrine of equivalents, which played no part in the judgment of infringement in the original litigation.

Since the district court believed that *Interdynamics I* and *II* precluded its consideration of the claim language and the evidence proffered by Jones with respect to prior art and the prosecution history, the court excluded such evidence and made no finding of infringement.

Under the standard we adopt, a judgment of contempt against an enjoined party for violation of an injunction against patent infringement by the making, using or selling of a modified device may not be upheld without a finding that the modified device falls within the admitted or adjudicated scope of the claims and is, therefore, an infringement. Since the judgment holding Jones in contempt of court does not satisfy this standard, it must be vacated.

C.

The standard for the initial question, that is, whether infringement should be adjudicated in contempt proceedings, is difficult to articulate with precision, since it involves, to a large extent, the exercise of judicial discretion. Such discretion is not, however, unlimited.

There is, as previously indicated, uniformity in the circuits in so far as all have expressed the view that proceedings by way of contempt should not go forward if there is more than a "colorable difference" in the accused and adjudged devices.

The explanation by the Tenth Circuit in *McCullough Tool Co. v. Well Surveys, Inc., supra*, identifies the conflicting interests to be considered in this initial question:

> The question is presented as to how a patentee should be allowed to proceed when following a successful infringement suit the infringer modifies the infringing structure and continues as before. Allowing the patentee to proceed by a summary contempt proceeding in all cases would unnecessarily deter parties from marketing new devices that are legitimately outside the scope of the patent in question. On the other hand, to require in each instance the patentee to institute a new infringement suit diminishes the significance of the patent and the order of the court holding the patent to be valid and infringed. Obviously there must be a dividing point between those cases which should be handled by a summary contempt proceeding and those cases which should be more fully viewed in an infringement proceeding. Courts have uniformly held that the standard to be applied in determining the dividing point is whether the alleged offending device is "merely 'colorably' different from the enjoined device or from the patent."

Id. at 233, 158 USPQ at 84 (citations omitted). However, stating that the "difference" must be more than "colorable" provides little guidance to the appropriateness of contempt proceedings. The standard for determining a "colorable" difference is critical, and an examination of case law indicates wide variance.

The *American Foundry* court ... defined "colorable" by the "fair ground of doubt" language from *California Artificial Stone Paving* and endorsed the Second Circuit view that:

> Where the alteration in the device is "merely colorable" and obviously was made for the purpose of evading the decree without essential change in the nature of the device, the courts will try the question of infringement by the new device in proceedings for contempt for violation of the injunction. But where infringement by the new device is not clear on the face of the matter, and there are substantial issues for the determination of the court, the plaintiff may not have them determined in contempt proceedings, but must bring a supplemental bill for an injunction covering the new device, or institute a wholly new suit for such an injunction.

Under the above standard for determining a colorable difference, a party may seek relief by way of contempt proceedings only if the issues are appropriate for summary disposition. If substantial issues need to be litigated, particularly if expert and other testimony subject to cross-examination would be helpful or necessary, the court may properly require a supplemental or new complaint. The question to be answered under such standard is essentially a procedural one. Must substantial new issues be litigated to determine infringement?

Some courts, on the other hand, take a different view of the scope of a contempt proceeding, deeming it the proper context within which to litigate complex questions of infringement, including the *Graver Tank* doctrine of equivalents and prosecution history estoppel. Thus, the initial question under this view of contempt is essentially bypassed, although overall this view has the virtue of a proper determination of the issue of infringement. We agree, however, with the *McCullough* and *American Foundry* courts that the question whether the alleged infringement should be determined in contempt at all deserves careful scrutiny.

With respect to the issue of when contempt proceedings will be allowed, we conclude that the procedural analysis used by the majority of courts should be adopted as the general rule. A standard based on procedural considerations is more likely to meet due process requirements, considering the usual summary nature of contempt proceedings. Under a procedural standard, the district court is able to utilize principles of claim and issue preclusion (*res judicata*) to determine what issues were settled by the original suit and what issues would have to be tried. Such a determination may vary depending upon whether the original suit was settled by consent or fully litigated. If there are substantial open issues with respect to infringement to be tried, contempt proceedings are inappropriate. *Accord California Paving*, 113 U.S. at 618 (proceeding by way of a new suit "is by far the most appropriate one where it is really a doubtful question whether the new process adopted is an infringement or not"). The presence of such disputed issues creates a fair ground for doubt that the decree has been violated. So long as the district court exercises its discretion to proceed or not to proceed by way of contempt proceedings within these general constraints, this court must defer to its judgment on this issue.

IV.

In sum, the initial question to be answered in ruling on a motion for contempt is whether contempt proceedings are appropriate. That question is answered by the trial court's judging whether substantial disputed issues must be litigated. The second question, whether an injunction against infringement has been violated, requires, at a minimum, a finding that the accused device is an infringement.

VACATED AND REMANDED.

PAULINE NEWMAN, Circuit Judge, concurring in part.

I agree that this case should be remanded for further findings on the question of equivalency, but I do not endorse the sweeping rules of law and procedure espoused by the majority.

The question before the court is the law to be applied in the contempt action brought by KSM against Jones, an adjudged infringer that had modified its infringing insulation device in an attempt to avoid an existing injunction against infringement. On the facts of this case, it is a narrow question.

Careful analysis of the decisions of the various circuits shows how fact-dependent these decisions have been. I know of no reason to withdraw from trial courts the authority, in their discretion, to find contempt summarily when a modified device is "merely colorably different" from the prior adjudicated device. Most of the circuits have heretofore recognized the need for discretion in district courts to handle contempt cases simply and expeditiously, when the facts warrant. The majority ruling limits this discretion.

The majority holds that it is always error simply to compare the devices and to determine whether they are "merely colorably different". The majority holds that it is always necessary to return to the claims and to consider any questions raised of claim interpretation, prior art, and prosecution history estoppel. I agree that this is at times necessary or advisable. But I do not think it is proper for this court to impose this procedure upon courts and parties in all circumstances, including those where a trial court in its discretion does not deem it necessary to relitigate these questions, or where res judicata may apply.

The majority view makes it harder for a court to invoke the summary procedures by which courts normally enforce their judgments. In the case before us, the majority directs the district court on remand "to reconsider whether, under the standard set forth herein, infringement with respect to the ULTRA–LOK devices should be tested in contempt proceedings" or some other way—presumably a full infringement trial. However, the "standard set forth herein" requires so thorough a legal reanalysis that it does not accommodate simple procedures.

The majority states that determination of whether to conduct a contempt proceeding is discretionary with the trial judge, but does not provide guidance as to what the majority considers would be an abuse of that discretion. In *MAC Corporation of America v. Williams Patent Crusher & Pulverizer Co.*, 767 F.2d 882, 226 USPQ 515 (Fed. Cir. 1985), this court affirmed that it is within the discretion of the district court to decide not to handle a contempt case summarily, when the modified device is so changed that it raises a "fair ground of doubt" as to whether the injunction was violated. I agree.

* * *

I agree that when it is necessary to invoke the doctrine of equivalents to determine whether a modified device is in violation of an injunction against infringement, this may raise a fair ground of doubt as to whether differences between the devices are "merely colorable". It is then proper to review the claims, the specification, and the prosecution history if appropriate in the specific circumstances, with due regard to matters that are res judicata between the parties. If on remand infringement is found, literally or by equivalents, contempt is an appropriate remedy.

Notes

1. In *KSM*, the Federal Circuit created a two step analysis for determining whether the defendant is in contempt of an injunction: (1) the court looks at the scope of the injunction; and (2) the court determines whether the new product actually infringes the patent. In *KSM*, the Court held that when it is not "clear on the face of the matter" that the new device infringes and there are "substantial issues for determination," the patentee must institute an entirely new suit for infringement in order to enjoin the infringer from making, using or selling this new device. What are "substantial open issues?" Does a new question of claim construction constitute a "substantial open issue" of infringement? The next case considers this very issue.

2. **Who can the injunction be enforced against**? Who can be held in violation of a contempt proceeding? The following case considers who can be held in contempt.

ADDITIVE CONTROLS & MEASUREMENT SYSTEMS, INC. v. FLOWDATA, INC.
154 F.3d 1345, 47 USPQ2d 1906 (Fed. Cir. 1998)

Before CLEVENGER, Circuit Judge, SKELTON, Senior Circuit Judge, and BRYSON, Circuit Judge.

BRYSON, Circuit Judge.

Following a trial, the United States District Court for the Southern District of Texas issued an injunction prohibiting Additive Controls &

Measurement Systems, Inc., (AdCon) from selling certain positive displacement flowmeters that were determined to infringe Flowdata's United States Patent No. 4,815,318. Appellants Galen M. Cotton, Jack D. Harshman, and Truflo Instrumentation, Inc., (Truflo) were subsequently determined to be in contempt of that injunction and were assessed civil contempt penalties in the amount of Flowdata's damages and attorney fees. We affirm the district court's contempt findings with respect to Cotton and Truflo, but reverse the portion of the court's order holding Harshman in contempt.

I

At one time, AdCon and Flowdata were competitors in the market for positive displacement flowmeters, which are used to measure the flow of liquids. Following a trial, AdCon was found to have willfully infringed Flowdata's patent and engaged in unfair competition. The district court subsequently entered an injunction barring AdCon from further sales of its infringing meter or any colorable imitations.

Shortly after the injunction was issued in August 1993, Flowdata began investigating sales of a redesigned positive displacement flowmeter by AdCon's president and majority stockholder, Galen Cotton. Flowdata requested that the district court institute contempt proceedings to determine whether the new meter was being marketed in violation of the injunction. Ultimately, Cotton and the other two appellants, Harshman and Truflo, were found to be in contempt of the injunction for their roles in developing and marketing the new flowmeter.

The sequence of events preceding the contempt findings is complicated and requires some additional explanation. In February 1994, the district court held a three-day show-cause hearing with testimony from Cotton and experts for both AdCon and Flowdata. The testimony adduced at the hearing established that Cotton had designed the new flowmeter during the pendency of the patent infringement suit and had enlisted Harshman to develop the engineering drawings for the new meter. Cotton then participated in forming two companies, Truflo and TruGear, Inc., to produce and manufacture the new meters, which were to be marketed as "TruGear meters." Cotton maintained a majority interest in Truflo, with Harshman receiving a 10% share for his efforts. Neither Harshman nor Truflo participated in the February 1994 contempt proceeding.

Following the February 1994 hearing, the district court concluded that the TruGear meters were merely colorable variations of the infringing AdCon meter and held Cotton in contempt of the 1993 injunction. In an order issued in October 1994, Harshman, Truflo, and several other non-parties were enjoined from disposing of inventory of the TruGear meter and ordered to show cause why they should not be held in contempt for actively participating with Cotton in violating the court's injunction. The part of the court's order enjoining the non-parties was later vacated by this court in *Additive Controls & Measurement Systems, Inc. v. Flowdata, Inc.*, 96 F.3d 1390, 40 USPQ2d 1106 (Fed. Cir. 1996).

The show cause hearing was held in March 1995. The non-parties, including Harshman and Truflo, appeared and presented evidence regarding the extent of their participation with Cotton in designing and selling the TruGear meter. In September 1997, the district court issued an order dismissing several non-parties, including TruGear, Inc., from the contempt action but finding that Harshman and Truflo had actively participated with Cotton in violating the injunction. Harshman and Truflo were made jointly and severally liable with Cotton for Flowdata's damages and attorney fees, an amount in excess of $350,000. This appeal followed.

II

The first issue in this appeal is whether it was permissible for the district court to try issues relating to the TruGear meter in a contempt proceeding. Appellants argue that the contempt findings in this case must be vacated because the contempt proceeding should never have been convened. Instead, according to appellants, Flowdata should have been required to litigate its claims regarding the TruGear meter in a separate infringement action. We review the district court's decision to proceed via a contempt hearing for abuse of discretion. *See KSM Fastening Sys., Inc. v. H.A. Jones Co.*, 776 F.2d 1522, 1530, 227 USPQ 676, 682 (Fed. Cir. 1985).

Before entering a finding of contempt of an injunction in a patent infringement case, a district court must address two separate questions. The first is whether a contempt hearing is an appropriate forum in which to determine whether a redesigned device infringes, or whether the issue of infringement should be resolved in a separate infringement action. That decision turns on a comparison between the original infringing product and the redesigned device. If the differences are such that "substantial open issues" of infringement are raised by the new device, then contempt proceedings are inappropriate. If contempt proceedings are appropriate, the second question the district court must resolve is whether the new accused device infringes the claims of the patent. Within those general constraints, the district court has broad discretion to determine how best to enforce its injunctive decrees.

The district court in this case recognized its responsibility to compare the TruGear meter both to the original AdCon meter and to the patent claims. Following the testimony of Flowdata's expert, the court denied Cotton's motion to dismiss the contempt proceedings. Subsequently, after considering all the evidence, the court issued an opinion characterizing the TruGear meter as a mere colorable variation of the AdCon meter. In the same opinion, the court compared the TruGear meter to the patent claims and found infringement. Although our case law suggests that the need for expert testimony counsels against the use of contempt proceedings to try infringement, the district court satisfied the procedural requirements of *KSM* by separately analyzing the questions whether contempt proceedings were appropriate and whether the redesigned device infringed the patent.

On the merits, the district court did not abuse its discretion in finding that the TruGear meter raised no substantial open questions of infringement and infringed the claims of Flowdata's patent. The Tru-Gear meter differs from the AdCon meter principally by including a ball-bearing sleeve and by using different-sized rotors to measure flow. In addition, the main chamber of the TruGear meter is round rather than oval-shaped. The court found that those differences did not raise a substantial new question of infringement because the configuration of the main chamber and the relative size of the two rotors were not elements of the pertinent patent claim, and because the evidence at the hearing suggested that the bearings in the TruGear meter were not necessary for its operation and were included merely in an attempt to disguise the actual operation of the device.

The appellants argued that the preamble to the pertinent claim of Flowdata's patent referred to the claimed meter as "bearingless," and that the TruGear meter did not infringe because it was not "bearing-less." The district court, however, concluded that the term "bearingless" in the preamble was not a limitation of the claim. That question of claim construction was a new issue in the case, because in the original infringement trial AdCon had stipulated that its flowmeter met every limitation of Flowdata's patent. The presence of a new issue, however— even a new issue of claim construction—does not necessarily require that a separate infringement action be brought to determine whether the accused device infringes the patent in suit. Contempt proceedings are appropriate as long as the new issue does not raise a substantial question of infringement.

In this instance, the district court found that the issue of the proper construction of the term "bearingless" in Flowdata's claim did not give rise to a substantial question of infringement. The court's conclusion in that regard was supported by evidence at the hearing that the term "bearingless," as used in the patent, simply meant that bearings were not necessary for the operation of the claimed meter. Under the circumstances, it was therefore permissible for the court to resolve the claim construction issue in the course of the contempt proceedings and to conclude that the sale of the TruGear meter violated the injunction and infringed Flowdata's patent.

Appellants also argue that the contempt proceeding was inappropriate because AdCon did not contest infringement or the validity of Flowdata's patent in the underlying action. For that reason, the appellants contend that they are not subject to issue preclusion on those issues and that "substantial open questions" of infringement and validity necessarily remain, which cannot properly be addressed in a contempt proceeding. The judgment against AdCon, however, established for purposes of this litigation that Flowdata's patent was valid and that the AdCon meter infringed the patent. In a contempt proceeding to enforce the injunction entered as a part of that judgment, the only available defense for anyone bound by the injunction was that the TruGear meter did not infringe (or that it was more than a colorable variation of the first meter, thus requiring that the issue of infringement be resolved through a separate infringement action). Validity and infringement by the original device were not open to challenge. Thus, the fact that AdCon did not contest infringement at the original trial did not bar the district court from concluding that there were no substantial open issues of infringement and that it was appropriate to proceed by way of contempt.

Finally, Cotton argues that because he had secured a patent on the TruGear device, there were necessarily "substantial open issues" presented that were not appropriate for resolution in a contempt proceeding. We agree that in some instances a showing that a redesign has resulted in the issuance of a patent would be sufficient to require a separate lawsuit to litigate any potential infringement by the redesigned device. The file history of Cotton's patent, however, shows that neither the original AdCon meter nor the Flowdata patent was submitted to the patent examiner. In fact, only two references, patents from 1968 and 1976, were cited as prior art as a result of the examiner's own search. Under those circumstances, the fact that the TruGear meter design was patented does not demonstrate that the redesigned meter was more than colorably different from the AdCon meter.

III

Appellants next contend that the injunction entered by the district court did not cover their activities with respect to the TruGear meter. Flowdata's suit was brought against AdCon, and AdCon was the only entity named in the district court's August 1993 injunction. Appellants argue that the injunction therefore reaches only conduct by AdCon or by others acting in concert with AdCon. Because all parties agree that AdCon has been inactive since the entry of the injunction and has no interest in the TruGear meter, appellants conclude that they cannot be held in contempt.

In an earlier appeal in this case, we addressed the basic rules concerning enjoining non-parties. *See Additive Controls & Measurement Sys., Inc. v. Flowdata, Inc.*, 96 F.3d 1390, 40 USPQ 2d 1106 (Fed. Cir. 1996). This appeal, by contrast, involves holding non-parties in contempt of an injunction. The two are quite different. As a general matter, a court may not enjoin a non-party that has not appeared before it to have its rights legally adjudicated. Non-parties may be held in contempt, however, if they "either abet the defendant, or [are] legally identified with him." *Alemite Mfg. Co. v. Staff*, 42 F.2d 832, 833 (2d Cir. 1930). That common-law principle is reflected in the text of Rule 65(d), Fed. R. Civ. Proc., which states that an injunction is binding on parties and "their officers, agents, servants, employees, and attorneys, and upon those persons in active concert and participation with them who receive actual notice of the order by personal service or otherwise." As the Supreme Court has stated, the effect of an injunction on non-parties "depends on an appraisal of [their] relations and behavior [with the enjoined party] and not upon mere construction of terms of the order." *Regal Knitwear Co. v. NLRB*, 324 U.S. 9, 15 (1945). We therefore address the contempt orders entered against Cotton, Harshman, and Truflo individually. We conclude that while there is sufficient evidence to find Cotton and Truflo in contempt of the injunction, the contempt finding against Harshman must be reversed.

A

Cotton was held in contempt of the August 1993 injunction for his actions in developing and marketing the TruGear meter. The district court's finding of contempt was predicated on its determination that Cotton was "legally identified" with AdCon and thus subject to the injunction even though he was not a named party to the suit. We review that decision and other subsidiary factual findings in contempt proceedings for clear error.

As an initial matter, it is clear that Cotton was bound by the injunction when it was entered against AdCon in August 1993, even though Cotton was not a named party to the underlying infringement suit. Rule 65(d) specifically names "officers" of a defendant as among those who are bound by an injunction, and there is a substantial body of case law in support of that proposition. *See Wilson v. United States*, 221 U.S. 361, 376 (1911) ("A command to the corporation is in effect a command to those who are officially responsible for the conduct of its affairs."); *Reich v. Sea Sprite Boat Co.*, 50 F.3d 413, 417 (7th Cir. 1995) ("An order issued to a corporation is identical to an order issued to its officers, for incorporeal abstractions act through agents."). At the time the August 1993 injunction was issued, Cotton was the president of AdCon, and he has remained its majority shareholder.

Although directed at AdCon, the injunction did not necessarily lapse with the cessation of AdCon as a working business. An injunction may survive the dissolution of the corporation at which it is directed and continue to bind any successor in interest to the original defendant. *See Walling v. James V. Reuter, Inc.*, 321 U.S. 671, 674 (1944) (injunction may be enforced "against those to whom the business may have been transferred, whether as a means of evading the judgment or for other reasons"). Such a rule is necessary to prevent an enjoined defendant from "nullify[ing] a decree by carrying out prohibited acts through aiders and abettors, although they were not parties to the original proceeding." *Regal Knitwear*, 324 U.S. at 14.

Cotton asserts that once he resigned as an officer of AdCon and acted "independently" in developing the TruGear meter, the August 1993 injunction no longer regulated his conduct. Cotton is correct in asserting that an employee of an enjoined corporation is usually not bound by an injunction after severing relations with the corporation. In *Alemite Manufacturing Corp. v. Staff,* 42 F.2d 832 (2d Cir. 1930), for example, the court held that an injunction in a patent infringement case entered against a corporation did not bind an employee who resigned from the company and committed infringing acts identical to those adjudicated in the original suit. The court's rationale in *Alemite*, however, was that the employee acted independently after his resignation and was not legally identified with the defendant corporation. Thus, Cotton's reliance on *Alemite* is availing only if the district court erred in finding that he was legally identified with AdCon.

The question whether a corporate officer is "legally identified" with a corporation is a case-specific inquiry. In general, an officer is legally identified with a corporation if the officer is "so identified in interest with those named in the decree that it would be reasonable to conclude that [his] rights and interests have been represented and adjudicated in the original injunction proceeding." 11A CHARLES ALAN WRIGHT, FEDERAL PRACTICE AND PROCEDURE § 2956, at 340–41 (2d ed. 1995). *See also G. & C. Merriam Co. v. Webster Dictionary Co.*, 639 F.2d 29, 37 (1st Cir. 1980) (officer is legally identified with the corporation if the officer "had such a key role in the corporation's participation in the injunction proceedings that it can be fairly said that he has had his day in court in relation to the validity of the injunction"). Factors that may be pertinent to the inquiry are the officer's position and responsibilities in the enjoined corporation, his participation in the litigation that preceded the entry of the injunction, and the degree of similarity between his activities in the old and new businesses.

The district court made a number of factual findings relevant to its conclusion that Cotton was legally identified with AdCon. Cotton was the incorporator and sole shareholder of AdCon when it was formed. At all times Cotton owned at least 90% of AdCon's stock. Cotton served as president of AdCon throughout the litigation with Flowdata, and he represented AdCon's interests in that litigation. The district court also found that AdCon had operated out of Cotton's home for some period of time, the same location from which Cotton started and operated Truflo. Cotton's testimony indicated that the reason for forming Truflo to market the TruGear meter was that "AdCon was not in a position to obtain partners for [the] purpose of manufacturing anything." The court also noted that Cotton's work on the TruGear meter began while Cotton was still serving as AdCon's president.

Based on those findings, which Cotton does not dispute, we see no clear error in the district court's conclusion that Cotton was legally identified with AdCon and therefore remained subject to contempt sanctions for violating the injunction even after resigning from his position as AdCon's president. The factual context outlined above is similar to that described in *Reich v. Sea Sprite Boat Co.*, 50 F.3d 413 (7th Cir. 1995). In that case, a closely held corporation was enjoined by the Department of Labor from committing certain safety violations. Rather than comply, the corporation's owner and president caused the corporation to cease operating and started a new corporation to continue the same activity. *Id.* at 417. The Seventh Circuit held that both the owner and the new corporation were bound by the injunction entered against the old corporation. In this action as well, Cotton's legal identification with AdCon precluded him from acting independently in the field of flowmeters of the type subject to the injunction.

Apart from asserting that he is not liable for contempt because he was not a party to the underlying action, Cotton also argues that previous mandates of this court and the district court show that the contempt finding is erroneous. We address those issues briefly.

First, Cotton contends that the district court found him in contempt based on his actions "in active concert or participation" with AdCon, although AdCon has been dormant for years. If that were the basis for the contempt finding, we would agree; one cannot act in concert with an inactive corporation. Cotton's liability, however, stems from the district court's finding that he was legally identified with AdCon. Under that theory of liability, Cotton was bound by the injunction against AdCon just as if it had been directed to him personally.

Cotton also argues that an opinion of this court, issued in a separate infringement action brought by Flowdata against Cotton personally, demonstrates that before being held in contempt Cotton was entitled to an opportunity to litigate the questions whether the AdCon meter infringed Flowdata's patent and whether Flowdata's patent was valid. In that opinion, we held that Cotton was not bound by the findings in the AdCon suit because the issues of infringement and validity had not been "actually litigated." *See Flowdata, Inc. v. Cotton*, No. 95–1013, slip op. at 4 (Fed. Cir. Jun. 5, 1995) (unpublished opinion). Issue preclusion, however, only determines what issues may or may not be raised in a separate proceeding. The findings concerning validity and infringement of Flowdata's patent were binding in the case in which they were entered, and the district court had the power to hold Cotton in contempt for violating the injunction entered in that case.

Finally, Cotton argues that our previous opinion in this case addressing the power of a district court to enjoin non-parties somehow prohibits the district court from holding him in contempt. In that opinion, however, we simply stated that the district court could not enter an injunction restraining the independent conduct of non-parties who had not appeared before the court. Here, Cotton has been held in contempt of an injunction that was lawfully entered and that bound him personally. Nothing in our prior opinion prevented the district court from taking that action if the facts so warranted, as they did in this case.

B

Harshman was also found in contempt for his actions taken with respect to the TruGear meter. Because Harshman had no relationship with AdCon, his contempt finding can be sustained only if he acted "in active concert and participation" with Cotton to violate the injunction. In view of the applicable requirements for finding active concert and participation in the Fifth Circuit, we conclude that the contempt sanctions against Harshman must be reversed.

The general rule in civil contempt is that a party need not intend to violate an injunction to be found in contempt. Non-parties are differently situated. Non-parties are subject to contempt sanctions if they act with an enjoined party to bring about a result forbidden by the injunction but only if they are aware of the injunction and know that their acts violate the injunction, *See Waffenschmidt v. MacKay*, 763 F.2d 711, 723–26, 726 (5th Cir. 1985) ("Although good faith is irrelevant as a defense to a civil contempt order, good faith is relevant to whether [a non-party] aided or abetted [an enjoined party] in dissipating the funds with knowledge that it was violating the court's orders.").

Harshman argues that because he did not work with AdCon during the period the injunction was in effect, he cannot be liable for acting in active concert and participation with an enjoined party. That assertion is incorrect, because Harshman dealt with Cotton, and Cotton was subject to the injunction by virtue of his legal identification with AdCon. Harshman's contention is more properly directed at the scienter requirement for acting in active concert and participation. For Harshman to be aware that he was acting in violation of the injunction, he would have to be aware both that his acts were proscribed and that Cotton was bound by the injunction.

In determining that Harshman had acted knowingly and in concert with Cotton to violate the injunction, the district court relied on Harshman's course of conduct throughout this extended litigation. Harshman testified as an expert witness for AdCon at the first trial for a minimal fee. Harshman also produced the engineering drawings for the TruGear meter, working from a prototype developed by Cotton. As partial compensation for his work on the drawings, Harshman received a 10% interest in Truflo. He also served as Truflo's director of engineering. Finally, Harshman accepted a $25,000 payment for the drawings on July 12, 1994, the day that the court issued its first injunction against the TruGear meter. Despite the deference we accord to the district court in light of that court's familiarity with this extended litigation, we do not believe that the evidence summarized above supports the court's conclusion that Harshman knowingly acted in concert with Cotton to violate the injunction, particularly in light of the timing of the injunction and the evidence regarding when Harshman learned of it.

Although the injunction issued in August 1993, Harshman did not receive actual notice of the injunction until December 29, 1993. Because actual notice is a requirement for contempt based on active concert and participation with an enjoined party, only those acts of Harshman that took place after December 29, 1993, can serve as a basis for contempt. Evidence at the March 1995 contempt hearing established that all of the drawings that Harshman produced for the TruGear meter, with the possible exception of a three-inch diameter meter that was never manufactured, were done before Harshman received notice of the injunction. Similarly, Harshman's service to AdCon as an expert witness and his long association with Cotton do not establish contempt of the court's order. At most, that evidence tended to show that Harshman was aware that Cotton was legally identified with AdCon.

Other evidence adduced at the contempt hearing further suggests that Harshman did not act in knowing violation of the injunction. Harshman testified that when he learned of the injunction, he questioned both Cotton and a patent attorney as to whether the TruGear meter was affected by the injunction. Both assured Harshman that the meter was not covered by Flowdata's patent and did not violate the injunction. Although those opinions turned out to be incorrect, that evidence would tend to indicate that Harshman did not knowingly violate the injunction.

The only acts that can be ascribed to Harshman after he learned of the AdCon injunction are his receipt of the $25,000 payment and his occasional contacts with TruGear, Inc., the company that made the TruGear meters, to discuss manufacturing difficulties. Harshman's acceptance of the $25,000 does not suggest knowing complicity with Cotton in view of the large amount of time Harshman spent preparing the drawings, and Flowdata does not argue that Harshman was aware of the court's order enjoining the TruGear meter when Harshman accepted that money. Finally, there was nothing about Harshman's acts of providing advice to the manufacturer that would indicate that he acted with knowledge that his conduct violated the injunction. We therefore reverse that aspect of the district court's order holding Harshman in contempt.

C

Truflo was held in contempt of the August 1993 injunction on a theory of successor liability. Following the March 1995 contempt hearing, the district court found that Cotton had formed Truflo as a means of evading the court's injunction against AdCon, and that Truflo was therefore acting in active concert and participation with Cotton to avoid the injunction.

An injunction would be of little value if its proscriptions could be evaded by the expedient of forming another entity to carry on the enjoined activity. For that reason, courts have consistently held that "successors" are within the scope of an injunction entered against a corporation and may be held in contempt for its violation.

Truflo argues that it cannot be a successor to AdCon because it inherited none of AdCon's assets and as such would not have been regarded as a successor corporation under Texas law. That argument misses the mark, however, because the question of the extent to which a federal injunction applies to non-parties is governed by Federal Rule of Civil Procedure 65(d), not by state law. Prior to the adoption of the Rules of Civil Procedure, federal courts applied general principles of equity, or federal common law, to determine the scope of an injunction. Rule 65(d) codified the pre-rules precedents as to what constitutes privity and courts have continued to look to federal law in determining the reach of federal injunctions under Rule 65(d). We therefore reject the argument that Texas corporate law governs the question whether Truflo is a successor to AdCon for purposes of deciding if Truflo is subject to the district court's injunction.

In a series of cases, the Supreme Court described successorship liability as turning on whether there is a "substantial continuity of identity" between the two organizations. Although the original formulation of the test arose in the labor relations context, the "substantial continuity of identity" test has been adopted as a general expression of the degree of closeness that Rule 65(d) requires for a non-party successor to be subject to the injunction. We apply that standard in reviewing the district court's finding that Truflo was a successor to AdCon.

In making its finding on that issue, the district court properly recognized that Cotton was the incorporator, president, and majority stockholder of both AdCon and Truflo, and that both entities shared phone lines and office space at his home. In our previous opinion, we noted that any entity "created in order to evade the original injunction" could be subject to contempt under Rule 65(d). The facts as found by the district court adequately support its conclusion that Truflo was such an entity formed to evade the injunction.

Truflo raises the additional claim that it was not afforded procedural due process in the proceedings leading to the contempt citation against it, because it was never served with process under Rule 4(a), Fed. R. Civ. Proc., nor made a party to a lawsuit. Truflo's first contention fails because it is well established that formal service is not required in a contempt proceeding. *See* 11A WRIGHT, *supra*, § 2956, at 338 ("the amenities of original process need not be followed" if the person charged with contempt has actual knowledge of the injunction).

Truflo is correct, however, in asserting that parties to a contempt proceeding are entitled to adequate notice and an opportunity to be heard. In order to show that Truflo was in contempt of the injunction, Flowdata was required to prove by clear and convincing evidence that the TruGear meter was produced in violation of the injunction and that Truflo itself was subject to the injunction, either as a successor to AdCon or as an instrumentality of Cotton formed to evade the injunction. Truflo was entitled to an opportunity to challenge Flowdata's showing and present its own evidence on those issues.

The contempt proceedings in this case included two extended hearings held to address the conduct that was alleged to constitute contempt. In February 1994, Cotton appeared before the court, and issues pertaining to the violation of the injunction by the TruGear meter were litigated. Although Truflo was not a party to those proceedings, the district court made a factual finding after the hearing that "Cotton caused the formation of Truflo ... for the purpose of thwarting and avoiding the Court's August 2, 1993, injunctive Order."

On its own, that finding would not provide a sufficient basis for holding Truflo in contempt, because Truflo was not given notice prior to the February 1994 hearing that it was subject to contempt sanctions based on evidence introduced at that hearing. The district court remedied that problem, however, by holding an additional hearing in March 1995. At that hearing, Truflo presented evidence concerning the extent of its involvement with Cotton in developing and marketing the TruGear meter. After that hearing, the district court indicated that it intended to reconsider its previous rulings regarding contempt liability. Subsequently, the district dismissed several non-parties from the contempt proceeding, but it reconfirmed its earlier factual findings that Truflo was a mere successor to AdCon that had been formed for the purpose of evading the injunction.

Those proceedings satisfied Truflo's rights to notice and an opportunity to be heard. Truflo argues that it did not have a sufficient opportunity to be heard because it did not have the opportunity to contest infringement and violation of the injunction by the TruGear meter. The district court's findings regarding Truflo's status as a successor entity, however, establish that Truflo had no independent identity outside of Cotton and AdCon. For that reason, it was not error for the district court to deny Truflo an opportunity to contest the other elements of the contempt charge. Accordingly, we uphold the district court's finding that Truflo was subject to contempt sanctions because, as a successor to AdCon, it was bound by the injunction.

IV

Appellants also raise a separate challenge to the terms of amendments to the injunction that the district court issued in September 1997. In broad terms, the injunction, as amended, prohibits Cotton and those found to have acted in active concert and participation with him from undertaking any activities with respect to positive displacement flowmeters without first obtaining leave of court. Appellants argue that the amended injunction does not comply with the specificity requirements of Rule 65(d), Fed. R. Civ. Proc., and must be vacated for that reason.

In entering the expanded injunctive provisions, the district court relied on the decision of this court in *Spindelfabrik Suessen–Schurr v. Schubert & Salzer Maschinenfabrik Aktiengesellschaft*, 903 F.2d 1568, 14 USPQ2d 1913 (Fed. Cir. 1990). In that case, the district court entered a similarly broad injunction "to secure future compliance" with the court's orders. The district court considered the broad injunction to be necessary in light of the repeated past violations of the original injunction. On appeal, this court upheld the broad injunction as within the district court's discretion.

Given the district court's familiarity with the proceedings in this lengthy case, we are persuaded that the district court properly exercised its discretion when it entered an injunction similar to that used in *Spindelfabrik*. Although such broad injunctions should be used only in exceptional cases, the district court reasonably concluded that such measures were necessary in this case to compel compliance with the court's orders. Should Cotton wish to reenter the positive displacement flowmeter market with a non-infringing product, we are confident that his application for relief from the injunction will receive fair consideration from the district court.

One provision of the injunction appears to restrict the ability of Cotton or any person who has been found to have acted in active concert and participation with him to challenge the validity or interpretation of Flowdata's patent in a subsequent proceeding without obtaining prior leave of court. We interpret that provision to apply only to further contempt proceedings in the instant case. In a separate infringement action, the ability of Cotton (or any other party) to challenge the validity or construction of Flowdata's patent would be governed by the principles of issue or claim preclusion. Indeed, we have previously held that Cotton is not subject to issue preclusion with respect to the validity of Flowdata's patent. We do not interpret the injunction to bar Cotton or any other party from litigating such issues in a separate infringement action in which they would not be subject to issue or claim preclusion.

Notes

1. **Summary or Evidentiary Contempt Proceedings**. Although contempt proceedings are generally summary, the court can allow a full evidentiary hearing. The court can permit the parties to introduce exhibits, affidavits or live testimony—making a contempt proceeding like a mini-trial.

2. **Who is subject to the Court's Contempt Powers?** As we see from the preceding case, there are three groups who are subject to the court's contempt powers: (1) the defendants from the original proceeding; (2) the officers, agents, employees and lawyers of the defendants from the original proceedings; and (3) those who have received actual notice of the injunction and who act in concert or participation with (1) and (2). Hence, when the injunction issues, the patentee should send a copy by certified mail to all people whom the patentee believes may fall into group (3).

3. **Defenses Available to those Charged with Contempt.** An advantage of a contempt proceeding is that the defendant cannot defend by claiming that the patent is invalid. Validity or unenforceability of the patent and infringement by the original device are considered law of the case and may not be challenged by a defendant in a contempt proceeding. What defenses can the defendant raise? The defendant can argue: (1) she never received notice of the injunction; (2) there are substantial open issues with regard to infringement of the modified device (i.e., it is more than a mere "colorable variation" of the device found to infringe) or the modified device does not contain all of the claim elements; and (3) the defendant has not made, used, or sold the device after entry of the permanent injunction or after she received notice of the injunction.

4. **Broader Injunction Issued After Contempt is Found.** Notice that after the district court found contempt in *Additive Controls*, it modified the injunction to prevent those in contempt from undertaking any activities with respect to the positive displacement flowmeter without first receiving permission from the court. The Federal Circuit affirmed this modified injunction. Similarly in *Spindelfabrick Suessen–Schurr v. Schubert & Salzer Maschinenfabrick Aktiengesellschaft*, 903 F.2d 1568, 14 USPQ2d 1913 (Fed.

Cir. 1990), the Court upheld an injunction entered after a finding of contempt where the injunction:

1. enjoined Schubert from making using or selling the infringing device or inducing others to infringe;

2. enjoined Schubert from "directly engaging in any activity in any way related to the manufacture, sale, use, servicing, exhibition, demonstration, promotion or commercialization of any automated rotor spinning machines;"

3. Schubert must file a verified petition seeking relief from this injunctive order which would clearly and convincingly show that any new and substantially redesigned automated spinning machine would not infringe; and

4. Schubert's CEO must file quarterly sworn statements with the trial court certifying compliance with the order.

Problems

Problem 1

You represent Mike's Fishing who sells a commercial embodiment of his '835 patent (see Chapter Eight for the patent and Chapter Ten for the prosecution history) called The Perch Troller. Mike's business and his sales have been extremely successful, but they have been limited to the Midwest region—the Great Lakes area. He has a manufacturing plant in Gary, Indiana, which employs 300 people in the manufacture of various trolling motors including The Perch Troller.

Mike tells you that at a trade show on November 1, 1995, he encountered two companies selling bow-mounted trolling motor with electronic autopilot systems. The Easy Troller, manufactured and sold by Mark's Boats exclusively in the Pacific Northwest (Washington state, Oregon and northern California) and the Bass Troller sold by LL Green exclusively in New England. Mike's Fishing sent cease-and-desist letters to both companies on January 1, 1996.

The Bass Troller Dispute

The letter to LL Green accused its Bass Troller of infringing the '835 patent and offered to discuss licensing terms. LL Green refused to take a license and Mike's Fishing sued it for patent infringement in the Western District of Massachusetts. After a jury found that LL Green infringed the '835 patent under the doctrine of equivalents, the companies settled (6 months ago). You obtain a copy of the licensing agreement which says "LL Green agrees to pay Mike's Fishing a royalty of 20% for the sale of all Bass Trollers until the expiration of the '835 patent and agrees to waive its right to appeal the jury's determination that the Bass Troller infringes in exchange for an exclusive license to sell the patented invention in New England (Massachusetts, Connecticut, Maine, Vermont, and Rhode Island)." You purchase a Bass Troller and discover that it is identical to The Easy Troller except that it does not have a manual override switch. You also notice that it is not marked with any patent numbers.

The Easy Troller

The January 1, 1996 cease-and-desist letter to Mark's Boats accused The Easy Troller of infringing the '835 patent and offered to discuss licensing terms. Mark and Mike met at the Boat House on February 1, 1996 to discuss licensing terms. Mark refused to take a license saying that he does not think The Easy Troller infringes. Mike responded, "I think your motor does infringe my patent and if you don't take a license within 10 days, I am going to consult a patent attorney and sue you. In fact, I am in the process of suing another company right now which makes a motor almost identical to yours."

You discover that Mark's Boats is a small company with a lot of capital and very little overhead. Mark's Boats currently has 100 employees manufacturing Easy Trollers in his Portland factory (in fact, that is the only thing that is made in this factory). You also discover that several other companies sell motors like the Easy Troller including Kulpa Motors and Moore Motors, neither of which are licensed under the '835 patent. Moore sells a motor identical to The Easy Troller and Kulpa Motors is selling a traditional stern-mounted trolling motor with an electronic autopilot system. In fact, there are lots of stern-mounted trolling motors with electronic autopilot systems on the market.

With the start of the fishing season right around the corner, Mike says he would like to move quickly to stop Mark's Boats from infringing. Mike also tells you that his company just posted an Internet site so that customers from all over can order Perch Trollers. How are you going to advise Mike?

Problem 2

Mike's Fishing wins its suit against Mark's Boats, the Court has asked you to submit a proposed order enjoining Mark's Boats from infringement. How will you draft the injunction and who will you serve it on?

Problem 3

Mark's Boats went out of business after the injunction was entered. A year after the injunction was entered you discover that Mark and his friend Bob formed a corporation, Bob's Motors which manufactures and sells trolling motors with autopilots. The trolling motors are just like the ones that Mark's Boats was selling except they are stern-mounted motors which happen to pull the boat. What options does Mike have?

Chapter Fourteen

DAMAGES

INTRODUCTION

STATUTORY PROVISION—35 U.S.C. § 284:

Upon finding for the claimant the court shall award the claimant damages adequate to compensate for the infringement, but in no event less than a reasonable royalty for the use made of the invention by the infringer, together with interest and costs as fixed by the court.... The court may receive expert testimony as an aid to the determination of damages or of what royalty would be reasonable under the circumstances.

STATUTORY PROVISION—35 U.S.C. § 286:

Except as otherwise provided by law, no recovery shall be had for any infringement committed more than six years prior to the filing of the complaint or counterclaim for infringement in the action.

Once liability for infringement has been established, the patent owner must prove damages. The damages phase of the trial is often bifurcated from the liability phase. *See* Chapter Seven. A damages award will be based upon lost profits or a reasonably royalty. As the statute indicates, a reasonable royalty is the floor for a damage award. The patent owner usually prefers to recover lost profits. Damages awards are generally accompanied by interest and costs. The patent owner may also allege that the infringement was willful, and that she should be entitled to enhanced damages and attorneys fees.

Both parties will usually present a damages expert to explain how the fact-finder should calculate damages and to testify on a variety of factors which underlie the determinations of lost profits or a reasonable royalty (fixed or variable costs, availability of competing products, licensing arrangements, manufacturing capability, price fluctuations in the relevant market, price elasticity, demand for the patented product, or motivations for price cutting). Of course, a variety of fact witnesses, including the inventor and corporate officers, will have testified on many of these subjects throughout the trial. The damages expert ties these factors together and presents a believable explanation for the damage award the party thinks is appropriate.

The damages expert is often an accounting expert (e.g., a CPA) or an economist. It is important that the damages expert have an understanding of the law of patent damages. This witness will review the financial records of the parties and opine on issues including lost profits, fixed or variable costs, and market information. Since this is often the last witness to testify, it is important to chose a damages expert who is dynamic and credible. Good credentials are important, but a Harvard degree is meaningless if the jury sleeps through the expert's testimony.

A. LOST PROFITS—THE PANDUIT "BUT FOR" TEST

A patentee is entitled to lost profits if she can prove that "but for" the infringer's conduct, she would have made the sales and earned a particular profit. In *Panduit Corp. v. Stahlin Bros. Fibre Works, Inc.*, 575 F.2d 1152, 1156, 197 USPQ 726, 730 (6th Cir. 1978), the Court articulated a four-factor test for proving lost profits which has subsequently been adopted by the Federal Circuit. Under the *Panduit* test, the patentee must prove:

(1) demand for the patented product;

(2) absence of acceptable non-infringing substitutes;

(3) manufacturing and marketing capability to exploit the demand; and

(4) the amount of the profit it would have made "but for" the infringement.

RITE-HITE CORP. v. KELLEY CO.
56 F.3d 1538, 35 USPQ2d 1065 (Fed. Cir. 1995)

Before ARCHER, Chief Judge, RICH, Circuit Judge, SMITH, Senior Circuit Judge and NIES, NEWMAN, MAYER, MICHEL, PLAGER, LOURIE, CLEVENGER, RADER, and SCHALL, Circuit Judges.

LOURIE, Circuit Judge.

Kelley Company appeals from a decision of the United States District Court for the Eastern District of Wisconsin, awarding damages for the infringement of U.S. Patent 4,373,847, owned by Rite–Hite Corporation. The district court determined, *inter alia*, that Rite–Hite was entitled to lost profits for lost sales of its devices that were in direct competition with the infringing devices, but which themselves were not covered by the patent in suit. The appeal has been taken *in banc* to determine whether such damages are legally compensable under 35 U.S.C. § 284. We affirm in part, vacate in part, and remand.

BACKGROUND

On March 22, 1983, Rite–Hite sued Kelley, alleging that Kelley's "Truk Stop" vehicle restraint infringed Rite–Hite's U.S. Patent 4,373,-

847 ("the '847 patent"). The '847 patent, issued February 15, 1983, is directed to a device for securing a vehicle to a loading dock to prevent the vehicle from separating from the dock during loading or unloading. Any such separation would create a gap between the vehicle and dock and create a danger for a forklift operator.

Rite–Hite distributed all its products through its wholly-owned and operated sales organizations and through independent sales organizations (ISOs). During the period of infringement, the Rite–Hite sales organizations accounted for approximately 30 percent of the retail dollar sales of Rite–Hite products, and the ISOs accounted for the remaining 70 percent. Rite–Hite sued for its lost profits at the wholesale level and for the lost retail profits of its own sales organizations.

The district court bifurcated the liability and damage phases of the trial and, on March 5, 1986, held the '847 patent to be not invalid and to be infringed by the manufacture, use, and sale of Kelley's Truk Stop device. The court enjoined further infringement. The judgment of liability was affirmed by this court.

On remand, the damage issues were tried to the court. Rite–Hite sought damages calculated as lost profits for two types of vehicle restraints that it made and sold: the "Manual Dok–Lok" model 55 (MDL–55), which incorporated the invention covered by the '847 patent, and the "Automatic Dok–Lok" model 100 (ADL–100), which was not covered by the patent in suit. The ADL–100 was the first vehicle restraint Rite–Hite put on the market and it was covered by one or more patents other than the patent in suit. The Kelley Truk Stop restraint was designed to compete primarily with Rite–Hite's ADL–100. Both employed an electric motor and functioned automatically, and each sold for $1,000–$1,500 at the wholesale level, in contrast to the MDL–55, which sold for one-third to one-half the price of the motorized devices. Rite–Hite does not assert that Kelley's Truk Stop restraint infringed the patents covering the ADL–100.

Of the 3,825 infringing Truk Stop devices sold by Kelley, the district court found that, "but for" Kelley's infringement, Rite–Hite would have made 80 more sales of its MDL–55; 3,243 more sales of its ADL–100; and 1,692 more sales of dock levelers, a bridging platform sold with the restraints and used to bridge the edges of a vehicle and dock. The court awarded Rite–Hite as a manufacturer the wholesale profits that it lost on lost sales of the ADL–100 restraints, MDL–55 restraints, and restraint-leveler packages. It also awarded to Rite–Hite as a retailer and to the ISOs reasonable royalty damages on lost ADL–100, MDL–55, and restraint-leveler sales caused by Kelley's infringing sales. Finally, pre-judgment interest, calculated without compounding, was awarded. Kelley's infringement was found to be not willful.

On appeal, Kelley contends that the district court erred as a matter of law in its determination of damages. Kelley does not contest the award of damages for lost sales of the MDL–55 restraints; however, Kelley argues that (1) the patent statute does not provide for damages based on Rite–Hite's lost profits on ADL–100 restraints because the ADL–100s are not covered by the patent in suit; (2) lost profits on unpatented dock levelers are not attributable to demand for the '847 invention and, therefore, are not recoverable losses; (3) the ISOs have no standing to sue for patent infringement damages; and (4) the court erred in calculating a reasonable royalty based as a percentage of ADL–100 and dock leveler profits. Rite–Hite and the ISOs challenge the district court's refusal to award lost retail profits and its award of prejudgment interest at a simple, rather than a compound, rate.

We affirm the damage award with respect to Rite–Hite's lost profits as a manufacturer on its ADL–100 restraint sales, affirm the court's computation of a reasonable royalty rate, vacate the damage award based on the dock levelers, and vacate the damage award with respect to the ISOs because they lack standing. We remand for dismissal of the ISOs' claims and for a redetermination of damages consistent with this opinion. The issues raised by Rite–Hite are unpersuasive.

DISCUSSION

A.   Kelley's Appeal

I.   Lost Profits on the Adl–100 Restraints

The district court's decision to award lost profits damages pursuant to 35 U.S.C. § 284 turned primarily upon the quality of Rite–Hite's proof of actual lost profits. The court found that, "but for" Kelley's infringing Truk Stop competition, Rite–Hite would have sold 3,243 additional ADL–100 restraints and 80 additional MDL–55 restraints. The court reasoned that awarding lost profits fulfilled the patent statute's goal of affording complete compensation for infringement and compensated Rite–Hite for the ADL–100 sales that Kelley "anticipated taking from Rite–Hite when it marketed the Truk Stop against the ADL–100." The court stated, "[t]he rule applied here therefore does not extend Rite–Hite's patent rights excessively, because Kelley could reasonably have foreseen that its infringement of the '847 patent would make it liable for lost ADL–100 sales in addition to lost MDL–55 sales." The court further reasoned that its decision would avoid what it referred to as the "whip-saw" problem, whereby an infringer could avoid paying lost profits damages altogether by developing a device using a first patented technology to compete with a device that uses a second patented technology and developing a device using the second patented technology to compete with a device that uses the first patented technology.

Kelley maintains that Rite–Hite's lost sales of the ADL–100 restraints do not constitute an injury that is legally compensable by means of lost profits. It has uniformly been the law, Kelley argues, that to recover damages in the form of lost profits a patentee must prove that, "but for" the infringement, it would have sold a product covered by the patent in suit to the customers who bought from the infringer. Under the circumstances of this case, in Kelley's view, the patent statute provides only for damages calculated as a reasonable royalty. Rite–Hite, on the other hand, argues that the only restriction on an award of actual lost profits damages for patent infringement is proof of causation-in-fact. A patentee, in its view, is entitled to all the profits it would have made on any of its products "but for" the infringement. Each party argues that a judgment in favor of the other would frustrate the purposes of the patent statute. Whether the lost profits at issue are legally compensable is a question of law, which we review *de novo*.

Our analysis of this question necessarily begins with the patent statute. Implementing the constitutional power under Article I, section 8, to secure to inventors the exclusive right to their discoveries, Congress has provided in 35 U.S.C. § 284 as follows:

> Upon finding for the claimant the court shall award the claimant damages adequate to compensate for the infringement, but in no event less than a reasonable royalty for the use made of the invention by the infringer, together with interest and costs as fixed by the court.

35 U.S.C. § 284 (1988). The statute thus mandates that a claimant receive damages "adequate" to compensate for infringement. Section 284 further instructs that a damage award shall be "in no event less than a reasonable royalty"; the purpose of this alternative is not to direct the form of compensation, but to set a floor below which damage awards may not fall. *Del Mar Avionics, Inc. v. Quinton Instrument Co.*, 836 F.2d 1320, 1326, 5 USPQ2d 1255, 1260 (Fed. Cir. 1987). Thus, the language of the statute is expansive rather than limiting. It affirmatively states that damages must be adequate, while providing only a lower limit and no other limitation.

The Supreme Court spoke to the question of patent damages in *General Motors*, stating that, in enacting § 284, Congress sought to "ensure that the patent owner would in fact receive full compensation for 'any damages' [the patentee] suffered as a result of the infringement." *General Motors*, 461 U.S. at 654. Thus, while the statutory text states tersely that the patentee receive "adequate" damages, the Supreme Court has interpreted this to mean that "adequate" damages should approximate those damages that will fully compensate the patentee for infringement. Further, the Court has cautioned against imposing limitations on patent infringement damages, stating: "When Congress wished to limit an element of recovery in a patent infringement action, it said so explicitly." *General Motors*, 461 U.S. at 653 (refusing to impose limitation on court's authority to award interest).

In *Aro Mfg. Co. v. Convertible Top Replacement Co.*, 377 U.S. 476 (1964), the Court discussed the statutory standard for measuring patent infringement damages, explaining:

> The question to be asked in determining damages is how much had the Patent Holder and Licensee suffered by the infringement. And that question [is] primarily: had the Infringer not infringed, what would the Patentee Holder–Licensee have made?

377 U.S. at 507 (plurality opinion) (citations omitted). This surely states a "but for" test. In accordance with the Court's guidance, we have held

that the general rule for determining actual damages to a patentee that is itself producing the patented item is to determine the sales and profits lost to the patentee because of the infringement. *See State Indus., Inc. v. Mor–Flo Indus., Inc..,* 883 F.2d 1573, 1577, 12 USPQ2d 1026, 1028 (Fed. Cir. 1989) (award of damages may be split between lost profits as actual damages to the extent they are proven and a reasonable royalty for the remainder). To recover lost profits damages, the patentee must show a reasonable probability that, "but for" the infringement, it would have made the sales that were made by the infringer. *King Instrument Corp. v. Otari Corp..,* 767 F.2d 853, 863, 226 USPQ 402, 409 (Fed. Cir. 1985).

Panduit Corp. v. Stahlin Bros. Fibre Works, Inc.., 575 F.2d 1152, 197 USPQ 726 (6th Cir. 1978), articulated a four-factor test that has since been accepted as a useful, but non-exclusive, way for a patentee to prove entitlement to lost profits damages. The *Panduit* test requires that a patentee establish: (1) demand for the patented product; (2) absence of acceptable non-infringing substitutes; (3) manufacturing and marketing capability to exploit the demand; and (4) the amount of the profit it would have made. A showing under *Panduit* permits a court to reasonably infer that the lost profits claimed were in fact caused by the infringing sales, thus establishing a patentee's prima facie case with respect to "but for" causation. A patentee need not negate every possibility that the purchaser might not have purchased a product other than its own, absent the infringement. The patentee need only show that there was a reasonable probability that the sales would have been made "but for" the infringement. When the patentee establishes the reasonableness of this inference, e.g., by satisfying the *Panduit* test, it has sustained the burden of proving entitlement to lost profits due to the infringing sales. The burden then shifts to the infringer to show that the inference is unreasonable for some or all of the lost sales.

Applying *Panduit,* the district court found that Rite–Hite had established "but for" causation. In the court's view, this was sufficient to prove entitlement to lost profits damages on the ADL–100. Kelley does not challenge that Rite–Hite meets the *Panduit* test and therefore has proven "but for" causation; rather, Kelley argues that damages for the ADL–100, even if in fact caused by the infringement, are not legally compensable because the ADL–100 is not covered by the patent in suit.

Preliminarily, we wish to affirm that the "test" for compensability of damages under § 284 is not solely a "but for" test in the sense that an infringer must compensate a patentee for any and all damages that proceed from the act of patent infringement. Notwithstanding the broad language of § 284, judicial relief cannot redress every conceivable harm that can be traced to an alleged wrongdoing. For example, remote consequences, such as a heart attack of the inventor or loss in value of shares of common stock of a patentee corporation caused indirectly by infringement are not compensable. Thus, along with establishing that a particular injury suffered by a patentee is a "but for" consequence of infringement, there may also be a background question whether the asserted injury is of the type for which the patentee may be compensated.

Judicial limitations on damages, either for certain classes of plaintiffs or for certain types of injuries have been imposed in terms of "proximate cause" or "foreseeability." Such labels have been judicial tools used to limit legal responsibility for the consequences of one's conduct that are too remote to justify compensation. The general principles expressed in the common law tell us that the question of legal compensability is one "to be determined on the facts of each case upon mixed considerations of logic, common sense, justice, policy and precedent." *See* 1 STREET, FOUNDATIONS OF LEGAL LIABILITY 110 (1906) (quoted in W. PAGE KEETON ET AL., PROSSER & KEETON ON THE LAW OF TORTS § 42, at 279 (5th ed. 1984)).

We believe that under § 284 of the patent statute, the balance between full compensation, which is the meaning that the Supreme Court has attributed to the statute, and the reasonable limits of liability encompassed by general principles of law can best be viewed in terms of reasonable, objective foreseeability. If a particular injury was or should have been reasonably foreseeable by an infringing competitor in the relevant market, broadly defined, that injury is generally compensable absent a persuasive reason to the contrary. Here, the court determined that Rite–Hite's lost sales of the ADL–100, a product that directly competed with the infringing product, were reasonably foreseeable. We agree with that conclusion. Being responsible for lost sales of a competitive product is surely foreseeable; such losses constitute the full compensation set forth by Congress, as interpreted by the Supreme Court, while staying well within the traditional meaning of proximate cause. Such lost sales should therefore clearly be compensable.

Recovery for lost sales of a device not covered by the patent in suit is not of course expressly provided for by the patent statute. Express language is not required, however. Statutes speak in general terms rather than specifically expressing every detail. Under the patent statute, damages should be awarded "where necessary to afford the plaintiff full compensation for the infringement." *General Motors*, 461 U.S. at 654. Thus, to refuse to award reasonably foreseeable damages necessary to make Rite–Hite whole would be inconsistent with the meaning of § 284.

Kelley asserts that to allow recovery for the ADL–100 would contravene the policy reason for which patents are granted: "[T]o promote the progress of . . . the useful arts." U.S. Const., art. I, § 8, cl. 8. Because an inventor is only entitled to exclusivity to the extent he or she has invented and disclosed a novel, nonobvious, and useful device, Kelley argues, a patent may never be used to restrict competition in the sale of products not covered by the patent in suit. In support, Kelley cites antitrust case law condemning the use of a patent as a means to obtain a "monopoly" on unpatented material.

These cases are inapposite to the issue raised here. The present case does not involve expanding the limits of the patent grant in violation of the antitrust laws; it simply asks, once infringement of a valid patent is found, what compensable injuries result from that infringement, i.e., how may the patentee be made whole. Rite–Hite is not attempting to exclude its competitors from making, using, or selling a product not within the scope of its patent. The Truk Stop restraint was found to infringe the '847 patent, and Rite–Hite is simply seeking adequate compensation for that infringement; this is not an antitrust issue. Allowing compensation for such damage will "promote the Progress of . . . the useful Arts" by providing a stimulus to the development of new products and industries.

Kelley further asserts that, as a policy matter, inventors should be encouraged by the law to practice their inventions. This is not a meaningful or persuasive argument, at least in this context. A patent is granted in exchange for a patentee's disclosure of an invention, not for the patentee's use of the invention. There is no requirement in this country that a patentee make, use, or sell its patented invention. *See Continental Paper Bag Co. v. Eastern Paper Bag Co.*, 210 U.S. 405, 424–30 (1908) (irrespective of a patentee's own use of its patented invention, it may enforce its rights under the patent). If a patentee's failure to practice a patented invention frustrates an important public need for the invention, a court need not enjoin infringement of the patent. *See* 35 U.S.C. § 283 (1988) (courts may grant injunctions in accordance with the principles of equity). Accordingly, courts have in rare instances exercised their discretion to deny injunctive relief in order to protect the public interest. Whether a patentee sells its patented invention is not crucial in determining lost profits damages. Normally, if the patentee is not selling a product, by definition there can be no lost profits. However, in this case, Rite–Hite did sell its own patented products, the MDL–55 and the ADL–100 restraints.

Kelley next argues that to award lost profits damages on Rite–Hite's ADL–100s would be contrary to precedent. Citing *Panduit*, Kelley argues that case law regarding lost profits uniformly requires that "the intrinsic value of the patent in suit is the only proper basis for a lost profits award." Kelley argues that each prong of the *Panduit* test focuses on the patented invention; thus, Kelley asserts, Rite–Hite cannot obtain damages consisting of lost profits on a product that is not the patented invention.

Generally, the *Panduit* test has been applied when a patentee is seeking lost profits for a device covered by the patent in suit. However, *Panduit* is not the *sine qua non* for proving "but for" causation. If there are other ways to show that the infringement in fact caused the patentee's lost profits, there is no reason why another test should not be acceptable. Moreover, other fact situations may require different means of evaluation, and failure to meet the *Panduit* test does not *ipso facto* disqualify a loss from being compensable.

In any event, the only *Panduit* factor that arguably was not met in the present fact situation is the second one, absence of acceptable non-infringing substitutes. Establishment of this factor tends to prove that the patentee would not have lost the sales to a non-infringing third party rather than to the infringer. That, however, goes only to the question of proof. Here, the only substitute for the patented device was the ADL–100, another of the patentee's devices. Such a substitute was not an "acceptable, non-infringing substitute" within the meaning of *Panduit* because, being patented by Rite–Hite, it was not available to customers except from Rite–Hite. Rite–Hite therefore would not have lost the sales to a third party. The second *Panduit* factor thus has been met. If, on the other hand, the ADL–100 had not been patented and was found to be an acceptable substitute, that would have been a different story, and Rite–Hite would have had to prove that its customers would not have obtained the ADL–100 from a third party in order to prove the second factor of *Panduit*.

Kelley's conclusion that the lost sales must be of the patented invention thus is not supported. Kelley's concern that lost profits must relate to the "intrinsic value of the patent" is subsumed in the "but for" analysis; if the patent infringement had nothing to do with the lost sales, "but for" causation would not have been proven. However, "but for" causation is conceded here. The motive, or motivation, for the infringement is irrelevant if it is proved that the infringement in fact caused the loss. We see no basis for Kelley's conclusion that the lost sales must be of products covered by the infringed patent.

Kelley has thus not provided, nor do we find, any justification in the statute, precedent, policy, or logic to limit the compensability of lost sales of a patentee's device that directly competes with the infringing device if it is proven that those lost sales were caused in fact by the infringement. Such lost sales are reasonably foreseeable and the award of damages is necessary to provide adequate compensation for infringement under 35 U.S.C. § 284. Thus, Rite–Hite's ADL–100 lost sales are legally compensable and we affirm the award of lost profits on the 3,283 sales lost to Rite–Hite's wholesale business in ADL–100 restraints.

II.   *Damages on the Dock Levelers*

Based on the "entire market value rule," the district court awarded lost profits on 1,692 dock levelers that it found Rite–Hite would have sold with the ADL–100 and MDL–55 restraints. Kelley argues that this award must be set aside because Rite–Hite failed to establish that the dock levelers were eligible to be included in the damage computation under the entire market value rule. We agree.

When a patentee seeks damages on unpatented components sold with a patented apparatus, courts have applied a formulation known as the "entire market value rule" to determine whether such components should be included in the damage computation, whether for reasonable royalty purposes. Early cases invoking the entire market value rule required that for a patentee owning an "improvement patent" to recover damages calculated on sales of a larger machine incorporating that improvement, the patentee was required to show that the entire value of the whole machine, as a marketable article, was "properly and legally attributable" to the patented feature. *See Garretson v. Clark*, 111 U.S. 120, 121 (1884). Subsequently, our predecessor court held that damages for component parts used with a patented apparatus were recoverable under the entire market value rule if the patented apparatus "was of such paramount importance that it substantially created the value of the component parts." *Marconi Wireless Telegraph Co. v. United States*, 53 USPQ 246, 250 (Ct. Cl. 1942), *aff'd in part and vacated in part*, 320 U.S. 1 (1943). We have held that the entire market value rule permits recovery of damages based on the value of a patentee's entire apparatus containing several features when the patent-related feature is the "basis for customer demand." *State Indus.*, 883 F.2d at 1580, 12 USPQ2d at 1031; *TWM Mfg. Co. v. Dura Corp.*, 789 F.2d 895, 900–01, 229 USPQ 525, 528 (Fed. Cir. 1986).

The entire market value rule has typically been applied to include in the compensation base unpatented components of a device when the unpatented and patented components are physically part of the same machine. The rule has been extended to allow inclusion of physically separate unpatented components normally sold with the patented components. However, in such cases, the unpatented and patented components together were considered to be components of a single assembly or parts of a complete machine, or they together constituted a functional unit.

In *Paper Converting*, this court articulated the entire market value rule in terms of the objectively reasonable probability that a patentee would have made the relevant sales. *See* 745 F.2d at 23, 223 USPQ at 599–600. Furthermore, we may have appeared to expand the rule when we emphasized the financial and marketing dependence of the unpatented component on the patented component. In *Paper Converting*, however, the rule was applied to allow recovery of profits on the unpatented components only because all the components together were considered to be parts of a single assembly. The references to "financial and marketing dependence" and "reasonable probability" were made in the context of the facts of the case and did not separate the rule from its traditional moorings.

Specifically, recovery was sought for the lost profits on sales of an entire machine for the high speed manufacture of paper rolls comprising several physically separate components, only one of which incorporated the invention. The machine was comprised of the patented "rewinder" component and several auxiliary components, including an "unwind stand" that supported a large roll of supply paper to the rewinder, a "core loader" that supplied paperboard cores to the rewinder, an "embosser" that embossed the paper and provided a special textured surface, and a "tail sealer" that sealed the paper's trailing end to the finished roll. Although we noted that the auxiliary components had "separate usage" in that they each separately performed a part of an entire rewinding operation, the components together constituted one functional unit, including the patented component, to produce rolls of paper. The auxiliary components derived their market value from the patented rewinder because they had no useful purpose independent of the patented rewinder.

Similarly, our subsequent cases have applied the entire market value rule only in situations in which the patented and unpatented components were analogous to a single functioning unit. *See, e.g., Kalman v. Berlyn Corp.*., 914 F.2d 1473, 1485, 16 USPQ2d 1093, 1102 (Fed. Cir. 1990) (affirming award of damages for filter screens used with a patented filtering device); *TWM*, 789 F.2d at 901, 229 USPQ at 528 (affirming award of damages for unpatented wheels and axles sold with patented vehicle suspension system).

Thus, the facts of past cases clearly imply a limitation on damages, when recovery is sought on sales of unpatented components sold with patented components, to the effect that the unpatented components must function together with the patented component in some manner so as to produce a desired end product or result. All the components together must be analogous to components of a single assembly or be parts of a complete machine, or they must constitute a functional unit. Our precedent has not extended liability to include items that have essentially no functional relationship to the patented invention and that may have been sold with an infringing device only as a matter of convenience or business advantage. We are not persuaded that we should extend that liability. Damages on such items would constitute more than what is "adequate to compensate for the infringement."

The facts of this case do not meet this requirement. The dock levelers operated to bridge the gap between a loading dock and a truck. The patented vehicle restraint operated to secure the rear of the truck to the loading dock. Although the two devices may have been used together, they did not function together to achieve one result and each could effectively have been used independently of each other. The parties had established positions in marketing dock levelers long prior to developing the vehicle restraints. Rite–Hite and Kelley were pioneers in that industry and for many years were primary competitors. Although following Rite–Hite's introduction of its restraints onto the market, customers frequently solicited package bids for the simultaneous installation of restraints and dock levelers, they did so because such bids facilitated contracting and construction scheduling, and because both Rite–Hite and Kelley encouraged this linkage by offering combination discounts. The dock levelers were thus sold by Kelley with the restraints only for marketing reasons, not because they essentially functioned together. We distinguish our conclusion to permit damages based on lost sales of the unpatented (not covered by the patent in suit) ADL–100 devices, but not on lost sales of the unpatented dock levelers, by emphasizing that the Kelley Truk Stops were devices competitive with the ADL–100s, whereas the dock levelers were merely items sold together with the restraints for convenience and business advantage. It is a clear purpose of the patent law to redress competitive damages resulting from infringement of the patent, but there is no basis for extending that recovery to include damages for items that are neither competitive with nor function with the patented invention. Promotion of the useful arts, *see* U.S. Const., art. I, § 8, cl. 8, requires one, but not the other. These facts do not establish the functional relationship necessary to justify recovery under the entire market value rule. Therefore, the district court erred as a matter of law in including them within the compensation base. Accordingly, we vacate the court's award of damages based on the dock leveler sales.

IV. *Computation of Reasonable Royalty*

The district court found that Rite–Hite as a manufacturer was entitled to an award of a reasonable royalty on 502 infringing restraint or restraint-leveler sales for which it had not proved that it contacted the Kelley customer prior to the infringing Kelley sale. The court awarded a royalty equal to approximately fifty percent of Rite–Hite's estimated lost profits per unit sold to retailers. Further, the court found that Rite–Hite as a retailer was entitled to a reasonable royalty amounting to approximately one-third its estimated lost distribution income per infringing sale. Kelley challenges the amount of the royalty as grossly excessive and legally in error.

A patentee is entitled to no less than a reasonable royalty on an infringer's sales for which the patentee has not established entitlement to lost profits. 35 U.S.C. § 284 (1988); *Hanson v. Alpine Valley Ski Area, Inc.*, 718 F.2d 1075, 1078, 219 USPQ 679, 681–82 (Fed. Cir. 1983) ("If actual damages cannot be ascertained, then a reasonable royalty must be determined."). The royalty may be based upon an established royalty, if there is one, or if not, upon the supposed result of hypothetical negotiations between the plaintiff and defendant.[13] The hypothetical negotiation requires the court to envision the terms of a licensing agreement reached as the result of a supposed meeting between the patentee and the infringer at the time infringement began. "One challenging only the court's finding as to amount of damages awarded under the 'reasonable royalty' provision of § 284, therefore, must show that the award is, in view of all the evidence, either so outrageously high or so outrageously low as to be unsupportable as an estimation of a reasonably royalty." *Lindemann Maschinenfabrik GmbH v. American Hoist & Derrick Co.*, 895 F.2d 1403, 1406, 13 USPQ2d 1871, 1874 (Fed. Cir. 1990).

The district court here conducted the hypothetical negotiation analysis. It determined that Rite–Hite would have been willing to grant a competitor a license to use the '847 invention only if it received a royalty

---

13. The hypothetical negotiation is often referred to as a "willing licensor/willing licensee" negotiation. However, this is an inaccurate, and even absurd, characterization when, as here, the patentee does not wish to grant a license. *See Hanson v. Alpine Valley Ski Area, Inc.*, 718 F.2d 1075, 1081, 219 USPQ 679, 684 (Fed. Cir. 1983) (The willing licensee/licensor concept is "employed by the court as a means of arriving at reasonable compensation and its validity does not depend on the actual willingness of the parties to the lawsuit to engage in such negotiations[; t]here is, of course, no actual willingness on either side.").

of no less than one-half of the per unit profits that it was foregoing. In so determining, the court considered that the '847 patent was a "pioneer" patent with manifest commercial success; that Rite–Hite had consistently followed a policy of exploiting its own patents, rather than licensing to competitors; and that Rite–Hite would have had to forego a large profit by granting a license to Kelley because Kelley was a strong competitor and Rite–Hite anticipated being able to sell a large number of restraints and related products. It was thus not unreasonable for the district court to find that an unwilling patentee would only license for one-half its expected lost profits and that such an amount was a reasonable royalty. The fact that the award was not based on the infringer's profits did not make it an unreasonable award. *See State Indus.*, 883 F.2d at 1580, 12 USPQ2d at 1031 ("The determination of a reasonable royalty ... is based not on the infringer's profit margin[; t]here is no rule that a royalty be no higher than the infringer's net profit margin."); *Stickle v. Heublein, Inc.*, 716 F.2d 1550, 1563, 219 USPQ 377, 387 (Fed. Cir. 1983) (royalty need not be less than price of infringing unit). Furthermore, the fact that the award was based on and was a significant portion of the patentee's profits also does not make the award unreasonable. The language of the statute requires "damages adequate to compensate," which does not include a royalty that a patentee—who does not wish to license its patent—would find unreasonable. *See Del Mar*, 836 F.2d at 1328, 5 USPQ2d at 1261 ("[The] imposition on a patent owner who would not have licensed his invention for [a certain] royalty is a form of compulsory license, against the will and interest of the person wronged, in favor of the wrongdoer."). Moreover, what an infringer would prefer to pay is not the test for damages. *See TWM*, 789 F.2d at 900, 229 USPQ at 528 (that the parties might have agreed to a lesser royalty is of little relevance, for to look only at that question would be to pretend that the infringement never happened; it would also make an election to infringe a handy means for competitors to impose a compulsory license policy upon every patent owner).

We conclude that the district court made no legal error and was not clearly erroneous in determining the reasonable royalty rate. Accordingly, we affirm the trial court's calculation of a reasonable royalty rate. However, because we vacate the court's decision to include dock levelers in the royalty base, we remand for a redetermination of damages based only on the sale of the infringing restraints and not on the restraint-leveler packages.

CONCLUSION

On Kelley's appeal, we affirm the district court's decision that Rite–Hite is entitled to an award of lost profit damages based on its lost business in ADL–100 restraints. We affirm the court's determination of the reasonable royalty rate. We vacate the awards to the ISOs and vacate the damage award based on the dock levelers. We remand for the court to dismiss the ISOs as plaintiffs and recalculate damages to Rite–Hite.

NIES, Circuit Judge, with whom ARCHER, Chief Judge, SMITH, Senior Circuit Judge, and MAYER, Circuit Judge join, dissenting-in-part.

I.

SUMMARY

The majority uses the provision in 35 U.S.C. § 284 for "damages" as a tool to expand the property rights granted by a patent. I dissent.

No one disputes that Rite–Hite is entitled to "full compensation for any damages suffered as a result of the infringement." *General Motors Corp. v. Devex Corp.*, 461 U.S. 648, 653–54 (1983). "Damages," however, is a word of art. "Damages in a legal sense means the compensation which the law will award for an injury done." Thus, the question is, "What are the injuries for which full compensation must be paid?".

The majority divorces "actual damages" from injury to patent rights. The majority holds that a patentee is entitled to recover its lost profits caused by the infringer's competition with the patentee's business in ADL restraints, products not incorporating the invention of the patent in suit but assertedly protected by other unlitigated patents. Indeed, the majority states a broader rule for the award of lost profits on any goods of the patentee with which the infringing device competes, even products in the public domain.

I would hold that the diversion of ADL–100 sales is not an injury to patentee's property rights granted by the '847 patent. To constitute legal injury for which lost profits may be awarded, the infringer must interfere with the patentee's property right to an exclusive market in goods embodying the invention of the patent in suit. The patentee's property rights do not extend to its market in other goods unprotected by the litigated patent. Rite–Hite was compensated for the lost profits for 80 sales associated with the MDL–55, the only product it sells embodying the '847 invention. That is the totality of any possible entitlement to lost profits. Under 35 U.S.C. § 284, therefore, Rite–Hite is entitled to "damages" calculated as a reasonable royalty on the remainder of Kelley's infringing restraints.

G. "Foreseeability" Is Not the Test for Patent Damages

The majority agrees that the types of compensable injury for patent infringement are not unlimited. The majority draws the line against recovery for an inventor's heart attack or for the decrease in the value of stock of a corporate patentee.

In the majority's view, the consideration of patent rights ends upon a finding of infringement. The separate question of damages under its test does not depend on patent rights but only on foreseeable competitive injury. This position cannot be squared with the premise that compensation is due only for injury to patent rights. Thus, the majority's foreseeability standard contains a false premise, namely, that the "relevant market" can be "broadly defined" to include all competitive truck restraints made by the patentee. The relevant market for determining damages is confined to the market for the invention in which the patentee holds exclusive property rights. The injury, thus, must be to the protected market in goods made in accordance with the patent, not unprotected truck restraints. In sum, patent rights determine not only infringement but also damages.

The majority simply has the rule backwards. Heretofore, the first requirement to establish a patentee's entitlement to actual damages in the form of lost profits has been proof that the patentee exercised its market place monopoly for its patented invention. Evidence of a patentee's business losses not due to an infringer's interference with the patentee's marketing of the invention was immaterial in assessing damages. The patent affords no property rights which can be injured outside the market in goods protected by the asserted patent.

The majority goes on to find the award of damages for lost sales of ADL–100s a foreseeable injury for infringement of the '847 patent. This is a remarkable finding. The facts are that Rite–Hite began marketing its ADL–100 motorized restraint in 1980. Kelley put out its Truk Stop restraint in June 1982. There is no dispute in this case that Kelley "designed around" the protection afforded by any patent related to the ADL–100 with which Kelley's Truk Stop restraint was intended to compete. Two years later, the '847 patent in suit issued on the later-developed alternative hook technology used in the MDL–55. Kelley would have to have had prescient vision to foresee that it would be held an infringer of the unknown claims of the subsequently issued '847 patent and that its lawful competition with the ADL–100 would be transformed into a compensable injury.

The basic flaw in the majority's ruling is its rejection of the premise that recovery must be tied to profits from the invention itself. Here the patentee would have made no profits from the patented invention by additional sales of the unprotected ADL–100. There is no reason for the entire market value analysis if a patentee is entitled to compensation for "competitive damages" to its business generally. The '847 patent discloses and claims particular hook technology for a truck restraint. No part of the invention relates to motors. Indeed, the specification states that an advantage of the invention is that it requires no motor. No doubt the motorized features of the ADL–100 and the Truk–Stop which added to their price, by the same token, contributed to their profitability and salability as well. But because Rite–Hite did not use the '847 invention in the ADL–100 restraint, it escaped having to prove consumer demand for the motorized restraint was attributable to the '847 invention of an improved hook. It simply was awarded lost profits based on unpatented features and features protected by other patents. None of the lost profits on the ADL–100s are the fruit of the '847 invention. It cannot be the law that they are recoverable.

It cannot be disputed that Congress intended that the patent grant provide an incentive to make investments in patented products during the patent term. If a patentee is rewarded with lost profits on its established products, the incentive is dulled if not destroyed. Why make the investment to produce and market a new drug if the patent on the new discovery not only protects the status quo in the market but also provides lost profits for the old?

For the foregoing reasons, I would hold that an injury to the patentee's marketing of products protected only by other patents—if at all—does not fall within the grant of rights protected by the '847 patent in suit and is not compensable. Thus, I would vacate the award of lost profits on 3,283 sales based on Rite–Hite's loss of business in ADL–100 restraints and remand for damages to be assessed on the basis of a reasonable royalty for those infringements.

Notes

1. Do you think this case would have been resolved the same way if Rite–Hite did not have a patent on the ADL–100?

2. *Rite-Hite* stands for the proposition that a patentee may receive lost profits for the lost sales of devices that were in competition with infringing goods (so long as these lost sales were reasonably foreseeable), even if the devices were not covered by the patent-in-suit. The lost profits analysis in *Rite-Hite* was expanded to include situations where a competitor's product infringes a patent which the patent owner has chosen not to manufacture at all. In *King Instruments, Inc. v. Perego*, 65 F.3d 941, 36 USPQ2d 1129 (Fed. Cir. 1995), King Instruments patented a magnetic tape splicer for automated cassette loading but did not manufacture the device. King and Tapematic marketed competing machines that automatically splice and wind magnetic tape into completed video cassettes. Tapematic's product infringed the King patent, King's product which was quite different from Tapematic's did not fall within the patent claims. The Federal Circuit affirmed the award of lost profits for forty-nine sales made by Tapematic. Unlike *Rite-Hite* where the patentee did commercialize the patented invention (MDL–100), King Instruments never manufactured a commercial embodiment of its patented magnetic tape splicer and the splicer which it did sell was not covered by a valid patent. The Court explained its reasoning for this holding as follows:

> The market may well dictate that the best use of a patent is to exclude infringing products, rather than market the invention. A patentee, perhaps burdened with costs of development, may not produce the patented invention as efficiently as an infringer. Indeed, the infringer's presence in the market may preclude a patentee from beginning or continuing manufacture of the patented product. Thus, as apparent in this case, the patentee may acquire better returns on its innovation investment by attempting to exclude infringers from competing with the patent holder's nonpatented substitute.

> Under this situation, the Patent Act is working well. The patentee is deriving proper economic return on its investment in acquiring a patent right. The public benefits from the disclosure of the invention and the ability to exploit it when the patent term expires.

A hypothetical example shows how an infringer could profit from such a rule. A hypothetical patentee could market a product covered by a patent and efficiently supply all demand for the product. A competitor seeking a license under the patent would not succeed. The patentee profits more by supplying the demand itself than by granting a license on terms which would allow the competitor to reasonably operate. In this situation, no reasonable royalty exists. Willing negotiators, assuming they both act in their own best interests, would not agree to any royalty. The value of exercising the right to exclude is greater than the value of any economically feasible royalty. If the competitor infringes in this situation and the patentee can recover only a "reasonable royalty," the patentee does not receive "adequate compensation" as the statute requires. The same reasoning applies anytime the patent owner benefits more by excluding others than by licensing.

In such situations, if lost profits are not available simply because the patent holder does not market a product pursuant to its patent, infringement may actually be profitable. If licensing (rather than excluding) competitors would have proven more rewarding to the patentee, the patentee would have licensed. Instead, the market dictated that exclusion was the best way to recover innovation investments. Limiting the patentee's recovery to a reasonable royalty, however, would give the infringer what the market denied—a license. Fortunately the Patent Act does not create such incentives to infringe. Rather, it guarantees damages adequate to compensate for infringement—which include provable lost profits.

Id. at 950–51, 36 USPQ2d at 1135–36. Do you agree that lost profits should extend to situations where the patentee sells a competing product which is not itself patented and does not embody the patented invention? Should lost profits be reserved for those who commercialize the patented invention?

3. **Can a patent owner receive lost profits where it cannot prove that it would have made all the sales the infringer made?** Proving lost profits is easy where the only products which compete for sales are the one manufactured by the infringer and the patent owner. In the two-supplier market, the patent owner can argue that she is entitled to lost profits on all of the infringer's sales because she would have made all of these sales if there was no infringement. What should be done where there are non-infringing alternatives in the market? If the patentee can prove what her share of the market is, she can claim that she is entitled to lost profits on a portion of the infringer's sales and a reasonable royalty on the rest. For example, in *State Indus., Inc. v. Mor–Flo Indus., Inc.*, 883 F.2d 1573, 1578–80, 12 USPQ2d 1026, 1029–1032 (Fed. Cir. 1989), the patent owner's share of the market was 40% because there were competing non-infringing substitutes available. The Court upheld the award to the patent owner of a *pro rata* share of lost profits—the patent owner received lost profits on 40% of the infringer's sales—and a reasonable royalty (3%) on the remaining 60% of the infringer's sales. Should the proportional share of the market be the only factor that the court considers? *See BIC, infra.*

4. **Entire Market Value Rule.** The entire market value rule recognizes that the economic value of a patent may be greater than the value of the sales of the patented part alone. Under this rule, courts have allowed recovery of lost profits or a reasonable royalty based not only on the profit from the patented part, but also on non-patented parts. *See, e.g., State Indus., Inc. v. Mor–Flo Indus., Inc.*, 883 F.2d 1573, 1580, 12 USPQ2d 1026, 1031 (Fed. Cir. 1989). The entire market value rule typically arises where the patented invention is a component of a larger machine. The issue is whether the patentee can recover lost profits based on the sale of the entire machine. For example, if the patented invention is a semiconductor imaging chip used in camcorders; can the patentee recover lost profits on the sale of camcorders or should the lost profits be limited to the sale of the chip? The test used to resolve this issue is whether the patentee has proven that the patented feature is the basis for customer demand for the unpatented parts to which it seeks to extend its damages. One way to prove that the patented feature or component is the basis for the customer's demand is to look to the infringer's own brochures, instructions, technical literature, and advertising materials. If the infringer's materials tout the advantage achieved by the patented part of the device, this is evidence that this part is responsible for the customer demand for the whole product. *See, e.g., Fonar Corp. v. General Elec. Co.*, 107 F.3d 1543, 1552–53, 41 USPQ2d 1801, 1808 (Fed. Cir. 1997) (GE's own technical literature emphasized the value of the patented feature). The entire market value rule has also been applied where the parts are separate, but sold together and considered part of a single assembly or machine, where they constitute a "functional unit."

5. **Convoy Sales/Derivative Sales.** Should the entire market value rule permit the patentee to obtain damages on the sale of unpatented accessories or spare parts sold with a patented invention? Convoyed sales are sales that the patentee would have made simultaneously with the patented device but for the infringement, such as accessories. Derivative sales are sales that are not simultaneous with the patented device, however, the patentee would have made them but for the infringement, such as replacement or spare parts. The Federal Circuit has applied the entire market value rule to convoyed sales and derivative sales in certain circumstances.

The Federal Circuit has upheld the application of the entire market value rule when the unpatented features are not part of a single machine, but are separate units capable of separate usage. *See Paper Converting Machine Co. v. Magna–Graphics Corp.*, 745 F.2d 11, 23, 223 USPQ 591, 599 (Fed. Cir. 1984). The claimed invention in *Paper Converting Machine* was a machine called an automatic rewinder used to manufacture rolls of densely wound industrial tissue and paper toweling. The separate units were an unwind stand which supported the large roll of paper, a core loader which supplied paperboard cores to the rewinder, an embosser, and a tail sealer. The Federal Circuit held that the patentee was entitled to lost profits for all these items:

> The present case differs from the usual one in which the patented and unpatented components are part of a single machine. Here, the mechanism for the high speed manufacture of paper rolls

comprises several components, only one of which incorporates the invention claimed in the '353 patent. The auxiliary equipment includes an "unwind stand" which supports the large roll of paper which is supplied to the rewinder for cutting and rewinding, a "core loader" which supplies paperboard cores to the rewinder, an "embosser" which when located between the unwind stand and the rewinder embosses the paper and provides a special textured surface, and a "tail sealer" which seals the paper's trailing end (the tail) to the consumer-sized roll.

None of the auxiliary units here are integral parts of the rewinder; rather, they each have separate usage. Paper Converting therefore obviously cannot prevent the manufacture or sale of these auxiliary units. This fact, however, does not control our decision. The deciding factor, rather, is whether "[n]ormally the patentee (or its licensee) can anticipate sale of such unpatented components as well as of the patented" ones. If in all reasonable probability the patent owner would have made the sales which the infringer has made, what the patent owner in reasonable probability would have netted from the sales denied to him is the measure of his loss, and the infringer is liable for that.

The district court found that Paper Converting adduced sufficient evidence at trial to sustain its burden of showing that if Magna–Graphics had not infringed the '353 patent, Paper Converting would have sold its entire rewinder line to Scott and Fort Howard. Substantial evidence showed, for instance, that the entire industry routinely purchased a complete rewinder line from the seller of the rewinder machine so as to ensure a single source of responsibility. Fort Howard and Scott exemplify this industry practice: every time Paper Converting sold a highspeed automatic rewinder to either of them, they purchased the entire rewinder line including auxiliary equipment. Moreover, in the two infringing sales which Magna–Graphics made, both Fort Howard and Scott again purchased the entire rewinder line including auxiliary equipment. Indeed, of Paper Converting's 572 rewinder sales, only nine involved rewinders alone.

Whether a patentee could anticipate additional income from the auxiliary parts is a question of fact which we cannot and will not disturb unless clearly erroneous. Fed. R. Civ. P. 52(a). The evidence amply supports the district court's finding that Paper Converting would have made these sales but for Magna–Graphics' infringing sales. We affirm.

Id. at 23, 223 USPQ at 599–600 (citations omitted). "The controlling touchstone in determining whether to include the non-patented spare part in a damage award is whether the patentee can normally anticipate the sale of the non-patented component together with the sale of the patented components." *King Instrument Corp. v. Otari Corp.*, 767 F.2d 853, 865, 226 USPQ 402, 411 (Fed. Cir. 1985). The financial and marketing dependence of the convoyed sales is also evidence that the entire market value rule should apply to these sales and that the patentee should therefore recover lost profits or a reasonable royalty on them as well. *See TWM Mfg. Co. v. Dura Corp.*, 789 F.2d 895, 901, 229 USPQ 525, 528 (Fed. Cir. 1986).

6. **The functional test for convoyed sales.** In *Rite-Hite*, the Federal Circuit held that the convoyed sales must bear a functional relationship with the patented goods. 56 F.3d at 1550, 35 USPQ2d at 1073. Lost profits were awarded for the patentee's lost sales of truck restraints, a device which holds a vehicle to a loading dock and lost profits were denied on convoyed sales of a loading dock leveler. The Court held that "[a]lthough the two devices may have been used together, they did not function together to achieve one result and each could effectively have been used independently of each other." *Id.* at 1551, 35 USPQ2d at 1073–74. What does it mean for two items to function together?

7. **Accelerated Market Reentry**. It is not infringement to make, use, sell, or offer to sell a patented device after the patent expires. However, accelerated reentry damages may arise when a patentee claims that the infringer will reenter the market after the patent expires at a level accelerated by the earlier infringement—customers who purchase the product from the infringer after the patent expires were actually diverted from the patent owner to the infringer by the infringing conduct. *Amsted Indus. Inc. v. National Castings Inc.*, 16 USPQ2d 1737, 1754 (N.D. Ill. 1990) (permitting the patent owner to introduce evidence of accelerated reentry damages because damages "based upon the defendant's accelerated reentry were actually compensation for the defendant's past infringement, not its post-expiration conduct."); *T.P. Orthodontics Inc. v. Professional Positioners Inc.*, 17 USPQ2d 1497, 1504–05 (E.D. Wis. 1990) (awarding damages for lost sales after the expiration of the patent, reasoning that the infringer made more sales after the patent's expiration by initiating sales prior to the expiration of the patent); *BIC Leisure Prods., Inc. v. Windsurfing Int'l, Inc.*, 687 F. Supp. 134, 9 USPQ2d 1152 (S.D. N.Y. 1988) (post-expiration damages based upon the accelerated reentry theory are recoverable because they are actually compensation for the defendant's past infringement, not its post-expiration conduct). In these cases, the patent owner argues that as a result of the infringement, the infringer has a "headstart" in gaining a client base and thus can enter the market more quickly upon expiration of the patent. Is it fair for the infringer to get this sort of headstart? Can a company gear-up to manufacture a patented product (build a manufacturing facility which has no other use and train employees) close to the expiration of the patent, so that it can begin making and selling the product as soon as the patent expires?

After reading *Rite-Hite* and *King Instruments,* it may seem that an award of lost profits is guaranteed to a patent holder. *BIC Leisure Products* demonstrates that this is not the case. If a patent holder can not satisfy its burden of proof, lost profits are not available.

BIC LEISURE PRODS. v. WINDSURFING INT'L, INC.

1 F.3d 1214, 27 USPQ2d 1671 (Fed. Cir. 1993)

Before NIES, Chief Judge, SMITH, Senior Circuit Judge, and RADER, Circuit Judge.

RADER, Circuit Judge.

The United States District Court for the Southern District of New York awarded Windsurfing International, Inc. lost profits for BIC Leisure Products, Inc.'s infringement of U.S. Reissue Patent No. 31,167. The court refused to award lost profits for alleged price erosion.

Assuming BIC had not been in the market, Windsurfing did not show that BIC's customers would have purchased sailboards from Windsurfing and other manufacturers in proportion to their market shares. Therefore, this court reverses the award of lost profits based upon Windsurfing's market share. Otherwise, this court affirms.

BACKGROUND

BIC infringed Windsurfing's Reissue Patent No. 31,167, which covers sailboards. Windsurfing seeks damages from BIC for the period from March 8, 1983 (the reissue date of Windsurfing's patent) to September 30, 1985 (the date the district court enjoined BIC from further infringement).

Windsurfing primarily manufactured and marketed sailboards embodying its patented invention for the "One–Design Class." The One–Design Class refers to a uniform competition class as defined by a sailboarding association. A sailboarding association sponsors regattas in which sailboarders compete against each other on boards of uniform weight and shape. Most of Windsurfing's sailboards fit within the weight and shape requirements for the One–Design competition class.

One–Design sailboards lost favor with most sailboarders, however, with the advent of faster, more maneuverable, and more versatile "funboards" and "wave boards." These newer boards had a lighter hull design. Despite the rising popularity of these newer boards in the early 1980s, Windsurfing decided to continue to concentrate on its One–Design boards.

Windsurfing licensed its patented technology extensively. Windsurfing licensed at least twelve companies in Europe. At least one of the European licensees granted sublicenses to other European manufacturers. Windsurfing also granted licenses in the United States. Eventually, Windsurfing licensed twelve companies in the United States. With few exceptions, Windsurfing charged 7.5% of net sales for the U.S. licenses. All of the U.S. licensees, as well as some of the European licensees, competed against Windsurfing in the United States.

Windsurfing manufactured its boards using a rotomolding process. During the early 1980s, many of Windsurfing's competitors reduced their production costs with a new blowmolding process. Instead of switching to the more efficient blowmolding process, Windsurfing invested one million dollars in an unsuccessful attempt to improve its rotomolding process. Windsurfing controlled 29.2% of the sailboard market in 1983, 25.6% in 1984, and 13.6% in 1985.

BIC began selling sailboards in 1981. BIC manufactured with the more efficient blowmolding process. BIC did not sell sailboards with the One Design hull form. Rather, BIC's sailboards differed from Windsurfing's products. BIC instead sold boards at the lower end of the market's price spectrum, reflecting its decision to target the entry level segment of the sailboard market.

In comparison, Windsurfing priced its sailboards at the upper end of the sailboard price spectrum. During the years covered by the damages period, U.S. sailboard dealers charged the following average prices:

1983		1984		1985	
Marker	837	Brockhaus	753	Mistral	804
Brockhaus	753	Mistral	741	Marker	774
Mistral	750	Marker	674	Brockhaus	750
Windsurfing	670	SAN/Romney	623	SAN	623
SAN/Romney	643	Windsurfing	589	Schutz	575
Alpha	574	Schutz	575	Windsurfing	571
Wayler	550	HiFly	527	HiFly	570
HiFly	518	Wayler	500	Wayler	500
SAN/Schaeffer	441	Alpha	450	O'Brien	477
O'Brien	436	O'Brien	412	Alpha	450
BIC	407	SAN/Schaeffer	388	AMF Inc.	380
AMF Inc.	377	AMF Inc.	384	BIC	312
Ten Cate	366	BIC	335	Ten Cate	253
AMF Mares	244	Ten Cate	299	AMF Mares	244
		AMF Mares	234		

The Patent and Trademark Office reissued Windsurfing's patent on March 8, 1983. On that date, BIC had 5,245 sailboards in its inventory and another 5,625 on order. BIC confirmed its purchase of the boards on order with a February 10, 1983 telex.

The district court applied the *Panduit* test to determine whether Windsurfing lost profits. The district court required Windsurfing to show (1) a demand for the patented product, (2) the absence of acceptable noninfringing substitutes, (3) its capacity to exploit the demand, and (4) the profits lost due to the infringement. The district court modified the *Panduit* test by presuming that Windsurfing would have captured a share of BIC's sales in proportion to Windsurfing's share of the sailboard market. Relying on *State Industries, Inc. v. Mor–Flo Industries, Inc.*, 883 F.2d 1573, 12 USPQ2d 1026 (Fed. Cir. 1989), the district court awarded Windsurfing lost profits based upon its pro rata percentage of BIC's sales for each year of the damages period. In addition, the district court awarded Windsurfing lost royalties for the boards its licensees would have sold absent BIC's infringement. The court calculated the amount of lost royalties based upon a weighted average price of the boards sold by the licensees.

DISCUSSION

Lost Profits

The finding of the amount of damages for patent infringement is a question of fact on which the patent owner bears the burden of proof. Where the district court fixes the amount of damages, this court reviews that finding under the clearly erroneous standard of Federal Rule of Civil Procedure 52(a).

To recover lost profits as opposed to royalties, a patent owner must prove a causal relation between the infringement and its loss of profits. The patent owner must show that "but for" the infringement, it would have made the infringer's sales. An award of lost profits may not be speculative. Rather the patent owner must show a reasonable probability that, absent the infringement, it would have made the infringer's sales.

The district court clearly erred by failing to apply the "but for" test before awarding lost profits. The record in this case does not evince a reasonable probability that Windsurfing would have made its pro rata share of BIC's sales had BIC not been in the market. During the period in question, at least fourteen competitors vied for sales in the sailboard market with prices ranging from $234 to $837. BIC's boards sold for $312 to $407; Windsurfing's boards sold for $571 to $670—a difference of over $250 or about 60–80% above BIC's selling range. Because Windsurfing concentrated on the One Design class hull form and BIC did not, Windsurfing's boards differed fundamentally from BIC's boards.

The record contains uncontradicted evidence that demand for sailboards is relatively elastic. The record further contains uncontradicted evidence that the sailboard market's entry level, in which BIC competed, is particularly sensitive to price disparity. By purchasing BIC sailboards, BIC's customers demonstrated a preference for sailboards priced around $350, rather than One–Design boards priced around $600. Therefore, without BIC in the market, BIC's customers would have likely sought boards in the same price range.

Several manufacturers offered sailboards at prices much closer to BIC than to Windsurfing. At least two of Windsurfing's licensees, O'Brien and HiFly, sold boards resembling BIC's in the same distribution channels as BIC. On this record, Windsurfing did not show with reasonable probability that BIC's customers would have purchased from Windsurfing in proportion with Windsurfing's market share. The record shows rather that the vast majority of BIC's customers would have purchased boards from O'Brien or HiFly if BIC's boards had not been available. The district court erred in assuming that, without BIC in the market, its customers would have redistributed their purchases among all the remaining sailboards, including Windsurfing's One Design boards at a price $200 to $300 more than BIC's.

Moreover, Windsurfing's sales continued to decline after the district court enjoined BIC's infringement. This aspect of the record shows as well that Windsurfing did not capture its market share of the sales replacing BIC's market sales. According to the record, the principal beneficiary of BIC's exit appears to be O'Brien.

The district court applied the *Panduit* test for lost profits. Properly applied, the *Panduit* test is an acceptable, though not an exclusive, test for determining "but for" causation. The *Panduit* test, however, operates under an inherent assumption, not appropriate in this case, that the patent owner and the infringer sell products sufficiently similar to compete against each other in the same market segment. If the patentee's and the infringer's products are not substitutes in a competitive market, *Panduit*'s first two factors do not meet the "but for" test—a prerequisite for lost profits.

The first *Panduit* factor—demand for the patented product—presupposes that demand for the infringer's and patent owner's products is interchangeable. Under this assumption, evidence of sales of the infringing product may suffice to show *Panduit*'s first factor, "demand for the patented product." *E.g., Gyromat Corp. v. Champion Spark Plug Co.,* 735 F.2d 549, 552, 222 USPQ 4, 6 (Fed. Cir. 1984). This analysis assumes that the patent owner and the infringer sell substantially the same product. In *Gyromat,* for instance, the patent owner's and the infringer's products were similar in price and product characteristics. If the products are not sufficiently similar to compete in the same market for the same customers, the infringer's customers would not necessarily transfer their demand to the patent owner's product in the absence of the infringer's product. In such circumstances, as in this case, the first *Panduit* factor does not operate to satisfy the elemental "but for" test.

Similarly, the second *Panduit* factor—absence of acceptable, noninfringing alternatives—presupposes that the patentee and the infringer sell substantially similar products in the same market. To be acceptable to the infringer's customers in an elastic market, the alleged alternative "must not have a disparately higher price than or possess characteristics significantly different from the patented product." *Kaufman Co. v. Lantech, Inc.,* 926 F.2d 1136, 1142, 17 USPQ2d 1828, 1832 (Fed. Cir. 1991) (citing *Gyromat,* 735 F.2d at 553). In *Kaufman,* for instance, the patent owner and the infringer sold substantially the same product. Thus *Panduit*'s second factor, properly applied, ensures that any proffered alternative competes in the same market for the same customers as the infringer's product. *See Yarway Corp. v. Eur–Control USA, Inc.,* 775 F.2d 268, 276, 227 USPQ 352, 357 (Fed. Cir. 1985) (alternative products did not possess features of the patent owner's and the infringer's products, nor compete in the same " 'special niche' or mini-market").

This court has held that a patent owner may satisfy the second *Panduit* element by substituting proof of its market share for proof of the absence of acceptable substitutes. This market share approach allows a patentee to recover lost profits, despite the presence of acceptable, noninfringing substitutes, because it nevertheless can prove with reasonable probability sales it would have made "but for" the infringement. Like *Panduit*'s second prong, however, this market share test also assumes that the patent owner and the infringer compete in the same market. In *State Industries*, for instance, the patent owner, infringer, and the other manufacturers sold substantially similar products. This similarity of products is necessary in order for market share proof to show correctly satisfaction of *Panduit*'s second factor.

The assumption underlying *Panduit*, *Gyromat*, and *State Industries* is not appropriate in this case. Instead, the record reveals that during the damages period the sailboard market was not a unitary market in which every competitor sold substantially the same product. Windsurfing and BIC sold different types of sailboards at different prices to different customers. As noted, their sailboards differed significantly in terms of price, product characteristics, and marketing channels. On the facts of this case, Windsurfing did not show "but for" causation under a correct application of *Panduit* or otherwise. The district court erred in awarding lost profits.

Moreover, Windsurfing itself set the value of its patent rights by licensing its technology to nearly every company supplying sailboards in the United States without competing itself in most sailboard submarkets. Windsurfing valued its patent in terms of licensing royalties, not in terms of profits it could make by excluding others from the market. Without evidence to support Windsurfing's claim to lost profits, this court reverses the district court's award.

Price Erosion

The district court evaluated the documentary and testimonial evidence on price erosion and found it too speculative to support an award of price erosion lost profits. This court finds nothing clearly erroneous in the district court's finding.

The record shows that other market forces, not BIC, forced Windsurfing to lower its prices. The record is replete with evidence that funboards, wave boards, and other designs replaced One Design boards as the sailboard of choice for many practitioners. Besides reducing the demand for One Design boards, consumer choices also caused many companies to discount their stock of One Design boards to make room for the newer boards.

Furthermore, Windsurfing licensed many competitors who produced boards at less cost. The more efficient blowmolding process allowed Windsurfing's competitors to cut prices. Windsurfing's own licensing policies exacerbated this problem. When the European market peaked in the early 1980s, Windsurfing's European licensees sold their excess inventory in the United States. The influx of European boards increased the supply of sailboards and further reduced prices. In light of these facts, the district court correctly found that Windsurfing failed to meet its burden of proof. Simply put, Windsurfing did not prove that it could have sold its boards at higher prices "but for" BIC's infringement.

Notes

1. **Price Erosion.** The patentee can argue that the defendant's infringing activities forced her to sell the patented product at a lower price than she would have in the absence of the defendant's infringement. When the defendant enters the market, she can undercut the patentee's price for the patented product because she does not have to recoup the costs of the research, development and patenting of the product. The argument is that the defendant's activities eroded the price for the patented item and in order to compete the patent owner was forced to sell the product at a lower price than she would have if the defendant had not been infringing. Although the patent owner may have been able to charge a higher price in the absence of the infringer, would she sell as many products at this higher price? Consider *Minnesota Mining & Mfg. Co. v. Johnson & Johnson Orthopaedics, Inc.*, 976 F.2d 1559, 1578–79, 24 USPQ2d 1321, 1337–38 (Fed. Cir. 1992) (citations omitted), where the Federal Circuit awarded lost profits based on price erosion:

> The Master also awarded 3M $28,923,219 in lost profits due to price erosion caused by JJO. The Master determined that 3M would have been able to increase its prices 2% per annum during the period of infringement if JJO had not been competing in the market.[11] JJO argues that there is "not a shred" of evidence in the record to support the 2% figure and that the Master should not have awarded these damages. We disagree.

> The Master made several findings of fact indicating that, among other things, 3M and JJO engaged in vigorous price competition over equivalent products which caused a steady decline in the price of casting tape during the infringement period and 3M would have charged higher prices absent JJO's infringement. Although other companies also engaged in price competition, they had a small effect on the downward trend of prices because they offered inferior products and their market share continually declined over the course of the infringement period to the point where 3M and JJO together had approximately 85% of the market. The Master also found that 3M would have commanded 70–80% of the casting tape market with JJO gone and would have experienced little or no price competition from other competitors.

> In addition, 3M's witnesses testified and presented documents to show that 3M would have raised prices approximately 4% per year to match the rate of inflation. 3M compared these figures with JJO's practice of raising prices 4% per year in the plaster casting market where JJO held a similar market share and had no patent protection.

> JJO argued that there would have been zero inflation on synthetic casting tapes. After considering the evidence, the Master concluded that if JJO were not in the market, 3M could have and

---

11. Based on the 2% figure, 3M's lost profit would have been $38,723,219. The Master, however, subtracted $9.8 million which she determined would be the market contraction that would result from 3M's price increases, arriving at the final figure of $28,923,219.

would have taken annual price increases of 2%. Although damages may not be based on speculation, they need not be proved with unerring precision either. The Master is not restricted from choosing a figure other than that advocated by either party and may substitute an intermediate figure as a matter of judgment from all the evidence. We find that the Master's decision to award the 2% increment rate based on all the evidence was not clearly erroneous.

Price erosion is difficult to prove as it requires some degree of speculation. If the patent owner is successful in proving price erosion, she may be able to recover damages for both past price erosion and future price erosion. It is common sense that the patent owner will not be able to effectuate a large increase in price the minute that the infringer is enjoined from selling the patented invention. Customers would not stand for it. The defendant will likely argue that factors other than its infringement are responsible for the low price of the patented good. Can you think of things that could be responsible for keeping the patent owner's price low?

B.   REASONABLE ROYALTIES

Test: The determination of a reasonable royalty is arguably a legal fiction based upon the hypothetical negotiation between a willing patent holder and willing licensee. A reasonable royalty should consider both the amount the licensee would be willing to pay to make and sell the patented article and the amount the patent owner would demand for a license (which could be more than the licensee's profit). The following district court opinion sheds some light on this highly factual inquiry and lists the types of facts that a fact finder should consider in arriving at what would be a reasonable royalty.

GEORGIA-PACIFIC CORP. v. UNITED STATES PLYWOOD-CHAMPION PAPERS, INC.

318 F. Supp. 1116, 166 USPQ 235 (S.D. N.Y. 1970).

TENNEY, District Judge.

By opinion dated October 26, 1956, entered in an action by Georgia–Pacific Corporation (hereinafter referred to as "GP") for a declaratory judgment of invalidity and non-infringement of three patents held by United States Plywood Corporation (hereinafter referred to as "USP") and upon a counterclaim by USP for patent infringement and unfair competition, my late brother Judge Herlands found USP's three patents (one Deskey and two Bailey patents) invalid for lack of invention, not infringed by GP's product and further, that there was no proof that GP engaged in acts of unfair competition. The Court of Appeals reversed and remanded in 1958, holding that Claim 1 of USP's Deskey Patent No. 2,286,068 covering "Weldtex" striated fir plywood valid and infringed by GP.

While the parties agree upon the doctrinal criteria of a reasonable royalty, they differ sharply in their application of those principles to the hard specifics of the evidence. The extreme divergence of the parties is reflected in the difference between GP's submission that the reasonable royalty herein should be fixed at a figure somewhere between a dollar and one-half to three dollars per thousand square feet and USP's claim that the minimum reasonable royalty should be the rate of fifty dollars per thousand square feet.

A comprehensive list of evidentiary facts relevant, in general, to the determination of the amount of a reasonable royalty for a patent license may be drawn from a conspectus of the leading cases. The following are some of the factors *mutatis mutandis* seemingly more pertinent to the issue herein:

1. The royalties received by the patentee for the licensing of the patent in suit, proving or tending to prove an established royalty.

2. The rates paid by the licensee for the use of other patents comparable to the patent in suit.

3. The nature and scope of the license, as exclusive or non-exclusive; or as restricted or non-restricted in terms of territory or with respect to whom the manufactured product may be sold.

4. The licensor's established policy and marketing program to maintain his patent monopoly by not licensing others to use the invention or by granting licenses under special conditions designed to preserve that monopoly.

5. The commercial relationship between the licensor and licensee, such as, whether they are competitors in the same territory in the same line of business; or whether they are inventor and promoter.

6. The effect of selling the patented specialty in promoting sales of other products of the licensee; that existing value of the invention to the licensor as a generator of sales of his non-patented items; and the extent of such derivative or convoyed sales.

7. The duration of the patent and the term of the license.

8. The established profitability of the product made under the patent; its commercial success; and its current popularity.

9. The utility and advantages of the patent property over the old modes or devices, if any, that had been used for working out similar results.

10. The nature of the patented invention; the character of the commercial embodiment of it as owned and produced by the licensor; and the benefits to those who have used the invention.

11. The extent to which the infringer has made use of the invention; and any evidence probative of the value of that use.

12. The portion of the profit or of the selling price that may be customary in the particular business or in comparable businesses to allow for the use of the invention or analogous inventions.

13. The portion of the realizable profit that should be credited to the invention as distinguished from non-patented elements, the manufacturing process, business risks, or significant features or improvements added by the infringer.

14. The opinion testimony of qualified experts.

15. The amount that a licensor (such as the patentee) and a licensee (such as the infringer) would have agreed upon (at the time the infringement began) if both had been reasonably and voluntarily trying to reach an agreement; that is, the amount which a prudent licensee—who desired, as a business proposition, to obtain a license to manufacture and sell a particular article embodying the patented invention—would have been willing to pay as a royalty and yet be able to make a reasonable profit and which amount would have been acceptable by a prudent patentee who was willing to grant a license.

The parties agree that there was no "established" royalty for USP's Weldtex or GP striated. Consequently, it is necessary to resort to a broad spectrum of other evidentiary facts probative of a "reasonable" royalty.

The parties rely upon the traditional array of facts probative of a reasonable royalty. But, in addition, USP places heavy reliance upon a later formulation called "the willing buyer and willing seller" rule. The rule is pronounced in *Horvath v. McCord Radiator & Mfg. Co.*, 100 F.2d 326, 335 (6th Cir. 1938), in these terms:

> In fixing damages on a royalty basis against an infringer, the sum allowed should be reasonable and that which would be accepted by a prudent licensee who wished to obtain a license but was not so compelled and a prudent patentee, who wished to grant a license but was not so compelled.

The rule is more a statement of approach than a tool of analysis. It requires consideration not only of the amount that a willing licensee would have paid for the patent license but also of the amount that a willing licensor would have accepted. What a willing licensor and a willing licensee would have agreed upon in a suppositious negotiation for a reasonable royalty would entail consideration of the specific factors previously mentioned, to the extent of their relevance. Where a willing licensor and a willing licensee are negotiating for a royalty, the hypothetical negotiations would not occur in a vacuum of pure logic. They would involve a market place confrontation of the parties, the outcome of which would depend upon such factors as their relative bargaining strength; the anticipated amount of profits that the prospective licensor reasonably thinks he would lose as a result of licensing the patent as compared to the anticipated royalty income; the anticipated amount of net profits that the prospective licensee reasonably thinks he will make; the commercial past performance of the invention in terms of public acceptance and profits; the market to be tapped; and any other economic factor that normally prudent businessmen would, under similar circumstances, take into consideration in negotiating the hypothetical license.

As pointed out in an earlier decision herein by this Court, the very definition of a reasonable royalty assumes that, after payment, "the infringer will be left with a profit." It is necessary to consider, as an element in determining the amount of the reasonable royalty, the fact that GP would be willing hypothetically to pay a royalty which would produce "a reasonable profit" for GP.

It is evidence, therefore, that the formulation called the willing seller and willing buyer rule represents an attempt to colligate diverse evidentiary facts of potential relevance. In applying the formulation, the Court must take into account the realities of the bargaining table and subject the proofs to a dissective scrutiny.

Certain basic statistics are not in dispute. GP's sales of the infringing striated plywood totalled 15,899,000 square feet and amounted to sales proceeds to GP of $2,547,393. The period of the infringement was March 1955 through September 1958.

The manufacturing part of the infringement began in February 1955. The hypothetical negotiations are, therefore, time-placed in February 1955 and the relevant factors are viewed in that frame of time-reference.

USP's undeviating policy was to maintain its patent monopoly on sales of striated fir plywood in the United States. Its exploitation of the Deskey patent through the sale of Weldtex was extremely successful and profitable. The Court of Appeals characterized the commercial success of Weldtex as a factor of "very great significance."

USP manufactured and sold Weldtex in substantial quantities since 1946. From April 30, 1951 to January 31, 1955, the annual average sales of Weldtex was approximately $6,000,000. During the last six quarter-annual periods before the infringement, extending up to January 31, 1955, sales of Weldtex totalled $9,325,022, the quarterly average being $1,554,170, compared with quarterly average sales of $1,456,605 during the period from April 30, 1951 to January 31, 1955. During the quarter ending April 30, 1955, the Weldtex sales amounted to $1,601,814.

[In] February 1955, USP had no reason to anticipate that there would be a significant decline in the demand for Weldtex in the foreseeable future. In fact, no such decline took place for two years subsequent to February 1955.

The commodity most relevant to the subject of USP's monopoly was striated fir plywood. GP argues that the relevant commodity is "decorative plywood" as a class, of which striated fir plywood (exemplified by USP's Weldtex) was only one of many; that USP's monopoly was diluted by the competition of other decorative plywoods with Weldtex; and that this competition in February 1955 was a factor that significantly tended to reduce the royalty for Weldtex that would have been negotiated hypothetically at that time. In fact, GP contends that the competition that Weldtex faced was so keen that only a minimal royalty can be justified.

Noteworthy is the fact that, despite the allegedly fierce competition between Weldtex and other decorative plywoods, GP deliberately decided to duplicate Weldtex notwithstanding the caveat of GP's own counsel that an expensive infringement suit was inevitable. GP's calculated infringement of Weldtex is an admission by conduct that it regarded Weldtex as occupying a uniquely favorable position in the market.

In this connection, it is also important to consider that, without a license from USP, GP could not legitimately manufacture striated fir plywood and, on the other hand, the granting of a license by USP to GP would place GP in direct and active competition with USP in the United States with respect to striated fir plywood. Obviously, only an adequate royalty would make this proposition palatable to USP.

The separate question—whether there were other competing decorative plywood panels—poses an inquiry into the extent of that competition and its ultimate bearing upon the determination of the amount of a reasonable royalty.

The evidence that, in February 1955, Weldtex was without keen competition is corroborated by admissions from GP's own files relating to times both before and after the hypothetical negotiations. For example, GP's attorney, in a letter dated July 23, 1953, said that Weldtex "has been without any substantial competition." Five years later, on May 13, 1958, a ranking representative of GP (Leonardson) wrote that Weldtex "is certainly one product on which they (USP) have very little competition."

While in a generalized sense Weldtex was only one of a number of decorative wall panels that were competitive (e.g., brushed fir plywood, Philippine mahogany plywood and embossed plywood) the Court accepts Mr. Heilpern's testimony that, to determine whether and to what extent various plywood and similar products were competitive with each other, it is necessary to know their respective price ranges and the respective markets that had been developed for them. The Court is convinced that, in February 1955, the commercial value of Weldtex was not undermined by competition.

The master found and this Court approved the finding, that Weldtex and GP's infringing striated plywood were competitive with each other to a greater degree than with other decorative panels. Competition in the form of imported products was not significant in February 1955. Such competition assumed substantial proportions only in 1957 or thereabouts. Mr. Heilpern's testimony proves that, while there were a number of other competitive decorative wall panels on the market during the period of infringement, they were not substantially significant as competitive items with Weldtex. This is corroborated by the fact that USP was able to maintain the volume of its sales at original prices. Mr. Antoville's credible testimony proves that, in 1955, the other decorative plywoods did not constitute a substantial competitive factor.

It follows that, in February 1955, the time of the hypothetical negotiations, the determination of a reasonable royalty would have been strongly influenced by the then dominant market position of Weldtex. While this element cannot be converted into commensurable arithmetical terms, it is a highly significant fact in the mix of factors.

The evidence referred to must be considered in conjunction with USP's policy not to license anyone to sell Weldtex in the United States or in any other area where USP was capable of making its own sales. In the licenses that USP did grant for the manufacture of Weldtex in the United States, USP stipulated that the licensee could sell only to USP or USP's designee.

The master found that USP had the financial and physical capacity to market an additional amount of striated fir plywood equaling 80% of the amount infringingly sold by GP. While the master and the Court found that USP had possessed that capacity, the master found, and the Court approved the finding, that the proof was insufficient to establish that USP would have in fact manufactured and sold any measurable quantity of Weldtex between February 1955 and September 1958, in addition to the quantities of Weldtex which they did actually manufacture and sell during that period.

What is pertinent for present purposes is that, at the time of the hypothetical negotiations, USP did have the physical and financial capacity to market an additional 12,784,000 square feet of Weldtex between March 1955 and September 1958 and that, when it would have entered into the hypothetical licensing agreement with GP, it was not doing so because it could not have produced additional Weldtex itself.

Next to be considered is the matter of the market demand for Weldtex in or about February 1955 and the then reasonable anticipation as to the continuance of that customer popularity. GP argues that Weldtex had passed its apogee just before GP began its infringing sales of striated plywood. Citing sales statistics, GP claims that Weldtex lost standing in each succeeding year since early 1955.

The more persuasive fact is that, in February 1955, there was no reason to anticipate any significant decline in the foreseeable future in the demand for the striated fir plywood on which USP had a legal monopoly. USP executives in fact anticipated no such decline.

The Court, therefore, finds that, in or about February 1955 and for approximately two years thereafter, the popularity of striated fir plywood was still a choice commodity; that it was viewed by USP and GP as one that would bring in substantial profits; that it was desirable in the eyes of GP; and that because GP coveted it, it deliberately proceeded to manufacture its own striated fir plywood imitation of Weldtex. Consequently, in considering the ultimate question of reasonable royalty, striated fir plywood must be evaluated in the foregoing context.

The entire and actual sales picture of striated plywood during the period from February 1955 through September 19, 1958 has been considered as a circumstance together with all of the other evidence in the case. Taking all of the historical facts into consideration the Court finds that, for purposes of determining a reasonable royalty, striated fir plywood was considered by the parties as a readily salable and highly profitable commodity; and that striated fir plywood had not lost its commercial value as a popular product at the time of the hypothetical negotiations.

The circumstance that the Deskey patent (which had issued on June 9, 1942) had only a little over four years to run from February 1955 until it expired on June 9, 1959 and the argument of GP that the reasonable royalty should therefore be minimal, are neutralized by certain practical business considerations: (1) because striated fir plywood was a product of demonstrated great commercial success, GP did not assume any risk in this respect; (2) a royalty calculated as a percentage of footage actually sold or volume of actual sales, as distinguished from a license fee expressed in advance as a flat amount of dollars, would mean that GP did not assume any fixed financial obligation; (3) the opportunity to engage in the sale of a patented product even several years before the patent's expiration would constitute a definite advantage to GP who intended to market the product after the expiration of the patent; and (4) GP could get into the profitable production of striated fir plywood with only the modest investment required for a striating machine, amounting to approximately $12,000 to $15,000.

The amount of profits that USP was making and could (in February 1955) reasonably expect to continue to make on its sales of Weldtex by licensing no one to sell Weldtex in the United States is of major relevance to the determination of the amount of royalty that USP would accept from GP and that GP would offer. USP was enjoying the profits of a readily salable product. USP was in a position to retain the entire market on striated fir plywood for itself. The result of GP's infringement was to interfere with that monopoly and, as planned, to put GP in direct competition with USP's Weldtex throughout the period of infringement. The hypothetical license would have been one whereby GP would have been permitted to market striated fir plywood throughout the United States (as GP infringingly did).

In the hypothetical negotiations, USP would have been reasonable in taking the position that it would not accept a royalty significantly less than the profit it was making by its policy of licensing no one to sell striated fir plywood in the United States.

During the years 1952 to 1958, Weldtex was manufactured to two sources: the contract mills where approximately 80 per cent of USP's total Weldtex was produced and sold to USP by said mills; and USP's own Seattle plant where approximately 20 per cent of the Weldtex was produced. On an incremental or differential cost accounting basis (as distinguished from an absorption-cost accounting basis), USP made an average profit of $54.25 per thousand square feet with respect to the Weldtex produced by USP from the contract mills; and USP made an average profit of $86.16 per thousand square feet with respect to the Weldtex produced at USP's Seattle plant. When these two profit figures are weighed on the basis of the 80 per cent to 20 per cent production ratio, the ultimate result is $60.63 as the average rate of profit per thousand square feet earned by USP on all its Weldtex sales at the time of the infringement, computed on an incremental cost accounting basis.

Incremental cost accounting, however, is not considered by the Court as appropriate in determining the actual profitability of Weldtex during the years prior to and up to February 1955. Arguably, that method of cost accounting might be appropriate in evaluating the factor of suppositions profit on additional hypothetical sales that USP would anticipate and preserve for itself by not licensing GP. But the absorption cost-basis is more reliable and pertinent to a determination of the historical profitability of Weldtex during the years prior to and up to February 1955.

Computed by the absorption method, USP's average rate of profit on its Weldtex sales was $48.64 per thousand square feet at the time of the infringement.

Another element emphasized by USP as one that it would have taken into account in the hypothetical negotiations to fix a reasonable royalty was the profits it was making on collateral or convoyed sales of other USP products that were generated by Weldtex sales. [Although USP failed to prove the specific amount of additional profits on collateral sales, it would have considered such sales in determining a reasonable royalty.] The record therefore leads to the finding that consideration of the collateral sales factor by both parties would have tended to increase significantly the amount of the reasonable royalty hypothetically negotiated between them; and the Court so finds.

GP would not have been at a significant competitive disadvantage in marketing striated plywood because (1) GP's striated plywood was exactly the same product as Weldtex for which USP had developed the market; (2) GP had contacts with all of USP's customers; and (3) GP's striated plywood would have been welcomed by the trade as an additional source of supply that would make the market competitive.

GP was willing to assume substantial risks and costs in order to make and sell striated fir plywood without authority from USP. The Court finds that GP would have been willing to pay a substantial royalty to USP in order to obtain reasonably anticipated large profits without the risk of infringement liability.

The Court has considered the evidence in order to quantify the amount of profits that GP would reasonably have expected, at the time of the hypothetical negotiations, to earn on its production and sale of striated fir plywood. This is a different question from the amount of infringing profits that GP actually did make—$685,837, according to the special master.

GP took, as its own guide for the purpose of profit expectations, the profit that USP was then making on its Weldtex sales. The evidence supports the inference that GP was able to estimate, fairly accurately, the amount of USP's costs on Weldtex; and that GP knew that its own costs would not be significantly higher.

It is undisputed that GP was also well aware of both the warehouse and the direct mill prices of Weldtex. GP would have expected to sell its own striated fir plywood at the same prices (as, in fact, it did).

In any event, since the Court has found that USP's average rate of profit on its Weldtex sales was $48.64 per thousand square feet at the time of the infringement, the Court also finds that GP would reasonably have expected to earn on its manufacture and sale of striated fir plywood profits at least approximately the same rate.... Moreover, this figure of $48.64 per thousand square feet must be amplified by virtue of the collateral sales factor insofar as that factor would have reasonably entered into GP's thinking at the time of the hypothetical royalty negotiations.

THE AMOUNT OF THE REASONABLE ROYALTY.

b) The significance of the decorative appearance of Weldtex and GP striated in relation to the question of the amount of a reasonable royalty.

Of course, Weldtex had a pleasing appearance and decorative effect. The Court of Appeals, in alluding to "the decorative appearance of Weldtex" as having "contributed toward this (Weldtex's) commercial success", observed that "this commercial success may in considerable measure be due to the decorative appeal of Weldtex and the effectiveness of the striation in masking joints and checks." It is necessary to determine the relationship of these facts to the issue of reasonable royalty.

The decorative appearance or "decorative effect" of Weldtex was not per se a patented element of the Deskey invention. Upon that circumstance as a foundation fact, GP erects the argument that whatever value of Weldtex may be attributable to its decorative appearance must be disregarded in determining the amount of a reasonable royalty for the use of the Deskey patent because "decorative appearance" is a feature beyond the scope of that patent.

The face of GP's infringing striated fir plywood was, from the viewpoint of deep striations and appearance, structurally and esthetically a replica of USP's Weldtex. This was the inevitable result of the infringement because the decorative effect or appearance of Weldtex and GP striated is an inherent, indivisible, and inextricable characteristic of Deskey's deep and random striations.

The Court has considered the evidence stressed by GP, that many purchasers of striated fir plywood were motivated to buy it only by its decorative appearance. This evidence does not tend to diminish or deflate the amount of a reasonable royalty in any significant fashion. Without the Deskey patent, GP could not lawfully have sold one square inch striated fir plywood. The Deskey patent created a new article, something that GP had never been able to sell before. GP was seeking the substantial profits it could obtain from the sale of striated fir plywood and of collateral products. To obtain any of those profits legitimately, GP would have had to have a license under the Deskey patent. The fact—as we now know it in retrospect, according to the evidence of the motives of the purchasers of striated fir plywood—that the buyers of that product were attracted to it by its decorative appearance is irrelevant to the hypothetical negotiations of a reasonable royalty where GP's expectations of profits could be lawfully fulfilled only by a license of the Deskey patent and where the rate of profit could be estimated by both USP and GP on the basis of a long and recognized record of past performance. In this setting of the relative bargaining positions of the parties and the economic realities of this particular situation, the Court rejects GP's argument based on the decorative appearance of striated fir plywood.

c) Absence of a prevailing royalty or royalties in generally comparable circumstances.

GP claims that the amount of a reasonable royalty is strongly evidenced by the proofs concerning (1) the financial arrangements between USP and Deskey; (2) the royalties payable under the five licenses granted by USP to its contract or "captive" mills; (3) the royalties payable under the three licenses granted by USP outside the United States; (4) eight or more miscellaneous other licenses cited by GP; and (5) the opinion testimony of GP's experts.

Accepting GP's proofs as possessing sufficient probative value to render them admissible, the Court finds that evidence does not significantly tend to indicate the amount of a reasonable royalty in the present situation. In each instance, the royalty or other payment cited by GP was made under circumstances that are sharply and fundamentally different from the congeries of controlling facts presently before the Court.

USP's original agreement with Deskey was made in 1940. The royalty originally provided for was 5 per cent of the mill price. At that time no patent had been issued. As assignee of the patent application, USP prosecuted the application, paying all the expenses involved, and actually obtaining the patent. At the time the agreement was made with Deskey "it was a gamble"; no one knew whether striated fir plywood "would sell or not sell" or whether the patent would be obtained.

The circumstances and arrangements between Deskey, the inventor, and USP, the promoter, were basically different from those that would be applicable to the negotiation of a reasonable royalty between two keen competitors like USP and GP in February 1955, when striated fir plywood was already a firmly-established and widely-recognized success.

In February 1955, Weldtex was at the height of its "amazing success". Its sales since 1951 totaled more than $23 million and averaged almost $6 million per year. USP "paid out to Deskey in the period 1940–1956 over $533,000 in royalties." "The large profits to be made as a result of the strong commercial appeal of a product like Weldtex were well recognized." Cornelius Reckers, GP's laboratory chief, testified that GP began the manufacture of striated plywood because it was "extremely advantageous from a profit standpoint." GP's attorney described Weldtex as "extremely successful."

The preponderant weight of the credible evidence demonstrates convincingly that the commercial circumstances and economic relationships prevailing between Deskey and USP in 1939 or 1940 and in 1946 have no significant probative bearing upon the issue of a reasonable royalty as between USP and GP.

(2) The royalties payable under the five licenses granted by USP to its contract or "captive" mills.

In the years 1946 and 1950, USP granted licenses—providing for the payment of a royalty to it of $2.00 per thousand square feet—to five "captive" mills.

These licenses were limited to the right of the "captive" mills to manufacture Weldtex for sale only to USP, in effect, to manufacture for USP's account. It was USP that made the substantial profits (of about $54.25 per thousand square feet) by selling the Weldtex that the "captive" mills produced for it. There is, therefore, a world of difference between a restricted license to a non-competitive "captive" mill to manufacture (and only to manufacture) exclusively for USP and, on the other hand, an unrestricted license that would have enabled GP to manufacture and sell for its own account in competition with USP in the very same markets.

Manifestly, the royalty prescribed by USP for its captive mills has hardly any relevance to the issue of the amount of a reasonable royalty to be negotiated by USP and GP nor does it afford any indication of what the Deskey patent was worth to USP.

(3) The royalties payable under the three licenses granted by USP outside the United States.

The three foreign licenses were: a license on November 26, 1946 by USP to Canadian Forest Products, Ltd. and providing for a royalty of $3.00 per one thousand square feet of Weldtex; a license on December 23, 1947 by USP to Proofwood, Ltd., in Australia, and providing for a royalty of $3.00 per one thousand square feet of Weldtex; and a license on August 22, 1947 by USP to Fletcher Holdings, Ltd., in New Zealand, and providing for a royalty of $3.00 per one thousand square feet of Weldtex.

The significance of these royalties is largely neutralized by the credible evidence that these licenses were granted by USP outside the United States, in areas where USP itself had no established sales facilities. As to the Australian and New Zealand licenses, USP had no idea what kind of a market could be established there for Weldtex, which was a new product in those remote countries; and, therefore, USP fixed a minimum royalty. USP's purpose in granting the licenses was not so much to obtain royalty income as to establish relationships with the licensees.

Because there is no sound basis for a meaningful comparison, the amounts of the royalties payable under the foreign licenses do not carry any significant weight with respect to the issue of a reasonable royalty between USP and GP.

5) The opinion testimony of GP's experts.

GP also relies upon the opinion testimony of four experts as to the amount of royalty which they thought "would be fair to both of the parties."

Mr. Heilpern testified that the range of royalties that USP would have considered accepting in negotiating the hypothetical royalty was between $50.00 and $54.00 per thousand square feet of striated fir plywood manufactured and sold by GP, with $50.00 representing "the cheapest rate we (USP) would have consented to" and that, in his judgment, GP would have been willing to pay at least that minimum rate. Mr. Antoville's testimony is that USP "would have asked for $55.00 to $65.00 per thousand."

In their opinion, they regarded those figures as representing a reasonable royalty that should be awarded by this Court for GP's infringement. It is USP's submission "that the minimum amount of the reasonable royalty to be awarded by the Court should be $50 per thousand square feet of the infringing product made and sold by GP."

The Court accepts the substance of the Heilpern–Antoville testimony (and finds as facts) that a royalty of $50.00 per thousand square feet payable by GP to USP would have enabled GP to realize a reasonable profit; that GP's average realization on all its striated fir plywood sales throughout the infringement period was $159.41 per one thousand square feet; that, after paying $50.00 per one thousand square feet to USP, the remainder of about $109.41 would enable GP to make a substantial profit; and that, in addition, GP would have the benefit of profits on collateral sales, though that amount cannot be quantified.

CONCLUSION

The Court finds and concludes that $50.00 per thousand square feet of the patented product, striated fir plywood, made and sold by GP, represents a fair reasonable royalty that should be paid by GP. This amounts to $800,000, which is hereby awarded to USP, together with interest on the said award computed from the date of the last infringement, September 1, 1958, to the date of payment of the award, at the rate of 6 per cent per annum.

Notes

1. Does the infringer have to be left with a profit for the royalty to be reasonable? The District Court in *Georgia-Pacific* seemed to think so. Do you agree?

2. Should the fact finder consider offers to license made by the patentee during settlement negotiations in settling a reasonable royalty? *See*

Hanson v. Alpine Valley Ski Area, Inc., 718 F.2d 1075, 219 USPQ 679 (Fed. Cir. 1983)

3. **Licensing rates to others.** The rates that the patent owner has licensed others can be persuasive evidence on what the reasonable royalty rate should be. However, the patent owner likely will be seeking a higher royalty rate in litigation. The patent owner should argue that the royalty rate which it receives from one or more licensees should not apply to this infringer because they are differently situated. For example, if the licensee is selling a higher volume of the patented product, the patent owner can argue that it is entitled to a lower royalty rate than the infringer.

4. **Panduit Kicker.** A reasonable royalty only awards the patent owner the royalty rate it would have received before the litigation; what about the costs of the lawsuit the patent owner had to bring to obtain its royalty? Should these litigation expenses be factored into a reasonable royalty? In the next case, *Mahurkar v. C.R. Bard, Inc.*, 79 F.3d 1572, 1580–81, 38 USPQ2d 1288, 1293–94 (Fed. Cir. 1996), the Court considered this very question.

MAHURKAR v. C.R. BARD, INC.

79 F.3d 1572, 38 USPQ2d 1288 (Fed. Cir. 1996)

Before ARCHER, Chief Judge, MICHEL, and RADER, Circuit Judges.

RADER, Circuit Judge.

The trial court fixed the total reasonable royalty rate at 34.88%. This total rate comprises a 25.88% rate with a 9% "kicker." When engaging in its judicially-sanctioned speculation as to the results of a hypothetical negotiation, the trial court appears to have considered evidence of Bard's actual net profit, the profit margin Bard would have been able to negotiate, and Bard's research and development savings. The court specifically found Bard was entitled to a 10% profit margin. It also determined that Bard realized a net profit of 29.16% on its sales of the Hickman catheters and saved 6.72% in research and development costs.

The trial court then calculated an initial royalty rate of 25.88%.[1] The district court apparently arrived at this figure by subtracting the 10% profit factor from the actual net profit of 29.16% and adding the savings of 6.72% in research and development. This award falls within the boundaries of reasonableness, and thus the trial court did not clearly err in calculating this much of the award.

To this reasonable royalty, however, the trial court added an additional 9%. It labeled this addition a "*Panduit* kicker," citing *Panduit*

---

1. Bard contends that the district court's royalty award did not leave Bard with adequate profit. However, courts have employed methodologies in calculating reasonable royalties in which the royalties exceed the infringer's profit. *See, e.g., Radio Steel & Mfg. Co. v. MTD Prods., Inc.*, 788 F.2d 1554, 1557, 229 USPQ 431, 433 (Fed. Cir. 1986).

Corp. v. Stahlin Bros. Fibre Works, Inc., 575 F.2d 1152, 197 USPQ 726 (6th Cir. 1978). The district court reasoned:

> Bard's cost for research and development were nonexistent. That then leads to the question of the *Panduit* kicker.... [T]he fact remains that the *Panduit* kicker and the reasons given ... for the *Panduit* kicker apply to this case. There is even less guidance for setting a *Panduit* kicker than there is for setting a reasonable royalty. But I have looked closely at the figures, and I believe that a *Panduit* kicker in this case of 9 percent is appropriate. So I, therefore, set the royalty rate at 34.88 percent....

With this reasoning and its 9% addition, however, the trial court abused its discretion.

In *Panduit,* the Sixth Circuit held that a patentee could recover damages if the patentee proved: (1) a demand for the patented product; (2) the absence of acceptable, noninfringing substitutes; (3) the patentee's capacity to exploit the demand; and (4) the profits lost due to infringement. This four-step test is "an acceptable, though not an exclusive" test for determining "but for" causation for lost profits. In other words, *Panduit* supplied one method of proving damages. *Panduit* is not the exclusive test for proving damages.

Although one method for proving damages, the *Panduit* methodology does not include a "kicker" to account for litigation expenses or for any other expenses. In *Panduit,* the Sixth Circuit noted that the patentee had incurred more than $400,000 in litigation expenses battling with the infringer for over thirteen years. Suggesting that the damages awarded by the trial court seemed unfair in light of the extensive litigation, the court observed that:

> The setting of a reasonable royalty after infringement cannot be treated, as it was here, as the equivalent of ordinary royalty negotiations among truly "willing" patent owners and licensees. That view would constitute a pretense that the infringement never happened. It would also make an election to infringe a handy means for competitors to impose a "compulsory license" policy upon every patent owner.

Panduit, 575 F.2d at 1158. However, the *Panduit* court specifically stated that it "express[es] no view respecting the applicability of rules governing willful infringement, treble damages, or attorneys' fees, none of which have been made of issue here."

In this case, the district court invoked *Panduit* out of context. This case did not feature a lost profits award at all, but instead reasonable royalties. To apply the *Panduit* test, the trial court would have needed to ascertain whether Bard's and Mahurkar's products competed for the same customers, whether the market included acceptable noninfringing substitutes, and whether Dr. Mahurkar had the capacity to exploit the demand. Without such evidence in this record, the trial court invoked *Panduit* out of context.

More important, *Panduit* does not authorize additional damages or a "kicker" on top of a reasonable royalty because of heavy litigation or other expenses. In sections 284 and 285, the Patent Act sets forth statutory requirements for awards of enhanced damages and attorney fees. The statute bases these awards on clear and convincing proof of willfulness and exceptionality. *Panduit* at no point suggested enhancement of a compensatory damage award as a substitute for the strict requirements for these statutory provisions. The district court's "kicker," on the other hand, enhances a damages award, apparently to compensate for litigation expenses, without meeting the statutory standards for enhancement and fees. Therefore, the district court abused its discretion in awarding a 9% "*Panduit* kicker."

MINCO, INC. v. COMBUSTION ENGINEERING, INC.

95 F.3d 1109, 40 USPQ2d 1001 (Fed. Cir. 1996)

Before RADER, Circuit Judge, COWEN, Senior Circuit Judge, and SCHALL, Circuit Judge.

PER CURIAM.

In this patent infringement case, Combustion Engineering, Inc. (CE) appeals and Minco, Inc. cross-appeals a final decision of the United States District Court for the Eastern District of Tennessee. The patent at issue, 4,217,462 (the '462 patent), claims a rotary furnace for fusing minerals. The district court found CE willfully infringed claims 3 and 4 of the '462 patent. The court awarded damages of $3,455,329 and a reasonable royalty of $7,408,179.40. Because the infringement was willful, the court doubled the damages for an overall award of $21,727,-016.80 plus attorneys fees and pre-judgment interest. Because the record supports the district court's findings and conclusions, this court affirms.

Background

As one way to fuse silica, an operator first puts high purity sand into a barrel-shaped, rotary furnace. External drive wheels then rotate the furnace to throw the sand against the furnace walls. Graphite electrodes then enter the furnace through openings at either end. These rods create a high energy arc which heats and fuses the silica. Finally, the operator dumps the ingot of fused silica out of the furnace. Once crushed, the fused silica has many applications, particularly in semiconductor technology.

CE and its predecessor produced fused silica and fused magnesia. During 1976–1977, CE used a rotary "jumbo kiln" to fuse these minerals. In July 1977, CE released Ken Jenkins, who then began experimenting in his barn to solve problems in fusion furnaces, such as CE's jumbo kiln. With input from another former CE employee, William Rawles, Jenkins developed the claimed furnace. This new furnace more efficiently produced a better quality of fused silica than CE's jumbo kiln.

In September 1977, Jenkins and his sister Verneil Richards formed Minco, Inc. to produce fused silica. Ultimately, they used their new rotary furnace in that endeavor. Fused silica from their invention enjoyed substantial commercial success. The new furnace produced fused silica with less discoloration and lower iron contamination than CE's product. Many purchasers found these qualities commercially attractive. Minco's net sales increased annually from 1979 through 1985.

In May 1978, Jenkins and Rawles filed a patent application claiming, in claims 1 and 2, their rotary furnace. In April 1979, they filed a continuation-in-part application adding claims 3 and 4. These added claims covered a rotary furnace in combination with crane supports for lifting and tilting the furnace housing. In August 1980, the '462 patent issued.

Minco's early success cut into CE's market. In 1985, for instance, CE's sales dropped approximately 20%. In response, CE tried to develop a comparable furnace but failed. In December 1983, CE obtained a copy of the '462 patent. Later CE hired an outside consultant, Nick Valk, to design a kiln capable of matching Minco's high quality silica. In an initial meeting with Valk, CE showed him a drawing similar to one in the '462 patent. With Valk's assistance, CE developed the accused RT kiln. In February of 1986, CE began to manufacture fused silica in its RT kiln. With fused silica from the RT kiln, CE's sales volume increased annually.

DISCUSSION

Damages

CE appeals the trial court's damages award and finding of willful infringement. Minco, in turn, appeals that court's refusal to award lost profits for price erosion in the fused silica market and for compensatory damages for CE's sale of its business, including the infringing RT kilns.

The Patent Act provides for "damages adequate to compensate for the infringement but in no event less than a reasonable royalty for the use made of the invention by the infringer." 35 U.S.C. § 284 (1994). This court has clarified that adequate damages can include lost profits due to diverted sales, price erosion, and increased expenditures caused by infringement. Because fashioning an adequate damages award depends on the unique economic circumstances of each case, the trial court has discretion to make important subsidiary determinations in the damages trial, such as choosing a methodology to calculate damages.

To recover lost profits, however, the patent holder must show that the infringer actually caused the economic harm for which the patentee seeks compensation. In the context of lost profits, causation requires evidence of "a reasonable probability that [the patent holder] would have made the asserted profits absent infringement." This court reviews a trial court's finding of causation for clear error.

In addition to causation, the patent holder bears the burden of proving the amount of the award. Quantum is an issue of fact, which this court reviews for clear error. Once a patentee shows causation, however, the trial court may resolve doubts underlying the precise measurement of damages against the infringer. Nevertheless, the burden remains on the patentee to prove the amount by a preponderance of the evidence.

In awarding both lost profits and a reasonable royalty, the trial court used the sale of fused silica as the baseline for measuring damages. The assessment of adequate damages under section 284 does not limit the patent holder to the amount of diverted sales of a commercial embodiment of the patented product. Rather, the patent holder may recover for an injury caused by the infringement if it "was or should have been reasonably foreseeable by an infringing competitor in the relevant market, broadly defined." In this case, the invention produced marketable fused minerals. Both CE and Minco used the invention to compete in that market. Therefore, CE should have reasonably foreseen that infringement of the '462 patent would harm Minco's sales in the fused silica market. This court accordingly upholds the trial court's determination to use that measure of damages.

Lost Profits

The district court found that Minco showed entitlement to lost profits on diverted sales of fused silica. In determining quantum, that court found that CE's infringement caused Minco to lose the sales of 26,201,956 pounds of fused silica, over the period from May 1988 through July 1990. These lost sales amounted to $3,455,329 in lost profits.

CE challenges these findings by asserting that the market featured non-infringing alternatives to the '462 patent. A non-infringing alternative in the fused silica market would make it less likely that the patentee would have made the sales to CE's customers without the infringement. The district court, however, found that Minco's fused silica product from the '462 patent was in significant demand. The record shows a preference for Minco's quality, fused silica in the market. Indeed, the record shows that two other primary fused silica manufacturers had bowed out of the market "in deference" to the '462 patent. Before use of the infringing RT kiln, the record shows that the market considered CE a source of "last resort." Thus, the record amply supports the district court's finding that Minco had a reasonable probability of making these sales but for the infringement.

CE's damages expert testified that CE could easily have designed around the patent by employing a cradle apparatus that could tip the furnace after a clamp removed the detachable end. However, testimony that an infringer might have been able to design around a patent does not, in itself, defeat a claim for lost profits. In spite of CE's litigation protestations, evidence showed it chose to copy the Minco kiln rather than pursue one of the plentiful, hypothetical, post hoc, non-infringing alternatives. In this case, CE's expert based his opinion on the testimony of a CE witness who testified that CE knew that cradle support systems could substitute for the crane supports. The record, however, does not show the marketplace use of this purported substitute either by CE or any other fused silica manufacturer.

Based on the record in its entirety, the trial court did not err in concluding that absent the infringement, CE would not have been able to compete effectively against Minco. The record also supports the district court's finding that Minco would have been able to make the additional sales of 26,201,956 pounds of fused silica during the 1987–1990 period. With these findings in place, the trial court properly awarded lost profits.

Reasonable Royalty

The Patent Act permits damages awards to encompass both lost profits and a reasonable royalty on that portion of an infringer's sales not included in the lost profit calculation. A segment of the infringer's sales may not warrant a lost profits award because the patentee cannot establish causation for that segment. For instance, a patent owner may not operate in the specific geographical area covered by the infringer or may not have had the manufacturing or marketing capacity to make the infringer's sales. However, the patentee would still be entitled to a reasonable royalty on each of those sales.

In this case, the district court awarded a reasonable royalty on CE sales beyond 95% of Minco's manufacturing capacity from May 1988 through July 1990. Minco also received a reasonable royalty on CE sales from 1986 through April 1988, during which CE produced a blended fused silica. In total, the district court awarded a reasonable royalty on approximately 122,329,000 pounds of fused silica.

A district court may calculate a reasonable royalty by postulating a hypothetical negotiation between a willing licensor and licensee at the time infringement commenced. This hypothetical construct seeks the percentage of sales or profit likely to have induced the hypothetical negotiators to license use of the invention. In this case, the district court awarded Minco a royalty rate of 20% on the gross value of CE's applicable sales. The district court based this relatively high royalty on a number of findings. First, Minco and CE competed head-to-head. Second, at the time of infringement, CE had an inferior product. Third, the market contained no non-infringing alternatives. Fourth, CE itself regarded the invention as a significant advance. Fifth, the industry enjoyed high rates of profit. The trial court found that CE realized an earnings before interest and taxes rate of 22.4% of sales under the jumbo kiln technology. Sixth, CE's earnings before taxes increased substantially after its use of the accused furnaces.

In addition to the court's other findings, because the industry enjoyed high profitability and the invention produced higher quality fused silica, this court detects no clear error in the district court's royalty award. The economic evidence on this point supports the finding that these hypothetical negotiators might have entered a license calculated at 20% of sales.

Price Erosion Damages

Minco sought and the trial court denied further lost profits based on the decrease in the price of fused silica. To prove price erosion damages, a patentee must show that, but for the infringement, it would have been able to charge higher prices.

The record discloses price fluctuations in the fused silica market. For instance, Minco's average price for fused silica in 1988 was $0.269 per pound, an increase from $0.2530 in 1987. However, the price of fused silica decreased in 1989 to $0.255 and to $0.220 in 1990. CE converted to infringing kilns in November 1987. By April 1988, CE sold only fused silica from the RT kilns. Nevertheless, Minco's average selling price increased in 1988. This evidence permits the inference that market forces other than infringement influenced the price of fused silica. Furthermore, the record suggests that Minco was the market leader in cutting prices. Although the trial court might have found that Minco cut prices in response to CE's infringement, the record allows other inferences as well. Moreover, the record lacks probative economic evidence that consumers would have tolerated higher prices in 1989 and 1990. Thus, the record supports the district court's finding that price erosion damages were too speculative.

Minnesota Mining & Mfg. Co. v. Johnson & Johnson Orthopaedics, Inc., 976 F.2d 1559, 24 USPQ2d 1321 (Fed. Cir. 1992), does not compel a different result. In *Minnesota Mining*, the fact finder determined that the patentee could have increased prices 2% per annum without infringement. With that record and that finding, this court affirmed price erosion damages. *Minnesota Mining*, however, does not compel price erosion damages whenever prices decrease in a market consisting primarily of the patent holder and the infringer.

In sum, the district court weighed the record evidence on the economic factors influencing price and determined that infringement did not cause those price decreases which occurred during the infringement period. This court detects no clear error in that finding.

Lost Profits on CE's Sale of its Business

Finally, Minco challenges the district court's denial of compensatory damages for CE's sale of its fused silica business to Imetal, a French corporation, on July 31, 1990. Minco seeks as damages the difference between the sales price of CE's business and its expert's valuation of CE's business without the infringing kilns. On this theory, Minco seeks an additional $34,634,527. Alternatively, Minco claims some damages on the sale to Imetal. The district court denied any recovery "based upon the lack of evidence in this case to support this element of damages."

Minco's theory values the sale of the infringing kilns, only a portion of CE's assets, at approximately $34 million. According to Minco, had CE not infringed its patent, Imetal would have purchased Minco instead. While in theory Minco might have been entitled to some recovery from CE's sale of its business because it included the infringing kilns, the district court specifically determined that Minco did not show that the infringing kilns were an important factor in the sale. Indeed, upon acquiring CE's business, Imetal switched to its own patented furnace in December 1991. This switch undermines Minco's claim that the kilns drove the sale. The record contains no probative evidence of Imetal's business motivations or the industry context. For example, Imetal might have paid a large premium for entry into the market or for CE's trademark. Thus, Minco did not prove Imetal would have purchased it absent CE's infringement.

Furthermore, assuming that CE profited through its sale from the goodwill built up through the use of the infringing kilns, Minco did not show entitlement to compensation beyond its proofs of lost profits and reasonable royalties. The district court's reasonable royalty award already compensates Minco for any goodwill CE garnered by infringement. The district court awarded Minco a generous royalty rate precisely because Minco and CE were head-to-head competitors. The district court reasoned that "CE's desire to maintain its market share would compel [it] to accept [a high royalty]." Thus, the district court already acknowledged in its retroactive, hypothetical license that CE was paying in part for the goodwill acquired by infringement.

The danger that an award stemming from the sale of CE would constitute a double recovery is apparent from an examination of the evidence relied on by Minco's expert. In proffering his assessment of CE's enhanced value, Minco's expert relied on the increase in CE's gross profit percentage during infringement. However, the district court had already factored the invention's ability to increase profits into its reasonable royalty calculation. Minco's theory for recovery based on the sale of CE, presented at trial, ignored the goodwill that would have naturally inhered from CE's licensing of the patent for the majority of its sales.

Viewed another way, the trial court determined that, under a hypothetical royalty negotiation in 1986, CE might have paid a high royalty to Minco for its use of the kilns in exchange for Minco's agreement to receive no additional royalty should CE sell its business. Of course, Minco could sue any purchaser who used the infringing kilns. This view of the negotiations corresponds with the evidence and the theories forwarded by Minco.

Accordingly, this court detects no clear error in the trial court's finding that Minco did not show a basis for additional damages from CE's sale of its business. Minco has the burden of proving the amount, if any, of its entitlement. Minco did not carry that burden.

Notes

1. If given a chance, and if able to satisfy the burden of proof, a patent holder would always prefer receiving lost profits over reasonable royalties. Reasonable royalties represent the "floor" amount that will compensate the patent holder for the infringement.

2. For an attempt by the Federal Circuit in defining a "reasonable royalty equation," (reasonable royalty equals gross profit minus overhead minus standard industry profit). *See TWM Mfg., Co. v. Dura Corp.*, 789 F.2d 895, 229 USPQ 525 (Fed. Cir. 1986) (reasonable royalty of 30% is calculated by taking the infringer's anticipated profits (52.7%) minus overhead expenses (10.7–15.7%) minus industry standard profit (6.56–12.5%)).

3. *See Hanson v. Alpine Valley Ski Area, Inc.*, 718 F.2d 1075, 219 USPQ 679 (Fed. Cir. 1983), for a discussion of reasonable royalties based on the estimated cost savings between an infringing product and its noninfringing (but less efficient) counterpart.

C. ENHANCED DAMAGE AWARDS

1. WILLFUL INFRINGEMENT

STATUTORY PROVISION—*35 U.S.C. § 284:*

When the damages are not found by a jury, the court shall assess them. In either event the court may increase the damages up to three times the amount found or assessed.

The primary consideration in determining whether the infringer willfully infringed is whether the infringer acted in *good faith* once she had actual knowledge of the patent and whether she determined after a sound inquiry that she had a reasonable basis to believe that her actions did not infringe a valid, enforceable patent. Once an infringer has actual notice of a patent, she has an affirmative duty to avoid infringement. Typically, an infringer will assert that she reasonably relied upon advice of counsel. Such a defense waives the attorney-client privilege with respect to the advice.

In a trial on willfullness, the parties usually provide expert testimony on the competency of the attorney opinion and the reasonableness of the infringer's reliance on the opinion. Accused infringers will often want to bifurcate the willfulness issue from the liability phase of the trial to avoid allowing the patentee to poison the jury against the defendant with evidence that the acts were taken "willfully." The patentee should generally move to compel production of documents related to any defenses the infringer intends to bring with respect to willful infringement. The patentee will want to know early in the discovery process whether the accused infringer intends to use an advice of counsel defense to ensure adequate time for investigation of the facts surrounding the opinion.

a. *Willful Infringement Factors*

READ CORP. v. PORTEC, INC.

970 F.2d 816, 23 USPQ2d 1426 (Fed. Cir. 1992)

Before NIES, Chief Judge, ARCHER, and MICHEL, Circuit Judges.

NIES, Chief Judge.

Portec, Inc., appeals from the May 25, 1990, final judgment, entered upon a jury verdict, of the United States District Court for the District of Delaware, holding Portec liable for infringement of U.S. Patent No. 4,197,194 (the '194 patent) and U.S. Design Patent No. 263,836 (the '836 patent), and awarding The Read Corporation and F.T. Read & Sons, Inc. (collectively Read) treble damages and attorney fees. We affirm the judgment with respect to liability for infringement of the '194 patent, reverse the judgment with respect to liability for infringement of the '836 patent and the enhancement of damages, vacate the award with respect to attorney fees, and remand for modification of the injunction and reconsideration of the award of Read's attorney fees in light of this opinion.

D. ENHANCED DAMAGES

Under section 284 of Title 35, damages may be enhanced up to three times the compensatory award. An award of enhanced damages for infringement, as well as the extent of the enhancement, is committed to the discretion of the trial court. While no statutory standard dictates the circumstances under which the district court may exercise its discretion, this court has approved such awards where the infringer acted in wanton disregard of the patentee's patent rights, that is, where the infringement is willful. On the other hand, a finding of willful infringement does not mandate that damages be enhanced, much less mandate treble damages.

The paramount determination in deciding to grant enhancement and the amount thereof is the egregiousness of the defendant's conduct based on all the facts and circumstances. The court must consider factors that render defendant's conduct more culpable, as well as factors that are mitigating or ameliorating. *Compare IVAC Corp. v. Terumo Corp.*, 18 USPQ2d 1637, 1639–40, 1990 WL 180202 (S.D. Cal. 1990) (Treble damages are appropriate when it is clear that defendant showed no good faith at the time infringement commenced, made no effort to follow the advice of patent counsel or alter the infringing device, and showed bad faith in litigation.); *with Datascope Corp. v. SMEC, Inc.*, 14 USPQ2d 1071, 1074 (D.N.J. 1990) ("A fifty-percent enhancement of damages is appropriate here. Although SMEC's infringement was willful, it was not blatant."); *and Chisum v. Brewco Sales & Mfg.*, 726 F. Supp. 1499, 13 USPQ2d 1657, 1668 (W.D. Ky. 1989) ("The lost profits will however be doubled rather than tripled, since we find that Brewer's actions were willful, but not so egregious as to warrant trebling of the damages."). In *Bott v. Four Star Corp.*, 807 F.2d 1567, 1572, 1 USPQ2d 1210, 1213 (Fed. Cir. 1986), three factors were identified for consideration in determining when an infringer "acted in [such] bad faith as to merit an increase in damages awarded against him":

(1) whether the infringer deliberately copied the ideas or design of another;

(2) whether the infringer, when he knew of the other's patent protection, investigated the scope of the patent and formed a good-faith belief that it was invalid or that it was not infringed; and

(3) the infringer's behavior as a party to the litigation.

The Bott factors are not all inclusive. In addition, other circumstances which courts appropriately have considered, particularly in deciding on the extent of enhancement, are:

(4) Defendant's size and financial condition. *St. Regis Paper Co. v. Winchester Carton Corp.*, 410 F. Supp. 1304, 1309, 189 USPQ 514, 518 (D. Mass. 1976) ("[D]ouble damages [appropriate]. If defendant were the giant and plaintiff the small independent, I would make it treble....").

(5) Closeness of the case. *Modine Mfg. Co. v. The Allen Group*, 917 F.2d at 543, 16 USPQ2d at 1626 (No abuse of discretion to award no enhanced damages on the ground that willfulness was "sufficiently close on the evidence."); *Crucible, Inc. v. Stora Kopparbergs Bergslags AB*, 701 F. Supp. 1157, 1164, 10 USPQ2d 1190, 1196 (W.D. Pa. 1988) ("[B]ecause the court still considers the [willfulness] question to be a close one ... double, and not treble damages are appropriate.").

(6) Duration of defendant's misconduct. *Bott v. Four Star Corp.*, 229 USPQ 241, 255 (E.D. Mich. 1985) (For sales prior to the appellate court's affirmance of the liability judgment, damages increased by 20%; for sales after the affirmance, damages doubled.), vacated and remanded for clarification of damage amount, 807 F.2d 1567, 1 USPQ2d 1210 (Fed. Cir. 1986).

(7) Remedial action by the defendant. *Intra Corp. v. Hamar Laser Instruments, Inc.*, 662 F. Supp. 1420, 1439, 4 USPQ2d 1337, 1351 (E.D. Mich. 1987) (Damages only doubled because defendant "voluntarily ceased manufacture and sale of infringing systems during the pendency of this litigation...."), aff'd without opinion, 862 F.2d 320 (Fed. Cir. 1988).

(8) Defendant's motivation for harm. *American Safety Table Co. v. Schreiber*, 415 F.2d 373, 379, 163 USPQ 129, 133 (2d Cir. 1969) ("[D]efendants' infringing acts, although deliberate and with knowledge of plaintiff's rights, could not be termed pernicious due to prevailing 'economic pressure in the form of customer dissatisfaction.'").

(9) Whether defendant attempted to conceal its misconduct. *Russell Box Co. v. Grant Paper Box Co.*, 203 F.2d 177, 183, 97 USPQ 19, 23 (1st Cir. 1953) (Enhanced damages supported in part by findings "that the defendant had failed to preserve its records

and had failed to cooperate as it should at the trial on the issue of damages.'').

Inasmuch as a finding of willful infringement does not mandate enhancement of damages, the above factors taken together assist the trial court in evaluating the degree of the infringer's culpability and in determining whether to exercise its discretion to award enhanced damages and how much the damages should be increased. To enable appellate review, a district court is obligated to explain the basis for the award, particularly where the maximum amount is imposed. For the latter, the court's assessment of the level of culpability must be high.

In its award of enhanced damages, the district court here relied on Portec's "copying," the willful nature of Portec's infringement, and Portec's "manipulative" litigation strategy, which the court said was "reflective of the dubiousness of Portec's assertions that it produced its devices with a good faith belief in the innocence of its action."

Throughout its brief to this court, Read stresses Portec's "copying" of the Read Screen–All as evidence of willful and wanton infringement. The district court also characterized Portec's activity as "copying," and criticized Portec heavily for doing so. Such a characterization is unwarranted. Certainly the Read Screen–All served as the starting point for Portec's design efforts. And certainly the purpose of Portec's efforts was to make a device which would compete with the Read Screen–All. However, the undisputed evidence of record shows that Portec made specific changes deemed adequate by counsel to avoid infringement of both of Read's patents. We have often noted that one of the benefits of the patent system is the incentive it provides for "designing around" patented inventions, thus creating new innovations.

Of course, determining when a patented device has been "designed around" enough to avoid infringement is a difficult determination to make. One cannot know for certain that changes are sufficient to avoid infringement until a judge or a jury has made that determination. In the present case, the jury found that the changes made by Portec were not sufficient to avoid infringement of either patent, and we have herein reversed the judgment respecting infringement of the '836 patent and affirmed the judgment respecting infringement of the '194 patent. Portec is thus liable for damages caused by its miscalculation respecting infringement of the '194 patent. The question which must first be answered here with respect to enhanced damages is whether Portec proceeded without a reasonable belief that it would not be held liable for infringement.

Willfulness is a determination as to a state of mind. One who has actual notice of another's patent rights has an affirmative duty to respect those rights. That affirmative duty normally entails obtaining advice of legal counsel although the absence of such advice does not mandate a finding of willfulness. Those cases where willful infringement is found despite the presence of an opinion of counsel generally involve situations where opinion of counsel was either ignored or found to be incompetent. This precedent does not mean a client must itself be able to evaluate the legal competence of its attorney's advice to avoid a finding of willfulness. The client would not need the attorney's advice at all in that event. That an opinion is "incompetent" must be shown by objective evidence. For example, an attorney may not have looked into the necessary facts, and, thus, there would be no foundation for his opinion. A written opinion may be incompetent on its face by reason of its containing merely conclusory statements without discussion of facts or obviously presenting only a superficial or off-the-cuff analysis.

In the present case, Portec obtained at least two independent written detailed opinions of unrelated patent counsel and engaged in numerous conferences with its lawyers on the matter. The defenses put forth by Portec in this suit track defenses set forth in these opinions and required full trial, which supports their good faith.[9] Despite these facts, the jury found that Portec had willfully infringed both the '194 and the '836 patents. The district court, in its opinion granting Read's motion for treble damages and attorney fees, discussed at length Portec's conduct relating to the willfulness issue. Reviewing the "evidence" which the district court relied on as allegedly showing the willfulness of Portec's conduct, as well as other evidence cited by Read in support of the jury verdict, we can only conclude that the jury's finding of willfulness is not supported by substantial evidence. No reasonable juror could find the asserted proof of willfulness rose to the quantum of clear and convincing evidence.

The district court indicated that Portec failed to heed the advice of its counsel. In support of this contention, the district court cites the January 1985 opinion of Groff as advising Portec that he "doubted" whether a device sufficiently modified to avoid infringement would be "as efficient and commercially appealing." This appears to be a misunderstanding of Groff's opinion. Groff stated unequivocally the patents "could be circumvented," but said it was questionable whether a device modified to avoid infringement would be as efficient or commercially appealing. However, the fact is that at the time Groff rendered his opinion, Portec had not yet begun design of any device, and thus Groff had no idea whether Portec could design a commercially acceptable device that avoided infringement.

The district court criticized the opinion of Valiquet because Valiquet admitted at trial that he performed no specific legal research prior to rendering the opinion. The district court was also of the view that Valiquet's opinion was incompetent because it failed to discuss infringement under the doctrine of equivalents. Further, the district court criticized Portec for not giving Groff's opinion to Valiquet.

---

9. An opinion of counsel, of course, need not unequivocally state that the client will not be held liable for infringement. An honest opinion is more likely to speak of probabilities than certainties. A good test that the advice given is genuine and not merely self-serving is whether the asserted defenses are backed up with viable proof during trial which raises substantial questions, as here.

None of these criticisms are justified. Valiquet was a patent attorney with many years of experience. Failure to perform legal research on the basic concepts of literal infringement, the doctrine of equivalents, and prosecution history estoppel does not per se make the opinion of a lawyer who specializes in patents incompetent.

Moreover, the district court was incorrect when it stated that Valiquet did not consider the doctrine of equivalents. Valiquet's opinion included the following:

> During prosecution before the U.S. patent office, Read was required by the patent office to add the limitation to his claims that the short end extends to the ground. Also, Read voluntarily added to his patent claims the concept of moving the frame so that is could be flush on the ground through use of movable wheels. Since these distinctions were added in view of prior art cited by the Examiner, Read cannot argue that Portec has any type of equivalent structure.

The district court maintained that this portion of Valiquet's opinion was directed solely to the question of literal infringement. We disagree. The substance of this analysis with its reference to "prior art" and "equivalent structure" can only relate to infringement under the doctrine of equivalents.

Further, the failure to give the first lawyer's opinion to Valiquet is a plus, not a minus. Valiquet was not influenced thereby and was able to make his own independent evaluation.

The most important consideration, however, is that nothing in Valiquet's letter would alert a client to reject the letter as an obviously bad opinion. Indeed, his opinion on infringement of the '836 patent was on the mark. More importantly, the opinion was detailed not merely conclusory. On finalization of the drawings, Valiquet reviewed the matters again. Portec sought professional advice on making a competing device which avoided the patent. The monetary exposure of his client required no less from Valiquet than the soundest advice he could offer, not merely to avoid enhanced damages, but all damages. Counsel's opinion, in effect, has been treated inappropriately and unfairly as part of a scheme to avoid enhanced damages only.

In sum, upon review of the record before us, we hold that there is insufficient evidence from which a reasonable jury could find that Portec's infringement was willful. Inasmuch as there is no infringement of the '836 patent, a finding of willful infringement with respect to that patent necessarily drops out of the case. That counsel's opinion turned out to be contrary to our judgment with respect to the '194 patent does not make his advice regarding that patent incompetent. Read cannot point to any substantial evidence which indicates that Portec did not have a good faith belief that it was not infringing, because it had successfully "designed around" the '194 patent. Thus, the factors of willful infringement and copying are not present.

The district court also relied upon instances of what it characterized as Portec's improper litigation strategy which the court stated demonstrated Portec's lack of a good faith belief in its defenses. Absent willful infringement, however, there is no basis in this case for enhanced damages. As indicated, bad faith behavior as a party to the litigation is a factor to be weighed in assessing the level of a defendant's culpability where an infringement is found willful. While dicta suggest that infringement damages may be enhanced solely by reason of misconduct during litigation, such dictum is contrary to our precedent that "[i]f infringement [is] . . . innocent, increased damages are not awardable for the infringement." *Kloster Speedsteel*, 793 F.2d at 1580, 230 USPQ at 91. Thus, applying *Kloster Speedsteel* to this case, we reverse the award of enhanced damages.

E. ATTORNEY FEES

With respect to making its award of attorney fees under 35 U.S.C. § 285, the district court again relied on the willfulness of Portec's infringement to find the case was exceptional. Thus, this award cannot stand. However, litigation misconduct may in itself make a case "exceptional." The district court found misconduct first by reason of Portec's creation, during litigation, of what the district court termed as an "aberrant model" of its device in order to avoid infringement of the '836 design patent. Even had we not reversed the finding of infringement of the '836 patent, this basis for enhancement would be meritless. Although Portec already had an opinion of noninfringement from its counsel on the device in suit, Portec made further design changes in its device in order to make sure that it had a noninfringing device. Such a "litigation strategy" should be encouraged, not viewed as misconduct.

The second example concerned a screening device referred to at trial as the "Hoehn device." Portec introduced evidence of the Hoehn device, in an attempt to show that the claims of the '194 patent were invalid, including two spatially-consecutive photographs showing the Hoehn device. Read discovered that part of the first photograph had been covered by the second photograph so that it could not be seen that the device in the first photograph had no hitch. The missing hitch seriously undermined the testimony which had already been presented by Portec concerning the chronology of the development of the Hoehn device. Portec asked the district court to allow it to present surrebuttal evidence to explain the absence of the hitch, but the district court denied its request, explaining that Portec should have presented this evidence in its case in chief.

We cannot say that the district court abused its discretion in not allowing Portec to present additional evidence to explain away the missing hitch on the Hoehn exhibit in connection with the issue of validity. On the other hand, where the question is improper conduct to support an award of attorney fees, we conclude that the evidence must be considered by the court before finding misconduct and that the finding that this incident constituted improper litigation strategy cannot stand. Accordingly, we remand for a re-determination by the district court whether Portec did engage in litigation misconduct and, if so, whether it was sufficiently culpable as to make the case exceptional. We point out that, when attorney fees under 35 U.S.C. § 285 are awarded solely on the basis of litigation misconduct, the amount of the award must bear some relation to the extent of the misconduct.

Note

1. In cases of willful infringement, 35 U.S.C. § 284 provides that a court may, at its discretion increase the award of damages up to three times the amount found or assessed. Willful conduct (as in other areas of law) is a question of intent and notice. To be considered a "willful" infringer, there must be "evidence that the infringer deliberately disregarded the patent or flagrantly disregarded the patent laws and had no reasonable basis for believing it had the right to act as it did." *Polaroid Corp. v. Eastman Kodak Co.*, 16 USPQ2d 1481, 1535 (D. Mass. 1990) (citing *Stickle v. Heublein, Inc.*, 716 F.2d 1550, 1556, 219 USPQ 377, 381 (Fed. Cir. 1983)). The question of willfulness is fact-sensitive requiring the trial court to evaluate the "totality of the surrounding circumstances." *Graco, Inc. v. Binks Mfg. Co.*, 60 F.3d 785, 792, 35 USPQ2d 1255, 1260 (Fed. Cir. 1995).

b. *Opinion Letters of Counsel and Good Faith*

To determine whether the infringer *reasonably relied* upon an opinion of counsel in making manufacturing choices courts have generally considered three factors:

1. the timing of the opinion;

2. the content of the opinion; and

3. the qualifications of the person writing the opinion.

Courts look at the timing of the opinion. For example, if the infringer obtained the opinion prior to manufacturing a design that might have infringed or immediately upon receiving notice of the patent at issue, this tends to show good faith on the part of the infringer. "Prudent behavior generally requires that competent legal advice was obtained before the commencement of the infringing activity." *SRI Int'l, Inc. v. Advanced Tech. Labs., Inc.*, 127 F.3d 1462, 1468, 44 USPQ2d 1422, 1426 (Fed. Cir. 1997). If the infringer waits until the eve of trial to solicit the opinion, they cannot argue that their earlier infringement was not willful.

The content of the opinion is extremely important when deciding whether the infringer's reliance on the opinion was reasonable. Courts look at whether the opinion was oral or written. A written opinion is preferable because it is immutable. Oral opinions could become more detailed and more favorable as trial approaches. Courts look at whether the opinion is detailed, giving reasons for each conclusion or simply making conclusory statements. For example, an opinion which states: "In my opinion Company X's new design will not infringe the '000 patent," would be conclusory. Whereas an opinion that states: "In my opinion Company X's new design will not infringe the '000 patent because it does not contain elements 1 or 2 either literally or by equivalents." A detailed opinion should compare the infringer's device to the patent claims considering each claim limitation. A detailed opinion should address literal infringement and infringement under the doctrine of equivalents. Finally, the attorney writing the opinion should look at all of the relevant information in formulating the opinion. At a minimum, this would include: the infringer's device, the patent, the prosecution history, and the prior art cited in the prosecution history.

Courts also look at the qualifications of the opinion giver in determining whether reliance on an attorney opinion was reasonable. Courts will look at the credentials of the opinion giver and the objectivity of the opinion and the opinion giver. Is the person a registered patent attorney? What is their educational and practice background? Would an electrical engineer be qualified to give a detailed opinion as to whether a DNA sequence infringes a patent under the doctrine of equivalents? Can a company rely on the opinion given by its in-house counsel who is under pressure to conclude that the design is acceptable?

ORTHO PHARMACEUTICAL CORP. v. SMITH

959 F.2d 936, 22 USPQ2d 1119 (Fed. Cir. 1992)

Before NIES, Chief Judge, COWEN, Senior Circuit Judge, and MICHEL, Circuit Judge.

NIES, Chief Judge.

Ortho Pharmaceutical Corporation and Johnson & Johnson Corporation appeal from the judgment of the United States District Court for the Eastern District of Pennsylvania holding claims 5, 19, 40, and 43 of U.S. Patent No. 3,959,322 (the '322 patent) not invalid. 18 USPQ2d 1977, 1990 W 121353 (1990). Appellants concede infringement. American Home Products Corporation and Dr. Herchel Smith cross-appeal from (1) the district court's denial of attorney fees pursuant to 35 U.S.C. § 285 (1988), and (2) the district court's refusal to modify the language of its permanent injunction. We affirm the district court's judgment in all respects.

A.   WILLFUL INFRINGEMENT

AHP appeals the district court's denial of attorney fees and costs under 35 U.S.C. § 285 which provides: "The court in exceptional cases may award reasonable attorney fees to the prevailing party." AHP asserts that the district court's finding that Ortho's infringement was not willful is clearly erroneous and should be reversed, thereby providing a basis for entitlement to attorney fees.

The issue of willful infringement is resolved by evaluating the totality of the surrounding circumstances. Where an infringer has actual notice of a patentee's rights, the infringer has an affirmative duty of due care which normally includes the duty to seek and obtain competent legal advice from counsel regarding the potential infringement.

Whether infringement is "willful" is by definition a question of the infringer's intent. While an opinion of counsel letter is an important factor in determining the willfulness of infringement, its importance does not depend upon its legal correctness. Indeed, the question arises only where counsel was wrong. Rather, counsel's opinion must be thorough enough, as combined with other factors, to instill a belief in the infringer that a court might reasonably hold the patent is invalid, not infringed, or unenforceable. *Cf. Underwater Devices Inc. v. Morrison–Knudsen Co.*, 717 F.2d 1380, 1390, 219 USPQ 569, 576–577 (Fed. Cir. 1983) (infringement defendant may show that it was justified in relying on opinion of counsel letter despite negative inferences arising from circumstances, i.e., letter provided by non-patent, in-house counsel). Thus, Ortho's intent and reasonable beliefs are the primary focus of a willful infringement inquiry.

The district court, in finding no willful infringement, concluded that Ortho obtained and reasonably relied upon opinion letters rendered by counsel. This finding is not clearly erroneous. Ortho's opinion letters were obtained from experienced patent counsel. The first letter relates to the '911 patent and thoroughly discusses reasons supporting counsel's conclusion of invalidity. This letter also makes reference to potential divisional applications, concluding that any claims in the divisional applications broad enough to include Ortho's product would be invalid for the same reasons as the '911 patent.

Counsel's second letter relates to both the '911 and the '322 patents, and concludes that the only claims broad enough to include Ortho's products are invalid. While the opinion states that certain narrow claims of the '322 patent are valid, it indicates that these claims are specifically drawn to norgestrel and do not include Ortho's product.

AHP points to two "deficiencies" in the opinion letters as the basis for claiming error by the district court. First, AHP alleges that the letters do not contain a non-infringement analysis under the doctrine of equivalents. Second, AHP claims that the letters acknowledge potential infringement due to the conversion of Ortho's norgestimate into norgestrel and norgestrel acetate within the body.

AHP cites *Datascope Corp. v. SMEC, Inc.*, 879 F.2d 820, 11 USPQ2d 1321 (Fed. Cir. 1989), to support its proposition that lack of analysis under the doctrine of equivalents carries great weight in a willfulness determination. In *Datascope*, this court reversed the district court's finding of non-willfulness noting the conclusory nature of counsel's remarks. The character of the letter on its face defeated the *Datascope* infringer's claim to having had a reasonable belief that it was not infringing a valid patent, not the absence of an equivalence analysis per se.

Similarly, AHP's view that the opinion letters indicate potential infringement by reason of "pro-drug" conversion does not compel a finding of willfulness. A party is not guilty of ignoring patent rights because it resolves a close question of infringement in its favor.

The analysis of case law provided by Ortho's counsel, whether technically accurate or not, could have led Ortho to believe that its "prodrug" conversion was not an infringement. In light of the letter's overall tone, its discussion of case law, its analysis of the particular facts and its reference to inequitable conduct, we cannot say the district court clearly erred in finding that Ortho reasonably relied upon opinions by its counsel and, thus, Ortho's infringement was not willful. Therefore, the district court's denial of AHP's request for attorney fees was not an abuse of discretion and is affirmed.

Notes

1. **An infringer can reasonably rely on an attorney opinion letter which turns out to be wrong.** The Federal Circuit repeatedly has held that relying on an attorney opinion which turns out to be wrong can still insulate an infringer from a conclusion that the infringement was willful:

> Our case law makes clear that legal opinions that conclude (even if ultimately incorrectly) that an infringer would not be liable for infringement may insulate an infringer from a charge of willful infringement if such opinions are competent (and followed). A opinion is competent if it is "thorough enough, as combined with other factors, to instill a belief in the infringer that a court might reasonably hold the patent is invalid, not infringed, or unenforceable."

John Hopkins Univ. v. Cellpro, Inc., 152 F.3d 1342, 1364, 47 USPQ2d 1705, 1721 (Fed. Cir. 1998). It is important to take note of the Federal Circuit's statement that the importance of an opinion letter of counsel "does not depend on its legal correctness." *Ortho Pharmaceutical, supra*. Although an opinion letter may help the infringer avoid treble damages for willful infringement, it does not get the infringer out of paying damages (lost profits or a reasonable royalty). For a famous (and costly) example *see Polaroid Corp. v. Eastman Kodak Co.*, 16 USPQ2d 1481 (D. Mass. 1990) (awarded Polaroid $454 million in damages plus $455 million in pre-judgment and post-judgment interest). In *Polaroid*, the court held that Kodak did not willfully infringe because a qualified patent attorney gave a detailed opinion (which just turned out to be wrong on claim construction) before Kodak began any infringing activity. Unfortunately, such an opinion cannot insulate a company from lost profits or reasonable royalty awards. As this case demonstrates, especially where the company is seeking an infringement opinion before it begins the infringing conduct, it wants a genuine opinion. Companies are not simply looking for an attorney to tell them that their design will not infringe to avoid a willfulness finding; companies want an honest opinion in order to decide whether to proceed with a course of action or to decide whether to litigate, settle, or license.

2. Can an infringer avoid willful infringement by relying on an opinion of counsel where the infringer kept the best information available from the attorney writing the opinion and did not address the product that the company ultimately marketed? *See Comark Communications, Inc. v. Harris Corp.*, 156 F.3d 1182, 48 USPQ2d 1001 (Fed. Cir. 1998). In *Comark*, the

Federal Circuit held that the jury finding of willfulness was supported by substantial evidence where the infringer relied on an attorney opinion that did not examine the device which it ultimately sold:

> The reason a potential defendant obtains an opinion from counsel is to ensure that it acts with due diligence in avoiding activities which infringe the patent rights of others. Obtaining an objective opinion letter from counsel also provides the basis for a defense against willful infringement. In order to provide such a prophylactic defense, however, counsel's opinion must be premised upon the best information known to the defendant. Otherwise, the opinion is likely to be inaccurate and will be ineffective to indicate the defendant's good faith intent. Whenever material information is intentionally withheld, or the best information is intentionally not made available to counsel during the preparation of the opinion, the opinion can no longer serve its prophylactic purpose of negating a finding of willful infringement.

> Comark does not challenge the legal competence of Sundheim's opinion, but rather challenges Harris's own actions in directing the creation of this opinion as undermining any reasonable good faith belief of competency. According to Comark, Sundheim's opinion cannot be relied upon by Harris because Harris intentionally withheld important information that Harris believed would result in an unfavorable opinion. In support of its argument, Comark points to two facts that it asserts permitted the jury to find willful infringement by clear and convincing evidence. First, Comark points to evidence that Harris management directed Sundheim to work with Danielsons instead of Culling, the designer of the Harris correction circuit, to obtain information necessary in preparing his opinion. Second, Comark points to evidence presented at trial that Sundheim's opinion with respect to claim 14 expressly restricts its analysis to a waveform monitor and not a spectrum analyzer. Comark also argues that the jury was entitled to find willfulness by clear and convincing evidence in light of evidence that, although at the time of Sundheim's opinion letter Harris's design did not employ a spectrum analyzer, Harris reverted to this design after Sundheim's opinion was complete and failed to seek a revised opinion from counsel. Comark argues that this evidence permits the inference that Harris intentionally withheld information from Sundheim that it knew would produce an unfavorable opinion and that the opinion was thereby rendered incompetent and unreliable by Harris's own actions.

Id. at 1191, 48 USPQ2d at 1009. As this case demonstrates, it is advisable for a company to obtain a supplemental or a new opinion if they change their product design.

3. **Knowledge of the opinion seeker.** Courts also look at the qualifications and knowledge of the infringer who relies on the opinion to determine if such reliance is reasonable. If the infringer, who receives and relies on the opinion, is knowledgeable on patent law and the technology, it is less reasonable for her to rely on conclusory opinions which do not address all of

the issues. Whereas an infringer without any patent law knowledge may be justified in relying on less competent attorney opinions. In *John Hopkins Univ. v. Cellpro, Inc.*, 152 F.3d 1342, 47 USPQ2d 1705 (Fed. Cir. 1998), the Federal Circuit held a jury finding of willfulness was supported by substantial evidence because Cellpro could not reasonably rely on attorney opinions which had obvious shortcomings.

> Kiley, the CellPro representative who procured the opinion letters from Bloomberg, was highly sophisticated in matters of patent law and in the involved technology. Kiley had worked as a patent examiner and later was a partner at the law firm of Lyon & Lyon, where he handled patent prosecution and patent litigation. It is therefore reasonable to conclude that Kiley should have been on notice concerning the opinions' obvious shortcomings and accordingly of the impropriety of CellPro's course of action. The opinions did not attempt to link the disclosures of the prior art references relied upon to establish anticipation or obviousness with the limitations of the claims of the patents. For example, and as the district court recognized, none of the allegedly anticipatory references cited in the '680 opinion letter even refers to a cell suspension. The '204 opinion letter concluded that CellPro did not infringe claims 2, 3, 5, and 6 of the '204 patent, but conspicuously omitted any reference to claims 1 and 4, the claims asserted by Hopkins in this action. Further, the opinion letters are merely conclusory as to their allegations concerning inequitable conduct, and importantly make no mention that intent to deceive is a necessary component of this defense, a fact that is often difficult to establish. Such shortcomings should have been especially troublesome to a knowledgeable practitioner like Kiley, especially considering that the opinions did not express an opinion concerning infringement of the broadest claims.

152 F.3d at 1364, 47 USPQ2d at 1721–22.

4. **Attorney-client privilege and opinion letters.** What do you do if an attorney provides you with a written opinion that the patent is valid and your device infringes? What if the opinion concludes that your device infringes, but that the patent may be invalid. Do you think you will have to reveal this opinion to the patentee in an infringement action during discovery? Do you want the jury considering this opinion when it is deciding whether you do infringe? In *Fromson v. Western Litho Plate & Supply Co.*, 853 F.2d 1568, 1572–73, 7 USPQ2d 1606, 1610–11 (Fed. Cir. 1988), the Court considered the consequences of a refusal to produce such an opinion:

> Western refused to answer interrogatories on whether it obtained counsel's opinion before it began infringement in 1965 or on the content of any such opinion, saying it would disclose such matters only if it were found liable for infringement at trial, in essence suggesting a separate trial on willfulness, e.g., as part of a separate trial on damages. That approach may be useful in meeting the attorney-client privilege problem. Here, however, willfulness and damages were tried with liability, and Western did not offer an opinion of counsel. Where the infringer fails to introduce an exculpatory opinion of counsel at trial, a court must be free to infer that

either no opinion was obtained or, if an opinion were obtained, it was contrary to the infringer's desire to initiate or continue its use of the patentee's invention.

In *Quantum Corp. v. Tandon Corp.*, 940 F.2d 642, 643–44 (Fed. Cir. 1991), the Federal Circuit suggested *in camera* review by the court as a means of reconciling the conflict the defendant is placed in:

> Proper resolution of the dilemma of an accused infringer who must choose between the lawful assertion of the attorney-client privilege and avoidance of a willfulness finding if infringement is found, is of great importance not only to the parties but to the fundamental values sought to be preserved by the attorney-client privilege. An accused infringer, therefore, should not, without the trial court's careful consideration, be forced to choose between waiving the privilege in order to protect itself from a willfulness finding, in which case it may risk prejudicing itself on the question of liability, and maintaining the privilege, in which case it may risk being found to be a willful infringer if liability is found. Trial courts thus should give serious consideration to a separate trial on willfulness whenever the particular attorney-client communications, once inspected by the court in camera, reveal that the defendant is indeed confronted with this dilemma. While our court has recognized that refusal of a separate trial will not require reversal in every case involving attorney client communications bearing on willfulness, we have suggested the advisability of separate trials in appropriate cases.

Do you think that when the defendant waives his attorney-client privilege by relying on an advice of counsel defense, it waives privilege as to all communications with counsel which pertain to infringement, enforceability and validity or just this one opinion letter? What if the defendant asked counsel to prepare three separate opinions addressing infringement, validity and enforceability. Obviously, the defendant would only want to produce the ones that are favorable to their case. Should the defendant be permitted to produce the helpful opinion and keep confidential as privileged the negative opinions?

PROBLEMS

In which of the following scenarios do you think the infringement is willful? Should damages be enhanced and if so by how much?

1. ATL relies on three opinion letters. The first is a letter written by its in-house counsel in response to a cease-and-desist letter from the patentee. The letter states that ATL does not require a license because "[it does] not make use of a unitary, continuously variable, passband filter. Instead, our units make use of a pair of filters which act in series, each of which is made up of four discrete filters which are individually selected." At trial it is discovered that ATL's product did indeed use a unitary, continuously variable, passband filter. The second is an opinion obtained eighteen months later from outside patent counsel which concluded that ATL may infringe, but that the patent is obvious and unenforceable. The obviousness opinion was based upon a prior art reference (the Weighart reference) which had been

considered by the patent office during reexamination. The opinion parroted the rejection the examiner initially made in the reexamination which the patentee overcame. With respect to the conclusion regarding inequitable conduct, the opinion letter stated that the patentee made a material misrepresentation of the technical nature of the Weighart reference. The opinion letter did not mention the intent prong of the inequitable conduct inquiry. Finally a year later (a total of seven years after ATL began its infringement) and two days before SRI's infringement suit was filed, Mr. Yorks, ATL's legal counsel, sent an opinion letter to ATL management, stating that he had found an invalidating reference. He wrote that U.S. Patent No. 2,590,-822 to Minton anticipated several claims of the '750 patent, and that Minton together with Weighart rendered the other claims invalid for obviousness. Can ATL avoid a finding of willfulness by arguing that it relied in good faith on these three opinions? *See SRI Int'l, Inc. v. Advanced Technology Labs., Inc.*, 127 F.3d 1462, 1465–66, 44 USPQ2d 1422, 1424–26 (Fed. Cir. 1997).

2.   Becton Dickinson was aware of Critikon's patents and the potential for infringement. Becton obtained eight separate attorney opinions, all concluding that there was no infringement. Four of the opinion were received prior to placing the infringing product on the market. Becton changed its product design after these opinions (so none of the opinions considered whether the product actually marketed infringed). None of the four opinions contained any analysis of the claims or claim construction, and none discussed the means-plus-function limitations or the prosecution history. There is evidence that Becton copied the product it ultimately marketed from the patents at issue. *See Critikon, Inc. v. Becton Dickinson Vascular Access, Inc.*, 120 F.3d 1253, 43 USPQ2d 1666 (Fed. Cir. 1997).

3.   There is evidence that Aerosonic deliberately and meticulously copied the patented invention. Aerosonic delayed eight months after it received written notice of infringement prior to contacting patent counsel. The opinion of counsel concludes that the patent was invalid as obvious, but made no mention of Aerosonic's copying and other objective indicia of nonobviousness. Moreover, the patent was later upheld during reexamination on the same issue (four months before the patent's expiration) and Aerosonic continued to infringe. *See Sensonics, Inc. v. Aerosonic Corp.*, 81 F.3d 1566, 1571, 38 USPQ2d 1551, 1555 (Fed. Cir. 1996).

2.   ATTORNEYS FEES

STATUTORY PROVISION—35 U.S.C. § 285:

The court in exceptional cases may award reasonable attorney fees to the prevailing party.

BECKMAN v. LKB PRODUKTER AB

892 F.2d 1547, 13 USPQ2d 1301 (Fed. Cir. 1989)

Before RICH, Circuit Judge, MILLER, Senior Circuit Judge, and ARCHER, Circuit Judge.

RICH, Circuit Judge.

Defendants LKB Produkter AB, Wallac Oy, Pharmacia LKB Nuclear Microtomy, Inc., and Pharmacia LKB Biotechnology, Inc. (collectively

LKB) appeal from the judgment of the United States District Court for the District of Maryland entered upon a jury verdict that LKB infringed claims 2 and 4 of U.S. Patent No. 4,029,401 ('401). LKB also appeals from the district court's decision to deny LKB's motion for a new trial and to impose plaintiff's attorney fees and expenses on LKB under 35 U.S.C. § 285. Plaintiff Beckman Instruments, Inc. (Beckman) cross-appeals based upon the district court's decision not to include Beckman's fees and expenses for expert witnesses and consultants in its calculation of attorney fees.

BACKGROUND

Patent '401 to Nather is for methods and apparatus for improving the accuracy of counting techniques in liquid scintillation counters (LSC's). LSC's are used in biological and pharmacological research to measure the amount of a radioactive tracer isotope present in a liquid biological sample. They detect light flashes or scintillations caused by radioactive emissions within the sample and convert those light flashes into electronic pulses. The electronic pulses are then sorted according to their amplitude and frequency, and displayed in a characteristic distribution curve or spectrum for the isotope being measured. The amount of the isotope present can then be calculated.

Researchers have long known that LSC's suffer from a phenomenon known as "quench." Quench is an interference with an LSC's ability to detect the full number and intensity of the scintillations in a given sample due to the sample's chemical or color content. In the mid–1960's, several groups of researchers filed patent applications on methods and apparatus which would compensate for the effect of quench. One of these applications belonged to Nather, which, after an extended prosecution including an interference proceeding, issued as the '401 patent on June 14, 1977.

LKB is in the business of making LSC's, which it sells in the United States and elsewhere. One such LSC manufactured by LKB includes an "auto window" chip within its computer hardware. This auto window chip performs the function of automatically compensating for quench in the sample.

Beckman filed its complaint on July 23, 1985, alleging that the LKB models which contain the auto window feature infringe claims 3–7 of the '401 patent. Several defenses were raised, including invalidity of the patent, inequitable conduct, and lack of personal jurisdiction over co-defendant LKB Produkter. In addition, LKB filed an antitrust counterclaim. The personal jurisdiction defense and the antitrust counterclaim were eventually dropped by LKB. The inequitable conduct defense was severed for a separate bench trial following a jury trial of the validity and infringement issues.

The jury found the three apparatus claims in issue (3, 5 and 6) invalid and not infringed and found the two method claims (4 and 7) "valid" [sic, not proved invalid] and infringed. The jury also found that the infringement was not willful and awarded damages of $1,028,000.

Upon hearing further testimony concerning the inequitable conduct issue, the court found no basis for a holding of inequitable conduct, and so entered judgment for Beckman on the jury's verdict.

The judge also entered a permanent injunction prohibiting LKB from future infringement of the '401 patent. The exact wording of a portion of the injunction is as follows:

> Defendants are further ordered, within 30 days of the effective date of this order, to deliver to counsel for plaintiffs for destruction all [auto window chips] ... which are in the defendants' possession, custody, or control within the United States.

Counsel for LKB apparently concluded that the above language gave LKB the option to ship the auto window chips out of the United States within the 30–day period instead of surrendering them for destruction. Therefore, a great many of the auto window chips in the U.S. at the date of the injunctive order were shipped to LKB's business in Finland. Ten demonstrator LSC's which included the auto window feature were allowed to remain in the United States. The district court found these activities to be a deliberate and repeated violation of the injunction.

Finally, the district court found the case to be "exceptional", and so awarded attorney fees and litigation expenses to Beckman under 35 U.S.C. § 285. In holding the case exceptional, the court relied on both the alleged violations of the injunction and LKB's vexatious litigation strategy. The district court awarded all of Beckman's attorney fees and expenses (totalling $1,969,664.44) except for those relating to the fees and expenses of expert witnesses and consultants (totalling $409,406.10), which the court was not certain were awardable under 35 U.S.C. § 285.

OPINION

III.   The Award of Attorney Fees

(a) Exceptional Case

35 U.S.C. § 285 provides that the court in "exceptional cases may award reasonable attorney fees to the prevailing party." While the decision to award attorney fees is discretionary with the trial judge, the finding that a case is "exceptional" is a finding of fact reviewable under the "clearly erroneous" standard. Among the types of conduct which can form a basis for finding a case exceptional are willful infringement, inequitable conduct before the P.T.O., misconduct during litigation, vexatious or unjustified litigation, and frivolous suit. Such conduct must be supported by clear and convincing evidence.

The district court found the case exceptional because LKB's litigation strategy was vexatious and because LKB had deliberately and repeatedly violated the permanent injunction. The court gives three examples of LKB's vexatious conduct: the jurisdiction defense which was dropped, the antitrust counterclaim which was dropped, and the inequitable conduct defense which was found to be baseless. In arguing that the court erred in finding the case exceptional, LKB maintains that we should review only the three particular examples cited by the district court. We disagree. While it is necessary for the district court to articulate the particular factual findings on which the ultimate finding of "exceptional circumstances" is based when the court's finding of vexatious litigation is based on a "strategy", we do not feel that it is necessary for the district court to set forth every underlying fact which contributed to its conclusion.

Viewed individually, the specific examples of vexatious conduct recited by the district court are somewhat tenuous. In particular, we find it difficult to agree that the inequitable conduct defense was "baseless" when it survived a motion for summary judgment and was rejected only after findings were made on disputed facts with respect to the other defense and counterclaim which were dropped, the mere fact that an issue was pleaded and then dropped prior to trial does not in itself establish vexatious litigation.

However, the district court's finding of exceptional circumstances is based on a strategy of vexatious activity. The three specific examples discussed above are clearly indicated to be merely that—examples. There is certainly sufficient evidence in the record to support a finding that there was additional vexatious conduct on the part of LKB.[1] While it is difficult to infer bad faith on the part of LKB when each action is viewed individually, when viewed together, we cannot say that the district court's finding of vexatious litigation was clearly erroneous. This is especially true considering that the district judge was in much the best position to monitor LKB's litigation "strategy."[2]

LKB has characterized the district court's findings concerning violation of the injunction as further examples of their alleged "vexatious conduct." However, we are satisfied that a fair reading of the district court's opinion indicates that the violations of the injunction constituted an additional basis for finding exceptional circumstances. Such activity could certainly be said to fall under the category of "litigation misconduct." And while LKB contends that the violations of the injunction occurred through honest mistake and oversight, we agree with the district court that the injunction is clear on its face. We conclude that the district court's findings concerning the violations of the injunction are not clearly erroneous.

In view of the foregoing, we affirm the district court's finding that the case is "exceptional."

---

1. For example, there is evidence in the record that LKB pleaded further defenses which were of only marginal relevance to the case, and engaged in various discovery and trial abuses. It is difficult from the "cold record" before us to get a sense of the extent of the abuses or of the good or bad faith involved. Therefore, we defer to the opinion of the trial judge who was actively involved in the proceedings.

2. LKB also contends that it was improper for the district court to consider a non-patent claim, namely the antitrust counterclaim, in a recovery under 35 U.S.C. § 285. However, in an action having both patent and non-patent claims, recovery may be had under § 285 for the non-patent claims if the issues involved therewith are intertwined with the patent issues. Since LKB's antitrust claim was based on alleged inequitable conduct in the PTO, this is certainly the case in the present litigation.

(b) Amounts

The next step is to determine whether the district court abused its discretion in awarding fees and in setting the amount of the fees. The district court's decision will be upheld unless it is based on an error of law or clearly erroneous fact findings, or unless the district court committed a clear error of judgment. While we find no abuse of discretion in the district court's decision to award fees, we find that the amount of the fees awarded is unreasonable, and to that extent an abuse of discretion.

The purpose of § 285 when applied to accused infringers is generally said to be two-fold: one, it discourages infringement by penalizing the infringer; and two, it prevents "gross injustice" when the accused infringer has litigated in bad faith. However, we are aware of few cases in which a patent owner has been granted attorney fees solely on the basis of litigation misconduct, without a concurrent finding of willful infringement.[3] In the present case, the jury explicitly found the infringement to be not willful, a finding which the trial judge did not disturb.

There being no willful infringement in this case, the purpose of discouraging infringement is not relevant. Thus, the fee award can be justified solely by the need to prevent gross injustice. Since any injustice present in this case is based upon LKB's bad faith and misconduct during litigation, the penalty imposed must in some way be related to bad faith and misconduct. While we can certainly imagine a case in which litigation misconduct would justify an award of attorney fees for the entire litigation we are not persuaded that this is the case here.

The district court found that LKB was guilty of engaging in a vexatious litigation strategy and of deliberately violating the injunctive order. While, as related above, we do not consider this finding to be clearly erroneous, we are not satisfied that such conduct justifies imposing all of Beckman's attorney fees, totalling almost $2,000,000, on LKB. The present lawsuit was instigated by Beckman prior to any misconduct by LKB, and Beckman would have incurred substantial legal expenses regardless of LKB's misconduct. In this respect, the case differs from cases in which willful infringement on the part of an infringer or inequitable conduct on the part of a patentee led to the bringing of the lawsuit. It was only after the lawsuit was begun that LKB engaged in misconduct, requiring Beckman to expend extra legal effort to counteract their misconduct.

---

3. In *Livesay Window Co. v. Livesay Industries, Inc.*, 251 F.2d 469, 116 USPQ 167 (5th Cir. 1958), the court upheld an award of attorney fees against an infringer without a finding of willful infringement. However, in that case there was extensive evidence of litigation misconduct extending from the beginning of the lawsuit through 19 years of litigation. In *Philip v. Mayer,* *Rothkopf Industries, Inc.*, 204 USPQ 753 (E.D. N.Y. 1979), *aff'd*, 635 F.2d 1056, 208 USPQ 625 (2d Cir. 1980), the district court awarded partial attorney fees for litigation misconduct despite a finding that the infringement was not willful. However, the court limited recovery to the fees expended in responding to the infringer's misconduct.

To require Beckman to pay its attorneys to defend against LKB's vexatious litigation strategy and misconduct would be a gross injustice. However, that can be avoided by awarding Beckman the portion of its attorney fees which related to the vexatious litigation strategy and other misconduct. The determination of the amount of the award remains within the discretion of the trial court, since it is the trial judge who is in the best position to know how severely LKB's misconduct has affected the litigation. However, the trial judge here did not in any way consider the extent of LKB's misconduct in determining the amount of damages; once the trial judge determined that the case was "exceptional," he awarded all of Beckman's attorney fees, checking only to make sure that the sum was reasonable in relation to the entire lawsuit. Accordingly, we hold that the trial judge's failure to take into account the particular misconduct involved in determining the amount of fees was an abuse of discretion.

Furthermore, while the parties did not discuss the issue on appeal, § 285 provides only for attorney fees being paid to the prevailing party. In the present case, Beckman accused LKB of infringing five claims of the '401 patent; of these claims, only two were found not to be invalid and to be infringed. The other three claims were found invalid and not infringed. Therefore, there is some question whether Beckman can be considered altogether a "prevailing party" for the purpose of § 285. Once again, we are given very little assistance by the case law, since very few cases have involved an award of attorney fees after a "split" jury verdict. The commentators seem to suggest, however, that the correct approach is either to deny fees entirely, or to grant fees only to the extent that a party "prevailed." *See* 5 D. Chisum, Patents § 20.03[4] (1989).

When infringement is found to be willful, the policy behind § 285 of discouraging infringement might justify imposing all of the patent owner's attorney fees on the infringer, even if the infringer prevailed as to some of the claims in suit. However, we are of the opinion that when the sole basis for imposing attorney fees is "gross injustice," and one party prevails on some claims in issue while the other party prevails on other claims, this fact should be taken into account when determining the amount of fees under § 285. In other words, the amount of fees awarded to the "prevailing party" should bear some relation to the extent to which that party actually prevailed. We hold the failure of the district court to take into account this factor in assessing fees in the present case constituted an abuse of discretion.

Since the district court abused its discretion in determining the amount of fees to be awarded, we vacate the award of attorney fees, and remand for a new determination of reasonable fees upon consideration of the factors discussed above.

(c) Fees of Experts and Consultants

Finally, with respect to Beckman's cross-appeal, the district court refused to award Beckman's fees and expenses for experts and consultants, indicating that it was not clear to the court that such fees and expenses were awardable under § 285. In view of our decision in *Mathis v. Spears*, 857 F.2d 749, 758–59, 8 USPQ2d 1551, 1558–59 (Fed. Cir. 1988), it is now clear that such fees are awardable. Therefore, on remand, the district court should take these fees and expenses into account in determining reasonable fees under § 285, subject, of course, to consideration of the other factors set forth in section III of this opinion.

Notes

1. In *Beckman, supra*, the court stated that fees for expert witnesses can be awarded to the prevailing party, and on remand reasonable expert fees should be determined under 35 U.S.C. § 285. However, the Federal Circuit later limited the amount available for expert fees to those authorized by statute under 28 U.S.C. § 1821(b) which states:

> A witness shall be paid an attendance fee of $40 per day for each day's attendance. A witness shall also be paid the attendance for the time necessarily occupied in going to and returning from the place of attendance at the beginning and end of such attendance or at any time during such attendance. 28 U.S.C. § 1821(b) (Supp. IV 1992).

See Amsted Indus., Inc. v. Buckeye Steel Casting Co., 23 F.3d 374, 376, 30 USPQ2d 1470,1472 (Fed. Cir. 1994).

2. 35 U.S.C. § 285 provides that attorney fees may be awarded to the "prevailing party," but who is the prevailing party? In *Gentry Gallery, Inc. v. The Berkline Corp.*, 134 F.3d 1473, 1480, 45 USPQ2d 1498, 1505 (Fed. Cir. 1998), the court held that in an unsuccessful action for infringement, the patent holder was not entitled to attorney fees simply by defending the validity of the patent. In order to be awarded attorney fees, the party must be "the prevailing party" which requires it to receive some benefit from bringing suit such as being awarded damages or an injunction. *Id. See also Beckman, supra*, for a discussion of the relationship between the amount of fees awarded to the "prevailing party" and the extent to which that party actually prevailed.

3. In *Motorola, Inc. v. Interdigital Tech. Corp.*, 930 F. Supp. 952, 985–86 (D. Del. 1996), *aff'd*, 121 F.3d 1461, 43 USPQ2d 1481 (Fed. Cir. 1997), the district court declined to declare the case "exceptional" where the behavior of both parties was egregious and the court did not want either party to benefit from the award of attorney fees:

> A case is exceptional if "it would be grossly unfair for the prevailing party to bear the cost of litigation, or where the conduct of the losing party is marked by bad-faith or unfairness." *Interspiro USA, Inc. v. Figgie Int'l, Inc.*, 815 F. Supp. 1488, 1521 (D. Del. 1993), *aff'd*, 18 F.3d 927 (Fed. Cir. 1994). Factors to consider in determining whether a case is exceptional include the closeness of the case and the conduct of the parties, including evidence of bad faith.

> Each party presented positions which were for the most part reasonable, and the jury weighed the evidence and decided in favor

of Motorola. Having reviewed the evidence in this case on numerous occasions before, during, and after trial, the Court cannot characterize ITC's positions in this litigation as meritless or frivolous. Motorola's motion must rise or fall, therefore, on ITC's vexatious conduct.

Both parties have done an admirable job in the post-trial briefing of presenting each others transgressions. This summary was unnecessary because the Court witnessed all of it, and the Court sees no value in rehashing the deplorable conduct of both parties. The record amply reflects the Court's repeated conclusions that counsel's conduct in this litigation was the worst observed by this Court in more than 22 years on the bench. The record also reflects that both sides were at fault, and while the Court finds that ITC's conduct was indeed more egregious than Motorola's, the difference is not great enough to justify the windfall that would accrue to Motorola if the Court were to declare this case "exceptional." The message which the Court means to send with this ruling is not that ITC's counsel did nothing wrong, but rather that when both sides behave as counsel did in this case, no one side should benefit. The Court denies Motorola's motion for attorneys' fees.

Id. at 985–86.

4. A district court may find a case exceptional and still not award attorney fees. *See National Presto Indus., Inc. v. The West Bend Co.*, 76 F.3d 1185, 37 USPQ2d 1685 (Fed. Cir. 1996); *Graco, Inc. v. Binks Mfg. Co.*, 60 F.3d 785, 35 USPQ2d 1255 (Fed. Cir. 1995); *S.C. Johnson & Son, Inc. v. Carter–Wallace, Inc.*, 781 F.2d 198, 228 USPQ 367 (Fed. Cir. 1986). The decision whether or not to award attorney fees is at the discretion of the court. Why would a court find a case exceptional and not award attorney's fees?

5. Under § 285, the award of attorney fees must be reasonable. The district court has discretion in the awarding of fees and may use a variety of methods to determine what will qualify as a reasonable fee. *See* Donald S. Chisum, Chisum on Patents § 20.03[4] (1997). The court can use actual fees (*see Beckman, supra*) or set a discretionary award based on multiple factors such as the time required, novelty of the case, and attorney fees in similar cases. *See Structural Panels Inc. v. Elite Aluminum Inc.*, 16 USPQ2d 1474, 1476 (S.D. Fla. 1989). The amount of the fee is often calculated using the number of hours spent on the litigation multiplied by a reasonable hourly rate. A reasonable hourly rate is determined by comparison to similar firms in the same geographic region with similar expertise.

3. INTEREST

ALLEN ARCHERY INC. v. BROWNING MFG. CO.
898 F.2d 787, 14 USPQ2d 1156 (Fed. Cir. 1990)

Before RICH, Circuit Judge, FRIEDMAN, Senior Circuit Judge, and MILLS, District Judge.

FRIEDMAN, Senior Circuit Judge.

These are an appeal and a cross-appeal from a judgment of the United States District Court for the District of Utah in the accounting phase of a patent infringement suit awarding damages.

I

A. In 1977, the appellant Allen Archery, Inc. (Allen) filed suits against the appellees Browning and its wholly owned subsidiary Browning Manufacturing Company (Browning Mfg.) (collectively referred to as the Browning defendants) and three others. The suits charged that the defendants had infringed Allen's '495 patent covering an archery bow known in the trade as a "compound bow" and that Browning Mfg. had breached a patent licensing agreement with Allen.

After a further trial, the court held that the four claims of the Allen patent asserted in this case were valid and enforceable, and that the defendants had infringed those claims. It further ruled that Allen and Browning Mfg. had entered into an enforceable patent licensing agreement, that Browning Mfg. had breached the agreement, and that Allen was entitled to recover the royalties specified in the agreement.

The court held that Allen was entitled to prejudgment interest, except for the

> period of approximately three years in 1978–81 during which this case was stayed pending the outcome of the *Jennings* litigation in California. Responsibility for the three-year delay must be shared equally by both Allen and Browning/[Browning Mfg.], as the stay was granted by this court pursuant to a joint motion by the parties.

The court computed the prejudgment interest based on the annualized yield of three-month United States Treasury bills, compounded quarterly. It explained: "The three-month Treasury Bill represents a benchmark as the shortest term, risk-free investment available to ordinary investors and is a proper basis upon which to compensate Allen for the foregone use of the money."

The court's final judgment awarded Allen damages of $1,629,714 and prejudgment interest of $957,712.12. Both parties challenge the award of prejudgment interest.

A. In their cross-appeal, the Browning defendants contend that no prejudgment interest should have been awarded. Relying on the statement in *General Motors Corp. v. Devex Corp.*, 461 U.S. 648, 656 (1983), that a patent owner's damages from infringement "consist not only of the value of the royalty payments but also of the forgone use of the money between the time of infringement and the date of the judgment," they assert that because Allen's business consisted solely of licensing its patent, the loss of the royalty payments did not injure Allen by denying it the use of money that it otherwise would have had.

This contention rests upon a misreading of *Devex* and our cases applying that decision. *Devex* stated that "prejudgment interest should ordinarily be awarded under [35 U.S.C.A.] § 284," 461 U.S. at 656, and that "prejudgment interest should ordinarily be awarded absent some justification for withholding such an award." *Id.* at 657. *See also Nickson Indus., Inc. v. Rol Mfg. Co.*, 847 F.2d 795, 800, 6 USPQ2d 1878, 1881 (Fed. Cir. 1988) ("Generally, prejudgment interest should be awarded from the date of infringement to the date of judgment.").

The rationale of *Devex* is that "[i]n the typical case an award of prejudgment interest is necessary to ensure that the patent owner is placed in as good a position as he would have been had the infringer entered into a reasonable royalty agreement." 461 U.S. at 655. It would be inconsistent with that rationale to require that, in order to award prejudgment interest, the district court first would have to consider and determine what use the patentee would have made of the royalty payments it should have received.

B. The cross-appellees also argue that the district court erred in awarding compound interest. "The rate of prejudgment interest and whether it should be compounded or uncompounded are matters left largely to the discretion of the district court." *Bio-Rad Labs., Inc. v. Nicolet Instrument Corp.*, 807 F.2d 964, 969, 1 USPQ2d 1191, 1194 (Fed. Cir. 1986). The district court did not abuse its discretion in compounding post-judgment interest.

C. Allen argues that the district court erred in excluding from the period for which it awarded prejudgment interest the time during which the present case was stayed pending the decision in the *Jennings* case. The court stated that "[r]esponsibility for the three-year delay must be shared equally by both Allen and Browning/[Browning Mfg.], as the stay was granted by this court pursuant to a joint motion by the parties." The court concluded that "in its discretion" it would not "award interest to Allen for this period."

Devex recognized that section 284 "leaves the court some discretion in awarding prejudgment interest. For example, it may be appropriate to limit prejudgment interest, or perhaps even deny it altogether, where the patent owner has been responsible for undue delay in prosecuting the lawsuit." 461 U.S. at 656–57. *See also Nickson Industries*, 847 F.2d at 800, 6 USPQ2d at 1881 ("District courts have discretion to limit prejudgment interest where, for example, the patent owner has caused undue delay in the lawsuit, but there must be justification bearing a relationship to the award.").

In the present case, Allen cannot properly be denied prejudgment interest because it, jointly with the Browning defendants, sought a stay of this case pending the decision in *Jennings*. The stay originally was sought only by the Browning defendants, and Allen opposed it. Allen only joined in the stay request after the Panel on Multidistrict Litigation had denied Allen's motion to consolidate discovery proceedings and suggested that the parties seek a stay. In these circumstances, Allen cannot be said to have "caused" the three-year delay in the present case until *Jennings* was decided.

Furthermore, the delay in the present case was neither "undue" nor unjustified. To the contrary, the postponement of proceedings in this case until *Jennings* was decided was in the public interest because it furthered the possible and actual conservation of judicial and attorney resources. If the *Jennings* court had held all of the Allen claims invalid instead of just six, there would have been no need for this case to be tried. The invalidation of six of the Allen patent claims in *Jennings*, which claims Allen then disclaimed before the Patent Office, substantially simplified the trial of the present case.

In sum, although the district court has "some discretion in awarding prejudgment interest," *Devex*, 461 U.S. at 656–57, the district court here abused its discretion in declining to award prejudgment interest for the period during which the present case was stayed pending the decision in *Jennings*.

Notes

1. Prejudgment interest is generally awarded, absent a justification for withholding it, in order to put the patent holder in the same position as if a reasonable royalty agreement had been made with the infringer prior to the infringement. *General Motors v. Devex Corp.*, 461 U.S. 648, 655, 217 USPQ 1185, 1188 (1983). Prejudgment interest accrues from the date of infringement to the date of judgment. The trial court has discretion in setting the interest rate, although it is typically based on the statutory rate, the Treasury Bill Rate, or the prime rate. *See* Bradley J. Hulbert and Mary S. Consalvi, *Devexing Prejudgment Interest Awards in Patent Cases—At What Point Interest?*, 67 JPTOS 103 (1985).

2. Prejudgment interest should be awarded for damages based on either a reasonably royalty or lost profits, but it is not appropriate for enhanced damages for willfulness or attorneys fees.

3. Post-judgment interest, on the other hand, accrues from the date the clerk enters the final judgment and is calculated at the statutory rate provided in 28 U.S.C. § 1961(a). The rate is based on 52 week T-bills and is compounded annually.

4. **Costs**. Costs, as fixed by the court, may be awarded to the prevailing party. 35 U.S.C. § 284. Examples of items generally included as "costs" are clerk fees, fees for the court reporter, and docket fees.

D. MARKING

Statutory Provision—35 U.S.C. § 287:

(a) Patentees, and persons making, offering for sale, or selling within the United States any patented article for or under them, or importing any patented article into the United States, may give notice to the public that the same is patented, either by fixing thereon the word "patent" or the abbreviation "pat.", together with the number of the patent, or when, from the character of the article, this can not be done, by fixing to it, or to the package wherein one or more of them is contained, a label containing a like notice. In the event of failure so to mark, no damages shall be recovered by the patentee in any action for infringement, except on proof that the infringer was notified of the infringement and continued to infringe thereafter, in which event damages may be recovered only for infringement occurring after such notice. Filing of an action for infringement shall constitute such notice.

1. MARKING BY THE PATENT OWNER

AMERICAN MED. SYSTEMS, INC. v. MEDICAL ENG'G CORP.

6 F.3d 1523, 28 USPQ2d 1321 (Fed. Cir. 1993)

Before NIES, Chief Judge, MICHEL and RADER, Circuit Judges.

MICHEL, Circuit Judge.

American Medical Systems, Inc. (AMS) brought suit in the United States District Court for the Eastern District of Wisconsin against Medical Engineering Corporation (MEC) for willful infringement of United States Patent No. 4,597,765, issued to Klatt (the '765 patent). MEC counterclaimed for declaratory judgment of invalidity and noninfringement, for an alleged breach of warranty, and for intentional, negligent and fraudulent misrepresentation by AMS.

After a bench trial, the district court issued its Decision and Order on June 25, 1992, rejecting each of MEC's counterclaims and holding that the '765 patent was not invalid and was infringed. The court further found that MEC's infringement was willful and that AMS was entitled to an award of enhanced damages of 1.5 times its proven lost profits and reasonable royalties. The court limited AMS's recoverable damages to those incurred after the filing date of the lawsuit, however, due to AMS's initial failure to mark its patented articles under 35 U.S.C. § 287(a) (1988). On September 1, 1992, the district court entered judgment in accord with its decision and permanently enjoined MEC from any further infringement of the '765 patent.

BACKGROUND

AMS and MEC were vigorous competitors in the area of penile prostheses. Each company had its own commercial version of a fluid-filled prosthetic device. AMS's prosthesis was called the "Hydroflex" and MEC's equivalent device was the "Flexi–Flate." Both devices were initially sold unfilled in a "dry pack" configuration.

The present appeal involves AMS's '765 patent, which claims an apparatus and method for packaging a fluid-containing penile prosthesis in a pre-filled, sterile state. Both the Hydroflex and the Flexi–Flate are this type of device. The packaging comprises a sterile, fluid-filled inner package that holds the pre-filled prosthesis and a non-sterile outer package that contains the inner package in a sterile state. This packaging configuration is referred to in the industry as the "wet pack."

AMS filed its application claiming the combination of a prefilled prosthesis stored in the double layer packaging on December 27, 1984. The '765 patent issued from this application on July 1, 1986. Claims 1–

12 and 21–24 of the '765 patent are directed to the apparatus comprising the prefilled and presterilized packaged prosthesis. Claims 14–15 and 18–20 of the '765 patent are directed to the method of making and sterilizing a packaged pre-filled and presterilized prosthesis.

The prior art unfilled prosthesis, such as the dry-pack Hydroflex or dry-pack Flexi–Flate, required filling in the operating room prior to implantation. This was undesirable because it increased the operating time required to implant the prosthesis and could lead to certain problems due to improper filling or leaking.

The subject matter of the '765 patent solved the problems of the prior art dry-pack configuration devices by pre-filling the prosthesis with a saline solution and immersing it in a foil pouch filled with a saline solution having the same osmotic properties as the solution within the prosthesis. This allowed the liquid level within the device to be maintained at a precise level while in storage prior to implantation. This inner foil pouch was then sterilized and stored inside an outer non-sterile container. The two layer packaging configuration allowed for a non-sterile nurse to open the non-sterile outer package and present the sterile inner package containing the pre-filled prosthesis to a sterile nurse to open in the operating field. Because of these asserted advantages, there was a much greater demand in the market for a pre-filled, pre-sterilized prosthesis over an unfilled device.

MEC began to work on the problem of marketing a pre-filled, sterilized packaged version of its Flexi–Flate prosthesis in early 1984. MEC's original packaging concept involved placing the pre-filled prosthesis in a rigid vapor impermeable tube containing saline of the same osmolarity as that within the device. The rigid tube was then enclosed in a slightly larger tube or pouch. MEC also attempted reversing the relationship of the tube and the pouch. None of these attempts to design a pre-filled packaged prosthesis proved to be successful, however, due to problems with leaking and sterilization.

In May of 1985, MEC personnel saw AMS's pre-filled, sterilized Hydroflex prosthesis in the wet pack packaging configuration at the annual American Urological Association trade show. The AMS package at the trade show was not marked with any patent pending notice, and no representations were made at that time that any patent applications had been filed. MEC abandoned its previous packaging configurations after it obtained a sample of the Hydroflex device and packaging, which it referred to in creating its own double foil pouch wet pack packaging. MEC then introduced its own wet pack "Flexi–Flate" prosthesis in the market in May 1985.

MEC became aware of the '765 patent shortly after it issued in late July 1986, through the efforts of its in-house patent counsel, Stuart Krieger. AMS's patent counsel, James Elacqua, also called Krieger twice in August 1986, to advise MEC of the existence of the '765 patent. No accusation of infringement was made by AMS at that time, however. Krieger immediately contacted MEC's vice president for scientific affairs,

Garry Carter, to advise him of the patent. Krieger also testified that he authorized performance of several patent validity searches on the '765 patent. These opinions were withheld at trial, however. At the end of August or the beginning of September of 1986, Krieger informed MEC's president, Robert Helbling, in an oral opinion that the '765 patent was invalid for obviousness and that MEC's wet pack Flexi-Flate fell literally within the scope of the '765 patent claims.

Shortly after learning of AMS's '765 patent, MEC began work on an alternative packaging configuration for its pre-filled device, known as the "vacuum pack." MEC did not begin selling the vacuum pack in the market until about January 1988. Even after development of the vacuum pack, MEC continued to ship its remaining inventory of the wet pack Flexi–Flate throughout the remainder of 1988.

As damages, AMS asserted entitlement to lost profits for the period of July 1, 1986 (the issue date of the '765 patent), through December 1987, after which MEC's noninfringing "vacuum pack" Flexi–Flate entered the market. From January 1988 on, AMS claimed entitlement to a reasonable royalty for MEC's continued shipping of its remaining inventory of the wet pack Flexi–Flates.

In awarding damages, the district court noted that AMS did not begin to mark its Hydroflex device until two months after the patent issued and that AMS did not begin shipping those marked devices until October 15, 1986. From this, the district court concluded that more than a *de minimis* number of devices was shipped without any patent marking pursuant to 35 U.S.C. § 287(a). Accordingly, the district court held that AMS was only entitled to damages from the date that it gave MEC actual notice of infringement. The district court further found that actual notice was not given until the present lawsuit was filed on October 28, 1987. Therefore, the district court found that AMS was entitled to lost profits for the period of October 28, 1987 through December 1988, in the amount of $906,806.00, and to a reasonable royalty for the period of January 1988 to December 1988 in the amount of $46,264.24. This equals a total amount of $953,070.24 in lost profits and reasonable royalties, multiplied by 1.5, resulting in total damages of $1,429,605.30.

AMS cross-appeals the district court's limitation of recoverable damages because of its initial failure to mark its patented product pursuant to 35 U.S.C. § 287(a).

ANALYSIS

A. *Patent Marking*

AMS cross-appeals the district court's limitation of its recoverable damages to the period after the filing date of this lawsuit for failure to mark under 35 U.S.C. § 287(a), claiming that the district court erroneously construed the statute. Statutory construction is a legal question which we review *de novo*.

The district court found, and the parties do not dispute the following facts. The '765 patent issued on July 1, 1986. Prior to issuance of the '765 patent, AMS had already shipped 8,556 unmarked prostheses. AMS did not begin marking its product until about two months after issuance of the '765 patent, and did not begin shipping its marked products until October 15, 1986, three and one-half months after the patent issued. During the period after issuance of the patent, 1,939 prostheses were shipped without marking. Relying on *Hazeltine Corp. v. Radio Corp. of Am.*, 20 F. Supp. 668, 35 USPQ. 438 (S.D. N.Y. 1937), the district court concluded that, under section 287(a), AMS was "obliged to have marked all Hydroflexes subsequent to issue [sic] of the patent, except that it is allowed a relatively small number to be shipped unmarked as it readies the marking process." The district court found that AMS failed to comply with section 287(a) because it had shipped more than a *de minimis* number of products after the patent issued without the requisite marking.

AMS argues that the district court erroneously interpreted section 287(a). Under the correct interpretation of section 287(a), AMS asserts that it is entitled to damages from the time that it began consistently marking its product, thereby satisfying the statutory requirement. According to AMS, the district court's reliance on *Hazeltine* is misplaced, because that case was decided under Revised Statute 4900, ch. 67, 44 Stat. 1058–59 (1927), the predecessor statute to the current section 287(a). R.S. 4900 provided that "[i]t shall be the *duty* of all patentees . . . to give sufficient notice to the public that the same is patented. . . ." (emphasis added). In 1952, Congress amended R.S. 4900 to become the present section 287(a), changing the language to make marking permissive rather than mandatory, so that a "[p]atentee . . . may give notice to the public" by the specified marking. Although the legislative history does not shed much light on Congress's intent regarding this specific language change, it is clear that the amendments were meant to reorganize and clarify the prior provisions. AMS argues that since *Hazeltine* and the 1952 amendments, the courts have interpreted the new marking provision to allow damages from the point at which the statute is complied with by fully marking the patented device. AMS also argues that *Hazeltine* is not applicable to the present situation, because in that case, marking was haphazard and, therefore, the statute was never fully complied with at any time.

Specifically, AMS points to *Slimfold Manufacturing Co. v. Kinkead Indus., Inc.*, C.A. No. 1:78–CV–1978–JOF, 1990 WL 512961 (N.D. Ga. May 29, 1990), *aff'd*, 932 F.2d 1453, 18 USPQ2d 1842 (Fed. Cir. 1991). In *Slimfold*, the patentee commercialized the invention before the patent issued on May 14, 1974, but did not begin marking the patented product until November 1, 1977. The defendant began infringing in June 1977, the first actual notice of infringement was given in March 1978, and suit was filed in October 1978. The district court held that Slimfold was entitled to damages from November 1, 1977, when it began to consistently mark its patented products. In reaching this conclusion, the court reasoned that:

> The statute does not require marking within a particular time after issuance of a patent. Both the Fifth and Sixth Circuit Courts of Appeal have so held. "The Court points out that there is ' . . . nothing in the statute requiring marking or notice within any period after issue as a condition for recovery of damages for infringement . . . .' " Liability for infringement begins with marking (or actual notice) whenever that occurs.

On appeal, the Federal Circuit specifically affirmed the district court's award of damages as of the marking date, although the specific question of the proper interpretation of section 287(a) was not before the court.

As noted by the district court in *Slimfold*, both the Fifth and Sixth Circuits have in the past specifically interpreted section 287(a) to allow damages from the time that actual marking begins or from the time of actual notice of infringement, whichever comes first. In *Wm. Bros. Boiler & Manufacturing Co. v. Gibson–Stewart Co.*, 312 F.2d 385, 136 USPQ 239 (6th Cir. 1963), the Sixth Circuit held that although the patentee failed to mark its patented devices for nine months after the date that the patent issued, he was entitled to recovery of damages from the time of compliance with the marking provisions of the statute. The holding was based on the district court's reasoning that

> [U]nless and until the patentee marks his patent or serves actual notice upon an alleged infringer he can recover no damages, but . . . nothing in the statute require[s] marking or notice within any period after issue as a condition for recovery of damages for infringement . . . . [T]he penalty for failure to do either [is] limited to denial of damages for infringement at any time prior to compliance with the requirements of the statute.

Id. at 386, 136 USPQ at 240.

Similarly, in *Briggs v. M & J Diesel Locomotive Filter Corp.*, 228 F. Supp. 26, 63–64, 141 USPQ 96, 127 (N.D. Ill. 1964), *aff'd*, 342 F.2d 573, 144 USPQ 701 (7th Cir. 1965), the district court held that despite a two year delay in marking, the patentee was entitled to recover damages for infringement undertaken after marking began.

MEC fails to adequately distinguish these cases or to convince us that their rationale is unsound. MEC cites a number of authorities in support of the district court's interpretation of the statute that marking of all patented products must begin immediately after issuance of the patent, subject to the *de minimis* exception of *Hazeltine*. These cases were all decided under the predecessor statutes to section 287(a) and, therefore, are not controlling on the interpretation of the present statute. As discussed above, since the statute was amended in 1952, the cases which specifically address this issue have interpreted section 287(a) to allow damages from the time when marking begins in compliance with the statute or actual notice is given, whichever comes first.

Although not binding on this court, we find the reasoning of the post–1952 cases highly persuasive. The plain language of section 287(a) does not provide any time limit by which marking must begin, nor does the legislative history indicate any such limitation. Congress structured the statute so as to tie failure to mark with disability to collect damages, not failure to mark at the time of issuance with disability to collect damages. Furthermore, allowing recovery of damages from the point of full compliance with the marking statute furthers the policy of encouraging marking to provide notice to the public, even if initial marking after issuance of the patent is delayed. The sooner one complies with the marking requirements, the more likely one is to maximize the period of time for recoverable damages. To prevent recovery of damages for failure to immediately mark, however, provides no incentive for a patentee who inadvertently or unavoidably fails to mark initially to mark in the future.

Moreover, preventing recovery of damages for an initial failure to mark does not remedy the problem of having unmarked products in the marketplace. Any products entering the market prior to issuance of the patent will not be marked. Even the *Hazeltine* court recognized that "[i]t is not the number of articles seen by the defendant which is controlling on an issue of marking ... but whether the patentee performed this statutory duty which was a prerequisite to his *in rem* notice to the world." *Hazeltine*, 20 F. Supp. at 671, 35 USPQ at 442. Therefore, once marking has begun in compliance with the statute, *in rem* notice is provided and there is no reason to further limit damages on this account.

In light of the permissive wording of the present statute, and the policy of encouraging notice by marking, we construe section 287(a) to preclude recovery of damages only for infringement for any time prior to compliance with the marking or actual notice requirements of the statute. Therefore, a delay between issuance of the patent and compliance with the marking provisions of section 287(a) will not prevent recovery of damages after the date that marking has begun. We caution, however, that once marking has begun, it must be substantially consistent and continuous in order for the party to avail itself of the constructive notice provisions of the statute.

Applying this statutory construction to the facts of this case, AMS is entitled to damages from the time when it either began marking its products in compliance with section 287(a) or when it actually notified MEC of its infringement, whichever was earlier. AMS began marking its products about two months after issuance of the '765 patent and it began externally shipping those marked products on October 15, 1986. The district court found that actual notice of infringement was not given until the lawsuit was filed on October 28, 1987. AMS has not shown that the district court's finding as to actual notice was clearly erroneous.[18]

---

18. AMS argues that MEC was notified in August 1986 by its own counsel, Krieger, that MEC was infringing the '765 patent. This is clearly not what was intended by the marking statute. Section 287(a) requires a party asserting infringement to either provide constructive notice (through marking) or actual notice in order to avail

We hold that AMS is entitled to damages from the time that it began shipping its marked products, October 15, 1986, rather than the filing date of the lawsuit as found by the district court, because AMS was in compliance with the marking statute at that time. The date that AMS began marking its products is irrelevant for purposes of the statute, because marking alone without distribution provides no notice to the public where unmarked products are continuing to be shipped. The purpose of the constructive notice provision is "to give patentees the proper incentive to mark their products and thus place the world on notice of the existence of the patent." *Laitram Corp. v. Hewlett–Packard Co.*, 806 F. Supp. 1294, 1296, 25 USPQ2d 1827, 1834–35 (E.D. La. 1992). The world cannot be "put on notice" if the patentee marks certain products, but continues to ship unmarked products. Therefore, AMS was not in full compliance with the marking statute while it continued to ship its unmarked products, which continued to mislead the public into thinking that the product was freely available. Full compliance was not achieved until AMS consistently marked substantially all of its patented products, and it was no longer distributing unmarked products. We therefore remand this portion of the case to the district court for a proper determination of damages consistent with this decision.

B. *Patent Marking Relating to Method Claims*

AMS argues that the district court erred in limiting its recoverable damages from the infringed method claims of the '765 patent pursuant to section 287(a). The law is clear that the notice provisions of section 287 do not apply where the patent is directed to a process or method. The district court, however, relied on *Devices for Medicine, Inc. v. Boehl*, 822 F.2d 1062, 3 USPQ2d 1288 (Fed. Cir. 1987), in holding that "where there are both product and method claims being claimed infringed, the patentee must mark the product." 794 F. Supp. at 1391, 26 USPQ2d at 1095.

In *Devices for Medicine*, the court noted that in *Bandag* and *Hanson*, a distinction was made between cases "in which only method claims are asserted to have been infringed" and cases where a patentee alleges infringement of both the apparatus and method claims of the same patent. *Devices for Medicine*, 822 F.2d at 1066, 3 USPQ2d at 1292. The *Devices for Medicine* court further stated that because the method claims of the patent were directed to the use of the claimed product, "[h]aving sold the product unmarked, [the patentee] could hardly maintain entitlement to damages for its use by a purchaser uninformed that such use would violate [patentee's] method patent." *Id.*, 3 USPQ2d at 1292.

AMS contends that *Devices for Medicine* is inapposite, because in that case the patent contained product claims and claims covering the use of the same product. AMS asserts that the sale of a product carries

---

itself of damages. The notice of infringement must therefore come from the patentee, not the infringer. *Devices for Medicine, Inc. v. Boehl*, 822 F.2d 1062, 1066, 3 USPQ2d 1288, 1292 (Fed. Cir. 1987) ("Absent notice, [infringer's] 'knowledge of the patents' is irrelevant.").

an implied license to use it as a matter of law; therefore failing to mark a patented product rationally creates an expectation of receiving a right from the seller to use it for its customary purposes. By contrast, AMS argues that the '765 patent involves methods of making and sterilizing the patented product and that sale of a product does not grant any implied license to make an additional product or to use a particular manufacturing process to make it. Therefore, AMS asserts that the rationale of *Devices for Medicine* should not apply and that section 287(a) has no application to the instant method claims.

We find AMS's distinction of the claims in *Devices for Medicine* from those in the present action to be meaningless within the context of section 287(a). The purpose behind the marking statute is to encourage the patentee to give notice to the public of the patent. The reason that the marking statute does not apply to method claims is that, ordinarily, where the patent claims are directed to only a method or process there is nothing to mark. Where the patent contains both apparatus and method claims, however, to the extent that there is a tangible item to mark by which notice of the asserted method claims can be given, a party is obliged to do so if it intends to avail itself of the constructive notice provisions of section 287(a).

In this case, both apparatus and method claims of the '765 patent were asserted and there was a physical device produced by the claimed method that was capable of being marked. Therefore, we conclude that AMS was required to mark its product pursuant to section 287(a) in order to recover damages under its method claims prior to actual or constructive notice being given to MEC.

Notes

1. What damages is the patent owner entitled to in each of the following scenarios (assume a complaint for patent infringement was filed against an accused infringer yesterday):

   a. patentee sells a product covered by the patent claims and the product is marked;

   b. patentee sells a competing product which is not covered by her patent claims and the product is not marked;

   c. patentee sells a product made by the patented method and the product is not marked;

   d. patentee has a patent which contains both method and apparatus claims and sells a product which is made by the method and falls within the apparatus claims, the product is not marked;

   e. patentee sells an unmarked product which is covered by the patent; and

   f. patentee sells an unmarked product and sent a cease and desist letter to an infringer one year ago.

2. **Complaint**. The complaint filed by the patent owner must show that the patentee complied with the marking statute.

2. MARKING BY LICENSEES

MAXWELL v. J. BAKER INC.

86 F.3d 1098, 39 USPQ2d 1001 (Fed. Cir. 1996)

Before LOURIE, Circuit Judge, SKELTON, Senior Circuit Judge, and SCHALL, Circuit Judge.

LOURIE, Circuit Judge.

BACKGROUND

In retail shoe stores, pairs of shoes must be kept together to prevent them from becoming disorganized and mismatched. Typically, manufacturers connect pairs of shoes using plastic filaments threaded through each shoe's eyelets. However, some shoes do not have eyelets and cannot be connected in this manner. Thus, manufacturers have resorted to other methods of keeping the shoes together such as making a hole in the side of each shoe and threading a filament through these holes. This method creates problems for retailers and manufacturers because the shoes are damaged by the process.

Maxwell, an employee at a Target retail store, recognized this problem and invented a system for connecting shoes that do not have eyelets. She secured tabs along the inside of each shoe and connected the shoes with a filament threaded through a loop or hole in each tab. By securing the tabs inside the shoe, she preserved the integrity and appearance of the shoes.

Maxwell filed a patent application entitled "System for Attaching Mated Pairs of Shoes Together," which issued as the '060 patent on November 25, 1986.

Maxwell sued J. Baker on December 12, 1990, alleging infringement of the '060 patent. After a month long trial, a jury returned a special verdict finding that the '060 patent was valid; J. Baker infringed claims 1, 2, and 3 of the patent; and J. Baker's infringement was willful after June 1990, when it received actual notice of the '060 patent. The jury also determined that Maxwell complied with the marking requirements of 35 U.S.C. § 287(a) as of November 1987. Thus, it awarded over $1.5 million in damages based on its determination that a reasonable royalty for use of Maxwell's patent was $.05 per pair of shoes and J. Baker sold 31 million infringing pairs of shoes. In addition, the jury awarded Maxwell an additional $1.5 million based on its determination that Maxwell was damaged in excess of the $.05 royalty.

C. Marking

J. Baker also argues that the court erred by denying its JMOL motion on the issue of patent marking under 35 U.S.C. § 287(a). J. Baker asserts that, as a matter of law, no damages may be awarded for infringement occurring before it had actual notice of the alleged infringement in June 1990, and that substantial evidence does not support the jury's verdict that Maxwell complied with the marking statute as of

November 1987. In support, J. Baker relies on evidence that at least 5% of the shoes sold by Maxwell's licensee, Target, were not properly marked because Target failed to instruct some of its manufacturers to mark the patented systems.

In response, Maxwell argues that substantial evidence supports the jury's verdict. In particular, Maxwell asserts that she was diligent in enforcing Target's duty to mark, and Target successfully marked 95% of the shoes sold with the attachment system. Thus, she maintains that the court did not err when it denied J. Baker's JMOL motion on the issue of marking. We agree. [T]he statute defines that "[a patentee] is entitled to damages from the time when it either began marking its product in compliance with section 287(a)[, constructive notice,] or when it actually notified [the accused infringer] of its infringement, whichever was earlier." *American Medical Sys., Inc. v. Medical Eng'g Corp.*, 6 F.3d 1523, 1537, 28 USPQ2d 1321, 1331 (Fed. Cir. 1993). We have construed section 287(a) to require that "once marking has begun, it must be substantially consistent and continuous in order for the party to avail itself of the constructive notice provisions of the statute." *Id.* As the patentee, Maxwell had the burden of pleading and proving at trial that she complied with the statutory requirements. Compliance with section 287(a) is a question of fact, and we review the court's denial of JMOL on the jury's resolution of the issue for substantial evidence.

A patentee who makes, uses, or sells its own invention is obligated to comply with the marking provisions to obtain the benefit of constructive notice. The marking provisions also apply to "persons making or selling any patented article for or under [the patentees]." 35 U.S.C. § 287(a). Thus, licensees, such as Target, and other authorized parties, such as Target's manufacturers, must also comply. *See Amsted Industries, Inc. v. Buckeye Steel Castings Co.*, 24 F.3d 178, 185, 30 USPQ2d 1462, 1467–68 (section 287(a) applies to express and implied licensees). However, with third parties unrelated to the patentee, it is often more difficult for a patentee to ensure compliance with the marking provisions. A "rule of reason" approach is justified in such a case and substantial compliance may be found to satisfy the statute. Therefore, when third parties are involved, the number of shoes sold without proper marking is not conclusive of the issue whether the patentee's marking was "substantially consistent and continuous." When the failure to mark is caused by someone other than the patentee, the court may consider whether the patentee made reasonable efforts to ensure compliance with the marking requirements. The rule of reason is consistent with the purpose of the constructive notice provision—to encourage patentees to mark their products in order to provide notice to the public of the existence of the patent and to prevent innocent infringement.

Here, Maxwell, the patentee, made extensive and continuous efforts to ensure compliance by Target. There is evidence that Target, as licensee of Maxwell's patent, marked at least 95% of the shoes sold using the patented system. Because Target sold millions of pairs of shoes using the patented system, it is true that a numerically large number of shoes were sold without proper marking. Despite this, however, the evidence supports the jury's finding that Maxwell complied with the statute. Before the patent issued, Target agreed to mark "Patent Pending" on all pairs of shoes using Maxwell's shoe attachment system. After the patent issued on November 26, 1986, Maxwell notified Target to mark the patent number on all shoes using the patented system, as required by their license agreement. Initially, Target made no effort to change the marking from "Patent Pending" to recite the patent number. In response, Maxwell notified Target's manufacturers of the need to properly mark. Subsequently, Target agreed to properly mark shoes using the patented system by November 1987. Thereafter, on several occasions when Maxwell learned of Target's failure to properly mark shoes using the patented system after November 1987, she notified Target of the errors and requested that the shoes be properly marked in the future. Maxwell also presented evidence that, in response to her urging, Target used its best efforts to correct its failure to mark by instructing its manufacturers to properly mark in the future.

Thus, we find that substantial evidence supports the jury's determination that Maxwell complied with the marking statute as of November 1987. Most pairs of shoes using the patented attachment system were properly marked. Any deficiency in the marking was not due to Maxwell or any failure on her part to ensure compliance by her licensees; she diligently attempted to comply with the statutory marking requirements. Therefore, we affirm the district court's denial of J. Baker's JMOL motion on the issue of marking.

Notes

1. False marking under § 292 can be a very costly proposition. The infringer is fined up to $500 for each offense. If the infringer is manufacturing, for example microchips, each time a microchip is falsely marked, the infringer has committed another offense. To be found liable of false marking, the infringer must have the intent to deceive the public.

Problems

1. How could an attorney draft a cease-and-desist type letter that would be sufficient notice to receive damages under § 287, but not provide the reasonable apprehension necessary for the accused infringer to bring a declaratory judgment action?

2. You are employed as a patent attorney with the firm Moore, Michel & Lupo. You are asked to advise a client, Mike's Fishing, who sells a commercial embodiment of his '835 patent called The Perch Troller (*See* Chapter Eight for the '835 patent). Mike's business and his sales are limited to the Midwest region—the Great Lakes areas. However, with his new website, he thinks he can expand his sales market beyond the Midwest. The Perch Troller has been a commercially successful products. It outsells all of Mike's other trolling motors combined by 2–1. Mike has sold 100,000 Perch Trollers each year since the beginning of 1994. His plant is capable of

making 120,000 Perch Trollers per year. The trolling motor sells for $100. He makes a profit of $20/trolling motor. Mike believes that he could have sold the Perch Troller for $10 more if there were no infringers in the market. He also sells cases which the motor can be stored in during the winter. The cases have no other use and no other motors fit within the case. He sells 500,000 cases/year to customers who buy the Perch Troller at a profit of $10/case. Looking at The Perch Troller, you realize that it is not marked with the '835 patent number.

Mike tells you that at a trade show on November 1, 1995, he encountered two companies selling bow-mounted trolling motor with electronic autopilot systems. The Easy Troller, manufactured and sold by Mark's Boats exclusively in the Pacific Northwest (Washington state, Oregon and northern California) and the Bass Troller sold by LL Green exclusively in New England. Mike's Fishing sent cease-and-desist letters to both companies on January 1, 1996.

The Bass Troller Dispute

The letter to LL Green accused its Bass Troller of infringing the '835 patent and offered to discuss licensing terms. LL Green refused to take a license and Mike's Fishing sued them for patent infringement in the Western District of Massachusetts. After a jury found that LL Green infringed the '835 patent under the doctrine of equivalents, the companies settled. You obtain a copy of the licensing agreement which says "LL Green agrees to pay Mike's Fishing a royalty of 20% for the sale of all Bass Trollers until the expiration of the '835 patent and agrees to waive its right to appeal the jury's determination that the Bass Troller infringes in exchange for an exclusive license to sell the patented invention in New England (Massachusetts, Connecticut, Maine, Vermont, and Rhode Island)." You notice that the Bass Troller is not marked with any patent numbers.

The Easy Troller

The January 1, 1996 cease-and-desist letter to Mark's Boats accused The Easy Troller of infringing the '835 patent and offered to discuss licensing terms. Mark and Mike met at the Boat House on February 1, 1996 to discuss licensing terms. Mike offered Mark a license to sell the trolling motor for a royalty rate of 25%, which Mike claims is his standard royalty rate for licensing any of his trolling motor patents. Mark refused saying that he does not think The Easy Troller infringes and besides 25% is highway robbery, other companies typically license their trolling motor patents for about 10%.

Upon an examination of The Easy Troller and its sales literature you determine that The Easy Troller is almost identical to the Bass Troller and that it may infringes under the doctrine of equivalents (you think it could be a close case).

With Mike's permission, you contact Mark about the possibility of licensing the '835 patent. He calls you back and tells you that he is not interested in a license. He says that he does not think that his Easy Troller infringes. He also tells you he got an opinion from Hank Cheatum, a patent attorney with 25 years experience and a mechanical engineering degree, after he received your call. He tells you that Hank Cheatum looked at the patent and The Easy Troller and concluded that it did not infringe. You ask Mark for a copy of the opinion and he says it was an oral opinion that Hank gave him last Saturday when they went fishing. You ask him if Hank told him why the Easy Troller does not infringe. He laughs and says, "I'm no patent attorney, Hank said it did not infringe and that was all I needed to hear." Mark continues, "Besides, we discovered the '835 patent as soon as it issued and my engineers modified the Easy Troller design so that we would not infringe."

Mike freely tells you that he has sold 50,000 Easy Trollers each year since the beginning of 1994. He makes a profit of $30/per trolling motor. He has 100 employees manufacturing Easy Trollers in his Portland factory (in fact, that is the only thing that is made in this factory).

What remedies might Mike receive? What arguments will be raised by each side? Do you have any advise for Mike?

How would it affect your analysis if Mike told you that there is a non-infringing stern-mounted trolling motor on the market? It is sold by Kulpa Motors for $150. Kulpa sells 100,000 motors per year. In addition, Mike just discovered that Moore Motors is selling a trolling motor identical to the Easy Troller and Mike wants to sue them for infringement as soon as you resolve the suit against Mark's Boats. Moore sells about 100,000 trolling motors per year at $100/motor. How would you advise Mike?

Chapter Fifteen

JURY INSTRUCTIONS, SPECIAL VERDICT FORMS, AND POST–TRIAL MOTIONS

A. SPECIAL VERDICT AND JURY INSTRUCTIONS

FEDERAL RULES OF CIVIL PROCEDURE- Rule 49:

(a) Special Verdicts. The court may require a jury to return only a special verdict in the form of a special written finding upon each issue of fact. In that event the court may submit to the jury written questions susceptible of categorical or other brief answer or may submit written forms of the several special findings which might properly be made under the pleadings and evidence; or it may use such other method of submitting the issues and requiring the written findings thereon as it deems most appropriate. The court shall give to the jury such explanation and instruction concerning the matter thus submitted as may be necessary to enable the jury to make its findings upon each issue. If in so doing the court omits any issue of fact raised by the pleadings or by the evidence, each party waives the right to a trial by jury of the issue so omitted unless before the jury retires the party demands its submission to the jury. As to an issue omitted without such demand the court may make a finding; or, if it fails to do so, it shall be deemed to have made a finding in accord with the judgment on the special verdict.

This chapter addresses some of the special aspects that accompany a patent jury trial. More often than not, trials of patent infringement cases are conducted before juries. It is logical to ask whether the trials of matters so technical in nature can be effectively presented to a jury of lay persons. Yet, the jury trial is a matter of right and will be granted on demand made in accordance with the requirements of Rule 38 of the Federal Rules of Civil Procedure.

The jury trial itself is conducted differently from a bench trial. Most significantly, the court protects carefully what evidence is presented to the jury to minimize confusion and prevent undue prejudice. The accompanying arguments are most often not even heard by the jury and are conducted at "side bar," and thereby further enhance the mystery of the proceeding to the jury.

One can imagine the potential for confusion in a patent jury trial. Not only are the patent liability issues new, the technology unfamiliar, the claims and specification language potentially incomprehensible, the jurors are also asked to perform a job they have never done before, and may never do again. First and foremost then in importance, the jury must be told what its job is and how it is to be performed. This is the job of the court with significant input from counsel. It, therefore, becomes the essential role of respective counsel to do several things in both the presentation of the trial and in helping the court to properly instruct the jury.

First, effective jury trial advocacy requires presentation of all issues and disputed matters in a manner understandable to a typical juror. The technical parlance of the specification and claims and the accused subject matter must be "translated" to inform the jury of your client's story. This is particularly true for the defendant who must assure that the jury understands enough about the claimed invention so that it can be convinced as to why the accused subject matter is different; or as to why the claimed subject matter is anticipated or obvious over the prior art. It is likewise important for the plaintiff-patentee's story to be understandable if the jury is to be convinced that the claims are infringed by the accused subject matter and that the claimed invention is an important one worthy of a substantial damage award.

But even when the best adversarial presentation satisfies the need for simplicity and clarity, the entire process may still fail if the jury is not properly instructed on what it is to decide and how it is to do so. Proper jury instructions and the special verdict form become critical as the next case demonstrates.

AMERICAN HOIST & DERRICK CO. v. SOWA & SONS, INC.

725 F.2d 1350, 220 USPQ 763 (Fed. Cir. 1984)

Before RICH, Circuit Judge, COWEN, Senior Circuit Judge, and KASHIWA, Circuit Judge.

RICH, Circuit Judge.

American Hoist and Derrick Co. (AmHoist) appeals from the unpublished decision of the United States District Court for the District of Oregon holding for Sowa & Sons, Inc. (Sowa) on AmHoist's suit for infringement of claims 3, 5 and 7 of its Shahan U.S. Patent No. 4,079,584, issued March 21, 1978, for a "Heavy Duty Shackle." After a two and one-half day jury trial, the jury rendered a verdict for defendant by answering written interrogatories as to two legal issues, stating that each claim in suit was invalid for obviousness and for fraud in the prosecution of those claims in the United States Patent and Trademark Office (PTO).

In three separation opinions, the district court held (1) that it would adopt the jury's determination of obviousness, (2) that there was sufficient evidence to support the jury's "findings" of fraud, and, while the degree of fraud was insufficient to support Sowa's unfair competition and antitrust counterclaims, that it was sufficient to render this an exceptional case under 35 U.S.C. § 285 justifying an award to Sowa of its attorney fees, and (3) that Sowa was entitled to $50,000 in attorney fees rather than the $90,367.55 requested.

Because of erroneous jury instructions, and because there exist disputed issues of fact, we vacate and remand for a new trial. However, we reverse the trial court's determination that the jury could properly have found that no damages were proved.

BACKGROUND

As described in the "ABSTRACT" of the patent in suit, the invention relates to

> A heavy duty shackle for use under great loads, such as in anchor lines. The shackle is formed from a cylindrical bar rod by shaping the ends to a reduced diameter, and forging the central portion into a flattened shape having the cross-section of a wide shallow U shape. The bottom surface of the central section is in the form of a portion of a circular cylinder. The ends of the bar are flattened and a central opening is forged and based for a pin. The formed bar is then bent in the form of a bow to provide an eye for the shackle, with two parallel ears spaced a selected distance apart.

Figures 5 and 6 of the patent are reproduced below:

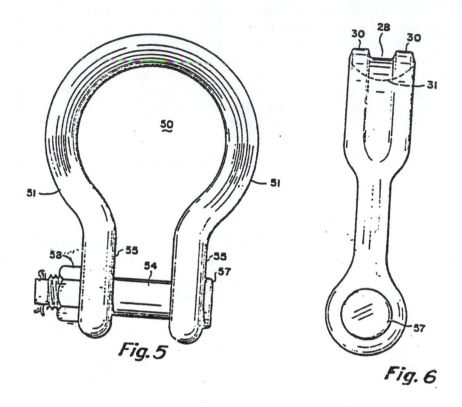

Fig. 5

Fig. 6

In Fig. 5, 50 is the "eye" of the shackle, 51 labels the "rein sections," 55 the "ears," and 54 and 57 designate parts of a pin that may be threaded and held on by a nut 58 and/or cotter pin as shown. Fig. 6 shows at 28 a depressed central portion, at 30 flat surfaces, and 31 indicates the cylindrical under surface of the shackle.

Claims 3, 5, and 7, all claims in suit, read as follows:

3.   A shackle bow for heavy duty use under large loads, as in anchor lines, comprising:

a.   a rein section adjacent the two ends of said shackle for a selected length and of diameter X', each said rein section being between a central cylindrical portion and a flattened ear portion;

b.   said central cylindrical portion being of a broadened flattened shape, having a U-shaped cross-section with a circular bottom surface, the radius of said bottom surface being at least substantially equal to X';

c.   said shackle being in the shape of a bow, with said U-shape of said central cylindrical portion directed outwardly, around a central eye, said ears being substantially parallel, spaced apart a distance less than the diameter of said eye, and having coaxial central openings therein to receive a pin there-through.

5.   A shackle bow having an approximately circular eye, with two rein sections leading to two substantially parallel ears;

the cross-section of said bow being in the form of a broad flat U section, with the bottom (inner) surface having as large a radius as possible;

the thickness of the cross-section of said bow substantially constant;

the cross-section of said rein section approximately circular;

the cross-section of said ears being broad and thin, with aligned central openings, and thick flanges formed by forging central depressions in said ears; said shackle bow being heat treated.

7.   The shackle bow of claim 5 including a locked pin through said central openings.

Defending against AmHoist's suit for infringement of these claims, Sowa denied infringement and counterclaimed for a declaratory judgment of invalidity. Sowa later brought to AmHoist's attention what it deemed new prior art, leading AmHoist to file an application for reissue of its patent. Sowa then amended its answer and counterclaimed for damages for unfair competition and for violation of federal antitrust law, asserting that AmHoist committed fraud in the PTO by not disclosing to the examiner the prior art that Sowa discovered.

Sowa stipulated in a pretrial order that its products infringed the claims in suit, Sowa's counterclaims were severed, and the issue of validity was tried to a jury. The jury returned its answers to two written interrogatories on ultimate legal issues, cf. Fed. R. Civ. P. 49(b), stating that each claim was invalid under § 103 and for "fraud on the Patent Office."

Shortly after the verdict, the PTO completed examination of the reissue application, allowing claims 1, 2, 5, 6, and 7 without change in the first Office Action. After AmHoist amended claim 3 to clarify the meaning of "diameter," and swore that the mistake in claim 3 occurred without deceptive intent, it too was allowed, as was claim 4 which had been objected to as depending from a rejected claim.

The district court stated:

Because the issue of obviousness under 35 U.S.C. § 103 is one of law rather than of fact, it is encumbent [sic] upon the court rather than the jury to make the final determination. Guided by the jury's findings and by the evidence, I hold the Shahan patent to be invalid under § 103.

In reaching its conclusion, the court first noted that because the PTO was not in possession of all "relevant prior art" the 35 U.S.C. 282 presumption of validity "disappears" because "the court is not entitled to rely upon the patent office expertise." After setting forth the scope and content of the prior art and stating that testimony of several experts indicated that a person of ordinary skill in the art of heavy-duty shackle design is "a skilled engineer capable of determining stress requirements, material, and shape designs and would have a high familiarity with the design, manufacturing, and performance characteristics of various types of rope fittings and fixtures," the court concluded a two-page opinion on validity as follows:

> The jury determined that the subject matter of the Shahan patent would have been obvious to one of ordinary skill in the art at the time of the claimed invention. I agree. The only difference other than size between the Shahan design and other cited, prior art is the presence of rein portions of either rectangular (Crosby–Laughlin and Nicro/Fico) or ellipsoidal (Schaefer Marine), rather than circular cross-section. Such circular cross-section design is not new, however, and can be found on the old and well-known anchor shackle design.

In another opinion, the court determined this to be an "exceptional case" within 35 U.S.C. § 285, although "the degree of fraud was insufficient to support defendant's unfair competition claim":

> A jury determined that AmHoist's patent was invalid. On each claim of the patent in issue, the jury determined that AmHoist committed fraud on the Patent Office. The fact that a reissue application was allowed by a Patent Office examiner makes this a harder case, but does not remove the finding of fraud by the jury.

* * *

> I find that plaintiff's actions taken to procure its Shahan patent were well within the range of activities sufficient to find the ensuing patent infringement case "exceptional" within the meaning of § 285. A jury properly concluded that AmHoist committed fraud on the Patent Office. Even assuming that AmHoist's conduct was short of fraud, I would find that it was in excess of simple negligence so as to support a finding of "exceptional."

> I further find that an award of attorney's fees in this case is appropriate. Defendant is a smaller company than plaintiff and enjoyed substantially less of the market share. The amount of potential damages for the alleged infringement was small—a factor which might have counseled Sowa's success in invalidating an unlawfully obtained patent accrues not only to its interests but also to the public interest. Under these circumstances, I find that it would be unjust for Sowa to bear the expense of its counsel's fees in successfully pursuing this case.

In its final opinion, the district court entered an award of $50,000 in attorney fees, but "only for work on the patent claims and not on the counterclaims [Sowa] pursued." Sowa had requested $90,367.55, but the court believed that to be "too high considering all relevant factors."

ARGUMENTS ON APPEAL

AmHoist argues that the court erred in submitting the fraud issue to the jury because there was no evidence of bad faith and intent to deceive the examiner or gross negligence representing such reckless disregard for the truth as to be tantamount to bad faith, and because there was insufficient evidence to show materiality of the undisclosed art by clear, unequivocal and convincing evidence; that the award of attorney fees based on the jury's finding of fraud must also be reversed; and that the jury's finding that AmHoist suffered no damage as a result of Sowa's admitted infringement must also be reversed because AmHoist's evidence as to damages was uncontroverted except as to calculation of profit from lost sales.

With respect to jury instructions, AmHoist argues that the court erred: in instructing the jury that AmHoist, the patentee, had the burden of proving nonobviousness if Sowa introduced at trial art more pertinent than the art cited by the examiner; in refusing to instruct the jury on the effect of the reissue proceedings on the quantum of proof necessary for Sowa to prove obviousness; in refusing to submit the factual inquiries underlying 35 U.S.C. § 103 to the jury in the form of special interrogatories under Fed. R. Civ. P. 49; and in instructing the jury that the invention described in AmHoist's patent must produce new and unexpected results to be considered nonobvious.

With respect to AmHoist's allegation that the court erred in submitting the fraud issue to the jury, Sowa responds that there was substantial evidence of fraud upon which the jury could have relied. Sowa also submits that the jury could have properly found, as it did, that AmHoist failed to establish any lost profits on the sale by Sowa of the accused shackles.

With respect to AmHoist's assertion that the court erred in instructing the jury that AmHoist bore the burden of proving nonobviousness, Sowa argues: (1) that AmHoist did not object to the instruction in question, see Fed. R. Civ. P. 51; (2) that the instruction was clearly in conformity with the law of the circuit in which the case was tried; (3) that, even if it was error to give the instruction in question, that error was harmless because there is another, independent ground upon which the judgment of the lower court was based, namely, that the claims in suit were obtained by fraud; and (4) that aside from the propriety of the instruction, independent review of the record by this court (it being asserted by Sowa that there is no dispute as to the underlying facts) will disclose that the claims are invalid under 35 U.S.C. § 103. However, Sowa's assertion that the underlying facts are undisputed is itself the subject of dispute.

AmHoist replies that it complied with Fed. R. Civ. P. 51 by submitting requested jury instructions and verdict forms placing the burden of proving obviousness on Sowa, and that it was not required to object at all to an instruction which properly set forth the law of the Ninth Circuit.

OPINION

While we regret having to order a new trial before an already overburdened district court, a new trial is mandated, and this case is a good illustration of the difficulties inherent, generally, in the use of juries to resolve patent disputes and, specifically, in allowing the use in such cases of general verdict forms unaccompanied by interrogatories on the controlling facts.

The verdict returned by the jury is reproduced in full below:

IN THE UNITED STATES DISTRICT COURT

FOR THE DISTRICT OF OREGON

AMERICAN HOIST & DERRICK COMPANY,

    Plaintiff,

    v.   Civil No. 79-981-PA

SOWA & SONS, INC.,

    Defendant.

VERDICT

1. Do you find that claim 3 of the patent is

    Valid

    Invalid X   [CHECK ONLY ONE]

2. If you have found that claim 3 of the patent is invalid, then state the reason or reasons why by checking the applicable item(s) below. [DO NOT ANSWER THIS IF YOU FOUND CLAIM 3 VALID]

    a. The subject matter of claim 3 would have been obvious to one of ordinary skill in the art at the time the claimed invention was made.

    b. Plaintiff committed fraud on the Patent Office in connection with claim 3.

    c. James M. Shahan is not the inventor of claim 3 and the patent office was intentionally deceived in this regard.

3. Do you find that claim 5 of the patent is

    Valid

    Invalid X   [CHECK ONLY ONE]

4. If you have found that claim 5 of the patent is invalid, then state the reason or reasons why by checking the applicable item(s) below. [DO NOT ANSWER THIS IF YOU FOUND CLAIM 5 VALID]

    a. The subject matter of claim 5 would have been obvious to one of ordinary skill in the art at the time the claimed invention was made.

    b. Plaintiff committed fraud on the Patent Office in connection with claim 5.

5. Do you find that claim 7 of the patent is

    Valid

    Invalid X   [CHECK ONLY ONE]

6. If you have found that claim 7 of the patent is invalid, then state the reason or reasons why by checking the applicable item(s) below. [DO NOT ANSWER THIS IF YOU FOUND CLAIM 7 VALID]

    a. The subject matter of claim 7 would have been obvious to one of ordinary skill in the art at the time the claimed invention was made.

    b. Plaintiff committed fraud on the Patent Office in connection with claim 7.

7. Regardless of your previous answers, what is the amount of the profits lost by plaintiff, if any, as the result of defendant's sales of 18 wide-body shackles?

    Damages $ 0

Dated the 13 day of November, 1981.

Before the jurors retired to reach this verdict, the trial court read to them twenty-six pages of instructions. AmHoist urges reversal on the ground that several of those instructions were erroneous. On consideration of those instructions, in light of all the instructions given, we are constrained to agree.

1. 35 U.S.C. § 282

With respect to the burden of proof, the court instructed the jury as follows:

> If you find the prior art references which defendant has cited are no more pertinent than the art utilized by the examiner when examining the Shahan patent[,] then defendant has the burden of establishing obviousness by "clear and convincing evidence." If, on the other hand, you find any of the prior art references which defendant has cited are more pertinent than the art utilized by the examiner when examining the Shahan patent, then that presumption of validity *disappears* as to that issue of obviousness and the *plaintiff has the burden of proof* by a preponderance of the evidence. [Emphasis ours.]

That instruction was erroneous in two respects. First, it misassigned the burden of proof. The final sentence of 35 U.S.C. § 282 mandates that "The burden of establishing invalidity of a patent or any claim thereof shall rest on the party asserting such invalidity." Precedent adopted by this court pursuant to *South Corp. v. United States*, 690 F.2d 1368, 1369, 215 USPQ 657, 658 (Fed. Cir. 1982), declares that burden to be permanent, emphasizing that § 282

> mandates not only a presumption shifting the burden of going forward in a purely procedural sense, but also *places the burden of persuasion on the party who asserts that the patent is invalid*. To speak of the presumption as "no longer attaching" is to risk a concomitant, and unspoken, assumption that the burden of persuasion is thereafter no longer upon him who asserts invalidity. That view is contrary to the meaning of § 282, for *the burden of persuasion is and remains always upon the party asserting invalidity*, whether the most pertinent prior art was or was not considered by the examine. [Emphasis ours.]

Solder Removal Co. v. U.S. International Trade Commission, 65 C.C.P.A. 120, 582 F.2d 628, 632–33, 199 USPQ 129, 133 (C.C.P.A. 1978) (footnotes omitted). On this point we, like the C.C.P.A., disagree with the Ninth Circuit position stated in *Tveter, supra* note 1, which was that because the examiner did not have certain prior art patents before him when examining the application for the patent in suit, which patents were closer art than he cited, the burden of proving non-obviousness was on the patentee. Our position is that this is never so because it would be contrary to the statute.

The second and more general error in the above jury instruction was that it failed to explain accurately the "presumption of validity," which is not surprising. The prevailing confusion in the cases over its meaning and effect has been engendered by assertions that under some circumstances the presumption is retained and under others it is destroyed, or that the presumption is strengthened or weakened, as a result of which, it has been said, the burden of proof shifts from one party to another or the standard of proof changes.

The presumption was, originally, the creation of the courts and was a part of the judge-made body of patent law when the Patent Act of 1952 was written. That act, for the first time, made it statutory in § 282, first paragraph, which, before the amendments of 1965 and 1975, was of the utmost simplicity. It read:

> A patent shall be presumed valid. The burden of establishing invalidity of a patent shall rest on the party asserting it.

To summarize on this point, § 282 creates a presumption that a patent is valid and imposes the burden of proving invalidity on the attacker. That burden is constant and never changes and is to convince the court of invalidity by clear evidence. Deference is due the Patent and Trademark Office decision to issue the patent with respect to evidence bearing on validity with respect to evidence it did not consider. All evidence bearing on the validity issue, whether considered by the PTO or not, is to be taken into account by the tribunal in which validity is attacked.

2. 35 U.S.C. § 103

In ending its jury charge on the § 103 nonobviousness requirement, the court said:

> You must next determine whether the differences between plaintiff's claimed invention and the prior art, if any, and as you have found them to be, produce a new and unexpected result. That is, you must determine whether the elements making up plaintiff's claimed invention combine so as to perform in some way or manner, a new and unexpected function in combination than they perform separately. The reason for this is that a patented invention which unites only old elements without producing either a new and unexpected result merely withdraws from the public's use that which was known before.

Instructing a jury that the presence of such a "new and unexpected function in combination" is a requirement of patentability—and reasoning that were the law otherwise a claimed combination of old elements would "merely [withdraw] from the public's use that which was known before"—is wholly erroneous.

We also agree with AmHoist that the district court should have submitted to the jury the factual inquiries underlying a § 103 determination in the form of special interrogatories. Fed. R. Civ. P. 49. While the form of jury verdict is normally a matter discretion with the trial court, one court has noted that the "failure to utilize this method in a patent case places a heavy burden of convincing the reviewing court that the trial judge did not abuse his discretion." *Baumstimler v. Rankin*, 677 F.2d 1061, 1071–72, 215 USPQ 575, 584 (5th Cir. 1982).

The use of special interrogatories, as noted by the Fifth Circuit, *id.*, facilitates appellate review (and review by the trial court on any motion for judgment notwithstanding the verdict), for such use frees the court from having to survey every possible basis for the jury's decision. Utilization of that verdict form may also help avoid lengthy retrials, e.g., by demonstrating in a particular case that implementation of the harmless error standard is appropriate. 28 U.S.C. § 2111 (1982).

Additionally, the use of special interrogatories "accords with the inherent divisional lines between the roles of judge and jury, the boundaries of which are so easily transgressed in patent cases tried to juries." *Baumstimler, supra* at 1071, 215 USPQ at 583. In this case, the district court began its opinion on whether Sowa had met its burden of demonstrating the Shahan patent to be invalid by noting that, "Because the issue of obviousness under 35 U.S.C. § 103 is one of law rather than of fact, it is encumbent [sic] upon the court rather than the jury to make the final determination." "Guided by the jury's *findings* and by the evidence [emphasis added]," the court held the claims invalid.

There were no express findings, however, by which the district court could have been guided, nor were the "findings" of the jury reexamined by the court, in writing, under the appropriate standard on AmHoist's motion for judgment n.o.v. *Cf. Control Components, Inc. v. Valtek, Inc.,* 609 F.2d 763, 768–69, 204 USPQ 785, 789–90 (5th Cir. 1980) (Court's "independent review of the record discloses competent substantial evidence to support the jury's findings on the factual inquiries underlying the determination of validity."). Further, the district court apparently set forth its own findings of fact with respect to the scope and content of the prior art, the level of ordinary skill in the art, and the differences between the claimed invention and the prior art.

In performing its role with respect to § 103, we assume that the district court recognized that it had no express findings of fact on which to base its legal conclusion. A district court may not solicit only a legal conclusion from the jury and then act as factfinder preliminary to expressing agreement with its legal determination.

After the jury returned its verdict in favor of Sowa, the court ordered each side to submit proposed findings of fact, conclusions of law, and judgment within ten days. After expressing its agreement with the jury's conclusion on obviousness, which is a conclusion of law, the court stated: "This opinion shall constitute findings of fact and conclusions of law pursuant to Fed. R. Civ. P. 52(a)." The court seems to have turned the respective roles of judge and jury upside down. We caution that the role of the jury as fact-finder must not be usurped. By its terms, Rule 52, titled "Findings by the Court," applies only to "actions tried upon the facts without a jury or with an advisory jury."

3. *Fraud in the PTO*

On the fraud issue, the court instructed the jury that

the law imposes upon an applicant for a patent and the applicant's attorney, an uncompromising duty to be completely candid and to fully disclose all pertinent facts which *may affect* the decision that the patent examiner has to make on the question of whether to grant a patent. [Emphasis ours.]

The court continued:

If an applicant intentionally and *fraudulently* withholds any information or makes *fraudulent* representations to the Patent Office [sic, PTO] which are false and have a *material* influence upon the examiner in deciding the question of whether to grant a patent on the invention, the patent is not enforceable. A good faith mistake does not constitute fraud. [Emphasis ours.]

The jury was also instructed that:

The applicant's duty to disclose all facts *pertinent* to the prosecution of an application requires disclosure to the [PTO] of all *pertinent* prior art or other *pertinent* information of which applicant is aware or *reasonably should be aware*. [Emphasis ours.]

The above instructions are defective both with respect to what was stated and by reason of what was not stated.

It is not correct to instruct a jury that an applicant for patent must "fully disclose all pertinent facts which may affect the decision" of the PTO. Such instruction is broad enough to include information which might persuade the examiner to allow claims, as opposed to rejecting them. Further, a jury should not be given instructions on "fraud in the PTO" that utilize phrases like "fraudulently withholds any information," or "makes fraudulent representations * * * which are false." Such instructions do not aid the jury in understanding "fraud," do not direct the jury to the relevant factual inquiries, and can only cause mental confusion.

Reverting to the court's recitation of a "duty to disclose all facts pertinent to the prosecution of an application," it is also clear that an applicant for patent is under no obligation to disclose "all pertinent prior art or other pertinent information" of which he is aware. *Digital Equipment Corp. v. Diamond*, 653 F.2d 701, 716, 210 USPQ 521, 538 (1st Cir. 1981).

Sowa argues that AmHoist may not complain of the court's instructions on materiality, for it lodged no objection below. While we recognize that "fraud in the PTO" is an area of law fraught with confusion and contradiction, to allow a jury verdict of fraud to stand on these instructions would be a great injustice. Additionally, and although mindful of the sometime tactic of counsel making a conscious decision not to object to an instruction known to be erroneous, thus allowing to stand, for purposes of appeal, an error that might warrant a new trial, we nevertheless would "reverse on the ground of plain error in a jury charge that was not objected to [because] such is necessary to correct a fundamental error."

4.   The Reissue Proceeding

As earlier noted, AmHoist also contends that the district court erred in refusing to instruct the jury on the effect of the reissue proceedings "on Sowa's burden of proof on the issue of obviousness." Sowa counters that "at the time this case was presented to the jury the Shahan reissue application was still pending as AmHoist had been required by the PTO to submit a new oath because the previously submitted oath failed to state that the applicant had claimed more than it was entitled to."

Thus, Sowa argues that "the district court properly refused to apply the presumption of validity to a pending reissue application. As the point is now moot, we need not decide the question.

Should the case be tried again to a jury, however, it is clearly appropriate that the jury be instructed that because the PTO has not held the claims in suit patentable in light of the additional art discovered by Sowa, its burden of proof of unpatentability has become more difficult to sustain—a fact likewise to be taken into account by the trial judge. With respect to the "fraud" issue, it is also manifest that the decision of the PTO may have an effect on determining the degree of materiality of the involved prior art under the standards previously discussed.

AmHoist asks for guidance regarding an appropriate instruction on the effect of reissue. Other than the consequences just noted, we perceive no further impact on instructing a future jury in this case.

Notes

1. **Preliminary Instructions.** Many courts give "preliminary jury instructions" at the beginning of trial as an introduction of the subject matter of the trial and of the jury's role. These instructions are often far less comprehensive than the jury instructions given at the end of the presentation of evidence.

2. **Avoid Technical or Legal Jargon.** It is important to draw a balance between the legal sufficiency and accuracy of the instructions in the sense of using the required legal terms and standards and trying to translate those terms into language that is understandable to the jury. Where possible, technical aspects should be described in plain language, not the language of the technical experts. In *Skidmore v. Baltimore & Ohio Railroad Co.*, 167 F.2d 54, 64–65 (2d Cir. 1948), the Court opined:

> The theory of the general verdict involves the assumption that the jury fully comprehends the judge's instructions concerning the applicable substantive legal rules. Yet, often the judge must state those rules to the jury with such niceties that many lawyers do not comprehend them, and it is impossible that the jury can. Judge Bok notes that 'juries have the disadvantage * * * of being treated like children while the testimony is going on, but then being doused with a kettleful of law during the charge that would make a third-year law-student blanch.' Nevertheless, the patently fictitious assumption that the jurors have more legal wisdom than third-year law-students requires the upper court to reverse when a trial judge fails to state the pertinent substantive rules with sufficient particularity. Such faulty instructions, it has been said, 'are the greatest single source of reversible error.'

The jury instructions should use the parties' names (Mike's Fishing) rather than plaintiff or patentee or assignee. They should mention who has the burden of proof and the evidentiary burden. They should explain how the law applies to the facts of the case rather than just reciting the statute. In *Structural Rubber Products Co. v. Park Rubber Co.*, 749 F.2d 707, 722–23, 223 USPQ 1264, 1276 (Fed. Cir. 1984), the following instruction on obviousness had been given by the district court:

> A patent may not be obtained if the differences between the claimed invention and the prior art are such that the claimed invention would have been obvious at the time it was made to a person having ordinary skill in the art of the subject matter of the claimed invention.
>
> The prior art includes earlier patents, any additional information admitted by the patent application to be prior art, and prior inventions described in printed publications more than one year before the application for the patent or before the actual invention was made by the person filing the application. Under the law an inventor is presumed to have knowledge of all the prior art relevant to his claimed invention.
>
> If you find that the differences between the products recited in any claim in the patents in suit and what is taught by the prior art would have been such that the claimed invention taken as a whole would have been obvious to a person skilled in the art at the time the claimed invention of each patent in suit was made, then the subject of the claim is said to be obvious from the prior art.
>
> If you find obviousness as described in these instructions, then the claims for that invention must be found invalid.

Is there any error in this instruction? The Federal Circuit held:

> The error in this type of instruction on obviousness is not that the court has misstated the law, but that, as indicated above, the court has abdicated its responsibility to inform the jury of how the statute applies to the particular case.
>
> As stated in 9 WRIGHT & MILLER, FEDERAL PRACTICE AND PROCEDURE: CIVIL, § 2556, at 658 (1971) on the subject of proper instructions: "To repeat statutory language is not sufficient unless its meaning and application to the facts are clear without explanation." "Obviousness", as used in patent law, is not a term readily understood by a jury. Indeed, the term is overladen with layman's meanings different from its legal connotation, which can only add confusion to the decision-making process by the most conscientious jury. In this case such confusion is demonstrated by the jury's anomalous answers that there is no prior art, that the inventions were not obvious, but that the inventions were lacking in novelty.
>
> We join other courts that have held that the duty of a trial court in any jury trial is to give instructions which are meaningful, not in terms of some abstract case, but which can be understood and given effect by the jury once it resolves the issues of fact which are in dispute. A reasoned resolution of the basis for upholding or

invalidating patents is mandated by *Graham*. Unlike a verdict on negligence to which the jury is expected to contribute the sense of the community, a decision on patent validity does not benefit from the jury's communal sense of patentability. A patentee, as well as an infringer, is entitled to have its position judged only by the standard which Congress has written into the statute. Thus, a party has a right (upon proper requests) to have the trial court delineate in its instructions what facts in the particular case must be found to reach a conclusion of obviousness and what facts require a contrary answer. On appeal, this court can then concentrate on those factors which the trial court indicated in its instructions were key to the obviousness decision and will not be forced to engage in shadowboxing the presumptions and assumptions underlying the decision which is necessary when the trial court does no more than read or paraphrase the statute as an instruction. Without the benefit of the trial court's reasoning in particularized instructions, the appeal takes on the character of an initial determination with respect to application of the law to the facts, rather than a review.

Id. at 723, 223 USPQ at 1276 (citations omitted).

3. Jury instructions and the special verdict form are usually the result of negotiation between the parties, each of whom proposed their preferred language. Where agreement is reached, the court will review the instructions and verdict form to assure legal sufficiency. Where agreement is not reached, the court will decide the language to be used. Rule 51 gives the court discretion in deciding when to instruct the jury. Most attorneys will want to use the jury instructions and special verdict forms in their closing arguments, so it is often better to have the jury instructed just prior to closing arguments.

4. **Special Verdicts.** For purposes of appeal, it is very important that the instructions be legally sufficient and that the special verdict form be clear, so that the reviewing court can determine that the jury did its job properly. As noted in *American Hoist*, the use of special interrogatories also "frees the court from having to survey every possible basis for the jury's decision." As the Federal Circuit instructed in *Structural Rubber Products*, 749 F.2d at 723–24, 223 USPQ at 1276–77:

Because of the many factual variables which may enter into the question of obviousness, and to an even greater extent into a general verdict, it is a formidable task to draft unobjectionable instructions which lay out alternative mandatory general verdicts if specific facts are found. However, Fed. R. Civ. P. 49(a), provides a viable alternative ... Resort to Rule 49(a) greatly simplifies the instructions which must be given and clearly separates the respective functions of judge and jury. As stated in MOORE'S MANUAL § 22.08[1], at 22–78 to 22–79 (1983):

Use of the special verdict eliminates the necessity for and use of complicated instructions on the law, which are a normal concomitant of the general verdict. Complicated instructions have always been ludicrous and unfair: ludicrous in that only the naive can believe lay juries are capable of absorbing all the legal elements involved; unfair in that lack of comprehension leads to confusion and ultimately, injustice. When the special verdict is used the court should give to the jury only such explanation and instructions as it deems necessary to enable the jury to make intelligent findings upon the issues of facts submitted.

The utilization of Rule 49(a) appears to us as a particularly useful tool in conserving judicial resources and in effectuating the Congressional policy expressed in the patent laws.

Which party (the patent owner or the accused infringer) would prefer special verdict forms for the jury resolution of obviousness? For an article discussing the importance of special verdict forms and jury instructions in patent cases to shine some light into the black box, *see* Paul R. Michel & Dr. Michelle Rhyu, *Improving Patent Jury Trials,* 6 FED. CIRCUIT B.J. 89 (1996).

5. **Review of General Verdict on Appeal.** The Federal Circuit has held that it will review a general verdict by the jury by presuming that the jury found for the winning party on all underlying fact issues as long as there is evidence in the record. For example, obviousness is a question of law with four underlying facts. Imagine that the jury is simply given the general verdict: "Was the invention claimed in the '835 patent obvious at the time the patent application was filed?" and the jury returns a verdict of "YES." The court will review the jury verdict on obviousness by presuming that the jury found the scope and content of the prior art to include all disputed prior art and the jury found that the elements in the claims of the '835 patent are all contained in this prior art and that the objective considerations (commercial success, long felt need) all favor the obviousness conclusion. *See, e.g., Richardson–Vicks Inc. v. Upjohn Co.*, 122 F.3d 1476, 1479, 44 USPQ2d 1181 (Fed. Cir. 1997).

6. **Objections to Instructions.** Parties must object to jury instructions which they disagree with in order to preserve the issue for appeal. Failure to object waives the issue. To protect your right to appeal, you should renew the jury instruction objections after the court has instructed the jury.

SAMPLE SPECIAL VERDICT FORMS*

IN THE UNITED STATES DISTRICT COURT
FOR THE WESTERN DISTRICT OF PENNSYLVANIA

PPG INDUSTRIES, INC.,	)	
Plaintiff,	)	
	)	
v.	)	Civil Action No. 94–1112
	)	
GUARDIAN INDUSTRIES CORP.,	)	
Defendant	)	

* These special verdict forms were supplied by Robert Krupka of Kirkland & Ellis and are reproduced with his permission.

VERDICT

1. Has PPG proved by a preponderance of the evidence that Guardian infringed claim 4 of PPG's '886 patent?

   YES _____   NO ____X____
       (for PPG)   (for Guardian)

   If NO, go no further and advise Mr. Palus that you have reached a verdict.

   If YES, go to question #2.

2. Has PPG proved by clear and convincing evidence that Guardian willfully infringed PPG's '886 patent?

   YES _____   NO _____
       (for PPG)   (for Guardian)

   Go to question #3.

3. Has Guardian proved by clear and convincing evidence that claim 4 of PPG's '886 patent is invalid for obviousness?

   YES_____   NO _____
       (for Guardian)   (for PPG)

   If YES, go no further and advise Mr. Palus that you have reached a verdict.

   If NO, go to question #4.

4. How much damages do you award PPG for Guardian's infringement?

   $_____

Date: _____

_____
           Foreperson

IN THE UNITED STATES DISTRICT COURT
FOR THE DISTRICT OF DELAWARE

ALLIEDSIGNAL INC.,	)	
Plaintiff,	)	
	)	
v.	)	Civil Action No. 96–540 (RRM)
	)	
COOPER AUTOMOTIVE, INC.,	)	
Defendant	)	

SPECIAL VERDICT FORM

We, the jury, unanimously find as follows:

A.   INFRINGEMENT

Doctrine of Equivalents

1.   For each step of claim 1, do you find that AlliedSignal proved by a preponderance of the evidence that Cooper's process for manufacturing spark plug electrodes includes a step which is equivalent? (A "Yes" answer to this question is a find for AlliedSignal. A "No" answer is a finding for Cooper.)

Claim 1

Steps for Claim 1	Allied Signal Proved that Cooper has an Equivalent Step	
1. A Method of Manufacturing Electrodes for a Spark Plug Comprising the Steps Of	Yes	No
(1) cutting a first piece of inconel wire from a source to define a cylindrical blank having a first end and second end;	X	
(2) placing said cylindrical blank in a first die forming an extruded tip on said first end;	X	
(3) placing said cylindrical blank in a second die, said second die forming an extruded cup in said cylindrical blank that extends from said second end toward said first end;	X	
(4) inserting a copper core in said cup;	X	
(5) placing said cylindrical blank and copper core in a die to extrude to predetermined length between said first and second end for a resulting center wire;	X	
(6) locating the axial center of said tip;	X	
(7) placing a first sphere of platinum from a source in a fixture;	X	
(8) positioning the axial center on said first sphere of platinum;	X	
(9) applying a compressive force to said center wire while applying electrical current to the center wire and first sphere of platinum, said electrical current causing thermal energy to be created at the junction of the axial center and first sphere, said thermal energy causing the inconel in the tip at the junction to melt and flow around said first sphere;	X	
(10) terminating the electrical current and compressive force when approximately fifty percent of said first sphere is covered with inconel; and	X	
(11) transporting said center wire to a die where said first sphere of platinum is flattened into a first disc having a dome which is metallurgically bonded to the tip of said center electrode.	X	

B.   INVALIDITY

Obviousness to a Person of Ordinary Skill in the Art

1.   Do you find that Cooper proved by clear and convincing evidence that claim 1 of the '220 patent is invalid because the subject matter

would have been obvious to one of ordinary skill in the art at the time of the invention? (A "Yes" anser to this question is finding for Cooper. A "No" answer to this question is finding for AlliedSignal.)

Claim 1 Invalid   Yes _____   No __X__

If you answer no, skip page 4. If you answer yes, a list of the items Cooper contends are prior art to consider is provided on page 3. Check the box of the items you find are prior art and you relied upon to reach this conclusion.

Items Cooper Intends Are Prior Art

	Items Cooper Contends are Prior Art	*Relied Upon*	
1.	The disclosure by National Machinery to Mr. Moore of using a sphere of platinum in a process for making precious metal tipped spark plug electrodes	Yes _____	No _____
2.	The disclosure of Taylor–Winfield to Mr. More of welding a ball directly to a flat surface of the electrode by projection welding in a process for making precious metal tipped spark plug electrodes	Yes _____	No _____
3.	Process developed by Taylor–Winfield for attaching a sphere of platinum to a spark plug electrode	Yes _____	No _____
4.	The AlliedSignal stake and weld technique using platinum slugs	Yes _____	No _____
5.	Japanese Kokai Patent Application No. Sho 59 (1984)—119692 (Yoshio)	Yes _____	No _____
6.	U.S. Patent 4,725,254 entitled "Method for Manufacturing a Center Electrode for a Spark Plug" issued to David J. Moore and William A. Barrett	Yes _____	No _____
7.	U.S. Patent 4,803,395 entitled "Process for the Manufacture of a Platinum–Tipped Bimetallic Central Electrode for an Ignition Plug and the Electrode Produced According to this Process" issued to Michael Matesco	Yes _____	No _____
8.	U.S. Patent 3,548,472 entitled "Ignition Plug and Method for Manufacturing a Center Electrode for the Same" issued to Hisashi Urushiwara, et al.	Yes _____	No _____
9.	U.S. Patent 4,705,486 entitled "Method for Manufacturing a Center Electrode for a Spark Plug" issued to Martin G. Myers and William A. Barrett	Yes _____	No _____
10.	U.S. Patent 4,893,051 entitled "Spark Plug and the Method of Manufacturing the Same" issued to Ryoji Kondo	Yes _____	No _____
11.	U.S. Patent 3,488,841 entitled "Method for Manufacturing Electrical Contact Elements" issued to Theodore L. Stern	Yes _____	No _____
12.	U.S. Patent 3,194,940 entitled "Ball Assembly Apparatus" issued to Arthur James Thomson, et al.	Yes _____	No _____
13.	U.S. Patent 4,699,600 entitled "Spark Plug and Method of Manufacturing the Same issued to Ryoji Kondo	Yes _____	No _____
14.	Other Patents, Publications (Specify) _____ _____ _____	Yes _____	No _____
15.	Other disclosures to the named inventor (specify) _____ _____ _____	Yes _____	No _____

Inventorship

2. Do you find that claim 1 of the '220 patent is invalid because Cooper proved by clear and convincing evidence that in addition to Mr. Moore, other individuals were co-inventors of the processes recited in the claim? (A "Yes" answer to this question is finding for Cooper. A "No" answer is a finding for AlliedSignal.)

Yes _____ No __X__

Best Mode

3. Do you find that claim 1 of the '220 patent is invalid because Cooper proved by clear and convincing evidence that Mr. Moore, AlliedSignal or its attorneys did not disclose in the '220 parent specifications the best mode of carrying out the invention known to Mr. Moore at the time he filed his patent application? (A "Yes" answer to this question if a finding for Cooper. A "No" answer is a find for AlliedSignal.)

Yes _____ No __X__

Enablement

4. Do you find that claim of the '220 patent is invalid because Cooper proved by clear and convincing evidence that the '220 patent specification does not provide a written description of the invention in full, clear, concise, and exact terms as to enable a person skilled in the art to which it pertains, or with which it is mostly nearly connected, to use the invention as claimed? (A "Yes" to this question is a finding for Cooper. A "No" answer is a find for AlliedSignal.)

Yes _____ No __X__

5. Do you find that claim 1 of the '220 patent is invalid because Cooper proved by clear and convincing evidence that the '220 patent claims do not particularly point out and distinctly claim the subject matter which Mr. Moore regarded as his invention? (A "Yes" to this question is a finding for Cooper. A "No" answer is a find for AlliedSignal.)

Yes _____ No __X__

If you find that claim 1 is infringed and valid, proceed to the questions in section C and D below. If you find that claim 1 is not infringed or is not valid, then you should skip the remaining question and sign and date this verdict.

C. DAMAGES

Verdict as to Damages

We, the jury, unanimously find as follows:

1. The total past damages caused to plaintiff, AlliedSignal, by infringement of the '220 patent by Cooper from 1994 to the present is $39,210,409.

Interrogatories as To Damages

a. In computing the total past damages (Verdict Question C1), did you determine a reasonable royalty for <u>all</u> of Cooper's sales?

Yes ____

No __X__

b. If you answer to the interrogatory above was "YES", then insert "0" in response to question i and ii below. If your answer to the interrogatory above was "NO", then answer question i and ii below.

   i. AlliedSignal's **Reasonable Royalty** on a <u>portion</u> of Cooper's Sales $1,561.086.

   ii. AlliedSignal's **Loss Profits** on a <u>portion</u> of Cooper's Sales $29,131,780.

c. Of the amount of total damages awarded in part 1 above, how much, if any, is a result of **Price Erosion** on AlliedSignal's sales to Ford as a result of Cooper's proposals to Ford $8,517,543.

D. WILLFUL INFRINGEMENT

1. If you find that claim 1 is valid and is infringed, do you also find that AlliedSignal has shown by clear and convincing evidence that Cooper has willfully infringed claim 1? (A "Yes" answer to this question is a finding for AlliedSignal. A "No" answer is a finding for Cooper.)

Yes __X__ No _____

You each must sign this Verdict Form:

Dated: <u>6–11–98</u>

_____

(Foreperson)

Notes

1. Compare the special verdict form in *PPG Indus. v. Guardian Indus. Corp.* with *Allied Signal Inc. v. Cooper Automotive, Inc.* Keep in mind that the purpose of special verdict forms is to record jury reasoning for their verdicts. Do both of these special verdict forms accomplish this task? For more information on the PPG. Indus. case, see *PPG Indus., Inc. v. Guardian Indus. Corp.*, 156 F.3d 1351, 48 USPDQ2d 1351 (Fed. Cir. 1998).

Problems

1. Do you think that it is more to the plaintiff-patentee's benefit, or to the accused infringer's benefit, that the jury understand the technology?

2. What is the role of the technical witnesses in presentation of the parties' positions; is it to simplify the explanation and technology or to make

a complete technical record for appeal? Is there any danger in making the technology sound too simple?

3.   Is it more important to try the case to win it before the jury at the expense of sacrificing some completeness on the technical infringement analysis, or to make a complete and thorough record for appeal at the expense of presenting a case that the jury may not understand? Is there a balance?

4.   You represent either Mike's Fishing or Mark's Boats. Draft jury instructions and verdict forms to submit to the court. Be prepared to argue why your instruction should be adopted rather than your opponents. Mike's Fishing sued Mark's Boats alleging that its Easy Troller infringed the '835 patent. The district court granted Mark's Boats summary judgment of no literal infringement. There was a trial on whether the Easy Troller infringed claim 1 and claim 3 under the doctrine of equivalents. See Problems at the end of Chapter Eight for the '835 patent and Chapters Eight and Nine for a description of The Easy Troller technology. After the court rendered its claim construction, the only disputed issues with respect to claim 1 are whether a compass is equivalent to a magnetometer and whether optical coupling is equivalent to electrical coupling. The only disputed issue with respect to claim 3 is whether the means for manually overriding the autopilot in the Easy Troller (bike-type handle) is equivalent to the structure disclosed in the '835 specification (brake pedal). Assume there is no prosecution history.

5.   You represent either Mike's Fishing or Mark's Boats. Draft jury instructions and verdict forms to submit to the court on the issues of invalidity of claim 1. Be prepared to argue why your instruction should be adopted rather than your opponents. Mark's Boats has argued that claim 1 of the '835 patent is invalid because of the public use and on-sale bar of § 102(b). Mike's Fishing argued that his uses were experimental. See Problems in the obviousness section in Chapter Eleven for a description of the invalidity issues.

B.   POST–TRIAL MOTIONS

Federal Rules of Civil Procedure— RULE 50:

RULE 50. Judgment as a Matter of Law in Jury Trials; Alternative Motion for New Trial; Conditional Rulings

(a) Judgment as a Matter of Law.

(1) If during a trial by jury a party has been fully heard on an issue and there is no legally sufficient evidentiary basis for a reasonable jury to find for that party on that issue, the court may determine the issue against that party and may grant a motion for judgment as a matter of law against that party with respect to a claim or defense that cannot under the controlling law be maintained or defeated without a favorable finding on that issue.

(2) Motions for judgment as a matter of law may be made at any time before submission of the case to the jury. Such a motion shall specify the judgment sought and the law and the facts on which the moving party is entitled to judgment.

(b) Renewing Motion for Judgment After Trial; Alternative Motion for New Trial. If, for any reason, the court does not grant a motion for judgment as a matter of law made at the close of all the evidence, the court is considered to have submitted the action to the jury subject to the court's later deciding the legal questions raised by the motion. The movant may renew its request for judgment as a matter of law by filing a motion no later than 10 days after entry of judgment—and may alternatively request a new trial or join a motion for a new trial under Rule 59. In ruling on a renewed motion, the court may:

    (1) if a verdict was returned:

        (A) allow the judgment to stand,

        (B) order a new trial, or

        (C) direct entry of judgment as a matter of law; or

    (2) if no verdict was returned;

        (A) order a new trial, or

        (B) direct entry of judgment as a matter of law.

(c) Granting Renewed Motion for Judgment as a Matter of Law; Conditional Rulings; New Trial Motion

    (1) If the renewed motion for judgment as a matter of law is granted, the court shall also rule on the motion for a new trial, if any, by determining whether it should be granted if the judgment is thereafter vacated or reversed, and shall specify the grounds for granting or denying the motion for the new trial. If the motion for a new trial is thus conditionally granted, the order thereon does not affect the finality of the judgment. In case the motion for a new trial has been conditionally granted and the judgment is reversed on appeal, the new trial shall proceed unless the appellate court has otherwise ordered. In case the motion for a new trial has been denied, the appellee on appeal may assert error in that denial; and if the judgment is reversed on appeal, subsequent proceedings shall be in accordance with the order of the appellate court.

    (2) Any motion for a new trial under Rule 59 by a party against whom judgment as a matter of law is rendered shall be filed no later than 10 days after entry of the judgment.

(d) Same: Denial of Motion for Judgment as a Matter of Law. If the motion for judgment as a matter of law is denied, the party who prevailed on that motion may, as appellee, assert grounds entitling the party to a new trial in the event the appellate court concludes that the trial court erred in denying the motion for judgment. If the appellate court reverses the judgment, nothing in this rule precludes it from determining that the appellee is entitled to a new trial, or from directing the trial court to determine whether a new trial shall be granted.

RULE 59. New Trials; Amendment of Judgments

(a) Grounds. A new trial may be granted to all or any of the parties and on all or part of the issues (1) in an action in which there has been a trial by jury, for any of the reasons for which new trials have heretofore been granted in actions at law in the courts of the United States; and (2) in an action tried without a jury, for any of the reasons for which rehearings have heretofore been granted in suits in equity in the courts of the United States. On a motion for a new trial in an action tried without a jury, the court may open the judgment if one has been entered, take additional testimony, amend findings of fact and conclusions of law or make new findings and conclusions, and direct the entry of a new judgment.

(b) Time for Motion. Any motion for a new trial shall be filed no later than 10 days after entry of the judgment.

(c) Time for Serving Affidavits. When a motion for new trial is based on affidavits, they shall be filed with the motion. The opposing party has 10 days after service to file opposing affidavits, but that period may be extended for up to 20 days, either by the court for good cause or by the parties' written stipulation. The court may permit reply affidavits.

(d) On Court's Initiative; Notice; Specifying Grounds. No later than 10 days after entry of judgment the court, on its own, may order a new trial for any reason that would justify granting one on a party's motion. After giving the parties notice and an opportunity to be heard, the court may grant a timely motion for a new trial for a reason not stated in the motion. When granting a new trial on its own initiative or for a reason not stated in a motion, the court shall specify the grounds in its orders.

(e) Motion to Alter or Amend Judgment. Any motion to alter or amend a judgment shall be filed no later than 10 days after entry of the judgment.

After the plaintiffs' case has been presented, the defendant may make a motion under Rule 50 for a "directed verdict," known as a motion for judgment as a matter of law (JMOL) on any and all issues upon which the plaintiff bears the burden of proof. This motion is made outside the presence of the jury. The motion requests that the court end the trial in whole or part by entering judgment for the defendant because the plaintiff failed to establish a *prima facie* case on all or some of the issues upon which it based its complaint. A JMOL motion must be reviewed by the trial court "in the light least favorable to the movant."

Thus, the granting of a JMOL motion most often arises in situations where the plaintiff failed to present any evidence on a particular issue during its case-in-chief. The denial of the motion is most often the result where the plaintiff has presented evidence on the issue. The court may also postpone decision on the motion. If the JMOL motion is granted, the jury will hear no further evidence on that issue. If denied or postponed, the defendant will need to present its counter proofs during its case-in-chief.

A similar opportunity arises at the end of the defendant's case-in-chief, when the plaintiff may file a JMOL motion on those issues for which the defendant bore the burden of proof because it pleaded them in its affirmative defenses and counterclaims. Similarly under Rule 50(b), following any rebuttal or surrebuttal presentations, plaintiff and defendant may "within 10 days after the entry of judgment" file a JMOL motion. The filing of a JMOL motion at this time is necessary to preserve the parties' rights to again move for judgment as a matter of law following the jury's verdict.

In all of these situations involving JMOL motions, the action to be taken by the court is "to assure enforcement of the controlling law and is not an intrusion on any responsibility for factual determinations conferred on the jury by the Seventh Amendment or any provision of federal law." Fed. R. Civ. P. 50 advisory committee notes (1991 Amendments).

With respect to the Rule 50(b) motion filed after entry of the order, the movant may also request in the alternative a new trial, or join a motion for a new trial under Rule 59. As indicated in Rule 59(c), if the court grants a motion for judgment as a matter of law under Rule 50(b), the court may also rule on the motion for new trial, and may conditionally grant or deny the motion based on whether the judgment is vacated or reversed on appeal.

DELTA-X CORP. v. BAKER HUGHES PRODUCTION TOOLS INC.

984 F.2d 410, 25 USPQ2d 1447 (Fed. Cir. 1993)

Before SKELTON, Senior Circuit Judge, and ARCHER and RADER, Circuit Judges.

RADER, Circuit Judge.

Delta–X Corporation sued Baker Hughes Production Tools, Inc. and Baker CAC (collectively Baker) for infringement of United States Patent No. 4,286,925 (the '925 patent). A jury found that Baker willfully infringed the '925 patent under the doctrine of equivalents. The United States District Court for the Western District of Texas, however, both set aside the jury's willfulness finding and denied Delta–X's request for enhanced damages, attorney fees, and costs. Delta–X appeals these decisions. Baker cross-appeals the infringement judgment, challenging the jury instructions.

Because Baker did not move for a directed verdict, the district court's grant of judgment notwithstanding the verdict (JNOV) was error. However, it was harmless error because the district court properly denied Delta–X's request for enhanced damages, attorney fees, and costs. Finally, this court finds no prejudicial error in the jury instructions. Therefore, this court affirms the district court's judgment.

Background

Delta–X is the assignee of the '925 patent, a "Control Circuit for Shutting Off the Electric Power to a Liquid Well Pump." The '925 patent discloses a mechanism for shutting off power to a well experiencing "fluid pound." Fluid pound occurs when the reciprocating rod of an oil pump, usually submerged, rises out of an abnormally low oil level within the well. As the rod cycles down the well hole, the rod end hits or "pounds" the fluid surface. Fluid pound can damage the reciprocating rod.

At trial Delta–X charged that Baker's rod pump controllers infringed claims 1 and 2 of the '925 patent. The parties sharply disagreed about the meaning of the term "electrical comparator" in claim 1. At the close of evidence, Baker objected to the jury instructions concerning infringement. Baker, however, did not move for directed verdict. The jury found that Baker willfully infringed the '925 patent under the doctrine of equivalents. After trial, Delta–X moved for entry of judgment in its favor, requesting enhanced damages and attorney fees under 35 U.S.C. §§ 284, 285 (1988). Baker moved for entry of judgment without enhanced damages or attorney fees, or in the alternative, JNOV. Delta–X did not file an opposition to Baker's JNOV motion.

On July 29, 1991, the district court granted Baker's JNOV motion and set aside the jury's finding of willful infringement and denied Delta–X's request for increased damages. On September 4, 1991, the district court denied Delta–X's request for attorney fees and ordered each party to bear its own costs.

Discussion

JNOV Ruling

This court reviews procedural matters without an essential relationship to its statutory mandate as a national court of appeals under the law of the district court's regional circuit. Therefore, this court looks to the law of the United States Court of Appeals for the Fifth Circuit to determine the import of Baker's failure to move for directed verdict.

Federal Rule of Civil Procedure 50 prevents a district court from entering JNOV unless the movant has first moved for directed verdict at the close of evidence. Without satisfying Rule 50, a party cannot challenge the sufficiency of the evidence through a JNOV motion. This requirement both enables the trial court to re-examine the sufficiency of evidence as a matter of law if the jury returns a verdict contrary to the movant and alerts the opposing party to insufficiencies in time to cure defects in proof.[2]

Baker concedes that it did not move for directed verdict. Thus, the district court erred in setting aside on JNOV the jury's finding of willfulness. Without compliance with Rule 50, Baker's JNOV motion was not properly before the trial court. Therefore, this court reverses the district court's grant of JNOV and reinstates the jury's finding of willfulness.

---

2. Delta–X did not oppose Baker's JNOV motion until after the motion was granted. Baker argues that this court should not allow Delta–X to challenge the JNOV motion for the first time on appeal. In *Texas v. United States*, 730 F.2d 339, 358, n. 35 (5th Cir.), *cert. denied*, 469 U.S. 892 (1984), the Fifth Circuit stated that it will not generally consider an issue for the first time on appeal. Application of this general rule, however, is within the appellate court's discretion on a case-by-case ba-sis. In particular, the Fifth Circuit may address an issue for the first time on appeal if it concerns a pure question of law or if the proper resolution of the issue is beyond doubt. *Id.* The implications of electing not to move for a directed verdict raise a pure question of law within a resolution beyond doubt. Applying the law of the Fifth Circuit, this court addresses the propriety of the JNOV motion in the absence of a directed verdict motion.

Enhanced Damages, Attorney Fees, and Costs

Because the trial court independently determined that Delta–X had not shown entitlement to enhanced damages, attorney fees, and costs, however, the district court's grant of Baker's JNOV motion was harmless error. In its July 29, 1991, Memorandum Opinion and Judgment, the district court concluded that Delta–X was not entitled to enhanced damages under 35 U.S.C. § 284. In its September 4, 1991, Order and Amended Judgment, the district court denied Delta–X's motion for costs and attorney fees. Absent an abuse of discretion, this court upholds decisions on award of enhanced damages.

Jury Instructions

Baker's cross-appeal seeks a new trial due to allegedly prejudicial jury instructions on the infringement doctrine. More specifically, Baker contends that a few isolated references in the instructions may have given the jury mixed messages about its role in interpreting the patent claims. Although correctly instructing the jury to compare the properly interpreted claims to the accused device, the instructions suggested that the judge would interpret the claims. Because of disputes over claim terms, the judge instead left resolution of these disputes to the jury.

This court reviews jury instructions for prejudicial legal error. After viewing instructions in their entirety, this court only orders a new trial when errors in the instructions as a whole clearly misled the jury. Moreover, to prevail on a challenge to jury instructions, a party must show both fatal flaws in the jury instructions and a request for alternative instructions which could have corrected the flaws.

At trial Baker objected to the jury instructions. Baker asked the judge to interpret the claims and resolve issues about the meaning of the word "comparator" in the claims. More specifically, Baker requested that the judge instruct the jury that, as a matter of law, a comparator and a computer are not the same thing. The district judge denied Baker's request and instead submitted the disputed matter to the jury. Baker now argues that the district court instructed the jury that the court would interpret the claims but never did so as promised. Baker argues, therefore, that the court cannot be certain that the jury properly interpreted the claims. This court disagrees.

Although excerpts from certain jury instructions suggest that the court might interpret the claims for the jury, the instructions are not misleading when viewed in their entirety. For example, Baker ignores the following jury instructions:

> [I]f Baker's Pump–Off controllers include all of the components or parts of either of these claims, as the words of the claim are interpreted by you in accordance with these instructions, then Baker's products literally infringe the claim.

* * *

You are instructed "literal" infringement of a patent claim occurs when the Baker product includes all of the elements recited in the claim, using the meaning and scope of the words of the claim as you have determined, in accordance with the instructions which I have given you.

* * *

In determining whether or not there is infringement, you must compare Baker's Pump–Off controllers alleged to infringe the '925 patent with the patent claims one and two, as interpreted.

In sum, these instructions make it clear that the court instructed the jury to resolve evidentiary disputes over claim terms. The court's instructions then advised the jury to determine whether Baker's products infringed. Because it returned a finding of infringement, the jury must have resolved the evidentiary dispute over the meaning of "electrical comparator." This court concludes that Baker did not show any error in the jury instructions, when read as a whole, so egregious as to mislead the jury and require a new trial.

CONCLUSION

Although the district court erred in granting Baker's JNOV motion in the absence of a motion for directed verdict, this error was harmless. Finally the trial court's jury instructions on infringement were not prejudicial. Therefore this court affirms the district court's decision.

Notes

1. As the above case indicates, the failure to move for judgment as a matter of law before the jury receives the case prevents the district court from setting aside the jury's verdict on a JMOL motion filed after the verdict. Thus, it should be standard practice to file JMOL motions with the district court at the time your opponent rests its case, and at the end of the presentation of all evidence, prior to the case going to the jury. Likewise, similar JMOL motions should be filed within 10 days of entry of judgment on all issues adversely decided by the jury.

2. Often the trial court will deny JMOL motions made at the close of evidence in order to give the jury a chance to properly resolve the case. If the jury verdict is in error the court can still grant the motion. If the jury verdict is proper, the Court need not address the motion. Allowing the jury to resolve the case avoids a possible new trial in the event that the Federal Circuit disagrees with the court's holdings. If the Court grants the JMOL and discharges the jury and the Federal Circuit reverses a new trial must be conducted.

Problems

1. What if you are representing the defendant and you failed to make a JMOL motion on infringement at the close of plaintiff's case-in-chief. Can you make the JMOL motion after you have presented your defense on the issues? Can you make the JMOL motion after the plaintiff has presented its rebuttal case on the issue?

2.   What are the similarities between a JMOL motion filed under Rule 50 and a motion for summary judgment filed under Rule 56?

Chapter Sixteen

THE APPEAL

INTRODUCTION

The United States Court of Appeals for the Federal Circuit has exclusive jurisdiction over all patent appeals from the district courts. Appeals may not be taken to the regional circuits in which the district courts reside, only the Federal Circuit decides appeals from patent cases. Why do you think a specialized appellate court was created to hear all patent appeals?

A patent appeal may be taken after a final judgment is entered by the district court or if the district court certifies the issue for an interlocutory appeal. An interlocutory appeal to the Federal Circuit is a matter of the discretion of the district court. Even when granted, such an appeal will result in delaying the eventual outcome of the case which will surely add significantly to the overall cost of the litigation. The Federal Circuit may also refuse to hear interlocutory appeals. What kinds of issues in a patent litigation are appropriate for interlocutory appeal? What would be the pros and cons of permitting interlocutory appeals?

STATUTORY PROVISION—28 U.S.C. § 1292:

Interlocutory Decisions

(b) When a district judge, in making in a civil action an order not otherwise appealable under this section, shall be of the opinion that such order involves a controlling question of law as to which there is substantial ground for difference of opinion and that an immediate appeal from the order may materially advance the ultimate termination of the litigation, he shall so state in writing in such order. The Court of Appeals which would have jurisdiction of an appeal of such action may thereupon, in its discretion, permit an appeal to be taken from such order, if application is made to it within ten days after the entry of the order: Provided, however, That application for an appeal hereunder shall not stay proceedings in the district court unless the district judge or the Court of Appeals or a judge thereof shall so order.

(c) The United States Court of Appeals for the Federal Circuit shall have exclusive jurisdiction—

(1) of an appeal from an interlocutory order or decree described in subsection (a) or (b) of this section in any case over which the court would have jurisdiction of an appeal under section 1295 of this title; and

(2) of an appeal from a judgment in a civil action for patent infringement which would otherwise be appealable to the United States Court of Appeals for the Federal Circuit and is final except for an accounting.

STATUTORY PROVISION—28 U.S.C. § 1295:

(a) The United States Court of Appeals for the Federal Circuit shall have exclusive jurisdiction—

(1) of an appeal from a final decision of a district court of the United States, the United States District Court for the District of the Canal Zone, the District Court of Guam, the District Court of the Virgin Islands, or the District Court for the Northern Mariana Islands, if the jurisdiction of that court was based, in whole or in part, on section 1338 of this title, except that a case involving a claim arising under any Act of Congress relating to copyrights, exclusive rights in mask works, or trademarks and no other claims under section 1338(a) shall be governed by sections 1291, 1292, and 1294 of this title;

A. APPEAL PROCEDURES

In order to appeal a judgment or order from a district court to the Federal Circuit, the appellant must comply with the Rules of Practice Before the United States Court of Appeals for the Federal Circuit and the Federal Rules of Appellate Procedure. As a preliminary matter, a notice of appeal must be filed with (received by) the district court within thirty days of the entry of the judgment or order.

FEDERAL RULES OF APPELLATE PROCEDURE—Rule 4:

Appeal as of Right—When Taken

(a) Appeal in a civil case.—

(1) Except as provided in paragraph (a)(4) of this Rule, in a civil case in which an appeal is permitted by law as of right from a district court to a court of appeals the notice of appeal required by Rule 3 must be filed with the clerk of the district court within 30 days after the date of entry of the judgment or order appealed from; but if the United States or an officer or agency thereof is a party, the notice of appeal may be filed by any party within 60 days after such entry. If a notice of appeal is mistakenly filed in the court of appeals, the clerk of the court of appeals shall note thereon the date when the clerk received the notice and send it to the clerk of the district court and the notice will be treated as filed in the district court on the date so noted.

(2) A notice of appeal filed after the court announces a decision or order but before the entry of the judgment or order is treated as filed on the date of and after the entry.

(3) If one party timely files a notice of appeal, any other party may file a notice of appeal within 14 days after the date when the first notice was

filed, or within the time otherwise prescribed by this Rule 4(a), whichever period last expires.

(4) If any party files a timely motion of a type specified immediately below, the time for appeal for all parties runs from the entry of the order disposing of the last such motion outstanding. This provision applies to a timely motion under the Federal Rules of Civil Procedure:

(A) for judgment under Rule 50(b);

(B) to amend or make additional findings of fact under Rule 52(b) whether or not granting the motion would alter the judgment;

(C) to alter or amend the judgment under Rule 59;

(D) for attorney's fees under Rule 54 if a district court under Rule 58 extends the time for appeal;

(E) for a new trial under Rule 59; or

(F) for relief under Rule 60 if the motion is filed no later than 10 days after the entry of judgment.

A notice of appeal filed after announcement or entry of judgment but before disposition of any of the above motions is ineffective to appeal from the judgment or order, or part thereof, specified in the notice of appeal, until the entry of the order disposing of the last such motion outstanding. Appellate review of an order disposing of any of the above motions requires the party, in compliance with Appellate Rule 3(c), to amend a previously filed notice of appeal. A party intending to challenge an alteration or amendment of the judgment must file a notice, or amended notice of appeal within the time prescribed by this Rule 4 measured from the entry of the order disposing of the last such motion outstanding. No additional fees will be required for filing an amended notice.

(5) The district court, upon a showing of excusable neglect or good cause, may extend the time for filing a notice of appeal upon motion filed not later than 30 days after the expiration of the time prescribed by this Rule 4(a). Any such motion which is filed before expiration of the prescribed time may be ex parte unless the court otherwise requires. Notice of any such motion which is filed after expiration of the prescribed time shall be given to the other parties in accordance with local rules. No such extension shall exceed 30 days past such prescribed time or 10 days from the date of entry of the order granting the motion, whichever occurs later.

(6) The district court, if it finds (a) that a party entitled to notice of the entry of a judgment or order did not receive such notice from the clerk or any party within 21 days of its entry and (b) that no party would be prejudiced, may, upon motion filed within 180 days of entry of the judgment or order or within 7 days of receipt of such notice, whichever is earlier, reopen the time for appeal for a period of 14 days from the date of entry of the order reopening the time for appeal.

(7) A judgment or order is entered within the meaning of this Rule 4(a) when it is entered in compliance with Rules 58 and 79(a) of the Federal Rules of Civil Procedure.

Federal Circuit Rule—Rule 4:

Appeal as of Right—When Taken

(a) Trial Court Mail Rule.—If, pursuant to statute, the trial court has adopted a rule that deems a document filed on the date it is transmitted by a specified type of mail, a notice of appeal shall be deemed filed as provided in that rule.

(b) Untimely Notice of Appeal.—The clerk may return a notice of appeal that is untimely on its face.

B.　WHAT CAN BE APPEALED

As provide in Rule 4 of the Federal Rules of Appellate Procedure, an appeal as a matter of right can be taken only upon the district court's entry of a judgment or order. A "judgment" includes: the granting of an injunction, summary judgment only if the grant of summary judgment has the effect of completely disposing of the suit, judgment as a matter of law, and of course a final judgment of liability. In addition to appeals as a matter of right, permission to appeal an interlocutory decision can be sought by filing a petition for permission to appeal with the clerk within 10 days after the district entered the order.

C.　THE STANDARDS OF REVIEW ON APPEAL

The standard of appellate review varies depending on: (1) the nature of the issue decided; and (2) who was the adjudicator. The standards of review are as follows (in order of least deference to most deference):

1.　*de novo;*

2.　clearly erroneous;

3.　substantial evidence; and

4.　abuse of discretion.

If the issue is one of fact, the Federal Circuit will review the finding with greater deference than it will an issue of law. Why do you think the Federal Circuit gives more deference to factual issues rather than legal issues? The following list provides the Federal Circuit's standard of review for various issues on appeal:

1) Questions of fact decided by a jury are reviewed under the substantial evidence standard. If a finding is supported by substantial evidence in the record then it must be affirmed.

2) Questions of fact decided by the district court are reviewed under the clearly erroneous standard. "A finding is 'clearly erroneous' when although there is evidence to support it, the reviewing court on the entire evidence is left with the definite and firm conviction that a mistake has been committed." *United States v. United States Gypsum Co.,* 333 U.S. 364, 395, 76 USPQ 430 (1948).

Questions of fact include: literal infringement; infringement under the doctrine of equivalents; whether a defendant's infringement was willful; each of the four factors underlying an obviousness determination (the scope and content of the prior art, level of ordinary skill in the art, comparison of the claims to the accused device, secondary considerations); whether a reference is material; and when the inventor conceived of her invention. Can you think of others?

3) Questions of law are reviewed *de novo* regardless of which decision-maker decided them. Questions of law include: claim construction; statutory construction; obviousness; whether a use is a "public use" pursuant to § 102(b); and whether prosecution history estoppel applies. Can you think of others?

4) Decisions in which a district court has discretion are reviewed under the abuse of discretion standard. A district court has abused its discretion if its determination "was based on a clear error of fact, an error of law, or a manifest error of judgment." *National Presto Indus., Inc. v. West Bend Co.*, 76 F.3d 1185, 1193, 37 USPQ2d 1685, 1691 (Fed. Cir. 1996). The district court has discretion in granting or denying a preliminary injunction or enhancing damages for willful infringement. All equitable decisions made by the district court, such as inequitable conduct, laches, equitable estoppel, unclean hands, are also review under an abuse of discretion. Can you think of any others?

Interesting things occur on appeal when a district court gives questions of law or equitable issues to a jury. The Federal Circuit has held that a court may allow a jury to resolve the legal issue of obviousness. When a jury resolves this legal issue, on appeal the Federal Circuit will presume that the jury found each of the underlying facts in favor of the verdict. For this reason, it is generally advantageous for the patent owner to request special verdict forms or special interrogatories for issues of this kind. *See* Chapter Fifteen.

The district court may also permit the jury to resolve (on an advisory basis) an equitable issue pursuant to Federal Rule of Civil Procedure 39(c). For example, the district court may permit the jury to consider whether the infringer has proven that inequitable conduct occurred in the prosecution of the patent. However, such a jury determination is merely an advisory opinion for the court which must still decide all equitable issues. Therefore, the court is free to disregard the jury's determination of inequitable conduct and the facts that underlie this decision (intent and materiality) . . "The disputed issues of fact underlying the issue of inequitable conduct are not jury questions, the issue being entirely equitable in nature. Thus, the facts are ordinarily for the court to resolve, accompanied by findings of fact in accordance with Rule 52(a)." *General Electro Music Corp. v. Samick Music Corp.*, 19 F.3d 1405, 1408, 30 USPQ2d 1149, 1152 (Fed. Cir. 1994).

D. BEWARE THE FRIVOLOUS APPEAL

Although your client may have an appeal as a matter of right because it was found to infringe a patent or because its patent was determined to be invalid, not every case should be appealed and the Federal Circuit has awarded sanctions against parties who bring frivolous appeals. Although you may be tempted to appeal in order to negotiate a more favorable settlement for your client, beware of the consequences of frivolous appeals. Federal Rule of Appellate Procedure 38 permits the awarding of sanctions for frivolous appeals. An appeal is frivolous if "the judgment by the tribunal below was so plainly correct and the legal authority contrary to appellant's position so clear that there really is no appealable issue." *Finch v. Hughes Aircraft Co.*, 926 F.2d 1574, 1579–80, 17 USPQ2d 1914, 1918 (Fed. Cir. 1991). Carefully consider whether your client has grounds for an appeal taking the applicable standards of review into account before filing an appeal.

> In light of the character of the conduct we are sanctioning, we hold that Bravo and its counsel shall be jointly and severally liable for payment of the damages assessed. An appeal is an entirely appropriate means of seeking to vindicate legal rights, but a frivolous appeal imposes substantial and gratuitous injury. Parties who inflict such injury should be held accountable for it, and in a case such as this one their attorneys should likewise be called upon to answer for the injury they inflict.

S. Bravo Systems, Inc. v. Containment Technologies Corp., 96 F.3d 1372, 1377, 40 USPQ2d 1140, 1145 (Fed. Cir. 1996) (citations omitted). As *S. Bravo* demonstrates, a frivolous appeal can be costly to both attorney and client.

Chapter Seventeen

ASSIGNMENTS AND LICENSING

A. ASSIGNMENT v. LICENSE

An assignment is a transfer of all rights under the patent for a fixed sum. A license is a grant of the right to operate under the patent for a royalty which is based upon the extent to which the invention is used. A license is not a transfer of ownership interest in the patent. It is merely an agreement not to sue the licensee for patent infringement. The manner in which payment is made is not determinative of whether a transfer is an assignment or a license. Thus, payment for an assignment may be made in the form of a royalty, and payment for a license may be made in a lump sum. Both assignments and licenses give the transferee immunity from suit for infringement of the patent.

The fundamental practical difference between assignments and licenses lies in the right or lack of right of the transferee to sue for infringement of the patent. Licenses can be either exclusive or non-exclusive. An exclusive license essentially includes a promise by the patent owner not to grant licenses to others. A non-exclusive licensee can never sue infringers. An exclusive licensee can sue infringers only by making the patent owner a party to the suit. An assignee can sue infringers on its own. Can the patent owner still sue infringers after an assignment? Do you think an exclusive licensee should be able to sue for past infringement, that is infringement that took place before the licensing agreement? Should an assignee be able to sue for past infringement? This chapter considers these and other questions concerning licenses and assignments. The book generally incorporates the information on licenses and assignments into the substantive chapters; however, there are a few unique issues that warrant attention here.

STATUTORY PROVISION— 35 U.S.C. § 261:

Applications for patent, patents, or any interest therein, shall be assignable in law by an instrument in writing. The applicant, patentee, or his assigns or legal representatives may in like manner grant and convey an exclusive right under his application for patent, or patents, to the whole or any specified part of the United States.

An assignment, grant or conveyance shall be void as against any subsequent purchaser or mortgagee for a valuable consideration, without notice, unless it is recorded in the Patent and Trademark Office within three months from its date or prior to the date of such subsequent purchase or mortgage.

Assignments should be recorded with the PTO. Assignments are reflected on the front of the patent document.

ORTHO PHARMACEUTICAL CORP.
v. GENETICS INSTITUTE, INC.

52 F.3d 1026, 34 USPQ2d 1444 (Fed. Cir. 1995)

Before ARCHER, Chief Judge, NIES and MICHEL, Circuit Judges.

NIES, Circuit Judge.

This appeal raises a question of a patent licensee's standing to sue an infringer in the name of the patentee/licensor. Ortho Pharmaceutical Corporation is a licensee of Amgen, Inc., owner of United States Patent No. 4,703,008 (the '008 patent). Ortho and its sublicensees filed suit against Genetics Institute for infringement of the '008 patent in the District Court for the District of Massachusetts. The district court dismissed Ortho's suit concluding that Ortho was a nonexclusive licensee and, therefore, lacked standing. We affirm.

I.

The '008 patent claims a product used for the production of erythropoietin (EPO), a hormone that stimulates the synthesis of red blood cells in bone marrow. The '008 patent claims a purified and isolated DNA sequence encoding human EPO and host cells transformed or transfected with a DNA sequence in a manner allowing host cells to express EPO. The claims do not claim the EPO product itself.

In 1984, three years prior to the issuance of the patent, Amgen and Kirin Brewery Co., Ltd., established a joint venture, Kirin–Amgen, Inc. At that time, Amgen, as owner of the then-pending application for the '008 patent, assigned certain rights to Kirin–Amgen. In 1985, Ortho entered into Product License Agreements (PLAs) with Kirin–Amgen and Amgen separately under which Ortho was allowed limited rights to manufacture in the United States and sell EPO in the United States and in certain foreign countries in which the licensors were seeking to obtain patents on various products and processes, including EPO itself.

On October 27, 1987, the date the '008 patent issued, Kirin–Amgen assigned the patent to Amgen. On the same date, Amgen brought suit for infringement against Genetics and Chugai. The trial of Amgen's suit was bifurcated into liability and damages phases. Shortly before trial on liability, Ortho attempted to intervene under Fed. R. Civ. P. 24, either as a matter of right or permissively, based on its rights under the license from Amgen. This motion was denied on the grounds of untimeliness and because Ortho's interests were adequately represented by Amgen respecting liability, a decision Ortho did not appeal. Following a bench trial on liability, claims 2, 4, and 6 of the '008 patent were held not to be invalid or unenforceable and found to be infringed by both Chugai and Genetics Institute. This court affirmed that judgment on interlocutory appeal.

Ortho and its European sublicensees then filed a suit against Genetics Institute in the same court. Before an answer was filed, they amended the complaint to name Amgen as a defendant and subsequently moved to realign Amgen as an involuntary plaintiff. Genetics and Amgen filed motions to dismiss or for summary judgment on the ground of the plaintiff's lack of standing or for failure to state a claim. Ortho and the co-plaintiffs cross-moved to intervene in the Amgen litigation for the purpose of securing part of the damages. Ortho's suit was consolidated with the Amgen suit.

In reply to the defendants' motions, Ortho again asserted its rights as a licensee of Amgen. In particular, Ortho relied on Paragraph 2.01 of the PLA license, which provides:

> (a) AMGEN hereby grants to ORTHO but not AFFILIATES, except as hereinafter provided, an exclusive license to make in one location, have made and use LICENSED KNOW–HOW, LICENSED PATENTS and LICENSED PRODUCTS in the LICENSED TERRITORY in the LICENSED FIELD and to sell LICENSED PRODUCTS in the LICENSED TERRITORY.

> (b) AMGEN, having received the consent of Kirin Brewery Co., Ltd., hereby grants to ORTHO but not AFFILIATES, an exclusive license, except as against AMGEN's rights under this AGREEMENT in the LICENSED TERRITORY, to make EPO in one location in the United States for use and sale outside the LICENSED TERRITORY but not including China and Japan. AMGEN shall provide to ORTHO all information and any assistance and know-how required to ORTHO to achieve the purposes of this paragraph.

The agreement defined the LICENSED TERRITORY as the United States and the LICENSED FIELD as "all indications for human use except dialysis and diagnostics." In return, Amgen received royalties on Ortho's resulting sales of EPO in the United States. Thus, one of the effects of paragraph 2.01(a), as interpreted by the court, was to grant Ortho the implied right to use the invention claimed in the '008 patent in one location to make EPO, for use or sale in the United States, for all human use except dialysis or diagnostics. Paragraph 2.01(b) repeated the implied grant to Ortho to use the '008 invention to make EPO in one location in the United States and, with Kirin-Amgen's consent, the right to make certain foreign sales of EPO.

The PLA executed by Ortho and Amgen also contains section 8.02 entitled "Infringement by Third Parties." Amgen argues that this section precludes Ortho's suit because Amgen exercised its right to sue alone, as provided therein. However, Ortho disputes that the provisions control to bar a second suit by Ortho in Amgen's name, even though Amgen has sued.

In ruling on the motion, the court first rejected Ortho's argument that it could premise standing based upon paragraph 2.01(a) of the license agreement. The court reasoned that because Amgen did not promise not to sublicense its own right to use its '008 invention to manufacture EPO in the United States, Ortho held a nonexclusive license under this provision. The court also found no merit in Ortho's argument that paragraph 2.01(b) granted it an exclusive field-of-use license for sales of EPO abroad. The court emphasized that the '008 patent did not cover sales of EPO itself. Thus, Ortho's right to sell EPO abroad could not be a right arising from or a license under the U.S. patent grant. As in paragraph 2.01(a), Ortho's license to use the '008 patented technology was held to be nonexclusive. The sole issue on appeal is whether Ortho's license gave it standing to sue.

II.

The Patent Act of 1952 provides "a patentee shall have remedy by civil action for infringement of his patent." 35 U.S.C. § 281 (1988). The term patentee includes "not only the patentee to whom the patent was issued but also the successors in title to the patentee." 35 U.S.C. § 100(d) (emphasis added). Thus, the statute requires that the parties to an infringement suit will have the patentee on one side and the accused infringer on the other. Without the patentee as plaintiff, the remedies provided in the patent statute are unavailable except in extraordinary circumstances "as where the patentee is the infringer, and cannot sue himself." *Waterman v. Mackenzie*, 138 U.S. 252, 255 (1891) (suit dismissed because not brought by record owner); *Crown Die & Tool Co. v. Nye Tool & Mach. Works*, 261 U.S. 24, 40–41 (1923) (plaintiff must have legal title to patent at the time of infringement); *see also Arachnid, Inc. v. Merit Indus., Inc.*, 939 F.2d 1574, 1579, 19 USPQ2d 1513, 1517 (Fed. Cir. 1991) (relying on Crown Die).

Courts look to the substance of an agreement to determine whether it has the effect of an assignment and, thus, satisfies the statutory requirement that the "patentee" must sue. Where a patentee makes an assignment of all significant rights under the patent, such assignee may be deemed the effective "patentee" under the statute and has standing to bring a suit in its own name for infringement. *Vaupel Textilmaschinen KG v. Meccanica Euro Italia S.P.A.*, 944 F.2d 870, 875, 20 USPQ2d 1045, 1049 (Fed. Cir. 1991) (transfer of substantially all rights held to be assignment). Any other party seeking enforcement of the patent can sue, if at all, only with the patentee or in the name of the patentee. "Any rights of the licensee must be enforced through or in the name of the owner of the patent," and "never in the name of the licensee alone, unless that is necessary to prevent an absolute failure of justice." *Waterman*, 138 U.S. at 255; *see Independent Wireless Telegraph Co. v. Radio Corp. of America*, 269 U.S. 459, 468 (1926) (patentee necessary to give jurisdiction in law or equity and to enable infringer to defeat all claims in one action or bar all other actions by satisfying one decree); *Abbott Labs. v. Diamedix Corp.*, 47 F.3d 1128 (Fed. Cir. 1995) (patentee has a right to intervene in licensee's suit).

Saying that a licensee must sue with or in the name of the patentee does not mean that every licensee under a patent has a rightful place in an infringement suit. A licensee must have "standing" under the patent statute. A license may amount to no more than a covenant by the patentee not to sue the licensee for making, using or selling the patented invention, the patentee reserving the right to grant others the same right. A holder of such a nonexclusive license suffers no legal injury from infringement and, thus, has no standing to bring suit or even join in a suit with the patentee. As explained in *Western Elec. Co. v. Pacent Reproducer Corp.*, 42 F.2d 116, 118 (2d Cir. 1930):

> In its simplest form, a license means only leave to do a thing which the licensor would otherwise have a right to prevent. Such a license grants to the licensee merely a privilege that protects him from a claim of infringement by the owner of the patent monopoly.... He has no property interest in the monopoly of the patent, nor any contract with the patent owner that others shall not practice the invention. Hence the patent owner may freely license others, or may tolerate infringers, and in either case no right of the patent licensee is violated. Practice of the invention by others may indeed cause him pecuniary loss, but it does him no legal injury.

The district court here relied on Judge Hand's analysis of standing in *A.L. Smith Iron Co. v. Dickson*, 141 F.2d 3, 6 (2d Cir. 1944), with which we agree:

> The key question for determining standing of a licensee is whether the licensee as a matter of law has an exclusive property interest in the patent itself, not whether the licensee in fact has been harmed by a third-party infringer. As Judge Learned Hand explained in *A.L. Smith Iron Co. v. Dickson*, 141 F.2d 3, 6 (2d Cir. 1944), there are strong policy reasons why patent law does not confer standing on a nonexclusive licensee to sue a third party for infringement even though the licensee has suffered due to the infringement:
>
> > It is indeed true that a mere licensee may have an interest at stake in such a suit; his license may be worth much more to him than the royalties which he has agreed to pay, and its value will ordinarily depend on his ability to suppress the competition of his rivals. The reason why he is not permitted to sue is not because he has nothing to protect. But against that interest is the interest of the infringer to be immune from a second suit by the owner of the patent; and also the interest of the patent owner to be free to choose his forum.... Indeed, the owner may have granted a number of licenses, and it would be exceedingly oppressive to subject him to the will of all his licensees. These two interests in combination have been held to overweigh any interest of the licensee.

808 F. Supp. at 904 n.11, 27 USPQ2d at 1585 n.11.

Thus economic injury alone does not provide standing to sue under the patent statute. To have co-plaintiff standing in an infringement suit, a licensee must hold some of the proprietary sticks from the bundle of patent rights, albeit a lesser share of rights in the patent than for an assignment and standing to sue alone. *See Weinar v. Rollform, Inc.*, 744 F.2d 797, 803, 223 USPQ 369, 374–75 (Fed. Cir. 1984) (exclusive licensee properly joined in suit; "two parties sharing the property rights represented by the patent may have respective rights protected").

The proprietary rights granted by any patent are the rights to exclude others from making, using or selling the invention in the United States. A patent license may have the effect between the parties to the license of transferring some of those proprietary rights from the patentee to its licensee. Such license then does more than provide a covenant not to sue, i.e., a "bare" license. In addition, the license makes the licensee a beneficial owner of some identifiable part of the patentee's bundle of rights to exclude others. Thus, a licensee with proprietary rights in the patent is generally called an "exclusive" licensee. But it is the licensee's beneficial ownership of a right to prevent others from making, using or selling the patented technology that provides the foundation for co-plaintiff standing, not simply that the word "exclusive" may or may not appear in the license. As stated in *Philadelphia Brief Case Co. v. Speciality Leather Prods. Co.*, 145 F. Supp. 425, 428, 111 USPQ 180, 182 (D. N.J. 1956), *aff'd*, 242 F.2d 511, 113 USPQ 100 (3d Cir. 1957):

> This so-called exclusive licensee, while only a licensee, comes so close to having truly proprietary interests in the patent, that the courts have held that he is equitably entitled to sue on the patent, provided he joins the true proprietor of the patent in such suit.

The consequence of recognizing co-plaintiff standing is that the licensee has a right to bring suit on the patent, albeit in the name of the licensor, whether or not the license so provides and regardless of the patentee's cooperation. Further, the patentee/licensor suffers the legal consequences of litigation brought in its name. As stated in *Independent Wireless Co.*, 269 U.S. at 469:

> It seems clear then on principle and authority that the owner of a patent who grants to another the exclusive right to make, use or vend the invention, which does not constitute a statutory assignment, holds the title to the patent in trust for such a licensee, to the extent that he must allow the use of his name as plaintiff in any action brought at the instance of the licensee in law or in equity to obtain damages for the injury to this exclusive right by an infringer or to enjoin infringement of it. Such exclusive licenses frequently contain express covenants by the patent-owner and licensor to sue infringers that expressly cast upon the former the affirmative duty of initiating and bearing the expense of the litigation. But without such express covenants, *the implied obligation of the licensor to allow the use of his name is indispensable to the enjoyment by the licensee of the monopoly which by personal contract the licensor has*

given. Inconvenience and possibly embarrassing adjudication in respect of the validity of the licensor's patent rights, as the result of suits begun in aid of the licensee, are only the equitable and inevitable sequence of the licensor's contract, whether express or implied. [Emphasis added.]

In the case at hand, the patentee has refused to let its licensee join in its suit against an infringer. However, co-plaintiff standing is determined by whether or not the licensee acquired proprietary rights in the patent under the contract with the patentee. The patentee's later second thoughts are irrelevant, either to confer standing or, as here, to deny standing. To resolve the issue of standing, we must examine the licensing agreement to determine whether the parties intended to effect a transfer of proprietary rights to the licensee as an incident to protection of its interests. *Vaupel*, 944 F.2d at 874 (intent of parties controlling).

III.

Ortho does not assert it has standing to sue alone. Moreover, on appeal, Ortho has abandoned paragraph 2.01(a) of the license as a basis for co-plaintiff standing and now relies only upon paragraph 2.01(b) of the license. The burden of demonstrating standing falls to Ortho, as "[i]t is well established . . . that before a federal court can consider the merits of a legal claim, the person seeking to invoke the jurisdiction of the court must establish the requisite standing to sue." *Whitmore v. Arkansas*, 495 U.S. 149, 154 (1990).

The trial court found Ortho had no proprietary interest in thc '008 patent based on its rights under either paragraph (a) or (b). It was a nonexclusive licensee. With respect to patent rights, Ortho had an implied license to use the '008 invention in one location in the United States. It is undisputed that that right was nonexclusive inasmuch as Amgen had the right to license others to do the same. Ortho concedes this point but argues that its additional right to sell EPO abroad as provided in paragraph (b) is an exclusive field of use of the '008 technology which provides standing. We disagree. Ortho commingles its consent from Kirin–Amgen to sell EPO abroad (as expressly stated in paragraph (b) to be necessary) with the rights it received from Amgen under the U.S. patent to use the '008 technology. U.S. patent '008 provides no rights respecting the product EPO per se. Moreover, a U.S. patent grants rights to exclude others from making, using and selling the patented invention only in the United States. 35 U.S.C. § 154. With respect to Ortho's right to sell unpatented EPO abroad, the court correctly held that Ortho's right was not a proprietary right arising from the '008 patent. Indeed, Amgen itself had no right to sell EPO abroad by reason of its obtaining the '008 patent and, thus, could not license that right to Ortho as an incident of patent ownership. With respect to rights under the '008 patent, Ortho had only a nonexclusive right to use the '008 invention at one location in the United States. Thus, considering only this right, Ortho is a bare, that is, nonexclusive, licensee and has no standing to bring or join a suit for infringement against Genetics.

The conclusion that Ortho held only nonexclusive rights under paragraph 2.01(b) would end our inquiry except for the provision in the license agreements which gave Ortho the right to bring appropriate suits if Amgen did not. As provided in paragraph 8.02:

> AMGEN shall have the right, but not the obligation, to bring, defend, and maintain any appropriate suit or action.... In the event AMGEN fails to take action with respect to such matters within a reasonable period, not more than six (6) months, following receipt of such notice and evidence, ORTHO shall have the right, but not the obligation, to bring, defend, and maintain any appropriate suit or action. Absent an agreement between the parties to jointly bring any action or suit hereunder and share the expenses thereof, any amount recovered in any such action or suit shall be retained by the party bearing its expenses thereof.

Other parts of the right to sue clause require that Amgen and Ortho consult and sue together if either "finds it necessary" to "join" the other and that each will "cooperate" with the other.

Ortho argues that the contract should be construed to give each party the right to bring its own action where cooperation is not forthcoming. Amgen argues that the contract provisions, under which Amgen exercised its right to sue alone and keep all damages, would control regardless of whether or not Ortho had an exclusive license. We conclude that the right to sue clause has no effect in this case.

First, a licensee with sufficient proprietary interest in a patent has standing regardless of whether the licensing agreement so provides. Express covenants may, of course, regulate the duties between the licensor and licensee to implement the rights of the parties. However, a contract cannot change the statutory requirement for suit to be brought by the "patentee." By the same token, a right to sue clause cannot negate the requirement that, for co-plaintiff standing, a licensee must have beneficial ownership of some of the patentee's proprietary rights. A patentee may not give a right to sue to a party who has no proprietary interest in the patent. *Crown Die & Tool Co. v. Nye Tool & Machine Works*, 261 U.S. 24, 44 (1923); *see also Life Time Doors, Inc. v. Walled Lake Door Co.*, 505 F.2d 1165, 1167–68, 184 USPQ 1, 2 (6th Cir. 1974) (bare licensee has no right to be in suit or to appeal; such authorization by patentee has no effect); *Overman Cushion Tire Co. v. Goodyear Tire & Rubber Co.*, 59 F.2d 998, 14 USPQ 104 (2d Cir.) (nonexclusive licensee has no right to sue or be joined in suit); *Philadelphia Brief Case Co.*, 145 F. Supp. at 429–30, 111 USPQ at 183 (contract clause cannot give right to sue where licensee would otherwise have no such right). Here, being only a nonexclusive licensee, Ortho has no inherent or implied right to sue which the clause regulates as between the parties. Thus, we conclude the right to sue clause has no effect on Ortho's standing, one way or the other.

Secondly, under the cited precedent, the requirement that a licensee sue in the name of the patentee is not merely a formality. The patentee is brought into the suit for substantive reasons, namely, to protect its own interests in connection with the charged acts of infringement and "to enable the alleged infringer to respond in one action to all claims of infringement for his act." *Independent Wireless Co.*, 269 U.S. at 468.

A licensee cannot stand by until a patentee's suit is concluded and then seek to vindicate its rights in a second suit. As stated in *Birdsell v. Shaliol*, 112 U.S. 485, 486–87 (1884):

> When a suit … has been brought and prosecuted, in the name of the patentee alone, with the licensee's consent and concurrence, to final judgment from which, if for too small a sum, an appeal might have been taken in the name of the patentee, we should hesitate to say merely because the licensee was not a formal plaintiff in that suit, that a new suit could be brought to recover damages against the same defendant for the same infringement.

While Ortho sought to become part of Amgen's suit at trial, on appeal Ortho seeks approval of an independent second suit in the name of Amgen against the same infringer for the same acts of infringement, namely, Genetics use of the patented '008 technology in the United States, which was the subject of Amgen's suit. Ortho does not claim it was a necessary or indispensable party to Amgen's suit, did not appeal the denials of intervention therein, and did not appeal the order deconsolidating this suit from Amgen's. Moreover, the parties advised the court at the hearing that the Amgen/Genetics litigation has been settled. Thus, Ortho has effectively consented and concurred to suit in the name of the patentee alone.

Notes

1. **Can a patent assignee sue for pre-assignment infringement?** If the agreement is silent on the issue of past infringement, that is, the right to sue for infringement that occurred prior to the assignment, the assignee does not have a right to sue for past infringement. *See Crown Die & Tool Co. v. Nye Tool & Mach. Works*, 261 U.S. 24, 43 (1923) (the assignee may sue for past infringement if the "owner assigns the patent and also the claim for past infringements to the same person"); *Mas-Hamilton Group v. LaGard, Inc.*, 156 F.3d 1206, 1210, 48 USPQ2d 1010, 1013 (Fed. Cir. 1998); *Minco, Inc. v. Combustion Eng'g, Inc.*, 95 F.3d 1109, 1117, 40 USPQ2d 1001, 1006 (Fed. Cir. 1996) ("the conveyance of the patent does not normally include the right to recover for injury occurring to the prior owner"). The right to sue a party for past infringement is not transferred to the assignee unless the assignment agreement manifests an intent to transfer this right. The agreement does not require a particular formula or set prescription of words in order to express that conveyance. The construction of an assignment agreement or a licensing agreement is generally governed by state contract law, except where state law "would be inconsistent with the aims of federal patent policy." *Lear, Inc. v. Adkins*, 395 U.S. 653, 673, 162 USPQ 1 (1969). *See also Minco, Inc. v. Combustion Eng'g, Inc.*, 95 F.3d 1109, 40 USPQ2d 1001 (Fed. Cir. 1996). In *Minco*, the court held that something less that an express conveyance of "the right to sue for past infringement" was sufficient to transfer this right:

The assignment documents show that Richards obtained by express language the right to sue for past infringement from Rawles. Therefore, both Jenkins and Richards held the right to sue for prior infringement when they entered into the transactions with MAC. Jenkins and Richards then assigned to MAC all of their rights in the '462 patent, including the right to sue for past infringement. MAC, in turn, assigned all of its interest to Minco. According to this chain of title, Minco possessed the right to sue for infringement which occurred before it acquired title.

CE challenges one link in this chain—the assignment to MAC. The long form assignment from Jenkins and Richards to MAC transferred "all of Assignors' right, title and interest." Under the general rule, the bare reference to all right, title, and interest does not normally transfer the right to sue for past infringement. The MAC assignment, however, expressly notes that Richards received all "right, title, and interest" from Rawles, including "all rights of action and damages for past infringement." The express reference to past infringement in the MAC assignment expanded the scope of the term "right, title, and interest" to encompass the right to sue for prior infringement. Indeed, paragraph 6 of the assignment confirms that Jenkins and Richards "do not retain any right to any recoveries for infringement . . . [or] to sue in their own name with regard to the [Patent]." In addition, the assignment expressly grants MAC all patent rights "as fully and entirely as the same would have been held and enjoyed by Assignors . . . [as if the] agreement had not been made." In sum, the entirety of the agreements establishes that the MAC assignment clearly conveyed the right to sue for past infringement.

Id. at 1117–1118, 40 USPQ2d at 1007.

2. **Are patent licenses assignable?** In *In re CFLC, Inc.*, 89 F.3d 673, 39 USPQ2d 1518 (9th Cir. 1996), the Ninth Circuit addressed the issue of whether a nonexclusive patent licensee may assign the license to a third party. During a bankruptcy proceeding, the licensee CFLC assigned its nonexclusive license under the patent to a third party, Everex Systems, Inc. The patent owner, Cadtrack Corporation, objected to the assignment arguing that under federal law patent license agreements are personal and may not be assigned. Everex, however, argued that the assignability of patent licenses should be a matter of state contract law which would support the assignability of the licensing agreement. The Ninth Circuit held that federal patent policy justifies the application of federal law which does not permit assignment of a licensing agreement absent the patent owner's consent:

Allowing free assignability—or, more accurately, allowing states to allow free assignability—of nonexclusive patent licenses would undermine the reward that encourages invention because a party seeking to use the patented invention could either seek a license from the patent holder or seek an assignment of an existing patent license from a licensee.

* * *

Federal law holds a nonexclusive patent license to be personal and nonassignable and therefore would excuse Cadtrak from accepting performance from, or rendering it to, anyone other than CFLC. "It is well settled that a non-exclusive licensee of a patent has only a personal and not a property interest in the patent and that this personal right cannot be assigned unless the patent owner authorizes the assignment or the license itself permits assignment."

Id. at 679, 39 USPQ2d at 1523 (citations omitted). Do you agree with this holding? Why should these agreements be considered personal? Would a patent owner license to just anyone? Would the terms of a license be the same regardless of who the patent owner was licensing or how much of the product they intended to sell? Can you think of other factors that would affect the patent owner's decision whether to license and the terms of the license?

Similarly, a nonexclusive patent license may not be sublicensed unless the patent owner gives specific permission. *See Rock-Ola Mfg. Corp. v. Filben Mfg. Co.*, 168 F.2d 919, 78 USPQ 175 (8th Cir. 1948). However, the holder of a license to make and use, or to make and sell, patented goods is permitted (in the absence of express language in the agreement) to have the goods made by a third party. *Radio-Craft Co. v. Westinghouse Elec. & Mfg. Co.*, 7 F.2d 432 (3d Cir. 1925). But if the third-party produces the goods for his own use or the use of someone other than the licensee, the arrangement will be deemed a sublicense and is not permitted unless the patent owner expressly authorized sublicensing. *Carey v. United States*, 326 F.2d 975, 140 USPQ 345 (Ct. Cl. 1964).

3. **Implied licenses:** In *De Forest Radio Telephone & Telegraph Co. v. United States*, 273 U.S. 236, 241 (1927), the Supreme Court stated:

No formal granting of a license is necessary in order to give it effect. Any language used by the owner of the patent or any conduct on his part exhibited to another, from which that other may properly infer that the owner consents to his use of the patent in making or using it, or selling it, upon which the other acts, constitutes a license.

The authorized sale of a patented article vests in the purchaser the right to use and re-sell the article. *Adams v. Burke*, 84 U.S. 453 (1873). Additionally, a licensee receives an implied license in any other patent owned by the licensor, to the extent necessary to enable him to operate under the licensed patent. *See Met–Coil Systems Corp. v. Korners Unlimited, Inc.*, 803 F.2d 684, 231 USPQ 474 (Fed. Cir. 1986). An implied license may also arise where the patent owner knows of the user's infringement and does not sue (the equitable doctrine of laches or equitable estoppel can bar the patent owner's recovery for such infringement).

4. **Shop rights:** Where an employee, during her hours of employment, working with her employer's materials and appliances, conceives and perfects an invention for which she obtains a patent, her employer can obtain a nonexclusive right to practice the invention, even though she may not be required under her employment contract to assign her rights to the employer. Such right is known as a shop right. *McElmurry v. Arkansas Power & Light Co.*, 995 F.2d 1576, 27 USPQ2d 1129 (Fed. Cir. 1993). The court applies the law of the state in which the activities took place and considers

factors such as whether the invention is in the employer's field, whether the employee worked on it during business hours, whether the employee used any of the employer's resources in the development of the invention and what the employee's position was.

5. **Life of the license cannot exceed the patent term.** In *Brulotte v. Thys Co.*, 379 U.S. 29, 143 USPQ 264 (1964), the Supreme Court held that licensing agreements that extend beyond the life of an issued patent are unlawful. In *Aronson v. Quick Point Pencil Co.*, 440 U.S. 257, 201 USPQ 1 (1979), the Supreme Court was faced with a situation in which the parties had agreed to a license for the use of a key holder for which a patent application was pending. The agreement stipulated that the royalty rate would be 5% of sales for the first five years, and that if, after five years, no patent had issued, the licensee would continue to pay royalties, albeit at the reduced rate of 2.5% of sales. The Court held that where no patent has issued, federal patent law does not preempt state contract law, and thus a license is allowable on an unpatented article for any number of years.

The contracting parties in *Meehan v. PPG Indus., Inc.*, 802 F.2d 881, 231 USPQ 400 (7th Cir. 1986), had entered into a license agreement in anticipation of applying for patents. As the patentee, Meehan, intended to apply for patents in multiple countries. The agreement called for royalties to be paid until the expiration of the last-expiring patent. The patent issued and the U.S. patent expired in January of 1983. The last-expiring patent, the Canadian patent, expired in December of 1984. The licensee, PPG, discontinued payment upon the expiration of the U.S. patent, relying on *Brulotte*. Meehan argued that because no patent application had yet been filed when the agreement was entered into, the contract did not involve a transfer of patent rights, and therefore the *Brulotte* rule did not apply. But the Seventh Circuit ruled that the payment of royalties beyond the expiration of the U.S. patent was unenforceable. The court held that it is the issuance of the patent that triggers application of the *Brulotte* rule, not the transfer of rights. Therefore the *Brulotte* rule applies to agreements entered into in anticipation of applying for a patent.

6. **Are best efforts required?** What happens if a company takes an exclusive license under the patent and never actually manufactures the product? What if the company took the license for the sole purpose of excluding others from manufacturing the invention? In *Dwight & Lloyd Sintering Co. v. American Ore Reclamation Co.*, 44 F.Supp. 391 (D.C. N.Y. 1937), the court held that there is an implied clause in exclusive patent license agreements that requires the licensee to use its best efforts to work the patent, i.e., bring in profits and revenues. The court held that such a best-efforts clause is implied even where the agreement contains a minimum royalty provision.

In contrast, in *Permanence Corp. v. Kennametal, Inc.*, 908 F.2d 98, 15 USPQ2d 1550 (6th Cir. 1990), the Sixth Circuit ruled that a best-efforts clause is implied in an exclusive patent license agreement only where the agreement does not provide for consideration beyond royalties as a percentage of sales (for example, minimum royalties, up-front fee or advance royalties). The Sixth Circuit opined that the *Dwight and Lloyd Sintering* court misapplied the *Wood* doctrine, which states that a best-efforts clause is implied *where it is necessary to provide mutuality of obligation*.

B.   WHO CAN CHALLENGE THE VALIDITY OF A PATENT?

1.   LICENSEE ESTOPPEL

LEAR, INC. v. ADKINS

395 U.S. 653, 162 USPQ 1 (1969)

Mr. Justice HARLAN delivered the opinion of the Court.

In January of 1952, John Adkins, an inventor and mechanical engineer, was hired by Lear, Incorporated, for the purpose of solving a vexing problem the company had encountered in its efforts to develop a gyroscope which would meet the increasingly demanding requirements of the aviation industry. The gyroscope is an essential component of the navigational system in all aircraft, enabling the pilot to learn the direction and altitude of his airplane. With the development of the faster airplanes of the 1950's, more accurate gyroscopes were needed, and the gyro industry consequently was casting about for new techniques which would satisfy this need in an economical fashion. Shortly after Adkins was hired, he developed a method of construction at the company's California facilities which improved gyroscope accuracy at a low cost. Lear almost immediately incorporated Adkins' improvements into its production process to its substantial advantage.

The question that remains unsettled in this case, after eight years of litigation in the California courts, is whether Adkins will receive compensation for Lear's use of those improvements which the inventor has subsequently patented. At every stage of this lawsuit, Lear has sought to prove that, despite the grant of a patent by the Patent Office, none of Adkins' improvements were sufficiently novel to warrant the award of a monopoly under the standards delineated in the governing federal statutes. Moreover, the company has sought to prove that Adkins obtained his patent by means of a fraud on the Patent Office. In response, the inventor has argued that since Lear had entered into a licensing agreement with Adkins, it was obliged to pay the agreed royalties regardless of the validity of the underlying patent.

The Supreme Court of California unanimously vindicated the inventor's position. While the court recognized that generally a manufacturer is free to challenge the validity of an inventor's patent, it held that 'one of the oldest doctrines in the field of patent law establishes that so long as a licensee is operating under a license agreement he is estopped to deny the validity of his licensor's patent in a suit for royalties under the agreement. The theory underlying this doctrine is that a licensee should not be permitted to enjoy the benefit afforded by the agreement while simultaneously urging that the patent which forms the basis of the agreement is void.'

Almost 20 years ago, in its last consideration of the doctrine, this Court also invoked an estoppel to deny a licensee the right to prove that his licensor was demanding royalties for the use of an idea which was in reality a part of the public domain. *Automatic Radio Manufacturing Co. v. Hazeltine Research, Inc.*, 339 U.S. 827, 836 (1950). We granted *certiorari* in the present case to reconsider the validity of the *Hazeltine* rule in the light of our recent decisions emphasizing the strong federal policy favoring free competition in ideas which do not merit patent protection.

I.

At the very beginning of the parties' relationship, Lear and Adkins entered into a rudimentary one-page agreement which provided that although "all new ideas, discoveries, inventions, etc., related to ... vertical gyros become the property of Mr. John S. Adkins," the inventor promised to grant Lear a license as to all ideas he might develop "on a mutually satisfactory royalty basis." As soon as Adkins' labors yielded tangible results, it quickly became apparent to the inventor that further steps should be taken to place his rights to his ideas on a firmer basis. On February 4, 1954, Adkins filed an application with the Patent Office in an effort to gain federal protection for his improvements. At about the same time, he entered into a lengthy period of negotiations with Lear in an effort to conclude a licensing agreement which would clearly establish the amount of royalties that would be paid.

These negotiations finally bore fruit on September 15, 1955, when the parties approved a complex 17–page contract which carefully delineated the conditions upon which Lear promised to pay royalties for Adkins' improvements. The parties agreed that if "the U.S. Patent Office refuses to issue a patent on the substantial claims (contained in Adkins' original patent application) or if such a patent so issued is subsequently held invalid, then in any of such events Lear at its option shall have the right forthwith to terminate the specific license so affected or to terminate this entire Agreement.... "

As the contractual language indicates, Adkins had not obtained a final Patent Office decision as to the patentability of his invention at the time the licensing agreement was concluded. Indeed, he was not to receive a patent until January 5, 1960. This long delay has its source in the special character of Patent Office procedures. The regulations do not require the Office to make a final judgment on an invention's patentability on the basis of the inventor's original application. While it sometimes happens that a patent is granted at this early stage, it is far more common for the Office to find that although certain of the applicant's claims may be patentable, certain others have been fully anticipated by the earlier developments in the art. In such a situation, the Patent Office does not attempt to separate the wheat from the chaff on its own initiative. Instead, it rejects the application, giving the inventor the right to make an amendment which narrows his claim to cover only those aspects of the invention which are truly novel. It often happens, however, that even after an application is amended, the Patent Office finds that some of the remaining claims are unpatentable. When this occurs, the agency again issues a rejection which is subject to further amendment. And so the process of rejection and amendment continues until the Patent Office Examiner either grants a patent or concludes that none of the inventor's claims could possibly be patentable, at which time a final rejection is entered on the Office's records. Thus, when Adkins made his original application in 1954, it took the average inventor more than three years before he obtained a final administrative decision on the patentability of his ideas, with the Patent Office acting on the average application from two to four times.

The progress of Adkins' effort to obtain a patent followed the typical pattern. In his initial application, the inventor made the ambitious claim that his entire method of constructing gyroscopes was sufficiently novel to merit protection. The Patent Office, however, rejected this initial claim, as well as two subsequent amendments, which progressively narrowed the scope of the invention sought to be protected. Finally, Adkins narrowed his claim drastically to assert only that the design of the apparatus used to achieve gyroscope accuracy was novel. In response, the Office issued its 1960 patent, granting a 17–year monopoly on this more modest claim.

During the long period in which Adkins was attempting to convince the Patent Office of the novelty of his ideas, however, Lear had become convinced that Adkins would never receive a patent on his invention and that it should not continue to pay substantial royalties on ideas which had not contributed substantially to the development of the art of gyroscopy. In 1957, after Adkins' patent application had been rejected twice, Lear announced that it had searched the Patent Office's files and had found a patent which it believed had fully anticipated Adkins' discovery. As a result, the company stated that it would no longer pay royalties on the large number of gyroscopes it was producing at its plant in Grand Rapids, Michigan (the Michigan gyros). Payments were continued on the smaller number of gyros produced at the company's California plant (the California gyros) for two more years until they too were terminated on April 8, 1959.

As soon as Adkins obtained his patent in 1960, he brought this lawsuit in the California Superior Court. He argued to a jury that both the Michigan and the California gyros incorporated his patented apparatus and that Lear's failure to pay royalties on these gyros was a breach both of the 1955 contract and of Lear's quasi-contractual obligations. Although Lear sought to raise patent invalidity as a defense, the trial judge directed a verdict of $16,351.93 for Adkins on the California gyros, holding that Lear was estopped by its licensing agreement from questioning the inventor's patent. The trial judge took a different approach when it came to considering the Michigan gyros. Noting that the company claimed that it had developed its Michigan designs independently of Adkins' ideas, the court instructed the jury to award the inventor recovery only if it was satisfied that Adkins' invention was novel, within the meaning of the federal patent laws. When the jury returned a verdict for Adkins of $888,122.56 on the Michigan gyros, the trial judge granted Lear's motion for judgment notwithstanding the verdict, finding that Adkins' invention had been completely anticipated by the prior art.

Neither side was satisfied with this split decision, and both appealed to the California District Court of Appeal, which adopted a quite different approach. The court held that Lear was within its contractual rights in terminating its royalty obligations entirely in 1959, and that if Adkins desired to recover damages after that date he was "relegated to an action for infringement" in the federal courts. So far as pre–1959 royalties were concerned, the court held that the contract required the company to pay royalties on both the California and Michigan gyros regardless of the validity of the inventor's patent.

Once again both sides appealed, this time to the California Supreme Court, which took yet another approach to the problem presented. The court rejected the District Court of Appeal's conclusion that the 1955 license gave Lear the right to terminate its royalty obligations in 1959. Since the 1955 agreement was still in effect, the court concluded, relying on the language we have already quoted, that the doctrine of estoppel barred Lear from questioning the propriety of the Patent Office's grant. The court's adherence to estoppel, however, was not without qualification. After noting Lear's claim that it had developed its Michigan gyros independently, the court tested this contention by considering "whether what is being built by Lear (in Michigan) springs entirely" from the prior art. Applying this test, it found that Lear had in fact "utilized the apparatus patented by Adkins throughout the period in question," and reinstated the jury's $888,000 verdict on this branch of the case.

II.

Since the California Supreme Court's construction of the 1955 licensing agreement is solely a matter of state law, the only issue open to us is raised by the court's reliance upon the doctrine of estoppel to bar Lear from proving that Adkins' ideas were dedicated to the common welfare by federal law. In considering the propriety of the State Court's decision, we are well aware that we are not writing upon a clean slate. The doctrine of estoppel has been considered by this Court in a line of cases reaching back into the middle of the 19th century. Before deciding what the role of estoppel should be in the present case and in the future, it is, then, desirable to consider the role it has played in the past.

While the roots of the doctrine have often been celebrated in tradition, we have found only one 19th century case in this Court that invoked estoppel in a considered manner. And that case was decided before the Sherman Act made it clear that the grant of monopoly power to a patent owner constituted a limited exception to the general federal policy favoring free competition. Curiously, a second decision often cited as supporting the estoppel doctrine points clearly in the opposite direction. *St. Paul Plow Works v. Starling*, 140 U.S. 184 (1891), did not even question the right of the lower courts to admit the licensee's evidence showing that the patented device was not novel. A unanimous Court merely held that, where there was conflicting evidence as to an invention's novelty, it would not reverse the decision of the lower court upholding the patent's validity.

In the very next year, this Court found the doctrine of patent estoppel so inequitable that it refused to grant an injunction to enforce a licensee's promise never to contest the validity of the underlying patent. "It is as important to the public that competition should not be repressed by worthless patents, as that the patentee of a really valuable invention should be protected in his monopoly.... " *Pope Manufacturing Co. v. Gormully*, 144 U.S. 224, 234 (1892).

Although this Court invoked an estoppel in 1905 without citing or considering *Pope's* powerful argument, *United States v. Harvey Steel Co.*, 196 U.S. 310 (1905), the doctrine was not to be applied again in this Court until it was revived in *Automatic Radio Manufacturing Co. v. Hazeltine Research, Inc.*, *supra*, at 836, which declared, without prolonged analysis, that licensee estoppel was "the general rule." In so holding, the majority ignored the teachings of a series of decisions this Court had rendered during the 45 years since *Harvey* had been decided. During this period, each time a patentee sought to rely upon his estoppel privilege before this Court, the majority created a new exception to permit judicial scrutiny into the validity of the Patent Office's grant. Long before *Hazeltine* was decided, the estoppel doctrine had been so eroded that it could no longer be considered the "general rule," but was only to be invoked in an evernarrowing set of circumstances.

It will simplify matters greatly if we first consider the most typical situation in which patent licenses are negotiated. In contrast to the present case, most manufacturers obtain a license after a patent has issued. Since the Patent Office makes an inventor's ideas public when it issues its grant of a limited monopoly, a potential licensee has access to the inventor's ideas even if he does not enter into an agreement with the patent owner. Consequently, a manufacturer gains only two benefits if he chooses to enter a licensing agreement after the patent has issued. First, by accepting a license and paying royalties for a time, the licensee may have avoided the necessity of defending an expensive infringement action during the period when he may be least able to afford one. Second, the existence of an unchallenged patent may deter others from attempting to compete with the licensee.

Under ordinary contract principles the mere fact that some benefit is received is enough to require the enforcement of the contract, regardless of the validity of the underlying patent. Nevertheless, if one tests this result by the standard of good-faith commercial dealing, it seems far from satisfactory. For the simple contract approach entirely ignores the position of the licensor who is seeking to invoke the court's assistance on his behalf. Consider, for example, the equities of the licensor who has obtained his patent through a fraud on the Patent Office. It is difficult to perceive why good faith requires that courts should permit him to recover royalties despite his licensee's attempts to show that the patent is invalid.

Even in the more typical cases, not involving conscious wrongdoing, the licensor's equities are far from compelling. A patent, in the last analysis, simply represents a legal conclusion reached by the Patent Office. Moreover, the legal conclusion is predicated on factors as to which reasonable men can differ widely. Yet the Patent Office is often obliged to reach its decision in an *ex parte* proceeding, without the aid of the arguments which could be advanced by parties interested in proving patent invalidity. Consequently, it does not seem to us to be unfair to require a patentee to defend the Patent Office's judgment when his licensee places the question in issue, especially since the licensor's case is buttressed by the presumption of validity which attaches to his patent. Thus, although licensee estoppel may be consistent with the letter of contractual doctrine, we cannot say that it is compelled by the spirit of contract law, which seeks to balance the claims of promisor and promisee in accord with the requirements of good faith.

Surely the equities of the licensor do not weigh very heavily when they are balanced against the important public interest in permitting full and free competition in the use of ideas which are in reality a part of the public domain. Licensees may often be the only individuals with enough economic incentive to challenge the patentability of an inventor's discovery. If they are muzzled, the public may continually be required to pay tribute to would-be monopolists without need or justification. We think it plain that the technical requirements of contract doctrine must give way before the demands of the public interest in the typical situation involving the negotiation of a license after a patent has issued.

We are satisfied that *Automatic Radio Manufacturing Co. v. Hazeltine Research, Inc., supra*, itself the product of a clouded history, should no longer be regarded as sound law with respect to its "estoppel" holding, and that holding is now overruled.

The case before us, however, presents a far more complicated estoppel problem than the one which arises in the most common licensing context. The problem arises out of the fact that Lear obtained its license in 1955, more than four years before Adkins received his 1960 patent. Indeed, from the very outset of the relationship, Lear obtained special access to Adkins' ideas in return for its promise to pay satisfactory compensation.

Thus, during the lengthy period in which Adkins was attempting to obtain a patent, Lear gained an important benefit not generally obtained by the typical licensee. For until a patent issues, a potential licensee may not learn his licensor's ideas simply by requesting the information from the Patent Office. During the time the inventor is seeking patent protection, the governing federal statute requires the Patent Office to hold an inventor's patent application in confidence. If a potential licensee hopes to use the ideas contained in a secret patent application, he must deal with the inventor himself, unless the inventor chooses to publicize his ideas to the world at large. By promising to pay Adkins royalties from the very outset of their relationship, Lear gained immediate access to ideas which it may well not have learned until the Patent Office published the details of Adkins' invention in 1960. At the core of this case, then, is the difficult question whether federal patent policy bars a State from enforcing a contract regulating access to an unpatented secret idea.

Adkins takes an extreme position on this question. The inventor does not merely argue that since Lear obtained privileged access to his ideas before 1960, the company should be required to pay royalties accruing before 1960 regardless of the validity of the patent which ultimately issued. He also argues that since Lear obtained special benefits before 1960, it should also pay royalties during the entire patent period (1960–1977), without regard to the validity of the Patent Office's grant. We cannot accept so broad an argument.

Adkins' position would permit inventors to negotiate all important licenses during the lengthy period while their applications were still pending at the Patent Office, thereby disabling entirely all those who have the strongest incentive to show that a patent is worthless. While the equities supporting Adkins' position are somewhat more appealing than those supporting the typical licensor, we cannot say that there is enough of a difference to justify such a substantial impairment of overriding federal policy.

Nor can we accept a second argument which may be advanced to support Adkins' claim to at least a portion of his post-patent royalties, regardless of the validity of the Patent Office grant. The terms of the 1955 agreement provide that royalties are to be paid until such time as the "patent . . . is held invalid," and the fact remains that the question of patent validity has not been finally determined in this case. Thus, it may be suggested that although Lear must be allowed to raise the question of patent validity in the present lawsuit, it must also be required to comply with its contract and continue to pay royalties until its claim is finally vindicated in the courts.

The parties' contract, however, is no more controlling on this issue than is the State's doctrine of estoppel, which is also rooted in contract principles. The decisive question is whether overriding federal policies would be significantly frustrated if licensees could be required to continue to pay royalties during the time they are challenging patent validity in the courts.

It seems to us that such a requirement would be inconsistent with the aims of federal patent policy. Enforcing this contractual provision would give the licensor an additional economic incentive to devise every conceivable dilatory tactic in an effort to postpone the day of final judicial reckoning. We can perceive no reason to encourage dilatory court tactics in this way. Moreover, the cost of prosecuting slow-moving trial proceedings and defending an inevitable appeal might well deter many licensees from attempting to prove patent invalidity in the courts. The deterrent effect would be particularly severe in the many scientific fields in which invention is proceeding at a rapid rate. In these areas, a patent may well become obsolete long before its 17–year term has expired. If a licensee has reason to believe that he will replace a patented idea with a new one in the near future, he will have little incentive to initiate lengthy court proceedings, unless he is freed from liability at least from the time he refuses to pay the contractual royalties. Lastly, enforcing this contractual provision would undermine the strong federal policy favoring the full and free use of ideas in the public domain. For all these reasons, we hold that Lear must be permitted to avoid the payment of all royalties accruing after Adkins' 1960 patent issued if Lear can prove patent invalidity.

Adkins' claim to contractual royalties accruing before the 1960 patent issued is, however, a much more difficult one, since it squarely raises the question whether, and to what extent, the States may protect the owners of unpatented inventions who are willing to disclose their ideas to manufacturers only upon payment of royalties. The California Supreme Court did not address itself to this issue with precision, for it believed that the venerable doctrine of estoppel provided a sufficient answer to all of Lear's claims based upon federal patent law. Thus, we do not know whether the Supreme Court would have awarded Adkins recovery even on his pre-patent royalties if it had recognized that previously established estoppel doctrine could no longer be properly invoked with regard to royalties accruing during the 17–year patent period. Our decision today will, of course, require the state courts to reconsider the theoretical basis of their decisions enforcing the contractual rights of inventors and it is impossible to predict the extent to which this reevaluation may revolutionize the law of any particular State in this regard. Consequently, we have concluded, after much consideration, that even though an important question of federal law underlies this phase of the controversy, we should not now attempt to define in even a limited way the extent, if any, to which the States may properly act to enforce the contractual rights of inventors of unpatented secret ideas. Given the difficulty and importance of this task, it should be undertaken only after the state courts have, after fully focused inquiry, determined the extent to which they will respect the contractual rights of such inventors in the future. Indeed, on remand, the California courts may well reconcile the competing demands of patent and contract law in a way which would not warrant further review in this Court.

Notes

1. In *Foster v. Hallco Mfg. Co.*, 947 F.2d 469, 20 USPQ2d 1241 (Fed. Cir. 1991), the parties had resolved prior litigation with the entry of a consent decree which granted a nonexclusive, royalty-bearing license to

Foster, and which stipulated that the patents at issue were valid. Hallco subsequently brought suit against Foster, alleging that Foster was operating under the patents without paying royalties. Despite the consent decree, Foster claimed that the patents were invalid, citing the *Lear* policy favoring patent challenges. The Federal Circuit held that normal principles of *res judicata* favoring finality of consent decrees outweigh the public policy expressed in Lear.

STUDIENGESELLSCHAFT KOHLE, M.B.H., v. SHELL OIL CO.

112 F.3d 1561, 42 USPQ2d 1674 (Fed. Cir. 1997)

Before MAYER, SCHALL, and BRYSON, Circuit Judges.

RADER, Circuit Judge.

The United States District Court for the Southern District of Texas determined that claims 1–6 and 14 of U.S. Patent No. 4,125,698 ('698 patent) are invalid, and that infringement of claim 13 by Shell Oil Company's (Shell) polypropylene operations and infringement of claims 7, 9–12, and 15 by Shell's polybutylene operations were not properly before the court. Studiengesellschaft Kohle m.b.H. (SGK), the owner of the '698 patent, appeals these decisions. Further, the district court certified the following question under 28 U.S.C. § 1292(b) (1994):

> Where the Court has found the relevant patent claims invalid, may the Licensor recover damages for breach of contract for past royalties due on processes allegedly covered by such claims, from the date of the alleged breach until the date that the Licensee first challenged validity of the claims?

Because an applicant cannot combine multiple prior applications to obtain an earlier filing date for an individual claim, this court affirms the district court's invalidity holding. Because infringement involving claim 13 and Shell's polybutylene operations was properly before the district court, this court reverses and remands. Finally, this court answers the certified question in the affirmative.

I.

SGK is the licensing arm of a famous, non-profit research and educational organization in Germany—the Max–Planck Institute for Coal Research. The '698 patent is part of a family of patents filed by Professor Karl Ziegler, a Nobel laureate and past director of the Max–Planck Institute, and various co-inventors. Ziegler and his co-workers initially discovered that combinations of reducing agents (most notably organoaluminum compounds) and heavy metal compounds would polymerize ethylene to form high molecular plastics. Ziegler extended this discovery to the polymerization of higher members of the ethylene series, such as propylene and butene. Ziegler, et al. filed the 770,484 application, which matured into the '698 patent, on October 29, 1958.

In another case, this court categorized the '698 patent as a continuation-in-part (CIP) because it was not limited to a single parent application. *See Studiengesellschaft Kohle mbH v. Northern Petrochemical Co.*, 784 F.2d 351, 352, 228 USPQ 837, 838 (Fed. Cir. 1986). The 770,484 CIP application, which was filed on October 29, 1958, combined Ziegler's 482,412 application, filed January 17, 1955, with his 514,068 application, filed June 8, 1955. On December 6, 1955, over a year before the filing of the 770,484 application, Belgian Patent No. 538,782 (the Belgian Patent) issued. Claims 1–6 and 14 of the '698 patent, both parties agree, cover a process disclosed in the Belgian Patent.

Shell and SGK first entered into an agreement involving the Ziegler family of patents in 1974. Under that agreement, SGK licensed Shell to polymerize propylene under the Ziegler patents. When the '698 patent issued in 1978, the 1974 agreement already authorized Shell to practice the claimed process. In 1987, after several disputes over this license, Shell and SGK renegotiated the license only with regard to the '698 patent. The new terms provided Shell a paid-up license to produce 450 million pounds of polypropylene per year, with a 1.5% running royalty on any polypropylene sales in excess of 450 million pounds. Further, the amended agreement obligated Shell to give a yearly accounting of its entire polypropylene production. In that yearly accounting, Shell was to "specify the amount of Polypropylene produced which it considers as falling outside of the license and ... provide SGK, in confidence, with sufficient information to allow SGK to independently evaluate whether or not said production is, in fact, outside of the scope of the license."

In 1987, Shell also began producing polypropylene by an alleged new process in Seadrift, Texas (the Seadrift Process). Because Shell contended that the '698 patent did not cover the Seadrift Process, Shell did not pay royalties on polypropylene produced by that process. Moreover, in its yearly accountings to SGK, Shell did not disclose its production of polypropylene by the Seadrift Process.

Ultimately, SGK terminated Shell's license and brought an action for unpaid royalties from 1987 through 1993. Additionally, SGK set forth claims for infringement of the '698 patent for the period 1993 through 1995. Shell moved for summary judgment of invalidity of claims 1–6 and 14 of the '698 patent based on anticipation by the Belgium patent. SGK responded by arguing that the '698 patent is not anticipated because it is entitled to an earlier filing date than the Belgian patent. To arrive at this earlier filing date, SGK relied on 35 U.S.C. § 120 (1994) to combine the disclosures of the two earlier patent applications (the 482,412 application and the 514,068 application).

The district court held that section 120 does not permit the combination of two earlier disclosures to acquire an earlier filing date, because "an earlier application must comply with the requirements of § 112 for each claim that seeks the benefit of the filing date of that earlier application." As none of the parent applications alone describes the invention recited in claims 1–6 and 14 of the '698 patent, the district court held that these claims were only entitled to the filing date of the continuation-in-part application (October 29, 1958). Thus, the district court determined that the Belgian Patent anticipated claims 1–6 and 14 of the '698 patent, and, therefore, granted summary judgment of invalidity under 35 U.S.C. § 102(b).

The district court further ruled that the only matter remaining before it was SGK's claim for royalties under the parties' license. In that regard, the district court held that a licensor could recover damages for breach of a license agreement where the validity of the underlying patent was not challenged until after the breach occurred. The district court certified the question of whether the invalidity determination on claims 1–6 and 14 would affect plaintiff's claim for unpaid royalties for the period before Shell challenged the validity of the patent ... This court affirms the district court's grant of summary judgment of invalidity under 35 U.S.C. § 102(b) of claims 1–6 and 14 of the '698 patent.

IV.

The district court also certified a question concerning the effect of an invalidity finding on unpaid royalties. See 28 U.S.C. § 1292(b) (1994). According to the 1987 licensing agreement, Shell agreed to pay SGK a 1.5% running royalty on the sale of any polypropylene, produced with a heavy metal catalyst as defined in claim 1 of the '698 patent, in excess of 450 million pounds per year. Further, as discussed above, this agreement obligated Shell to give a yearly accounting of its entire polypropylene production, specifying "the amount of Polypropylene produced which it considers as falling outside of the license." The agreement obligated Shell to provide SGK with sufficient information to allow independent evaluation of whether its production falls outside the scope of the license. The record shows that Shell breached this contract by producing polypropylene under the Seadrift Process, without either paying royalties or reporting the production as outside of the license.

Nothing in this license made payment of royalties contingent upon the validity of the '698 patent. Setting aside momentarily both federal patent law and policy, this contract—regardless of the patent's validity—obligates Shell to pay royalties on polypropylene produced in accordance with claim 1 of the '698 patent. In other words, contract law governs the enforcement of the license. Enforcement of these contract terms is not contingent upon validity of the patent which defines the subject matter of the license. Assuming that the Seadrift Process infringes claim 1 of the '698 patent and thus fits within the terms of the license, Shell breached the license by failing to pay royalties. Enforcement of the license, if the Seadrift Process infringes the '698 patent, would require Shell to pay back royalties.

With a patent licensing agreement at stake, this court examines the contract for rare, but potential, conflicts between state contract law and federal patent law. For example, in *Lear v. Adkins*, 395 U.S. 653 (1969), the Supreme Court prevented the enforcement of a valid royalty payment agreement to facilitate a determination of patent validity. Specifically, the Supreme Court declined to estop a patent licensee from contesting the validity of the licensed patent. In tones that echo from a past era of skepticism over intellectual property principles, the Court in *Lear* feared that

> licensees may often be the only individuals with enough economic incentive to challenge the patentability of an inventor's discovery. If they are muzzled, the public may continually be required to pay tribute to would-be monopolists without need or justification. We think it plain that the technical requirements of contract doctrine must give way before the demands of the public interest.

Lear, 395 U.S. at 670. Thus, in examining the interface between national patent policy and state contracts, the Supreme Court requires this court to consider "whether overriding federal policies would be significantly frustrated" by enforcing the license. *Id.*

This court encountered the *Lear* test when an assignor-inventor and his company sought to defend against an infringement action by challenging the validity of the assigned patents. *See Diamond Scientific Co. v. Ambico, Inc.*, 848 F.2d 1220, 6 USPQ2d 2028 (Fed. Cir. 1988). With careful consideration of the *Lear* test and policies, this court nonetheless estopped the assignor from challenging the validity of the patent:

> To allow the assignor to make that representation [of the worth of the patent] at the time of the assignment (to his advantage) and later to repudiate it (again to his advantage) could work an injustice against the assignee.... Despite the public policy encouraging people to challenge potentially invalid patents, there are still circumstances in which the equities of the contractual relationships between the parties should deprive one party ... of the right to bring that challenge.

Diamond Scientific, 848 F.2d at 1224–25.

As in *Diamond Scientific*, this court detects no significant frustration of federal patent policy by enforcing the 1987 license agreement between Shell and SGK, to the extent of allowing SGK to recover royalties until the date Shell first challenged the validity of the claims. First, as in *Diamond Scientific*, Shell executed a contractual agreement which produced significant benefits for the corporation and attested to the worth of the patent. Under the agreement (with its provision for Shell to notify SGK of all polypropylene production), Shell had the benefits of producing polypropylene insulated from unlicensed competition, insulated from investigations of infringement, and even insulated from royalties (until SGK's discovery of the Seadrift Process). To these benefits, Shell now seeks to add the benefit of abrogating its agreement and avoiding its breach of the contract. Following the reasoning of *Diamond Scientific*, this court must prevent the injustice of allowing Shell to exploit the protection of the contract and patent rights and then later to abandon conveniently its obligations under those same rights.

Just as important, however, Shell's apparent breach of its duty to notify under the agreement is itself more likely to frustrate federal patent policy than enforcement of the contract. As already noted, *Lear* focused on the "full and free use of ideas in the public domain." By abrogating its notification duty, Shell delayed a timely challenge to the validity of the '698 patent and postponed the public's full and free use of the invention of the '698 patent. Shell enjoyed the protection of the license from 1987 until SGK became aware of the Seadrift Process. Upon SGK's discovery of its Seadrift process, Shell suddenly seeks the protection of the *Lear* policies it flaunted for many years. However, a licensee, such as Shell, cannot invoke the protection of the *Lear* doctrine until it (i) actually ceases payment of royalties, and (ii) provides notice to the licensor that the reason for ceasing payment of royalties is because it has deemed the relevant claims to be invalid. Other circuits addressing this issue have arrived at the same conclusion.

In this factual setting, therefore, enforcement of the license according to its terms, even if this entails a determination of whether the Seadrift process infringes a now-invalidated patent, does not frustrate federal patent policy. Accordingly, this court remands this case to the district court for enforcement of the license (prior to the date Shell first challenged the validity of the claims) and, if necessary, computation of back royalties.

2.   ASSIGNOR ESTOPPEL

DIAMOND SCIENTIFIC CO. v. AMBICO, INC.

848 F.2d 1220, 6 USPQ2d 2028 (Fed. Cir. 1988)

Before FRIEDMAN, DAVIS and NEWMAN, Circuit Judges.

DAVIS, Circuit Judge.

This appeal from an order of the United States District Court for the Southern District of Iowa granting plaintiff's motion to strike three affirmative defenses is before us by permission, to decide whether the doctrine of assignor estoppel prevents this assignor-inventor and his company, who are sued for infringement, from challenging the validity of the patents previously assigned by him to the assignee. We affirm.

Appellee Diamond Scientific Co. (Diamond) employed Dr. Clarence Welter from 1959 until 1974. During that time, Dr. Welter invented a vaccine against gastroenteritis in swine, and filed a patent application for "Transmissible Gastroenteritis Vaccines and Methods of Producing the Same." While making this patent application, Dr. Welter assigned all of the rights in the patents to Diamond Laboratories, Inc. (the predecessor of Diamond). Eventually, Diamond's predecessor was awarded the following patents from this application: No. 3,479,430; No. 3,585,108; and No. 3,704,203.

In 1974 Dr. Welter left Diamond, where he had become a vice-president, and formed his own company, appellant Ambico, Inc. (Ambico). Ambico began manufacturing and selling a gastroenteritis vaccine for swine. Diamond began this patent infringement suit against Ambico and Dr. Welter, claiming infringement of the three patents that Dr. Welter had assigned to Diamond. The defendants' answer raised, among other defenses, three grounds for patent invalidity: 35 U.S.C. § 112 (inadequate disclosure); 35 U.S.C. § 102 (lack of novelty); and 35 U.S.C. § 103 (obviousness). Diamond's motion to strike these three defenses asserted the doctrine of assignor estoppel. The district court granted Diamond's motion and this appeal followed.

The central issue to be decided is whether in this case the assignor-inventor of the patents (or a company in privity with him) can defend the infringement suit brought by the assignee by challenging the validity of the patents previously assigned, or whether the equitable doctrine of assignor estoppel prevents the assignor from claiming that the patents are invalid.

Lear resolved the issue of licensee estoppel by writing its obituary. *Lear, Inc. v. Adkins*, 395 U.S. 653 (1969). But for courts wrestling with assignor estoppel it was less clear whether *Lear* had also sounded the death knell for that doctrine. Certainly, there was nothing in its holding that eliminated the doctrine. Beyond the questioning *dicta* in *Lear*, the Court has left assignment estoppel untouched for the past nineteen years.

In examining *Lear*, one important distinction between assignors and licensees becomes apparent—a distinction that cautions against the automatic application to assignment cases of the rationale underlying *Lear* and licensees. The public policy favoring allowing a licensee to contest the validity of the patent is not present in the assignment situation. Unlike the licensee, who, without Lear might be forced to continue to pay for a potentially invalid patent, the assignor who would challenge the patent has already been fully paid for the patent rights.

Assignor estoppel is an equitable doctrine that prevents one who has assigned the rights to a patent (or patent application) from later contending that what was assigned is a nullity. The estoppel also operates to bar other parties in privity with the assignor, such as a corporation founded by the assignor. The estoppel historically has applied to invalidity challenges based on "novelty, utility, patentable invention, anticipatory matter, and the state of the art." *Babcock v. Clarkson*, 63 F. 607, 609 (1st Cir. 1894).

The four most frequently mentioned justifications for applying assignor estoppel are the following: "(1) to prevent unfairness and injustice; (2) to prevent one [from] benefiting from his own wrong; (3) by analogy to estoppel by deed in real estate; and (4) by analogy to a landlord-tenant relationship." Cooper, *Estoppel to Challenge Patent Validity: The Case of Private Good Faith vs. Public Policy*, 18 Case W. Res. 1122 (1967). Although each rationale may have some utility depending on the facts presented by the particular case, our concern here is primarily with the first one.

Courts that have expressed the estoppel doctrine in terms of unfairness and injustice have reasoned that an assignor should not be permitted to sell something and later to assert that what was sold is worthless, all to the detriment of the assignee. Justice Frankfurter's dissent in

Scott Paper explained that the doctrine was rooted in the notion of fair dealing. "The principle of fair dealing as between assignor and assignee of a patent whereby the assignor will not be allowed to say that what he has sold as a patent was not a patent has been part of the fabric of our law throughout the life of this nation." *Scott Paper v. Marcalus Mfg. Co.*, 326 U.S. 249, 260 (1945) (Frankfurter, J., dissenting). "The essence of the principle of fair dealing which binds the assignor of a patent in a suit by the assignee, even though it turns out that the patent is invalid or lacks novelty, is that in this relation the assignor is not part of the general public but is apart from the general public." *Id.* at 261–62. In other words, it is the implicit representation by the assignor that the patent rights that he is assigning (presumably for value) are not worthless that sets the assignor apart from the rest of the world and can deprive him of the ability to challenge later the validity of the patent. To allow the assignor to make that representation at the time of the assignment (to his advantage) and later to repudiate it (again to his advantage) could work an injustice against the assignee.

Our holding is that this is a case in which public policy calls for the application of assignor estoppel. We are, of course, not unmindful of the general public policy disfavoring the repression of competition by the enforcement of worthless patents. Yet despite the public policy encouraging people to challenge potentially invalid patents, there are still circumstances in which the equities of the contractual relationships between the parties should deprive one party (as well as others in privity with it) of the right to bring that challenge.

Appellants argue that assignor estoppel is necessarily a variation of estoppel by conduct and should be governed by the traditional elements of equitable estoppel. But the Supreme Court has never analyzed assignor estoppel by reference to the elements of equitable estoppel and has explicitly recognized assignor estoppel to be the functional equivalent of estoppel by deed. *Westinghouse Elec. & Mfg. Co. v. Formica Insulation Co.*, 266 U.S. at 348–49 (1924). Estoppel by deed is a form of legal, not equitable, estoppel. *AMP, Inc., v. United States*, 389 F.2d 448, 452, 156 USPQ 647, 649 (1968). The *Westinghouse* Court did not specify whether assignor estoppel operates in precisely the same manner as estoppel by deed, which ordinarily prevents one from attacking any material fact found in the document (or deed) transferring the rights—whether assignor estoppel would prevent an assignor from attacking a material fact found in the assignment, thereby preventing the assignor's assertion of invalidity. But the extent to which the concept of an estoppel by deed may or may not shape the doctrine of assignor estoppel, though it may often play a significant role, need not confine our application of the doctrine. As noted above, we believe that the primary consideration in now applying the doctrine is the measure of unfairness and injustice that would be suffered by the assignee if the assignor were allowed to raise defenses of patent invalidity. Our analysis must be concerned mainly with the balance of equities between the parties.

We note first that Dr. Welter assigned the rights to his inventions to Diamond in exchange for valuable consideration (one dollar plus other unspecified consideration—presumably his salary over many years and other employment benefits). Dr. Welter also executed an inventor's oath, which stated his belief, *inter alia*, that he was the first and sole inventor, that the invention was never known or used before his invention and that it was not previously patented or described in any publication in any country. Furthermore, Dr. Welter apparently participated actively in the patent application process, including drafting the initial version of the claims and consulting on their revision.

Appellants would now defend against accusations of infringement by trying to show that the three patents in issue are invalid because the inventions either were inadequately disclosed by the specifications, lacked novelty, or would have been obvious to one of ordinary skill at the time the inventions were made. If appellants are permitted to raise these defenses and are successful in their proof, Dr. Welter will have profited both by his initial assignment of the patent applications and by his later attack on the value of the very subjects of his earlier assignment. In comparison, Diamond will have given value for the rights to Dr. Welter's inventions only to have him later deprive Diamond of the worth of those assigned rights.

We agree with the district court that the equities weigh heavily in favor of Diamond. Although the doctrine of assignor estoppel may no longer be a broad equitable device susceptible of automatic application, the case before us is appropriate for its use. When the inventor-assignor has signed the Oath, Power of Attorney and Petition, which attests to his belief in the validity of the patents, and has assigned the patent rights to another for valuable consideration, he should be estopped from defending patent infringement claims by proving that what he assigned was worthless. That is an implicit component of the assignment by Welter to Diamond which is immune from contradiction. The inventor's active participation in the prosecution and preparation of the patent applications, as is alleged here, would tilt the equities even more heavily in favor of the assignee, but consideration of this factor is not necessary to the result.

It is also irrelevant that, at the time of the assignment, Dr. Welter's patent applications were still pending and the Patent Office had not yet granted the patents. What Dr. Welter assigned were the rights to his inventions. That Diamond may have later amended the claims in the application process (a very common occurrence in patent prosecutions), with or without Dr. Welter's assistance, does not give appellants' arguments against estoppel any greater force. Our concern must be the balance of the equities. The fact is that Dr. Welter assigned the rights to his invention, irrespective of the particular language in the claims describing the inventions when the patents were ultimately granted. Appellants should not be allowed now to destroy those rights by derogating the patents' validity. *Cf. AMP, Inc.*, 389 F.2d at 452, 156 USPQ at 649–50 (legal estoppel, in context of implied license doctrine, prevents licensor (or assignor) who has licensed (or assigned) a definable property right for valuable consideration from attempting to derogate or detract from that right). In *Westinghouse*, the Court observed that the scope of the right conveyed in the assignment of patent rights before the granting of the patent "is much less certainly defined than that of a granted patent, and the question of the extent of the estoppel against the assignor of such an inchoate right is more difficult to determine than in the case of the patent assigned after its granting." *Westinghouse*, 266 U.S. at 352–53. However, the Court merely suggested that "this difference might justify the view that the range of relevant and competent evidence in fixing the limits of the subsequent estoppel should be more liberal than in the case of an assignment of a granted patent," and found it unnecessary to decide the question. *Id.* at 353.

Nevertheless, *Westinghouse* does allow for an accommodation in such circumstances. To the extent that Diamond may have broadened the claims in the patent applications (after the assignments) beyond what could be validly claimed in light of the prior art, *Westinghouse* may allow appellants to introduce evidence of prior art to narrow the scope of the claims of the patents, which may bring their accused devices outside the scope of the claims of the patents in suit. *Id.* at 350. This exception to assignor estoppel also shows that estopping appellants from raising invalidity defenses does not necessarily prevent them from successfully defending against Diamond's infringement claims.

CONCLUSION

Because we agree that the public policy behind the doctrine of assignor estoppel prevents these appellants from challenging the validity of the patents in issue, the district court's decision granting Diamond's motion to strike appellants' second, third and sixth affirmative defenses is affirmed.

Notes

1. **Assignor estoppel also applies to parties in privity.** Assignor estoppel also applies to parties in privity with the assignor, such as a corporation founded by the assignor. The test to determine privity is whether there is an identity of interests between parties such that it is equitable to place the party in the shoes of the assignor. In *Shamrock Tech., Inc., v. Medical Sterilization, Inc.*, 903 F.2d 789, 14 USPQ2d 1728 (Fed. Cir. 1990), the inventor had assigned his invention to his employer company A. The inventor subsequently left company A to join company B. The court said that:

> whether company B is in privity and thus bound by the doctrine will depend on the equities dictated by the relationship between the inventor and company B in light of the act of infringement. The closer that relationship, the more the equities will favor applying the doctrine to company B.

Id. at 793, 14 USPQ2d at 1732. In *Shamrock Tech.*, the court found that Shamrock (the assignor) and MSI were in privity (and therefore MSI was bound by assignor estoppel) where an employee left Shamrock to run MSI:

> The district court correctly determined that, considering the balance of equities and the relationship of Luniewski and MSI, no genuine issue of material fact exists regarding privity in this case. The undisputed facts are: (1) in July 1983 Luniewski left Shamrock to join MSI as Vice–President in charge of Operations; (2) Luniewski owns 50,000 shares of MSI stock; (3) MSI was formed in 1982 to sterilize surgical instruments and manufacture other medical goods; yet as soon as Luniewski was hired in 1983, MSI built facilities for processing PTFE with radiation; (4) Luniewski oversaw the design and construction of those facilities; (5) Luniewski was hired in part to start up MSI's infringing operations; (6) the decision to begin processing PTFE with radiation was made jointly by Luniewski and the president of MSI; (7) MSI began manufacturing PTFE with radiation in 1985; and (8) Luniewski was in charge of MSI's PTFE operation.

> MSI attempts to distinguish *Diamond Scientific*, citing *National Cash Register Co. v. Remington Arms Co.*, 283 F. 196, 202 (D. Del. 1922), *aff'd*, 286 F. 367 (3d Cir. 1923), and *Babcock & Wilcox Co. v. Toledo Boiler Works Co.*, 170 F. 81, 85 (6th Cir. 1909), for the proposition that there is no privity between a corporation and a mere employee thereof. However, as above indicated, Luniewski was far more than a mere employee of MSI and the undisputed facts establish MSI's direct involvement of Luniewski in MSI's infringing operations. MSI clearly availed itself of Luniewski's "knowledge and assistance" to conduct infringement. The district court committed no error in finding MSI in privity.

Id. at 794, 14 USPQ2d at 1732–33.

In *Mentor Graphics Corp. v. Quickturn Design Sys., Inc.*, 150 F.3d 1374, 47 USPQ2d 1683 (Fed. Cir. 1998), the Court held that assignor estoppel also prevents a party in privity with an estopped assignor from challenging the patents validity. In *Mentor*, Mentor assigned the '473 patent to Quickturn. After the sale Mentor acquired Meta, a French company that had been independently developing the technology of the '473 patent. The court held that Mentor's ownership of all of Meta's stock, the sharing of personnel, and the fact that Mentor approved Meta's budgets supported the finding that the two company's were in privity.

Do you think that there is privity such that assignor estoppel should apply where:

a. between assignor and co-developer of infringing device with company they formed to advance their interests in infringing device? *See United States Appliance Corp. v. Beauty Shop Supply Co.*, 121 F.2d 149, 151, 50 USPQ 40, 42–43 (9th Cir. 1941).

b. between assignor and company of which he was principal stockholder, president, and general manager? *See Stubnitz–Greene Spring*

Corp. v. Fort Pitt Bedding Co., 110 F.2d 192, 195, 45 USPQ 52, 55 (6th Cir. 1940).

c. between assignor and corporation over which he had control of policy but lacked voting control? *See Buckingham Prods. Co. v. McAleer Mfg. Co.*, 108 F.2d 192, 195, 44 USPQ 91, 95 (6th Cir. 1939).

2. What if the party seeking to challenge validity is both the assignor and a licensee of the same patent? In *Acoustical Design, Inc., v. Control Elec. Co.*, 932 F.2d 939, 18 USPQ2d 1707 (Fed. Cir. 1991), the Federal Circuit held that, where the assignor takes back or retains a license under the patent, *Diamond Scientific* wins out over *Lear*, and the assignor/licensee is estopped from challenging the patent's validity.

3. **Assignee Estoppel.** An assignee may be estopped from challenging the validity of the assigned patent. *See Roberts v. Sears, Roebuck & Co.*, 573 F.2d 976, 197 USPQ 516 (7th Cir. 1978). This doctrine serves to avoid placing the assignee in the legally awkward position of simultaneously attacking and defending the validity of the same patent.

4. **Requirements Contracts.** A requirements contract for a patented product does not amount to an exclusive license. *See Textile Productions Inc. v. Mead Corp..*, 134 F.3d 1481, 45 USPQ2d 1633 (Fed. Cir. 1998). In *Textile*, the Federal Circuit dismissed an infringement suit brought by an exclusive supplier against the patentee for lack of standing because the agreement between the patentee and the exclusive supplier did not qualify as an exclusive license. In an exclusive license, the patentee must promise to refrain from granting a license to anyone else. The agreement in this case, was silent on this point. The Court acknowledged the general rule that a licensee is not entitled to bring an infringement suit unless the licensee has "all substantial rights" under the patent (making it effectively an assignee). There is, however, an exception where an exclusive licensee does not have all substantial rights but standing is necessary to prevent an injustice, such as where the patentee is the infringer. The Court held that *Textile* did not fall within this exception because its requirement contract amounted to a bare license and the exception only applies to an exclusive license.

Chapter Eighteen

REEXAMINATION AND REISSUE

There are several strategic considerations in deciding whether to request a reexamination. Reexamination offers a seldom-explored option to have the PTO reconsider patent validity. The reexamination process was created to provide fast, relatively inexpensive determinations on patent validity in cases where prior art has been discovered that was not considered by the PTO during patent prosecution. Reexamination may be preferred because the PTO reconsiders validity rather than a judge or jury—an option that is sometimes more attractive to the patent owner or infringer because it is cheaper and faster. In general, the patent owner is more likely to seek reexamination than a possible infringer for the reasons discussed below.

A.   REEXAMINATIONS

Statutory Provisions—35 U.S.C. §§ 301–305:

§ 301.   Citation of prior art

Any person at any time may cite to the Office in writing prior art consisting of patents or printed publications which that person believes to have a bearing on the patentability of any claim of a particular patent. If the person explains in writing the pertinency and manner of applying such prior art to at least one claim of the patent, the citation of such prior art and the explanation thereof will become a part of the official file of the patent. At the written request of the person citing the prior art, his or her identity will be excluded from the patent file and kept confidential.

§ 302.   Request for reexamination

Any person at any time may file a request for reexamination by the Office of any claim of a patent on the basis of any prior art cited under the provisions of section 301 of this title. The request must be in writing and must be accompanied by payment of a reexamination fee established by the Commissioner of Patents pursuant to the provisions of section 41 of this title. The request must set forth the pertinency and manner applying cited prior art to every claim for which reexamination is requested. Unless the requesting person is the owner of the patent, the Commissioner promptly will send a copy of the request to the owner of record of the patent.

§ 303. Determination of issue by Commissioner

(a) Within three months following the filing of a request for reexamination under the provisions of section 302 of this title, the Commissioner will determine whether a substantial new question of patentability affecting any claim of the patent concerned is raised by the request, with or without consideration of other patents or printed publications. On his own initiative, and any time, the Commissioner may determine whether a substantial new question of patentability is raised by patents and publications discovered by him or cited under the provisions of section 301 of this title.

§ 304. Reexamination order by Commissioner

If, in a determination made under the provisions of subsection 303(a) of this title, the Commissioner finds that a substantial new question of patentability affecting any claim of a patent is raised, the determination will include an order for reexamination of the patent for resolution of the question. The patent owner will be given a reasonable period, not less than two months from the date a copy of the determination is given or mailed to him, within which he may file a statement on such question, including any amendment to his patent and new claim or claims he may wish to propose, for consideration in the reexamination. If the patent owner files such a statement, he promptly will serve a copy of it on the person who has requested reexamination under the provisions of section 302 of this title. Within a period of two months from the date of service, that person may file and have considered in the reexamination a reply to any statement filed by the patent owner. That person promptly will serve on the patent owner a copy of any reply filed.

§ 305. Conduct of reexamination proceedings

After the times for filing the statement and reply provided for by section 304 of this title have expired, reexamination will be conducted according to the procedures established for initial examination under the provisions of sections 132 and 133 of this title. In any reexamination proceeding under this chapter, the patent owner will be permitted to propose any amendment to his patent and a new claim or claims thereto, in order to distinguish the invention as claimed from the prior art cited under the provisions of section 301 of this title, or in response to a decision adverse to the patentability of a claim of a patent. No proposed amended or new claim enlarging the scope of a claim of the patent will be permitted in a reexamination proceeding under this chapter. All reexamination proceedings under this section, including any appeal to the Board of Patent Appeals and Interferences, will be conducted with special dispatch within the Office.

IN RE RECREATIVE TECHNOLOGIES CORP.

83 F.3d 1394, 38 USPQ2d 1776 (Fed. Cir. 1996)

Before ARCHER, Chief Judge, and RICH and NEWMAN, Circuit Judges.

PAULINE NEWMAN, Circuit Judge.

Recreative Technologies Corp. ("Recreative") appeals the decision of the Patent and Trademark Office ("PTO") Board of Patent Appeals and

Interferences holding claims 1, 2, and 4 of United States Patent No. 4,912,800 ("the '800 patent"), upon reexamination, to be unpatentable. We conclude that the Board exceeded the statutory authorization that governs reexamination. We reverse the decision of the Board, and remand for further proceedings consistent with this opinion.

BACKGROUND

The '800 patent is directed to a cleaning device for use by golfers. The device is structured to be secured to a golf bag for use to clean items such as golf clubs, balls, and shoes. The cleaning device is comprised of several elements including a water absorbent towel body, a brush member secured to the towel body and a mounting means to releasably mount the towel body/brush to a golf bag. After Recreative sued Preferred Response Marketing ("Preferred") for infringement, Preferred requested reexamination of the '800 patent, citing as new references five patents and three publications, and stating that these new references raised a substantial new question of patentability. The PTO granted the request for reexamination.

On reexamination the examiner rejected claims 1, 2, 4–7, and 17 as unpatentable on the ground of obviousness, 35 U.S.C. § 103, in view of a reference to Ota. The examiner did not reject any claim on any of the eight new references cited by Preferred, and did not cite any reference other than Ota. The examiner confirmed original claims 13–16 and 18–20 and held patentable original claims 3 and 8–12. The Ota reference had been cited in the original examination on the same ground, obviousness, and the claims had been held patentable over Ota.

Recreative appealed the reexamination rejection to the Board. The Board reversed the examiner's rejection of claims 1, 2, 4–7, and 17, holding that the claims were not obvious in view of Ota. However, the Board sua sponte rejected claims 1, 2, and 4 based on the same Ota reference, but now under 35 U.S.C. § 102, for lack of novelty. This appeal followed.

DISCUSSION

The Reexamination Statute

Recreative states that the PTO had no authority to reject the claims, on reexamination, on the same ground on which the application was examined and the claims allowed during the original prosecution. Recreative states that the reexamination statute limits reexamination to "a substantial new question of patentability," and does not authorize repetition of a rejection on the same grounds that had been resolved in favor of the applicant during the original examination. 35 U.S.C. § 303 requires the examiner to determine whether a "substantial new question of patentability" is raised by the reexamination request. Only if a new question of patentability is raised, can the patent be reexamined.

Recreative states that the examiner merely repeated the same rejection for obviousness, based on the same Ota reference, as during the initial examination. Recreative states that it had successfully traversed the rejection based on the Ota reference in the initial examination, and that the reexamination statute was written to limit reexamination to new questions.

The Commissioner argues that "[o]nce initiated, the scope of reexamination includes reexamination of the patent in view of any pertinent patents and printed publications," new or old. The Commissioner thus contends that the repeat examination on the same ground was proper practice. However, the reexamination statute was designed to exclude repeat examination on grounds that had already been successfully traversed. Thus, the statute, on its face, does not accommodate the Commissioner's position.

The statute authorizes reexamination only when there is a substantial new question of patentability. A second examination, on the identical ground that had been previously raised and overcome, is barred. Thus, once it becomes apparent that there is no new question of patentability, it is improper to conduct reexamination on an old question that had been finally resolved during the initial examination. The Commissioner's argument that a different interpretation should prevail, and that the PTO has authority to reach a different result on reexamination on the identical ground, has led us to review the considerations that underlay the statute at the time of enactment.

Legislative History of Public Law 96–517

The reexamination statute was an important part of a larger effort to revive the United States' competitive vitality by restoring confidence in the validity of patents issued by the PTO. *Patlex Corp. v. Mossinghoff*, 758 F.2d 594, 601, 225 USPQ 243, 248 (Fed. Cir. 1985). Congressman Robert Kastenmeier described the reexamination proposal as "an effort to reverse the current decline in U.S. productivity by strengthening the patent and copyright systems to improve investor confidence in new technology." 126 Cong. Rec. 29,895 (1980).

The proponents of reexamination anticipated three principal benefits. First, reexamination based on references that were not previously included in the patentability examination could resolve validity disputes more quickly and less expensively than litigation. Second, courts would benefit from the expertise of the PTO for prior art that was not previously of record. Third, reexamination would strengthen confidence in patents whose validity was clouded because pertinent prior art had not previously been considered by the PTO. *Patlex*, 758 F.2d at 602, 225 USPQ at 248–49. These benefits are achieved by authorizing the PTO to correct errors in the prior examination:

> The reexamination statute's purpose is to correct errors made by the government, to remedy defective governmental (not private) action, and if need be to remove patents that never should have been granted.... A defectively examined and therefore erroneously

granted patent must yield to the reasonable Congressional purpose of facilitating the correction of governmental mistakes.

Patlex, 758 F.2d at 604, 225 USPQ at 250.

However, Congress recognized that this broad purpose must be balanced against the potential for abuse, whereby unwarranted reexaminations can harass the patentee and waste the patent life. The legislative record and the record of the interested public reflect a serious concern that reexamination not create new opportunities for abusive tactics and burdensome procedures. Thus reexamination as enacted was carefully limited to new prior art, that is, "new information about pre-existing technology which may have escaped review at the time of the initial examination of the patent application." H.R. Rep. No. 96–1307, 96th Cong., 2d Sess. 3 (1980), reprinted in 1980 U.S.C.C.A.N. 6460, 6462. No grounds of reexamination were to be permitted other than based on new prior art and sections 102 and 103. As explained in the legislative history, matters that were decided in the original examination would be barred from reexamination:

> This "substantial new question" requirement would protect patentees from having to respond to, or participate in unjustified reexaminations. Further, it would act to bar reconsideration of any argument already decided by the Office, whether during the original examination or an earlier reexamination.

Id. at 7, reprinted in 1980 U.S.C.C.A.N. at 6466.

Thus the statute guarded against simply repeating the prior examination on the same issues and arguments. Commissioner Diamond explained the importance of this safeguard:

> [The proposed statute] carefully protects patent owners from reexamination proceedings brought for harassment or spite. The possibility of harassing patent holders is a classic criticism of some foreign reexamination systems and we made sure it would not happen here.

Industrial Innovation & Patent & Copyright Law Amendments: Hearings on H.R. 6933, 6934, 3806 & 214 Before the Subcomm. on Courts, Civil Liberties and the Administration of Justice of the House Comm. on the Judiciary, 96th Cong., 2d Sess. 594 (1980) (statement of Sidney Diamond, Cmr. of Patents & Trademarks).

In this case, the Commissioner points out that the Manual of Patent Examining Procedure authorizes the procedure that was followed. Section 2258 of the M.P.E.P. states that

> [O]nce initiated, the scope of reexamination includes reexamination of the patent in view of any pertinent patents or printed publications, including issues previously addressed by the Office.

Thus the Commissioner argues that it is within the examiner's authority to apply the old ground of rejection on the Ota reference, as the only ground of rejection. We can not agree. This is the very action against which the statute protects. The Commissioner's argument that reexamination, once begun, can be limited to grounds previously raised and finally decided, can not be accommodated by the statute, and is directly contravened by the legislative history. Although Congress may entrust the administrative agency with administration of a statute, the agency can not depart from the statutory purpose.

> [The courts] must reject administrative constructions of the statute, whether reached by adjudication or by rulemaking, that are inconsistent with the statutory mandate or that frustrate the policy that Congress sought to implement.

Patlex, 771 F.2d at 487, 226 USPQ at 989 (quoting *Federal Election Comm'n v. Democratic Senatorial Campaign Committee*, 454 U.S. 27, 31–32 (1981)).

We take note that § 2258 of the M.P.E.P. was not among the original reexamination rules that were adopted to implement the reexamination statute. See revision 7 to the 4th edition, July 1981. The current text of § 2258 appeared in subsequent editions of the M.P.E.P. We do not know its genesis, yet it plainly exceeds the statutory authorization. It is also in apparent conflict with other procedural instructions in the Manual. Compare M.P.E.P. § 2216, which states that requests for reexamination should point out how the questions of patentability newly raised are substantially different from those raised in the original prosecution. Also compare M.P.E.P. § 2242, which includes the following:

> If the prior art patents and printed publications raise a substantial new question of patentability of at least one claim of the patent, then a substantial new question of patentability is present, *unless it is clear to the examiner that the same question of patentability has already been decided* (1) [by a court] ... (2) by the Office either in the original examination, the examination of a reissue patent, or an earlier concluded reexamination.

(Emphasis added.) M.P.E.P. § 2242, which bars review of a question that "has already been decided," does not readily harmonize with M.P.E.P. § 2258, which permits reexamination of "issues previously addressed." Thus although the M.P.E.P. usefully implements the patent statute, when a section of the M.P.E.P. is inconsistent with the statute it must yield to the legislative purpose.

The statutory instruction that a new question of patentability must be raised is explicit in 35 U.S.C. § 303. Reexamination is barred for questions of patentability that were decided in the original examination. That power can not be acquired by internal rule of procedure or practice. The policy balance reflected in the reexamination statute's provisions can not be unilaterally realigned by the agency. To the extent that M.P.E.P. § 2258 enlarges the statutory authorization, it is void.

The Ota Reference

The question of patentability in view of the Ota reference was decided in the original examination, and thus it can not be a substantial new question. The Commissioner argues that the examiner failed to appreciate the Ota reference during the first examination, citing *Standard Havens Products, Inc. v. Gencor Industries, Inc.*, 897 F.2d 511, 13 USPQ2d 2029 (Fed. Cir. 1990). In *Standard Havens* the Commissioner ordered reexamination in view of a reference that had not been cited in the original examination, the Commissioner observing that it was uncertain whether the reference had been considered. *Id.* at 514, 13 USPQ2d at 2031. Ota, however, had been cited. It was the subject of extensive prosecution during the original examination, and the rejection had been overcome.

On the reexamination appeal to the Board, the Board had reversed the examiner's reexamination rejection under § 103, stating that obviousness had not been shown. The Board then spontaneously rejected claims 1, 2, and 4 for lack of novelty, again based on Ota. Recreative points out that "anticipation is the epitome of obviousness," and that the original examiner necessarily considered novelty when examining the claims for obviousness. We need not reach this aspect, for this procedure by the Board can not overcome the fact that reexamination should not have been granted or should have been dismissed at the examination stage when no new grounds of rejection were raised.

It can not have been the statutory intent that a patentee would not know whether there was a new ground of rejection, as required for reexamination, until the reexamination was completed on the old ground, was appealed to the Board, and was decided by the Board not on the old ground but on a possibly new ground that was not previously part of the reexamination. Thus even on the Commissioner's argument that a rejection on the same reference but styled as lack of novelty instead of obviousness is a "new ground"—an interesting question that we do not reach—the requirement of § 303 was not met. It would eviscerate the statutory safeguard to permit the Board to cure an improper reexamination with the creation of a new issue at the appellate stage of the reexamination proceeding.

In sum, the argument based on Ota did not present a new question of patentability. Recreative is correct that the reexamination should have been terminated when no other ground of rejection was raised.

REVERSED AND REMANDED.

Notes

1. Would it have made a difference to the court if the Examiner had rejected the claims of the '800 patent as obvious based on a specific combination of prior art that, although before the PTO in an earlier examination, had not been considered in combination by the examiner? In *In re Portola Packaging, Inc.*, 110 F.3d 786, 42 USPQ2d 1295 (Fed. Cir. 1997), the Federal Circuit held that the PTO could not reject patent claims during reexamination proceedings based solely on the combination of prior art patents that were before the PTO in an earlier examination, despite the fact that the earlier claims of the original application were never rejected based on the specific combination of those references. The Court held:

> Whether the earlier examination was correct or not, reexamination of the same claims in light of the same references does not create a substantially new question of patentability, which is the statutory criterion for reexamination.

Id. at 790, 42 USPQ2d at 1299. Could the examiner reject the claims of the '800 patent as obvious based on the combined teachings of the Ota reference and one of the five new patents previously not before the PTO?

2. What, if anything, should the PTO be allowed to consider during reexamination proceedings in addition to new prior art? Can the PTO consider patents and printed publications which are not prior art? The Federal Circuit held that they could if they are looking at double patenting issues. In *In re Lonardo*, 119 F.3d 960, 43 USPQ2d 1262 (Fed. Cir. 1997), the Federal Circuit held that the PTO is authorized to consider double patenting in a reexamination proceeding. The doctrine of double patenting is intended to prevent a patentee from obtaining an extension of a patent term by patenting the same invention or an obvious modification thereof in more than one application. In order to determine whether a patentee is trying to obtain such an extension, the PTO may need to look at patents other than those considered prior art, (i.e., other patents issued to the same patentee). In *In re Lonardo* the court held that, according to legislative history, such patents clearly fall within the scope of reexamination and are exactly the type of evidence Congress intended the PTO to consider during reexamination. *See id.* at 966, 43 USPQ2d at 1266.

3. **Patents and Printed Publications Only.** Notice that the PTO will only consider patents and printed publications during reexamination. The M.P.E.P also permits the submission of deposition or trial transcript in a reexam proceeding. What other forms of prior art might a competitor or accused infringer want considered? Do you think it is feasible to expand the reexamination proceedings to consider other forms of prior art?

4. **Third Party Participation in Reexam.** Third party participation in the reexamination process is very limited. The third-party who requests reexam cites the patents and printed publications and how they bear on the patentability. The Commissioner considers the third party request and determines (within three months) whether the request raises a substantial new question of patentability. If the Commissioner determines that a substantial new question of patentability is not raised, the reexam request is denied. This decision is final and not appealable. If, on the other hand, the Commissioner grants the reexam request finding that a substantially new question of patentability has been raised, then the patentee has two options: filing a statement responding to the Commissioner's finding or proceeding to reexamination. In practice, the patentee almost never files a responsive statement because that would allow the third party to file a reply brief. The patentee will generally prefer to shut the third party out of the proceedings by going straight to reexamination where the PTO and the patentee are the only participants. At that point, the third party who requested the reexamination is reduced to a mere witness and is completely excluded from the proceedings. When a reexamination is requested by the patent owner, third-parties have no opportunity to participate, even with knowledge of the patentee's submissions.

The district court cannot order the patentee to file the accused infringer's documents with the PTO in a reexamination proceeding as a condition of the stay of litigation. *Emerson Elec. Co. v. Davoil, Inc.*, 88 F.3d 1051, 1054, 39 USPQ2d 1474, 1476 (Fed. Cir. 1996). The district court cannot order the parties to a litigation to request reexamination. *In re Continental General Tire, Inc..*, 81 F.3d 1089, 1092, 38 USPQ2d 1365, 1368 (Fed. Cir. 1996).

Changes to the reexamination statute have been proposed in Congress for several years to permit greater third party participation. If potential infringers could participate in the reexamination, they would undoubtedly find this alternative more appealing.

5. **Commissioner's Decision to Grant Request.** Is the Commissioner's decision to grant a request for reexamination, finding a substantially new question of patentability appealable? What can the patentee do if the Commissioner finds a substantially new question of patentability based on prior art references that were already considered by the PTO? *See In re Hiniker Co.*, 150 F.3d 1362, 1368, 47 USPQ2d 1523 (Fed. Cir. 1998) (holding that an error by the Commissioner (which is not directly appealable to the Federal Circuit) in granting the request for reexamination is "washed clean" when the board rejects the patent on the basis of prior art that was not previously before the PTO).

6. **Stay District Court Proceeding During Reexam.** District courts will often be willing to stay their proceedings pending the PTO's reexamination decision. Since the PTO cannot consider issues other than validity, and can only consider patents and printed publications for validity challenges, should the district court automatically stay all proceedings when a reexamination request is granted? Courts consider a number of factors when determining whether to stay litigation. In *Agar Corp. Inc. v. Multi–Fluid, Inc.*, 983 F. Supp. 1126, 1127–28, 44 USPQ2d 1158, 1159–60 (S.D. Tex. 1997) (citations omitted), the court discussed the decision to grant a stay as follows:

> In determining whether to grant a Motion to Stay Pending Reexamination, the district court has considerable latitude. The district court will, in exercising its discretion, consider a number of factors, including: (1) the technical expertise of the Patent Office; (2) the probable effect on the litigation that granting a stay would have; and (3) the stage of the litigation at which the motion was filed.

> The expertise of the Patent Office is an important factor for the district court to consider in determining whether to stay its proceedings. Usually, a court will grant a stay when the Patent Office is perceived as the institution best able to assess the validity of the patent in view of the prior art. However, a court will be inclined to proceed to trial when it already has the benefit of a technical evaluation from the Patent Office arising out of a prior reexamination.

* * *

This Court's next consideration is the effect a stay pending reexamination would have on the litigation as a whole. If a stay would more likely than not delay the district court proceedings without any countervailing benefit, the court should proceed with the merits of the case without the benefit of the Patent Office reexamination.

Here, the Court has a definite concern about the delay that may result from a stay. Only the '680 patent has been granted a reexamination by the Patent Office. The requests for reexamination for the Plaintiff's other patents were refused by the Patent Office. Should the '680 patent be found invalid by the Patent Office's reexamination, the remaining claims of patent infringement might not be affected. This is particularly true when the Court considers that the Patent Office's basis for reexamining the '680 patent was an absence of certain references in the '680's prosecution history. Because those references were considered by the Patent Office in allowing Plaintiff's remaining patents, the reexamination of the '680 patent likely will not produce results that would affect the remaining patent infringement claims. Additionally, Plaintiff's unfair competition claim would not be affected by the reexamination.

In considering the stage of the litigation at which the motion to stay is requested, the earlier the motion is filed, the more the court will be inclined to suspend its proceedings and await the results of the reexamination proceeding. However, courts are inclined to deny a stay when the litigation is at a later stage, such as when the case has been set for trial and the discovery phase has almost been completed. This case has been pending for approximately one year and nine months. It is set for trial in the Spring of 1998. Although the discovery stage has not yet been completed, it has also not just begun. Thus, this case could be considered to be in its later stages of litigation, and granting a stay to allow the Defendant to await a reexamination would not be justified.

This Court concludes that a stay is not warranted here where the expertise of the Patent Office is not required, there is no countervailing benefit of staying the litigation pending reexamination by the Patent Office, discovery is well underway, and a trial date is set for Spring 1998.

Courts have cited a number of advantages in staying a litigation during PTO reexamination including:

1. All prior art presented to the Court will have been first considered by the PTO, with its particular expertise.

2. Many discovery problems relating to prior art can be alleviated by the PTO examination.

3. In those cases resulting in effective invalidity of the patent, the suit will likely be dismissed.

4. The outcome of the reexamination may encourage a settlement without the further use of the Court.

5. The record of reexamination would likely be entered at trial, thereby reducing the complexity and length of the litigation.

6. Issues, defenses, and evidence will be more easily limited in pre-trial conferences after a reexamination.

7. The cost likely will be reduced both for the parties and the Court.

Braintree Labs., Inc. v. Nephro–Tech, Inc., 1997 WL 94237 (D. Kan. 1997).

7. **Damages May be Limited After Reexam.** In *Bloom Eng'g Co. v. North American Mfg. Co.*, 129 F.3d 1247, 44 USPQ2d 1859 (Fed. Cir. 1997), the Federal Circuit held that no damages should be awarded for the period of time before the reexam certificate issued where the patentee made substantive changes to the claims being asserted against an infringer during reexam. In *Bloom Eng'g,* Bloom alleged that North American infringed its patent. During pretrial proceedings, North American directed Bloom's attention to a British patent that had not been cited during prosecution. This lead Bloom to seek reexamination of its patent. In the course of reexamination, original patent claims 2 and 13 were amended and the limitations from dependent claims 7 and 18 were incorporated into those claims. The Federal Circuit affirmed the trial court's determination that those changes were substantive because the claims were narrowed to distinguish Bloom's invention from the British patent. Accordingly, North American was free from liability for infringement during the period before the reexamination certificate was granted. The Court held:

> The effect of a reexamined patent during the period before issuance of the reexamination certificate is governed by 35 U.S.C. § 307(b), which provides that the rules established in § 252 for reissued patents shall apply to reexamined patents.... Sections 307 and 252 shield those who deem an adversely held patent to be invalid; if the patentee later cures the infirmity by reissue or reexamination, the making of substantive changes in the claims is treated as an irrebuttable presumption that the original claims were materially flawed. Thus the statute relieves those who may have infringed the original claims from liability during the period before the claims are validated.

Id. at 1249, 44 USPQ2d at 1861.

8. **Amending Claims During Reexam.** According to your reading of 35 U.S.C. §§ 301, 302, 304, and 305, should the patentee be allowed to amend claims or add new claims during the reexamination proceedings? Patentees are allowed to do exactly this; however, a fundamental rule is that no proposed amendment or new claim may enlarge the scope of any claim of the patent. Read the following excerpt from *Quantum Corp. v. Rodime, PLC*, 65 F.3d 1577, 1580–84, 36 USPQ2d 1162, 1165–68 (Fed. Cir. 1995) (citations omitted):

> 35 U.S.C. § 305 states, in relevant part, that "[n]o proposed amended or new claim enlarging the scope of a claim of the patent will be permitted in a reexamination proceeding." An amended or new claim has been enlarged if it includes within its scope any

subject matter that would not have infringed the original patent. "A claim that is broader in any respect is considered to be broader than the original claims even though it may be narrower in other respects." Accordingly, the claims at issue have been improperly broadened in violation of 35 U.S.C. § 305 if the track density limitation in the claims of the reexamined '383 patent—"at least approximately 600 tpi"—is broader than the track density limitation in the claims of the original '383 patent—"at least 600 tpi."

* * *

[W]e conclude that, as a matter of law, the district court arrived at the correct result. The purpose of the reexamination process is to provide a mechanism for reaffirming or correcting the PTO's action in issuing a patent by reexamining patents thought to be of doubtful validity. Consistent with this overall purpose, Congress enacted section 305 which, while allowing an applicant to amend his claims or add new claims to distinguish his invention over cited prior art, explicitly prohibits any broadening of claims during reexamination. If an applicant fails to claim as broadly as he or she could have, the proper recourse, if within two years of issuance of the patent, is to file a reissue application, see 35 U.S.C. § 251, not to remedy this problem in a reexamination proceeding.

See also Phillips Petroleum Co. v. Huntsman Polymers Corp., 157 F.3d 866, 877, 48 USPQ2d 1161, 1170 (Fed. Cir. 1998) (holding claims invalid that were broadened during reexamination).

B. STRATEGIC CONSIDERATIONS FOR REEXAMINATION

1. THE PATENTEE'S PERSPECTIVE

a. *Advantages of Requesting Reexamination*

i. *PTO is a friendly forum*

Reexamination offers the patentee several advantages to litigation. It is less expensive and quicker than litigation. Moreover, the same examiner within the PTO who originally granted the patent often reconsiders it during reexamination. Hence, the PTO is often viewed as a friendlier forum for the patentee who already received the patent office's imprimatur on her patent once before.

ii. *No participation by accused infringer*

In addition, reexamination is an *ex parte* proceeding. If the patent owner requests the reexamination, then no participation by accused infringers is permitted. In this case, the reexamination is essentially just a reopening of the prosecution of the patent in light of new prior art. The patent does not receive a presumption of validity during reexamination and the patentee is free to amend or narrow the claims to avoid the new prior art. The patentee will undoubtedly frame the prior art issues in a manner favorable to her patent. Unlike a reissue filed within two years of the patent issuance date, the patent owner cannot broaden the claims during a reexamination. The only difference between reexamination and original prosecution is that reexamination is a public proceeding; it is not a confidential exchange.

iii. Courts give extra deference to reexamined patents

Finally, the patent owner may prefer reexamination because courts often give special deference to patents that survive reexamination. In fact, reexamination by the PTO can launder the patent from any prior art not of record which is typically given more consideration during an invalidity challenge in federal courts. Accordingly, patent owners may prefer to request reexamination of the patent and stay a district court action when they are presented with prior art that could invalidate the patent in the patent infringement proceeding.

b. Disadvantages of Reexamination

i. No presumption of validity

The patent owner may prefer to have the court determine validity rather than the PTO in a reexamination proceeding because there is no presumption of validity in a reexamination. The PTO considers whether the claims are invalid by a preponderance of the evidence, not clear and convincing evidence as a litigation.

ii. Delays the litigation

The patentee generally does not want the litigation delayed for any reason. Courts routinely stay litigation during reexamination, which will delay the suit.

iii. Infringer could acquire intervening rights

In addition, if the claims are altered during reexamination, the accused infringer could obtain intervening rights. Section 307 provides that any "amended or new claim determined to be patentable and incorporated into a patent following reexamination proceedings will have the same effect as ... for reissued patents on the right of any person who made, purchased, or used within the United States ... anything patented by such proposed amended or new claim...." Section 252 provides for intervening rights as follows:

> A reissued patent shall not abridge or affect the right of any person or that person's successors in business who, prior to the grant of a reissue, made, purchased, offered to sell, or used within the United States, or imported into the United States, anything patented by the reissued patent, to continue the use of ... the specific thing so made ... unless the making ... infringes a valid claim of the reissued patent which was in the original patent. The court before which such matter is in question may provide for the continued manufacture, use, offer for sale, or sale of the thing made ... or for

the manufacture, use, offer for sale, or sale in the United States of which substantial preparation was made before the grant of the reissue, and the court may also provide for the continued practice of any process patented by the reissue that is practiced, or for the practice of which substantial preparation was made, before the grant of the reissue, to the extent and under such terms as the court deems equitable for the protection of investments made or business commenced before the grant of the reissue.

An intervening right allows the accused infringer to avoid liability for infringement if she began manufacturing a product prior to the grant of the reissued or reexamined patent and that product infringes the reissued or reexamined patent, but would not have infringed the original patent. *See Fortel Corp. v. Phone–Mate, Inc.*, 825 F.2d 1577, 3 USPQ2d 1771 (Fed. Cir. 1987). Would the narrowing of a claim to overcome prior art be a substantive change that would allow for intervening rights?

iv.   Materiality element for inequitable conduct

Finally, if the reexamination involves prior art which the patentee knew of at the time of the original application and did not disclose and the examiner relies on that art during reexamination, then the materiality element of inequitable conduct has been proven.

2.   THE ACCUSED INFRINGER'S PERSPECTIVE

a.   Advantages of Requesting Reexamination

i.   No presumption of validity

In a litigation, the accused infringer has the burden of proving invalidity by clear and convincing evidence because of the presumption of validity that attaches to issued patents. When the PTO grants a reexamination request, the patent loses its presumption of validity, and validity is considered under the preponderance of the evidence standard. Moreover, at the PTO claims are given their broadest interpretation for determining validity.

ii.   Stalls litigation

The accused infringer may prefer reexamination if she cannot afford a full-blown patent litigation. The accused infringer may be interested in requesting reexamination if the accused infringer wants to stall the litigation. Courts are often willing to stay a litigation, especially in early stages, while the PTO conducts reexamination proceedings. Accused infringers may be particularly interested in delaying litigation where they are concerned about a possible injunction or if the patent is about to expire. However, the court will likely take these considerations (like the patent nearing expiration) into account when determining whether to stay the litigation during the reexamination.

iii. Materiality element for inequitable conduct

If the accused infringer has a strong inequitable conduct defense, she may want to request reexamination. If the examiner relies on the withheld reference in rejecting the patent claims, the materiality element of inequitable conduct has been proven. Of course, this must be balanced against the possibility that the patent examiner may not rely on the reference, which could have a fatal effect on the inequitable conduct allegation.

iv. Accused infringer could acquire intervening rights

Reexamination which forces a patentee to amend patent claims could result in intervening rights for the accused infringer.

v. Confidentiality

Also keep in mind when counseling potential infringers that a reexamination can be requested anonymously, which means that it will not alert the patentee to the identity of potential infringers, but will provide a forum to contest the patent's validity. A competitor can also use reexamination to obtain an advisory opinion on patent validity before it invests time and money in possibly infringing activities. Could a competitor bring a declaratory judgment action to determine if such activities would infringe and if the patent is valid? *See* Chapter Two.

b. Disadvantages of reexamination

Reexamination has several drawbacks for the accused infringer, which generally weigh against requesting reexamination.

i. Limited participation

Unlike litigating validity where the infringer can argue why he believes the newly discovered references render the patent invalid, because of the *ex parte* nature of the reexamination proceeding, the accused infringer has limited participation. If the patent owner requests the reexamination, the accused infringer is not permitted to participate in the reexamination process at all. If the accused infringer requests the reexamination and the patent owner files a statement opposing the request for reexamination, then the accused infringer can file a reply responding to the patent owner's arguments. However, the patent owner will almost never file such a statement in order to keep the infringer from being involved. Once the PTO grants the reexamination request, the proceeding is limited to the patentee who will argue that the patent is valid over the prior art and the examiner who will determine whether the patent is valid. No participation by the accused infringer is permitted.

ii. Limited scope

Moreover, only patents and printed publications will be considered by the PTO on reexamination. Hence, if the accused infringer wishes to challenge a patent's validity based on public use or on-sale bar activities or prior invention, these challenges cannot be presented in the reexamination. Accordingly, most accused infringers prefer to take their chances with the judge or jury.

iii. No appeal rights

The accused infringer has no appeal rights if the PTO refuses to reexamine the patent or grants the patent after a reexamination. Although an accused infringer could still argue to the district court that the patent is invalid even if the PTO rejects the request for reexamination or allows the patent over the prior art after a reexamination proceeding, the accused infringer is not likely to fair well. If the PTO reconsidered the exact prior art reference raised by the infringer during a reexamination, it is not likely that a judge or jury will want to substitute its own judgment for that of the PTO, which would have just recently considered the issue. Patents are presumed valid. Patents that have successfully weathered reexamination end up getting even more deference—not that the legal presumption is any different, just that the more times the PTO decides that the patentee is entitled to a patent, the less likely it is that a judge or jury will conclude the PTO was wrong.

C. REISSUE

Statutory Provisions—35 U.S.C. § 251:

§ 251. Reissue of Defective Patents

Whenever a patent is, through error without any deceptive intention, deemed wholly or partly inoperative or invalid, by reason of a defective specification or drawing, or by reason of the patentee claiming more or less than he had a right to claim in the patent, the Commissioner shall, on the surrender of such patent and the payment of the fee required by law, reissue the patent for the invention disclosed in the original patent, and in accordance with a new and amended application, for the unexpired part of the term of the original patent. No new matter shall be introduced into the application for reissue.

* * *

No reissued patent shall be granted enlarging the scope of the claims of the original patent unless applied for within two years from the grant of the original patent.

"Reissue is essentially a reprosecution of all claims." *Hewlett-Packard Co. v. Bausch & Lomb Inc.*, 882 F.2d 1556, 1563, 11 USPQ2d 1750, 1756 (Fed. Cir. 1989). A reissue, like an ordinary patent application, undergoes substantive examination to determine patentability. The PTO can reconsider any of the claims in the application, and it need only prove them invalid by a preponderance of the evidence (the presumption of validity is gone). Only a patentee can utilize the reissue procedures and must make an oath that an error made without deceptive intent makes the patent wholly or partially inoperative or invalid. Reissue proceedings are advantageous for the patent owner because they are a less expensive alternative than litigation for correcting patent defects and are conducted in the PTO which previously granted the patent.

Why would a patentee file a reissue application? There are several reasons a patentee may file a reissue application, including:

1. To modify the claims to read literally on a competitor's product.

If a patentee discovers that a competitor has modified the patented invention to such a degree that infringement may not be able to be proved or may be difficult to prove, the patentee may want to institute a reissue proceeding. Through reissue, a patentee may amend or add claims to the patent. No new matter may be added unless it is supported by the original patent specification. So long as the changes are supported by the patentee's specification, then claims can be added which will literally read on the competitors product. This way the patentee will have a much easier infringement charge. If the added claims are broader than the original claims, the reissue must be filed within two years of the original issuance date.

2. To broaden unduly narrow claims.

For two years after the patent has issued, the patentee is permitted to enlarge the scope of the claims. However, reissue changes made after two years are only permitted to limit the scope of the claims. A reissue application to broaden claims must be filed within two years of the date the patent issued. The claims are deemed broader if they are broader in *any* respect. A good rule of thumb is that if the new claim would cover something that would not have been covered by the old claims, then the claim is broader. This could also include adding method claims where the original patent only contained apparatusclaims or vice versa (as long as the specification supports such claims). Do you think the addition of the word "substantially" to the word "rounded" in a claim broadens or narrows the claim? *See Ex parte Neuwirth*, 229 USPQ 71 (Bd. Pat. App. & Int'f 1985). If the patent owner is seeking to broaden the patent claims, the inventor must be involved; the assignee or owner cannot pursue broader claims alone.

3. To narrow claims to avoid prior art.

A patentee may also wish to institute reissue proceedings to add limitations to avoid possible invalidating prior art. "The basis for seeking narrowing reissue has generally been the belated discovery of partially-invalidating prior art." In re Amos, 953 F.2d 613, 616, 21 USPQ2d 1271, 1273 (Fed. Cir. 1991). *See also In re Harita*, 847 F.2d 801, 805, 6 USPQ2d 1930, 1932 (Fed. Cir. 1988); *General Elec. Co. v. Hoechst Celanese Corp.*, 698 F. Supp. 1181, 1185, 12 USPQ2d 1517, 1521 (D. Del. 1988) (change of "comprising" to "consisting essentially of" was a narrowing of the claim to avoid prior art); *White v. Fafnir Bearing Co.*, 389 F.2d 750, 754, 156 USPQ 657, 660 (2d Cir. 1968) (patent on Teflon lubricated bearings was narrowed from covering all compound cloths to just "compound cloth in a bearing to bind the Teflon fibers in the cloth in the proper position").

4. To fix claims to domestic or foreign priority.

What errors cannot be cured by reissue? There are several errors which the patentee cannot cure with a reissue application, including:

1. **New matter.** The patentee can never add new matter to a claim. New matter would be matter not already supported by the specification. If the accused infringer is challenging patent validity on the ground that the specification is not enabling of the broad claims or failure to satisfy the written description requirement, the patentee cannot cure these defects by adding matter to the specification. The patentee can, however, narrow the claims during reissue to cover only subject matter that is enabled and described in the specification.

2. **Correct inequitable conduct.** The patentee cannot cure earlier inequitable conduct by filing a reissue application.

3. **Correct Failure to Disclose the Best Mode**. The patentee cannot add a non-disclosed best mode during reissue.

4. **Recapture Rule.** The patentee cannot try to recapture during reissue matter which was surrendered during the original prosecution to overcome prior art. *See Hester Indus., Inc. v. Stein, Inc.*, 142 F.3d 1472, 46 USPQ2d 1641 (Fed. Cir. 1998) (recapture rule prevents the patentee from broadening claims during reissue in a manner which would recapture matter surrendered during the original prosecution by way of argument to overcome prior art). However, in *Ball Corp. v. United States*, 729 F.2d 1429, 221 USPQ 289 (Fed. Cir. 1984), the Court held valid claims added during reissue which contained a single feedline limitation even though applicant had cancelled claims to a single feedline and added the limitation "plurality of feedlines" to all the claims during the original prosecution to overcome the examiner's rejection based on prior art. In *Ball*, the Court determined that while the claims were broader in that one respect, they were significantly narrower than the cancelled claims in other respects and therefore were not barred by the recapture rule. 729 F.2d at 1437–38, 221 USPQ at 296–97. Is this an effective ruling? Should the recapture rule act like prosecution history estoppel to bar the applicant from broadening the claim scope in the exact manner in which she intentionally limited it to overcome prior art?

Reissue Oath. A reissue oath must be filed with the reissue application. The reissue oath is a dangerous document forthe patentee, and it must be carefully prepared. If the oath is defective, then the patentee has created a record admitting that the patent is defective but has not corrected the error. The reissue regulations (prior to 1997) required an applicant to file an oath with the reissue application. The Federal Circuit held that the oath or declaration filed with a reissue application must "specify every difference between the original and reissue claims." *Nupla Corp. v. IXL Mfg. Co.*, 114 F.3d 191, 193, 42

USPQ2d 1711, 1713 (Fed. Cir. 1997). Since reissue applications are only permitted when there is an error in the patent, the oath must describe in detail how the error arose and how it was discovered. If the claims are being narrowed to avoid prior art, the reissue oath must explain why. Supplemental reissue oaths will be required to explain claim changes that may be made during prosecution of the reissue application. *See Nupla*, 114 F.3d at 195, 42 USPQ2d at 1716. If the claims are being broadened, an oath must be filed by all of the inventors. Otherwise, the assignee of the entire interest can sign the oath. *See* 37 C.F.R. § 1.172.

However, in 1997, 37 C.F.R. § 1.175 was revised. It now requires that the patentee identify at least one error in the original patent rather than particularly and distinctly identifying all errors. The patentee is only required to make a general statement that the errors arose without deceptive intent rather than making a detailed showing of how each error arose. The patentee need not identify every error corrected during prosecution, but need only file a supplemental oath generally stating that all corrected errors arose without deceptive intent.

1.175   Reissue oath or declaration.

(a) The reissue oath or declaration . . . must also state that:

> (1) The applicant believes the original patent to be wholly or partly inoperative or invalid by reason of a defective specification or drawing, or by reason of the patentee claiming more or less than the patentee had the right to claim in the patent, stating at least one error being relied upon as the basis for reissue; and

> (2) All errors being corrected in the reissue application up to the time of filing of the oath or declaration under this paragraph arose without any deceptive intention on the part of the applicant.

(b)(1) For any error corrected, which is not covered by the oath or declaration submitted under paragraph (a) of this section, applicant must submit a supplemental oath or declaration stating that every such error arose without any deceptive intention on the part of the applicant. . . .

These changes to patent procedure were undertaken in an effort to simplify and streamline Patent Office filings.

Reissue is a dangerous proceeding. By filing a reissue application, the patent owner has admitted that the patent is wholly or partially inoperative or invalid. This can be very dangerous because prosecution history estoppel attaches to statements made during the reissue prosecution.

Inequitable conduct. The patentee has a continuing duty to disclose material prior art to the PTO during prosecution of a patent. This same duty applies to reissue applications. Therefore, if the patentee has learned of prior art since the patent issuance, all of it must be disclosed to the PTO. This includes prior art that may be brought to the patentee's attention by an accused infringer during litigation. In addition, during reissue the patentee must inform the PTO of pending litigations and allegations made during the litigation. Moreover, if the patentee discloses a prior art reference to the PTO during reissue and it is relied upon by the examiner, then materiality is established.

Third-party involvement. There is no formal third-party involvement in reissue proceedings. However, an accused infringer may wish to submit prior art and arguments under the protest procedure of 37 C.F.R. § 1.291. Under the procedure,the PTO is only obligated to acknowledge receipt of the protest. Thus, there is no guarantee that the merits of the protest will ever be considered.

Intervening rights. Under § 252, the accused infringer may acquire intervening rights. This would allow a competitor to continue business commenced before the reissue patent issued as long as that conduct would not have amounted to infringement of the original patent.

Problem

Problem 1

1.   Smith has sued Flow Instruments for infringement of its '000 patent which issued one year ago for a flowmeter with extended range. A flowmeter is a device which measures the rate of flow of liquid. It is a tube with a float inside. As the liquid flows through the tube, the float rises to measure the rate of flow. With floats of varying sizes, different ranges of flow can be measured. Smith's invention claims a flowmeter using more than one float to measure flow, thereby permitting an extended range of measurement without the need to purchase multiple flow meter tubes. Claim 1 reads:

> 1.   An apparatus for measuring an extended range of flow comprising
>
> [1]   floats of varying sizes, and
>
> [2]   a tube capable of containing floats.

The preferred embodiment of the '000 patent describes a single flowmeter which contains multiple floats in its tapered tube simultaneously to measure an extended range of flow.

Flow Instruments sells a flowmeter and extra replacement floats of varying sizes. Flow Instruments does not suggest that its users put multiple floats in the tube simultaneously to extend the range of flow measurements; rather it suggests that when the range of flow exceeds the smallest float's measurement capability (which occurs when the float is pinned against the top of the flowmeter by the water), the user remove that float from the tube and insert a larger float. Flow Instruments teaches extending the range of the flowmeter tube with multiple floats, but by inserting them in the tube in an alternating fashion rather than simultaneously.

Smith is concerned that her claims might be construed as being limited to a flowmeter with multiple floats contained in the tube simultaneously. Smith has very limited resources to enforce her patent. She is also concerned because Flow Instruments just filed a summary judgment motion of invalidity for prior invention under § 102(g), obviousness, and lack of enablement and noninfringement. Flow Instruments identified two prior art publications, one of which was before the PTO during prosecution of the '000 patent and one which was not. The publication that was not before the PTO was authored by Smith. Flow Instruments argued that the patent was not enabled for all tubes capable of containing floats, but only for tapered tubes. Finally, Flow Instruments argued that it cannot infringe because it extends flow by the method of using multiple floats in a single tapered tube in an alternating fashion. It does not sell an apparatus capable of extending flow range with multiple floats simultaneously.

Should either of the parties request reissue or reexamination? What can the PTO consider? Should the case be stayed while the PTO proceedings occur?

Problem 2

2. A United States patent issued to Kramer on November 1, 1999, based upon an application filed on January 29, 1998. The Kramer patent describes and claims a method of purifying water. Kramer's primary competitor, Newman, wishes to file a third-party request for reexamination. He is aware of the following possibilities for filing the request:

(A) Since November 15, 1996, the Jones Company has sold bottled water to consumers purified through the identical method claimed by Kramer. Jones has rigidly maintained its water-purifying method as a trade secret, however.

(B) An article written by Snyder and published on January 19, 1997, in a leading industry journal. The Snyder article is listed on the Kramer patent instrument itself as having been considered by the examiner. However, Newman believes that the Snyder article plainly anticipates the Kramer patent and that the examiner did not fully understand the teachings of the Snyder article.

(C) An independent inventor, Fitch, orally described a water purifying method to Kramer on September 5, 1994. Although the method claimed in the Kramer patent differs somewhat from what Fitch described to Kramer, the differences between the two would have been obvious to a skilled artisan as of 1994.

(D) Cline Limited, a corporation based in Chester, England, sold water purified by the precise method claimed by Kramer during the early 1980's. Employees of Cline Limited conducted daily tours through Cline's water-purifying plant during this period, allowing members of the public to observe the precise method described in the Kramer patent.

Can Newman file a request for reexamination with any chance of success?

Index

References are to Pages
